Staffing Organizations

Staffing Organizations

Herbert G. Heneman III
University of Wisconsin-Madison

Robert L. Heneman
The Ohio State University

Mendota House
Middleton, WI
Austen Press-Irwin
Homewood, IL

Note To The Instructor:

Mendota House and Austen Press have combined their respective skills to bring you *Staffing Organizations* in your classroom. This text is marketed and distributed by Richard D. Irwin, Inc. For assistance in obtaining information or supplementary material please contact your Irwin sales representative or the customer services division of Irwin at 800-323-4560.

AUTHOR PROFILES

Herbert G. Heneman III

Herb Heneman is the Dickson-Bascom Professor in Business at the University of Wisconsin-Madison. He also serves as the Chair of the Management and Human Resources Department, and as a participating faculty member in the Industrial Relations Research Institute. Herb has also served on the faculty at the University of Washington and The Ohio State University.

Herb's research and teaching interests are in the areas of staffing, employment law and equal employment opportunity, compensation, and union growth. He is the coauthor of four books. His research has been published in *Journal of Applied Psychology, Academy of Management Journal, Personnel Psychology, Industrial and Labor Relations Review,* and *Academy of Management Review.*

Herb is a member of the Academy of Management, and a former Chair of its Human Resources Division. He is also a member of the Industrial Relations Research Association, Society for Industrial and Organizational Psychology, Society for Human Resource Management, Employment Management Association, and the International Personnel Management Association.

Robert L. Heneman

Rob Heneman is Associate Professor of Management and Human Resources in the College of Business at The Ohio State University. He also serves as the Director of Graduate Programs in Labor and Human Resources. Prior to receieving his Ph.D. at Michigan State University, Rob was employed as a staffing and training specialist at Pacific Gas and Electric. He has served as a consultant to over 30 private and public organizations.

Rob's research and teaching interests are in the areas of performance assessment, individual and organizational compensation systems, and staffing. Rob is the author of *Merit Pay: Linking Pay Increases to Performance Ratings* (Addison-Wesley, 1992). His research has been published in *Personnel Psychology, Academy of Management Journal* and *Journal of Business and Psychology.*

Currently Rob is Chair-Elect of the Human Resources Division of the Academy of Management. He is also a member of American Psychological Society, Society for Industrial and Organizational Psychology, Industrial Relations Research Association, American Compensation Association, and the Employment Management Association.

Dedication
To Susan and Renẽe

PREFACE

Staffing is a process and function that plays a prominent role in an organization's Human Resource Management (HRM) system. At the heart of the process is an attempt to form matches between people and jobs that will result in an effective workforce for the organization. Since staffing involves the creation of the person/job match, it is the starting point for building workforce effectiveness. Other HRM activities, such as compensation and training, follow from the initial endeavor of bringing people and jobs together via staffing.

Designing and managing successful staffing processes is a major challenge for an organization. It requires multiple tools, techniques, activities, and participants. It must occur within a complex set of external influences beyond organizational control, such as labor markets and laws and regulations. Science, past experience, and gut feel must be carefully blended together to create a process that will maximize the likelihood of successful person/job matches as the employment relationship is established. This book seeks to both describe and prescribe staffing activities that can be undertaken in order to meet the staffing challenge. To do this, several features have been incorporated into the book.

First, the book is structured around the staffing organizations model. The model identifies key influences on, and components of, staffing. These include external forces, staffing support activities such as job analysis, external and internal recruitment activities, external and internal selection activities, and employment activities that represent the end point of the person/job match.

Second, the book is written from an organizational, managerial perspective. It emphasizes the role of staffing as an HR mechanism that can further the managerial purpose of achieving organizational effectiveness. However, since research increasingly reveals that applicants are vitally affected by the organization's staffing process, the applicant's perspective is not ignored. Rather, results of this research are incorporated into suggestions for how the organization can align its staffing practices in ways that will yield positive impacts on job applicants.

Third, as a logical outgrowth of the staffing organizations model there is a wide breadth of topical coverage. This is in contrast to most other books which focus on only a single, narrow aspect of staffing such as recruitment or selection. Staffing is a much more inclusive process than is implied in these types of books.

Fourth, accompanying this broad scope of topical coverage is reference to a diversity of literature. These references draw upon both academic and practitioner literature from behavioral, managerial, economic, and legal sources. The references were chosen in part to provide students with a useful starting point for further pursuit of topics that interest them.

Through use of the above features we seek to provide students and others with an appreciation for, and knowledge of, the multiple facets of staffing organizations. These facets must be designed, managed, and evaluated as components of the organization's overall staffing process. Our goal is to provide individuals with an understanding of this process and to help them function as effective practitioners within it.

ACKNOWLEDGEMENTS

We have benefitted from the inputs of many people in developing our knowledge and understanding of staffing. Several of them also provided direct assistance in the preparation of the book through their discussions and comments on the manuscript. To all of the following, we gratefully acknowledge your contributions:

Steve Abraham (University of Minnesota-Morris)
Alison Barber (Michigan State University)
John Blackburn (Ohio State University)
Wayne Cascio (University of Colorado-Denver)
Maria Castenada (SUNY-Albany)
Russ Cunningham (Pacific Gas and Electric)
Lee Dyer (Cornell University)
Rebecca Ellis (California Polytechnic-San Luis Obispo)
John Fossum (University of Minnesota)
Dennis Huett (State of Wisconsin)
Brian Klaas (University of South Carolina)
Howard Klein (Ohio State University)
Anthony Milanowski (University of Wisconsin-Madison)
Raymond Noe (University of Minnesota)
Judy Olian (University of Maryland)
Sara Rynes (University of Iowa)
Donald Schwab (University of Wisconsin-Madison)
Gale Varma (Deloitte Touche)
Phil Young (Ohio State University)

We wish to thank the following people for their excellent clerical support: Brenda Brugger, Janet Christopher, Joan Evans, Mary Feiner, Kathy McCord and Rona Velte. Production of the book was greatly aided by the work of Joyce Jackson and Jane Rundell at Impressions (a division of Edwards Bros., Inc.) in Madison, Wisconsin.

Finally, we owe a special thanks to Bill Schoof and John Weimeister at Austen Press. They have provided continual adventure and cooperation during our innovative joint undertaking.

BRIEF CONTENTS

CONTENTS

PART FIVE
STAFFING ACTIVITIES: EMPLOYMENT **431**

CHAPTER 11
Decision Making **433**

STAFFING ORGANIZATIONS MODEL

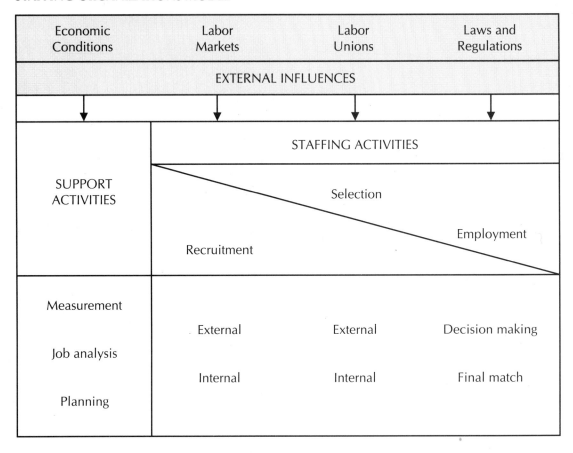

PART ONE

Staffing and External Influences

CHAPTER ONE

Overview and Models

S taffing is a critical human resource management (HRM) function for any organization. Through its staffing function and activities, the organization initially acquires its human resources from the external labor market. Individuals so acquired are matched to jobs with the goal of yielding a good fit between the two. A good fit, or person/job match, is one in which the person achieves and demonstrates effectiveness on various HR outcomes, such as performance, satisfaction, and retention.

Staffing also involves a parallel person/job matching process within the organization's internal labor market. Here, internal mobility (promotion and transfer) systems operate to fill job vacancies with members of the organization's current workforce.

When the person/job match occurs, an employment relationship is established that is first and foremost a legal or contractual one. The contract between an organization and the employee represents the agreed-upon terms and conditions (e.g., compensation, work rules, hours) that govern the employment relationship and its potential termination. But the relationship is also a psychological one, based in particular on feelings about the amount of commitment the individual has to the organization and vice versa. These feelings form a so-called psychological contract between the individual and the organization.

The staffing activities of an organization are intended to instigate, manage, and complete the person/job matching process. Results of a recent survey indicate that these activities play a crucial role in organizations' overall HRM activities. The survey was conducted among a nationwide, random sample of HR department individuals who are members of the Society for Human Resource Management (SHRM). These people were employed in organizations of widely differing size (from fewer than 100 to more than 5,000 employees), industrial composition, and geographic location. The respondents were asked to indicate the percentage of their HR department's budget and the percentage of their time that is spent on staffing and other activities. Results of the survey are shown in Exhibit 1.1. As can be seen, staffing received the greatest percentage (19%) of budget dollars and the second greatest percentage (15%) of time spent among the HR activities.

Having presented this brief introduction to the nature and importance of staffing, this chapter now turns to a more formal treatment of staffing organizations. It begins with a definition of the term ''staffing,'' followed by a discussion of several implications of that definition. Then, four models of staffing are presented that depict key elements of staffing activities and objectives. The last of these models serves as the general staffing model upon which the structure of the book is based. Finally, the chapter concludes with a brief description of the remainder of the book.

EXHIBIT 1.1   Survey Results Regarding Staffing and Other HR Activities

In the spring of 1993, the Society for Human Resource Management (SHRM) surveyed a random sample of its members on their views about a variety of human resource activities and their satisfaction with those activities as individual HR professionals.

The first section of the questionnaire was a general overview of respondents' involvement in human resource activities. Rough estimates were obtained of the allocation of budgetary and time resources across a variety of major human resource domains. As the table below indicates, more budget dollars are devoted to staffing than any other human resource function, while the most time is spent on employee and labor relations.

	% of Budget	% of Time
Staffing	19	15
Design/administration of employee benefits programs	15	10
Employee & labor relations	13	18
Training	11	9
Design/administration of employee compensation programs	9	10
Health, safety & security	8	6
Design/administration of programs in response to government regulations	6	7
Performance appraisal	5	7
Strategic planning	4	7
Conducting other activities	10	11

Source: "Human Resource Practices and Job Satisfaction" (Executive Summary), 1993.
Reprinted with the permission of the Society for Human Resource Management, Alexandria, VA.

THE NATURE OF STAFFING

Definition of Staffing

The following definition of *staffing* is offered and will be used throughout this book:

> Staffing is the mutual process by which the individual and the organization become matched to form the employment relationship.

This straightforward definition contains several implications, which are identified and explained next.

Implications of Definition

Organization and Individual Perspectives

Staffing is a mutual process that involves organizations seeking individuals (the traditional view of staffing) as well as individuals seeking organizations (a more recent view). Both the organization and the individual are thus active players in the staffing process, and both organizational and individual perspectives are important to reckon with and understand.[1]

The organizational perspective emphasizes staffing as activities undertaken to further the attainment of organizational goals, such as survival, profitability, and growth. The individual perspective stresses the fact that individuals seek jobs that they will find rewarding, and that these individuals are affected by their experiences in the staffing process (e.g., how fairly they feel they have been treated by the organization).

Throughout this book, the organizational perspective is dominant. Staffing is examined primarily through an organizational lens that focuses on how staffing may contribute to organizational effectiveness. The individual perspective is not ignored, however, since individuals' experiences with the staffing system may influence the effectiveness of that system. For example, applicants who are "turned off" by aspects of the staffing process may enter the organization as less than fully committed new hires, or they may actually opt out of even joining the organization at all.

Staffing as a Process or System

Staffing is not an event such as "we hired two new sales people today." Rather, staffing is a process or system composed of a series of interrelated activities such as recruitment, selection, decision making, and job offers. Actually hiring someone is the culmination of the staffing process.

It is best to think of staffing as a process that establishes and governs the flow of applicants into the organization (external staffing) and within the organization (internal staffing). There are many steps through which applicants flow from the time they first enter the system to the time they become new hires.

The steps begin with the organization's decision to fill a vacancy, which in itself is a decision derived from strategic HR and staffing planning exercises. Usually, recruitment activities are undertaken to identify and attract applicants for the position. These blend into selection activities in which various selection techniques, such as interviews and tests, are used to assess and evaluate applicants against the requirements of the job. Results of these evaluations are then used to make decisions about which applicants to reject and which to offer a job. The final step of the staffing process is the applicant's acceptance of the job offer.

In short, applicants flow through staffing systems. The processes used in the system must be planned and managed to facilitate the making of effective person/job matches. Staffing is a generic term that encompasses these processes, be they external or internal in focus.

Forming the Employment Relationship

An emphasis on forming or entering into the employment relationship includes certain staffing decisions and excludes others. Included are hiring, promotion, and transfer decisions since all lead to the creation of a new person/job match. Excluded are decisions and actions that sever or end the employment relationship, such as voluntary quits, layoffs, and discharges. Both the organization and the individual must act positively to create a person/job match. There must be both organization selection and self-selection as part of the formation of the employment relationship.

Only formation of the employment relationship is treated in this book. This will be apparent in the staffing models presented next, which pertain to the person/job match, specific components of staffing, and staffing and HRM. These three models are then combined into the staffing organizations model.

STAFFING MODELS

Person/Job Match

At the heart of staffing organizations is the person/job match. This match seeks to align characteristics of individuals and jobs in ways that will result in desired HR outcomes. Casual comments made about applicants often reflect awareness of the importance of the person/job match. "Clark just doesn't have the interpersonal skills that it takes to be a good customer service representative." "Mary has exactly the kinds of budgeting experience this job calls for; if we hire her there won't be any downtime while she learns our systems." "Gary says he was attracted to apply for this job because of its sales commission plan; he says he likes jobs where his pay depends on how well he performs." "Diane was impressed by the amount of challenge and autonomy she will have." "Jack turned down our offer; we gave him our best shot, but he just didn't feel he could handle the long hours and amount of travel the job calls for."

Comments such as these raise four important points about the person/job match. First, jobs are characterized by their requirements (e.g., interpersonal skills, previous budgeting experiences) and embedded rewards (e.g., commission sales plan, challenge and autonomy). Second, individuals are characterized by their level of qualification (e.g., few interpersonal skills, extensive budgeting experience) and motivation (e.g., need for pay to depend on performance, need for challenge and autonomy). Third, in each of the previous examples the issue was one of the likely degree of fit or match between the characteristics of the job and the person. Fourth, there are implied consequences for every match. For example, Clark may not perform very well in his interactions with customers; retention might quickly become an issue with Jack.

These points and concepts are shown more formally through the person/job match model in Exhibit 1.2. In this model, the job has certain requirements and

---

EXHIBIT 1.2   Person/Job Match Model

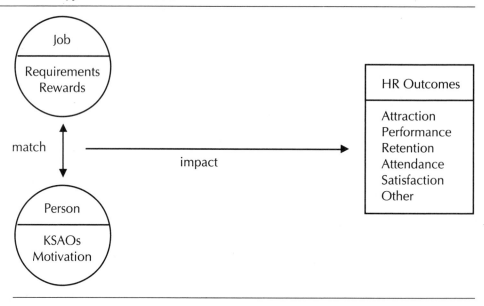

---

rewards associated with it. The person has certain qualifications, referred to as KSAOs (knowledges, skills, abilities, and other characteristics), and motivations. There is a need for a match between the person and the job. To the extent that the match is a good one, it will likely have positive impacts on HR outcomes, particularly attraction of job applicants, job performance, retention, attendance, and satisfaction.

There is actually a need for a dual match to occur: job requirements to KSAOs, and job rewards to individual motivation. In and through staffing activities, there are attempts to ensure both of these. Such attempts collectively involve what will be referred to throughout this book as the matching process.

Several points pertaining to staffing need be made about the person/job matching model. First, the concepts shown in the model are not new.[2] They have been used for decades as the dominant way of thinking about how individuals successfully adapt to their work environments. The view is that it is the positive interaction of individual and job characteristics that creates the most successful matches. Thus, a person with a given ''package'' of KSAOs is not equally suited to all jobs, because jobs vary in the KSAOs required. Likewise, an individual with a given set of needs or motivations will not be satisfied with all jobs, because jobs differ in the rewards they offer. Thus, in staffing, each individual must be assessed relative to the requirements and rewards of the job being filled.

Second, the model emphasizes that the matching process involves a dual match of KSAOs to requirements and motivation to rewards. Both matches require attention in staffing. For example, a staffing system may be designed to focus on the KSAOs/requirements match by carefully identifying job requirements and then thoroughly assessing applicants relative to these requirements. While such a staffing system may be one that will accurately identify the probable high performers, problems may arise with it. By ignoring or downplaying the motivation-rewards portion of the match, the organization may have difficulty getting people to accept job offers (an attraction outcome) or having new hires remain with the organization for any length of time (a retention outcome). It does little good to be able to identify the likely high performers if they cannot be induced to accept job offers or to remain with the organization.

Third, job requirements should usually be expressed in terms of both the tasks involved and the KSAOs thought necessary for performance of those tasks. Most of the time, it is difficult to establish meaningful KSAOs for a job without having first identified the job's tasks. KSAOs usually must be derived or inferred from knowledge of the tasks. An exception to this involves very basic or generic KSAOs, such as literacy and oral communication skills, that are reasonably deemed necessary for most jobs.

Fourth, even if tasks have not been fully identified and written down to guide the development of a staffing system, there is still a need to be concerned about the person/job match. For example, job descriptions frequently provide a listing of the job's specific tasks as well as a catchall phrase such as ''other tasks and duties as required.'' When these other tasks and duties actually are assigned, they become a part of the job. At that point, the person/job match for these other tasks and duties becomes an issue. In staffing, it is very difficult to anticipate what these other tasks and duties may turn out to be at the time applicants are considered for the job. These other tasks and duties may, in fact, turn out to be an important component of the job, but their KSAOs will not have been identified and built into the staffing system. Applicants will thus not be assessed for a portion of the person/job match, and this may have unfortunate implications for HR outcomes.

A fifth point that pertains to staffing entails the concept of job rewards, which should be viewed very broadly to encompass a wide variety of extrinsic and intrinsic rewards. This view recognizes the complexity and range of individuals' needs and the corresponding rewards that can be provided to satisfy those needs. Recently, for example, some people have suggested that the person/job match is too narrow a focus in looking at staffing because it ignores certain rewards that are part of the organization's broader culture and values.[3] Examples of such values include emphasis on achievement, honesty and integrity, and fairness of treatment. While these values may indeed transcend individual jobs as part of the overall milieu of the organization, they are most likely to be experienced by individuals through events that occur as part of their own jobs. In this sense, therefore, organizational values may be thought of as rewards offered by the job and thus may be incorporated into the person/job match model.

Finally, the matching process can yield only so much by way of impacts on the HR outcomes. The reason for this is that these outcomes are influenced by factors outside the realm of the person/job match. Retention, for example, depends not only on how close a match there is between job rewards and individual motivation, but also on the availability of suitable job opportunities in other organizations and labor markets. As another example, Total Quality Management proponents argue that it is characteristics of the production or service system that have the biggest impact on performance outcomes, not the person/job match.[4] According to this view, the system itself establishes a baseline level of performance that individuals achieve. Variations in performance are due to anomalies of the system, rather than problems with the person/job match. These examples suggest potential limitations on the usefulness of staffing (and the person/job match) for influencing HR outcomes.

Staffing Components

As noted, staffing encompasses managing the flows of people into and within the organization. The staffing process has several components that represent steps and activities that occur over the course of these flows. Exhibit 1.3 shows these components and the general sequence in which they occur.

EXHIBIT 1.3   Staffing Components Model

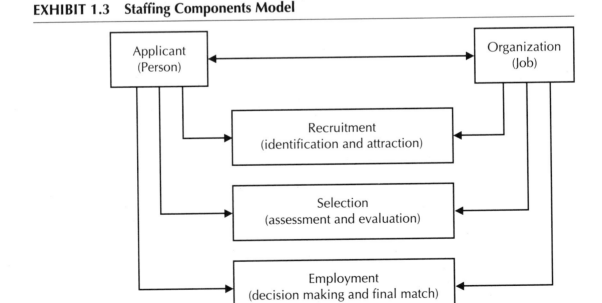

As shown in the exhibit, staffing begins with a joint interaction between the applicant and the organization. The applicant seeks the organization and job opportunities within it, and the organization seeks applicants for job vacancies it has or anticipates having. Both the applicant and the organization are thus involved as ''players'' in the staffing process from the very start, and they remain joint participants throughout the process.

At times, the organization may be the dominant player, such as in aggressive and targeted recruiting for certain types of applicants. At other times, the applicant may be the aggressor, such as when the applicant desperately seeks employment with a particular organization and will go to almost any length to land a job with it. Most of the time, staffing involves a more balanced and natural interplay between the applicant and the organization, which occurs over the course of the staffing process.

The initial stage in staffing is recruitment, which involves identification and attraction activities by both the organization and the applicant. The organization seeks to identify and attract individuals so that they become job applicants. Activities such as recruitment advertising, job fairs, use of recruiters, preparation and distribution of informational brochures, and ''putting out the word'' about vacancies among its own employees are undertaken. The applicant attempts to identify organizations with job opportunities through activities such as reading advertisements, contacting an employment agency, mass mailing resumes to employers, and so forth. These activities are accompanied by attempts to make one's qualifications (KSAOs and motivation) attractive to organizations, such as by personally applying for a job or preparing a carefully constructed resume that highlights significant skills and experiences.

Gradually, recruitment activities phase into the selection stage and its accompanying activities. Now, the emphasis is on assessment and evaluation. For the organization, this means the use of various selection techniques (interviews, application blanks, and so forth) to assess applicant KSAOs and motivation. Data from these assessments are then evaluated against job requirements to determine the likely degree of person/job fit. At the same time, the applicant is assessing and evaluating the job and organization. The applicant's assessment and evaluation are based on information gathered from organizational representatives (e.g., recruiter, manager with the vacancy, other employees); written information (e.g., brochures, employee handbook); informal sources (e.g., friends and relatives who are current employees); and visual inspection (e.g., a video presentation, a worksite tour). This information, along with a self-assessment of KSAOs and motivation, is evaluated against the applicant's understanding of job requirements and rewards to determine if there is likely to be a good person/job match.

The final component of staffing is employment, which involves decision-making and final match activities by the organization and the applicant. The organization must decide which applicants to reject from further consideration and which to allow to continue in the staffing process. This may involve multiple decisions over successive selection steps or hurdles. Some applicants ultimately become finalists for the job. At that point, the organization must decide to whom it will make the job offer, what will be the content of the offer, and how it will be drawn up and presented to the applicant. Upon the applicant's acceptance of the offer, the final match is complete, and the employment relationship is formally established.

For the applicant, the employment stage involves *self-selection,* a term that refers to decisions about whether to continue in or drop out of the staffing process. These decisions may occur anywhere along the selection process, up to and including the moment of the job offer. If the applicant continues as part of the process through the final match, the applicant has decided to be a finalist. The individual's attention now turns to a possible job offer, possible input and negotiation on its content, and making a final decision about the offer. The applicant's final decision is based on overall judgment about the likely suitability of the person/job match.

It should be noted that the staffing components apply to both external and internal staffing. While this may seem obvious in the case of external staffing, a brief elaboration may be necessary for internal staffing. In internal staffing, the applicant is a current employee, and the organization is the current employer. Job opportunities (vacancies) exist within the organization and are filled through the activities of the internal labor market. Those activities involve recruitment, selection, and employment, with the employer and employee as joint participants. For example, the employer may recruit through use of an internal job posting system. Employees who apply may be assessed and evaluated on the basis of supervisory recommendation, a formal promotability rating, and past job assignments for the employer. Decisions are made by both the employer and the employees who are applicants. Ultimately, the position will be offered to one of the applicants and, hopefully, accepted. When this happens, the final match has occurred, and a new employment relationship has been established.

Human Resource Management

Since staffing is only one of several activities that comprise HRM, its nature must be considered in the broader HRM context. A particular model of HRM, shown in Exhibit 1.4, depicts the nature of HRM and staffing's place within it. The model is discussed next.

Person/Job Match

As the model shows, the person/job match plays a central role in all of HRM. Indeed, it shows that all HR activities are directed toward creating and maintaining effective person/job matches as a way of having a positive impact on the HR outcomes.

EXHIBIT 1.4 Human Resource Management Model

Economic Conditions	Labor Markets	Labor Unions	Laws and Regulations

EXTERNAL INFLUENCES

HR ACTIVITIES		HR OUTCOMES

SUPPORT ACTIVITIES
  Measurement
  Job analysis
  Planning

FUNCTIONAL ACTIVITIES
  External staffing
  Internal staffing
  Training & development
  Compensation
  Labor relations
  Work environment

Job
Requirements
Rewards

Person
KSAOs
Motivation

Attraction
Performance
Retention
Attendance
Satisfaction
Other

Source: Adapted from H. G. Heneman, III, D. P. Schwab, J. A. Fossum, and L. Dyer, *Personnel/Human Resource Management,* fourth ed. (Homewood, IL: Irwin, 1989).

HR Activities

Each HR activity is classified as a support or functional activity. Support activities include measurement, job analysis, and planning. These three activities are not intended to directly influence the person/job match. Rather, they serve in a supportive role, providing input to the functional activities. This suggests that measurement, job analysis, and planning are logical prerequisites for staffing activities; their conduct should enhance the effectiveness of staffing activities.

Functional activities are undertaken to have a direct impact upon the person/job match, and thus, the HR outcomes. These activities include external staffing, internal staffing, training and development, compensation, labor relations, and work environment (e.g., physical and environmental conditions, hours of work schedules). Each of these activities has the potential for making important and unique contributions to the matching process. For this reason, they are typically administered as separate functional areas within HRM and the HR department.

Interrelationships Among Activities

While administered separately, the functional HR activities are highly interrelated and, hence, must work in concert with each other. For example, assume that the results of HR planning lead an organization to establish a goal of hiring 20 new management trainees over the next 12 months. Achieving this goal requires co-ordination among the functional HR activities. Will the trainees be sought from outside the organization, inside, or both? What will be the qualifications desired of external and internal applicants? What starting pay level and other terms will be necessary to attract sufficient numbers of applicants? What types of training and development will the trainees receive and when? What evening and weekend work will be required?

Answers to these questions must be coordinated in ways that have functional activities all working toward attaining the common hiring goal. This is difficult in practice because decisions made in one area may have consequences in other areas. Suppose, for example, that in order to control labor costs, the compensation staff recommends that there be (a) the same starting salaries for trainees as last year, and (b) elimination of hiring bonuses that were commonly used in past years. If implemented, these recommendations could make it difficult to attract new trainees, thus requiring new and stepped-up recruiting efforts relative to past years. Moreover, the qualifications of those recruited may be lower, necessitating revi-sions in the training and development curriculum. Finally, weekend work may have to be scaled back, or even curtailed, in order to compensate for the starting salary freeze and elimination of hiring bonus.

External Influences

At the top of Exhibit 1.4 are listed several external influences that affect HR activities, the person/job match, and HR outcomes. These influences are economic conditions, labor markets, labor unions, and laws and regulations.

Economic Conditions   Economic conditions influence the overall financial health of an organization. They have a direct bearing on the numbers and types of jobs the organization has, the numbers and types of people it will need in those jobs, and the types of rewards it will be able to offer in those jobs. In the preceding management trainee example, declining economic conditions may require a goal of hiring only ten trainees, accompanied by reducing starting pay relative to last year. Such changes will obviously carry over to and have an impact upon staffing activities for the job (e.g., college recruitment may be cut back).

Labor Markets   Labor markets represent the external arena in which the organ-ization seeks new employees (labor demand) and individuals offer their availability (labor supply). Staffing activities are very susceptible to labor market undercurrents in both numerical and qualitative terms. Numerically, ''tight'' labor markets (strong demand relative to supply) make recruiting adequate numbers of applicants both difficult and expensive. Alternatively, ''loose'' labor markets (weak demand relative to supply) create a more favorable environment for identifying and attracting sufficient numbers of applicants.

The qualitative aspect of labor demand and supply refers to the types of qualifications required by jobs and provided by job applicants. In the previous management trainee example, the numerical hiring goal will be accompanied by specifying the desired KSAOs and motivation characteristics of applicants. These are also a reflection of labor demand. On the labor supply side, obtaining applicants who can meet these qualitative specifications depends upon the actual availability of people with the desired qualifications.

Labor Unions   Labor unions negotiate with the organization about the terms and conditions of employment for their members, expressed in a written labor contract. The terms and conditions typically deal with both job requirements and rewards. For job requirements, the job tasks and duties, as well as the classification of jobs into a hierarchy (for promotion and transfer purposes), may be negotiated. Actual workings of the internal labor market, such as job posting and seniority systems, are almost always negotiated. For job rewards, virtually all extrinsic job rewards are negotiated and then ''locked in'' for the life of the contract. Establishment and flexibility of both job requirements and rewards are thus greatly affected by the union presence.

Laws and Regulations   Laws and regulations serve to define (a) the nature of the employment relationship, and (b) the limits of permissible and impermissible HR practices, including staffing ones. The employment relationship is specified as a contractual one that is entered into by the organization and the individual. The contract is determined either collectively (as with a labor union) or individually through a job offer/acceptance process. But the nature of the employment relationship is also established legally by subsequent HR policies and practices as well. Laws and regulations specify and clarify the boundaries between permissible and impermissible HR practices. This is particularly the case with equal employment opportunity and affirmative action (EEO/AA) laws and regulations. All support and functional HR activities are strongly and vitally affected by their content and enforcement.

In summary, staffing occurs within the framework and conduct of HRM generally. HR activities, including staffing, seek to influence the person/job match and (through it) the HR outcomes. Some of these activities influence the match indirectly (support activities), while others have a more direct impact (functional activities). External influences constrain and complicate these activities. Since the organization has little control over these external influences, it must modify its staffing and other activities to meet these conditions and changes in the external environment.

Staffing Organizations

The concepts and terminology from the discussions of staffing components and staffing within HRM may be drawn together to yield the staffing organizations model as shown in Exhibit 1.5. In that model, staffing is comprised of support activities, staffing activities, and external influences. The support activities are measurement, job analysis, and planning. Recruitment, selection, and employment form the staffing activities. External influences have an impact upon both the

EXHIBIT 1.5   Staffing Organizations Model

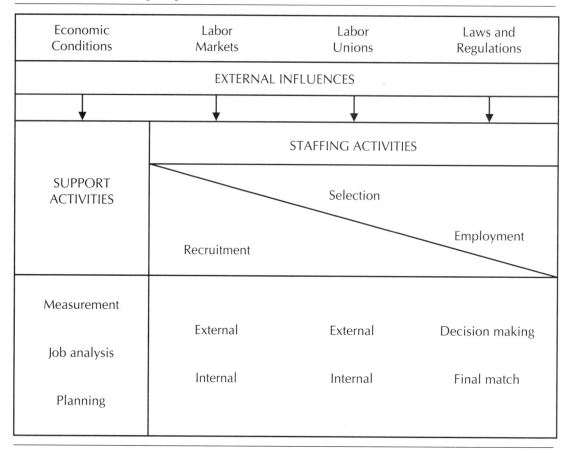

support and staffing activities, in the form of economic conditions, labor markets, labor unions, and laws and regulations.

The staffing model requires several comments. While it does not depict the person/job match and resultant HR outcomes, these remain the central, underlying focus of staffing organizations. The support activities, staffing activities, and external influences all combine and interact to implement the matching process.

The three support activities from the HRM model are included in the staffing model. This signifies and reinforces their importance to staffing organizations. Indeed, they are the foundations upon which effective, and legally defensible, staffing practices are built for an organization.

The diagonal line in Exhibit 1.5, cutting through the three staffing activities, signifies that there is no clear line of demarcation between them. In fact, all three activities may occur at the same time. While recruitment dominates staffing activities in the early stages of the process, selection and then employment activities become more prominent as the process unfolds. However, even recruitment does not formally end until the final match has been completed, and the applicant has "signed on the dotted line."

The recruitment, selection, and employment activities occur for both external and internal applicants. The fundamental purpose of these activities (identification and attraction, assessment and evaluation, decision making and final match) are identical for both external and internal staffing.

Staffing organizations requires more than recruitment and selection. Decision-making and final match activities are critical in bringing the results of recruitment and selection to fruition. Quite simply, without decision-making and final match activities, the recruitment and selection activities would yield no new hires for the organization.

Finally, external influences play prominent roles in both support and staffing activities. They set the external parameters and constraints within which staffing systems operate. So large and all-encompassing is their impact that external influences will be discussed prior to support and staffing activities.

The remainder of the book is structured around and built on the staffing organizations model shown in Exhibit 1.5.

PLAN FOR THE BOOK

The book is divided into five parts:

1. Staffing and External Influences
2. Support Activities
3. Staffing Activities: Recruitment
4. Staffing Activities: Selection
5. Staffing Activities: Employment

Each chapter in these five parts begins with a brief topical outline in order to help the reader quickly discern its general contents. The "meat" of the chapter comes next. A chapter summary then reviews and highlights points from the chapter. A set of discussion questions and detailed endnotes complete the chapter.

As noted, the importance of external influences is such that they are considered first in Chapter 2 (Economic Conditions, Labor Markets, and Labor Unions) and Chapter 3 (Laws and Regulations). The laws and regulations, in particular, have become so pervasive that they require special treatment. To do this, Chapter 3 reviews the basic laws affecting staffing, with an emphasis on the major federal laws and regulations pertaining to EEO/AA matters generally. Specific provisions relevant to staffing are covered in depth. Each subsequent chapter then has a separate section at its end labeled "Legal Issues" in which specific legal topics relevant to the chapter's content are discussed. This allows for a more focused discussion of legal issues, while not diverting attention from the major thrust of the book.

The endnotes at the end of each chapter are quite extensive. They are drawn from academic, practitioner, and legal sources with the goal of providing a balanced selection of references from each of these sources. Emphasis is on inclusion of recent references of high quality and easy accessibility. Too lengthy a list of references to each specific topic is avoided, with instead a sampling of only the best available included.

SUMMARY

Staffing is defined as "the mutual process by which the individual and the organization become matched to form the employment relationship." This definition suggests that staffing should be viewed, using both individual and organizational perspectives, as a process undertaken by the organization to manage the occurrence of the person/job match. Several models illustrate this point.

The person/job match model indicates there is a dual need to match (a) the person's KSAOs to job requirements, and (b) the person's motivation to the job's rewards. Managing the matching process effectively results in positive impacts on HR outcomes such as attraction, performance, and retention of employees.

The staffing components model shows that there are three basic activities in staffing. Those activities and their fundamental purposes are recruitment (identification and attraction of applicants), selection (assessment and evaluation of applicants), and employment (decision making and final match).

The human resource management model shows staffing within the broader framework of HRM. That framework has various support activities (e.g., job analysis) and functional activities (e.g., staffing, compensation) that influence the HR outcomes through their impact upon the person/job match. Importantly, the model also identifies several external influences on the conduct of HRM activities. These influences are economic conditions, labor markets, labor unions, and laws and regulations.

The staffing organizations model shows that staffing is comprised of three support activities (measurement, job analysis, and planning) and the three staffing activities (recruitment, selection, and employment). These activities occur for both external and internal staffing. Their fundamental purpose is to manage the person/job matching process. They do this, however, within the confines of the external influences previously identified.

The staffing organizations model serves as the structural outline for the remainder of the book. The first part treats external influences. This is followed by separate parts for support activities, recruitment, selection, and employment. Each chapter for support and staffing activities has a separate section at its end labeled "Legal Issues." Each chapter also has extensive references drawn from academic, practitioner, and legal sources.

ENDNOTES

1. J.A. Breaugh, *Recruitment: Science and Practice* (Boston: PWS-Kent, 1992); R.D. Gatewood and H.S. Feild, *Human Resource Selection,* third ed. (Chicago: Dryden, 1994); S.L. Rynes, "Recruitment, Job Choice, and Post-Hire Consequences: A Call for New Research Directions," in M.D. Dunnette and L.M. Hough (eds.), *Handbook of Industrial and Organizational Psychology,* vol. 2, second ed. (Palo Alto, CA: Consulting Psychologists Press, 1991); J.P. Wanous, *Organizational Entry,* second ed. (Reading, MA: Addison-Wesley, 1992).

2. D.F. Caldwell and C.A. O'Reilly III, "Measuring Person-Job Fit With A Profile-Comparison Process," *Journal of Applied Psychology,* 1990, 75, pp. 648–657; R.V. Dawis, "Person-Environment Fit and Job Satisfaction," in C.J. Cranny, P.C. Smith, and E.F. Stone, *Job Satisfaction* (New York: Lexington, 1992), pp. 69–88; R.V. Dawis, L.H. Lofquist, and D.J. Weiss, *A Theory of Work Adjustment (A Revision),* (Minneapolis: Industrial Relations Center, University of Minnesota, 1968).

3. D.E. Bowen, G.E. Ledford, Jr., and B.R. Nathan, "Hiring for the Organization and Not the Job," *Academy of Management Executive,* 1991, 5(4), pp. 35–51; T.A. Judge and R.D. Bretz, Jr., "Effects of Work Values on Job Choice Decisions," *Journal of Applied Psychology,* 1992, 77, pp. 001–0011; C.A. O'Reilly III, J. Chatman, and D.F. Caldwell, "People and Organizational Culture: A Profile Comparison Approach to Assessing Person-Organization Fit," *Academy of Management Journal,* 1991, 34, pp. 487–516.

4. G.H. Dobbins, R.L. Cardy, and K.P. Carson, "Examining Fundamental Assumptions: A Contrast of Person and System Approaches to Human Resource Management," in G.R. Ferris and K.M. Rowland, eds., *Research in Personnel and Human Resources Management* (Boston: JAI Press, 1991), pp. 1–38.

CHAPTER TWO

Economic Conditions, Labor Markets, and Labor Unions

I n the previous chapter, external influences were shown to have a vital impact upon the conduct of HR activities, as well as upon the person/job match and the HR outcomes. This chapter explores in more detail the nature of the first three of these external influences (economic conditions, labor markets, labor unions) and how they have a specific impact on staffing activities. A similar treatment for laws and regulations is provided in the following chapter.

The first section of this chapter deals with economic conditions. It shows that these conditions have both a positive and negative impact on job growth. Job growth, in turn, affects the movement of people into jobs, among jobs, and out of jobs, and occurs within the framework of current competitive standards for employers. Staffing activities manage these movements.

Job growth also directly involves labor markets. Labor markets are the mechanism by which organizational signals about job availability (labor demand) and individual signals about willingness to work (labor supply) converge and play themselves out. Both labor demand and supply involve numerical (numbers of people) and qualitative (KSAOs and individual motivation) aspects. This section describes the numerical and qualitative components of labor demand and supply, as well as their future trends. Implications for staffing activities are presented.

The final section of this chapter shows the role of labor unions vis-à-vis organizational staffing. Labor unions negotiate and help administer labor contracts. Each contract contains the terms and conditions of employment that will govern the employment relationship between labor and management in a workplace. The terms of the contract affect job requirements and rewards, and have a direct impact upon staffing activities through clauses dealing with staffing issues. The nature of these clauses, as well as their implications for management discretion and flexibility in staffing, are detailed.

ECONOMIC CONDITIONS

In Chapter 1, staffing was said to involve the managed movement of individuals. Economic conditions have a vital impact on such movement, particularly because of the influence they exert on job growth. The general nature of these relationships is shown in Exhibit 2.1.

The exhibit shows that organizations operate within, and must contend with, a multitude of general economic conditions. These include product and labor market competition (both national and international), inflation, interest rates, foreign exchange rates, and government regulations. From these forces emerge positive, neutral, or negative impacts on job growth. In response to these forces, organizations move people into (new hires), within (internal labor markets), and out of (exit) organizations.

Consider the case of job expansion. When new jobs are created, new hire rates begin to increase, for both entry level and higher level jobs. These new hires are

EXHIBIT 2.1   General Economic Conditions, Job Growth, HR Movement Impacts

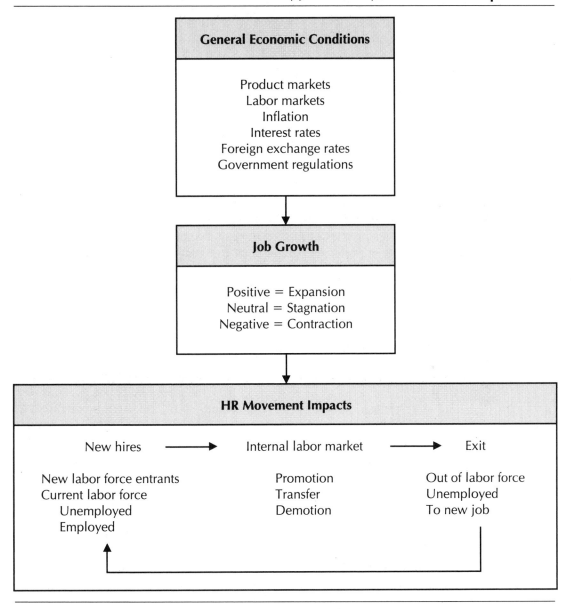

either new entrants into the labor force (e.g., recent college graduates) or current members of the labor force, both unemployed and employed. There will also be increased movement within organizations' internal labor markets through the operation of their promotion and transfer systems (there may also be occasional demotions). This movement will be necessitated by a combination of new jobs being created that will be filled internally and the exit of current employees from the organization. Most likely, the departure of employees will be due to their leaving the organization to take new jobs at other organizations. Some, however, may be temporarily unemployed (while they look for new job opportunities), and others may leave the labor force entirely.

With this example, it can be seen that job growth is like a spigot governing the flows of people among jobs, organizations, and labor force status. The greater the rate of job growth, the greater the likely impacts on such movement. Anticipation, accommodation, and management of these flows is part and parcel of staffing organizations.

Within this general framework, some specific comments about the private sector and the public sector elucidate the crucial role that economic conditions play in shaping the staffing of organizations. This is followed in this chapter by a brief review of a study that focused on implications of the business environment for HR practices, including staffing, in the year 2000.

Private Sector

The private sector is currently confronting and changing over to what has been called the "new economy." It is evolving from the mass production economy that started to develop at the end of the 19th century and emphasized production of a high volume of goods, coupled with high productivity standards for achieving it. The automobile industry epitomizes the mass production economy.

The new economy has a set of competitive standards that businesses must meet; these include, but extend beyond, the high volume and productivity standards of the mass production economy. In particular, the new economy is characterized by the following competitive standards:[1]

1. robust productivity levels and gains
2. heightened product and service quality
3. greater variety and choice in products and services
4. customization of goods to specific consumer tastes
5. increased convenience
6. timeliness in providing goods and services

These standards come into direct play with other forces. Particularly important are trends toward increased globalization and global competition, and rapid technological breakthroughs and automation of production methods.

The impact of these competitive standards and forces on organizations has been tremendous, requiring considerable organizational learning, adaptation, and change. The changes forced upon and required of organizations can be summarized as follows:

> The new competitive standards and flexible technologies of the new economy need to be housed in new kinds of organizations. Both large, top-down hierarchies typical of manufacturing and smaller, isolated and fragmented structures typical of services are being replaced by flexible networks.
>
> The new economy is creating a new structure of jobs. Organizations are using a mix of highly skilled but fewer production workers and more service workers to meet new competitive standards. The new economy also requires a highly skilled workforce. Workers' skills need to be both broader and deeper especially at the point of production, service delivery, and at the interface with the customer in order to meet new competitive standards and to complement flexible organizational structures and technologies.[2]

Public Sector

Public sector organizations have been buffeted by heightened taxpayer demands, particularly as pertains to education, health care, and welfare. At the same time, there have been large reductions in demand for military services, resulting in the loss of jobs for military personnel and associated civilian workers. The resulting "peace dividend," however, has been more illusory than real because of the need to pay for the increased demand for other services, as well as to finance the federal debt.

Increasingly, the public sector has been placed in competition with the private sector. In some instances, the private sector has provided services that reduce the demand for similar public ones. The United States Postal Service, for example, is being challenged by private overnight delivery of mail, as well as by the fax machine and electronic mail (E-mail). In other instances, the public sector is willing to turn over or to contract with the private sector for services that once were strictly in the public domain. Private trash collection and prison construction and administration are two examples of this. In many respects, the new economy of the private sector is spilling over into the public sector and applying its competitive standards to it in the process.

Gaining Competitive Advantage

Economic conditions and forces demand organizational response. As organizations change in response to these forces, so must their HR activities, including staffing.

An excellent illustration of this is provided by the IBM-Towers Perrin study that sought to assess the human resource implications of changes in the business environment to occur by the year 2000. Survey responses were gathered from over 2,900 line executives, human resource executives, consultants, business reporters, and academic faculty from organizations around the world. The responses collected indicate that the top three business environment factors that will influence HR management in the year 2000 are increased national/international competition, focus on total quality/customer satisfaction, and changing employee values/goals. The respondents also indicated the importance of various methods for meeting these environmental challenges. The third most important method is "attraction of a high quality workforce," with "high productivity/quality/customer satisfaction" and "linkage of HR to business strategies" the first and second most important methods, respectively.[3] Thus, these experts viewed staffing as a highly important strategy for helping organizations to cope with business environment forces acting on them.

LABOR MARKETS

In and through labor markets, employers express their demand for labor, and individuals express their willingness to participate in the labor force. In a macro sense, it is through these joint actions and decisions that person/job matches occur throughout the economy. In this section, the elements of labor demand and labor supply will be explored. This involves quantitative (e.g., numbers of employed) and qualitative (e.g., KSAO) characteristics of both demand and supply.

Labor Demand

Labor demand is a derived demand; it is a reflection or result of demands for the organization's goods and services. Conceptually, the demand for labor is expressed in terms of "units of labor," which is an abstraction of the total quantity and quality of labor demanded. The demand for labor can be made more operational and measurable as a way of learning more about the demand side of labor markets.

Quantity Demanded
The basic way of examining labor demand is to collect and analyze data about employment patterns and distribution, and to estimate their future occurrence. More specific instances reflecting labor demand, such as job displacement and a specific employer's actions to manage its labor demand, can also be examined.

Industry   The distribution of employment by industry in 1975, 1990, and 2005 (projected) is shown in Exhibit 2.2. As can be seen, the goods-producing sector

EXHIBIT 2.2   Employment Projections, by Industry

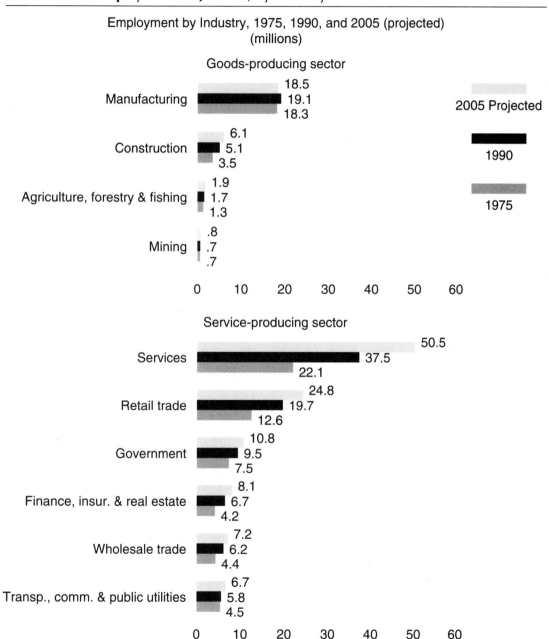

Employment by Industry, 1975, 1990, and 2005 (projected)
(millions)

Goods-producing sector

Manufacturing
18.5
19.1
18.3

Construction
6.1
5.1
3.5

Agriculture, forestry & fishing
1.9
1.7
1.3

Mining
.8
.7
.7

2005 Projected

1990

1975

0   10   20   30   40   50   60

Service-producing sector

Services
50.5
37.5
22.1

Retail trade
24.8
19.7
12.6

Government
10.8
9.5
7.5

Finance, insur. & real estate
8.1
6.7
4.2

Wholesale trade
7.2
6.2
4.4

Transp., comm. & public utilities
6.7
5.8
4.5

0   10   20   30   40   50   60

Source: Adapted from M. L. Carey and J. C. Franklin, ''Industry Output and Job Growth Continues Slow Into Next Century,'' *Monthly Labor Review*, 1991, 114 (11), p. 46.

has been stagnant or declining for the past two decades, while the service sector has been expanding. This expansion is projected to continue. There are also substantial industry differences within overall sector employment patterns. For example, manufacturing employment will actually decline by 2005, while there will be substantial growth in services, followed by growth in retail trade and government.

Occupation Employment by major occupational groups is shown in Exhibit 2.3. As can be seen, in 1990, the greatest number of occupations were in administrative support and services, followed (in order) by operator, fabricator, and laborer positions; professional specializations; precision production, craft and re-

---

EXHIBIT 2.3   Employment by Major Occupational Group

Employment by major occupational group, 1990 and 2005 (projected)

(Number in thousands)

Occupation	1990		2005		Percent Change	
	Number	Percent	Number	Percent	1975–90	1990–2005
Total, all occupations	122,573	100.0	147,191	100.0	37.4	20.1
Executive, administrative, and managerial	12,451	10.2	15,866	10.8	83.1	7.4
Professional specialty	15,800	12.9	20,907	14.2	59.9	32.3
Technicians and related support	4,204	3.4	5,754	3.9	75.7	36.9
Marketing and sales	14,088	11.5	17,489	11.9	55.1	24.1
Administrative support occupations, including clerical	21,951	17.9	24,835	16.9	33.9	13.1
Service occupations	19,204	15.7	24,806	16.9	36.1	29.2
Agricultural, forestry, fishing, and related occupations	3,506	2.9	3,665	2.5	−9.8	4.5
Precision production, craft, and repair	14,124	11.5	15,909	10.8	28.9	12.6
Operators, fabricators, and laborers ...	17,245	14.1	17,961	12.2	6.7	4.2

NOTE: The 1990 and 2005 employment data and the projected change 1990–2005 are derived from the industry-occupation employment matrices for each year. The data on 1975–90 percent change were derived from the Current Population Survey (CPS) because a comparable industry-occupation matrix for 1975 is not available. The CPS data represent estimates of employed persons and exclude the estimate of persons with more than one job that are included in the industry-occupation employment matrices. The CPS exclusion of dual jobholders affects the employment levels and trends of some occupational groups more than others. Therefore, the resulting comparisons of change between 1975–90 and 1990–2005 are only broadly indicative of trends.

Source: G. Silvertri and J. Lukasiewicz, "Occupational Employment Projections," *Monthly Labor Review*, 1991, 114 (11), p. 65.

pairs; marketing and sales; administration and management; technicians; and agricultural, forestry and fishing.

Projecting ahead to 2005, the data in Exhibit 2.3 indicate that occupations will have very different employment growth rates. The highest rates will be for technicians, professional specialists, and service providers. At the other extreme, there will be very low growth rates for operators, fabricators, and laborers, and for agricultural, forestry, and fishing workers.

More specific information on occupational employment distributions and growth is also available. Exhibits 2.4 and 2.5 show the data for specific occupations projected to have the largest job growth and largest job decline by 2005. Clearly, there will be some major occupational "winners" and "losers" over the next 10 to 15 years.

Employer Size   The vast majority of jobs and job growth occurs in small business. Two telling examples highlight this.[4] First, in 1991, the Fortune 500 employers (the top 500 private firms in terms of total sales) accounted for less than 11% of total nonfarm employment in the United States. This was down from a peak of 21% in 1969, and there is every reason to expect this decline to continue. Second, in 1991, 16% of jobs were found in businesses with ten or fewer employees.

Job Displacement   Jobs (and therefore employment opportunities) disappear as an employer responds to decreases in the demand for its goods and services. Survey data report the incidence of job displacement due to plant closings, employers going out of business, and layoffs without subsequent recall.[5] In 1984, there were 11.4 million such job displacements; this number had declined to 8.9 million in 1990. The incidence of job displacement also fell in manufacturing during this time period, but it increased in services. Thus, both employment and job displacement are increasing simultaneously in the services sector.

Specific Employer Actions   Employers engage in a variety of specific actions to manage their demand for labor besides employment expansion, contraction, and displacement. National data are hard to come by regarding these actions, and the numbers of people affected by them. Examples include "downsizing" and "restructuring," which can involve job creation, elimination, redesign, and reassignment all at the same time. Another example is "reengineering," which represents productivity improvements that increase the level of goods and services produced without any increase in labor input.[6] If employees work "harder" and "smarter," no new employees need be hired. Another example of reengineering is more flexible staffing patterns, which allow for rapid responses to changes in product demand and do not represent long-term commitments to employees. Illustrations of such "contingent staffing" include use of part-time and temporary workers, the incidence of which clearly appears to be increasing.[7]

EXHIBIT 2.4   Occupations with Largest Projected Job Growth

Occupations with the largest job growth, 1990–2005

(Number in thousands)

Occupation	Employment		Numerical Change	Percent Change
	1990	2005		
Salespersons, retail	3,619	4,506	887	24.5
Registered nurses	1,727	2,494	767	44.4
Cashiers	2,633	3,318	685	26.0
General office clerks	2,737	3,407	670	24.5
Truckdrivers, light and heavy	2,362	2,979	617	26.1
General managers and top executives	3,086	3,684	598	19.4
Janitors and cleaners, including maids and house cleaners	3,007	3,562	555	18.5
Nursing aides, orderlies, and attendants	1,274	1,826	552	43.4
Food counter, fountain, and related workers	1,607	2,158	550	34.2
Waiters and waitresses	1,747	2,196	449	25.7
Teachers, secondary school	1,280	1,717	437	34.2
Receptionists and information clerks	900	1,322	422	46.9
Systems analysts and computer scientists	463	829	366	78.9
Food preparation workers	1,156	1,521	365	31.6
Child care workers	725	1,078	353	48.8
Gardeners and groundskeepers, except farm	874	1,222	348	39.8
Accountants and auditors	985	1,325	340	34.5
Computer programmers	565	882	317	56.1
Teachers, elementary	1,362	1,675	313	23.0
Guards	883	1,181	298	33.7
Teacher aides and educational assistants	808	1,086	278	34.4
Licensed practical nurses	644	913	269	41.9
Clerical supervisors and managers	1,218	1,481	263	21.6
Home health aides	287	550	263	91.7
Cooks, restaurant	615	872	257	41.8
Maintenance repairers, general utility	1,128	1,379	251	22.2
Secretaries, except legal and medical	3,064	3,312	248	8.1
Cooks, short order and fast food	743	989	246	33.0
Stock clerks, sales floor	1,242	1,451	209	16.8
Lawyers	587	793	206	35.1

Source: G. Silvertri and J. Lukasiewicz, "Occupational Employment Projections," *Monthly Labor Review*, 1991, 114 (11), p. 65.

EXHIBIT 2.5   Occupations with Largest Projected Job Declines

Occupations with the largest job declines, 1990–2005

(Number in thousands)

Occupation	Employment		Numerical Change	Percent Change
	1990	2005		
Farmers	1,074	850	−224	−20.9
Bookkeeping, accounting, and auditing clerks	2,276	2,143	−133	−5.8
Child care workers, private household	314	190	−124	−39.5
Sewing machine operators, garment	585	469	−116	−19.8
Electrical and electronic assemblers	232	128	−105	−45.1
Typists and word processors	972	869	−103	−10.6
Cleaners and servants, private household	411	310	−101	−24.5
Farm workers	837	745	−92	−11.0
Electrical and electronic equipment assemblers, precision	171	90	−81	−47.5
Textile draw-out and winding machine operators and tenders	199	138	−61	−30.6
Switchboard operators	246	189	−57	−23.2
Machine forming operators and tenders, metal and plastic	174	131	−43	−24.5
Machine tool cutting operators and tenders, metal and plastic	145	104	−42	−28.6
Telephone and cable TV line installers and repairers	133	92	−40	−30.4
Central office and PBX installers and repairers	80	46	−34	−42.5
Central office operators	53	22	−31	−59.2
Statistical clerks	85	54	−31	−36.1
Packaging and filling machine operators and tenders	324	297	−27	−8.3
Station installers and repairers, telephone	47	21	−26	−55.0
Bank tellers	517	492	−25	−4.8
Lathe and turning machine tool setters and set-up operators, metal and plastic	80	61	−20	−24.4
Grinders and polishers, hand	84	65	−19	−22.5
Electromechanical equipment assemblers, precision	49	31	−18	−36.5
Grinding machine setters and set-up operators, metal and plastic	72	54	−18	−25.1
Service station attendants	246	229	−17	−7.1
Directory assistance operators	26	11	−16	−59.4
Butchers and meatcutters	234	220	−14	−5.9
Chemical equipment controllers, operators, and tenders	75	61	−14	−19.1
Drilling and boring machine tool setters and set-up operators, metal and plastic	52	39	−13	−25.6
Meter readers, utilities	50	37	−12	−24.8

Source: G. Silvertri and J. Lukasiewicz, ''Occupational Employment Projections,'' *Monthly Labor Review*, 1991, 114 (11), p. 65.

Quality Demanded

Qualitative characteristics (KSAOs, motivation) of employers' demand for labor are difficult to describe, given the paucity of data available. Surveys of employers' preferences regarding labor quality, and an attempt to develop a national taxonomy of skills necessary for jobs, provide a glimpse at patterns in this area.

Employer Preferences   A recent survey of more than 400 senior HR executives revealed a major concern with issues reflecting labor quality. Of particular salience for staffing was the "poor quality of education among new job applicants" that these executives reported. This factor was viewed as the second most important factor affecting their competitiveness, behind only "increased cost of health benefits."[8]

A more focused national survey of employers sought their opinions on the kinds of skills they felt needed enhancing in current and prospective employees. Presumably, these skills are of direct relevance to organizational goals and competitiveness. The results are shown in Exhibit 2.6. As can be seen, the top two skills needing enhancing are written and interpersonal skills. These are followed by customer service skills, basic computer literacy, relevant technical skills, organizational knowledge, and cross-cultural knowledge.

SCANS Report   The Department of Labor established a special commission (Secretary's Commission on Achieving Necessary Skills) to study the possibility of identifying a taxonomy of skills that would be applicable to jobs on a national basis. Such a taxonomy would represent a common way of describing jobs in terms of skill requirements, and it would make possible the development of skill measures that could then be used to gauge skill levels of the workforce. Employers could also use the taxonomy as a way of focusing on and developing their own qualitative demands for labor.

The commission presented such a skill taxonomy in the SCANS report.[9] The taxonomy contains two levels of skills—foundation skills (Exhibit 2.7) and competencies (Exhibit 2.8). The foundation skills involve the traditional basic skills, plus thinking and cognitive skills, and personal qualities. These core skills are prerequisites for the competencies, which pertain to resource, information, interpersonal, systems, and technology skills.

The foundation skills and competencies will be discussed in more detail in Chapter 5 (Job Analysis) where their possible incorporation into job analysis for purposes of establishing KSAO requirements for particular jobs is explored.

Labor Supply

Conceptually, the supply of labor is the number of "units of labor" offered by individuals at various compensation levels. This is reflected in the traditional,

EXHIBIT 2.6   Employer Opinions About Needed Skills Enhancement

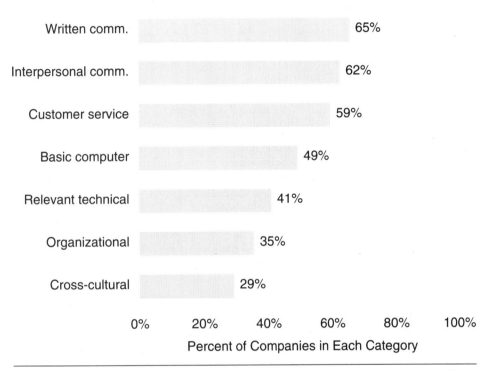

SKILLS NEEDING ENHANCEMENT
Among Current and Prospective Employees

Written comm.	65%
Interpersonal comm.	62%
Customer service	59%
Basic computer	49%
Relevant technical	41%
Organizational	35%
Cross-cultural	29%

0%   20%   40%   60%   80%   100%

Percent of Companies in Each Category

Source: Olsten Corporation, Westbury, NY. *Olsten Forum ™ on Human Resource Issues and Trends, Skills for Success: Training and Developing the Work Force of the 1990s*, p. 5. Reprinted with permission.

upward-sloping labor supply curve, which shows that as compensation increases, so do the number of units of labor offered by individuals in the labor market. At the more operational level, units of labor are studied and discussed in terms of both quantity of labor (numbers of workers) and quality of labor (KSAOs and motivation).

Quantity
Quantity of labor supplied is measured and reported periodically through a formal labor force survey process. The resulting data can then be combined with other data to study labor force trends.

EXHIBIT 2.7   SCANS Competencies and Skills: Foundation Skills

---

Basic Skills	Reading
	Writing
	Arithmetic
	Mathematics
	Listening
	Speaking
Thinking Skills	Creative thinking
	Decision making
	Problem solving
	Seeing things in the mind's eye
	Knowing how to learn
	Reasoning
Personal Qualities	Responsibility
	Self-esteem
	Social
	Self-management
	Integrity/honesty

Source: Secretary's Commission on Achieving Necessary Skills (SCANS), *Skills and Tasks for Jobs* (Washington, D.C.: U.S. Government Printing Office, 1992), pp. 1–5.

Measuring the Labor Force   The Bureau of Labor Statistics, housed in the Department of Labor, collects data through use of a monthly survey. It also conducts special labor force surveys, usually focusing on a labor force segment (e.g., older workers) or issue (e.g., part-time employment).

The monthly survey is the most fundamental tool for collecting labor force statistics. It is conducted among approximately 60,000 households throughout the United States each month, with 25% of the households being new inclusions each time. Based on their responses to a detailed set of questions, individuals are placed into certain categories for purposes of statistical calculation and reporting, using standard definitions of terms. The major categories and definitions used in this process are shown in Exhibit 2.9.

This exhibit shows that each individual is placed into one of four categories—employed, unemployed, not in the labor force, or institutionalized and/or less than 16 years of age. Though the definitions for each category are seemingly straightforward, there is a bit of fuzziness to them. For example, the line between being unemployed and not in the labor force (such as with unemployed workers who have become so discouraged in their job search that they quit looking for work) is a fine one.

Using the nomenclature shown in Exhibit 2.8, labor force statistics are reported on a monthly basis (the monthly unemployment rate has become a "hot" number

EXHIBIT 2.8   SCANS Competencies and Skills: Competencies

Resources	Allocates time
	Allocates money
	Allocates material and facility resources
	Allocates human resources
Information	Acquires and evaluates information
	Organizes and maintains information
	Interprets and communicates information
	Uses computers to process information
Interpersonal	Participates as a member of a team
	Teaches others
	Serves clients/customers
	Exercises leadership
	Negotiates to arrive at a decision
	Works with cultural diversity
Systems	Understands systems
	Monitors and corrects performance
	Improves and designs systems
Technology	Selects technology
	Applies technology to task
	Maintains and troubleshoots technology

Source: Secretary's Commission on Achieving Necessary Skills (SCANS), *Skills and Tasks for Jobs* (Washington, D.C.: U.S. Government Printing Office, 1992), pp. 1–5.

for the media to report and mull over). These data are also aggregated and reported on an annual basis. Examples of the annual figures for 1991 and 1992 are shown in Exhibit 2.10. The civilian noninstitutionalized population was just under 200 million, and, of those, about 66% participated in the labor force in both years. The unemployment rate jumped from 6.7% to 7.4% during that period. Both rates are considered high by historical standards.

Labor Force Trends   Three labor force trends have particular relevance for staffing organizations. These are the slow rate of labor force growth, increased demographic diversity, and growth of the contingent work force.

Labor force growth is slowing, going from an annual growth rate of around 2% in the early 1990s to a projected rate of 1% by the year 2005. There are increasingly fewer new entrants to the labor force. This trend, coupled with the severe KSAO deficiencies that many of the new entrants will have, creates major adaptation problems for organizations.[10] Part of their response to the impending labor shortage will likely be a staffing one. It will involve aggressive and targeted re-

---

EXHIBIT 2.9   Categories and Definitions for Labor Force Statistics

---

A. Categories

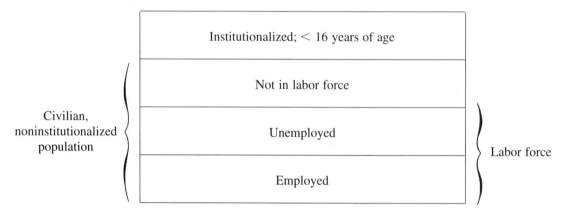

B. Definitions
  1. Employed—worked for pay one or more hours during survey week; temporarily absent from regular job; self-employed.
  2. Unemployed—no work during survey week; available for work; looked for work in last four weeks.
  3. Not in labor force—retired; homemaker; attending school; long-term illness; discouraged from seeking work because of personal or job-market factors; voluntarily idle.
  4. Institutionalized—inmate of penal or mental institution, sanitarium, home for aged, infirm, or needy; member of armed forces in U.S.
  5. Unemployment rate—percentage of labor force unemployed.
  6. Labor force participation rate—percentage of civilian noninstitutionalized population in the labor force.

---

cruitment for the relatively few qualified workers, coupled with increased starting pay rates and other job rewards. Moreover, once these new entrants have been hired, the organization will have to focus its attention on their retention.

Demographically, the labor force has become more diverse, and this trend will continue. The data in Exhibit 2.11 clearly show this. If current demographic levels are extrapolated to the year 2005, it can be seen that the composition of the labor force will include (a) fewer men and more women, (b) fewer whites, (c) more Blacks, Asians, and Hispanics, (d) fewer younger (16–24) workers, and (e) more older (55+) workers.

These demographic changes mean that organizations will be confronted with changing applicant populations. This will make it difficult for organizations to recruit who, and how, they did in the past. And with this increased diversity, organ-

EXHIBIT 2.10   Labor Force Statistics for 1991 and 1992

	1991	1992
Civilian noninstitutionalized population	189.8	191.6
Civilian labor force	125.3	127.0
participation rate	66.0%	66.3%
Employed	116.9	117.6
Employment-population ratio	61.6%	61.4%
Unemployed	8.4	9.4
Unemployment rate	6.7%	7.4%
Not in labor force	64.5	64.6

Note: Numbers in millions

Source: U.S. Department of Labor, *Monthly Labor Review*, 1993, 116 (5), p. 85.

izations may have to provide more diverse sets of job rewards in order to attract and retain those recruited. In addition, staffing efforts will have to be supplemented with actions designed to enhance the cultural and attitudinal assimilation of new entrants into the workforce. Organizations are now experimenting with what are called ''diversity programs'' to achieve this objective.

The contingent workforce is comprised of part-time and temporary employees, as well as self-employed individuals who work for organizations as independent contractors. Full-time, permanent employees are called the core workforce. There has been, and will continue to be, growth in the contingent workforce, and thus, decline in the size of the core workforce.[11]

The increased use of contingent workers provides organizations the flexibility they need to respond to new competitive standards. The mix of core and contingent workers, however, must be carefully thought through in HR and staffing planning.[12] The core may be restricted to workers with critical, difficult-to-find KSAOs, as well as those who occupy key jobs and are difficult to replace. On the other hand, contingent workers may be used for jobs with relatively low KSAOs and/or generic KSAOs that are not organization- or industry-specific.

Quality

Using the person/job matching model, the quality of labor may be thought of in KSAO and motivation terms. Each person possesses a bundle of KSAOs and motivation, and the labor force is nothing more than an aggregation of these individual bundles. The issue for study is what we know about these collective bundles that help us make characterizations about labor supply quality.

Ideally, we would have standard classifications or taxonomies of KSAOs and motivation, and measures to accompany them. We could then periodically survey

EXHIBIT 2.11   Labor Force Demographics: Current and Projected

Civilian labor force by sex, age, race, and Hispanic origin, 1975, 1990, and 2005

(Numbers in millions)

	Level			Change		Percent Distribution			Annual Growth Rate	
	1975	1990	2005	1975–90	1990–2005	1975	1990	2005	1975–90	1990–2005
Total, 16 years and over	93.8	124.8	150.7	31.0	25.9	100.0	100.0	100.0	1.9	1.3
Men, 16 years and over	56.3	68.2	79.3	11.9	11.1	60.0	54.7	52.6	1.3	1.0
Women, 16 years and over	37.5	56.6	71.4	19.1	14.8	40.0	45.3	47.4	2.8	1.6
16 to 24	22.6	21.3	24.0	−1.4	2.8	24.1	17.0	16.0	−0.4	0.8
25 to 54	56.9	88.1	104.6	31.3	16.4	60.6	70.6	69.4	3.0	1.1
55 and over	14.3	15.4	22.1	1.1	6.7	15.3	12.3	14.7	0.5	2.4
White, 16 years and over	82.8	107.2	125.8	24.3	18.6	88.3	85.9	83.4	1.7	1.1
Black, 16 years and over	9.3	13.5	17.8	4.2	4.3	9.9	10.8	11.8	2.5	1.9
Asian and other, 16 years and over (1)	1.7	4.1	7.2	2.4	3.1	1.8	3.3	4.8	6.2	3.8
Hispanic, 16 and over (2)		9.6	16.8		7.2		7.7	11.1	(3) 5.9	3.8

(1) The "Asian and other" group includes (a) Asians and Pacific Islanders, and (b) American Indians and Alaskan Natives. The historic data are derived by subtracting "Black" from the "Black and other" group; projections are made directly.

(2) Persons of Hispanic origin may be of any race. Data for Hispanics are not available before 1980.

(3) This growth rate is from 1976 to 1990.

Source: Adapted from H. N. Fullerton, Jr., "Labor Force Projections: The Baby Boom Moves On," *Monthly Labor Review*, 1991, 114 (11), p. 36.

KSAO and motivation characteristics of the labor force to learn about and track labor supply quality. Unfortunately, we do not have such taxonomies and measurements. Hence, we gather data in limited kinds of ways and use the results to try to derive some quality indications. We have some such data on KSAOs, and virtually none on motivation.

KSAOs   The most common, and broad, indicator of labor force quality is educational attainment level. Such data for 1992 are shown in Exhibit 2.12. It can be seen that about 27% of the population 25 and older had attained a college degree or higher, while 12% had less than a high school diploma; the remainder had education attainment levels within this band. The data also show differences in attainment level among whites, blacks, and hispanics, with whites generally having the highest level of formal education.

A second, related indication of labor force quality pertains to literacy. Here, studies of new labor force entrants suggest problems for employers. In these studies, literacy is defined and measured in terms of a capacity to deal with

1. prose or texts such as newspapers, articles, and stories
2. documents such as tables, charts, maps, and indexes
3. quantitative data embedded in prose or documents

EXHIBIT 2.12   Educational Attainment Levels of the Labor Force

Percent distribution of the labor force by educational attainment, race, and Hispanic origin, 1992 annual averages

(Numbers in millions)

Educational Attainment	Total	White	Black	Hispanic Origin
Total, 25 years and over	106,530	91,242	11,422	7,993
Percent	100.0	100.0	100.0	100.0
Less than a high school diploma	12.4	11.6	18.5	39.1
High school graduates, no college	35.7	35.6	39.4	29.5
Some college, no degree	18.0	18.0	19.3	14.3
Associate degree	7.4	7.5	7.0	5.6
College graduates, total	26.5	27.3	15.8	11.5
Bachelor's degree	17.2	17.7	10.9	7.8
Master's degree	6.5	6.7	3.9	2.5
Professional degree	1.8	1.9	.5	.8
Doctoral degree	1.1	1.1	.4	.4

Source: U.S. Department of Labor, *News*, July 10, 1993.

Scores for these skills were obtained for multiple samples and then divided into five categories measuring level of literacy. One-half to one-third of the new entrants fell into the bottom two categories.[13]

Results of education and literacy level studies are compared with what are felt to be the KSAO requirements of current or future jobs. These comparisons converge on a common conclusion, namely that there is a KSAO gap or skill shortage among workers, and that the gap will widen.[14] A recent example of such a conclusion is drawn from a massive study on workforce skill preparation by the Department of Labor.[15]

> The kinds of skills that people need to have—even if they hold the same job as before—have changed in the direction of higher skills, and more of them. The competitive work-place of today—regardless of the product or service—is a high skill environment designed around technology and people who are technically competent. Assembly line workers must now understand their work as part of a much larger whole. Many workers must be comfortable with computer-numerically-controlled equipment. Front-line supervisors must confront tasks like budgeting and fiscal planning; clerical and other support personnel must handle complex word-processing and spreadsheet functions. Relatively few of these workers are likely to have graduated from college, while not long ago most of those skills would have been demanded only of the college-educated.

Motivation   Direct data on the motivational levels of workers in the labor force are virtually nonexistent. Development of such measures presents thorny questions pertaining to definitions of motivational goals (e.g., performance, attendance, retention of workers) and measures of motivation (e.g., self-reporting; behavioral indicators such as productivity, attendance record, length of service).

Compounding these problems is a general recognition that levels of motivation among workers are very much a function of the work environment they are part of. Motivation is thus not a hard-and-fast, stable characteristic or some general energy level that individuals maintain over extended periods of time. Measurements of motivation, if they could be made, would thus be very unreliable and depend upon the samples from which they are drawn.

Implications for Staffing   Our knowledge of labor force quality is limited. We have very limited KSAO, and no motivational, measures that are gathered from workers across the labor force. Nor do workers have the equivalent of a generic KSAO or motivation certificate that they can use to ''represent'' their KSAOs and motivation to employers during their job search. Consequently, the organization must rely, to a considerable extent, on its own resources to become knowledgeable about the quality of its labor supply, and then act on that knowledge. Indeed, doing so is at the heart of staffing systems.

Recruitment activities help focus the organization on identifying and notifying potentially qualified segments of the labor force about employment needs and opportunities. Once identified, these applicants must be attracted to the organization through knowledge provided by the organization of specific job requirements and rewards, and then enter the applicant flow. Once a part of that flow, the organization must begin to assess the applicants' KSAOs and motivation, which is the major purpose of selection activities. Following that, hiring decisions must be made on the basis of the information gathered.

In all of these ways, the organization takes the initiative in attracting and assessing applicants from the labor force. It is through these staffing activities that individuals in the labor force become matched with jobs in the organization. Without specific staffing activities, person/job matches would likely be sporadic, chance-driven occurrences.

LABOR UNIONS

Labor union members are found across the spectrum in craft, production, professional, technical, clerical, transportation, maintenance, and sales jobs, as well as others. Managerial and supervisory employees, by law, are not permitted to be union members since they are involved in the establishment and administration of job requirements and rewards. If they were union members, they would have a conflict between allegiance to the union and their employer. Currently, about 15.8% of the labor force is unionized; the rates are 11.5% and 36.7% in the private and public sectors, respectively.[16]

Labor unions themselves are legally recognized and protected organizations whose purpose is to organize and to represent workers in matters affecting the employment relationship. It is the representation as opposed to organizing purpose of unions that is of most relevance to staffing organizations. Representation involves the establishment of the terms and conditions that will govern the employment relationship. It thus directly affects job requirements and rewards, as well as the person/job matching process.

Those effects are felt and expressed through provisions found in the labor contract. In terms of staffing, these provisions pertain to general characteristics of labor contracts, contract negotiation, contract clauses, and contract administration.

Labor Contracts

A labor contract is a legally enforceable, binding agreement between the organization and the union that represents the covered workers. It contains a set of terms and conditions that both parties have agreed to abide by during the duration of the contract. Those terms and conditions

1. apply to all covered workers
2. are to be uniform in their application to all workers
3. are the only terms and conditions permissible between employer and employees
4. may not be unilaterally changed by either party
5. are in effect for the duration of the contract

For management, the impact of a labor contract is twofold. First, it standardizes terms and conditions of employment, making them uniform for all covered employees. The contract is thus a collective one, and cannot be replaced or supplemented by individual contracts between employees and the organization. Second, the contract explicitly restricts management authority and flexibility. Management cannot unilaterally establish or change terms and conditions of employment. The labor contract thus establishes, and "locks in," many job requirements and rewards.

Contract Negotiation

Various federal and state laws govern collective bargaining and the labor-management relationship. Under those laws both parties generally have a mutual obligation to bargain in good faith over wages, hours, and other terms and conditions of employment.

As the law is interpreted, there are three types of issues that fall in the area of "terms and conditions"—those that are mandatory, those that are permissible, and those that are prohibited.[17] Mandatory issues include wages and hours as well as any issues regarding practices that have a direct and immediate effect on members' jobs and are strongly determined by labor cost factors. Prohibited issues are ones that labor and management are statutorily prohibited from bargaining over. Permissible issues are those that are neither mandatory nor prohibited. As regards staffing, most issues are mandatory subjects of bargaining because of their direct impact on jobs and labor costs.

Contract Clauses Affecting Staffing

Because of the mandatory nature of most staffing issues, contract clauses are negotiated for a wide array of staffing practices.[18] Several of the most prominent of these are discussed here.

Management Rights

A management rights clause specifies what rights management has to act unilaterally without prior consultation or negotiation with the union. Such a clause is found in almost every labor contract.

The clause may be a so-called savings clause, which says that management saves or retains all rights (including any regarding staffing) that are not explicitly covered by the contract. Or, the clause may contain explicit restrictions on management rights in certain areas. Examples of such areas are subcontracting, supervisory performance of union members' jobs, introduction of technological change, and plant shutdowns or relocations. All of these areas clearly pertain to matters having strong staffing overtones, particularly regarding labor demand.

Jobs and Job Structures

Individual job tasks and job titles are negotiable. An organization must decide what an electrician does, and whether it wants to use that title to describe a job. Also negotiable are job structures involving lines of task demarcation among jobs (e.g., does the electrician or carpenter rip out old wiring?), and internal mobility paths among jobs (into which jobs can someone be transferred or promoted?). Results of negotiations on jobs and job structures establish the structural features of the organization's internal labor market.

Recently, some organizations have tried to negotiate sweeping revisions in their contracts on matters relating to jobs and job structures. The reason for this is that jobs and structures had been too restrictive, giving management little flexibility in hiring, work assignments, and job transfers and promotions. For example, the GM Saturn automobile manufacturing plant, in order to create flexibility, has only one broad job classification—''operating technician''—instead of many narrow ones, for all nonskilled workers, and five job classifications for skilled trades workers. This is in comparison with the dozens of job classifications found in other GM plants. These job classifications for both Saturn and other GM plants are incorporated into the labor contracts between GM and the United Automobile Workers.[19]

External Staffing

Normally, external staffing is not an important topic of negotiation, and labor contracts are relatively void of contract clauses pertaining to it. The reason for this is that, by law, requiring union membership as a condition of employment (''closed shop'' practices) is prohibited, except in certain narrow circumstances. With this restriction, unions are relatively indifferent as to whom management hires, and how it goes about doing that. Unions do not want to negotiate about the types of people that management must hire, nor would management want to do this.

Occasionally, there will be contract clauses pertaining to external staffing. There may be a clause requiring a preference for hiring people in the local geographic area or in the industry (e.g., by contract clause, the new Saturn automobile manufacturing plant was staffed primarily by GM employees from other plants or on layoff). In other instances, the union may have a direct hand in the administration of the staffing system, including the making of selection decisions. This occurs in referral or hiring hall arrangements (common in construction), as well as through joint labor-management apprenticeship committees.

Internal Staffing

Unions are extremely active in negotiating and administering contract clauses pertaining to internal staffing. The nature of jobs and job rewards, and access to them, are matters of great concern to their membership. Specific contract clauses pertaining to job postings, lines of movement, and seniority are of great relevance to internal staffing.

Job Posting   Many contracts contain provisions requiring the posting of job vacancies, as well as specifying procedures for applying for those vacancies. Job posting creates a very open internal mobility system, one that allows employees an active role in gathering information about vacancies and deciding whether to apply for them.

Lines of Movement   Lateral and upward lines of movement among jobs, and the rules and procedures for governing that movement, receive considerable attention from both labor and management. These transfer and promotion systems contain plenty of grist for the negotiating mill. Union leadership and management must decide upon the operational or procedural characteristics of the internal labor market. For example: To which other jobs are employees eligible to move? Will there be restrictions upon movement by department, function, shift, or location of facility? Who will be eligible for job moves, and what factors will be taken into account in making promotion and transfer decisions? This latter question raises important seniority concerns.

Seniority   Seniority clauses in contracts treat both definitional and decision-making issues. They lay out when seniority begins (e.g., date of hire or date reporting for work); what happens when seniority is interrupted (e.g., due to medical leave or layoff); in what way one builds up seniority and may exercise seniority rights (department, division, plant, organization); and whether seniority may be carried across the normal seniority unit (e.g., from one department to another). Answers to these types of questions are negotiated and incorporated into contract clauses. The resultant clauses may create seniority calculation questions, and employees will want to know exactly how much seniority they have. In response, the contract may also contain a clause requiring posting of seniority lists or rosters.

In terms of seniority and decision making, the basic issue is what role seniority will play in transfer and promotion decisions and how much weight will be accorded seniority as opposed to other qualifications. Typically, a contract clause will specify seniority's weight.

Contract Administration

Terms of the contract need to be administered during its duration. This means addressing problems of interpretation and application of contract clauses. When interpretation and application problems arise, normally management and labor will attempt to handle and resolve them informally. Should they not be successful, there will, in all likelihood, be a grievance/arbitration process specified in the labor contract to which they can turn.[20] That process will be a formal one, specifying the steps that must be followed to resolve the grievance. Thus, aspects of the organization's staffing system are open not only to bargaining, but to grievance as well. Both of these facts restrict management's discretion and flexibility in staffing.

SUMMARY

Economic conditions are comprised of general economic forces that establish the overall economic environment in which the organization must function. That environment, in turn, affects the rate and direction of job growth. A positive rate of growth creates a positive impact on the movement of people into, within, and out of organizations. Staffing activities exist to anticipate and manage the "people flow" that comes about from job growth.

Labor markets are the external arena in which labor demand and supply forces interact. Labor demand may be measured along quantity and quality (KSAO and motivation) dimensions. Quantitative data show distribution and trends of labor movement by occupation, industry, and employer size, as well as in terms of job displacement. Anecdotal evidence shows specific actions employers take to manage their labor demand, such as restructuring, reengineering, and reliance on contingent workers. Qualitatively, relatively little is known about labor demand as it pertains to specific KSAOs. There is a general sense, however, that KSAO requirements of jobs are on the rise.

On the supply side, results of periodic labor force surveys provide solid numerical information about the labor force. The data show numbers of people employed, unemployed, not in the labor force, and institutionalized and under 16 years of age; these permit calculation of unemployment and labor force participation rates. Knowledge of qualitative characteristics of the labor force is sparse, except for educational attainment levels and literacy. It is generally perceived that KSAO levels of the labor force are low, relative to demand, thus creating a skills gap between ideal and actual employees. With such limited knowledge of qualities in the labor force, staffing activities have a crucial role to play in helping the organization identify, attract, assess, and select individuals who are most likely to result in effective person/job matches.

Labor unions affect staffing activities through their role as the employees' representative to negotiate and administer labor contracts. Contained in these contracts are the terms and conditions of employment that will govern the employment relationship for all represented employees over the life of the contract. Of particular importance to staffing are clauses pertaining to management rights, jobs and job structures, external staffing, and especially internal staffing. The contract also contains provisions for a grievance/arbitration process to resolve problems of interpretation and application of these and all other contract clauses.

DISCUSSION QUESTIONS

1. Think of an organization you have worked for and describe how economic conditions have influenced its staffing activities (Hint: use Exhibit 2.1 to help you).

2. What are some of the reasons there will be occupational "winners" (those who experience employment growth) and "losers" (those who experience employment decline) over the next decade?

3. Describe various ways you have experienced or seen a previous or current employer adjust staffing practices in order to best manage its labor demand.

4. How will a more demographically diverse workforce influence the person/job matching process in organizations?

5. Using the person/job matching model, why do unions seek to negotiate over job posting, lines of movement, and seniority?

ENDNOTES

1. A. P. Carevale, *America and the New Economy* (Washington, D.C.: American Society for Training and Development, U.S. Department of Labor, 1991), pp. 24–33.

2. A. P. Carevale, *America and the New Economy,* p. iii.

3. A. S. Richter and Associates, *Priorities for Competitive Advantage* (New York: Towers Perrin, 1992), pp. 11, 16.

4. D. Crispell, "People Patterns," *Wall Street Journal,* Aug. 6, 1993, p. B1; D. Hale, "For New Jobs, Help Small Business," *Wall Street Journal,* Aug. 10, 1992, p. B1.

5. M. Podgursky, "The Industrial Structure of Job Displacement, 1979–89," *Monthly Labor Review,* 1992, 115 (9), pp. 17–25.

6. A. Ehrbar, "Re-Engineering Gives Firms New Efficiency, Workers the Pink Slip," *Wall Street Journal,* Mar. 16, 1993, p. A1; M. Selz, "Firms Find Ways to Grow Without Expanding Staffs," *Wall Street Journal,* Mar. 18, 1993, p. B1; G. P. Zachary and B. Ortega, "Workplace Revolution Boosts Productivity at Cost of Job Security," *Wall Street Journal,* Oct. 1993, p. A1.

7. C. Ansberry, "Workers Are Forced to Fake More Jobs With Few Benefits," *Wall Street Journal,* Mar. 11, 1993, p. A1; R. Belous, "How Human Resource Systems Adjust to the Shift Toward Contingent Workers," *Monthly Labor Review,* 1989, 112 (3), pp. 7–12; C. Tilly, "Reasons for the Continuing Growth of Part-Time Employment," *Monthly Labor Review,* 1991, 114 (3), pp. 10–18.

8. A. A. Johnson and F. Linden, *Availability of a Quality Workforce* (New York: The Conference Board, 1992), p. 14.

9. Secretary's Commission on Achieving Necessary Skills (SCANS), *Skills and Tasks for Jobs* (Washington, D.C.: U.S. Government Printing Office, 1992).

10. W. B. Johnston, "The Coming Labor Shortage," *Journal of Labor Research,* 1992, 13, pp. 1–10.

11. R. Belous, "How Human Resource Systems Adjust to the Shift Toward Contingent Workers."

12. V. Scarpello and S. Motowidlo, "Workforce 2000: Assumptions, Trends, and Staffing Implications," *IRRA Proceedings,* 1989, pp. 518–526.

13. A. Packer, "Skill Deficiencies: Problems, Policies and Prospects," *Journal of Labor Research,* 1993, 14, pp. 227–247.

14. A. Packer, "Skill Deficiencies: Problems, Policies and Prospects."

15. U.S. Department of Labor, *Economic Change and The American Workforce* (Washington, D.C.: authors, 1992), p. 3.

16. United States Department of Labor, "Union Members in 1992," *News,* Feb. 8, 1993.

17. J. A. Fossum, *Labor Relations: Development, Structure, Process,* fifth ed. (Homewood, IL: Irwin, 1992), pp. 180–181.

18. Bureau of National Affairs, *Basic Patterns in Union Contracts,* thirteenth ed. (Washington, D.C.: author, 1992).

19. B. Geber, "Saturn's Grand Experiment," *Training,* June 1992, pp. 27–33.

20. J. A. Fossum, *Labor Relations: Development, Structure, Process,* pp. 408–434.

CHAPTER THREE

Laws and Regulations

L aws and regulations have assumed an importance of major proportions in the process of staffing organizations. Virtually all aspects of staffing are subject to their influence. No organization can or should ignore provisions of the law; in this case, ignorance truly is not bliss.

This chapter begins by introducing the employment relationship as a voluntary contract between employer and employee that is a logical extension or outgrowth of the person/job match. For many reasons, the employment relationship has become increasingly regulated. The need for this control, as well as the major sources of laws and regulations to accomplish it, is explained.

Equal employment opportunity and affirmative action (EEO/AA) laws and regulations have become dominant in the eyes of most who are concerned with staffing organizations. This dominance is illustrated first by a general discussion of EEO, AA, and quotas, as well as the two approaches for bringing forth and resolving discrimination charges. Following that, the general provisions of five major EEO/AA laws are summarized, along with indications of how these laws are administered and enforced.

For these same five laws, their specific (and numerous) provisions regarding staffing are then presented in detail. It is within this presentation that the true scope, complexity, and impact of the laws as regards to staffing become known.

Numerous regulations and guidelines have been issued to assist in interpretation, implementation, and enforcement of these five laws. The most prominent are the Uniform Guidelines on Employee Selection Procedures, Revised Order No. 4, and the Employment Regulations of the Americans With Disabilities Act. Each of these is introduced (their full text is found in Appendixes A, B, and C). Also, numerous information sources about EEO/AA laws and regulations are presented.

Attention then turns to other staffing laws and regulations. These involve a myriad of federal laws, state and local laws, and civil service laws and regulations. These laws, like federal EEO/AA ones, have major impacts on staffing activities.

Finally, the chapter concludes with an indication that each of the chapters that follows this one has a separate section, ''Legal Issues,'' at the end of it. In these sections, specific topics and applications of the law are presented. Their intent is to provide guidance and examples (not legal advise per se) regarding staffing practices that are permissable, impermissible, and required.

THE EMPLOYMENT RELATIONSHIP

The person/job matching process culminates in the establishment of an employment relationship between employer and employee. That relationship is defined formally through the establishment of an employment contract that is entered into voluntarily by the two parties and subject to numerous laws and regulations that affect and define the permissible and impermissible aspects of that relationship.

Before those laws and regulations are examined in detail, however, it is helpful to begin with a general elaboration on the nature of the employment relationship.

In this section, three topics regarding the employment relationship are discussed. First, the nature of employment contracts is indicated. Second, the need for laws to govern the employment relationship is treated, with an emphasis on the protective role of these laws for both employee and employer. Third, various sources of laws and regulations are identified.

Employment Contracts

The employment relationship that results from the person/job matching process is a contractual one, as shown in Exhibit 3.1. The employer and employee negotiate and agree upon the terms and conditions that will define and govern their relationship. Their formal agreement represents an *employment contract,* the terms and conditions of which represent the promises and expectations of the parties (job requirements and rewards, and KSAOs and motivation).[1] Over time, the initial contract may be modified due to changes in requirements or rewards of the current

EXHIBIT 3.1   Matching Process, Employment Contract, and Employment Relationships

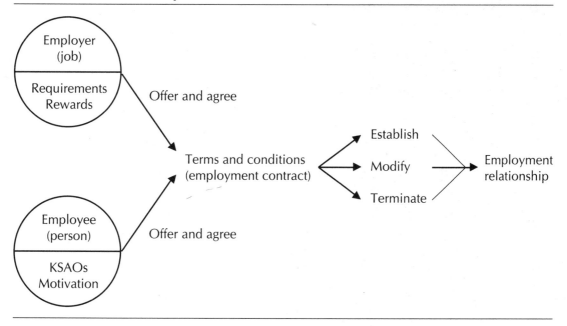

job or to employee transfer or promotion. The contract may also be terminated by either party, thus ending the employment relationship.

Employment contracts come in a variety of styles. They may be written or oral (both types are legally enforceable), and their specificity may vary from extensive to "bare bones." In some instances, where the contract is written, terms and conditions are described in great detail. Examples of such contracts are collective bargaining agreements and contracts for professional athletes, entertainers, and upper-level executives. At the other extreme, the contract may be little more than some simple oral promises about the job, such as promises about wages and hours, and agreed to on the basis of a handshake.

Keeping in mind two important employment contract issues is helpful to understanding the critical importance of the contractual relationship. The first issue is that of employment-at-will, which pertains to the right of the parties to terminate the employment relationship. The second issue is workplace torts, which deals with breaches of legal duty by the employer when establishing or modifying the initial employment relationship.

Employment-at-Will

One of the key issues about an employment contract is its length or duration.[2] A *set-term contract* has a definite duration and expiration date; however, it may be terminated prior to the expiration date for reasons such as "just cause" or "failure to perform."

An *indeterminate-term contract* has no expiration date or other limitation on its duration. This type of contract defines an employment relationship known as employment-at-will. Here, both the employer and the employee serve at the will of the other, and either may terminate the relationship at will, without penalty. Thus, the employer may fire the employee at will, and the employee may quit at will.

Most employment contracts are of the at-will variety. As such, they are governed by principles of common law as described later in this chapter. These contracts afford considerable freedom and discretion to both the employer and employee with regard to establishing and maintaining the employment relationship.

Workplace Torts

Another common law issue involving employment contracts and the employment relationship is that of *workplace torts*.[3] A tort is a civil wrong, meaning a violation of a duty by the employer that leads to harm or damages suffered by others, usually employees or customers. One example of a tort in staffing is the practice of *fraud and misrepresentation* by the employer. An employer may intentionally lie or make misleading statements about an employment situation when communicating terms and conditions of the job to a job applicant. The employer thus violates a duty to be truthful in the presentation of information. The misled applicant, who accepts a job offer, only to subsequently find out that the job is not as it was presented, might then file suit against the employer.

Another example of a workplace tort involves *negligent hiring* practices by the employer. Here, the employer hires incompetent, unsafe, dangerous, or untrustworthy employees, thereby violating a duty to protect employees and customers against unreasonable and foreseeable risk of harm. Actual examples of negligent hiring cases are described in the following headlines: "Hospital Settles $3.5 Million Suit for Negligently Hiring Kidney Transplant Coordinator," "Jury Awards $500,000 Against Employer Who Failed to Check Driving Record of Unsafe Employee," "Twenty Minute Interview of Delivery Person May Be Inadequate to Fulfill Supermarket's Duty of Care to Customers," and "Employer of Ex-Offenders Cannot Escape Liability by Relying on State-Licensed Agency to Screen Applicants."[4]

These workplace torts examples clearly indicate that staffing decisions have implications that far transcend employer concerns with the person/job match as a way of influencing HR outcomes, such as employee performance and satisfaction. Such decisions create the possibility of subsequent employer liability for employees acquired and retained through the organization's staffing system. This fact serves to heighten the importance the organization should attach to utilizing an effective matching process.

Need for Laws and Regulations

Establishment and maintenance of the employment relationship involves exercising discretion on the part of both the employer and the employee. Broadly speaking, laws affecting the employment relationship spring from a need to define the scope of permissible discretion and place limits on it. Their purpose is to create a reasonable balance of power between employer and employee, as well as to provide protections for each.

Balance of Power

Entering into and maintaining the employment relationship involves negotiating issues of power.[5] The employer has something desirable to offer the employee (a job with certain requirements and rewards), and the employee has something to offer the employer (KSAOs and motivation). Both parties seek to use to their own advantage what they have to offer in establishing the terms and conditions of employment.

Usually, the employer has the upper hand in this power relationship because the employer has more to offer, and more control over what to offer, than does the employee. It is the employer who controls the creation of jobs; the definition of jobs in terms of requirements and rewards; access to those jobs via staffing

systems; movement of employees among jobs over time; and ultimately, the retention or termination of employees. While employees participate in these processes and decisions to varying degrees, it is seldom as an equal or a partner of
the employer. Employment laws and regulations exist, in part, to reduce or limit
the employer's power in the employment relationship. Laws pertaining to wages,
hours, equal employment opportunity, and so forth, all seek to limit employer
discretion in the establishment of the terms and conditions of employment.

Protection of Employees

Laws and regulations seek to provide specific protections to employees that they
could conceivably, though improbably, acquire individually in an employment
contract.[6] These protections pertain to employment standards, individual workplace rights, and consistency of treatment.

Employment Standards   Employment standards usually represent minimum acceptable terms and conditions of employment. Examples of these standards include
minimum wage laws, overtime pay requirements, and safety and health standards.
Sometimes employment standards represent maximums, such as maximum permissible hours of work for minors and maximum permissible levels of exposure
to work environment elements (e.g., noise and toxic substances).

Individual Rights   Laws and regulations provide employees with individual
rights that they could not acquire alone in a contract with their employers. An
example of these are the organizing and collective bargaining rights granted employees under the Railway Labor Act and the National Labor Relations Act. Another, more recent, example are civil rights protections afforded employees by the
various civil rights laws discussed in following sections.

A final example are the protections given employees through constraints that
have been developing on employment-at-will. These constraints place limits on
the right of the employer to unilaterally terminate the employment relationship.
Laws prohibit discharge on the basis of union preference, race, sex, disability, and
so forth. Common law also increasingly recognizes limits or exceptions to employment-at-will as the norm in employment contracts. For example, statements
about job security for employees in an employee handbook may be treated as an
implied contract that restricts the right of the employer to terminate employees at
will.

Consistency of Treatment   As the previous examples show, laws and regulations, in effect, provide guarantees of consistency of treatment among employees.
They constitute a constraint on the employer to treat employees differently from
one another in terms and conditions of employment and afford employees some
measure of procedural justice, or fairness in the process whereby decisions are

made about them. Hiring and promotion decisions, for example, cannot be made on the basis of protected employee characteristics (e.g., race, sex). Ensuring this in essence requires the employer to develop and implement standardized staffing systems (e.g., all job applicants receive the same interview and must provide the same biographical data about themselves).

Protection of Employers

While the preceding discussion suggests a general pro-employee tenor or slant to employment laws and regulations, employers also gain protections in the process.

Permissible/Impermissible Practices   Given the inherent fuzziness of the employment relationship and the ground rules surrounding it, laws and regulations provide guidance to employers as to what are permissible practices as well as impermissible practices. The Civil Rights Act, for example, not only forbids certain types of discrimination on the basis of race, color, religion, sex, and national origin, but also specifically mentions employment practices that are permitted. One of those practices, for example, is the use of professionally developed ability tests, a practice that has major implications for external and internal selection.

Administrative Predictability and Stability   New laws and regulations initially create uncertainty and turbulence for an employer. What do the laws mean, and exactly what do they require? Over time, these questions are clarified through many avenues—court decisions, policy statements from government agencies, informal guidance from enforcement officials, and networking with other employers. The result is increasing convergence upon what is required in order to comply with the laws. This allows the employer to implement needed changes, which then become standard operating procedure in staffing systems. In this manner, for example, affirmative action programs have developed and been incorporated into the administrative mainstream for many employers.

Sources of Laws and Regulations

There are numerous sources of law and regulation that govern the employment relationship. Exhibit 3.2 provides examples of these as they pertain to staffing. Each of these is commented on next.

Common Law

Common law, which has its origins in England, is court-made law, as opposed to law from other sources such as the state. It consists of the case-by-case decisions of the court, which determine over time permissible and impermissible practices, as well as their remedies. There is a heavy reliance in common law on the prec-

---

EXHIBIT 3.2   Sources of Laws and Regulations

SOURCE	EXAMPLES
Common law	Employment-at-will Workplace torts
Constitutional	Fifth Amendment Fourteenth Amendment
Statutory	Civil Rights Act Age Discrimination in Employment Act Americans With Disabilities Act Rehabilitation Act Immigration Reform and Control Act Immigration Act Employee Polygraph Protection Act State and local laws Civil service laws
Executive order	11246 (nondiscrimination under federal contracts)
Agencies	Equal Employment Opportunity Commission (EEOC) Department of Labor (DOL) Office of Federal Contract Compliance Programs (OFCCP) State Fair Employment Practice (FEP) agencies

---

edence established in previous court decisions. Each state develops and administers its own common law. Employment-at-will and workplace tort cases, for example, are treated at the state level.

Constitutional Law
Constitutional law is derived from the U.S. Constitution and its amendments. It supersedes any other source of law or regulation. Its major application is in the area of the rights of public employees, particularly their due process rights.

Statutory Law
Statutory law is derived from written statutes that are passed by legislative bodies. These bodies are federal (Congress), state (legislatures and assemblies), and local (municipal boards and councils). Legislative bodies may create, amend, and eliminate laws and regulations. They may also create agencies to administer and enforce the law.

Agencies
Agencies exist at the federal, state, and local level. Their basic charge is to interpret, administer, and enforce the law. At the federal level, the two major agencies

of concern to staffing are the Department of Labor (DOL) and the Equal Employment Opportunity Commission (EEOC). Housed within DOL are several separate units for administration of employment law, notably the Office of Federal Contract Compliance Programs (OFCCP).

Agencies rely heavily on written documents to perform their functions. These documents are variously referred to as rules, regulations, guidelines, and policy statements. Rules, regulations, and guidelines are published in the *Federal Register,* as well as incorporated into the Code of Federal Regulations (CFR), and have the weight of law. Policy statements are somewhat more benign in that they do not have the force of law. They do, however, represent the agency's official position on a point or question.

EEO/AA: PRELIMINARY ISSUES

The numerous and complex equal employment opportunity and affirmative action (EEO/AA) laws and regulations are major sources of influence on staffing. Understanding them requires familiarity first with some preliminary issues that set the context for the specifics of the laws and regulations.

EEO, AA, and Quotas

The terms equal employment opportunity (EEO), affirmative action (AA), and quotas are encountered frequently, and often lead to confusion. There are conceptual, semantic, and practical differences among these three terms as they apply to staffing.[7] What follows is a brief overview of the distinctions to help clarify their meaning and usage.

EEO

As applied to staffing, EEO refers to practices that are designed and used in a "facially neutral" manner, meaning that all applicants and employees are treated similarly without regard to protected characteristics such as race and sex. Consistent application of and adherence to these practices is thought to create an equal opportunity for everyone to obtain a job or promotion.

To illustrate, consider a simple example where an organization is filling a vacant position and uses both a written job knowledge test and an interview in assessing job applicants. Anyone is free to apply for the position, and all that do so will be given both the test and the interview. How well each performs on the test and in the interview determines who is hired. Thus, all applicants have an equal chance or opportunity to be considered for the job, and which applicant receives the job offer depends upon an unbiased assessment of applicants' job qualifications.

AA

AA requirements in staffing must be placed in the context of past practices that were discriminatory against minorities and women, as well as other groups. Through changing existing staffing practices and adding new ones, AA seeks to rectify the discriminatory effects of these past practices. In this sense, AA is less than completely facially neutral. AA may be voluntarily undertaken by an employer, without anyone "pointing a finger" at specific actions. AA may also be court-ordered, or agreed to, as a remedy for past actions that indeed were discriminatory.

Consider again the preceding staffing example, and assume that the staffing system has operated in the same way for many years. Several features of the system may have created potentially unequal employment opportunities for women and minorities, resulting in their being numerically underrepresented relative to their availability and qualifications in the labor market. For example, there may have been an outright refusal to recruit women and minorities, or the recruitment methods used—referrals from current, mostly male, employees—may have greatly favored male applicants. As another example, women and minorities may have scored poorly on the job knowledge test because of lack of access to the types of training and/or job experience necessary to acquire that job knowledge. Special affirmative actions, voluntary or court-imposed, seek to enhance the employment of women and minorities and help deal with these sorts of historical problems.[8]

What might these actions entail? The organization might undertake special recruiting methods, other than just employees' referral, to identify and attract women and minority applicants. Management might establish specific hiring goals and timetables for achieving those goals for women and minorities. The organization would make good faith efforts to meet the hiring goals and timetables. Also, the organization could place less weight on the job knowledge test when making hiring decisions and create a training program for new job entrants to provide them the types of job knowledge they need in order to perform effectively on the job.

Quotas

Quotas represent rigid hiring and promotion requirements that must be adhered to. Quotas do not leave staffing to the somewhat ill-defined concept of affirmative action; quotas focus on and demand staffing results.

If a quota staffing system were applied in the previous example, a hiring formula would be established that specifies the number or percentage of women and minorities to be hired so that their numerical representation in the workplace reflects the percentage of potentially qualified women and minorities in the population. Quota staffing systems of this kind are legally permissible as a judicial remedy for past discrimination. Though quotas may be sanctioned and/or imposed by the courts, there are limitations on their usage and features.[9] For example, the quota system must be only temporary, and abandoned once quotas have been reached.

Disparate Treatment and Disparate Impact

Claims of discrimination in staffing ultimately require evidence and proof, particularly as these charges pertain to the staffing system itself and its specific characteristics as it has operated in practice. Toward this end, there are two different avenues or paths to follow—disparate treatment and disparate impact.[10]

Disparate Treatment

Claims of disparate treatment involve allegations of intentional discrimination where it is alleged that the employer knowingly and deliberately discriminated against people on the basis of specific characteristics such as race or sex. Evidence for such claims may be of several sorts.

First, the evidence may be direct. It might, for example, involve reference to an explicit, written policy of the organization such as one stating that "women are not to be hired for the following jobs . . ."

The situation may not involve such blatant action, however, but may consist of what is referred to as a mixed motive. Here, both a prohibited characteristic (e.g., sex) and a legitimate reason (e.g., job qualifications) are mixed together to contribute to a negative decision about a person, such as a failure to hire or promote. If an unlawful motive, such as sex, plays any part in the decision, it is illegal, despite the presence of a lawful motive as well.

Finally, the discrimination may be such that evidence of a failure to hire or promote because of a protected characteristic must be inferred from several situational factors. Here, the evidence involves four factors:

1. The person belongs to a protected class.
2. The person applied for, and was qualified for, a job the employer was trying to fill.
3. The person was rejected despite being qualified.
4. The position remained open and the employer continued to seek applicants as qualified as the person rejected.

Most disparate treatment cases involve and require the use of these four factors to initially prove a charge of discrimination.

Disparate Impact

Disparate impact is also known as *adverse impact* and focuses on the effect of employment practices, rather than on the motive or intent underlying them. Accordingly, the emphasis here is on the need for direct evidence that, as a result of a protected characteristic, people are being adversely affected by a practice. Statistical evidence must be presented to support a claim of adverse impact.[11] Three types of statistical evidence may be used, and these are shown in Exhibit 3.3.

EXHIBIT 3.3 Types of Disparate Impact Statistics

A. FLOW STATISTICS

Definition:

Significant differences in selection rates between groups

Example

Job Category: Customer Service Representative

No. of Applicants		No. Hired		Selection Rate (%)	
Men	**Women**	**Men**	**Women**	**Men**	**Woman**
50	45	25	5	50%	11%

B. STOCK STATISTICS

Definition:

Underutilization of women or minorities relative to their availability in the relevant population

Example

Job Category: Management Trainee

Current Trainees (%)		Availability (%)	
Nonminority	**Minority**	**Nonminority**	**Minority**
90%	10%	70%	30%

C. CONCENTRATION STATISTICS

Definition:

Concentration of women or minorities in certain job categories

Example

	Job Category			
	Clerical	**Production**	**Sales**	**Managers**
% Men	3%	85%	45%	95%
% Women	97%	15%	55%	5%

Shown first in the exhibit are *applicant flow statistics,* which look at differences in selection rates (proportion of applicants hired) among different groups for a particular job. If the differences are large enough, this suggests that the effect of the selection system is discriminatory. In the example, the selection rate for men is .50 (or 50%) and for women it is .11 (or 11%), suggesting the possibility of discrimination.

A second type of statistical evidence, shown next in the exhibit, involves the use of *stock statistics.* Here, the percentage of women or minorities actually employed in a job category is compared with their availability in the relevant population. Relevant is defined in terms of such things as "qualified," "interested," or "geographic." In the example shown, there is a disparity in the percentage of minorities employed (10%) compared with their availability (30%), which suggests their underutilization.

The third type of evidence involves use of *concentration statistics.* Here, the percentages of women or minorities in various job categories are compared to see if women are concentrated in certain workforce categories. In the example shown, there is a concentration of women in clerical jobs (97%), a concentration of men in production (85%) and managerial (95%) jobs, and roughly equal concentrations of men and women in sales jobs (45% and 55%, respectively).

EEO/AA LAWS: GENERAL PROVISIONS AND ENFORCEMENT

In this section, the major federal EEO/AA laws are summarized in terms of their general provisions. Mechanisms for enforcement of the laws are also discussed.[12]

General Provisions

The federal EEO/AA laws that are major follow:

1. Civil Rights Acts (1964, 1991)
2. Age Discrimination in Employment Act (1967)
3. Americans With Disabilities Act (1990)
4. Rehabilitation Act (1973)
5. Executive Order 11246 (1965)

Exhibit 3.4 contains a summary of the basic provisions of these laws, pertaining to coverage, prohibited discrimination, enforcement agency, and important rules, regulations, and guidelines.

Inspection of Exhibit 3.4 suggests that these laws are appropriately labeled major for several reasons. First, the laws are very broad in their coverage of employers. Second, they specifically prohibit discrimination on the basis of several individual characteristics (race, color, religion, sex, national origin, age, disability, handicap). Third, separate agencies have been created for their administration and enforcement. Finally, these agencies have issued numerous rules, regulations, and guidelines to assist in interpretating, implementing, and enforcing the law.

Enforcement: EEOC

As shown in Exhibit 3.4, the EEOC has responsibility for enforcing the Civil Rights Act, Age Discrimination in Employment Act, and Americans With Disabilities Act. While each law requires separate enforcement mechanisms, some generalizations about their collective enforcement are possible.[13]

Initial Charge and Conciliation

Enforcement proceedings begin when a charge is filed by an employee or job applicant (the EEOC itself may also file a charge). In states where there is an EEOC-approved fair enforcement practice (FEP) law, the charge is initially de-

EXHIBIT 3.4 Major Federal EEO/AA Laws: General Provisions

Law or Executive Order	Coverage	Prohibited Discrimination	Enforcement Agency	Important Rules, Regulations, and Guidelines
Civil Rights Act (1964, 1991)	Private employers with 15 or more employees Federal, state, and local governments Educational institutions Employment agencies Labor unions	Race, color, religion, national origin, sex	EEOC	Uniform Guidelines on Employee Selection Procedures Sex Discrimination Guidelines Religious Discrimination Guidelines National Origin Discrimination Guidelines
Age Discrimination in Employment Act (1967)	Private employers with 20 or more employees Federal, state, and local governments Employment agencies Labor unions	Age (40 or over)	EEOC	Interpretations of the Age Discrimination in Employment Act
Americans with Disabilities Act (1990)	Private employers with 15 or more employees State and local governments	Qualified individual with a disability	EEOC	ADA—Employment Regulations
Rehabilitation Act (1973)	Federal contractors with contracts in excess of $2,500	Individual with a handicap	DOL (OFCCP)	Affirmative Action Regulations on Handicapped Workers
Executive Order 11246 (1965)	Federal contractors with contracts in excess of $10,000	Race, color, religion, national origin, sex	DOL (OFCCP)	Sex Discrimination Guidelines Affirmative Action Guidelines— Revised Order, No. 4

NOTE: Full text of the laws and Executive Order, as well as the important rules, regulations, and guidelines, may be found in the Bureau of National Affairs, *Fair Employment Practices*, Volume 1 (Washington, D.C.: author, periodically updated).

ferred to the state. An investigation of the charge occurs to determine if there is "reasonable cause" to assume discrimination has occurred. If such reasonable cause is not found, the charge is dropped. If reasonable cause is found, however, the EEOC attempts *conciliation* of the charge. Conciliation is a voluntary settlement process that seeks agreement by the employer to stop the practice(s) in question and abide by proposed remedies. This is the EEOC's preferred method of settlement.

Litigation

Should conciliation fail, suit is filed in federal court. The ensuing litigation process is shown in Exhibit 3.5. As can be seen, the charge of the *plaintiff* (charging party) will follow either a disparate treatment or disparate impact route. In either event, the plaintiff has the initial burden of proof. Such a burden requires the plaintiff to establish a *prima facie case* that demonstrates reasonable cause to assume discrimination has occurred. Assuming this case is successfully presented, the defendant must rebut the charge and accompanying evidence.

In disparate treatment cases, the *defendant* must provide nondiscriminatory reasons during rebuttal for the practice(s) in question. In disparate impact cases, the

EXHIBIT 3.5   Basic Litigation Process: EEOC

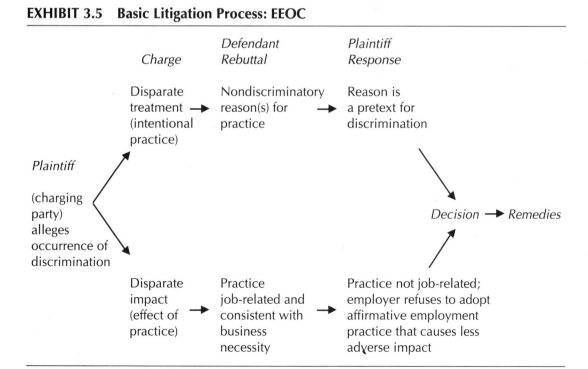

employer must demonstrate that the practices in question are job-related and consistent with business necessity.

Following rebuttal, the plaintiff may respond to the defense provided by the defendant. In disparate treatment cases, that response hinges on a demonstration that the defendant's reasons for a practice are a pretext, or smokescreen, for the practice. In disparate impact cases, the plaintiff's response will focus on showing that the defendant has not shown its practices to be job-related and/or that the employer refuses to adopt a practice that causes less adverse impact.

Who bears the final, or ultimate, burden of proof? In disparate treatment cases it is the plaintiff who must ultimately prove that the defendant's practices are discriminatory. For disparate impact cases, on the other hand, the burden is on the defendant. That is, it is the defendant who must prove that its practices are not discriminatory.

Decision and Remedies   The plaintiff and defendant have an opportunity to end their dispute through a *consent decree.* This is a voluntary, court-approved agreement between the two parties. The consent decree may contain not only an agreement to halt certain practices, but also an agreement to implement certain remedies, such as various forms of monetary relief and affirmative action programs. A rather dramatic example of a consent decree—atypical in terms of size—is shown in Exhibit 3.6 and involves an agreement between black applicants and employees, and Shoney's (a restaurant chain) for $105 million in monetary relief (back pay) plus implementation of an affirmative action plan.

In the absence of a consent decree, the court will fashion its own remedies from those permitted under the law. There are several remedies available. First, the court may enjoin certain practices, which means requiring the defendant to halt the practices. Second, the court may order the hiring or reinstatement of individuals. Third, the court may fashion various forms of monetary relief, such as back pay, front pay, attorney's fees, and compensatory and punitive damages. These compensatory and punitive damages may be applied only in cases involving disparate treatment, and there is a cap of $300,000 on them. Finally, under the Civil Rights Act and Americans With Disabilities Act, the court may order "such affirmative action as may be appropriate," as well as "any other equitable relief" that the court deems appropriate. Through these provisions, the court has considerable latitude in the remedies it imposes. Note that this court's prerogative includes imposition of affirmative action plans, as well as hiring and promotion quota systems.

Enforcement: OFCCP

Enforcement mechanisms used by the OFCCP are very different from those used by the EEOC.[14] Most covered employers are required to develop and implement

---

EXHIBIT 3.6   Example of Consent Decree (Summary)

SHONEY'S, INC. SETTLES 36-STATE JOB BIAS SUIT FOR $105 MILLION

NASHVILLE, TN—Shoney's, Inc. announced a $105 million settlement November 6th of a race discrimination class action filed on behalf of black employees and job applicants at more than 1,700 company-owned and franchised restaurants in 36 states (*Haynes v. Shoney's, Inc.,* DC NFla, No. 89-30093, 11/3/92).

"The claims fund will provide payments to persons who claim to have suffered discrimination in hiring, discharge or promotion or who claim to have suffered harassment or retaliation during the class period," dating back to February 1985, the Nashville-based company said.

In a complaint filed in the U.S. District Court for the Northern District of Florida in 1989, the class members originally sought $530 million in damages. The settlement covers discrimination claims against restaurants operated under the Shoney's name, its subsidiary restaurant chains under the names of Captain D's, Lee's Famous Recipe Chicken, Pargo's, and Fifth Quarter, and at Shoney's corporate headquarters in Nashville. Judge Roger Vinson, who approved the settlement in Pensacola, FL, will retain jurisdiction to determine eligible claimants.

Certifying a class of black employees, former employees, and applicants last June, Vinson said they had established sufficient evidence that a policy emanating from Raymond L. Danner, the company's founder and former chief executive officer, had a significant impact on the everyday employment practices in the company's restaurants (122 DFLA-3, 6/23/92).

The company said it could not accurately estimate the number of claims that will be filed under the settlement because of the size of its workforce and high turnover. Shoney's alone has some 30,000 employees and issues more than 100,000 federal income tax forms annually to workers at company-owned restaurants and corporate headquarters. The figures do not include employees at franchised restaurants.

The settlement calls for Shoney's to "adopt specific practices and to make specific actions" to increase total Black employment in certain jobs and positions where they may be underrepresented, according to the company. The agreement would also ban retaliation against Shoney employees "who opposed illegal employment practices."

Company Pledges Affirmative Action

"We regret any mistakes that occurred in the past with respect to employment practices," said Leonard H. Roberts, the current chairman and CEO of Shoney's, Inc.

"An important aspect of this settlement is an attempt to right any wrongs to the extent possible through payments to individuals whom the court determines eligible," he added. "But even more important is where we go from here. The company's goal is to maximize its effectiveness in affirmative action, including employment, minority franchise participation, supplier programs and other business development."

Compliance with the settlement and future affirmative action efforts will be directed and monitored by a new committee of company directors, Roberts said.

Tommy Warren, a Tallahassee, FL, attorney for the plaintiffs, said claimants will come from among some 100,000 current or former black employees who had worked for Shoney's restaurants or franchisees or had applied for jobs since 1985. He said the actual number of claimants would be

(continued)

EXHIBIT 3.6 Continued

---

significantly less than that figure because some may not see published notices of the settlement and others may not have suffered discrimination. Payments will be determined on a point basis, including the time of the alleged discrimination and its nature, Warren said.

"We are very pleased with the settlement," Warren told The Bureau of National Affairs November 4th. It puts an end to highly contentious litigation. It also allows this company to be committed to a new process for carrying forward equal employment opportunities for our class, and it allows the company to prosper even more greatly than it has in the past."

Warren said the settlement agreement also included Danner, from whom the original complaint had sought $100 million in damages. "Whatever contribution he made to Shoney's, that's between him and them," he said.

In addition to damage payments to claimants, the $105 million will cover plaintiffs' legal fees, payroll taxes, and costs of administering the settlement, the company said. Shoney's, Inc. operates and franchises a total of 1,803 restaurants in the United States and Canada.

Source: Reprinted with permission from *Daily Labor Report,* No. 215, pp. A-3–A-4 (Nov. 5, 1992). Copyright 1993 by Bureau of National Affairs, Inc. (800-372-1033).

written affirmative action plans for women and minorities. Specific affirmative action plan requirements for employers under EO 11246 are spelled out in Revised Order No. 4.

To enforce these requirements, the OFCCP conducts employer site visits and compliance reviews of employers' AA plans. It also investigates complaints charging noncompliance. Employers found to be in noncompliance are urged to change their practices through a conciliation process. An example of a conciliation agreement summary is shown in Exhibit 3.7. Should conciliation not be successful, employers are subject to various penalties that affect their status as a federal contractor. These include cancellation of contracts and debarment from bidding on future contracts.

EEO/AA LAWS: SPECIFIC STAFFING PROVISIONS

Each of the major laws covered in the previous section contains specific provisions pertaining to staffing practices by organizations. This section summarizes those specific provisions.[15] Phrases in quotation marks are direct quotations from the laws themselves. Applications of these provisions to staffing policies, practices, and actions occur throughout the remainder of the book.

Civil Rights Acts (1964, 1991)

The provisions of the Civil Rights Acts of 1964 and 1991 are combined for discussion purposes here. The 1991 law is basically a series of amendments to the 1964 law, though it does contain some provisions unique to it.

EXHIBIT 3.7   Example of Conciliation Agreement (Summary)

G.E. APPLIANCES REACHES $273,000 EQUAL EMPLOYMENT OPPORTUNITY SETTLEMENT WITH U.S. LABOR DEPARTMENT

G.E. Appliances, Decatur, AL, has agreed to pay more than $273,000 to 73 qualified applicants in an equal employment opportunity (EEO) settlement with the U.S. Labor Department.

The settlement follows a compliance review begun in June 1992 by the department's office of Federal Contract Compliance Programs (OFCCP). Following its review, OFCCP alleged that from January 1, 1991, G.E. discriminated against qualified minority and female applicants for assembler positions. G.E.'s affirmative action plan also was alleged to have reporting deficiencies.

While not admitting to any violation of federal EEO laws, G.E. agreed to equally divide $273,226 among 73 affected applicants, and to offer 12 assembler positions to five black females, five white females, and two black males chosen from the list of affected class members. In addition, G.E. will consult an affirmative action list of the remaining class members when there are openings for entry level assemblers.

"We are pleased that a reasonable settlement has been reached," said OFCCP Acting Director Len Biermann. "OFCCP is strongly committed to assuring equal employment opportunity for all qualified applicants regardless of gender or race.

G.E.'s Decatur facility is part of the appliance division which supplies refrigerators and other appliances to the federal government.

Part of the department's Employment Standards Administration, OFCCP is responsible for enforcing Executive Order 11246 and other laws requiring federal contractors to guarantee equal employment opportunity without regard to race, gender, religion, color, national origin, disability or Vietnam-era veteran status.

Source: U.S. Department of Labor, *News* (Washington, D.C.: author, 4/14/93).

Unlawful Employment Practices

This section of the law contains a comprehensive statement regarding unlawful employment practices. Specifically, it is unlawful for an employer

1. "to fail or refuse to hire or to discharge any individual, or otherwise discriminate against any individual with respect to his compensation, terms, conditions, or privileges of employment, because of such individual's race, color, religion, sex, or national origin"; or

2. "to limit, segregate, or classify his employees or applicants for employment in any way which would deprive or tend to deprive any individual of employment opportunities or otherwise adversely affect his status as an employee because of such individual's race, color, religion, sex, or national origin."

These two statements are the foundation of civil rights law. They are very broad and inclusive, applying to virtually all staffing practices by an organization. There are also separate such statements for employment agencies and for labor unions.

Establishment of Disparate Impact

As discussed previously, a claim of discrimination may be pursued via a disparate impact or disparate treatment approach. The law makes several points regarding the former approach.

First, staffing practices that do not cause adverse impact are not illegal (assuming, of course, that no intention to discriminate underlies them). Thus, while certain practices may somehow seem unfair, outrageous, or of dubious value to the employer, they are a matter of legal concern only if their usage causes disparate impact.

Second, staffing practices that the plaintiff initially alleges to have caused adverse impact are unlawful unless the employer can successfully rebut the charges. To do this, the employer must show that the practices are "job related for the position in question and consistent with business necessity." Practices that fail to meet this standard are unlawful.

Third, the plaintiff must show adverse impact for each specific staffing practice or component. For example, if an employer has a simple selection system in which applicants first take a written test, and those who pass it are interviewed, the plaintiff must show adverse impact separately for the test and the interview, rather than for the two components combined.

Disparate Treatment

Intentional discrimination with staffing practices is prohibited, and the employer may not use a claim of business necessity to justify intentional use of a discriminatory practice.

Mixed Motives

An employer may not defend an action by claiming that while a prohibited factor, such as sex, entered into a staffing decision, other factors, such as job qualifications, did also. Such "mixed motive" defenses are not permitted.

Bona Fide Occupational Qualification (BFOQ)

An employer may attempt to justify use of a protected characteristic, such as national origin, as being a bona fide occupational qualification, or BFOQ. The law permits such claims, but only for sex, religion, and national origin—not race or color. The employer must be able to demonstrate that such discrimination is "a bona fide occupational qualification reasonably necessary to the normal operation of that particular business or enterprise." Thus, a maximum security prison with mostly male inmates might hire only male prison guards on the grounds that by doing so it ensures the safety, security, and privacy of inmates. However, it must be able to show that doing so is a business necessity.

Testing

The law explicitly permits the use of tests in staffing. The employer may "give and act upon the results of any professionally developed ability test, provided that such test, its administration, or action upon the basis of results is not designed, intended, or used to discriminate because of race, color, religion, sex, or national origin."

Interpretation of this provision has been difficult. What exactly is a "professionally developed ability test"? How does an employer use a test to discriminate? Not discriminate? The need for answers to such questions gave rise to the Uniform Guidelines on Employee Selection Procedures (UGESP), which will be discussed later in this book.

Test Score Adjustments

Test scores are not to be altered or changed in order to somehow make them more fair; test scores should speak for themselves. Specifically, it is an unlawful employment practice "to adjust the scores of, use different cutoff scores for, or otherwise alter the results of employment related tests on the basis of race, color, religion, sex, or national origin." This provision bans so-called *race norming* in which people's scores are compared only to members of their own racial group and separate cutoff or passing scores are set for each group.

Seniority or Merit Systems

The law explicitly permits the use of seniority and merit systems as a basis for applying different terms and conditions to employees. However, the seniority or merit system must be a "bona fide" one, and it may not be the result of an intention to discriminate.

This provision has particular relevance to internal staffing systems. It in essence allows the employer to take into account seniority (experience) and merit (e.g., KSAOs, promotion potential assessments) when making internal staffing decisions.

Employment Advertising

Discrimination in employment advertising is prohibited. Specifically, the employer may not indicate "any preference, limitation, specification, or discrimination based on race, color, religion, sex, or national origin." An exception to this is if sex, religion, or national origin is a BFOQ.

Preferential Treatment and Quotas

The law does not require preferential treatment or quotas. Thus, the employer is not required to have a balanced workforce, meaning one whose demographic composition matches or mirrors the demographic makeup of the surrounding population from which it draws its employees.

Note that the law does not prohibit preferential treatment, affirmative action, and quotas. It merely says they are not required. Thus, they may be used in certain instances, such as a voluntary affirmative action plan or a court-imposed remedy.

Age Discrimination in Employment Act (1967)

Prohibited Age Discrimination

The law explicitly and inclusively prohibits discrimination against those 40 and older. It is unlawful for an employer

1. "to fail or refuse to hire or to discharge any individual or otherwise discriminate against any individual with respect to his compensation, terms, conditions or privileges of employment, because of such individual's age''; and

2. "to limit, segregate, or classify his employees in any way which would deprive or tend to deprive any individual of employment opportunities or otherwise adversely affect his status as an employee, because of such individual's age.''

Bona Fide Occupational Qualification (BFOQ)

Like the Civil Rights Act, the law contains a BFOQ provision. Thus, it is not unlawful for an employer to differentiate among applicants or employees on the basis of their age "where age is a bona fide occupational qualification reasonably necessary to the normal operation of the particular business.''

Factors Other Than Age

Normally, unlawful practices may be permitted if "the differentiation is based on reasonable factors other than age.'' This provision is vague in meaning. It seems to suggest that if reasonable factors, such as KSAOs and job performance, are the basis for decision making, where decisions have an adverse impact on the basis of age, there is not a violation of the law.

Seniority Systems

The law permits the use of seniority systems (merit systems are not mentioned). Thus, the employer is permitted "to observe the terms of a bona fide seniority system that is not intended to evade the purposes'' of the act.

Employment Advertising

Age discrimination in employment advertising is prohibited. Ads may not indicate "any preference, limitation, specification, or discrimination based on age.''

Americans With Disabilities Act (1990)

The ADA is a new and sweeping piece of legislation whose application to employment did not occur until mid-1992. Its basic purpose is to prohibit discrimination against qualified individuals with disabilities, and to require the employer to make reasonable accommodation for such individuals unless that would cause undue hardship for the employer.

Prohibited Discrimination

The law contains a broad prohibition against disability discrimination. It specifically says that an employer may not "discriminate against an individual with a disability because of the disability of such individual in regard to job application procedures, the hiring, advancement or discharge of employees, employee compensation, job training, and other terms, conditions, and privileges of employment."

The law does not apply to all disabled people, only those who are "otherwise qualified." It therefore does not require the hiring, promotion, or retention of unqualified people. There is thus an important emphasis on the determination of qualifications for decision-making purposes. This emphasis is very consistent with the person/job matching model. Also, the law does not require preferential treatment, affirmative action, or quotas for disabled people.

Definition of Disability

Disability refers to both physical and mental impairments that limit a major life activity of the person (e.g., breathing, walking, working). It also refers to persons who have a record of such impairment in the past or are regarded by others as having such an impairment.

Disability refers not only to obvious impairments, such as blindness, but to many others as well—for example, cancer, AIDS, and many mental illnesses. Current users of illegal drugs are excluded from coverage. Recovering former drug users, though, are covered, as are both practicing and recovering alcoholics.

Qualified Individual with a Disability

A qualified individual with a disability is "an individual with a disability who, with or without reasonable accommodation, can perform the essential functions of the employment position that such individual holds or desires."

Essential Job Functions

The law provides little guidance as to what are essential job functions. It would seem that they are the major, nontrivial tasks required of an employee. The employer has great discretion in such a determination. Specifically, "consideration shall be given to the employer's judgement as to what functions of a job are essential, and if an employer has prepared a written description before advertising or interviewing applicants for the job, this description shall be considered evidence of the essential functions of the job.'' For staffing purposes, this seems to create a major responsibility for job analysis as the process for identifying essential job functions.

Reasonable Accommodation and Undue Hardship

Unless it would pose an ''undue hardship'' on the employer, the employer must make ''reasonable accommodation'' to the ''known physical or mental impairments of an otherwise qualified, disabled job applicant or employee.'' The law provides actual examples of such accommodation. They include changes in facilities (e.g., installing wheelchair ramps); job restructuring; changes in work schedules; employee reassignment to a vacant position; purchase of adaptive devices; provision of qualified readers and interpreters; and adjustments in testing and training material. In general, only accommodations that would require significant difficulty or expense are considered to create an undue hardship.

Selection of Employees

The law deals directly with discrimination in the selection of employees. Prohibited discrimination includes

1. ''using qualification standards, employment tests or other selection criteria that screen out or tend to screen out an individual with a disability or a class of individuals with disabilities unless the standard, test, or other selection criteria, as used by the covered entity, is shown to be job related for the position in question and is consistent with business necessity''; and

2. ''failing to select and administer tests concerning employment in the most effective manner to ensure that, when such a test is administered to a job applicant or employee who has a disability that impairs sensory, manual, or speaking skills, such results accurately reflect the skills, aptitude or whatever other factor of such applicant or employee that such test purports to measure, rather than reflecting the impaired sensory, manual, or speaking skills of such employee or applicant (except where such skills are the factors that the test purports to measure).''

These provisions seem to make two basic requirements of staffing systems. First, if selection procedures cause disparate impact against people with disabilities, the employer must show that the procedures are job-related and consistent with business necessity. The requirement is similar to that for selection procedures under the Civil Rights Act. Second, the employer must ensure that employment tests are accurate indicators of the KSAOs they attempt to measure.

Medical Exams for Job Applicants

The employer may not conduct medical exams of job applicants, or inquire whether or how severely a person is disabled. Specific inquiries about a person's ability to perform essential job functions, however, are permitted.

After a job offer has been made, the employer may require the applicant to take a medical exam. The job offer may be contingent upon the applicant successfully passing the exam. Care should be taken to ensure that all applicants are required to take and pass the same exam. Medical records should be confidential and maintained in a separate file.

Affirmative Action

There are no affirmative action requirements for employers.

Rehabilitation Act (1973)

This law has many similarities to the ADA. Indeed, the ADA draws heavily on it and complements it in providing similar coverage to employers who are not federal contractors. Hence, its provisions are mentioned only briefly.

Prohibited Discrimination

According to the law, ''no otherwise qualified individual with handicaps . . . shall, solely by reason of his handicaps, be excluded from participation in, or denied the benefits of, or be subjected to discrimination under any program or activity receiving federal assistance. . . .'' The term ''handicaps'' is used in a similar fashion and with similar meaning to the term ''disability'' under the ADA. There are other similarities between the two laws as well. Both, for example, use the terms ''otherwise qualified,'' ''essential job functions,'' and ''reasonable accommodation.''

Affirmative Action

The law explicitly requires employers to undertake affirmative action. It says that the federal contractor ''shall take affirmative action to employ and advance in employment qualified individuals with handicaps.''

Executive Order 11246 (1965)

Prohibited Discrimination

The federal contractor is prohibited from discrimination on the basis of race, color, religion, sex, and national origin. (A similar prohibition against age discrimination by federal contractors is contained in Executive Order 11141).

Affirmative Action

The order plainly requires affirmative action. It says specifically that "the contractor will take affirmative action to ensure that applicants are employed, and that employees are treated during employment, without regard to their race, color, religion, sex, or national origin. Such actions shall include, but not be limited to the following: employment, upgrading, demotion, or transfer; recruitment or recruitment advertising; layoff or termination; rates of pay or other forms of compensation; and selection for training, including apprenticeship." (Executive Order 11141 does not require affirmative action.)

EEO/AA: REGULATIONS AND INFORMATION

As noted previously, and in Exhibit 3.4, numerous regulations and guidelines have been issued to further implement the enforcement of the EEO/AA law. Three major sets of these, with particular relevance to staffing, are briefly mentioned in the following sections. Also briefly mentioned are various information sources that are useful to consult regarding EEO/AA regulations and guidelines.

Regulations and Guidelines

Staffing policies and practices are most directly affected by the Uniform Guidelines on Employee Selection Procedures (UGESP), Revised Order No. 4, and Employment Regulations for the Americans With Disabilities Act. The general content of each of these is indicated next. The full text of each is contained in Appendixes A (UGESP), B (Revised Order No. 4), and C (Employment Regulations for the ADA).

UGESP

The UGESP deals with adverse impact issues, requiring the organization to keep detailed records about the demographics of its applicants and new hires, and to use these data to generate applicant flow statistics (selection rates). If significant differences in selection rates between protected groups are found—that is, there is adverse impact—the UGESP requires the organization to take steps to eliminate it, or to justify it through the conduct of validation studies. Detailed technical standards for these studies are provided. The UGESP also indicates the relationship between its requirements and AA obligations of the organization.

Revised Order No. 4

This order applies to most federal contractors. It requires them to conduct *utilization analysis.* The analysis is to use stock statistics to identify if, and in what jobs, women and minorities are underutilized relative to their availability in the population. Eight availability factors or criteria are provided for use in the utilization analysis. The contractor is also required to develop and implement AA plans and programs (AAPs) that address identified underutilization. The AAP must include hiring and promotion goals and timetables for their achievement. A thorough review must be conducted of all HR activities to ensure that they will not hinder, but in fact further, the attainment of AA goals. The contractor is required to put forth a good faith effort to achieve AA goals and timetables, and compliance with the order will be judged—at least partially—on the extent to which such efforts are shown.

Employment Regulations for ADA

These regulations seek to clarify the meanings of terms used in the ADA, such as ''disability,'' ''qualified individual with a disability,'' and ''reasonable accommodation.'' There are several sections explicitly dealing with selection of new employees. These pertain to the use and administration of tests and other selection procedures, as well as hiring standards. Medical examinations also receive detailed treatment. Employer defenses to discrimination charges, both disparate treatment and disparate impact, are specified. Finally, the regulations contain a lengthy appendix providing additional interpretive guidance.

Information Sources

The sheer volume and complexity of EEO/AA laws and regulations is staggering. Several key information sources are available that collect, categorize, and summarize the information in very understandable, user-friendly ways. Each of these sources is described next, and the reader is well advised to become familiar with these sources and consult them for assistance.

Information Services

The Bureau of National Affairs publishes *Fair Employment Practices,* a three-volume loose-leaf reference manual that is continually updated.[16] The first volume is the most useful overall and contains the following:

1. text of federal laws and executive orders
2. text of federal rules, regulations, and guidelines
3. text of federal policy statements
4. federal law—who is covered
5. federal law—what discrimination is forbidden
6. federal law—administration and enforcement
7. federal law—reports, records

The other two volumes contain a section on affirmative action, plus the full text of states' fair employment practice (FEP) laws.

The Bureau of National Affairs also publishes *FEP Cases.* It provides the text of federal and state court rulings, as well as summaries of decisions. In a similar vein, the Commerce Clearing House publishes *Employment Practice Decisions.*[17]

Compliance Manuals

Various compliance manuals are published that provide very practical, hands-on suggestions and guidance for employers' compliance attempts. The Bureau of National Affairs publishes the *EEOC Compliance Manual,* covering the Civil Rights Acts, the Age Discrimination in Employment Act, and the Americans With Disabilities Act, and the *Affirmative Action Compliance Manual for Federal Contractors,* covering Executive Order 11246 and the Rehabilitation Act. The Equal Employment Opportunity Commission publishes the *Technical Assistance Manual,* covering the Americans With Disabilities Act.[18]

Reference Books

There are certain books that review and summarize permissible and impermissible practices, as well as court cases pertaining to them. Examples include *Federal Law of Employment Discrimination, Employment Discrimination Law, Employment Law Manual,* and *Fair Employment Practices.*[19] These books contain a wealth of summarized and condensed material.

Professional Associations

Most professional associations provide informational services to their members. For example, the Society for Human Resource Management publishes *HR Magazine,* a monthly journal frequently containing staffing and EEO/AA articles. The society also puts out a monthly newsletter, which often contains EEO/AA material. The Employment Management Association publishes its own journal, the *EMA Journal,* and it, too, provides a newsletter to members pertaining to staffing issues.

OTHER STAFFING LAWS

In addition to the EEO/AA laws, there are a variety of other laws and regulations affecting staffing. At the federal level are the Immigration Reform and Control Act, and the Employee Polygraph Protection Act. At the state and local level are a wide array of laws pertaining to EEO, as well as a host of other areas. Finally, there are civil service laws and regulations that pertain to staffing practices for federal, state, and local government employers.

Federal Laws

Immigration Reform and Control Act (1986)

The purpose of this law is to prohibit the employment of unauthorized aliens, and to provide civil and criminal penalties for violations of this law. The law was amended by the Immigration Act of 1990, and those amendments are incorporated into the discussion that follows.

Prohibited Discrimination   The law prohibits the initial or continuing employment of unauthorized aliens. Specifically,

1. "it is unlawful for a person or other entity to have, or to recruit or refer for a fee, for employment in the United States an alien knowing the alien is an unauthorized alien with respect to such employment"; and
2. "it is unlawful for a person or other entity, after hiring an alien for employment . . . to continue to employ the alien in the United States knowing the alien is (or has become) an unauthorized alien with respect to such employment." (This does not apply to the continuing employment of aliens hired before November 6, 1986.)

The law also prohibits employment discrimination on the basis of national origin or citizenship status. The purpose of this provision is to discourage employers from attempting to comply with the prohibition against hiring unauthorized aliens by simply refusing to hire applicants who are foreign-looking in appearance or have foreign-sounding accents.

Employment Verification System   The employer must verify that the individual is not an unauthorized alien and is legally eligible for employment. This is accomplished by the examination of one or more documents that serve to establish employment verification (e.g., U.S. passport, certificate of U.S. citizenship, certificate of naturalization, unexpired foreign passport, or resident alien card).

The individual seeking employment must attest to being an authorized alien. There is a particular form (commonly referred to as the I-9 form) that the individual and employer must then sign, indicating employment verification. This form must be retained by the employer and made available for enforcement inspection.

Enforcement   The law is enforced by the Department of Justice. Noncompliance may result in fines of up to $10,000 for each unauthorized alien employed, as well as imprisonment for up to six months for a pattern or practice of violations.

Employee Polygraph Protection Act (1988)

The purpose of this law is to prevent most private employers from using the polygraph or lie detector on job applicants or employees. The law does not apply to other types of "honesty tests," such as paper-and-pencil ones.

Prohibited Practices   The law prohibits most private employers (public employers are exempted) from (a) requiring applicants or employees to take a polygraph test, (b) using the results of a polygraph test for employment decisions, and (c) discharging or disciplining individuals for refusal to take a polygraph test.

There are three explicit instances in which the polygraph may be used. First, it may be used by employers who manufacture, distribute, or dispense controlled substances, such as drugs. Second, the polygraph may be used by private security firms that provide services to businesses affecting public safety or security, such as nuclear power plants or armored vehicles. Third, the polygraph may be used in an investigation of theft, embezzlement, or sabotage that caused economic loss to the employer.

Enforcement   The law is enforced by the Department of Labor. Penalties for noncompliance are fines of up to $10,000 per individual violation. Also, individuals may sue the employer, seeking employment, reinstatement, promotion, and back pay.

State and Local Laws

The emphasis in this book is on federal laws and regulations. It should be remembered, however, that an organization is subject to law at the state and local level as well.[20] This greatly increases the array of applicable laws to which the organization must attend.

EEO/AA Laws

These laws are often patterned after federal law. Their basic provisions, however, vary substantially from state to state. Compliance with federal EEO/AA law does not ensure compliance with state and local EEO/AA law, and vice versa. Thus, it is the responsibility of the organization to be explicitly knowledgeable of the laws and regulations that apply to it. The text of relevant state (but not local) law is located in *Fair Employment Practices* (volumes 2 and 3).

Of special note is the fact that state and local EEO/AA laws and regulations often provide protections beyond those contained in the federal laws and regulations. State laws, for example, may apply to employers with fewer than 15 employees, which is the cutoff for coverage under the Civil Rights Act. State laws may also prohibit certain kinds of discrimination not prohibited under federal law, for example, sexual preference. The law for the District of Columbia prohibits 13 kinds of discrimination, including sexual orientation, physical appearance, matriculation, and political affiliation. Finally, state law may deviate from federal law with regard to enforcement mechanisms and penalties for noncompliance.

Other State Laws

Earlier reference was made to employment-at-will and workplace torts as they apply to negligent hiring, and fraud and misrepresentation. These are primarily matters of common law, which, in turn, is governed at the level of state law. The common law pertaining to staffing and employment has been characterized as fractured, and the following explanation has been provided for this characterization:

> Each state has adopted and adapted the common law to its own needs. The success of common law in the United States is attributable, in significant part, to its ability to draw upon the ingenuity of individuals and courts and on the experience of individual states in advancing the law of any particular jurisdiction. Each jurisdiction acts, in effect, as a laboratory in which new legal rights are tested. While generally not bound by the decisions of courts in other states, courts may review those decisions and are free to adopt the reasoning of those decisions that they find persuasive.[21]

Statutory state laws applicable to staffing, in addition to EEO/AA laws, are also plentiful. Examples of areas covered in addition to EEO/AA include criminal record inquiries by the employer, polygraph and ''honesty testing,'' drug testing, AIDS testing, and employee access to personnel records.

Civil Service Laws and Regulations

Federal, state, and local government employers are governed by special statutory laws and regulations collectively referred to as civil service. Civil service is guided by so-called *merit principles* that serve as the guide to staffing practices. Following these merit principles results in notable differences between public and private employers in their staffing practices.

Merit Principles and Staffing Practices

The essence of merit principles relevant to staffing is fourfold:

1. to recruit, select, and promote employees on the basis of their KSAOs
2. to provide for fair treatment of applicants and employees without regard to political affiliation, race, color, national origin, sex, religion, age, or handicap
3. to protect the privacy and constitutional rights of applicants and employees as citizens
4. to protect employees against coercion for partisan political purposes[22]

Merit principles are codified in civil service laws and regulations. In the state of Wisconsin, for example, Chapter 230 of the Wisconsin Statutes governs state employment relations. The merit policy of the state at the beginning of that Chapter, as well as its topical contents, is shown in Exhibit 3.8. The Chapter 230 statutes, in turn, are implemented and interpreted through the Wisconsin Administrative Code.

Comparisons with Private Sector

The merit principles and civil service laws and regulations combine to shape the nature of staffing practices in the public sector. This leads to some notable differences between the public and private sectors. Examples of public sector staffing practices are:

1. open announcement of all vacancies, along with the content of the selection process that will be followed
2. very large numbers of applicants due to applications being open to all persons
3. legal mandate to test applicants only for KSAOs that are directly job-related
4. limits on discretion in the final hiring process, such as number of finalists, ordering of finalists, and affirmative action considerations
5. rights of applicants to appeal the hiring decision, testing process, or actual test content and method[23]

EXHIBIT 3.8 Example of Civil Service Statutes—State of Wisconsin

Statement of Merit Policy

(1) It is the purpose of this chapter to provide state agencies and institutions of higher education with competent personnel who will furnish state services to citizens as fairly, efficiently, and effectively as possible.

(2) It is the policy of the state and the responsibility of the secretary and the administrator to maintain a system of personnel management which fills positions in the classified service through methods which apply the merit principle, with adequate civil service safeguards. It is the policy of this state to provide for equal employment opportunity by ensuring that all personnel actions including hire, tenure or term, and condition or privilege of employment be based on the ability to perform the duties and responsibilities assigned to the particular position without regard to age, race, creed or religion, color, handicap, sex, national origin, ancestry, sexual orientation or political affiliation. It is the policy of this state to take affirmative action which is not in conflict with other provisions of this chapter. It is the policy of the state to ensure its employees opportunities for satisfying careers and fair treatment based on the value of each employee's services. It is the policy of this state to encourage disclosure of information under subchapter III and to ensure that any employee employed by a governmental unit is protected from retaliatory action for disclosing information under subchapter III. It is the policy of this state to correct pay inequities based on gender or race in the state civil service system.

(continued)

EXHIBIT 3.8 Continued

Contents of Chapter 230

State Employment Relations

SUBCHAPTER I
ADMINISTRATIVE SERVICES

230.01	Statement of policy
230.02	Liberal construction of statutes
230.03	Definitions
230.04	Powers and duties of the secretary
230.046	Training programs
230.047	Temporary interchange of employees
230.048	Daycare for children of state employees

SUBCHAPTER II
CIVIL SERVICE

230.05	Powers and duties of the administrator
230.06	Powers and duties of appointing authorities
230.08	Classification of civil service
230.09	Classification
230.10	Compensation plan coverage
230.12	Compensation
230.13	Closed records
230.14	Recruitment
230.147	Employment of aid recipients
230.148	Unclassified service reappointments
230.15	Appointments, promotions, changes in classified service
230.16	Applications and examinations
230.17	Applicants and eligibles may be barred; bonds may be required
230.18	Discrimination prohibited
230.19	Promotion
230.20	Recommendations
230.21	Unskilled labor and critical recruitment selection
230.215	Part-time employment and flexible-time schedules
230.22	Entry profession selection
230.24	Career executive selection
230.25	Certification, appointments and registers
230.26	Limited term appointments
230.27	Project positions
230.28	Probationary period
230.29	Transfers
230.30	Employing units; establishment and revision
230.31	Restoration of employment and reinstatement privileges
230.32	Restoration after military leave
230.33	Leave of absence and pay while serving in unclassified position
230.335	Rights of unclassified division administrators
230.337	Rights of employees: corrections or parole
230.34	Demotion, suspension, discharge and layoff
230.35	State office hours; standard workweek; leaves of absence; holidays
230.36	Hazardous employment, injuries, pay continued
230.37	Standards of performance and ratings
230.40	Political activities; public office
230.41	Invalid appointments
230.43	Misdemeanors; how punished
230.44	Appeal procedures
230.45	Powers and duties of personnel commission
230.46	Duties of council on affirmative action
230.48	State employees' suggestion board

SUBCHAPTER III
EMPLOYEE PROTECTION

230.80	Definitions
230.81	Employee disclosure
230.82	Processing of information
230.83	Retaliatory action prohibited
230.85	Enforcement
230.86	Discipline based on surveillance
230.87	Judicial review
230.88	Payment of award, judgment or settlement; effect of order, arbitration award or commencement of court action
230.89	Rule making and reporting

Source: Wisconsin Statutes, Chapter 230 (State Employment Relations).

These examples are unlikely to be encountered in the private sector. Moreover, they are only illustrative of the many differences in staffing practices and context between the private and public sectors. A more thorough summary of the differences between the two sectors is shown in Exhibit 3.9.

LEGAL ISSUES IN REMAINDER OF BOOK

The laws and regulations applicable to staffing practices by organizations are multiple in number and complexity. The emphasis in this chapter has been on an understanding of the need for law, the sources of law, general provisions of the law, and a detailed presentation of specific provisions that pertain to staffing activities. Little has been said about practical implications and applications.

In the remaining chapters of the book, the focus shifts to the practical, with guidance and suggestions on how to align staffing practices with legal requirements. The last section of each remaining chapter is devoted to ''Legal Issues'' and discusses major issues from a compliance perspective. The issues so addressed, and the chapter in which they occur, are shown in Exhibit 3.10. Inspection of the exhibit should reinforce the importance accorded laws and regulations as an external influence on staffing activities.

It should be emphasized that there is a selective presentation of the issues in Exhibit 3.10. Only certain issues have been chosen for inclusion, and only a summary of their compliance implications is presented. It should also be emphasized that the discussion of these issues does not constitute professional legal advice.

SUMMARY

The person/job match becomes reality through the establishment of the employment relationship. That relationship is a contractual one, in which the employee and organization agree on the terms and conditions that will govern their relationship.

Over time, a myriad of laws and regulations have come forth from several sources to place constraints on the contractual relationship between employee and employer. These constraints seek to ensure a balance of power in the relationship, as well as provide specific protections to both employee and employer. Through common law, employment-at-will (termination of relationship), and workplace torts (employer liability for negligent or fraudulent staffing practices), issues are addressed.

Statutory federal laws pertaining to EEO/AA prohibit discrimination on the basis of race, color, religion, sex, national origin, age, and disability. This prohibition applies to staffing practices intentionally used to discriminate (disparate treatment), as well as to staffing practices that have a discriminatory effect (dis-

EXHIBIT 3.9 Staffing Differences Between Private and Public Sector

Area	Private Sector	Public Sector
Goal	Select good people	Allow all to apply and select the best among them
Laws	State/federal law on discrimination	State/federal law on discrimination State/federal/municipal law on merit and civil service (CS)
Ethics	Corporate principles and policies	State ethics laws on conflict of interest and patronage Executive orders banning discrimination
Fairness	Fairness is an ideal goal Patronage is inefficient	Fairness is legally mandated Patronage is illegal
Appeals and reviews	Internal review by personnel/AA office Review by federal agencies	Internal review by agency personnel/AA office Review by federal agencies Appeals by individuals Routine audits by central CS
Speed	Speed in hiring possible	Speed difficult to achieve
Power	Centralized in CEO and board of directors Unions	Three equal branches of government News media Unions Special interest groups
Ease of change	Procedures and policies based on consensus or fiat Easy to innovate Change controlled by managers Exceptions to procedures possible Few legal ramifications or exceptions Flexible Change to corporate policy or union contracts most difficult	Procedures and policies based on law Difficult to innovate Change controlled by legislature and executive Exceptions to rules, policy and procedure are difficult and may be subject to appeal/review Exceptions may be grounds for appeal Appeal at each step by persons involved Little flexibility
Public interest	Public has little interest in personnel matters	Public has great interest in personnel matters
Central control	Degree of central control varies	Degree of central control varies
Recruitment	Area often local, may be countrywide Period may be arbitrarily short	Area usually jurisdiction-wide, may be countrywide Recruitment period act by law, rule or regulation
Paperwork	Documentation desirable	Documentation required

Source: J. P. Wiesen, N. Abrams, and S. A. McAttee, *Employment Testing: A Public Sector Viewpoint,* 1990. Reprinted with permission of the International Personnel Management Association Assessment Council, Monograph Vol. 2 #3.

EXHIBIT 3.10   Legal Issues Covered in Other Chapters

Chapter		Topic
Measurement	(4)	Disparate impact statistics Standardization and validation
Job Analysis	(5)	Job-relatedness and court cases Job analysis and the UGESP Essential job functions
Planning	(6)	Affirmative action plans (AAPs) and Revised Order No. 4 Diversity programs
External Recruitment	(7)	Definition of job applicant Disclaimers Targeted recruitment Recruitment sources Job advertisements Fraud and misrepresentation
Internal Recruitment	(8)	Revised Order No. 4 Bona fide seniority systems The glass ceiling
External Selection	(9)	Uniform Guidelines on Employee Selection Procedures Selection under the ADA Bona fide occupational qualifications Preemployment inquiries
Internal Selection	(10)	Uniform Guidelines on Employee Selection Procedures Revised Order No. 4 The glass ceiling
Decision Making	(11)	Uniform Guidelines on Employee Selection Procedures Choices among finalists
Final Match	(12)	Authorization to work Negligent hiring Employment-at-will

parate or adverse impact). Equal employment opportunity, affirmative action, and quotas are each general attempts to bring staffing practices into compliance with these legal requirements.

Such attempts must occur within the specific provisions of the laws pertaining to staffing, which specify both prohibited and permissible practices. In both instances, the emphasis is on use of staffing practices that are job-related and focus on the person/job match.

Interpretation and implementation of the major EEO/AA laws occur through federal guidelines and regulations. The most prominent of these regarding staffing are the Uniform Guidelines on Employee Selection Procedures, Revised Order No. 4, and the Employment Regulations for the ADA.

Other laws and regulations also affect staffing practices. At the federal level, there is a prohibition on the employment of unauthorized aliens, and on the use of the polygraph (lie detector). State and local EEO/AA laws supplement those found at the federal level. Many other staffing practices are also addressed by state and local law. Finally, civil service laws and regulations govern staffing practices in the public sector. Their provisions create marked differences in certain staffing practices between public and private employers.

Legal issues will continue to be addressed throughout the remainder of this book. The emphasis will be on explanation and application of the laws' provisions to staffing practices.

DISCUSSION QUESTIONS

1. Do you agree that "the employer usually has the upper hand" when it comes to establishing the employment relationship? When might the employee have maximum power over the employer?

2. What is the nature of the distinction between AA and quotas?

3. What are the limitations of disparate impact statistics as indicators of potential staffing discrimination?

4. Why is each of the four situational factors necessary to establishing a claim of disparate treatment?

5. What factors would lead an organization to enter into a consent agreement rather than continue to pursue a suit in court?

6. What are the differences between staffing in the private and public sectors? Why would private employers probably resist adopting many of the characteristics of public staffing systems?

ENDNOTES

1. C. J. Bakaly, Jr., and J. M. Grossman, *The Modern Law of Employment Relationships* (Englewood Cliffs, NJ: Prentice-Hall, 1992), pp. 1–23; A. G. Feliu, *Primer on Individual Employee Rights* (Washington, D.C.: Bureau of National Affairs, 1992), pp. 1–9.

2. C. J. Bakaly, Jr., and J. M. Grossman, *The Modern Law of Employment Relationships,* pp. 1–23; G. P. Panaro, *Employment Law Manual* (Boston: Warren, Gorham and Lamont, 1990), pp. 7–1 to 7–51.

3. R. M. Green and R. J. Reibstein, *Employer's Guide to Workplace Torts* (Washington, D.C.: Bureau of National Affairs, 1992), pp. 3–62.

4. R. M. Green and R. J. Reibstein, *Employer's Guide to Workplace Torts,* pp. 8–37.

5. A. G. Feliu, *Primer on Individual Employee Rights,* pp. 1–8.

6. A. G. Feliu, *Primer on Individual Employee Rights,* pp. 1–8.

7. Bureau of National Affairs, *Fair Employment Practices,* Vols. 1 and 2 (Washington, D.C.: author, periodically updated); Commerce Clearing House, *1991 Guidebook to Fair Employment Practices* (Chicago: author, 1991), pp. 15–73, 153–162; B. S. Gamble, ed., *Sex Discrimination Handbook* (Washington, D.C.: Bureau of National Affairs, 1992), pp. 149–174; M. A. Player, *Federal Law of Employment Discrimination* (St. Paul, MN: West, 1992), pp. 47–49, 59–66, 217–225.

8. Bureau of National Affairs, *Fair Employment Practices,* Vols. 1 and 2 (Washington, D.C.: author, periodically updated); Commerce Clearing House, *1991 Guidebook to Fair Employment Practices* (Chicago: author, 1991), pp. 15–73, 153–162; B. S. Gamble, ed., *Sex Discrimination Handbook* (Washington, D.C.: Bureau of National Affairs, 1992), pp. 149–174; M. A. Player, *Federal Law of Employment Discrimination* (St. Paul, MN: West, 1992), pp. 47–49, 59–66, 217–225.

9. Bureau of National Affairs, *Fair Employment Practices,* Vol. 1, pp. 431:363–374; T. Johnson, ''The Legal Use of Racial Quotas and Gender Preference by Private and Public Employees,'' *Labor Law Journal,* 1989, 40, pp. 419–425.

10. Bureau of National Affairs, *Fair Employment Practices,* Vol. 1, pp. 431:225–250; M. A. Player, *Federal Law of Employment Discrimination,* pp. 67–114.

11. R. D. Arvey and R. H. Faley, *Fairness in Selecting Employees,* second ed. (Reading, MA: Addison-Wesley, 1988), pp. 73–80; J. C. Cook, ''Preparing for Statistical Battles under the Civil Rights Act,'' *HR Focus,* May 1992, pp. 12–13.

12. Bureau of National Affairs, *Fair Employment Practices,* Vol. 1, pp. 401:1–4241; R. C. West, ed., *U.S. Labor and Employment Laws* (Washington, D.C.: author, 1991).

13. Bureau of National Affairs, *Fair Employment Practices,* Vol. 1, pp. 431:1–55, 151–170, 301–375; P. E. Varca and P. Pattison, ''Evidentiary Standards in Employment Discrimination: A View Toward the Future,'' *Personnel Psychology,* 1993, 40, pp. 239–258.

14. Bureau of National Affairs, *Fair Employment Practices,* Vol. 1, pp. 431:55–64, 481–490.

15. Bureau of National Affairs, *Fair Employment Practices,* Vol. 1, pp. 401:1–4241; R. C. West, ed., *U.S. Labor and Employment Laws.*

16. Bureau of National Affairs, *Fair Employment Practices,* Vols. 1, 2, and 3.

17. Commerce Clearing House, *Employment Practice Decisions* (Chicago: author, periodically updated).

18. Bureau of National Affairs, *EEOC Compliance Manual* and *Affirmative Action Compliance Manual for Federal Contractors* (Washington, D.C.: author, periodically updated); Equal Employment Opportunity Commission, *Technical Assistance Manual of the Employment Provisions of the Americans With Disabilities Act* (Washington, D.C.: author, 1992).

19. Commerce Clearing House, *1991 Guidebook to Fair Employment Practices;* G. P. Panaro, *Employment Law Manual;* M. A. Player, *Federal Law of Employment Discrimination;* B. L. Schlei and P. Grossman, *Employment Discrimination Law* (Washington, D.C.: Bureau of National Affairs, 1987).

20. R. M. Green and R. J. Reibstein, *Employer's Guide to Workplace Torts.*

21. A. G. Feliu, *Primer on Individual Employee Rights,* p. 284.

22. J. P. Wiesen, N. Abrams, and S. A. McAttee, *Employment Testing: A Public Sector Viewpoint* (Alexandria, VA: International Personnel Management Association Assessment Council, 1990), pp. 2–3.

23. J. P. Wiesen, N. Abrams, and S. A. McAttee, *Employment Testing: A Public Sector Viewpoint,* pp. 3–7.

STAFFING ORGANIZATIONS MODEL

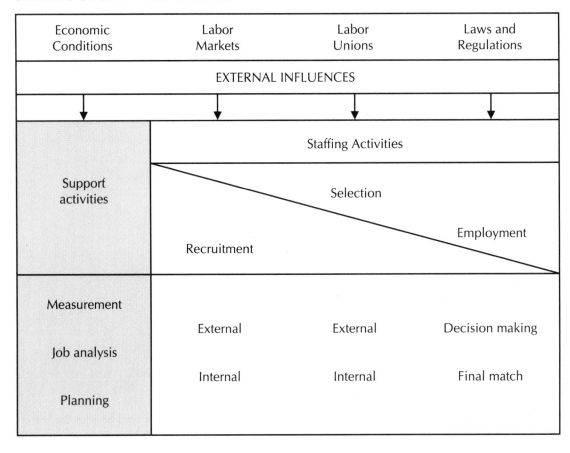

PART TWO

Support Activities

CHAPTER FOUR

Measurement

Importance and Use of Measures
　Measurement and Staffing
　Specific Uses of Measures in Staffing

Key Concepts
　Measurement
　Scores
　Correlation Between Scores

Quality of Measures
　Reliability of Measures
　Validity of Measures
　Validation of Measures in Staffing
　Validity Generalization

Legal Issues
　Disparate Impact Statistics
　Standardization and Validation

Summary

In staffing, measurement is a process used to gather and express information about persons and jobs in numerical form. A common example where management employs measurement is to administer a test to job applicants and evaluate their responses to determine a test score for each of them. The first part of this chapter presents a view of the process of measurement, then provides several specific examples of how measures are used in staffing.

After showing the vital importance and uses of measurement in staffing activities, three key concepts are then discussed. The first concept is that of measurement itself, along with the issues raised by it—standardization of measurement, levels of measurement, and the difference between objective and subjective measures. The second concept is that of scoring and how to express scores in ways that aid in their interpretation. The final concept is that of correlations between scores, particularly as expressed by the correlation coefficient and its significance. Calculating correlations between scores is a very useful way to learn even more about the meaning of scores.

What is the quality of the measures used in staffing? How sound an indicator of the attributes measured are they? Answers to these questions lie in the reliability and validity of the measures and the scores they yield. There are multiple ways of doing reliability and validity analysis; these are discussed in conjunction with numerous examples drawn from staffing situations. As these examples show, the quality of staffing decisions (e.g., who to hire or reject) depends heavily on the quality of measures and scores used as inputs to these decisions.

Measurement concepts and procedures are directly involved in legal issues, particularly EEO/AA ones. Organizations must perform various statistical analyses to help determine if disparate or adverse impact in staffing is occurring. This requires collection and analysis of applicant flow and stock statistics. Requirements for doing these analyses, as expressed in the Uniform Guidelines on Employee Selection Procedures (UGESP) and Revised Order No. 4, are reviewed. Also reviewed are implications of the results of disparate impact analysis for standardization and validation of measures, particularly as required by the UGESP.

IMPORTANCE AND USE OF MEASURES

Measurement is one of the key ingredients for, and tools of, staffing organizations. A general illustration of this is shown next, followed by a discussion of the major specific uses of measurement: measuring jobs, measuring individuals, measuring HR outcomes, monitoring and recordkeeping, and research and evaluation.

Measurement and Staffing

Staffing organizations is highly dependent upon the availability and use of measures. Indeed, it is virtually impossible to have any type of systematic staffing process that does not use measures and an accompanying measurement process.

Measures are methods or techniques for describing and assessing attributes of objects that are of concern to us. Examples include tests of applicant KSAOs, evaluations of employees' job performance, and applicants' ratings of their preferences for various types of job rewards. These assessments of attributes are gathered through the measurement process. That process consists of (a) choosing an attribute of concern, (b) developing an operational definition of the attribute, (c) constructing a measure of the attribute (if no suitable measure is available) as it is operationally defined, and (d) using the measure to actually gauge the attribute.

Results of the measurement process are expressed as numbers or scores—for example, applicants' scores on an ability test, employees' performance evaluation rating scores, or applicants' ratings of rewards in terms of their importance. These scores become the indicators of the attribute. Through the measurement process, the initial attribute and its operational definition have been transformed into a numerical expression of the attribute.

An example of these points, in a staffing context, is shown in Exhibit 4.1. The process starts with identification of an attribute of concern, in this case knowledge of mechanical principles. Once the attribute has been chosen, the measurement process unfolds, culminating in the use of actual scores generated by the measure to make hiring decisions about job applicants.

Specific Uses of Measures in Staffing

The example in Exhibit 4.1 has embedded within it several specific uses of measurement in staffing. Each of these uses is described.

Measuring Jobs

In the person/job matching model, jobs are said to have both requirements and rewards associated with them. These requirements and rewards need to be identified, defined, and measured in order to make the matching concept come to life for staffing purposes. This occurs through the process of job analysis, which is discussed in Chapter 5.

Through job analysis, job requirements become specified in terms of tasks and the KSAOs thought to be necessary for the performance of those tasks. Throughout the job analysis process, measurement processes are used.[1] For example, a task questionnaire might be administered to job incumbents where they are asked to rate the importance of each of a set of tasks for the performance of their job. The resultant scores would then be analyzed to develop a numerical profile of task requirements. This profile, in turn, could be used to identify the types of KSAOs likely to be necessary for the job.

To understand, refer again to the example in Exhibit 4.1. Assume that the job involved is that of maintenance mechanic in a food processing plant. A job analysis may have revealed that the job involves troubleshooting and diagnosis of equip-

---

EXHIBIT 4.1   Use of Measures in Staffing

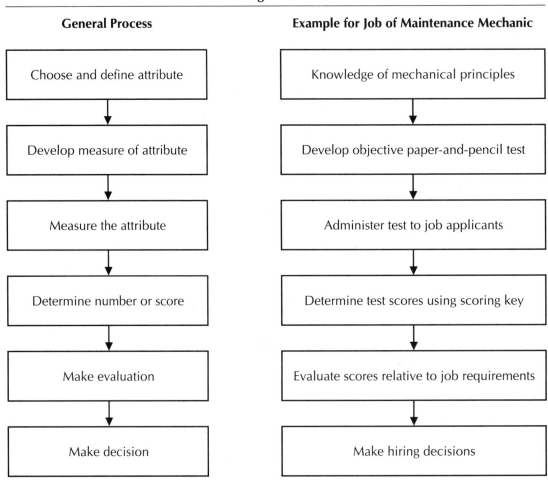

General Process	Example for Job of Maintenance Mechanic
Choose and define attribute	Knowledge of mechanical principles
Develop measure of attribute	Develop objective paper-and-pencil test
Measure the attribute	Administer test to job applicants
Determine number or score	Determine test scores using scoring key
Make evaluation	Evaluate scores relative to job requirements
Make decision	Make hiring decisions

---

ment failure, and that 30% of the job involves these tasks. With this task knowledge, it was inferred that knowledge of mechanical principles is an essential KSAO for the job. Furthermore, the specific sets of principles necessary for this particular job may have been specified, and their relative importance to job performance may have been rated by a group of job incumbents and their supervisors. In these ways, an attribute to measure has been chosen, and an operational definition of it has been developed.

Measuring Individuals

People possess a vast number of KSAOs. Some of these KSAOs will be of particular importance to the organization because they match identified KSAO requirements of jobs. Selecting individuals who possess these KSAO requirements as employees is greatly facilitated by having and using measures of individual applicants' job-relevant KSAOs.

There are a multitude of KSAOs to measure, and a corresponding multitude of measures of them that have been developed. Refinements of existing measures, as well as construction of new ones, occur on a continual basis. For example, tests of word processing skills were nonexistent 20 years ago, and the newly developed tests are revised constantly as changes in word processing technology occur.

The study of people's KSAOs has revealed two facts about people that have major staffing implications.[2] First, there are typically substantial *interindividual differences,* or differences among people, for any particular KSAO. Thus, if a particular ability test is administered to a group of people, inspection of their scores reveals substantial differences among them in performance on the test and, by inference, how much or little of the measured ability they possess.

The second fact revealed by studying KSAOs is that there are substantial *intraindividual differences,* or differences within an individual, as well. If a battery of ability tests, measuring several different abilities, were administered to a particular individual, inspection of the person's scores would show that the person scored better on some of the tests than on others.

The concept of inter- and intraindividual differences is illustrated in Exhibit 4.2. Notice that for any given ability there are differences in scores among people, and that for any given person there are differences in scores among abilities.

The importance of these pervasive differences to staffing should be apparent in the context of the person/job matching model. For KSAOs that are job-relevant, the existence of interindividual differences means that, for any particular KSAO, some individuals will be more qualified (better matched to job requirements) than will others. In terms of intraindividual differences, not all jobs have the same KSAO requirements, and thus, any given person will be more suited to perform some jobs than others. As a result of inter- and intraindividual differences, it is

---

EXHIBIT 4.2   Illustration of Inter- and Intraindividual Differences in Ability

	Ability Test Scores			
Person	**Verbal Comprehension**	**Word Fluency**	**Number Aptitude**	**Inductive Reasoning**
A	85	112	95	93
B	125	102	103	98
C	93	85	95	91
D	101	98	120	112
E	117	125	78	96
F	99	102	87	100

crucial that the organization be able to measure KSAOs so that applicants can be hired for jobs for which they are best suited.

In staffing, measures of KSAO characteristics of individuals are referred to as *predictors*, or tests. These predictors, and scores derived from them for individuals, serve as fundamental guides for staffing activities. In recruitment, for example, applicants may be informed that the selection process will require taking and passing a particular test; they may use this knowledge to help decide whether they truly want to apply for the position or want to self-select out of the staffing process. In the selection process, the predictor is administered to applicants, and then scored. These test score results are then fed into the employment activities, which require setting a passing (cutoff) score on the test, determining which applicants actually passed the test, and making job offers.

These types of staffing activities, driven by measurement concerns, are clearly illustrated in Exhibit 4.1. In this example, a test of knowledge of mechanical principles is developed, and applicants are informed that this predictor will be administered to them. For those who choose to take the test, it is administered and scored. Their scores are evaluated relative to job requirements (the passing or cutoff score), and this information serves as input to the hiring decisions made about the applicants.

Measuring Outcomes

Outcomes of the person/job matching process include factors such as job performance and retention. In order to determine and track the levels being attained on these outcomes, measures of them must be developed and used. In staffing, these outcome measures are referred to as *criterion measures*.[3] Scores on criterion measures include performance ratings and turnover rates, and may be used to help the organization decide if outcomes are occurring at acceptable levels, and if not, what corrective actions are necessary. These actions may include staffing activities.

Return again to the example in Exhibit 4.1. Perhaps the organization had a performance appraisal system that measured and tracked the performance of its maintenance mechanics. Appraisal results (criterion scores) may have indicated unacceptably low levels of performance. Diagnosis of the situation may have indicated that employees were deficient in their knowledge of mechanical principles. Based on this diagnosis, the organization could develop strategies for remedying the knowledge deficiency. One alternative would be to develop a training program for current employees and new hires for the job. A different strategy would be to impose a stringent knowledge requirement for new hires. If this alternative were chosen, it might necessitate the flow of events shown in the exhibit.

Monitoring and Record Keeping

Monitoring and record keeping are (or should be) an integral part of any staffing system. Through these activities, the organization gathers and records numerical information that may be used for numerous staffing-related purposes. These purposes include determining how well staffing activities conform to staffing policies and procedures, tracking numerically how applicant pools are reduced as applicants proceed through the staffing process (so-called applicant flow statistics), and determining compliance with legal requirements.

In the example in Exhibit 4.1, the organization could have developed a monitoring and record keeping program as part of the overall staffing system for the job of maintenance mechanic. The program might record information such as (a) date of initial application; (b) gender, age, and ethnicity of applicants; (c) scores on the test of knowledge of mechanical principles; (d) whether an offer was extended, and if so, if and when it was accepted; and (e) total elapsed time from date of application to date of acceptance or rejection. These data could then be analyzed periodically to provide indications of such things as (a) demographic composition of the applicant pool; (b) average and range of applicant test scores; (c) overall pass rate on the test, as well as specific pass rates for gender and ethnicity categories (in order to collect adverse impact statistics); and (d) speed in processing applicants.

Research and Evaluation

The maintenance and availability of staffing data leads naturally into more formal staffing research and evaluation activities. Such activities are primarily concerned with rigorously determining the effectiveness of specific staffing activities, as well as the overall effectiveness of the staffing system.

Consider once again the example in Exhibit 4.1. There are several types of research and evaluation projects the organization might wish to undertake. First, it might decide to investigate the reliability and validity of the results of its test of knowledge of mechanical principles. Conducting this evaluation project would require several types of research and data analysis, the nature of which is discussed in sections that follow. A second project might involve an analysis of pass rates on the test for the various gender and ethnic categories of job applicants. This is called adverse impact analysis, and it, too, is discussed. A third project might involve an assessment of the more routine processing aspects of the staffing system, with an eye toward efficiency, as well as reasonable treatment from the applicants' point of view (e.g., no excessive time delays in scheduling appointments or providing feedback).

KEY CONCEPTS

This section covers a series of key concepts in three major areas: measurement, scores, and correlation between scores.

Measurement

In the preceding discussion, the essence of measurement and its importance and use in staffing were described. It is now important to define the term "measurement" more formally and explore implications of that definition.

Definition

Measurement may be defined as the process of assigning numbers to objects to represent quantities of an attribute of the objects.[4] In the example in Exhibit 4.1, the attribute being measured is knowledge of mechanical principles, and the objects being measured are job applicants. Each job applicant received a number or score based on rules that had been determined in advance to measure correct and incorrect responses to each question on the test.

Several implications follow from this definition and example of measurement. First, the *attribute,* which is also called a *construct,* represents the concept to be measured. Second, the attribute is a particular characteristic of the object chosen for measurement, and it is the attribute, not the object, that is measured. Third, a particular method is selected to measure an attribute, such as a paper-and-pencil test. The numbers or scores that result are thus a direct function of the particular method of measurement used.

Fourth, the amount of an attribute possessed by an object is expressed numerically, and that number is determined through the use of rules that have been developed. Ideally, those rules are determined in advance and are agreed upon as reasonable. If these conditions do not hold, then there will be disagreements about the scores that should be assigned. There may also be disagreement over the meaning of the scores that are assigned.

Standardization

The hallmark of sound measurement practice is *standardization.*[5] Standardization is a means of controlling the influence of outside or extraneous factors on the scores generated by the measure, and ensuring that, as much as possible, the scores obtained are a reflection of the attribute measured.

A standardized measure has three basic properties:

1. The content is identical for all objects measured (e.g., all job applicants take the same test).
2. The administration of the measure is identical for all objects (e.g., all job applicants have the same time limit on a test).
3. The rules for assigning numbers are clearly specified and agreed upon in advance (e.g., a scoring key for the test is developed before it is administered).

These seemingly simple and straightforward characteristics of standardization of measures have substantial implications for the conduct of many staffing activities. These implications will become apparent throughout the remainder of this text. For example, assessment devices, such as the employment interview and letters of reference, often fail to meet the requirements for standardization, and organizations must undertake steps to make them more standardized.

Levels of Measurement

There are varying degrees of precision in measuring attributes and in representing differences among objects in terms of attributes. Accordingly, there are different *levels* or *scales of measurement.*[6] It is common to classify any particular measure as falling into one of four levels of measurement: *nominal, ordinal, interval,* or *ratio.*

Nominal   With nominal scales, a given attribute is categorized and numbers are assigned to the categories. With or without numbers, however, there is no order or level implied among the categories. The categories are merely different, and none is higher or lower than the other. For example, each job title could represent a different category, with a different number assigned to it: managers = 1, clericals = 2, sales = 3, and so forth. Clearly, the numbers do not imply any ordering among the categories.

Ordinal   With ordinal scales, objects are rank-ordered according to how much of the attribute they possess. Thus, objects may be ranked from ''best'' to ''worst,'' or from ''highest'' to ''lowest.'' For example, five job candidates, each of whom has been evaluated in terms of overall qualification for the job, might be rank-ordered from 1 to 5, or highest to lowest, according to their job qualifications.

Rank orderings only represent relative differences among objects, and they do not indicate the absolute levels of the attribute. Thus, the rank ordering of the five job candidates does not indicate exactly how qualified each of them is for the job, nor are the differences in their ranks necessarily equal to the differences in their qualifications. The difference in qualifications between applicants ranked 1 and 2 may not be the same as the difference between those ranked 4 and 5.

Interval   Like ordinal scales, interval scales allow us to rank order objects. However, the differences between adjacent points on the measurement scale are now equal in terms of the attribute. If an interval scale is used to rank order of the five job candidates, the differences in qualifications between those ranked 1 and 2 are equal to the differences between those ranked 4 and 5.

It should be pointed out that there are many instances in which the level of measurement falls somewhere between an ordinal and interval scale. That is, objects can be clearly rank-ordered, but the differences between the ranks are not necessarily equal throughout the measurement scale. In the example of the five job candidates, the difference in qualifications between those ranked 1 and 2 might be slight compared with the distance between those ranked 4 and 5.

Unfortunately, this in-between level of measurement is characteristic of many of the measures used in staffing. While it is not a major problem, it does signal caution in interpreting the meaning of differences in scores among people.

Ratio   Ratio scales are like interval scales in that there are equal differences between scale points for the attribute being measured. In addition, however, ratio scales have a logical or absolute true zero point. Because of this, how much of the attribute each object possesses can be stated in absolute terms.

Normally, ratio scales are involved in counting or weighing things. There are many such examples of ratio scales in staffing. Assessing how much weight a candidate can carry over some distance for physically demanding jobs such as firefighting or general construction is an example of this. Perhaps the most common example is counting how much previous job experience, general or specific, job candidates have had.

Objective and Subjective Measures

Frequently, staffing measures are described as being either "objective" or "subjective." Often, the term subjective is used in disparaging ways ("I can't believe how subjective that interview was; there's no way they can rate me fairly on the basis of it"). Exactly what is the difference between so-called objective and subjective measures?

The difference, in large part, pertains to the rules used to assign numbers to the attribute being assessed. With *objective measures,* the rules are predetermined and usually communicated and applied via some sort of scoring key or system. Most paper-and-pencil tests are considered objective. The scoring systems in *subjective measures* are more elusive, and often involve a rater or judge who assigns the numbers. Many employment interviewers fall in this category, especially those with an idiosyncratic way of evaluating people's responses, one that is not known or shared by other interviewers.

In principle, any attribute can be measured objectively, subjectively, or both. Research shows that when an attribute is measured by both objective and subjective means, there is often relatively low agreement between scores from the two types of measures. A case in point pertains to the attribute of "job performance." It may be measured objectively through quantity of output, and it may be measured subjectively through performance appraisal ratings. A review of the research shows that there is very low correlation between scores from the objective and subjective performance measures.[7] Undoubtedly, the raters' lack of sound scoring systems for rating job performance was a major contributor to the lack of obtained agreement.

It thus appears that whatever type of measure is being used to assess attributes in staffing, serious attention should be paid to the scoring system or key that is used. This requires nothing more, in a sense, than having a firm knowledge of exactly what the organization is trying to measure in the first place. This is true for both paper-and-pencil (objective) measures and judgmental (subjective) measures such as the employment interview. It is simply another way of emphasizing the importance of standardization in measurement.

Scores

Measures yield numbers or scores to represent the amount of the attribute being assessed. Scores thus are the numerical indicator of the attribute. Once scores have been derived, they can be manipulated in various ways to give them even greater meaning, and to help better describe characteristics of the objects being scored.[8]

Central Tendency and Variability

Assume that a group of job applicants was administered the test of knowledge of mechanical principles shown in Exhibit 4.1. The test is scored, using a scoring key, and each applicant receives a score on the test, known as a *raw score*. Their scores are shown in Exhibit 4.3.

Some features of this set of scores may be summarized through the calculation of summary statistics. These pertain to central tendency and variability in the scores and are also shown in Exhibit 4.3.

The indicators of central tendency are the *mean, median,* and *mode.* Since it was assumed that the data were interval level data, it is permissible to compute all three indicators of central tendency. Had the data been ordinal, the mean should not be computed. For nominal data, only the mode would be appropriate.

The variability indicators are the *range* and the *standard deviation.* The range shows lowest to highest actual score for the job applicants. The standard deviation shows, in essence, the average amount of deviation of individual scores from the average score. It summarizes the amount of "spread" in the scores. The larger the standard deviation, the greater the variability, or spread, in the data.

Percentiles

A *percentile score* for an individual is the percentage of people scoring below the individual in a distribution of scores. Refer again to Exhibit 4.3, and consider applicant C. That applicant's percentile score is the 10th percentile ($2/20 \times 100$). Applicant S is in the 90th percentile ($18/20 \times 100$).

Standard Scores

When interpreting scores, it is natural to compare individuals' raw scores to the mean, that is, to ask whether scores are above, at, or below the mean. But a true understanding of how well an individual did relative to the mean takes into account the amount of variability in scores around the mean (the standard deviation). That

EXHIBIT 4.3   Central Tendency and Variability: Summary Statistics

Data		Summary Statistics
Applicant	**Test Score (x)**	
A	10	A. Central tendency
B	12	Mean ($\bar{x}$) = 338/20 = 16.9
C	14	Median = middle score = 17
D	14	Mode = most frequent score = 15
E	15	
F	15	B. Variability
G	15	Range = 10 to 24
H	15	Standard deviation (SD) =
I	15	
J	17	
K	17	$\sqrt{\dfrac{\Sigma\,(\chi-\bar{\chi})^2}{N}} = 3.52$
L	17	
M	18	
N	18	
O	19	
P	19	
Q	19	
R	22	
S	23	
T	24	
Total (Σ) = 338		
N = 20		

is, the calculation must be "corrected" or controlled for the amount of variability in a score distribution to accurately present how well a person scored relative to the mean.

Calculation of the *standard score* for an individual is the way to accomplish this correction. The formula for calculation of the standard score, or Z, is as follows:

$$Z = \frac{X - \bar{X}}{SD}$$

Applicant S in Exhibit 4.3 had a raw score of 23 on the test; the mean was 16.9 and the standard deviation was 3.52. Substituting into the above formula, applicant S has a Z score of 1.7. Thus, applicant S scored about 1.7 standard deviations above the mean.

Standard scores are also useful for determining how a person performed, in a relative sense, on two or more tests. For example, assume the following data for a particular applicant:

	Test 1	Test 2
Raw score	50	48
Mean	48	46
SD	2.5	.80

On which test did the applicant do better? To answer that, simply calculate the applicant's standard scores on the two tests. The Z score on test 1 is .80, and the Z score on test 2 is 2.5. Thus, while the applicant got a higher raw score on test 1 than on test 2, the applicant got a higher Z score on test 2 than on test 1. Viewed in this way, it is apparent that the applicant did better on the second of the two tests.

Correlation Between Scores

Frequently, in staffing there are scores on two or more measures for a group of individuals. One common occurrence is to have scores on two (or often even more than two) KSAO measures. For example, there could be a score on the test of knowledge of mechanical principles and also an overall rating of the applicant's probable job success based on the employment interview. In such instances, it is logical to ask whether there is some relation between the two sets of scores. Is there a tendency for an increase in knowledge test scores to be accompanied by an increase in interview ratings?

As another example, an organization may have scores on a particular KSAO measure (e.g., the knowledge test) and a measure of job performance (e.g., performance appraisal ratings) for a group of individuals. Is there a correlation between these two sets of scores? If there is, then this would provide some evidence about the probable validity of the knowledge test as a predictor of job performance. This evidence would help the organization decide whether to incorporate the use of the test into the selection process for job applicants.

Investigation of the relationship between two sets of scores proceeds through the plotting of scatter diagrams, and through calculation of the correlation coefficient.

Scatterdiagrams

Assume two sets of scores for a group of people, scores on a test and scores on a measure of job performance. A *scatterdiagram* is simply the plot of the joint distribution of the two sets of scores. Inspection of the plot provides a visual representation of the type of relationship that exists between the two sets of scores. Exhibit 4.4 provides three different scatter diagrams for the two sets of scores.

EXHIBIT 4.4   Scatterdiagrams and Corresponding Correlations

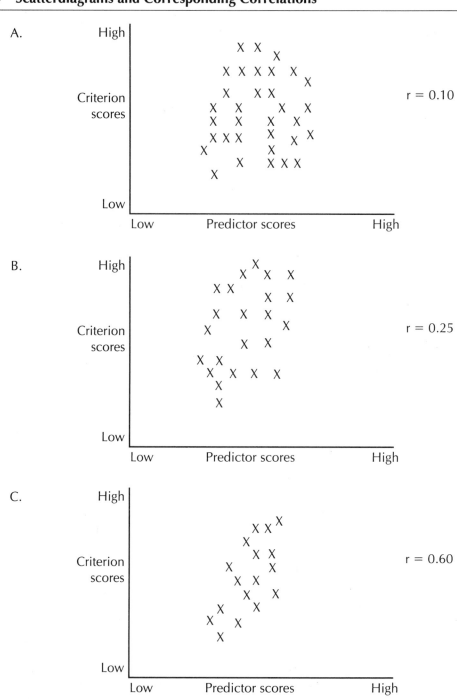

Each X represents a test score and job performance score combination for an individual.

Example A in Exhibit 4.4 suggests very little relationship between the two sets of scores. Example B shows a modest relationship between the scores, and example C shows a somewhat strong relationship between the two sets of scores.

Correlation Coefficient

The relationship between two sets of scores may also be investigated through calculation of the *correlation coefficient.* The symbol for the correlation coefficient is r. Numerically, r values can range from $r = -1.0$ to $r = 1.0$. The larger the absolute value of r, the stronger the relationship. When an r value is shown without the plus or minus sign, the value is assumed to be positive.

Naturally, the value of r bears a close resemblance to the scatter diagram. As a demonstration of this, Exhibit 4.4 also shows the approximate r value for each of the three scatter diagrams. In example A, a low r is indicated ($r = .10$). The r in example B is moderate ($r = .25$), and the r in example C is high ($r = .60$).

Actual calculation of the correlation coefficient is straightforward. An example of this calculation, and the formula for r, are shown in Exhibit 4.5. In the exhibit, there are two sets of scores for n = 20 people. The first set of scores is the set of test scores for the 20 individuals in Exhibit 4.3. The second set of scores is an overall job performance rating (on a 1–5 rating scale) for these people. As can be seen from the calculation, there is a correlation of $r = .58$ between the two sets of scores.

The calculation of the correlation coefficient is straightforward. The resultant value of r is a value that succinctly summarizes both the strength of the relationship between two sets of scores and the direction of the relationship. Despite the simplicity of its calculation, there are several notes of caution to sound regarding the correlation.

First, the correlation does not connote a proportion or percentage. An $r = .50$ between variables X and Y does not mean that X is 50% of Y, or that Y can be predicted from X with 50% accuracy. The appropriate interpretation is to square the value of r, for r^2, and then say that the two variables share that percentage of common variation in their scores. Thus, the proper interpretation of $r = .50$ is that the two variables share 25% ($.5^2 \times 100$) common variation in their scores.

Second, the value of r is affected by how much variation there actually is in each set of scores. Other things being equal, the less variation there is in either or both sets of scores, the smaller will be the calculated value of r. At the extreme, if there is no variation in one of the sets of scores, the correlation will be $r = .00$. That is, for there to be a correlation there must be variation in both sets of scores. The lack of variation in scores is called the problem of *restriction of range.*

Third, the formula used to calculate the correlation in Exhibit 4.5 is based on the assumption that there is a linear relationship between the two sets of scores. This may not always be a good assumption; something other than a straight line

EXHIBIT 4.5   Calculation of Product-Moment Correlation Coefficient

Person	Test Score (X)	Performance Rating (Y)	(X²)	(Y²)	(XY)
A	10	2	100	4	20
B	12	1	144	1	12
C	14	2	196	4	28
D	14	1	196	1	14
E	15	3	225	9	45
F	15	4	225	16	60
G	15	3	225	9	45
H	15	4	225	16	60
I	15	4	225	16	60
J	17	3	289	9	51
K	17	4	289	16	68
L	17	3	289	9	51
M	18	2	324	4	36
N	18	4	324	16	72
O	19	3	361	9	57
P	19	3	361	9	57
Q	19	5	361	25	95
R	22	3	484	9	66
S	23	4	529	16	92
T	24	5	576	25	120
	$\Sigma X = 338$	$\Sigma Y = 63$	$\Sigma X^2 = 5948$	$\Sigma Y^2 = 223$	$\Sigma XY = 1109$

$$r = \frac{N\Sigma XY - (\Sigma X)(\Sigma Y)}{\sqrt{[N\Sigma X^2 - (\Sigma X)^2][N\Sigma Y^2 - (\Sigma Y)^2]}} = \frac{20(1109) - (338)(63)}{\sqrt{[20(5948) - (338)^2][20(223) - (63)^2]}} = .58$$

may best capture the true nature of the relationship between scores. To the extent that two sets of scores are not related in a linear fashion, use of the formula for calculation of the correlation will yield a value of r that understates the actual strength of the relationship.

Finally, the correlation between two variables does not imply causation between them. A correlation simply says how two variables co-vary or co-relate; it says nothing about one variable necessarily causing the other one.

Significance of the Correlation Coefficient

Once the correlation coefficient is calculated, questions frequently arise as to the significance of the correlation. These questions may be addressed through consideration of a correlation's practical and statistical significance.

Practical Significance   The *practical significance* of the correlation refers to its size, regardless of its sign. The larger the r, the greater its practical significance.

This interpretation is a very appealing one. Recall that the correlation is really the amount of common or shared variation between two variables. The greater the degree of that covariation, the more we can use one variable to help us understand or predict another variable.

Consider again the correlation between the knowledge of mechanical principles test and the job performance ratings. The greater the r between those two variables, the greater the certainty that knowledge of mechanical principles is a key underlying KSAO of job performance, and that scores on this test are useful in predicting the likely performance of individuals at the time they are job applicants. Indeed, prediction such as this is a major purpose of staffing systems. Calculation and use of correlations is thus an extremely important tool for staffing activities.

Statistical Significance   When a correlation is computed for a particular group of individuals, it describes the relationship between two variables for that group only. However, to the extent that the group is drawn from, or representative of, some larger population, there may also exist a correlation in that population. For example, if there were a correlation between test scores and subsequent job performance ratings for a sample of current job applicants, it is possible to infer that there is a correlation in the population of future job applicants as well. Having made this inference, the organization could use the test to help select future applicants from that population.

The *statistical significance* of a correlation refers to the likelihood that a correlation exists in a population, based on knowledge of the actual value of r in a sample from that population. Concluding that a correlation is indeed statistically significant means that there is most likely a correlation in the population.

More formally, r is calculated in an initial group, called a *sample*. From this piece of information, the question arises whether to infer that there is also a correlation in the *population*. To do this, compute the t value of our correlation using the following formula,

$$t = \frac{r}{\sqrt{(1-r^2)/n-2}}$$

where r is the value of the correlation and n is the size of the sample.

A t distribution table in any elementary statistics book shows the significance level of r.[9] The significance level is expressed as p < some value, for example, p < .05. This p level tells the probability of concluding that there is a correlation in the population when, in fact, there is not a relationship. Thus, a correlation with p < .05 means there are fewer than 5 chances in 100 of concluding that there is a relationship in the population when, in fact, there is not. This is a relatively small probability, and usually leads to the conclusion that a correlation is indeed statistically significant.

It is important to avoid concluding that there is a relationship in the population when in fact there is not. Because of this, one usually chooses a fairly conservative or stringent level of significance that the correlation must attain before concluding that it is "significant." Typically, a standard of $p < .05$ or less (another common standard is $p < .01$) is chosen. The actual significance level (based on the t value for the correlation) is then compared to the desired significance level, and a decision reached whether the correlation is statistically significant or not. Here are some examples:

Desired Level	Actual Level	Conclusion about Correlation
$p < .05$	$p < .23$	Not significant
$p < .05$	$p < .02$	Significant
$p < .01$	$p < .07$	Not significant
$p < .01$	$p < .009$	Significant

Both the practical and statistical significance of the correlation are of concern in interpreting its significance. For example, if $r = .25$ and $p < .05$, the following kind of interpretation is made about significance. The correlation has moderate practical significance ($r^2 = .06$), and it meets a normal threshold for statistical significance. There is thus likely a relationship between the two variables in the population, based on what was found to be the relationship in this particular sample.

QUALITY OF MEASURES

Measures are developed and used to gauge attributes of objects. Results of measures are expressed in the form of scores, and various manipulation may be done to them. Such manipulations lead to better understanding and interpretation of the scores, and thus the attribute represented by the scores.

For practical reasons, in staffing the scores of individuals are treated as if they were, in fact, the attribute itself, rather than merely indicators of the attribute. For example, scores on a mental ability test are interpreted as being synonymous with how intelligent individuals are. Or, individuals' job performance ratings from their supervisors are viewed as indicators of their true performance.

Treated in this way, scores become a major input to decision making about individuals. For example, scores on the mental ability test are used and weighted heavily to decide which job applicants will receive a job offer. Or performance ratings may serve as a key factor in deciding which individuals will be eligible for an internal staffing move, such as a promotion. In these, and numerous other ways, management acts on the basis of scores to guide the conduct of staffing activities in the organization. This is illustrated through such phrases as "let the numbers do the talking," "we manage by the numbers," and "never measured, never managed."

The quality of the decisions and actions taken are unlikely to be any better than the quality of the measures on which they are based. Thus, there is a lot at stake in the quality of the measures used in staffing. Such concerns with the quality of measures are best viewed in terms of reliability and validity of measures.[10]

Reliability of Measures

Reliability of measurement refers to the consistency of measurement of an attribute.[11] A measure is reliable to the extent that it provides a consistent set of scores to represent an attribute. Rarely is perfect reliability achieved, because of the occurrence of measurement error. Reliability is thus a matter of degree.

Consistency of measurement is of concern both within a single time period in which the attribute is being measured, and between time periods. Moreover, reliability is of concern for both objective and subjective measures. These two concerns help create a general framework for better understanding reliability.

General Framework

The key concepts pertaining to reliability are best understood through use of a general operational framework. This framework is shown in Exhibit 4.6. In the exhibit, a single attribute, "A," (e.g., knowledge of mechanical principles) is being measured. Scores are available for $n = 15$ individuals, and scores range from 1 to 5. A is being measured in time period 1 (T_1) and time period 2 (T_2). In each time period. A may be measured objectively, with two test items, or subjectively, with two raters. The same two items or raters are used in each time period. (In reality, more than two items or raters would probably be used to measure A, but for simplicity's sake, only two are used here.) Each test item or rater in each time period is a submeasure of A. There are thus four submeasures of A—designated X_1, X_2, Y_1, and Y_2—and four sets of scores. In terms of reliability of measurement, the concern is with the consistency or similarity in the sets of scores. This requires various comparisons of the scores.

Comparisons Within T_1 or T_2   Consider the four sets of scores as coming from the objective measure, which used test items. Comparing sets of scores from these items in either T_1 or T_2 is called *internal consistency reliability*. The relevant comparisons are X_1 and Y_1, and X_2 and Y_2. It is hoped that the comparisons will show high similarity, because both the items are intended to measure A within the same time period.

Now treat the four sets of scores as coming from the subjective measure, which relied upon raters. Comparisons of these scores involve what is called *interrater reliability*. The relevant comparisons are the same as with the objective measure scores, namely X_1 and Y_1, and X_2 and Y_2. Again, it is hoped that there will be

---

EXHIBIT 4.6   Framework for Reliability of Measures

Scores on Attribute A

Person	Time Period 1 (T_1) Test Item or Rater		Time Period 2 (T_2) Test Item or Rater	
	X_1	Y_1	X_2	Y_2
A	5	5	4	5
B	5	4	4	3
C	5	5	5	4
D	5	4	5	5
E	4	5	3	4
F	4	4	4	3
G	4	4	3	4
H	4	3	4	3
I	3	4	3	4
J	3	3	5	3
K	3	3	2	3
L	3	2	4	2
M	2	3	4	3
N	2	2	1	2
O	1	2	3	2

NOTE: X_1 and X_2 are the *same* test item or rater; Y_1 and Y_2 are the *same* test item or rater. The subscript "1" refers to T_1, and the subscript "2" refers to T_2.

---

high agreement between the raters, because they are focusing on a single attribute at a single moment in time.

Comparisons Between T_1 and T_2   Comparisons of scores between time periods involve assessment of measurement stability. When scores from an objective measure are used, this is referred to as *test-retest reliability*. The relevant comparisons are X_1 and X_2, and Y_1 and Y_2. To the extent that A is not expected to change between T_1 and T_2, there should be high test-retest reliability.

When subjective scores are compared between T_1 and T_2, the concern is with *intrarater reliability*. Here the same rater evaluates individuals in terms of A in two different time periods. To the extent that A is not expected to change, there should be high intrarater reliability.

In summary, reliability is concerned with consistency of measurement. There are multiple ways of treating reliability, depending on whether scores from a measure are being compared for consistency within or between time periods, and depending on whether the scores are from objective or subjective measures. These points are summarized in Exhibit 4.7. Ways of actually computing agreement

---

EXHIBIT 4.7   Summary of Types of Reliability

	Compare scores within T_1 or T_2	Compare scores between T_1 and T_2
Objective measure (test items)	Internal consistency	Test–retest
Subjective measure (raters)	Interrater	Intrarater

---

between scores will be dealt with shortly, after the concept of measurement error is explored.

Measurement Error

Rarely will any of the comparisons among scores discussed previously yield perfect similarity or reliability. Indeed, none of the comparisons in Exhibit 4.7 visually shows complete agreement among the scores. The lack of agreement among the scores may be due to the occurrence of measurement error. This type of error represents "noise" in the measure and measurement process. Its occurrence means that the measure did not yield perfectly consistent scores, or so-called true scores, for the attribute.

The scores actually obtained from the measure thus have two components to them, a true score and measurement error. That is,

$$\text{actual score} = \text{true score} + \text{error}$$

The error component of any actual score, or set of scores, represents unreliability of measurement. Unfortunately, unreliability is a fact of life for the types of measures used in staffing. To help understand why this is the case, the various types or sources of error that can occur in a staffing context must be explored. These errors may be grouped under the categories of deficiency and contamination error.[12]

Deficiency Error   *Deficiency error* occurs when there is failure to measure some portion or aspect of the attribute assessed. For example, if knowledge of mechanical principles involves gear ratios, among other things, and our test does not have any items (or an insufficient number of items) getting at this aspect, then the test is deficient. As another example, if an attribute of job performance is "planning and setting work priorities," and the raters fail to rate people on that dimension during their performance appraisal, then the performance measure is deficient.

Deficiency error can occur in several related ways. First, there can be an inadequate definition of the attribute in the first place. Thus, the test of knowledge of mechanical principles may fail to get at familiarity with gear ratios because it was never included in the initial definition of mechanical principles. Or, the performance measure may fail to require raters to rate their employees on "planning and setting work priorities" because this attribute was never considered to be an important dimension of their work.

A second way that deficiency error occurs is in the construction of measures used to assess the attribute. Here, the attribute may be well defined and understood, but there is a failure to construct a measure that adequately gets at the totality of the attribute. This is akin to poor measurement by oversight, which happens when measures are constructed in a hurried, ad hoc fashion.

Deficiency error also occurs when the organization opts to use whatever measures are available because of ease, cost considerations, sales pitches and promotional claims, and so forth. The measures so chosen may turn out to be deficient.

Contamination Error   *Contamination error* represents the occurrence of unwanted or undesirable influence on the measure and on individuals for whom the measure is being used. These influences muddy the scores and make them difficult to interpret.

Sources of contamination abound, as do examples of them. Several of these sources and examples are shown in Exhibit 4.8, along with some suggestions for how they might be controlled. These examples show that contamination error is multifaceted, making it difficult to minimize and control.

EXHIBIT 4.8   Sources of Contamination Error and Suggestions for Control

Source of Contamination	Example	Suggestion for Control
Content domain	Irrelevant material on test	Define domain of test material to be covered
Standardization	Different time limits for people on test	Have same time limits for everyone
Chance response tendencies	Guessing by test taker	Impossible to control in advance
Rater	Rater gives inflated ratings to people	Train rater in rating accuracy
Rating situation	Interviewees asked different questions	Ask all interviewees same questions

Calculation of Reliability Estimates

There are numerous procedures available for calculating actual estimates of the degree of reliability of measurement.[13] The first two of these (coefficient alpha, interrater agreement) assess reliability within a single time period. The other two procedures (test-retest, intrarater agreement) assess reliability between time periods.

Coefficient Alpha   *Coefficient alpha* may be calculated in instances where there are two or more items (or raters) for a particular attribute. Its formula is

$$\alpha = \frac{n\,(\bar{r})}{1 + \bar{r}\,(n-1)}$$

where $\bar{r}$ is the average intercorrelation among the items (raters) and n is the number of items (raters). For example, if there are five items (n = 5), and the average correlation among those five items is $\bar{r}$ = .80, then coefficient alpha is .94.

It can be seen from the formula and example that coefficient alpha depends on just two things—the number of items and the amount of correlation between them. This suggests two basic strategies for increasing the internal consistency reliability of a measure—increase the number of items and increase the amount of agreement between the items (raters). It is generally recommended that coefficient alpha be at least .80 for a measure to have an acceptable degree of reliability.

Interrater Agreement   When raters serve as the measure, it is often convenient to talk about interrater agreement, or the amount of agreement among them. For example, if members of a group or panel interview and independently rate a set of job applicants on a 1–5 scale, it is logical to ask how much they agreed with each other.

A simple way to determine this is to calculate the percentage of agreement among the raters. An example of this is shown in Exhibit 4.9.

There is no commonly accepted minimum level of interrater agreement that must be met in order to consider the raters sufficiently reliable. Normally, a fairly high level should be set, 75% or higher. The more important the end use of the ratings, the greater should be the agreement required. Critical uses, such as hiring decisions, demand very high levels of reliability, well in excess of 75% agreement.

Test-Retest Reliability   To assess test-retest reliability, the test scores from two different time periods are correlated through calculation of the correlation coefficient. The r may be calculated on total test scores, or a separate r may be calculated for scores on each item. The resultant r provides an indication of the stability of measurement; the higher the r, the more stable the measure.

Interpretation of the r is made difficult by the fact that the scores are gathered at two different points in time. Between those two time points, the attribute being measured has an opportunity to change. Interpretation of test-retest reliability thus

---

EXHIBIT 4.9   Calculation of Percentage Agreement Among Raters

---

Person (ratee)	Rater 1	Rater 2	Rater 3
A	5	5	2
B	3	3	5
C	5	4	4
D	1	1	5
E	2	2	4

$$\% \text{ Agreement } = \frac{\text{\# agreements}}{\text{\# agreements } + \text{ \# disagreements}} \times 100$$

% Agreement
   Rater 1 and Rater 2 = 4/5 = 80%
   Rater 1 and Rater 3 = 0/5 = 0%
   Rater 2 and Rater 3 = 1/5 = 20%

---

requires some feeling for how much the attribute may be expected to change, and what the appropriate time interval between tests is. Usually, for very short time intervals (hours or days), most attributes are quite stable, and a large test-retest r ($r = .90$ or higher) should be expected. Over longer time intervals, it is usual to expect much lower r's, depending upon the attribute being measured. For example, over six months or a year, individuals' knowledge of mechanical principles might change. If so, there will be lower test-retest reliabilities (e.g., $r = .50$).

Intrarater Agreement   To calculate intrarater agreement, scores assigned the same people by a rater in two different time periods are compared. The calculation could involve computing the correlation between the two sets of scores, or it could involve use of the same formula as for interrater agreement (see Exhibit 4.9).

Interpretation of intrarater agreement is made difficult by the time factor. For short time intervals between measures, a fairly high relationship is expected (e.g., $r = .80$, or percentage agreement $= 90\%$). For longer time intervals, the level of reliability may reasonably be expected to be lower.

Implications of Reliability

The degree of reliability of a measure has two implications. The first of these pertains to interpreting individuals' scores on the measure and the standard error of measurement. The second implication pertains to the effect that reliability has on the measure's validity.

Standard Error of Measurement   Measures yield scores, which, in turn, are used as critical inputs for decision making in staffing activities. For example, in

Exhibit 4.1 a test of knowledge of mechanical principles was developed and administered to job applicants. The applicants' scores then were used as a basis for making hiring decisions.

The discussion of reliability suggests that measures and scores will usually have some amount of error in them. Hence, scores on the test of knowledge of mechanical principles most likely reflect both true knowledge and error. Since only a single score is obtained from each applicant, the critical issue is how accurate that particular score is as an indication of each applicant's true level of knowledge of mechanical principles alone.

The *standard error of measurement* addresses this issue. It provides a way to state, within limits, a person's likely score on a measure. The formula for the standard error of measurement (SEM) is

$$SEM = SD_x \sqrt{1 - r_{xx}}$$

where SD_x is the standard deviation of scores on the measure and r_{xx} is an estimate of the measure's reliability. For example, if $SD_x = 10$, and $r_{xx} = .75$ (based on coefficient alpha), then $SEM = 5$.

With the SEM known, the range within which any individual's true score is likely to fall can be estimated. That range is known as a *confidence interval* or limit. There is a 95% chance that a person's true score lies within ± 2 SEM of his or her actual score. Thus, if an applicant received a score of 22 on the test of knowledge of mechanical principles, the applicant's true score is most likely to be within the range of $22 \pm 2(5)$, or 12–32.

Recognition and use of the SEM allows for care in interpreting people's scores, as well as differences between them in terms of their scores. For example, using the preceding data, if the test score for applicant 1 = 22, and the score for applicant 2 = 19, what should be made of the difference between the two applicants? Is applicant 1 truly more knowledgeable of mechanical principles than applicant 2? The answer is probably not. This is because of the standard error of measurement and the large amount of overlap between the two applicants' intervals (12–32 for applicant 1, and 9–29 for applicant 2).

In short, there is not a one-to-one correspondence between actual scores and true scores. Most measures used in staffing are sufficiently unreliable that small differences in scores are likely to be due to error of measurement and should be ignored.

Relationship to Validity   The *validity* of a measure is defined as the degree to which it measures the attribute it is supposed to be measuring. For example, the validity of the test of knowledge of mechanical principles is the degree to which it measures that knowledge. There are specific ways to investigate validity, and these are discussed in the next section. Here, it simply needs to be recognized that the reliability with which an attribute is measured has direct implications for the validity of the measure.

The relationship between reliability and validity of a measure is

$$r_{xy} \leq \sqrt{r_{xx}}$$

where r_{xy} is the validity of a measure and r_{xx} is the reliability of the measure. For example, it had been assumed previously that the reliability of the test of knowledge of mechanical principles was $r = .75$. The validity of that test thus cannot exceed $\sqrt{.75} = .86$.

Thus, the reliability of a measure places an upper limit on the possible validity of a measure. It should be emphasized that this is only an upper limit. A highly reliable measure is not necessarily a valid one. Reliability does not guarantee validity; it only makes validity possible.

Validity of Measures

The *validity* of a measure is defined as the degree to which it is measuring the attribute it is intended to measure.[14] Refer back to Exhibit 4.1, which involved the development of a test of knowledge of mechanical principles that was then to be used for purposes of selecting job applicants. The validity of that test is the degree to which it truly measures the attribute or construct "knowledge of mechanical principles."

Judgments about the validity of a measure occur through the process of gathering data and evidence about the measure to assess how it was developed, and whether accurate inferences can be made from scores on the measure. This process can be illustrated in terms of concepts pertaining to accuracy of measurement and accuracy of prediction. These concepts may then be used to demonstrate how validation of measures occurs in staffing.

Accuracy of Measurement

How accurate is the test of knowledge of mechanical principles? This question asks for evidence about the accuracy with which the test portrays individuals' true levels of that knowledge. This is akin to asking about the degree of overlap between the attribute being measured and the actual measure of the attribute.

Refer to Exhibit 4.10. It shows the concept of accuracy of measurement in Venn diagram form. The circle on the left represents the construct "knowledge of mechanical principles," and the circle on the right represents the actual test of knowledge of mechanical principles. The overlap between the two circles represents the degree of *accuracy of measurement* for the test. The greater the overlap, the greater the accuracy of measurement.

Notice that there is not perfect overlap shown in Exhibit 4.10. This signifies the occurrence of measurement error with the use of the test. These errors, as indicated in the exhibit, are the errors of deficiency and contamination previously discussed.

EXHIBIT 4.10   Accuracy of Measurement

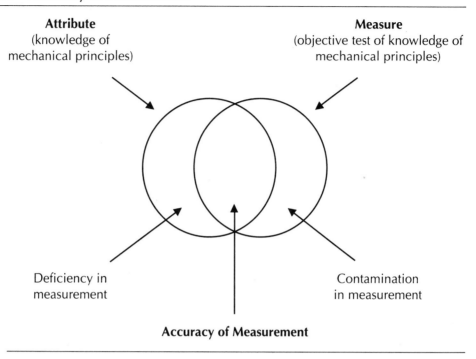

Attribute
(knowledge of
mechanical principles)

Measure
(objective test of knowledge of
mechanical principles)

Deficiency in
measurement

Contamination
in measurement

Accuracy of Measurement

So how does accuracy of measurement differ from reliability of measurement, since both are concerned with deficiency and contamination? There is disagreement among people on this question. Generally, the difference may be thought of as follows. Reliability refers to consistency among the scores on the test, as determined by comparing scores as previously described. Accuracy of measurement goes beyond this to assess the extent to which the scores truly reflect the attribute being measured—the overlap shown in Exhibit 4.10. Accuracy requires reliability, but it also requires more by way of evidence. For example, accuracy requires knowing something about how the test was developed. Accuracy also requires some evidence concerning how test scores are influenced by other factors—for example, how do test scores change as a result of employees attending a training program devoted to providing instruction in mechanical principles? Accuracy thus demands greater evidence than reliability.

Accuracy of Prediction
Measures are often developed because they provide information about people that can be used to make predictions about those people. In Exhibit 4.1, the knowledge test was to be used to help make hiring decisions, which are actually predictions

about which people will be successful at a job. Knowing something about the accuracy with which a test predicts future job success requires examining the relationship between scores on the test and scores on some measure of job success for a group of people.

Accuracy of prediction is illustrated in the upper half of Exhibit 4.11. Where there is an actual job success outcome (criterion) to predict, the test (predictor)

EXHIBIT 4.11 Accuracy of Prediction

A. General Illustration

		D	A
Actual criterion	High	Errors in predictions	Correct predictions
		C	B
	Low	Correct predictions	Errors in predictions
		Low	High

Predicted criterion

$$\text{Accuracy} = \frac{A+C}{A+B+C+D} \times 100$$

B. Selection Example (n=100 job applicants)

Actual Performance	High	20	45
	Low	25	10
		Low	High

Predicted performance
(based on test scores)

$$\text{Accuracy} = \frac{45+25}{45+10+25+20} \times 100 = 70\%$$

will be used to predict the criterion. Each person is classified as high or low on the predictor and high or low on the criterion, based on predictor and criterion scores. Individuals falling into cells A and C represent correct predictions, and individuals falling into cells B and D represent errors in prediction. Accuracy of prediction is the percentage of total correct predictions. Accuracy can thus range from 0% to 100%.

The bottom half of Exhibit 4.11 shows an example of the determination of accuracy of prediction using a selection example. The predictor is the test of knowledge of mechanical principles, and the criterion is an overall measure of job performance. Scores on the predictor and criterion measures are gathered for $n = 100$ job applicants, and dichotomized into high or low scores on each. Each individual is placed into one of the four cells. The accuracy of prediction for the test is 70%.

Validation of Measures in Staffing

In staffing, there is concern with the validity of predictors in terms of both accuracy of measurement and accuracy of prediction. It is important to have and use predictors that are accurate representations of the KSAOs to be measured, and those predictors need to be accurate in their predictions of job success. The validity of predictors is explored through the conduct of validation studies.

There are two types of validation studies typically conducted. The first of these is criterion-related validation, and the second is content validation. A third type of validation study, known as *construct validation,* involves components of reliability, criterion-related validation, and content validation. Each component is discussed separately in this book, and no further reference is made to construct validation.

Criterion-Related Validation

Exhibit 4.12 shows the components of criterion-related validation and their usual sequencing.[15] The process begins with job analysis. Results of job analysis are then fed into criterion and predictor measures. Scores on the predictor and criterion are obtained for a sample of individuals; the relationship between the scores is then examined to make a judgment about the predictor's validity.

Job Analysis and Job Requirements Matrix
Job analysis is undertaken to identify and define important tasks (and broader task dimensions) of the job. The KSAOs and motivation thought to be necessary for performance of these tasks are then inferred. Results of the process of identifying tasks and underlying KSAOs are expressed in the form of the job requirements matrix. The matrix is a task $\times$ KSAO matrix; it shows the tasks required, combined with the relevant KSAOs

EXHIBIT 4.12 Criterion-Related Validation

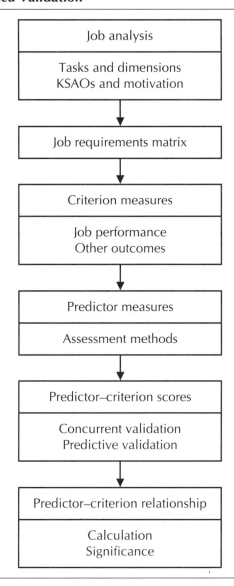

for each task. This job analysis process and the matrix are described in detail in Chapter 5.

Criterion Measures Measures of performance on tasks and task dimensions are needed. These may already be available as part of an ongoing performance appraisal system, or they may have to be developed. However gathered, the critical requirement is that the measures be as free from measurement error as possible.

Criterion measures need not be restricted to performance measures. Others may be used, such as measures of attendance, retention, safety, and customer service. As with performance-based criterion measures, these alternative criterion measures should also be as error-free as possible.

Predictor Measure   The predictor measure is the measure whose criterion-related validity is being investigated. Ideally, it taps one or more of the KSAOs identified in job analysis. Also, it should be the type of measure most suitable to assess the KSAOs. Knowledge of mechanical principles, for example, is probably best assessed with some form of written, objective test.

Predictor-Criterion Scores   Predictor and criterion scores must be gathered from a sample of current employees or job applicants. If current employees are used, this involves use of a *concurrent validation* design. Alternatively, if job applicants are used, a *predictive validation* design is used. The nature of these two designs is shown in Exhibit 4.13.

Concurrent validation has some definite appeal. Administratively, it is convenient and can often be done quickly. Moreover, results of the validation study will be available soon after the predictor and criterion scores have been gathered.

Unfortunately, some serious problems can arise with use of a concurrent validation design. One problem is that if the predictor is a test, current employees may not be motivated in the same way that job applicants would be in terms of desire to perform well on the test. Yet, it is future applicants for whom the test is intended to be used.

In a related vein, current employees may not be similar to, or representative of, future job applicants. Current employees may differ in terms of demographics such as age, race, sex, disability status, education level, and previous job experience. Hence, it is not certain that the results of the study will generalize to future job applicants. Also, some unsatisfactory employees will have been terminated, and some high performers may have been promoted. This leads to restriction of range on the criterion scores, which in turn will lower the correlation between the predictor and criterion scores.

Finally, current employees' predictor scores may be influenced by the amount of experience and/or success they have had on their current job. For example, scores on the test of knowledge of mechanical principles may reflect not only that knowledge, but how long people have been on the job and how well they have performed it. This is undesirable because we want predictor scores to be predictive of the criterion, rather than a result of it.

Predictive validation overcomes the potential limitations of concurrent validation, since the predictor scores are obtained from job applicants. Applicants will be motivated to do well on the predictor, and they are more likely to be represen-

---

EXHIBIT 4.13   Concurrent and Predictive Validation Designs

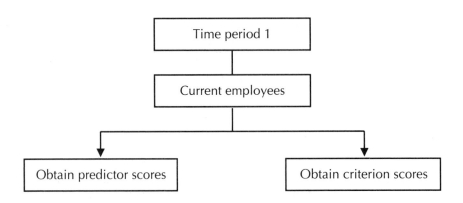

Concurrent Validation Design

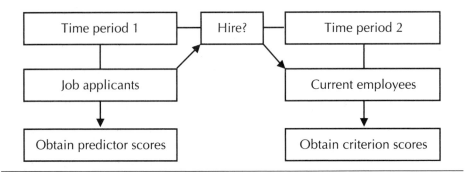

Predictive Validation Design

---

tative of future job applicants. And applicants' scores on the predictor cannot be influenced by success and/or experience on the job, since the scores were gathered prior to their being on the job.

Predictive validation is not without potential limitations, however. It is neither administratively easy nor quick. Moreover, results will not be available immediately, since some time must lapse before criterion scores can be obtained. Despite these limitations, predictive validation is considered the more sound of the two designs.

Predictor-Criterion Relationship   Once predictor and criterion scores have been obtained, the correlation r, or some variation of it, must be calculated. Then, the practical and statistical significance of the r should be determined. Only if the r meets desired levels of practical and statistical significance should the predictor be consider "valid," and thus potentially usable in the selection system.

Illustrative Study A study involving $n = 52$ law enforcement agency managers, holding ranks of sergeant through major, used a predictive validation design.[16] Predictor data were gathered in 1977, and criterion data in 1979, 1981, and 1984.

There were two predictors: assessment center ratings and subordinate ratings. Assessment center ratings were gathered during a two-day assessment. Managers participated in four exercises (leaderless group discussion, in-basket, subordinate counseling, and oral presentation). Upper-level managers rated participants' performance in the exercises on several dimensions (e.g., quality of ideas, interpersonal relations, and organization and planning). Ratings were summed up to form an overall assessment rating (OAR) for each participant. Subordinates also anonymously rated their managers annually on several performance dimensions. Ratings were summed up to form an overall subordinate rating.

There were three criterion measures, as follows:

1. Subordinate performance ratings, as already described, were gathered in 1979, 1981, and 1984.
2. Supervisory performance ratings were the sum of ratings on several performance dimensions.
3. Promotions were whether or not the manager was promoted in the time period. Decision makers had access to the OAR when making promotion decisions, so there was criterion contamination by knowledge of the OAR. This was not a problem with the other two criteria.

Results of the study are shown in Exhibit 4.14. The OAR significantly predicted near (1977) and long-term (1984) supervisory and subordinate performance ratings, as well as promotions (not unexpected, due to criterion contamination). Subordinate ratings significantly predicted all four sets of supervisory performance ratings, as well as all three sets of future subordinate ratings. These validities for the ratings were much more significant (both statistical and practical) than were those for the promotion criterion.

Content Validation

Content validation differs from criterion-related validity in one important respect: there is no criterion measure used in content validation. Thus, predictor scores cannot be correlated with criterion scores as a way of gathering evidence about a predictor's validity. Rather, a judgment is made about the probable correlation, had there been a criterion measure. For this reason, content validation is frequently referred to as judgmental validation.[17]

Content validation is most appropriate, and most likely to be found, in two circumstances—when there are too few people to form a sample for purposes of

EXHIBIT 4.14   Results of Validation Study for Law Enforcement Managers

Concurrent and Predictive Validity Coefficients for Two Predictors and Three Criteria over Seven Years

Criteria[a]

1977 Predictors	Supervisory Performance Ratings				Ratings by Subordinates				Promotions		
	1977	1979	1981	1984	1977	1979	1981	1984	1979	1981	1984
Assessment center OAR	.38**	.19***	.21	.41**	.29*	.19	−.14	.43**	.69***b	.69***b	.68***b
	(41)	(47)	(48)	(32)	(45)	(44)	(43)	(35)	(49)	(48)	(49)
Ratings by subordinates	.26*	.46***	.39**	.27*	NAc	.64***	.33**	.37*	.17	.20	.22*
	(49)	(56)	(54)	(38)		(51)	(48)	(37)	(.59)	(54)	(58)

[a]Numbers in parentheses are sample sizes.
[b]As noted in the text of the article, these very very high correlations should not be interpreted as predictive validity coefficients because of the direct use of OARs in promotion decisions.
[c]NA = Not Applicable
*p < .05; **p < .01; ***p < .001

Source: G. M. McEvoy and R. W. Beatty, "Assessment Centers and Subordinate Appraisals of Managers: A Seven-Year Examination of Predictive Validity," *Personnel Psychology*, 1989, 42, p. 46.

criterion-related validation, and when criterion measures are not available, or they are available but are of highly questionable quality. At an absolute minimum, an n = 30 is necessary for criterion-related validation.

Exhibit 4.15 shows the three basic steps in content validation—conducting a job analysis, constructing a job requirements matrix, and choosing or developing a predictor. These steps are commented on next. Comparing the steps in content validation with those in criterion-related validation (see Exhibit 4.12) shows that the steps in content validation are a part of criterion-related validation. Because of this, the two types of validation should be thought of as complementary, with content validation being a subset of criterion-related validation.

Job Analysis and Job Requirements Matrix   As with criterion-related validation, content validation begins with job analysis, which, in both cases, is undertaken to identify and define tasks and task dimensions, and to infer the necessary KSAOs and motivation for those tasks. Results are expressed in the job requirements matrix.

Predictor Measures   Sometimes the predictor will be one that has already been developed and is in use. An example here is a commercially available test, interviewing process, or biographical information questionnaire. Other times, there will not be such a measure available. This occurs frequently in the case of job knowledge, which is usually highly specific to the particular job involved in the validation.

EXHIBIT 4.15   Content Validation

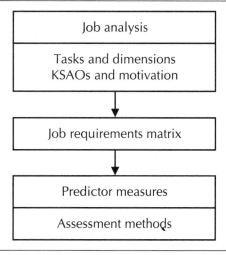

Lacking a readily available, or modifiable, predictor means that the organization will have to construct its own predictors. At this point, the organization has built predictor construction into the predictor validation process. Now, content validation and the predictor development processes occur simultaneously. The organization becomes engaged in test construction, a topic beyond the scope of this book.[18]

It should be emphasized that content validation procedures can be applied to any type of predictor, or combination of predictors, as illustrated in a content validation study involving police emergency telephone operators.[19] A job analysis identified six critical KSAO requirements for the job (communication skills, emotional control, judgment, cooperativeness, memory, and clerical/technical skills). The predictors included

1. a spelling test in which applicants received ten tape-recorded telephone calls and had to accurately record the pertinent information from each call on a form
2. a test in which applicants had to accurately record information received from monitoring police units
3. a typing test measuring both speed and accuracy
4. a situational interview in which applicants were asked how they would behave in a series of job-related situations
5. a role-playing exercise in which applicants assumed the role of police and telephone operators taking calls from complainants

This example makes clear that content validation is a flexible process for establishing task-KSAO-predictor linkages. At the same time that these linkages are being established administratively, validation evidence is emerging from a built-in process of content validation.

A final note about content validation emphasizes the importance of continually paying attention to the need for reliability of measurement and standardization of the measurement process. While these are always matters of concern in any type of validation effort, they are of paramount importance in content validation. The reason for this is that without an empirical correlation between the predictor and criterion, only the likely r can be judged. It is important, in forming that judgment, to pay considerable attention to reliability and standardization.

Illustrative Study   This study is concerned with the development of a computerized testing procedure for the selection of secretarial applicants to a large manufacturing organization.[20] The first phase of the study involved job analysis. Interviews were conducted with n = 110 experienced secretaries (so-called subject matter experts or SMEs) and focused on the identification of tasks, KSAOs, and linkages between the two. Tasks were grouped into task dimensions; interrater reliability of the SMEs in this process was very acceptable, with an r = .90. KSAOs were rated by the SMEs in terms of their importance to successful task perform-ance (from 1 = not at all important to 5 = critical). The task dimensions and KSAOs were placed in a job requirements matrix, shown in Exhibit 4.16. Each X repre-sents a KSAO receiving an average importance rating of 3 or higher for a given task dimension. The matrix then serves as the blueprint for test development.

In the test development phase, eight test components were identified to form the total test portion of the overall selection procedure. These test components were derived from the previously identified KSAOs and matched to them. The components deal with word processing, corrections, data bases, letters, travel ex-pense forms, mail logs, electronic mail messages, and telephone messages.

Tests were tailor-made for the eight selection components. Care was taken to ensure a strong fidelity between test content and actual job content (e.g., type of computer, software commands). Also, 30 secretaries from a secretarial help agency were hired to go through a dry run of the selection procedure and provide reactions to it. These were used to fine-tune the tests. All tests were highly standardized in their construction and administration, as were their scoring keys.

The procedure was then tested on a sample of 43 individuals. Results of this test showed that (a) there were relatively high standard deviations in test scores, indicating good interindividual differences; (b) the intercorrelations among the test components were low, indicating they were measuring different KSAOs, as intended; and (c) there was high interrater reliability in the scoring of people's responses to the tests, indicating that the scoring keys could be used in a consistent fashion by multiple raters.

Validity Generalization

In the preceding discussions of validity and validation, an implicit premise is being made that validity is situation-specific and therefore validation of predictors must occur in each specific situation. All of the examples involve specific types of measures, jobs, individuals, and so forth. Nothing is said about generalizing va-lidity across those jobs and individuals. For example, if a predictor is valid for a particular job in organization X, would it be valid for the same type of job in organization Y? Or, is validity specific to the particular job and organization?

The situation-specific premise is based on the following scenario, which, in turn, has its origins in findings from decades of previous research. Assume a large number of criterion-related validation studies have been conducted. Each study involves various predictor measures of a common KSAO attribute (e.g., general mental ability) and various criterion measures of a common outcome attribute (e.g., job performance). The predictor will be designated "X," and the criterion will be designated "Y." The studies are conducted in many different situations (types of jobs, types of organizations), and they involve many different samples (sample sizes, types of employees). In each study, r_{xy} is calculated. The results

EXHIBIT 4.16   Content Validation Study: Secretarial Job

JOB REQUIREMENTS MATRIX

Task Dimension	KSA															
	1	2	3	4	5	6	7	8	9	10	11	12	13	14	15	16
1. Maintaining and developing databases and spreadsheets, including collecting and entering information. Using databases and spreadsheets to obtain summaries and answer questions.		X[a]	X	X					X	X	X	X				X
2. General computer activities. Working with data files and preparing printed documents. Answering questions about computer use and printing options.		X		X				X	X	X		X			X	X
3. Creating and completing various company forms and insuring that they are filed and/or distributed to appropriate personnel.	X	X		X	X		X		X		X					X
4. General clerical activities including answering phone, filing, handling mail, and duplicating.	X	X		X	X	X	X	X	X		X		X	X		X
5. Note-taking, typing, and letter preparation, including editing and revising.	X	X		X	X	X	X		X	X	X	X	X	X	X	X
6. Handling travel arrangements, securing reimbursements, and completing travel expense reports.	X	X	X	X	X	X	X	X	X		X			X		X

(continued)

EXHIBIT 4.16   Continued

JOB REQUIREMENTS MATRIX

Task Dimension	1	2	3	4	5	6	7	8	9	10	11	12	13	14	15	16
7. Personnel related record keeping and handling payroll duties, including auditing and resolving discrepancies. Maintaining unit personnel files.	X	X	X	X	X	X	X		X		X					X
8. Coordinating office and building functions and maintaining equipment/supplies. Scheduling meetings and conferences, insuring that necessary people and equipment arrive.	X	X		X	X	X	X	X	X					X		X
9. Generating reports, charts, and graphs from notes/data and insuring their accuracy.		X	X	X	X		X		X	X		X				X
10. Coordinating and administering training and substituting activities.				X		X		X						X		X
11. Using electronic communication systems to send and receive information (file, messages, data, etc.).		X					X		X	X		X	X		X	X

(column header span label: **KSA**)

[a]X = Those KSAs for which performance of a task was considered important by expert judges, that is, mean ratings were 3.00 or above.

NOTE: The KSAs are (1) ability to follow oral directions, (2) ability to read and follow manuals, (3) ability to perform basic arithmetic operations, (4) ability to organize, (5) judgment/decision making, (6) oral communication, (7) written communication, (8) interpersonal skills, (9) typing skills, (10) knowledge of computer software, (11) knowledge of company policies, (12) knowledge of basic computer operations, (13) knowledge of how to use office machines, (14) flexibility in dealing with job demands, (15) knowledge of communication software, (16) ability to attend to detail.

Source: N. Schmitt, S. W. Gilliland, R. S. Landis, and D. Devine, ''Computer-Based Testing Applied to Selection of Secretarial Applicants,'' *Personnel Psychology*, 1993, 46, p. 152.

from all the studies reveal a wide range of different size r_{xy}'s, though the average is $\bar{r}_{xy} = .25$. These results suggest that while on average there seems to be some validity to X, the validity varies substantially from situation to situation. Based on these findings, the best conclusion is that validity most likely is situation-specific, and thus cannot be generalized across the situations.

The concept of validity generalization questions this premise.[21] It says that much of the variation in the r_{xy}'s is due to the occurrence of a number of methodological and statistical differences across the studies. If these differences were controlled for statistically, the variation in r_{xy}'s would shrink and converge toward an estimate of the true validity of X. If that true r is significant (practically and statistically), one can indeed generalize validity of X across situations. Validity thus is not viewed as situation-specific. The logic of this validity generalization premise is shown in Exhibit 4.17.

The distinction between situation-specific validity and validity generalization is important for two related reasons. First, from a scientific viewpoint, it is important to identify and make statements about X and Y relationships in general, without always having to say that everything depends on the sample, criterion measure, and so forth. In this regard, validity generalization clearly allows greater latitude than does situation specificity. Second, from a practical standpoint, it would be convenient and less costly not to have to conduct a separate validation study for predictor X in every situation in which its use was a possibility. Validity generalization allows that to happen, while situation specificity does not.

Evidence is beginning to surface that is supportive of the validity generalization premise. For example, evidence suggests that tests of general mental ability have meaningful, practical validity for predicting job performance across a wide variety of types of employees and jobs. Until more is known about validity generalization, however, caution is called for in its use in either scientific or practical terms. In this light, the following recommendations are offered as guides to staffing practice:

1. At a minimum, all predictors should routinely be subject to content validation.
2. When feasible, criterion-related validation studies should be conducted unless there is sufficient validity generalization evidence available to support use of a predictor without prior validation.

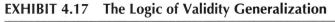

EXHIBIT 4.17   The Logic of Validity Generalization

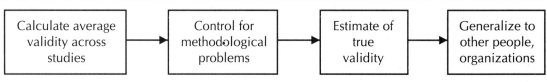

| Calculate average validity across studies | → | Control for methodological problems | → | Estimate of true validity | → | Generalize to other people, organizations |

3. Any claims of validity or validity generalization that are based on no criterion-related validity studies, or only a small number of them, should be suspect.

4. Organizations should become involved in various cooperative arrangements devoted to validation research in order to explore the extent to which validity may be generalized.

LEGAL ISSUES

Staffing laws and regulations, particularly EEO/AA laws and regulations, place great reliance on the use of measurement concepts and processes. Here, measurement is an integral part of (a) judging an organization's compliance through the conduct of disparate impact analysis, and (b) requiring standardization and validation of measures.

Disparate Impact Statistics

In Chapter 3, disparate (adverse) impact was introduced as a way of determining whether staffing practices were having potentially illegal impacts on individuals because of race, sex, and so forth. Such a determination requires the compilation and analysis of statistical evidence, primarily applicant flow and applicant stock statistics.

Applicant Flow Statistics

Applicant flow statistical analysis requires the calculation of selection rates (proportions or percentages of applicants hired) for groups, and the subsequent comparison of those rates to determine if they are significantly different from one another.[22] This may be illustrated by taking the example from Exhibit 3.4:

	Applicants	**Hires**	**Selection Rate**
Men	50	25	.50 or 50%
Women	45	5	.11 or 11%

It may be seen in this example that there is a sizeable difference in selection rates between men and women (.50 as opposed to .11). Does this difference indicate adverse impact?

The Uniform Guidelines on Employee Selection Procedures (UGESP) speak directly to this question (see Appendix A). Several points need to be made regarding the determination of disparate impact analysis.

First, the UGESP requires the organization to keep records that will permit calculation of such selection rates, also referred to as applicant flow statistics.

These statistics are a primary vehicle by which compliance with the law (Civil Rights Act) is judged.

Second, the UGESP requires calculation of selection rates (a) for each job category, (b) for both external and internal selection decisions, (c) for each step in the selection process, and (d) by race and sex of applicants. In order to meet this requirement, the organization must keep detailed records of its staffing activities and decisions. Such record keeping should be built directly into the organization's staffing system routines.[23]

Third, comparisons of selection rates among groups in a job category for purposes of compliance determination should be based on the 80% rule in the UGESP, which states that "a selection rate for any race, sex or ethnic group which is less than four-fifths (4/5) (or eighty percent) of the rate for the group with the highest rate will generally be regarded by federal enforcement agencies as evidence of adverse impact, while a greater than four-fifths rate will generally not be regarded by federal enforcement agencies as evidence of adverse impact."

If this rule is applied to the previous example, the group with the highest selection rate is men (.50). The rate for women should be within 80% of this rate, or .40 (.50 × .80 = .40). Since the actual rate for women is .11, this suggests the occurrence of adverse impact.

Fourth, the 80% rule is truly only a guideline. Note the use of the word "generally" in the rule with regard to differences in selection rates. Also, the 80% rule goes on to provide for other exceptions, based on sample size considerations and issues surrounding statistical and practical significance of difference in selection rates. Despite these exceptions, organizations are encouraged to use the 80% rule with stringency for purposes of self-analysis. Deviations from the rule should be treated as red flags that trigger an examination into possible reasons for their occurrence.

Applicant Stock Statistics

Applicant stock statistics require the calculation of the percentages of women and minorities (a) employed, and (b) available for employment in the population.[24] These percentages are compared to search for disparities in the percentages. This is referred to as *utilization analysis.*

To illustrate, the example from Exhibit 3.4 is shown here:

	Employed	**Availability**
Nonminority	90%	70%
Minority	10%	30%

It can be seen that 10% of employees are minorities, while their availability in the population is 30%. A comparison of these two percentages suggests an underutilization of minorities.

Utilization analysis of this sort is an integral part of not only compliance assessment, but affirmative action plans (AAPs). Indeed, utilization analysis is the starting point for the development of AAPs. This may be illustrated by reference to Revised Order No. 4 (see Appendix B), which specifies the affirmative action requirements for federal contractors.

The order requires the organization to conduct a formal utilization analysis of its workforce. That analysis must be (a) conducted by job category, and (b) done separately for women and minorities. While calculation of the numbers and percentages of persons employed is relatively straightforward, determination of their availability in the population is not. The order requires that the availabilities take into account eight factors, such as proximity to the organization and KSAO qualifications (these eight factors, and utilization analysis, are also covered in Chapter 6). Accurate measurement and/or estimation of availabilities that take into account these eight factors is extremely difficult. In large part, this is a reflection of difficulties in measuring characteristics of the labor force more generally.

Despite these measurement problems, the order requires comparison of the percentage of women and minorities employed with their availability. Based on this comparison, the organization must then determine if, and where, it is underutilizing these two groups. Unfortunately, the order does not provide any specific guidance to help determine how big a difference in percentages is tolerable before concluding that underutilization is occurring. Thus, the organization must exercise considerable discretion in the determination of adverse impact through the use of applicant stock statistics.

Standardization and Validation

When it has been determined that an organization is in noncompliance with the law, such as through adverse impact statistics, it must take certain steps to move toward compliance. While the specific steps will obviously depend on the situation, measurement activities invariably will be actively involved in them. These activities will revolve around standardization and validation of measures.

Standardization

A lack of consistency in treatment of applicants is one of the major factors contributing to the occurrence of discrimination in staffing. This is partly due to a lack of standardization in measurement, in terms of both what is measured and how it is evaluated or scored.

An example of inconsistency in what is measured is that the types of background information required of minority applicants may differ from that required of nonminority applicants. Minority applicants may be asked about credit ratings and criminal conviction records, while nonminority applicants are not. Or, the type of interview questions asked male applicants may be different from those asked female applicants.

Even if information is consistently gathered from all applicants, it may not be evaluated the same for all applicants. A male applicant who has a history of holding several different jobs may be viewed as a "career builder," while a female with the same history may be evaluated as an unstable "job hopper." In essence, different scoring keys are being used for men and women applicants.

Reducing, and hopefully eliminating, such inconsistency requires a straightforward application of the three properties of standardized measures discussed previously. Through standardization of measurement comes consistent treatment of applicants, and with it, the possibility of lessened adverse impact.

Validation

Even with standardized measurement, adverse impact may occur. Under these circumstances, the question is whether adverse impact is still justified. The UGESP addresses this issue directly. When there is adverse impact, the organization must either eliminate it or justify it through presentation of validity evidence regarding the measure(s) causing the adverse impact.

The types of validity evidence required under the UGESP are precisely those presented in this chapter. There are also detailed technical standards governing the conduct of these validation studies in the UGESP. The purpose of these requirements is to ensure that, if an organization's staffing system is causing adverse impact, it is for job-related reasons. Evidence of job-relatedness thus becomes the employer's rebuttal to the plaintiff's charges of discrimination. In the absence of such validation evidence, the employer must take steps to eliminate the adverse impact. These steps will involve various recruitment, selection, and employment activities that will be discussed throughout the remainder of the book.

SUMMARY

Measurement is an integral part of the foundation of staffing activities. Measures are used in staffing to assess job requirements and rewards, individuals' KSAOs, and HR outcomes; they are also used in monitoring and record keeping, as well as research and evaluation.

Measurement is defined as the process of using rules to assign numbers to objects to represent quantities of an attribute of the objects. Standardization of the measurement process is sought. This applies to each of the four levels of measurement—nominal, ordinal, interval, and ratio. Standardization is also sought for both objective and subjective measures.

Measures yield scores that represent the amount of the attribute being measured. Scores are manipulated in various ways to aid in interpreting the scores. Typical manipulations involve central tendency and variability, percentiles, and standard scores. Scores are also correlated to learn about the strength and direction of the relationship between two attributes. The significance of the resultant correlation coefficient is then judged in statistical and practical terms.

The quality of measures involves issues of reliability and validity. Reliability refers to consistency of measurement, both at a moment in time and between time periods. Various procedures are used to estimate reliability, including coefficient alpha, interrater and intrarater agreement, and test-retest. Reliability places an upper limit on the validity of a measure.

Validity refers to accuracy of measurement and accuracy of prediction, as reflected by the scores obtained from a measure. Criterion-related and content validation studies are conducted to help learn about the validity of a measure. In criterion-related validation, scores on a predictor (KSAO) measure are correlated with scores on a criterion (HR outcome) measure. In content validation, there is no criterion measure, so judgements are made about the content of a predictor relative to the HR outcome it is seeking to predict. Traditionally, results of validation studies have been treated as situation-specific, meaning that the organization ideally should conduct a new and separate validation study for any predictor in any situation in which the predictor is to be used. Recently, however, results from validity generalization studies have suggested that the validity of predictors may generalize across situations, meaning that the requirement of conducting costly and time-consuming validation studies in each specific situation could be relaxed.

Measurement is also an integral part of an organization's EEO/AA compliance activities, as the Uniform Guidelines on Employee Selection Procedures (UGESP) and Revised Order No. 4 make clear. The organization must calculate disparate impact statistics of both applicant flows and applicant stocks. These statistics are then used to help determine if and where the organization's staffing activities are causing disparate (adverse) impact. When adverse impact is found, changes in measurement practices may be legally necessary. As specified in the UGESP and Revised Order No. 4, these changes will involve movement toward standardization of measurement and the conduct of validation studies.

DISCUSSION QUESTIONS

1. Imagine and describe a staffing system for a job in which there were no measures used.

2. Describe how you might go about determining scores for applicants' responses to (a) interview questions, (b) letters of recommendation, and (c) questions about previous work experience.

3. Describe examples of when you would want the following for a written job knowledge test: (a) a low coefficient alpha (e.g., $\alpha = .35$), and (b) a low test-retest reliability.

4. Assume you gave a general ability test, measuring both verbal and computational skills, to a group of applicants for a specific job. Also assume that because of severe hiring pressures, you hired all of the applicants, regardless of their test scores. How would you investigate the criterion-related validity of the test?

5. Using the same example as in question four, how would you go about investigating the content validity of the test?

ENDNOTES

1. E. T. Cornelius III, "Analyzing Job Analysis Data"; E. L. Levine, J. N. Thomas, and F. Sistrunk, "Selecting a Job Analysis Approach," both in S. Gael (ed.), *The Job Analysis Handbook for Business, Industry and Government,* Vol. 1 (New York: Wiley, 1988), pp. 353–368 and pp. 339–352.

2. P. L. Ackerman and L. G. Humphreys, "Individual Difference Theory in Industrial and Organizational Psychology," in M. D. Dunnette and L. M. Hough (eds.), *Handbook of Industrial and Organizational Psychology,* Vol. 1 (Palo Alto, CA: Consulting Psychologists Press, 1990), pp. 223–282.

3. W. C. Borman, "Job Behavior, Performance, and Effectiveness," in M. D. Dunnette and L. M. Hough (eds.), *Handbook of Industrial and Organizational Psychology,* Vol. 2 (Palo Alto, CA: Consulting Psychologists Press, 1991), pp. 271–326. See also M. A. Campion, "Meaning and Measurement of Turnover: Comparison of Alternative Measures and Recommendations for Research," *Journal of Applied Psychology,* 1991, 76, pp. 19–212; D. L. Deadrick and R. M. Madigan, "Dynamic Criteria Revisited: A Longitudinal Study of Performance Stability and Predictive Validity," *Personnel Psychology,* 1990, 43, pp. 717–744; C. H. Campbell, P. Ford, M. G. Rumsey, E. D. Pulakos, W. C. Borman, D. B. Felker, M. V. D. Vera, and B. J. Riegelhaupt, "Development of Multiple Job Performance Measures in a Representative Sample of Jobs," *Personnel Psychology,* 1990, 43, pp. 277–300; K. R. Murphy and J. L. Cleveland, *Performance Appraisal* (Boston: Allyn and Bacon, 1991); A. K. Wigdor and B. F. Green, Jr., *Performance Assessment in the Workplace,* Vols. 1 and 2 (Washington, D.C.: National Academy Press, 1991).

4. E. F. Stone, *Research Methods in Organizational Behavior* (Santa Monica, CA: Goodyear, 1978), pp. 35–36.

5. F. G. Brown, *Principles of Educational and Psychological Testing* (Hinsdale, IL: Dryden, 1970), pp. 38–45.

6. E. F. Stone, *Research Methods in Organizational Behavior,* pp. 36–40.

7. R. L. Heneman, "The Relationship Between Supervisory Ratings and Results-Oriented Measures of Performance: A Meta-Analysis," *Personnel Psychology,* 1986, 39, pp. 811–826.

8. This section draws on F. G. Brown, *Principles of Educational and Psychological Testing,* pp. 158–197; L. J. Cronbach, *Essentials of Psychological Testing,* fourth ed. (New York: Harper and Row, 1984), pp. 81–120; N. W. Schmitt and R. J. Klimoski, *Research Methods in Human Resources Management* (Cincinnati: Southwestern, 1991), pp. 41–87.

9. J. T. McClave and P. G. Benson, *Statistics for Business and Economics,* third ed. (San Francisco: Dellan, 1985).

10. For an excellent review, see N. W. Schmitt and R. J. Klimoski, *Research Methods in Human Resources Management,* pp. 88–114.

11. This section draws on E. G. Carmines and R. A. Zeller, *Reliability and Validity Assessment* (Beverly Hills, CA: Sage, 1979).

12. D. P. Schwab, "Construct Validity in Organization Behavior," in B. Staw and L. L. Cummings (eds.), *Research in Organizational Behavior* (Greenwich, CT: JAI Press, 1980), pp. 3–43.

13. E. G. Carmines and R. A. Zeller, *Reliability and Validity Assessment;* J. M. Cortina, "What is Coefficient Alpha? An Examination of Theory and Application," *Journal of Applied Psychology,* 1993, 78, pp. 98–104; N. W. Schmitt and R. J. Klimoski, *Research Methods in Human Resources Management,* pp. 89–100.

14. This section draws on R. D. Arvey, "Constructs and Construct Validation," *Human Performance,* 1992, 5, pp. 59–69; W. F. Cascio, *Applied Psychology in Personnel Management,* fourth ed. (Englewood Cliffs, NJ: Prentice-Hall, 1991), pp. 149–170; H. G. Heneman III, D. P. Schwab, J. A. Fossum, and L. Dyer, *Personnel/Human Resource Management,* fourth ed. (Homewood, IL: Irwin, 1989), pp. 300–329; N. Schmitt and F. J. Landy, "The Concept of Validity," in N. Schmitt, W. C. Borman and Associates, *Personnel Selection in Organizations* (San Francisco: Jossey-Bass, 1993), pp. 275–309; D. P. Schwab, "Construct Validity in Organization Behavior."

15. H. G. Heneman III, D. P. Schwab, J. A. Fossum, and L. Dyer, *Personnel/Human Resource Management,* pp. 300–310.

16. G. M. McEvoy and R. W. Beatty, "Assessment Centers and Subordinate Appraisals of Managers: A Seven-Year Examination of Predictive Validity," *Personnel Psychology,* 1989, 42, pp. 37–52.

17. I. L. Goldstein, S. Zedeck, and B. Schneider, "An Exploration of the Job Analysis-Content Validity Process," in N. Schmitt, W. C. Borman, and Associates, *Personnel Selection in Organizations* (San Francisco: Jossey-Bass, 1993), pp. 3–34; H. G. Heneman III, D. P. Schwab, J. A. Fossum, and L. Dyer, *Personnel/Human Resource Management,* pp. 311–315; P. R. Sackett and R. D. Arvey, "Selection in Small N Settings," in N. Schmitt, W. C. Borman and Associates, *Personnel Selection in Organizations,* pp. 418–447; D. A. Joiner, *Content Valid Testing for Supervisory and Management Jobs: A Practical/Common Sense Approach* (Alexandria, VA: International Personnel Management Association, 1987).

18. R. S. Barrett, "Content Validation Form," *Public Personnel Management,* 1992, 21, pp. 41–52; E. E. Ghiselli, J. P. Campbell, and S. Zedeck, *Measurement Theory for the Behavioral Sciences* (San Francisco: W. H. Freeman, 1981).

19. N. Schmitt and C. Ostroff, "Operationalizing the Behavioral Consistency Approach: Selection Test Development Based on a Content-Oriented Strategy," *Personnel Psychology,* 1986, 39, pp. 91–108.

20. N. Schmitt, S. W. Gilliland, R. S. Landis, and D. Devine, "Computer-Based Testing Applied to Selection of Secretarial Applicants," *Personnel Psychology,* 1993, 46, pp. 149–165.

21. R. M. Guion, "Personnel Assessment, Selection and Placement," in M. D. Dunnette and L. M. Hough (eds.), *Handbook of Industrial and Organizational Psychology,* Vol. 2, pp. 360–365; F. L. Schmidt and J. E. Hunter, "Development of a General Solution to the Problem of Validity Generalization," *Journal of Applied Psychology,* 1977, 62, 529–540; N. Schmitt, W. C. Borman, and Associates, *Personnel Selection in Organizations,* pp. 295–296.

22. R. D. Arvey and R. H. Faley, *Fairness in Selecting Employees,* (Reading, MA: Addison-Wesley, 1988), pp. 73–78; J. Ledvinka and V. G. Scarpello, *Federal Regulation of Personnel and Human Resource Management,* second ed. (Boston: PWS-Kent, 1991), pp. 142–151.

23. J. C. Cook, ''Preparing For Statistical Battles Under the Civil Rights Act,'' *HR Focus,* 1992 (May), pp. 12–13.

24. Bureau of National Affairs, *Fair Employment Practices* (Washington, D.C.: author, periodically updated), pp. 443: 201, 209; J. Ledvinka and V. Scarpello, *Federal Regulation of Personnel and Human Resource Management,* pp. 124–142.

CHAPTER FIVE

Job Analysis

This chapter begins with a brief overview of job analysis and design. Job design creates job content, and job analysis captures and describes that content. Since job content is defined in terms of both job requirements and job rewards, job analysis must focus on both. The job requirements and job rewards approaches to job analysis are presented conceptually to show how they lead to reflections of job content. Each approach is then described in operational, practical ways in the bulk of the chapter.

The job requirements approach to job analysis is guided by the job requirements matrix, which contains three basic components (tasks, KSAOs, job context) that must be considered during a job analysis. Each of these components is described in some detail. Once the job requirements matrix has been completed, the results can be expressed in job descriptions and job specifications.

Collecting the necessary information for the job requirements matrix requires considering multiple job analysis methods, sources, and processes. All are described, along with indications of each one's advantages and disadvantages. Through this presentation, it is shown that there is no best or right way to conduct a job requirements job analysis.

Attention then shifts to the job rewards approach, which is guided by the job rewards matrix. It contains information about the extrinsic and intrinsic rewards of a job, along with indications about their amount, differentials among employees, and stability. Methods, sources, and processes for collecting this information are described.

Finally, three legal issues pertaining to job analysis are treated. All three issues involve the job requirements approach to job analysis as it applies to EEO/AA under the Civil Rights Acts and the Americans With Disabilities Act.

GENERAL ISSUES

Job Design and Structure

Jobs are the building blocks of an organization, in terms of both job content and the hierarchical relationships that emerge among them.[1] They are explicitly designed and aligned in ways that enhance the production of the organization's goods and services. Job analysis thus must be considered within the broader framework of the design of jobs, for it is through their design that jobs acquire their requirements and rewards in the first place.

Terminology

Certain terms are used frequently in discussions of job analysis and design. Definitions of some of the key terms, and examples of them, are provided in Exhibit 5.1. Note that the terms are presented in a logically descending hierarchy, starting with job category, or family, and proceeding downward through job, position, task dimension, task, and element.

EXHIBIT 5.1   Terminology Commonly Used in Job Analysis

TERM	DEFINITION
Job family	A grouping of jobs, usually according to function (e.g., production, finance, human resources, marketing)
Job category	A grouping of jobs according to generic job title or occupation (e.g., managerial, sales, clerical, maintenance), within or across job families
Job	A grouping of positions that are similar in their tasks and task dimensions
Position	A grouping of tasks/dimensions that constitute the total work assignment of a single employee; there are as many positions as there are employees
Task dimension	A grouping of similar types of tasks: sometimes called "duty," "area of responsibility," or "key results area"
Task	A grouping of elements to form an identifiable work activity that is a logical and necessary step in the performance of a job
Element	The smallest unit into which work can be divided without analyzing separate motions, movements, and mental processes

Traditional Job Design

The traditional way of designing a job is to identify and define its elements and tasks precisely, and then incorporate them into a job description. This task core includes virtually all tasks associated with the job, and from it a fairly inclusive list of KSAOs flows. Thus defined, there are clear lines of demarcation between jobs in terms of both tasks and KSAOs, and there is little overlap between jobs on either basis. Each job also has its own set of extrinsic and intrinsic rewards. Such job design is marked by formal organization charts, clear and precise job descriptions and specifications, and well-defined relationships between jobs in terms of mobility (promotion and transfer) paths. Traditional job design, as characterized here, is the dominant mode of design in most organizations.

Evolving Job Design

Traditionally designed and administered jobs may gradually change or evolve over time. These changes are not radical, are usually intentional, and are often due to technological and workload changes. An excellent example of such an evolving job is that of "secretary."[2] Traditional or core tasks associated with the job include typing, filing, taking dictation, and answering phones. However, the job has evolved in many organizations to include word processing tasks and the management of multiple projects, and thus requires new managerial skills such as planning and coordination and new KSAOs for these tasks. Accompanying these job design changes is a title change to "administrative assistant." Such evolving job design is normally incorporated into the job analysis process of the organization.

Nontraditional Job Design

Nontraditional job design represents a more substantial departure from traditional and evolving job design. This departure is best illustrated through several examples.[3] The first example is that of autonomous, self-managing work teams. Here, the job consists of the collective tasks of the team, and these tasks are varied and changing in nature. Each team member does not occupy a "position" in the traditional sense of the word, and team members are differentiated according to KSAO levels, rather than tasks performed.

In a typical manufacturing plant, for example, all nonmanagers may share the same job title (e.g., technician) and be classified into five skill (KSAO) levels. Employees progress through the skill (and corresponding pay) levels on the basis of company-provided training. With increases in skill come increases in the number of different tasks the employee is qualified to perform. The plant has explicit job specifications for the five KSAO levels, but does not have detailed job descriptions specifying detailed sets of tasks.

A second example of nontraditional job design involves jobs with a core set of tasks, plus an emergent set of tasks as add-ons. The latter tasks emerge sporadically, may not be part of the job for very long, and may never be formally recognized as part of the job. An example here is the job of registered nurse, where tasks frequently emerge and disappear in response to changes in technology, legal requirements, and patient load.

A third example of a nontraditional job is the "loose canon" one. Such jobs are defined by a broad job title (e.g., director, program manager, scientist), accompanied by a cursory summary statement of job tasks or duties. Within this fairly elastic title-task combination, the employee is free to rattle and roll around.

The final example involves idiosyncratic jobs.[4] Such jobs are unique and created in response to the known (or anticipated) availability of a specific person with highly valued skills. The person may be a current employee or an outsider to the organization. The person for whom the position is created may in fact even be the instigator of its creation. He or she may approach the organization and explicitly communicate availability and the type of position (both requirements and rewards) desired. Former politicians and high-level government employees are often hired into such idiosyncratically designed jobs.

This discussion of job design suggests several themes. First, jobs are intentionally created and designed by organizations to serve organizational purposes. Second, jobs are defined, designed, and aligned in a multitude of ways. Third, regardless of these differences, the common thread regarding jobs is a concern with job requirements and rewards. Fourth, job analysis is the administrative process that is appropriately used for identifying and describing these requirements and rewards. Finally, dealing with evolving and nontraditional jobs presents special challenges to job analysis and the staffing systems that are built upon it.

What Is Job Analysis

Job analysis may be defined as the process of studying jobs in order to gather, analyze, synthesize, and report information about job content.[5] Two things need to be emphasized in this definition. First, job analysis is a process, as opposed to a specific method or technique. While there are many such methods and techniques used in job analysis (and they will be discussed extensively in this chapter), they appropriately are thought of as a part of an overall process, rather than as the process per se.

A second important point of emphasis is that job analysis seeks to uncover and then report information about jobs in ways that will be useful to the organization. In staffing, useful information is that which assists the organization in matching persons to jobs. More specifically, the information must focus on job requirements and job rewards, which combine to form overall job content. Armed with such information, the organization is able to conduct staffing activities, such as communicating with job applicants about job vacancies (recruitment); determining appropriate assessment devices for measuring applicant qualifications (selection); and deciding which applicants will receive job offers, as well as determining the content of the offers (employment).

Job analysis and the information it provides thus serves as basic input to the totality of staffing activities for an organization. In this sense, job analysis is a support activity to the various functional staffing activities. Indeed, without thorough and accurate information about job requirements and rewards, the organization is greatly hampered in its attempts to acquire a workforce that will be effective in terms of HR outcomes such as performance, satisfaction, and retention. Job analysis thus is the foundation upon which successful staffing systems are constructed.

Some job analysis processes focus on the job requirements portion of job content; other job analyses concentrate on the job rewards part. Before discussion of specifics, however, it is useful to view the processes conceptually. The fundamental concepts in the job requirements approach are presented next,[6] followed by a similar presentation of the job rewards approach.[7]

Job Requirements Approach: Conceptual Overview

Any job has two related requirements that must be met by individuals in order for the job to be performed. These are (a) the job tasks, and (b) the underlying knowledge, skill, ability, and other characteristics (KSAOs) necessary for the performance of the tasks. Some processes of job analysis focus on the task component of job requirements, and these are referred to as *task-oriented* approaches. Other forms of job analysis, while not ignoring tasks, place emphasis on KSAOs, and these are referred to *KSAO-oriented* in nature. Each of these approaches, and the logical relationships between them, are shown in Exhibit 5.2.

Task-Oriented   As demonstrated in Exhibit 5.2, job analysis is first used to identify job tasks and the context in which these tasks are performed, such as the physical working environment. The results of this job analysis are typically reported in a *job description*. This document then becomes the written source of information that is incorporated into the HR activities of the organization, particularly staffing activities. Stated somewhat differently, the job description becomes the organization's operational indicator of tasks required for the job. These documents taken together are likely to be incorporated into job information manuals that will be maintained by the HR function of the organization, as well as provided to individual managers and employees.

KSAO-Oriented   As Exhibit 5.2 displays, job analysis may proceed beyond identification of tasks and job context. In particular, job analysis may seek to infer

EXHIBIT 5.2   Job Requirements Approach to Job Analysis

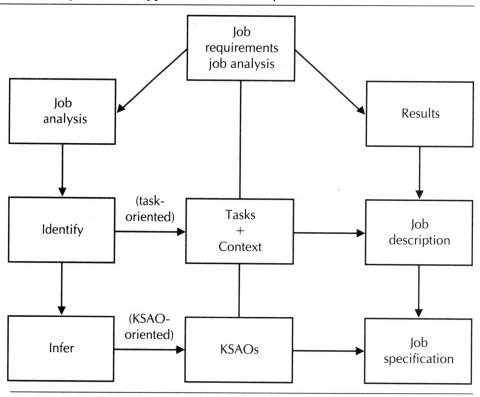

the KSAOs that are likely to be required for successful performance of job tasks, taking into account characteristics of the job context. For example, assume a task-oriented job analysis for the job of management trainee in a retail store, such as K-Mart or Sears, reveals that the job entails a number of tasks that may be grouped together into a broader task dimension labeled "customer service." Using this specific task information, a KSAO-oriented job analysis seeks to infer the specific types of KSAOs necessary for a management trainee in order to provide effective customer service. The resultant KSAOs might involve such things as product knowledge, interpersonal skills, verbal ability, and other characteristics pertaining to educational background (e.g., a major or specific courses).

The results of a KSAO-oriented job analysis, just like a task-oriented one, yield results that are reported in written documents, notably a *job specification.* In turn, these documents serve as basic sources of information that are stored, communicated throughout the organization, and used as input to the myriad staffing activities.

Job Rewards Approach: Conceptual Overview

Broadly speaking, every job has an array of rewards associated with it. Some of these rewards are external to the job itself and the tasks that comprise the job. Examples of such rewards include pay, benefits, promotion opportunities, and type of supervision. Collectively, these are referred to as *extrinsic rewards.* Other rewards, however, are internal to the job itself. They are usually a direct outgrowth of the tasks themselves and the feelings that an employee experiences while performing and completing the tasks. Feelings of autonomy, utilization of skills, and achievement of tasks and related goals are examples of these types of rewards. The label generally attached to these is *intrinsic rewards.*

The job rewards approach to job analysis focuses on both extrinsic and intrinsic rewards, as shown in Exhibit 5.3. As can be seen, job analysis first seeks to identify the extrinsic rewards associated with the job. Usually this is a straightforward process since the extrinsic rewards have already been established by the organization as part of regular HR functional activities. As an example, the pay is specified as part of the organization's compensation activities, which detail starting pay and pay range. The result of this job analysis is specification of extrinsic terms and conditions of employment. These terms are recorded and reported in a variety of ways, such as HR policy manuals, employee handbooks, labor contracts, and recruitment literature.

A second form of analysis is concerned with inferring the intrinsic rewards associated with the job, as seen in Exhibit 5.3. These inferences are made by studying the tasks identified during the job analysis; for example, the extent of repetitive tasks in a job says something about how challenging it is.

Inferences also are (and probably should be) made on the basis of responses from job incumbents to questionnaires designed to reveal their sense of on-the-job achievement, utilization of skills, and so forth. Results of analysis of intrinsic

EXHIBIT 5.3   Job Rewards Approach to Job Analysis

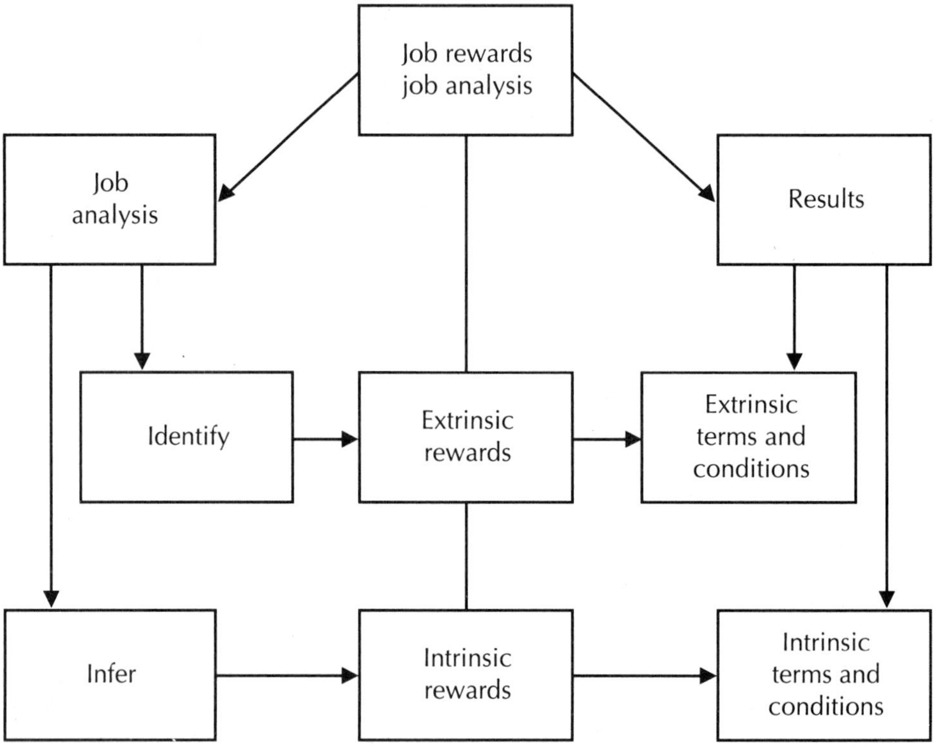

rewards is communicated as intrinsic terms and conditions of employment. They may be used as a basis for redesigning jobs (and thus task and KSAO requirements), developing recruitment information, and designing promotion systems that provide increases in both extrinsic and intrinsic rewards as employees advance upward in the organization's hierarchy.

Specific, detailed treatments of job analysis are presented next. The job requirements approach is discussed first, starting with task-oriented job analysis; following that, KSAO-oriented job analysis is dealt with. Then, attention is devoted to the job rewards approach.

JOB REQUIREMENTS JOB ANALYSIS

The job requirements approach to job analysis requires the organization to identify tasks and underlying KSAOs for jobs. This is no small undertaking. There are multiple jobs, tasks, KSAOs, potential job analysts, methods and techniques, and administrative processes to be concerned with. It is easy to get caught up in each of these issues and its complexities and to obscure the overall purpose, process, and results of the analysis.

The conceptual framework in Exhibit 5.2 can be transformed into a general operational framework, or *job requirements matrix,* that identifies the key components and results of job requirements job analysis. A job requirements matrix serves as a general guide to the design and conduct of job analysis, and it functions as an overlay to various methods, techniques, analysts, and so forth.

The job requirements matrix is presented first in this section. It is then followed by a discussion of key components and issues embedded within the matrix. Following that, potential methods of collecting job information and individuals who function as possible sources of job information are dealt with. This is followed by some general suggestions regarding the conduct of job analysis as a process.

Job Requirements Matrix

Job requirements job analysis is best conceptualized by referring to the job requirements matrix shown in Exhibit 5.4. The matrix shows the key components of job requirements job analysis, each of which must be explicitly considered for inclusion in any job requirements job analysis. Completion of the cell entries in

EXHIBIT 5.4   Job Requirements Matrix

Job Title:

Job Summary:

Tasks			KSAOs							
			Nature				Importance			
Tasks	**Dimensions**	**Importance**	**K**	**S**	**A**	**O**	**K**	**S**	**A**	**O**
1	A									
2										
3										
4	B									
.	.									
.	.									
.	.									
N	Z									

Job Context: Physical and environmental

the matrix represents the information that must be gathered, analyzed, synthesized, and expressed in usable written form.

At the top of Exhibit 5.4 are entered a "job title" and a "job summary." A job summary is an overall, general statement of major tasks or duties associated with the job. The section dealing with "tasks" contains three columns. The first column is for a listing (from 1 to N) of tasks expressed in the form of task statements (e.g., takes and records orders from customers). The second column is for "dimensions," which are groupings (A,B, . . . Z) of similar tasks into more abstract, but meaningful categories (e.g., planning and customer service). Column three indicates the "importance" of tasks and/or dimensions. "Importance" is a generic term used to indicate the significance attached to tasks/dimensions in terms of such attributes as frequency, time spent, and criticalness. This section of the matrix, when completed, will provide a representation of job task requirements in terms of their nature, groupings into dimensions, and indications about their relative importance.

The KSAO section of the matrix contains columns for "nature" and for "importance" of KSAOs. The nature of the KSAOs are derived by inference from the task section of the matrix. That is, for each task and associated task dimension, the underlying KSAOs necessary for performance of the tasks are inferred by various participants (sources) in the job analysis process. The importance of KSAOs represents judgments about their weight in terms of impact on, or contribution to, task performance.

Turning to the bottom of the job requirements matrix, the "job context" is represented as encompassing both tasks and KSAOs, for both of these occur within a particular job context. That context is usually analyzed and described in terms of physical demands and environmental characteristics (e.g., noise) surrounding the job.

When a job requirements job analysis process is finished, the final result or output is a completed job requirements matrix, an example of which is shown in Exhibit 5.5 for the job of administrative assistant. This matrix serves as the basic informational source or document for any job in terms of its job requirements. Often, the task and job context parts of the matrix are converted to a job description, and the KSAO portion is converted to a job specification. However it is expressed exactly, the resultant information serves as a basic input and guide to all subsequent staffing activities.

As just noted, the job requirements matrix contains major sections, each of which represents a basic component of job requirements job analysis. We turn now to a fuller discussion of each of those components.

Task Statements
The task-oriented approach to job analysis begins with the development of *task statements,* whose objective is to identify and record a set of tasks that both includes all of the job's major tasks and excludes nonrelevant or trivial tasks.[8] Task

EXHIBIT 5.5   Portion of Job Requirements Matrix for Job of Administrative Assistant

Tasks			KSAOs	
Specific Tasks	Task Dimensions	Importance (% time spent)	Nature	Importance to Tasks (1–5 rating)
1. Arrange schedules with office assistant/volunteers to assure that office will be staffed during prescribed hours	A. Supervision	30%	1. Knowledge of office operations and policies	4.9
			2. Ability to match people to tasks according to their skills and hours of availability	4.6
2. Assign office tasks to office assistant/volunteers to assure coordination of activities	A. Supervision		3. Skill in interaction with diverse people	2.9
			4. Skill in determining types and priorities of tasks	4.0
3. Type/transcribe letters, memos, and reports from handwritten material or dictated copy to produce final copy, using word processor	B. Word processing	20%	1. Knowledge of typing formats	3.1
			2. Knowledge of spelling and punctuation	5.0
			3. Knowledge of graphics display software	2.0
4. Prepare graphs and other visual material to supplement reports, using word processor	B. Word processing		4. Ability to proofread and correct work	5.0
			5. Skill in use of WordPerfect (most current version)	5.0
5. Proofread typed copy and correct spelling, punctuation, and typographical errors in order to produce high quality materials	B. Word processing		6. Skill in creating visually appealing and understandable graphs	4.3
				3.4

Job Context: No excessive physical demands; safe, occasionally noisy, work environment.

statements should thus be free from deficiency and contamination; they serve as the building blocks for the remainder of the job requirements job analysis.

Identification and recording of tasks begins with the construction of task statements. These statements are objectively written descriptions of the behaviors or work activities engaged in by employees in order to perform the job. The statements are made in simple declarative sentences.

Ideally, each task statement will show several things. These are

1. what the employees does, using a specific action verb at the start of the task statement
2. to whom or what the employee does what he or she does, stating the object of the verb
3. what is produced, indicating the expected output of the verb
4. what materials, tools, procedures, or equipment are used

Use of the *sentence analysis technique* is very helpful for writing task statements that conform to these four requirements. An example of the technique is shown in Exhibit 5.6 for several tasks from very different jobs.

In addition to meeting the preceding four requirements, there are several other suggestions for effectively writing task statements. First, use specific action verbs that have only one meaning. Examples of verbs that do not conform to this suggestion include "supports," "assists," and "handles."

Second, focus on recording tasks, as opposed to specific elements that comprise a task. This requires use of considerable judgment, since the distinction between a task and an element is relative and often fuzzy. A useful rule to keep in mind here is that most jobs can be adequately described within a range of 15–25 task statements. Should a task statement list exceed this range, it is a warning that it may be too narrow in terms of activities defined.

Third, do not include minor or trivial activities in task statements; focus only on major tasks and activities. An exception to this recommendation occurs when a so-called minor task is judged to have great importance to the job (see the following discussion).

Fourth, take steps to ensure that the list of task statements is content valid and reliable.[9] The basic way to conform to this suggestion is to have two or more people ("analysts") independently evaluate the task statement list in terms of (a) inclusiveness, and (b) clarity. High agreement between people signifies high reliability and content validity, meaning that job content is consistently described in ways not deficient or contaminated. Should disagreements between people be discovered, the nature of the disagreements can be discussed and appropriate modifications to the task statements made.

Fifth, have at least the manager and a job incumbent serve as the analysts, providing the content validity and reliability checks. It is important to have the manager participate in this process in order to verify that the task statements are

EXHIBIT 5.6   Use of the Sentence Analysis Technique for Task Statements

Sentence Analysis Technique

What does the worker do?		Why does the worker do it? What gets done?	What is the final result or technological objective?
Worker action		Purpose of the worker actions	Materials, products, subject matter, and/or services
(Worker function)	(Work devices, people or information)	(Work field)	(MPSMS)
Verb	Direct object	Infinitive phrase	
		Infinitive	Object of the infinitive
Sets up *(setting up)*	Various types of metal-working machines *(work device)*	to machine *(machining)*	metal aircraft parts. *(material)*
Persuades *(persuading)*	customers *(people)*	to buy *(merchandising)*	automobiles. *(product)*
Interviews *(analyzing)*	clients *(people)*	to assess *(advising–counseling)*	skills and abilities. *(subject matter)*
Drives *(driving–operating)*	bus *(work device)*	to transport *(transporting)*	passengers. *(service)*

Source: Vocational Rehabilitation Institute, *A Guide to Job Analysis* (Menominee, WI: University of Wisconsin-Stout, 1982), p. 8.

inclusive and accurate. For the job incumbent, the concern is not only that of verification, but also acceptance of the task statements as adequate representations that will guide incumbents' performance of the job. Ideally, there should be multiple managers and job incumbents, along with a representative of the HR department, serving as analysts. This would expand the scope of input and allow for more precise content validity and reliability checks.

Finally, recognize that the accuracy or validity of task statements cannot be evaluated against any external criterion, such as in an empirical validation study. The reason for this is that there is no external criterion available for use. Task descriptions are accurate and meaningful only to the extent that people agree on them. Because of this, the preceding recommendation regarding checks on content validity and reliability takes on added importance.

Task Dimensions

Task statement lists may be maintained in list form and subsequently incorporated into the job description. Often, however, it is useful to group sets of task statements into *task dimensions,* and then attach a name to each such dimension. Other terms for task dimensions are "duties," "accountability areas," "responsibilities," and "performance dimensions."

A useful way to facilitate the grouping process is to create a *task dimension matrix.* Each column in the matrix represents a potential task dimension, and a label is tentatively attached to it. Each row in the matrix represents a particular task statement. Cell entries in the matrix represent the assignment of task statements to task dimensions (the grouping of tasks). The goal is to have each task statement assigned to only one task dimension. The process is complicated by the fact that the dimensions and labels must be created prior to grouping; the dimensions and labels may have to be changed or rearranged in order to make task statements fit as one progresses through the assignment of task statements to dimensions.

Several things should be borne in mind about task dimensions. First, their creation is optional and should occur only if they will be useful. Second, there are many different grouping procedures, ranging from straightforward judgmental ones to highly sophisticated statistical ones.[10] For most purposes, a simple judgmental process is sufficient, such as having the people who participated in the creation of the task statements also create the groupings as part of the same exercise. As a rule, there should be 4–8 dimensions, depending on the number of task statements, regardless of the specific grouping procedure used. Third, it is important that the grouping procedure yield a reliable set of task dimensions acceptable to managers, job incumbents, and other organizational members. Finally, as with task statements, it is not possible to empirically validate task dimensions against some external criterion; for both task statements and dimensions, their validity is in the eyes of their definers and beholders.

Importance of Tasks/Dimensions

Rarely are all tasks/dimensions of a job thought to be of equal "weight" or importance. In some general sense, it is thus felt that these differences must be captured, expressed, and incorporated into job information, especially the job description. Normally, assessments of importance are made just for task dimensions, though it is certainly possible to make them for individual tasks as well.

Before actual weighting can occur, two decisions must be made. First, the specific attribute to be assessed in terms of importance must be decided (e.g., time spent on the task/dimension). Second, a decision is required regarding whether the attribute will be measured in categorical (e.g., essential-nonessential) or continuous (e.g., % of time spent, 1–5 rating of importance) terms. Exhibit 5.7 shows examples of the results of these two decisions in terms of commonly used importance attributes and their measurement.

EXHIBIT 5.7   Examples of Ways to Assess Task/Dimension Importance

A.   **Relative Time Spent**

For each task/dimension, rate the amount of time you spend on it, relative to all other tasks/dimensions of your job.

1	2	3	4	5
Very small amount		Average amount		Very large amount

B.   **Percentage (%) Time Spent**

For each task/dimension, indicate the percentage (%) of time you spend on it (percentages must total to 100%).

Dimension _____   % Time spent _____

C.   **Importance to Overall Performance**

For each task/dimension, rate its importance to your overall job performance.

1	2	3	4	5
Minor importance		Average importance		Major importance

D.   **Need for New Employee Training**

Do new employees receive a standard, planned course of training for performance of this task, other than a customary job orientation?

_____ Yes

_____ No

Once these decisions are made, it is possible to proceed with the actual process of assessing or weighting the tasks/dimensions in terms of importance. It should be noted here that if the tasks/dimensions are not explicitly assessed in such a manner, all tasks/dimensions end up being equally weighted by default.

If possible, it is desirable for the assessments to be done initially by independent analysts (e.g., incumbents and managers). In this way, it will be possible to then check for the degree of reliability among raters. Where differences are found, they can be discussed and resolved. Just as it is desirable to have high reliability in the identification of tasks and dimensions, it is desirable to have high reliability in judgments of their importance.[11]

KSAOs

KSAOs are inferred or derived from knowledge of the tasks and task dimensions themselves. The inference process requires that the analysts explicitly think in specific cause-and-effect terms. For each task or dimension, the analyst must in essence ask, "Exactly what KSAOs do I think will be necessary for (will cause) performance on this task or dimension?" Then the analyst should ask "Why do I think this?" in order to think through the soundness of the inferential logic. Discussions among analysts about these questions are to be encouraged.

When asking and answering these questions, it is useful to keep in mind what is meant by the terms "knowledge," "skill," "ability," and "other characteristics." It is also very helpful to refer to research results that help us better understand the nature and complexity of these concepts.

Knowledge   *Knowledge* is a body of information (conceptual, factual, procedural) that can be directly applied to the performance of tasks. It tends to be quite focused or specific in terms of job, organization, or occupation. Generally, research has not been concerned with identifying and defining bodies of knowledge required for specific tasks, dimensions, or jobs. Because of this, a heavy responsibility is placed on the analysts to infer the specific knowledges actually required for task performance. Analysts should be particularly wary of using global or shorthand terms such as "knowledge of accounting principles." Here, it would be better to indicate which accounting principles are being utilized, and why each is necessary for task performance.

Skill   *Skill* refers to an observable competence to perform a particular task or closely related set of tasks. Skill requirements are directly inferred from observation or knowledge of tasks performed.

Considerable research has been devoted to identifying particular job-related skills and to organizing them into taxonomies. Job analysts should begin the skills inference process by referring to the results of this research.

An excellent example of such useful research is found in the SCANS project.[12] It identifies two types of skills: competency and foundation. The *competency skills* are generic skills required for successful job performance in most if not all jobs, and the *foundation skills* are more basic skills or qualities underlying the competencies. Detailed definitions of each competency and foundation skill are contained in the report itself.

The SCANS report also identifies 35 jobs representative of the entire job spectrum in this country. They fall into five categories: health and human services; office, financial services, and government; accommodations and personal services; manufacturing, agribusiness, mining and construction; and trade, transportation, and communication. For each of these jobs there is provided a detailed statement of the specific competency and foundation skills as they apply to that job, as well as a listing of all of the skills and their rated (1–5 rating scale) importance to the job. An example of the listing and importance ratings for the job of dietary manager is shown in Exhibit 5.8.

EXHIBIT 5.8   Dietary Manager: Job Summary, Competencies, Foundation Skills

---

Job Summary: Duties performed by the dietary manager combine clinical and administrative services. The managers are responsible for meal planning and preparation on a large scale. Some of the services include supervising and training staff, preparing budgets, purchasing food and equipment, and establishing policy.

Competencies	Mean	Standard Deviation
Interprets and communicates information	4.75	.50
Exercises leadership	4.75	.50
Acquires and evaluates information	4.50	.58
Understands systems	4.50	.58
Serves clients/customers	4.50	.58
Teaches others	4.50	.58
Participates as a member of a team	4.25	.96
Allocates human resources	4.25	.50
Improves and designs systems	4.25	.50
Negotiates to arrive at a decision	4.25	.50
Selects technology	4.00	.82
Works with cultural diversity	4.00	.82
Allocates time	4.00	.82
Allocates money	3.75	1.50
Monitors and corrects performance	3.75	.96
Organizes and maintains information	3.50	1.00
Allocates material and facility resources	3.50	.58
Uses computers to process information	3.25	1.50
Applies technology to tasks	2.50	1.29
Maintains and troubleshoots technology	2.25	.96

(continued)

EXHIBIT 5.8   Continued

Foundation Skills	Mean	Standard Deviation
Listening	4.75	.50
Integrity/honesty	4.75	.50
Responsibility	4.75	.50
Reading	4.75	.50
Problem solving	4.50	1.00
Speaking	4.50	1.00
Writing	4.50	.58
Reasoning	4.50	.58
Decision making	4.25	.96
Self-management	4.25	.96
Arithmetic	4.00	.82
Social	4.00	.82
Self-esteem	3.75	.96
Knowing how to learn	3.75	1.26
Creative thinking	3.50	.58
Mathematics	3.25	.50
Seeing things in the mind's eye	3.25	.50

NOTE: Mean and standard deviation calculated on 1–5 importance rating scale.

Source: U.S. Department of Labor, *Skills and Tasks for Jobs: A SCANS Report for America 2000* (Washington, D.C.: author, 1992), pp. 3–27 to 3–37.

Ability   An *ability* is an underlying capacity to perform a task. This capacity is possessed by the person at the time the task is first performed.

Substantial research has been conducted on the nature and classification of human abilities. Analysts should consult the results of that research when doing ability inference. Recent research suggests a taxonomy of 52 specific abilities, grouped into four major ability categories (cognitive, psychomotor, physical, and sensory/perceptual).[13] These are shown in Exhibit 5.9.

Each of these 52 specific abilities is accompanied by a definition, examples of specific tasks requiring the ability, titles of jobs commonly requiring these tasks, and examples of selection tests that assess the ability. An example for the cognitive ability "written comprehension" is shown in Exhibit 5.10.

There may be instances in which standard taxonomies may not be sufficient to cover all the specific abilities required for a particular job. Such gaps in coverage will need to be closed by the analysts conducting the ability inferences. When doing so, they should seek to follow the format shown in Exhibit 5.10, particularly those sections pertaining to definition, tasks, and jobs (test examples are not necessary at this point; they become relevant during the selection process).

EXHIBIT 5.9   Taxonomy of Human Abilities

Cognitive Abilities

1. Oral comprehension
2. Written comprehension
3. Oral expression
4. Written expression
5. Fluency of ideas
6. Originality
7. Memorization
8. Problem sensitivity
9. Mathematical reasoning
10. Number facility
11. Deductive reasoning
12. Inductive reasoning
13. Information ordering
14. Category flexibility
15. Speed of closure
16. Flexibility of closure
17. Spatial orientation
18. Visualization
19. Perceptual speed
20. Selective attention
21. Time sharing

Psychomotor Abilities

22. Control precision
23. Multi-limb coordination
24. Response orientation
25. Rate control
26. Reaction time
27. Arm-hand steadiness
28. Manual dexterity
29. Finger dexterity
30. Wrist-finger speed
31. Speed-of-limb movement

Physical Abilities

32. Static strength
33. Explosive strength
34. Dynamic strength
35. Trunk strength
36. Extent flexibility
37. Dynamic flexibility
38. Gross body coordination
39. Gross body equilibrium
40. Stamina

Sensory/Perceptual Abilities

41. Near vision
42. Far vision
43. Visual color discrimination
44. Night vision
45. Peripheral vision
46. Depth perception
47. Glare sensitivity
48. Hearing sensitivity
49. Auditory attention
50. Sound localization
51. Speech recognition
52. Speech clarity

EXHIBIT 5.10 Written Comprehension Ability: Definition, Tasks, Jobs, and Test Examples

---

Definition: Written comprehension is the ability to understand written sentences and paragraphs. This ability involves reading and understanding the meaning of words, phrases, sentences, and paragraphs. It involves reading; it does not involve writing, listening to, or understanding spoken information.

Tasks: Written comprehension may be used in reading books, articles, technical manuals, written instructions, work orders, and apartment leases.

Jobs: Jobs that require high levels of written comprehension include those of an administrator, lawyer, reporter, scientist, translator, and journal editor.

Test Examples: Tests of written comprehension usually present subjects with one or more passages of information. They then answer multiple-choice questions about the information. The emphasis of the test may be on following directions, understanding the general meaning of paragraphs, or understanding the meaning of specific words. Other tests of written comprehension are strictly vocabulary-oriented, focusing on identifying definitions, synonyms, or antonyms.

Source: Modified and reproduced by special permission of the Publisher, Consulting Psychologists Press, Inc., Palo Alto, CA 94303 from *Handbook of Human Abilities: Definitions, Measurements, and Job Task Requirements* by Edward A. Fleishman and Maureen E. Reilley. Copyright 1992 by Consulting Psychologists Press, Inc. All rights reserved. Further reproduction is prohibited without the Publisher's written consent.

Other Characteristics This is a catchall category for factors that do not fit neatly into the K, S, and A, categories. Common examples here include licensure requirements (e.g., car, occupation), work-shift availability (e.g., night or day), appearance requirements, and general personality characteristics (e.g., sociable, assertive). Care should be taken to ensure that factors placed in the "other" category truly are job requirements, as opposed to whimsical and ill-defined preferences of the organization.

KSAO Importance

As suggested in the job requirements matrix (Exhibit 5.4), the KSAOs of a job may differ in their weight or contribution to task performance. Hence, their relative importance must be explicitly considered, defined, and indicated. Failure to do so means that all KSAOs will be assumed to be of equal importance by default.

As with task importance, deriving KSAO importance requires two decisions. First, what will be the specific attribute(s) on which importance is judged? Second, will the measurement of each attribute be categorical (e.g., required-preferred) or continuous (e.g., 1–5 rating scale)? Examples of formats for indicating KSAO importance are shown in Exhibit 5.11.

EXHIBIT 5.11   Examples of Ways to Assess KSAO Importance

A. **Importance to (acceptable) (superior) task performance**

1 = minimal importance
2 = some importance
3 = average importance
4 = considerable importance
5 = extensive importance

B. **Should the KSAO be assessed during recruitment/selection?**

☐ Yes
☐ No

C. **Is the KSAO required, preferred, or not required for recruitment/selection?**

☐ Required
☐ Preferred
☐ Not required (obtain on job and/or in training)

Job Context

As shown in the job requirements matrix, tasks and KSAOs occur within a broader job context. A job requirements job analysis should include consideration of the job context and the factors that are important in defining it. Such consideration is necessary because these factors may have an influence on tasks and KSAOs, and further, information about the factors may be used in the recruitment and selection of job applicants.

Consider, for example, a job context factor such as physical demands, which includes lifting and kneeling. These types of demands may influence how jobs and tasks are designed and subsequently performed. As such, consideration of these factors will have to be incorporated into the KSAO assessment procedures to be used in the selection of job applicants. In addition, information about the physical demands of a job may be communicated to job applicants in order to provide a realistic description of what the total job is like.

Two frequently considered job context factors are physical demands and environmental conditions. Physical demands refer to demands of the job per se, and not to the physical capacities or requirements of employees (these could obviously be derived as a part of the KSAO inference process). Environmental conditions refer to the surroundings in which a job is performed. They must be specific and have identifiable effects on tasks and/or employees performing them. Organization "climate" factors, such as trust and team spirit, are not included as environmental conditions and are more appropriately candidates for consideration under job rewards.

EXHIBIT 5.12   Job Context Factors: Physical Demands and Environmental Conditions

Physical Demands	Environmental Conditions
Strength	Exposure to weather
Balancing	Extreme cold
Stooping	Extreme heat
Kneeling	Wet and/or humid
Crouching	Noise intensity level
Crawling	Vibration
Climbing	Atmospheric conditions
Reaching	Moving mechanical parts
Handling	Electric shock
Fingering	High, exposed places
Feeling	Radiation
Talking	Explosives
Hearing	Toxic/caustic chemicals
Tasting/smelling	Other
Near acuity	
Far acuity	
Depth perception	
Accommodation	
Color vision	
Field of vision	

Example: Climbing	Example: Atmospheric Conditions
Ascending or descending ladders, stairs, scaffolding, ramps, poles and the like, using feet and legs or hands and arms. Bodily agility is emphasized.	Exposure to conditions such as fumes, noxious odors, dusts, mists, gases, and poor ventilation that affect the respiratory system, eyes, or skin.

Source: U.S. Department of Labor, *The Revised Handbook for Analyzing Jobs* (Washington, D.C.: author, 1991), pp. 12–1 to 12–18.

The physical demands of jobs may be defined in terms of 20 specific factors, and environmental conditions defined in terms of 14 factors.[14] Both sets of factors are shown in Exhibit 5.12 along with the information provided as an example for one physical demand factor ("climbing") and one environmental condition ("atmospheric conditions"). When these factors are used in job analysis, the importance of the factor is assessed in terms of a categorical judgment about frequency (does not exist, exists up to 1/3 of the time, exists from 1/3 to 2/3 of the time, exists 2/3 or more of the time).

Job Descriptions and Job Specifications

For administrative purposes, it is common practice to express the output or results of job requirements job analysis in written job descriptions and job specifications.[15]

A *job description* is a document containing information about job tasks and context; a *job specification* is a document containing information about KSAOs. Referring back to the job requirements matrix, note that its sections pertaining to tasks and job context are similar to a job description, and the section dealing with KSAOs is similar to a job specification. The job requirements matrix thus not only provides an operational framework for job analysis, but also indicates the operational output for job analysis in the form of the information to be included in job descriptions and job specifications.

There are no standard formats or other requirements for either job descriptions or job specifications. In terms of content, however, a job description should usually include the following: job family, job title, job summary, task statements and dimensions, importance indicator(s), job context indicators, and date job analysis conducted. A job specification should usually include job family, job title, job summary, KSAOs (separate section for each), importance indicators, and date conducted. An example of a combined job description/specification is shown in Exhibit 5.13.

Collecting Job Information

Job analysis involves not only consideration of the types of information (tasks, KSAOs, and job context) to be collected, but also the methods, sources, and processes to be used for such collection. These issues are discussed next, and as will be seen, there are many alternatives to choose from for purposes of developing an overall job analysis system for any particular situation.[16]

Methods

Job analysis methods represent procedures or techniques for collecting job information. There have been many specific techniques and systems developed and named (e.g., Functional Job Analysis, Position Analysis Questionnaire). Rather than discuss each of the many techniques separately, we will concentrate on the major generic methods that underlie all specific techniques and applications. There are many excellent descriptions and discussions of the specific techniques available.[17]

Prior Information   For any job, there is usually some prior information available about it that could and should be consulted. Indeed, this information should routinely be searched for and used as a starting point for a job analysis.

There are many possible organizational sources of job information available, including current job descriptions and specifications, job-specific policies and procedures, training manuals, and performance appraisals. Externally, job information may be available from other employers, as well as trade and professional associations. The most important and public external source of information is the *Dictionary of Occupational Titles,* published by the Department of Labor.[18] It contains

---

EXHIBIT 5.13   Example of Combined Job Description/Specification

---

FUNCTIONAL UNIT: CHILDREN'S REHABILITATION
JOB TITLE: REHABILITATION SPECIALIST
DATE: 12/5/93

JOB SUMMARY

Works with disabled small children and their families to identify developmental strengths and weaknesses, develop rehabilitation plans, deliver and coordinate rehabilitation activities, and evaluate effectiveness of those plans and activities.

PERFORMANCE DIMENSIONS AND TASKS   Time Spent (%)

1. Assessment   **10%**

Administer formal and informal motor screening and evaluation instruments to conduct assessments. Perform assessments to identify areas of strengths and need.

2. Planning   **25%**

Collaborate with parents and other providers to directly develop the individualized family service plan. Use direct and consultative models of service in developing plans.

3. Delivery   **50%**

Carry out individual and small group motor development activities with children and families. Provide service coordination to designated families. Work with family care and child care providers to provide total services. Collaborate with other staff members and professionals from community agencies to obtain resources and specialized assistance.

4. Evaluation   **15%**

Observe, interpret and report on client in order to monitor individual progress. Assist in collecting and reporting intervention data in order to prepare formal program evaluation reports. Write evaluation reports to assist in developing new treatment strategies and programs.

JOB SPECIFICATIONS

1. License: License to practice physical therapy in the state
2. Education: B.S. in physical or occupational therapy required; M.S. preferred
3. Experience: Prefer (not required) one year experience working with children with disabilities and their families
4. Skills: Listening to and interacting with others (children, family members, coworkers)
                Developing treatment plans
                Organizing and writing reports

generic job summaries in the form of task statements for over 20,000 separate job titles, with accompanying occupational and industry (if relevant) designations. The DOT should be available and consulted for any job analysis. An example of the type of information provided in the DOT for the job title ''job analyst'' is shown in Exhibit 5.14.

The ready availability of prior job information needs to be balanced with some possible limitations. First, there is the general issue of completeness. Usually, prior information will be deficient in some important areas of job requirements, as in evolving or nontraditional types of jobs. Sole reliance upon prior information thus should be avoided. A second limitation is that there will be little indication of exactly how the information was collected, and relatedly, how accurate it is. These limitations suggest that while prior information should be the starting point for job analysis, it should not be the stopping point.

Observation   Simply observing job incumbents performing the job is an obviously excellent way to learn about tasks, KSAOs, and context. It provides a thoroughness and richness of information unmatched by any other method. It is also the most direct form of gathering information since it does not rely on intermediary information sources, such as would be the case with other methods (e.g., interviewing job incumbents and supervisors).

The following potential limitations to observation should be borne in mind. First, it is most appropriate for jobs with physical (as opposed to mental) components, and ones with relatively short job cycles (i.e., amount of time required to complete job tasks before repeating them). Second, the method may involve

---

EXHIBIT 5.14   Job of "Job Analyst": As Defined in *Dictionary of Occupational Titles*

Collects, analyzes, and prepares occupational information to facilitate personnel, administration, and management functions of organization. Consults with management to determine type, scope, and purpose of study. Studies current organizational occupational data and compiles distribution reports, organization and flow charts, and other background information required for study. Observes jobs and interviews workers and supervisory personnel to determine job and worker requirements. Analyzes occupational data, such as physical, mental, and training requirements of jobs and workers and develops written summaries, such as job descriptions, job specifications, and lines of career movement. Utilizes developed occupational data to evaluate or improve methods and techniques for recruiting, selecting, promoting, evaluating, and training workers, and administration of related personnel programs. May specialize in classifying positions according to regulated guidelines to meet job classification requirements of civil service system and be known as Position Classifier.

Source: U. S. Department of Labor, *Dictionary of Occupational Titles,* fourth ed. (Washington, D.C.: Author, 1991), p. 11.

substantial time and cost. Third, the ability of the observer to do a thorough and accurate analysis is open to question; it may be necessary to train observers prior to the job analysis. Fourth, the method will require coordination with, and approval from, many people (e.g., supervisors and incumbents). Finally, the incumbents being observed may distort their behavior during observation in self-serving ways, such as making tasks appear more difficult or time-consuming than they really are.

Interviews   Interviewing job incumbents and others, such as managers, has many potential advantages. It respects the interviewee's vast source of information about the job. And, the interview format allows the interviewer to explain the purpose of the job analysis, how the results will be used, and so forth, thus enhancing likely acceptance of the process by the interviewees. It can be structured in format to ensure standardization of collected information.

As with any job analysis method, the interview is not without potential limitations. It is time-consuming and costly, and this may cause the organization to skimp on it in ways that jeopardize the reliability and content validity of the information gathered. The interview, not providing anonymity, may lead to suspicion and distrust on the part of interviewees. The quality of the information obtained, as well as interviewee acceptance, depends upon the skill of the interviewer. Careful selection, and possible training, of interviewers should definitely be considered when the interview is the method chosen for collecting job information. Finally, the success of the interview also depends on the skill and abilities of the interviewee, such as verbal communication skills and ability to recall tasks performed.

Task Questionnaire   A typical *task questionnaire* contains a lengthy list of task statements that cut across many different job titles, and is administered to incumbents (all or samples of them) in these job titles. For each task statement, the respondent is asked to indicate (a) whether or not the task applies to the respondent's job (respondents should always be given a DNA—does not apply—option), and (b) task importance (e.g., a 1–5 scale rating difficulty or criticalness).

The advantages of task questionnaires are numerous. They are standardized in content and format, thus yielding a standardized method of information gathering. They can obtain considerable task information from large numbers of people. They are economical to administer and score, and the availability of scores creates the opportunity for subsequent statistical analysis. Finally, task questionnaires are (also should be) completed anonymously, thus enhancing respondent participation, honesty, and acceptance.

A task questionnaire is potentially limited in certain ways. The most important limitation pertains to task statement content. Care must be taken to ensure that the questionnaire contains task statements of sufficient content relevance, representativeness, and specificity. This suggests that if a tailor-made questionnaire is to be used, considerable time and resources must be devoted to its construction to ensure accurate inclusion of task statements. If a preexisting questionnaire (e.g., the Position Analysis Questionnaire) is considered, its task statement content should be assessed relative to the task content of the jobs to be analyzed prior to any decision to use the questionnaire.

A second limitation of task questionnaires pertains to potential respondent reactions. Respondents may react negatively if they feel the questionnaire does not contain task statements covering important aspects of their jobs. Respondents may also find completion of the questionnaire to be both tedious and boring, and this may cause them to commit rating errors (e.g., halo, central tendency). Interpretation and understanding of the task statements may be problematic for some respondents who have reading and comprehension skill deficiencies.

Finally, it should be remembered that a typical task questionnaire focuses on tasks. Other job requirement components, particularly KSAOs and those related to job context, may be ignored or downplayed if the task questionnaire is relied upon as the method of job information collection.

Combined Methods   Only in rare instances does a job analysis involve use of only a single method. Much more likely is a "mix-and-match" eclectic approach using multiple methods. This makes job analysis a more complicated process to design and administer than implied by a description of each of the methods alone.

Criteria for Choice of Methods   Some explicit choices regarding methods of job analysis need to be made. One set of choices involves decisions to use or not use a particular method of information collection. An organization must decide, for example, whether to use an "off-the-shelf" method or its own particular method that is suited to its own needs and circumstances. A second set of choices involves how to blend together a set of methods that will all be used, in varying ways and degrees, in the actual job analysis. Some criteria for guidance in such decisions are shown in Exhibit 5.15.

Sources to Be Used

Choosing sources of information involves considering who will be used to provide the information sought. While this matter is not entirely independent of job analysis methods (e.g., use of a task questionnaire normally requires use of job incumbents as the source), they are treated as such in the sections that follow.

Job Analyst   A job analyst is someone who, by virtue of job title and training, is available and suited to conduct job analyses and to guide the job analysis process (refer back to Exhibit 5.14 for a job summary). The job analyst is also "out of the loop," being neither manager nor incumbent of the jobs analyzed. As such, the job analyst brings a combination of expertise and neutrality to the work.

EXHIBIT 5.15 Criteria for Guiding Choice of Job Analysis Methods

---

1. Degree of suitability/versatility for use across different types of jobs
2. Degree of standardization in the process and in the reporting of results
3. Acceptability of process and results to those who will serve as sources and/or users
4. Degree to which method is operational and may be used off-the-shelf without modification, as opposed to method requiring tailor-made development and application
5. Amount of training required for sources and users of job information
6. Costs of the job analysis, both in terms of direct administrative costs and opportunity costs of time involvement by people
7. Quality of resultant information in terms of reliability and content validity
8. Usability of results in recruitment, selection, and employment activities.

Source: Adapted from E. L. Levine, R. A. Ash, H. Hall, and F. Sistrunk, "Evaluation of Job Analysis Methods by Experienced Job Analysts," *Academy of Management Journal*, 1983, 26, 339–348.

Despite such advantages and appeals, reliance upon a job analyst as the job information source is not without potential limitations. First, the analyst may be perceived as an outsider by incumbents and supervisors, a perception that may eventuate in questioning the analyst's job knowledge and expertise, as well as trustworthiness. Second, the job analyst may, in fact, lack detailed knowledge of the jobs to be analyzed, especially in an organization with many different job titles. Lack of knowledge may cause the analyst to bring inaccurate job stereotypes to the analysis process. Finally, having specially designated job analysts (either as employees or outside consultants) tends to be expensive.

Job Incumbents Job incumbents seem like a natural source of information to be used in job analysis, and indeed they are relied upon in most job analysis systems. The major advantage to working with job incumbents is their familiarity with tasks, KSAOs, and job context. In addition, job incumbents may become more accepting of the job analysis process and its results through their participation in it.

Some skepticism should be maintained about job incumbents as a source of workplace data, as is true for any source. They may lack the knowledge or insights necessary to provide inclusive information, especially if they are probationary or part-time employees. Some employees also may have difficulty in describing the tasks involved in their job, or in being able to infer and articulate the underlying KSAOs necessary for the job. Another potential limitation of job incumbents as an information source pertains to their motivation to be a willing and accurate source. Feelings of distrust and suspicion may greatly hamper employees' willingness to function capably as sources. For example, incumbents may intentionally fail to report certain tasks as part of their job so that those tasks are not incorporated into the formal job description. Or, incumbents may purposely inflate the importance ratings of tasks in order to make the job appear more difficult than it actually is.

Supervisors   Supervisors could and should be considered excellent sources for use in job analysis. They not only supervise employees performing the job to be analyzed, they may also have played a major role in defining it and later in adding/deleting job tasks (as in evolving and nontraditional jobs). Moreover, supervisors ultimately have to accept the resultant descriptions and specifications for jobs they supervise, and inclusion of them as a source seems a way to ensure such acceptance.

Subject Matter Experts   Often times, the sources previously mentioned are called *subject matter experts* or SMEs.[19] Individuals other than those mentioned may also be used as SMEs. These people bring particular expertise to the job analysis process, an expertise thought not to be available through standard sources. While the exact qualifications for being designated an SME are far from clear, examples of sources so designated are available. These include previous jobholders (e.g., recently promoted employees), private consultants, customer/clients, and citizens-at-large for some public sector jobs, such as superintendent of schools for a school district. Whatever the sources of SMEs, a common requirement for them is that they have recent, firsthand knowledge of the job being analyzed.

Combined Sources   Combinations of sources, like combinations of methods, are most likely to be used in a typical job analysis. This is not only likely, but desirable. As noted previously, each source has some potentially unique insight to contribute to job analysis, as well as some limitations. It is through a pooling of such sources, and the information they provide, that an accurate and acceptable job analysis is most likely to result.

Job Analysis Process

Collecting job information through job analysis requires development and use of an overall process for doing so. Unfortunately, there is no set or best process to be followed; the process has to be tailor-made to suit the specifics of the situation in which it occurs. There are, however, many key issues to be dealt with in the construction and operation of the process.[20] Each of these is briefly commented on next.

Purpose   The purpose(s) of job analysis should be clearly identified and agreed upon. Since job analysis is a process designed to yield job information, the organization should ask exactly what job information is desired and why. Here, it is useful to refer back to the job requirements matrix to review the types of information that can be sought and obtained in a job requirements job analysis. Management must decide exactly what types of information are desired (task statements, task dimensions, and so forth), and in what format. Once the desired output and results of job analysis have been determined, the organization can then plan a process that will yield the desired results.

Scope   The issue of scope involves which job(s) to include in the job analysis. Decisions about actual scope should be based on consideration of (a) the importance of the job to the functioning of the organization, (b) the number of job applicants and incumbents, (c) whether the job is entry level and thus subject to constant staffing activity, (d) the frequency with which job requirements (both tasks and KSAOs) change, and (e) the amount of time lapsed since the previous job analysis.

Internal Staff or Consultant   The organization may conduct the job analysis using its own staff, or it may procure external consultants. This is a difficult decision to make since it involves not only the obvious consideration of cost, but many other considerations as well. Exhibit 5.16 highlights some of these concerns and the trade-offs involved.

Organization and Coordination   Any job analysis project, whether conducted by internal staff or external consultants, requires careful organization and coordination. There are two key steps to take to help ensure that this is achieved. First, an organizational member should be appointed to function as a project manager for the total process (if consultants are used, they should report to this project manager). The project manager should be assigned overall responsibility for the total project, including its organization and control. Second, the roles and relationships for the various people involved in the project—HR staff, project staff, line managers, and job incumbents—must be clearly established.

Communication   Clear and open communication with all concerned facilitates the job analysis process. Job analysis will be thought of by some employees as analogous to an invasive, exploratory surgical procedure, which, in turn, naturally raises questions in their minds about its purpose, process, and results. These questions and concerns need to be anticipated and addressed forthrightly.

Work flow and Time frame   Job analysis involves a mixture of people and paper in a process in which they can become entangled very quickly. The project manager should develop and adhere to a work-flow chart that shows the sequential ordering of steps to be followed in the conduct of the job analysis. This should be accompanied by a time frame showing critical completion dates for project phases, as well as a final deadline.

EXHIBIT 5.16   Factors to Consider in Choosing Between Internal Staff or Consultants for Job Analysis

Internal Staff	Consultant
Cost of technical or procedural failure is low	Cost of technical or procedural failure is high
Project scope is limited	Project scope is comprehensive and/or large
Need for job data ongoing	Need for job data is a one-time, isolated event
There is a desire to develop internal staff skills in job analysis	There is a need for assured availability of each type and level of job analysis skill
Strong management controls are in place to control project costs	Predictability of project cost can depend on adhering to work plan `
Knowledge of organization's norms, ''culture,'' and jargon are critical	Technical innovativeness and quality are critical
Technical credibility of internal staff is high	Leverage of external ''expert'' status is needed to execute project
Process and products of the project are unlikely to be challenged	Process and products of the project are likely to be legally, technically, or politically scrutinized
Rational or narrative job analysis methods are desired	Commercial or proprietary job analysis methods are desired
Data collected are qualitative	Data collection methods are structured, standardized, and/or quantitative

Source: D. M. Van De Vort and B. V. Stalder, ''Organizing for Job Analysis,'' in S. Gael (ed.), *The Job Analysis Handbook for Business, Industry, and Government.* Copyright © 1988 by John Wiley & Sons, Inc. Reprinted by permission of John Wiley & Sons, Inc.

Analysis, Synthesis, and Documentation   Once collected, job information must be analyzed and synthesized through use of various procedural and statistical means. These should be planned in advance and incorporated into the work-flow and time-frame requirements. Likewise, provisions need to be made for preparation of written documents, especially job descriptions and job specifications, and their incorporation into relevant policy and procedure manuals.

Maintenance of the System   Job analysis does not end with completion of the project. Rather, mechanisms must be developed and put into place to maintain the job analysis and information system over time. This is critical because the system will be exposed to numerous influences requiring response and adaptation. Examples of these influences include: (a) changes in job tasks and KSAOs—additions, deletions, and modifications; (b) job redesign, restructuring, and realignment; and (c) creation of new jobs, especially of the evolving and nontraditional varieties. In short, job analysis must be thought of and administered as an ongoing organizational process.

JOB REWARDS JOB ANALYSIS

As shown in Exhibit 5.3, job rewards job analysis involves identifying the job's extrinsic rewards conceptually and inferring the intrinsic rewards. Complexities abound in this seemingly straightforward process. For example, exactly what will be the domain of rewards on which the job is to be analyzed, and how will this domain be determined? How does the organization measure job rewards, especially intrinsic ones?

Answers to these and other questions are aided by use of an operational framework that specifies the key components of a job rewards job analysis, much as an operational framework aids in a job requirements job analysis. Such a framework for the analysis of job rewards is presented next, followed by discussions of its key components. Issues regarding methods and sources are incorporated directly into the discussion of the components, rather than treated separately.

Before proceeding, it should be noted that the treatment of job rewards job analysis will be relatively brief. This brevity is the result of two related factors. First, organizations typically pay little or no formal attention to this type of job analysis; whatever energy and resources are devoted to job analysis are usually given to the job requirements variety. Second, the research and knowledge base from which to draw our discussion of job rewards job analysis is quite recent and limited. Hopefully, these circumstances will change in the future. In the meantime, the discussion that follows should be viewed as tentative, but promising, in terms of job analysis practice and research.

Job Rewards Matrix

The operational framework for job rewards job analysis is specified in the job *rewards matrix,* shown in Exhibit 5.17. The matrix shows the key components to be addressed by the job analysis and the type of information that must be collected and reported.

At the top of the matrix is space for a job title and a job summary, just as in the job requirements approach. The far left column is labeled "rewards," and calls for a listing (from 1 to N) of the rewards associated with the job. The next column is labeled "dimensions," and in it are placed the names of groupings (A,B, . . . Z) of broader reward dimensions. The remaining columns are used to indicate "reward characteristics," which are ways of describing the nature of rewards. There are three such characteristics in the matrix—"amount," "differ-

EXHIBIT 5.17   Job Rewards Matrix

Job Title:

Job Summary:

		Reward Characteristics		
Reward	**Dimensions**	**Amount**	**Differential**	**Stability**
1	A			
2				
3				
4	B			
.	.			
.	.			
.	.			
N	Z			

ential," and "stability." When completed, the job requirements matrix shows a virtual catalogue of information about a job's rewards. An example of a completed job rewards matrix for the job of administrative assistant is shown in Exhibit 5.18.

Bearing the job rewards matrix in mind, we now turn to a brief discussion of its components. Blended into this discussion are ideas regarding methods (e.g., interviews, questionnaires) and sources (e.g., incumbents, managers) for collecting the rewards information.

Rewards

This portion of the job analysis requires development of an inclusive set or list of rewards that are a part of the job and are experienced by job incumbents. Research has been quite successful in identifying sets or taxonomies of relatively independent rewards through the development of job reward measures. The two most prominent of these measures are the Minnesota Job Description Questionnaire (MJDQ) and the Job Diagnostic Survey (JDS).[21] The MJDQ provides information about 20 different rewards, and covers the spectrum of both extrinsic and intrinsic rewards. The JDS, alternatively, measures a total of seven rewards (five "core" job characteristics plus two others), all of which are intrinsic in nature. Exhibit 5.19 shows listings of the rewards measured by the MJDQ and the JDS.

Reward sets such as those included on the MJDQ and JDS are a useful starting point for any job rewards job analysis. The sets could be amended by inclusion of additional rewards not covered by either of these measures, but clearly asso-

EXHIBIT 5.18   Portion of Job Rewards Matrix for Job of Administrative Assistant

Reward	Dimension	Amount	Reward Characteristics		
			Differential	Stability
1. Starting pay	A. Individual pay (extrinsic)	$2,000/month minimum	May exceed minimum, depending on KSAOs	Changes according to market conditions
2. Pay raises	A. Individual pay (extrinsic)	Typically, 2–3%	Across the board (same % for all)	Range from 0% to 10%, annually
3. Bonuses	A. Individual pay (extrinsic)	2.5% average	Range from 0% to 10%, depending on performance	Will vary each year, depending on size of bonus pool
4. Doing different tasks	B. Skill variety (intrinsic)	$\bar{x} = 4.8$*	SD = .73*	Frequent change
5. Using complex skills	B. Skill variety (intrinsic)	$\bar{x} = 3.9$*	SD = 1.54*	No recent changes; none anticipated
6. Doing simple and repetitive tasks	B. Skill variety (intrinsic)	$\bar{x} = 5.4$*	SD = .37*	Will continue to be part of job

*Rating scale (1–7) values, based on the three skill variety items from the Job Diagnostic Survey (JDS).

EXHIBIT 5.19   Rewards Assessed by the Minnesota Job Description Questionnaire (MJDQ) and the Job Diagnostic Survey (JDS)

MJDQ	JDS
1. Ability utilization	1. Skill variety*
2. Achievement	2. Task identity*
3. Activity	3. Task significance*
4. Advancement	4. Autonomy*
5. Authority	5. Feedback from job*
6. Company policies and procedures	6. Feedback from agents
7. Compensation	7. Dealing with others
8. Co-workers	*Core job characteristics
9. Creativity	
10. Independence	
11. Moral values	
12. Recognition	
13. Responsibility	
14. Security	
15. Social service	
16. Social status	
17. Supervision-human relations	
18. Supervision-technical	
19. Variety	
20. Working conditions	

---

ciated with the job. Such modifications could come about through consultation with various SMEs (e.g., incumbents, supervisors, HR staff representatives), using a variety of methods (e.g., interviews, questionnaires, observation). The desired end product of this part of the job analysis is a set of rewards that are agreed upon by all sources and methods as inclusive in scope and acceptable for purposes of capturing the reward domain of jobs.

Reward Dimensions

Once a reward set has been identified, the resulting list of rewards either must stand alone or must somehow be collapsed into a set of more general reward dimensions. Either choice is acceptable, and the decision made should be based on the ease with which the rewards are likely to be classified, as well as the usefulness of having rewards so cast.

It is probably useful, and relatively easy, to distinguish rewards as either "extrinsic" or "intrinsic." *Extrinsic rewards* are those that are established and changed (usually by management) without any direct, intended effect on job requirements (tasks or KSAOs). *Intrinsic rewards,* alternatively, are inherent to the nature of the job itself and thus flow from job tasks and the KSAOs required to perform the tasks. As noted, all of the rewards on the JDS are considered intrinsic. The MJDQ, however, contains a mixture of extrinsic and intrinsic rewards.

It is possible to go beyond the straightforward extrinsic/intrinsic dichotomy. Extrinsic rewards may be classified into a series of dimensions such as direct compensation, benefits, work hours, and internal job mobility. Intrinsic rewards may be classified into dimensions having to do with breadth of tasks, utilization of KSAOs, and task goals/challenges. Any such classification is possible; the key consideration is whether it meets the tests of ease and usefulness mentioned earlier. It should also be noted that these considerations are compounded by the fact that little is known about how various methods and sources can most effectively be used to form reward dimensions.

Reward Characteristics

In the job rewards matrix it is suggested that the organization analyze and record three particular characteristics of rewards: amount, differential, and stability. Each of these characteristics is considered next.

Amount of Reward   Clearly, any analysis of job rewards would seek to provide some indication about their amount or level. For external rewards, this is a relatively straightforward process because the reward amounts are externally defined and specified (e.g., starting pay, hours of work, number of vacation days). Intrinsic reward amounts, by their very nature, are not so easily analyzed and specified. They are not externally established, and there are no objective measures of their amount (e.g., how does one objectively measure amount of task challenge?). The amount of an intrinsic reward thus must be inferred from what various sources (e.g., incumbents, supervisors) tell about it.

Subjective methods or measures thus are used to gather the desired information about intrinsic reward amounts. Here is where the MJDQ and JDS again are very useful, for both have a solid history of research supporting their reliability and validity as measures.[22] Both use a questionnaire method of measurement. For the MJDQ, respondents are asked to indicate how well 20 job rewards describe their job, using a unique ranking procedure. For the JDS, respondents rate the amount of each reward on a 1–7 rating scale. Respondents for the MJDQ are usually supervisors, and for the JDS, they are incumbents. Exhibit 5.20 shows one set of the rating scales for the seven rewards measured by the JDS (the full instrument contains two more sets of items for these same seven rewards as well). After respondents have completed the JDS, the average rating score for each reward is computed, and those averages then represent the amounts of the rewards present in the job.

Unless the organization uses the MJDQ or JDS to measure intrinsic reward amounts, it must develop its own measure. If this is done, considerable care and

EXHIBIT 5.20   Set of Items from the Job Diagnostic Survey

1. To what extent does your job require you to *work closely with other people* (either "clients," or people in related jobs in your own organization)?

   1
   Very little; dealing with other people is not at all necessary in doing the job.

   2

   3

   4
   Moderately; some dealing with others is necessary.

   5

   6

   7
   Very much; dealing with other people is an absolutely essential and crucial part of doing the job.

2. How much *autonomy* is there in your job? That is, to what extent does your job permit you to decide *on your own* how to go about doing the work?

   1
   Very little; the job gives me almost no personal say about how and when the work is done.

   2

   3

   4
   Moderate autonomy; many things are standardized and not under my control, but I can make some decisions about the work.

   5

   6

   7
   Very much; the job gives me almost complete responsibility for deciding how and when the work is done.

3. To what extent does your job involve doing a *whole and identifiable piece of work?* That is, is the job a complete piece of work that has an obvious beginning and end? Or is it only a small *part* of the overall piece of work, which is finished by other people or by automatic machines?

   1
   My job is only a tiny part of the overall piece of work; the results of my activities cannot be seen in the final product or service.

   2

   3

   4
   My job is a moderate-sized chunk of the overall piece of work; my own contribution can be seen in the final outcome.

   5

   6

   7
   My job involves doing the whole piece of work, from start to finish; the results of my activities are easily seen in the final product or service.

4. How much *variety* is there in your job? That is, to what extent does the job require you to do many different things at work, using a variety of your skills and talents?

   1
   Very little; the job requires me to do the same routine things over and over again.

   2

   3

   4
   Moderate variety.

   5

   6

   7
   Very much; the job requires me to do many different things, using a number of different skills and talents.

EXHIBIT 5.20   Continued

5. In general, how *significant or important* is your job? That is, are the results of your work likely to significantly affect the lives or well-being of other people?

    1   2   3   4   5   6   7

    Not very significant; the outcomes   Moderately significant.   Highly significant; the outcomes
    of my work are *not* likely to have   of my work can affect other
    important effects on other people.   people in very important ways.

6. To what extent do *managers or co-workers* let you know how well you are doing on your job?

    1   2   3   4   5   6   7

    Very little; people almost never let   Moderately; sometimes people may   Very much; managers or co-
    me know how well I am doing.   give me feedback; other times they   workers provide me with almost
                                                 may not.   constant feedback about how well
                                                                                        I am doing.

7. To what extent does *doing the job itself* provide you with information about your work performance? That is, does the actual *work itself* provide clues about how well you are doing aside from any feedback co-workers or supervisors may provide?

    1   2   3   4   5   6   7

    Very little; the job itself is set up   Moderately; sometimes doing the   Very much; the job is set up so
    so I could work forever without   job provides feedback to me;   that I get almost constant
    finding out how well I am doing.   sometimes it does not.   feedback as I work about how
                                                                                        well I am doing.

caution should be exercised regarding the measure's development, reliability, and validity.

Reward Differential   This characteristic refers to the relative differences in reward amount that may be received or experienced by job incumbents. Do all have the same salary? Do all experience the same amount of skill variety? Such questions are at the heart of the reward differential issue.

Analyzing extrinsic job rewards in terms of their differential is quite straightforward. The analyst simply consults the relevant HR policies and activities to determine whether there are reward differentials or not, and if so, how many and how much. Consider the case of wage or salary. The analyst can look at the compensation policies for a job and determine whether all employees receive the same rate of pay, and if they do not, the range of pay rates (minimum and maximum) that are possible.

Analyzing intrinsic reward differentials is more difficult. Even though all employees on a given job may perform roughly the same tasks, they differ in how they perceive or experience the intrinsic rewards that flow from these tasks. The job analysis must be prepared to capture these differentials among employees for each intrinsic reward.

Measurement of reward differentials with questionnaire instruments such as the MJDQ and the JDS is easily accomplished. The analyst simply computes the standard deviation of ratings assigned to each reward by the respondents. The greater the standard deviation, the greater the variability in reward, as experienced and reported by the respondents. In the absence of a measure such as the MJDQ or JDS, the organization will have to build its own method of assessing reward differentials. For example, it may interview job incumbents about various intrinsic rewards, and based on their responses, classify each intrinsic reward as "high," "medium," or "low." Naturally, the reliability of this classification process is important to determine.

Reward Stability   Does the amount of a reward remain stable over time, or does it change? This is the matter of reward stability. For extrinsic rewards, assessment of stability is made by inspection of HR policies and activities that are explicitly designed to create stability or instability. Consider the extrinsic reward "pay raise." Analysis of the organization's pay raise policies will show whether or not pay raises are given, and if so, how frequently.

Assessing intrinsic reward stability will require gauging employees' perceptions of, or experiences with, these types of rewards over time. Perceptions of skill variety, for example, may change due to changes in actual task content, as occurs in evolving and nontraditional jobs.[23] Or, changes in employees themselves (e.g., KSAO changes due to new training and/or educational experiences) may lead them to perceive their intrinsic rewards differently over time.

Capturing the effects of these types of changes on employees and their perceptions of rewards may require a substantial commitment from the organization. For example, it may mean establishing and maintaining an intrinsic reward tracking system for employees in each particular job. This might require, for example, periodic (annual) administrations of the JDS to employees, followed by the necessary statistical analysis and interpretation of results as they pertain to trends in perceptions of rewards. Alternatively, in a more casual mode, summary written statements about stability may be made (and changed when necessary), as was done in Exhibit 5.18.

Results of Job Rewards Job Analysis

The job analysis produces a thorough description of the structure and pattern of rewards for a particular job. It is a description of the extrinsic and intrinsic terms and conditions of the job. The organization will thus have identified and defined such features as (a) the domain of relevant rewards; (b) broader groupings or dimensions of rewards, both extrinsic and intrinsic; (c) indications about the amount of each reward present; (d) how much difference there is among employees in the amounts of rewards they receive and experience; and (e) how stable or fluctuating are the rewards that employees receive.

Unfortunately, this wealth of job reward information may be difficult to translate into directly usable form. There are no standard procedures or formats for expressing the information. The job rewards matrix, as shown in Exhibit 5.17, and the completed matrix in Exhibit 5.18, however, are good starting points for recording and communicating the job reward information that has been collected.

In addition, the organization can use its own creativity to develop its own unique and useful ways of putting the information into usable formats and then incorporating it into policy manuals, employee handbooks, recruitment literature, college relations programs, and the like. As will be discussed, having and using job rewards information in these ways may play a key role in the multitude of recruitment, selection, and employment activities.

LEGAL ISSUES

This chapter has emphasized the crucial role that job analysis plays in establishing the foundations for staffing activities. That crucial role continues from a legal perspective. Job analysis becomes intimately involved in court cases involving the job-relatedness of staffing activities. It also occupies a prominent position in the Uniform Guidelines on Employee Selection Procedures (UGESP). Finally, the Americans With Disabilities Act requires that the organization determine the essential functions of each job, and job analysis can play a pivotal role in that process. As these issues are discussed in the following sections, note the direct relevance of the job requirements matrix and its development to them.

Job-Relatedness and Court Cases

In EEO/AA court cases, the organization is confronted with the need to justify its challenged staffing practices as being job-related. Common sense suggests that this requires first and foremost that the organization conduct some type of job analysis as a way of identifying job requirements and rewards. In addition, it also is the case that specific features or characteristics of the job analysis make a difference in the organization's defense. Specifically, an examination of court cases indicates that for purposes of legal defensibility the organization should conform to the following recommendations:

1. "Job analysis must be performed and must be for the job for which the selection instrument is to be utilized.
2. Analysis of the job should be in writing.
3. Job analysts should describe in detail the procedure used.
4. Job data should be collected from a variety of current sources by knowledgeable job analysts.
5. Sample size should be large and representative of the jobs for which the selection instrument is used.
6. Tasks, duties, and activities should be included in the analysis.
7. The most important tasks should be represented in the selection device.
8. Competency levels of job performance for entry-level jobs should be specified.
9. Knowledge, skills, and abilities should be specified, particularly if a content validation model is followed."[24]

These recommendations are very consistent with our more general discussion of job analysis as an important tool and basic foundation for staffing activities. Moreover, even though these recommendations were made several years ago, there is little reason to doubt or modify any of them on the basis of more recent court cases.

Job Analysis and the UGESP

The UGESP (see Appendix A) places great emphasis on job analysis in the conduct of validation studies. In general, these guidelines indicate that any validation study should begin with a job analysis. More specifically, here is their exact language regarding job analysis for criterion-related and content validation studies:

1. Criterion-related validation: "Validity studies should be based on review of information about the job for which the selection procedure is to be used. The review should included a job analysis except as provided in section 14B(3) below with respect to criterion-related validity. Any method of job analysis may be used if it provides the information required for the specific validation strategy used.

There should be a review of job information to determine measures of work behavior(s) or performance that are relevant to the job or group of jobs in question. These measures or criteria are relevant to the extent that they represent critical or important job duties, work behaviors, or work outcomes as developed from the review of job information."

2. Content validation: "There should be a job analysis which includes an analysis of the important work behavior(s) required for successful performance and their relative importance and, if the behavior results in work product(s), an analysis of the work product(s). Any job analysis should focus on the work behavior(s) and the tasks associated with them. If work behaviors are not observable, the job analysis should identify and analyze those aspects of the behavior(s) that can be observed and the observed work products. The work behavior(s) selected for measurement should be critical work behavior(s) and/or important work behavior(s) constituting most of the job.

For any selection procedure measuring a knowledge, skill or ability the user should show that (a) the selection procedure measures and is a representative sample of that knowledge, skill or ability and (b) that knowledge, skill or ability is used in and is a necessary prerequisite to critical or important work behavior(s)."

Reflection on these statements reveals the crucial role accorded job analysis in the conduct of validation studies. It is essential for derivation of the content of both criterion and predictor measures and for establishment of links between tasks and KSAOs.

Essential Job Functions

Recall that under the ADA, the organization must not discriminate against a qualified individual with a disability who can perform the "essential functions" of the job, with or without reasonable accommodation. This requirement raises three questions—what are essential functions? what is evidence of essential functions? and what is the role of job analysis?

What Are Essential Functions?

The ADA employment regulations (see Appendix C) provide the following statements about essential functions:

1. "The term essential functions refers to the fundamental job duties of the employment position the individual with a disability holds or desires. The

term essential function does not include the marginal functions of the position; and

2. A job function may be considered essential for any of several reasons, including but not limited to the following:

- The function may be essential because the reason the position exists is to perform the function;

- The function may be essential because of the limited number of employees available among whom the performance of that job function can be distributed; and/or

- The function may be highly specialized so that the incumbent in the position is hired for his or her expertise or ability to perform the particular function.''

Evidence of Essential Functions

The employment regulations go on to indicate what constitutes evidence that any particular function is in fact an essential one. That evidence includes, but is not limited to,

1. the employer's judgement as to which functions are essential
2. written job descriptions, prepared before advertising or interviewing applicants for the job
3. the amount of time spent on the job performing the function
4. the consequences of not requiring the incumbent to perform the function
5. the terms of a collective bargaining agreement
6. the work experience of past incumbents in the job
7. the current work experience of incumbents in similar jobs

Role of Job Analysis

What role(s) might job analysis play in identifying essential functions and establishing evidence of their being essential? The employment regulations are silent on this question. However, the EEOC has provided substantial and detailed assistance to organizations to deal with this, and many other issues, under the ADA.[25] The specific statements regarding job analysis and essential functions of the job are shown in Exhibit 5.21.

Examination of the statements in Exhibit 5.21 suggests the following. First, while job analysis is not required by law as a means of establishing essential functions of a job, it is strongly recommended. Second, the job analysis should focus on tasks associated with the job. Where KSAOs are also studied or specified, they should be derived from an explicit consideration of their probable links to the essential tasks. Finally, with regard to tasks, the focus should be on the tasks

---

EXHIBIT 5.21 Job Analysis and Essential Functions of the Job

Job Analysis and the Essential Functions of a Job

The ADA does not require that an employer conduct a job analysis or any particular form of job analysis to identify the essential functions of a job. The information provided by a job analysis may or may not be helpful in properly identifying essential job functions, depending on how it is conducted.

The term ''job analysis'' generally is used to describe a formal process in which information about a specific job or occupation is collected and analyzed. Formal job analysis may be conducted by a number of different methods. These methods obtain different kinds of information that is used for different purposes. Some of these methods will not provide information sufficient to determine if an individual with a disability is qualified to perform ''essential'' job functions.

For example: One kind of formal job analysis looks at specific job tasks and classifies jobs according to how these tasks deal with data, people, and objects. This type of job analysis is used to set wage rates for various jobs; however, it may not be adequate to identify the essential functions of a *particular* job, as required by the ADA. Another kind of job analysis looks at the kinds of knowledge, skills, and abilities that are necessary to perform a job. This type of job analysis is used to develop selection criteria for various jobs. The information from this type of analysis sometimes helps to measure the importance of certain skills, knowledge and abilities, but it does not take into account the fact that people with disabilities often can perform essential functions using other skills and abilities.

Some job analysis methods ask current employees and their supervisors to rate the importance of general characteristics necessary to perform a job, such as ''strength,'' ''endurance,'' or ''intelligence,'' without linking these characteristics to *specific* job functions or specific tasks that are part of a function. Such general information may not identify, for example, whether upper body or lower body strength is required, or whether muscular endurance or cardiovascular endurance is needed to perform a particular job function. Such information, by itself, would not be sufficient to determine whether an individual who has particular limitations can perform an essential function with or without an accommodation.

As already stated, the ADA does not require a formal job analysis or any particular method of analysis to identify the essential functions of a job. A small employer may wish to conduct an informal analysis by observing and consulting with people who perform the job, or have previously performed it, and their supervisors. If possible, it is advisable to observe and consult with several workers under a range of conditions, to get a better idea of all job functions and the different ways they may be performed. Production records and workloads also may be relevant factors to consider.

(continued)

EXHIBIT 5.21   Continued

To identify essential job functions under the ADA, a job analysis should focus on the purpose of the job and the importance of actual job functions in achieving this purpose. Evaluating importance may include consideration of the frequency with which a function is performed, the amount of time spent on the function, and the consequences if the function is not performed. The analysis may include information on the work environment (such as unusual heat, cold, humidity, dust, toxic substances or stress factors). The job analysis may contain information on the manner in which a job currently is performed, but should not conclude that ability to perform the job in that manner is an essential function, unless there is no other way to perform the function without causing undue hardship. A job analysis will be most helpful for purposes of the ADA if it focuses on the results or outcome of a function, not solely on the way it customarily is performed.

For example:

- An essential function of a computer programmer job might be described as ''ability to develop programs that accomplish necessary objectives,'' rather than ''ability to manually write programs.'' Although a person currently performing the job may write these programs by hand, that is not the essential functions, because programs can be developed directly on the computer.

- If a job requires mastery of information contained in technical manuals, this essential function would be ''ability to learn technical material,'' rather than ''ability to read technical manuals.'' People with visual and other reading impairments could perform this function using other means, such as audiotapes.

- A job that requires objects to be moved from one place to another should state this essential function. The analysis may note that the person in the job ''lifts 50-pound cartons to a height of 3 or 4 feet and loads them into truck-trailers 5 hours daily,'' but should not identify the ''ability to *manually* lift and load 50-pound cartons'' as an essential function unless this is the only method by which the function can be performed without causing an undue hardship.

A job analysis that is focused on outcomes or results also will be helpful in establishing appropriate qualification standards, developing job descriptions, conducting interviews, and selecting people in accordance with ADA requirements. It will be particularly helpful in identifying accommodations that will enable an individual with specific functional abilities and limitations to perform the job.

Source: Equal Employment Opportunity Commission, *Technical Assistance Manual for the Employment Provisions (Title I) of the Americans With Disabilities Act* (Washington, D.C.: author, 1992), pp. II-18 to II-20.

themselves and the outcome or results of the tasks, rather than the methods by which they are performed.

SUMMARY

Organizations design jobs in various ways to serve as the building blocks for a structure that will facilitate achievement of organizational goals. These design approaches (traditional, evolving, nontraditional) all result in job content in the form of job requirements and rewards. Job analysis is the process used to gather, analyze, synthesize, and report information about job content. The job requirements approach to job analysis focuses on tasks, KSAOs, and job context. The job rewards approach is concerned with extrinsic and intrinsic job rewards and various characteristics of them.

The job requirements approach is guided by the job requirements matrix. The matrix calls for information about tasks and task dimensions, as well as their importance. In a parallel fashion, it requires information about KSAOs required for the tasks, plus indications about the importance of those KSAOs. The final component of the matrix deals with the job context, both physical demands and environmental conditions.

When gathering the information called for by the job requirements matrix, the organization is confronted with a multitude of choices. Those choices revolve around various job analysis methods, sources, and processes. The organization must pick and choose from among these; all have advantages and disadvantages associated with them. The choices should be guided by a concern for the accuracy and acceptability of the information that is being gathered.

The job rewards matrix is suggested for use in a job rewards job analysis. The matrix indicates a need to identify the extrinsic and intrinsic rewards offered by the job. It also requires indication of the rewards' amounts, differences among employees, and stability. Instruments and processes for collecting the necessary information are in their infancy, as is the formal incorporation and use of the information in staffing activities.

From a legal perspective, job analysis assumes major importance in creating staffing systems and practices that are in compliance with EEO/AA laws and regulations. The employer must ensure (or be able to show) that its practices are job-related. This requires not only having conducted a job requirements job analysis, but also using a process that itself has defensible characteristics. The UGESP clearly accords job analysis a prominent place in the conduct of validation studies. Indeed, it is required as an initial step in both criterion-related and content validation. Under the ADA, the organization must identify the essential functions of the job. While this does not require a job analysis, the organization should strongly consider it as one of the tools to be used. Over time, we will learn more about how job analysis is treated under the ADA.

DISCUSSION QUESTIONS

1. How should task statements be written, and what sorts of problems might you encounter in asking a job incumbent to write these statements?

2. Would it be better to first identify task dimensions and then create specific task statements for each dimension, or should task statements be identified first and then used to create task dimensions?

3. What would you consider when trying to decide what criteria (e.g., % time spent) to use for gathering indications about task importance?

4. How might existing skill (e.g., SCANS) and ability (e.g., Fleishman and Reilly) taxonomies be used to help identify KSAOs in a job analysis?

5. What are the advantages and disadvantages to using multiple methods of job analysis for a particular job? Multiple sources?

6. Why might an organization resist doing a job rewards job analysis and using the results in staffing activities?

ENDNOTES

1. D. R. Ilgen and J. R. Hollenbeck, ''The Structure of Work: Job Design and Roles,'' in M. D. Dunnette and L. M. Hough (eds.), *Handbook of Industrial and Organizational Psychology,* Vol. 2 (Palo Alto, CA: Consulting Psychologists Press, 1991), pp. 165–207.

2. L. S. Vines, ''The New Clerical,'' *Human Resource Executive,* 1992, 6(10), pp. 57–79.

3. S. Drake, ''Teaming Up,'' *Human Resource Executive,* 6(8), pp. 39–42; Ilgen and Hollenbeck, ''The Structure of Work: Job Design and Roles;'' M. Moravec and R. Tucker, ''Job Descriptions for the 21st Century,'' *Personnel Journal,* 1992, pp. 37–44.

4. A. S. Miner, ''Idiosyncratic Jobs in Formalized Organizations,'' *Administrative Science Quarterly,* 1987, 32, pp. 327–351.

5. For excellent overviews and reviews, see S. Gael (ed.), *The Job Analysis Handbook for Business, Industry and Government,* Vols. 1 and 2 (New York: Wiley, 1988); J. V. Ghorpade, *Job Analysis* (Englewood Cliffs, NJ: 1988); R. J. Harvey, ''Job Analysis,'' in Dunnette and Hough, *Handbook of Industrial and Organizational Psychology,* pp. 71–163.

6. M. A. Campion, ''Ability Requirement Implications of Job Design: An Interdisciplinary Perspective,'' *Personnel Psychology,* 1989, 42, pp. 1–24; R. D. Gatewood and H. S. Feild, *Human Resource Selection,* second ed. (Chicago: Dryden, 1990), pp. 251–282; Harvey, ''Job Analysis.''

7. F. H. Borgen, ''Occupational Reinforcer Patterns,'' in S. Gael, *The Job Analysis Handbook for Business, Industry and Government,* Vol. 2, pp. 902–916; R. V. Dawis, ''Person-Environment Fit and Job Satisfaction,'' in C. J. Cranny, P. C. Smith, and E. F. Stone (eds.), *Job Satisfaction* (New York: Lexington, 1992); C. T. Kulik and G. R. Oldham, ''Job Diagnostic Survey,'' in S. Gael, *Handbook for Analyzing Jobs in Business, Industry and Government,* Vol. 2, pp. 936–959.

8. U.S. Department of Labor, *Revised Handbook for Analyzing Jobs* (Washington, D.C.: author, 1991), pp. 13–1 to 13–13.

9. For a summary of research on these points and on job analysis in general, see E. T. Cornelius III, "Practical Findings from Job Analysis Research," in S. Gael, *Handbook of Job Analysis for Business, Industry and Government,* Vol. 1, pp. 48–70.

10. C. J. Cranny and M. E. Doherty, "Importance Ratings in Job Analysis: Note on the Misinterpretation of Factor Analysis," *Journal of Applied Psychology,* 1988, 73, 320–322.

11. Gatewood and Feild, *Human Resource Selection,* pp. 252–254; Harvey, "Job Analysis," in Dunnette and Hough, pp. 75–79.

12. U.S. Department of Labor, Secretary's Commission on Achieving Necessary Skills, *Skills and Tasks for Jobs* (Washington, D.C.: author, 1992).

13. E. A. Fleishman and M. E. Reilly, *Handbook of Human Abilities* (Palo Alto, CA: Consulting Psychologists Press, 1992).

14. U.S. Department of Labor, *Revised Handbook for Analyzing Jobs,* pp. 12–1 to 12–18.

15. S. Gael, "Job Descriptions," in S. Gael, *Handbook of Job Analysis for Business, Industry and Government,* pp. 71–89.

16. For detailed treatments, see Gael, *The Job Analysis Handbook for Business, Industry and Government,* pp. 315–468; Harvey, "Job Analysis," in Dunnette and Hough; E. Levine, *Everything You Always Wanted to Know About Job Analysis But Were Afraid to Ask* (Tampa, FL: Mariner, 1983).

17. These are described in the sources cited in endnote 16.

18. U.S. Department of Labor, *Dictionary of Occupational Titles,* fourth ed. (Washington, D.C.: author, 1991).

19. F. J. Landy and J. Vasey, "Job Analysis: The Composition of SME Samples," *Personnel Psychology,* 1991, 44, pp. 27–50.

20. See Gael, *Job Analysis Handbook for Business, Industry and Government*, pp. 315–390.

21. See the citations in endnote 7.

22. See the citations in endnote 7, plus T. D. Taber and E. Taylor, "A Review and Evaluation of the Psychometric Properties of the Job Diagnostic Survey," *Personnel Psychology,* 1990, 43, pp. 467–500.

23. Campion, "Ability Requirement Implications of Job Design: An Interdisciplinary Perspective."

24. D. E. Thompson and T. A. Thompson, "Court Standards for Job Analysis in Test Validation," *Personnel Psychology,* 1982, 35, pp. 865–874.

25. Equal Employment Opportunity Commission, *Technical Assistance Manual on the Employment Provisions (Title 1) of the Americans With Disabilities Act,* (Washington, D.C.: author, 1992), pp. II–19 to II–21.

CHAPTER
SIX

Planning

Human Resource Planning
General Model
Operational Format

Components of HR Planning
Initial Decisions
Forecasting HR Requirements
Forecasting HR Availabilities
External and Internal Environmental Scanning
Reconciliation and Gaps
Action Planning

Staffing Planning
Staffing Planning Process
Staffing Philosophy
Staffing Flows

Legal Issues
Affirmative Action Plans (AAPs)
Legality of AAPs
Diversity Programs

Summary

Human resource planning (HRP) is the process of anticipating an organization's future employment needs and then developing sets of action plans for fulfilling identified needs. In this chapter, the basic elements of HRP are shown as five sequential steps in a general HRP model. These steps are then placed in an operational format utilizing the example of the sales and customer service unit of a company and providing a hypothetical illustration of HRP.

Based on this example, the major components of HRP are presented in detail. These components consist of making initial planning decisions, forecasting HR requirements, forecasting HR availabilities, scanning the external and internal environment, reconciling requirements and availabilities, and action planning. For each of these components, specific and detailed examples are provided that draw from, and build on, the initial example of the sales and customer service unit.

Staffing planning is addressed as a logical outgrowth of the general HRP process. The process is shown to involve setting staffing objectives, generating alternative staffing activities, assessing alternatives, and choosing alternatives. Following this process, implementation of staffing plans must begin. This involves reviewing issues involving staffing philosophy, recruitment, selection, and employment, as well as developing policies that guide the staffing plans.

Implementation of staffing plans is aided by designing specific staffing systems that show the sequential steps and flows of events that the organization and applicants follow. Staffing flowcharts are presented, and described, as a tool for constructing and illustrating the flows of applicants through the staffing process, from initial application to final match.

The major legal issue for HRP is that of affirmative action plans and programs (AAPs). The three basic components of AAPs are described and illustrated. Those components are utilization analysis, staffing goals and timetables, and action plans. An illustration of these components is given, accompanied by indications of the AAP requirements for federal contractors contained in Revised Order No. 4. Finally, the legality of AAPs and their specific characteristics are discussed.

HUMAN RESOURCE PLANNING

Human resource planning (HRP) is a process and set of activities undertaken to forecast an organization's labor demand (requirements) and internal labor supply (availabilities), to compare these projections to determine employment gaps, and to develop action plans for addressing these gaps. Action plans include staffing planning.

A general model depicting the elements of HRP is presented first in this chapter. Following this, an operational format for HRP is presented; it casts the general model into an administrative mode that can be used by organizations to guide the conduct of actual HRP.[1]

General Model

The basic elements of virtually any organization's HRP are shown in Exhibit 6.1. As can be seen, the HRP process involves five sequential steps:[2]

1. determining future human resource requirements
2. determining future human resource availabilities
3. conducting external and internal environmental scanning
4. reconciling requirements and availabilities—that is, determining gaps (shortages and surpluses) between the two
5. developing action plans to close the projected gaps

Future HR Requirements

Future HR requirements represent the number and types (in terms of qualities or KSAOs) of employees that the organization will need in the future to produce its goods and services. The requirements represent the organization's desired workforce of the future.

These projections are derived from knowledge of the overall business plan of the organization, as well as accompanying organizational plans regarding structure and hierarchy. Business and organizational plans thus drive the future HR requirements of the organization. In many organizations, however, the process is reciprocal; tentative projections about HR requirements help shape the establishment of business and organizational plans.

Future HR Availabilities

Availability projections focus on the organization's current internal workforce. Their concern is with estimating the numbers and types of current employees that will be available in the future. More specifically, these estimates are concerned with the loss or exit of employees from the organization, the resulting distribution of employees who remain within the organization's internal labor market (promotions, transfers, and demotions), and the number of accessions (new hires) during the planning time frame.

External and Internal Environmental Scanning

The external portion of scanning involves tracking trends and developments in the external environment, discerning implications of these trends for HRM, and ensuring that these implications receive attention during the HRP process. Referring back to the general HR model, note that external scanning focuses on the external forces of economic conditions, labor markets, labor unions, and laws and regulations.

Internal scanning involves assessing the organization's internal environment as it relates to the workforce and the conduct of HR activities. It is important to be aware of the composition and diversity of the organization's workforce, and the

EXHIBIT 6.1   Human Resource Planning (HRP) Process

Requirements Analysis
(demand)

Availability Analysis
(supply)

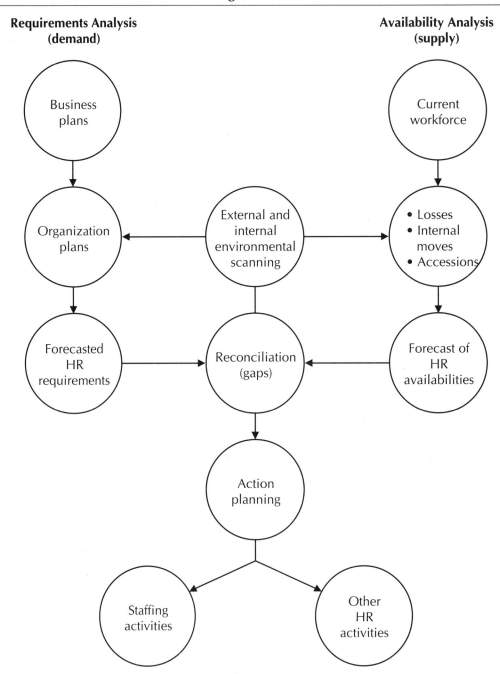

types of HR policies and programs that have been developed, or need to be developed, in order to accommodate and encourage diversity. Also important is awareness of employees' changing preferences for certain job rewards (e.g., parental leave, day care) and their likely responses to such new rewards. In both of these examples, knowledge derived from internal scanning could be useful in the prediction of losses, internal moves, and accessions.

Reconciliation (Gaps)

Armed with estimates of future requirements and availabilities—estimates tempered with assessments based on external and internal environmental scanning—the organization must reconcile all of the data it has collected in order to arrive at predicted employment gaps. Gaps represent shortages and surpluses of employees, primarily in terms of numbers of employees. Gaps may also be thought of in more qualitative terms pertaining to shortages or surpluses of KSAOs. The discussion here, and in the remainder of the chapter, however, will focus on gaps in the numerical sense only.

Identification of, and agreement on, gap estimates are the "bottom line" objective of forecasting activities. With some sense of impending shortages and surpluses, the organization has the opportunity to begin planning how to best cope with them. In this way, the organization can be proactive in its HR policies and programs, and can avoid a reactive approach to HR problems involving shortages (e.g., "Mary just quit; find me a replacement immediately!") and surpluses (e.g., "Sales keep falling; we have no choice but to lay off some employees").

Action Plans

Action plans spring forth and begin to take shape from identified employment gaps. They represent careful, intentional responses to likely future events. Many of these responses involve staffing activities. Shortages, for example, usually lead to the development and implementation of external staffing activities that yield sufficient numbers and types of new employees to meet the shortage challenge.

Other HR activities also flow from gap figures, usually in concert with staffing activities, or sometimes as substitutes for staffing. If the response to a predicted shortage is to increase hiring, for example, particular attention may need to be paid to starting pay and benefit issues in order to augment the staffing plan. As another example, shortages may be met by implementing a productivity improvement program involving current employees, rather than by hiring new employees.

Operational Format

The key elements of HRP, as shown in Exhibit 6.1 and discussed in the preceding sections, may be placed into a general operational format. That format may serve as the guiding template for the actual conduct of HRP by an organization. The format, including hypothetical results from forecasting requirements and availabilities, is shown in Exhibit 6.2.

The exhibit shows a partial HRP being conducted by an organization for a specific unit (sales and customer service). It involves only two job categories (A or sales, and B or customer service) and two hierarchical levels for each category (1 or entry level, and 2 or manager level). All of the HRP steps are confined to this particular organizational unit and its job categories/levels, as shown.

The current workforce size (number of employees) is given for each job category/level. Requirements and availabilities are forecast for a one-year time frame, and the results are shown in the relevant columns. After the reconciliation process, final gap figures are agreed upon and entered into the gap column. It can be seen that in total there is an estimated shortage of n $= -145$ employees. This overall shortage is very unevenly distributed across the four job categories/levels. In three of these, there are shortages projected (n $= -39$, n $= -110$, and n $= -3$), and in the remaining one, there is a projected surplus (n $= +7$).

These gap data serve as the basic input to action planning. Because the gaps show both shortages and a surplus, and because the gaps vary in severity relative to the current workforce, a specific action plan will likely have to be developed and implemented for each job category/level. The resultant four staffing (and other) plans will hopefully bring staffing into an orderly balance of requirements and availabilities over the course of the planning period.

COMPONENTS OF HR PLANNING

The operational format and example serve to identify and illustrate the rudiments of HRP. Within the format are several distinct HRP components that require elaboration. We turn now to these components, emphasizing that each component represents a factor that must be considered in HRP, and that there are specific choices to be made regarding the operational details for each component.

Initial Decisions

Before HRP per se can be undertaken, there are several critical decisions that must be made.[3] These decisions will shape the nature of the resultant HRP process, and they will influence the output of the process, namely the gap estimates. The quality and potential effectiveness of the action plans developed from the gap estimates are thus at stake when these initial decisions are confronted and made.

Comprehensiveness of Planning
Often, HRP takes place as an integral part of an organization's business planning process; this is referred to as *plan-based HRP*. This is a logical approach since most organizations do business planning, and these plans almost always have HR

EXHIBIT 6.2   Operational Format and Example for Human Resource Planning (HRP)

Organizational Unit: Sales and Customer Service

Job Category and Level	Current Workforce	Forecast for Workforce—One Year		Reconciliation and Gaps	Action Planning
		Requirements	Availabilities		
A1 (Sales)	100	110	71	−39 (shortage)	Staffing activities
A2 (Sales manager)	20	15	22	+7 (surplus)	Recruitment Selection Employment
B1 (Customer service representative)	200	250	140	−110 (shortage)	Other HR activities Compensation
B2 (Customer service manager)	15	25	22	−3 (shortage)	Training & development
	335	400	255	−145 (shortage)	

implications. It is always a good idea to have a close, reciprocal linkage between business and HR plans.

Not all important business developments are captured in formal business plans, however, particularly if they occur rapidly or unexpectedly. Sudden changes in consumer preferences, or in legal requirements, for example, can wreak havoc on business plans. Organizational responses to these changes often occur in the form of special projects, rather than in changes in the total business plan. Part of each response requires consideration of HR implications, however, resulting in what is called *project-based HRP*. This type of planning helps ensure that the necessary creation of new jobs, changes in requirements and rewards for existing jobs, and employee job changes are undertaken systematically and without undue interruption.

In addition, many organizations do HRP outside the formal planning cycle for critical groups of employees on a regular basis. This often occurs for jobs in which there are perennial shortages of employees, both externally and internally. Examples here include nurses in health care organizations, faculty in certain specialized areas at colleges and universities, and until recently, teachers in elementary and secondary schools. Planning focused on a specific employee group is referred to as *population-based HRP*.

Planning Time Frame

Since planning involves looking into the future, the logical question for an organization to ask is, How far into the future should our planning extend? Typically, plans are divided into long-term (three plus years), intermediate (one to three years), and short-term (one year or less). Organizations vary in their planning time frame, often depending upon which of the three types of HRP is being undertaken.[4]

For plan-based HRP, the time frame will be the same as that of the business plan. In most organizations, this is between three and five years for so-called strategic planning and something less than three years for operational planning. Planning horizons for project-based HRP vary depending on the nature of the projects involved. Solving a temporary shortage of, say, salespeople for the introduction of a new product might involve planning for only a few months, while planning for the start-up of a new facility could involve a lead time of two or more years. Population-based HRP will have varying time frames, depending on the time necessary for labor supply (internal as well as external) to become available. As an example, for top-level executives in an organization, the planning time frame will be lengthy.

Job Categories and Levels

The unit of HRP and analysis is comprised of job categories and hierarchical levels among jobs. These job category/level combinations, and the types and paths of employee movement among them, form the structure of an internal labor market. Management must choose which job categories and which hierarchical levels to use for HRP. In Exhibit 6.2, for example, the choice involves two jobs (sales and customer service) and two levels (entry and manager) for a particular organizational unit.

Job categories are created and used on the basis of the unit of analysis for which projected shortages and surpluses are being investigated. These categories should be consistent with results of the job analysis. Major attention should also be paid to EEO/AA activities and commitments.

Hierarchical levels should be chosen so that they are consistent with or identical to the formal organizational hierarchy. The reason for this is that it is these formal levels which define employee *promotions* (up levels), *transfers* (across levels), and *demotions* (down levels). Having gap information by level facilitates planning of internal movement programs within the internal labor market. For example, it is difficult to have a systematic promotion-from-within program without knowing probable numbers of vacancies and gaps at various organizational levels.

Head Count (Current Workforce)

Exactly how does an organization count or tally the number of people in its current workforce for forecasting and planning purposes? Simply counting the number of employees on the payroll at the beginning of the planning period may be adequate for intended purposes. It ignores, however, two important distinctions.

First, it ignores the amount of scheduled time worked by each employee relative to a full workweek. For example, it treats full-time employees as synonymous with part-time employees. To rectify this, an employee head count may be made and stated in terms of *full-time equivalents,* or "FTEs." To do this, simply define what constitutes full-time work in terms of hours per week (or other time unit), and count each employee in terms of scheduled hours worked relative to a full workweek. If full-time is defined as 40 hours per week, a person who normally works 20 hours per week is counted as a .50 FTE, a person normally working 30 hours per week is a .75 FTE, and so on.

A second problem with current payroll head count is that it ignores vacancies that exist at the time of the count. Since most of such vacancies are probably so-called authorized ones, derived from previous HRP, they are better added into any head count tallies for the current workforce.

Roles and Responsibilities

Both line managers and staff specialists (usually from the HR department) become involved in HRP, so the roles and responsibilities of each must be determined as part of HRP. Most organizations take the position that line managers are ultimately responsible for the completion and quality of HRP. But the usual practice is to have HR staff assist with the process.

Initially, the HR staff take the lead in proposing which types of HRP will be undertaken and when, and in making suggestions with regard to comprehensiveness, planning time frame, job categories and levels, and head counts. Final decisions on these matters are usually the prerogative of line management. Once an approach has been decided upon, task forces of both line managers and HR staff people are assembled to design an appropriate forecasting and action planning process and to do any other preliminary work.

Once these processes are in place, the HR staff typically assumes responsibility for collecting, manipulating, and presenting the necessary data to line management, and for laying out alternative actions plans (including staffing plans). Action planning usually becomes a joint venture between line managers and HR staff people, particularly as they gain experience with, and trust for, each other.

Forecasting HR Requirements

Forecasting HR requirements is a direct derivative of business and organizational planning. As such, it becomes a reflection of projections about a variety of factors, such as sales, production, technological change, productivity improvement, and the regulatory environment. Many specific techniques may be used to forecast HR requirements; these are either statistical or judgmental in nature, and are usually tailor-made by the organization.

Statistical Techniques

A wide array of statistical techniques is available for use in HR forecasting. Prominent among these are regression analysis, ratio analysis, time series analysis, and stochastic analysis. Brief descriptions of two of these techniques, *regression analysis* and *ratio analysis,* are given in Exhibit 6.3.

We will not elaborate on these techniques for several reasons. First, their very complexity would lead away from a staffing focus. Second, all of these techniques are designed simply to project the past into the future. These techniques thus have limited applicability in organizations whose immediate past and/or future forecast are characterized by significant alterations in products and services, technologies, or organizational structures. (Obviously, this includes a large percentage of organizations of varying size today.) Third, as they are dependent upon the discovery of historical relationships between certain so-called leading indicators (e.g., sales or production volume) and head count, often these relationships are difficult to find, and if found, they may not hold up in the future.

Judgmental Techniques

Judgmental techniques represent human decision-making models that are used for forecasting HR requirements. Unlike statistical techniques, it is the decision maker who collects and weighs the information subjectively and then turns it into forecasts of HR requirements. The decision maker's forecasts may or may not agree very closely with those derived from statistical techniques.

Implementation of judgmental forecasting can proceed from either a ''top-down'' or ''bottom-up'' approach.[5] In the former case, top managers of the or-

---

EXHIBIT 6.3   Examples of Statistical Techniques to Forecast HR Requirements

---

(A)   Ratio Analysis

1. Examine historical ratios involving workforce size

$$\text{Example: } \frac{\$ \text{ sales}}{1.0 \text{ FTE}} = ? \quad \frac{\text{No. of new customers}}{1.0 \text{ FTE}} = ?$$

2. Assume ratio will be true in future
3. Use ratio to predict future HR requirements

$$\text{Example: (a) } \frac{\$4,000 \text{ sales}}{1.0 \text{ FTE}} \text{ is past ratio}$$

     (b)   Sales forecast is $4,000,000

     (c)   HR requirements = 100 FTEs

(B)   Regression Analysis

1. Statistically identify historical predictors of workforce size

    Example: FTEs = a + b_1 sales + b_2 new customers

2. Only use equations with predictors found to be statistically significant
3. Predict future HR requirements, using equation

    Example: (a) FTEs = 7 + .0004 sales + .02 new customers

        (b)   Projected sales = $1,000,000

           Projected new customers = 300

        (c)   HR requirements = 7 + 400 + 6 = 413

---

ganization, organizational units, or functions rely on their knowledge of business and organizational plans to make predictions about what future head counts will be. At times, these projections may, in fact, be dictates rather than estimates, necessitated by strict adherence to the business plan. Such dictates are common in organizations undergoing significant change, such as restructuring, mergers, and cost-cutting actions.

In the bottom-up approach, lower-level managers make initial estimates for their unit (e.g., department, office, or plant) based on what they have been told, or presume, are the business and organizational plans. These estimates are then consolidated and aggregated upward through successively higher levels of management. It is then top management that establishes the HR requirements in terms of numbers.

Forecasting HR Availabilities

In Exhibit 6.2 head count data are given for the current workforce, and their availability as forecast, in each job category/level. These forecast figures take into account movement into each job category/level, movement out of each job category/level, and exit from the organizational unit or the organization. Exhibit 6.4 shows this.

Numerous techniques could have been used, alone or in combination, to generate the availabilities forecast from the current workforce figures shown in Exhibit 6.2. As with HR requirements, these techniques can be classified as statistical or judgmental.[6]

Statistical Techniques

Statistical techniques seek to predict availabilities on the basis of historical patterns of job stability and movement among employees. Referring again to Exhibit 6.4, note that between any two time periods, the following possibilities exist for each employee in the internal labor market:

1. job stability (remain in A1, A2, B1, B2)
2. promotion (move to a higher level: A1 to A2, A1 to B2, B1 to B2, B1 to A2)
3. transfer (move at the same level: A1 to B1, B1 to A1, A2 to B2, B2 to A2)
4. demotion (move to a lower level: A2 to A1, A2 to B1, B2 to B1, B2 to A1)
5. exit (move to another organizational unit or leave the organization)

These possibilities may be thought of in terms of flows, and rates of flow or movement rates. Past flows and rates may be measured, and then used to forecast the future availability of current employees, based on assumptions about the extent to which past rates will continue unchanged into the future. For example, if it is known that the historical promotion rate from A1 to A2 is .10 (10% of A1 employees are promoted to A2), we might predict that A1 will experience a 10% loss of employees due to promotion to A2 over the relevant time period.

To be beneficial, the study and use of flows and rates must capture all of them simultaneously within the internal labor market. That is, we must know all of the job stability, promotion, transfer, demotion, and exit rates for an internal labor market before we can forecast future availabilities. *Markov Analysis* is a statistical technique that accomplishes this, and it is discussed next. Other possible techniques, not discussed here, include renewal and goal programming models.

Markov Analysis The elements of Markov Analysis are shown in Exhibit 6.5 for the organizational unit originally presented in Exhibit 6.2. Refer first to part A of the exhibit. There are four job category/level combinations for which movement rates are calculated between two time periods (T and T + 1). This is accomplished as follows. For each job category/level, take the number of employees who were in it at T, and use that number as the denominator for calculating job stability and movement rates. Then, for each of those employees determine which job category/level they were employed in at T + 1. Then sum up the number of

EXHIBIT 6.4 A Forecast of Future Human Resource Availabilities

Job Category and Level	Current Work-force	Movement In		Movement Out			Exit		Availability
		Promotion	Transfer	Demotion	Promotion	Transfer	Demotion	Unit	Org.	
A1	100									71
A2	20			[specific cell entries not shown]						22
B1	200									140
B2	15									22
	335									255

EXHIBIT 6.5 **Use of Markov Analysis to Forecast Availabilities**

A.	**Transition Probability Matrix**				**T + 1**		
	Job Category and Level		**A1**	**A2**	**B1**	**B2**	**Exit**
	A1		.60	.10	.20	.00	.10
T	A2		.05	.60	.00	.00	.35
	B1		.05	.00	.60	.05	.30
	B2		.00	.00	.00	.80	.20

B.	**Forecast of Availabilities**					
		Current Workforce				
	A1	100	60	10	20	0
	A2	20	1	12	0	0
	B1	200	10	0	120	10
	B2	15	0	0	0	12
			71	22	140	22

employees in each job category/level at T + 1, and use these as the numerators for calculating stability and movement rates. Finally, divide each numerator separately by the denominator. The result is the stability and movement rates expressed as proportions, also known as *transition probabilities*. The rates for any row (job category/level) must add up to 1.0.

For example, consider job category/level A1. Assume that at time T in the past there were a total of 400 people in it. Further assume that at T + 1, 240 of these employees were still in A1, 40 had been promoted to A2, 80 had been transferred to B1, 0 had been promoted to B2, and 40 had exited the organizational unit or the organization. The resultant transition probabilities, shown in the row for A1, are .60, .10, .20, .00, and .10. Note that these rates sum to 1.00.

By referring to these figures, and the remainder of the transition probabilities in the matrix, an organization can begin to understand the workings of the unit's internal labor market. For example, it becomes clear that 60–80% of employees experienced job stability and that exit rates varied considerably, ranging from 10% to 35%. Promotions occurred only within job categories (A1 to A2, B1 to B2), and not between job categories (A1 to B2, B1 to A2). Transfers were confined to the lower of the two levels (A1 to B1, B1 to A1). Only occasionally did demotions occur, and only within a job category (A2 to A1). Presumably, these stability and movement rates are a reflection of specific staffing policies and procedures that were in place between T and T + 1.

With these historical transitional probabilities, it becomes possible to forecast the future availability of the current workforce over the same time interval, T and T + 1, assuming that the historical rates will be repeated over the time interval and that staffing policies and procedures will not change. Refer now to part B of Exhibit 6.5. To forecast availabilities, simply take the current workforce column and multiply it by the transition probability matrix shown in part A. The resulting availability figures (note these are the same as those shown in Exhibits 6.2 and 6.3) appear at the bottom of the columns: A1 = 71, A2 = 22, B1 = 140, B2 = 22. The remainder of the current workforce (n = 145) are forecast to exit and will not be available at T + 1.

Limitations of Markov Analysis   Markov Analysis is an extremely useful way to capture the underlying workings of an internal labor market and then use the results to forecast future HR availabilities. Markov Analysis, however, is subject to some limitations that must be kept in mind.[7]

The first and most fundamental limitation is that of sample size, or the number of current workforce employees in each job category/level. As a rule, it is desirable to have n = 20 or more employees in each job category/level. Since this number serves as the denominator in the calculation of transition probabilities, with small sample sizes there can be substantial differences in the values of transition probabilities, even though the numerators used in their calculation are not that different (e.g., 2/10 = .20 and 4/10 = .40). Thus, transition probabilities based on small samples yield unstable estimates of future availabilities.

A second limitation of Markov Analysis is that it does not detect multiple moves by employees between T and T + 1; it only classifies employees and counts their movement according to their beginning (T) and ending (T + 1) job category/level, ignoring any intermittent moves. To minimize the number of undetected multiple moves, therefore, it is necessary to keep the time interval relatively short, probably no more than two years.

A third limitation pertains to the job category/level combinations created to serve as the unit of analysis. These must be meaningful to the organization for HRP purposes, both forecasting and action planning. Thus, extremely broad categories (e.g., managers, clericals) and categories without any level designations, should be avoided. It should be noted that this recommendation may conflict somewhat with HRP for affirmative action purposes, as discussed later.

Finally, the transition probabilities reflect only gross, average employee movement, and not the underlying causes of the movement. Stated differently, all employees in a job category/level are assumed to have an equal probability of movement. This is unrealistic, since organizations take many factors into account (e.g., seniority, performance appraisal results, and KSAOs) when making movement decisions about employees. Because of these factors, the probabilities of movement may vary among specific employees.

Judgmental Techniques

There are three judgmental techniques for forecasting availabilities that enjoy widespread acceptance: executive reviews, succession planning, and vacancy analysis. In this context, the main difference between statistical and judgmental techniques is that the former treat employees as numbers and forecast their movements based on probabilities. The latter treat them as individuals and forecast their movements person by person.

Executive Reviews   Executive reviews focus on small and unique groups of employees, most commonly top executives and other managers and professionals judged to have the potential to be top executives. Thus, executive reviews are a form of population-based HRP. The actual reviews are carried out through a series of meetings at which the top executives in a given unit consider anticipated human resource requirements and then thoroughly discuss each person under review to determine who is likely to be, or should be, promoted, reassigned, developed for future assignments, or drummed out of the organization. Determinations are made based on judgments about performance, promotability, and potential, taking into account the long-term career interests of the employee being considered. The process produces a clear indication of where the organization can expect to have managerial shortages or surpluses. It also provides career and development plans for individuals.

Succession Planning   This planning is often an adjunct to executive reviews.[8] It helps to identify backup candidates who are, or soon will be, qualified to replace current executives or upper-level managers. Succession planning results are typically summarized on charts such as the one shown in Exhibit 6.6. These greatly facilitate the planning of likely retirements, terminations, promotions, and transfers within and across organizational units. These charts also show which managers are in need of further development to become ready to fill job(s) for which they are (or might be) considered as replacements.

Vacancy Analysis   In vacancy analysis, judgments are made about likely employee movement on an individual basis, as in executive reviews and succession planning. Because large numbers of employees are usually involved, the results may be aggregated and summarized statistically. Vacancy analysis is akin to judgmental Markov Analysis; employee movement is "guesstimated" through managerial judgment rather than estimated statistically through calculation and use of transition probabilities.

Exhibit 6.7 shows a vacancy analysis, using the same four job categories/levels, current workforce numbers, and forecast of requirements, as in Exhibits 6.2, 6.4, and 6.5. Vacancy analysis begins with a forecast about numbers of exits from each job category/level. This yields an effective internal labor supply, which can then be compared to a forecast of demand to arrive at a gross shortage or surplus number for each job category/level. These numbers are then adjusted for likely movement into and out of the job category/levels, resulting in final gap figures. These gaps serve as the input to action planning. Since both shortages and sur-

EXHIBIT 6.6   Employee Replacement Chart for Succession Planning

Organizational Unit _____

Date _____

Position	
Incumbent _____	Current job: years: ___ Total service: years: ___
Promote to _____	Date ready: _____
Replacement (1) _____	Current job: years: ___ Total service: years: ___
Present position _____	Date promotable: _____
Replacement (2) _____	Current job: years: ___ Total service: years: ___
Present position _____	Date promotable: _____

Position	
Incumbent _____	Current job: years: ___ Total service: years: ___
Promote to _____	Date ready: _____
Replacement (1) _____	Current job: years: ___ Total service: years: ___
Present position _____	Date promotable: _____
Replacement (2) _____	Current job: years: ___ Total service: years: ___
Present position _____	Date promotable: _____

Position	
Incumbent _____	Current job: years: ___ Total service: years: ___
Promote to _____	Date ready: _____
Replacement (1) _____	Current job: years: ___ Total service: years: ___
Present position _____	Date promotable: _____
Replacement (2) _____	Current job: years: ___ Total service: years: ___
Present position _____	Date promotable: _____

Position	
Incumbent _____	Current job: years: ___ Total service: years: ___
Promote to _____	Date ready: _____
Replacement (1) _____	Current job: years: ___ Total service: years: ___
Present position _____	Date promotable: _____
Replacement (2) _____	Current job: years: ___ Total service: years: ___
Present position _____	Date promotable: _____

EXHIBIT 6.7   Vacancy Analysis for Sales and Customer Service Unit

Job Category and Level	Current Work-force	Exit Forecast Org.	Exit Forecast Unit	Effective Supply	Forecast of Demand	(Shortages) or Surpluses	Movements Within Unit Into	Movements Within Unit Out	Gap/Net Shortage or Surplus	Accessions From Other Units	Accessions External New Hires	Reductions
A1	100	8	2	90	110	(20)	11	30	(39)			
A2	20	4	3	13	15	(2)	10	1	7	Action planning		
B1	200	25	15	160	250	(90)	0	20	(110)			
B2	15	2	1	12	25	(13)	10	0	(3)			

pluses were forecast in Exhibit 6.2, these plans are likely to involve both accessions (internal and external) and workforce reductions in head count and/or hours of work.

It should be noted that the data in Exhibit 6.7 were constructed to yield the same availability results and employment gaps as shown in Exhibits 6.2 and 6.4. Referring to Exhibit 6.7, note that A1 may be calculated as $(90 + 11 - 30 = 71)$, A2 as $(13 + 10 - 1 = 22)$, B1 as $(160 + 0 - 20 = 140)$, and B2 as $(12 + 10 - 0 = 22)$. In essence, the results of judgmental forecasting have been "rigged" to yield the same results as statistical forecasting. In actual practice, such a result is extremely unlikely. But our example does illustrate that if decision makers are knowledgeable about their internal labor markets, their judgments may yield results similar to those that would have been obtained from statistical forecasting, such as Markov Analysis.

External and Internal Environmental Scanning

External Scanning

This is the term applied to the process of tracking trends and developments in the outside world, documenting their implications for the management of human resources, and ensuring that these implications receive attention in the HRP process. Many large corporations maintain fairly elaborate networks of line managers, technical specialists, and human resource specialists, who monitor large numbers of publications, broadcast media, futurist think tanks, and conferences for relevant data. Periodically, these data are assembled and trend reports are prepared and made available to those responsible for HRP. These reports usually include a summary of the major environmental trends and their implications for human resource management. Exhibit 6.8 shows an example of an environmental scan and its use at the First Chicago Corporation.

Of the various areas monitored through external scanning, the labor market is most directly relevant to staffing planning. For a start-up organization in genetic engineering, for example, the future availability of geneticists, biologists, and other types of scientists and engineers is an important strategic contingency. If tight labor markets for these skills are expected, the organization must plan to put considerable time and money into attracting and retaining the needed talent (for example, by raising salaries or offering day care programs) or into developing alternative means of accomplishing its key research and development work (for instance, by using technicians wherever possible, thus reducing the need for scientists and engineers).

Clearly, then, an organization's grasp of impending developments in the outside world is very helpful to human resource planners. It puts them in an excellent position to influence the nature of business plans (and thus the nature of future

---

EXHIBIT 6.8   Example of an Environmental Scan and Its Use

First Chicago's HR Strategic Diagnostic

Pablo Picasso was known for painting in haptic style—that is, he painted the way people feel. If his portrait was one of a person with an injured finger, the finger would be painted disproportionately large to indicate pain.

According to Jim Alef, senior vice president and head of human resources at First Chicago Corporation, HR professionals often work in much the same fashion by giving their individual challenges a disproportionately large share of attention. The human resources strategic diagnostic is First Chicago's way of overcoming such tunnel vision and objectively prioritizing all issues related to HR management.

"As I looked at our HR activity, I saw a lot of well-intentioned people working on recommendations related to individual issues," he explains. "What I didn't see was an attempt to pull those recommendations together."

In 1989, under Alef's direction, the HR staff worked in concert to identify and prioritize all its HR issues. Extensive input was sought from other departments including corporate strategy, economics, government and legal affairs and the line areas. The resulting diagnostic was the company's first comprehensive, objective list of HR challenges.

Alef's staff uses the diagnostic to anticipate upcoming challenges and take early, decisive action on HR issues. What staff members may intuitively think are issues, the diagnostic confirms. By making decisions based on fact, not suspicion, the bank not only avoids potential problems, it experiences greater program success. Specifically, the document:

(1) Identifies and examines the major external and internal forces that have or will have implications for the management of First Chicago's human resources

(2) Establishes a sound data base that describes First Chicago's total work force as well as the work force composition of each major line of business

(3) Promotes possible courses of action for upcoming human resources challenges

(4) Crafts a time-phased agenda that reflects opportunities to put First Chicago ahead of those challenges

(5) Helps determine an appropriate organizational structure for the HR department, as well as corresponding staff and budget requirements.

The diagnostic, which is constantly being updated, measures the company's corporate business objectives against political, educational, demographic, economic, judicial and social issues. This "living document" is used as a strategic HR roadmap, allowing HR professionals to act on changing circumstances, rather than react to them.

Among the HR programs developed as a result of information revealed in the diagnostic are enhanced basic skills training efforts, a revised pensioner health care program, and stepped-up recruitment for entry-level, non-exempt positions.

"Upon compiling the diagnostic," says Alef, "we learned there are a vast number of things going on in this world that are HR-related, and, if we could do human resources right, what a tremendous competitive advantage we would have."

Source: S. Caudran, "Strategic HR at First Chicago," *Personnel Journal*, 1991, pp. 50–56.

human resource requirements) and to ensure that planned HR activities are both realistic and supportive of these business plans.

Internal Scanning

Also important is a firm grasp of an organization's internal environment. Thus, planners must be out and about in their organizations, taking advantage of opportunities to learn what is going on. Informal discussions with key managers can help, as can employee attitude surveys, special surveys, and the monitoring of key indices such as employee performance, absenteeism, turnover, and accident rates. Of special interest is the identification of nagging personnel problems, as well as prevailing managerial attitudes concerning human resources.

Nagging personnel problems refer to recurring difficulties that threaten to interfere with the attainment of future business plans or other important organizational goals. High turnover in a sales organization, for example, is likely to threaten the viability of a business plan that calls for increased sales quotas or the rapid introduction of several new products.

The values and attitudes of managers, especially top managers, toward human resources are also important to HRP. Trouble brews when these are inconsistent with the organization's business plans. For example, a mid-sized accounting firm may have formulated a business plan calling for very rapid growth through aggressive marketing and selected acquisitions of smaller firms, but existing management talent may be inadequate to the task of operating a larger, more complex organization. Moreover, there may be a prevailing attitude among the top management against investing much money in management development and against bringing in talent from outside the firm. This attitude conflicts with the business plan, requiring a change in either the business plan or attitudes.

Reconciliation and Gaps

The reconciliation and gap determination process is best examined by means of an example. Exhibit 6.9 presents intact the example in Exhibit 6.2. Attention is now directed to the reconciliation and gaps column. It represents the results of bringing together requirements and availability forecasts with the results of external and internal environmental scanning. Gap figures must be decided upon and entered into the column, and the likely reasons for the gaps need to be identified.

Consider first job category/level A1. A relatively large shortage is projected, due to a mild expansion in requirements coupled with a substantial drop in availabilities. This drop is not due to an excessive exit rate, but to losses through promotions and job transfers (refer back to the availability forecasts in Exhibits 6.5 and 6.7).

For A2, decreased requirements coupled with increased availabilities lead to a projected surplus. Clearly, changes in current staffing policies and procedures will

EXHIBIT 6.9 Operational Format and Example for Human Resource Planning (HRP)

Organizational Unit: Sales and Customer Service

Job Category and Level	Current Workforce	Forecast for Workforce—One Year		Reconciliation and Gaps	Action Planning
		Requirements	Availabilities		
A1 (Sales)	100	110	71	−39 (shortage)	Staffing activities
					Recruitment
A2 (Sales manager)	20	15	22	+7 (surplus)	Selection
					Employment
B1 (Customer service representative)	200	250	140	−110 (shortage)	Other HR activities
					Compensation
B2 (Customer service manager)	15	25	22	−3 (shortage)	Training & development
	335	400	255	−145 (shortage)	

have to be made in order to stem the availability tide, such as a slowdown in the promotion rate into A2 from A1 or an acceleration in the exit rate, through an early retirement program.

Turning to B1, note that a huge shortage is forecast. This is due to a major surge in requirements and a substantial reduction in availabilities. To meet the shortage, the organization could increase the transfer of employees from A1. While this would worsen the already projected shortage in A1, it might be cost-effective to do this and would beef up the external staffing for A1 to cover the exacerbated shortage. Alternatively, a massive external staffing program could be developed and undertaken for B1 alone. Or, a combination of internal transfers and external staffing for both A1 and B1 could be attempted. To the extent that external staffing becomes a candidate for consideration, this will naturally spill over into other HR activities, such as establishing starting pay levels for A1 and B1.

Finally, for B2 there is a small projected shortage. This gap is so small, however, that for all practical purposes it can be ignored. The HRP process is too imprecise to warrant concern over such small gap figures.

In short, the reconciliation and gap phase of HRP involves coming to grips with projected gaps and likely reasons for them. Quite naturally, thoughts about future implications begin to creep into the process.[9] Even in the simple example shown, it can be seen that considerable action will have to be contemplated and undertaken in order to respond to the forecasting results for the organizational unit. That will involve mixtures of external and internal staffing, with compensation as another likely HR ingredient. It is through action planning that these possibilities become real.

Action Planning

Action planning involves four basic sequential steps:[10]

1. Set objectives
2. Generate alternative activities
3. Assess alternative activities
4. Choose alternative activities

Movement through these steps is a logical outgrowth of HRP and is greatly enhanced by its occurrence. Indeed, without HRP the organization rarely has the luxury of doing action planning. Instead, reaction becomes the mode of operation, leading to crash or crisis activities and programs.

These general statements apply to virtually all HR activities that are in any way dependent upon the existence of employment gaps and the need to close them. The focus in this chapter is on staffing planning as a specific form of action planning.

STAFFING PLANNING

The four stages of action planning are directly translatable into a staffing planning process. These steps are melded together at the operational level through the development of an implementation plan, and through the development of staffing flow processes that summarize and guide the operational staffing process.

Staffing Planning Process

Staffing Objectives

Staffing objectives are derived from identified gaps between requirements and availabilities. As such, they involve objectives responding to both shortages and surpluses. They may require the establishment of quantitative and qualitative targets.

Quantitative targets should be expressed in head count or FTE form for each job category/level and will be very close in magnitude to the identified gaps. Indeed, to the extent that the organization believes in the gaps as forecast, the objectives will be identical to the gap figures. A forecast shortage of $n = 39$ employees in A1, for example, should be transformed into a staffing objective of $n = 39$ accessions (or something close to it) to be achieved by the end of the forecasting time interval. Exhibit 6.10 provides an illustration of these points regarding quantitative staffing objectives.

Qualitative staffing objectives refer to the types or qualities of people, usually in KSAO-type terms. For external staffing objectives, these may be stated in terms of averages, such as average education level for new hires and average scores on ability tests. Internal staffing objectives of a qualitative nature may also be established. These may reflect desired KSAOs in terms of seniority, performance ap-

---

EXHIBIT 6.10   Setting Numerical Staffing Objectives

Job Category and Level	Gap	Objectives					Total
		New Hires	Promotions	Transfers	Demotions	Exits	
A1	−39						+39
A2	+7	For each cell, enter a positive number for head count					−7
B1	−110	additions and a negative number for head count					+110
B2	−3	subtractions.					+3
Total							

Note: Assumes objective is to close each gap exactly.

praisal record over a period of years, types of on- and off-the-job training, and so forth.

Qualitative (KSAO) staffing concerns are usually not a part of the previously described forecast process. Gaps are thus not likely to be identified or expressed in qualitative terms. Hence, establishment of qualitative staffing objectives involves considerable judgment on the part of the organization. Ideally, the organization will have conducted job analysis and have available formal job specifications that it can use to guide it in establishing qualitative objectives.

Generating Alternative Staffing Activities

With quantitative and, possibly, qualitative objectives established, it is necessary to begin identifying possible ways of achieving them. This requires an identification of the fullest possible range of alternative activities, which, if pursued, might lead to achievement of the objectives. Three different approaches to generating staffing alternatives are (a) generic shortage and surplus activities, (b) contract or flexible staffing activities, and (c) alternative scheduling activities.

Generic Shortages and Surpluses   There is a wide array of possible activities for addressing both shortages and surpluses. Some of these will be short-term, and others long-term. At the beginning stages of generating alternatives, it is wise not to prematurely close the door on any alternatives. Exhibit 6.11 provides an excellent list of the full range of options available for initial consideration.

Contract or Flexible Staffing Alternatives   Organizations are increasingly viewing their workforces as divided into two components—*core workers* and *contingent workers*.[11] Core workers are generally regarded as full-time, permanent employees with whom the organization desires to have a long-term employment relationship. These employees are the ''guts and glue'' of the workforce. Contingent workers, on the other hand, are those who, by organization intent, have marginal attachments to it, either in terms of hours worked or length of the employment relationship.

Having both core and contingent workers increases the options available to organizations in terms of staffing activities. The organization can first of all decide to move toward development of a contingent component to its workforce, if it has not already done so. Within the contingent workforce, numerous flexible or contract staffing activities are available for consideration as staffing alternatives.

The Olsten Corporation, a major provider of temporary employees, conducted a large-scale survey (n = 427 companies) of flexible staffing and alternative staffing practices.[12] The companies surveyed were diverse in terms of size, annual revenues, industry type, and geographic region. The following flexible staffing alternatives were investigated: external temporary employees, in-house temporary employees, employee leasing, outsourcing/vendor-on-premises, and independent

EXHIBIT 6.11   Staffing Alternatives to Deal with Employee Shortages and Surpluses

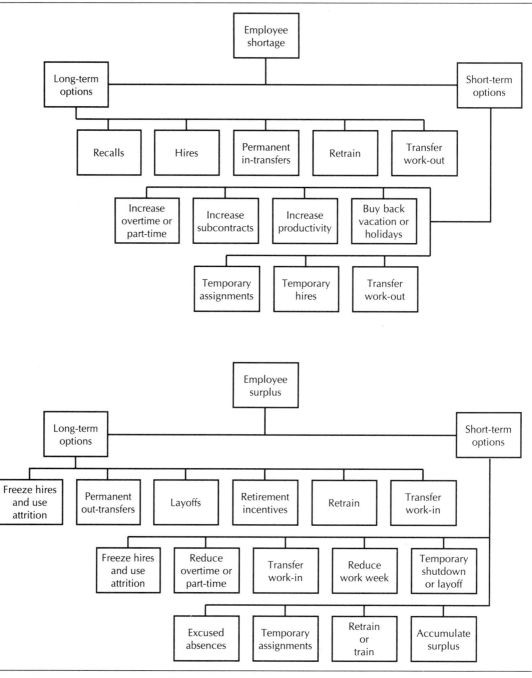

Source: Compliments of Dan Ward, GTE Corporation.

contractors. Definitions of these alternatives, and their current usage by the companies, is shown in Exhibit 6.12.

It should also be noted that 30% of the companies reported that they planned on increasing their use of flexible staffing alternatives. Contributing to the current and anticipated increase in flexible staffing were the following forces, all cost-driven:

1. Economic and competitive pressures, leading to downsizing (hours reductions, layoffs, hiring freezes) of the core workforce
2. The need to contain cost (core employees represent fixed costs in the form of direct pay and benefits, while contingent employees represent variable costs)
3. Difficulties in recruiting qualified core employees for many positions, leading to hiring contingent workers as the alternative for filling employment gaps
4. Increased workforce diversity and employee preferences for alternatives to core employment

Alternative Scheduling   Alternative scheduling refers to alternatives to the so-called normal 5-day, 40-hour week. The Olsten Corporation survey also examined

---

EXHIBIT 6.12   Contract or Flexible Staffing Alternatives

Alternative	Percent Using (N = 427 companies)
The following definitions were used in this survey for contract or flexible staffing strategies:	
● **Temporary employees (through an outside service firm):** A flexible staff for traditional strategic staffing services assigned to a client employed by the service firm.	83%
● **In-house temporary employees:** Members of a flexible staff drawn from an in-house pool employed by the company itself.	38%
● **Employee leasing:** Dedicated staff (usually servicing, on a full-time basis, specific areas from individual departments to an entire company) employed by an outside service firm.	11%
● **Outsourcing/vendor-on-premises:** The contracting of entire business functions or departments to outside service firms.	28%
Independent contractors: Self-employed individuals, such as consultants, freelancers, or commissioned representatives.	61%

Source: © Olsten Corporation, Westbury, NY. *Olsten Forum ™ on Human Resource Issues and Trends, New Staffing Strategies for the 90's*, pp. 5–6. Reprinted with permission.

company practices regarding the following alternative scheduling options: part-time, flextime, compressed workweek, job sharing, and work-at-home. Definitions of these options, and the usage of the options by the companies, is shown in Exhibit 6.13.

The survey also found that use of scheduling alternatives was primarily employee-driven. That is, alternatives were adopted in direct response to applicant and employee scheduling needs. This is an excellent example of the ways in which organizations alter job rewards in the face of applicants' needs in order to continue to have effective person/job matching.

Assessing Alternatives

As should be apparent, there is a veritable smorgasbord of alternative staffing activities available to address staffing gaps. Each of these alternatives needs to be systematically assessed in order to help decision makers choose from among the alternatives.

The goal of such assessment is to identify one or more preferred activities. A preferred activity is one offering the highest likelihood of attaining the staffing objective, within the time limit established, at the least cost or tolerable cost, and with the fewest negative side effects. There are no standard or agreed upon programs or formats for conducting these assessments. Thus, the organization will need to develop its own internal mechanisms for assessment. Whatever overall

---

EXHIBIT 6.13   Alternative Scheduling Options

Alternative	Percent Using (N = 427 companies)
The following definitions were used in this survey for alternative scheduling strategies:	
• **Part-time:** A regular employee who works fewer than 35 hours a week.	84%
• **Flextime:** A system that enables employees to vary their schedules. Usually, the flexibility applies to starting and finishing times.	40%
• **Compressed workweek:** A full-week schedule (usually 40 hours) that occurs in fewer than five days, such as four 10-hour days.	23%
• **Job sharing:** Two or more employees split a full-time position, dividing the responsibilities, and, to some degree, the compensation.	18%
• **Work-at-home:** A program that enables employees to complete work at home (or at a remote office closer to home) on a regular basis. It is often referred to as "flexplace" or "telecommuting."	13%

Source: © Olsten Corporation, Westbury, NY. *Olsten Forum* ™ *on Human Resource Issues and Trends, New Staffing Strategies for the 90's,* pp. 8–9. Reprinted with permission.

mechanism is developed, it should ensure that two things occur. First, a common set of assessment criteria (e.g., time for completion, cost, probability of success) should be identified and agreed upon. Second, each alternative should be assessed according to each of these criteria. In this way, all alternatives will receive equal treatment, and tendencies to jump at an initial alternative will be minimized.

Choosing Alternatives

Responsibility for scrutinizing the proposed package of staffing alternatives and making final decisions rests with top management. Inconsistencies between positions and overlaps among them must be ferreted out, and the alternatives must be realistically placed within the context of the emerging business and organizational plans. The alternatives must be seen as viable by top management in terms of the budget and people likely to be available to implement them.

Top management's decisions form the basis of staffing strategy. The strategy is derived from a systematic process of identifying employment gaps, establishing staffing objectives to address the gaps, generating alternative programs for achieving the objectives, assessing each of these programs according to a set of common criteria, and then presenting the information (and usually recommendations) to top management for final decision making. Once final decisions have been made, the chosen staffing plans must be implemented.

Staffing Philosophy

In conjunction with the staffing planning process, the organization's staffing philosophy should be reviewed. Results of this review help shape the direction and character of the specific staffing systems implemented. The review should focus on the following issues: internal versus external staffing, EEO/AA practices, and applicant reactions.

The relative importance to the organization of external or internal staffing is a critical matter because it so greatly shapes the nature of the staffing system, as well as sends signals to applicants and employees alike about the organization as an employer. For example, at the extreme, an exclusively external focus will require the organization to devote considerable resources to looking outward in order to identify applicant pools to activate and process. For potential applicants, this external focus will likely cause them to perceive any job as fair game, and will enhance the external reputation of the organization as a desirable place to seek employment at any level. Current employees, however, will perceive a lack of internal mobility possibilities, and this may cause such reactions as high turnover and negative feelings toward new external hires. Exhibit 6.14 highlights the advantages and disadvantages of external and internal staffing.

In terms of EEO/AA, the organization must be sure to consider, or develop, a sense of importance attached to being an EEO/AA-conscious employer, and the

---

EXHIBIT 6.14   Staffing Philosophy: Internal versus External Staffing

---

	Advantages	Disadvantages
Internal	• Positive employee reactions to promotion from within • Quick method to identify job applicants • Less expensive • Little orientation time required	• No new KSAOs into the organization • May perpetuate current underrepresentation of minorities and women • Small labor market to recruit from • Employees may require more training time
External	• Brings employees in with new KSAOs • Larger number of minorities and women to draw upon • Large labor market to draw from • Employees may require less training time	• Negative reaction by internal applicants • Time consuming to identify applicants • Expensive to search external labor market • New employees require more orientation time

---

commitment it is willing to make in incorporating EEO/AA elements into all phases of the staffing system. Attitudes toward EEO/AA can range all the way from outright hostility and disregard, to benign neglect, to aggressive commitment and support. As should be obvious, the stance that the organization adopts will have major effects on its operational staffing system, as well as on job applicants and employees.

As a final point about staffing philosophy, planners must continue to bear in mind that staffing is an interaction involving both the organization and job applicants as participants.[13] Just as organizations recruit and select applicants, so, too, do applicants recruit and select organizations (and job offers). Through their job search strategies and activities, applicants exert major influence on their own staffing destinies. Once the applicant has decided to opt into the organization's staffing process, the applicant is confronted with numerous decisions about whether to continue on in the staffing process or withdraw from further consideration. This process of self-selection is inherent to any staffing system. During staffing planning, those within the organization must constantly consider how the applicant will react to the staffing system and its components, and whether they want to encourage or discourage applicant self-selection.

Staffing Flows

Staffing an organization requires not only decisions about discrete staffing system characteristics (for example, which recruitment sources to use and what type of interviews to conduct), but also decisions about the overall flow of events that comprise a staffing system. This flow may be described in general terms or in specific terms. Organizations may use flowcharts to plan and designate the precise nature of the staffing system.

General Staffing Flows

There are several discrete, but sequential, phases that comprise a general staffing flow—a flow that involves an applicant reduction process and consists of the following:

1. Eligible labor force—At the national level, this includes the employed, the unemployed, discouraged workers, new labor force entrants, and labor force reentrants. Eligible labor forces also exist at the level of state, region, county, SMSA (standard metropolitan statistical area), and so forth.

2. Potential applicant population—These are individuals from the eligible labor force with at least the minimum qualifications (KSAOs) for the job or jobs for which staffing is occurring.

3. Applicants—These are the individuals who formally become identified as job applicants, by a process of organization and/or self identification.

4. Candidates—These are the applicants who survive the initial screening and remain interested in the organization.

5. Finalists—These are the candidates who survive all but the final selection activities.

6. Offer receiver—This is the finalist(s) who receives the offer of a job.

7. New hire(s)—The offer receiver who accepts the offer and formally begins the employment relationship.

This general staffing flow has external staffing activities as its apparent referent. However, it also may be used to describe the process entailed in promotion and transfer systems. The eligible labor force is the organization's total workforce, comprised of those employed, otherwise hired (e.g., temporary workers), and on layoff. The potential applicant population consists of those eligible individuals who also have the required KSAOs, including seniority and experience minimums. Applicants are those individuals who formally apply for the vacancy (such as through a job posting system) or are identified as candidates for the position by the organization (such as through succession planning and replacement charts). Candidates are those who survive initial screening. Finalists are those who remain in contention for the post after organization and self selection. The offer receiver is the person offered the promotion or the transfer. The new hire is the person who actually assumes the new position and becomes a job incumbent.

Specific Staffing Flows

General staffing flow operations may be expanded to take into account all the specific methods, techniques, and decision points that operationally define a staffing system. Moreover, these flows can be (and should be) visualized and charted from both organizational and applicant viewpoints. Developing such flowcharts represents the final stage of staffing planning.

Organization Staffing Flowchart   An example of a staffing flowchart from an organizations perspective is shown in Exhibit 6.15. It is a flowchart that depicts the staffing system of a medium-sized (n = 580 employees) high-tech printing and lithography company. It shows the actual flow of staffing activities, and both organization and applicant decision points, from the time a vacancy occurs until the time it is filled with a new hire.

A detailed inspection of the chart reveals the following sorts of information about the company's staffing system:

1. It is a generic system used for both entry-level and higher-level jobs.
2. For higher-level jobs, vacancies are first posted internally (thus showing a recruitment philosophy emphasizing a commitment to promotion from within). Entry-level jobs are filled externally.
3. External recruitment sources (colleges, newspaper ads, employment agencies) are used only if the current applicant file yields no qualified applicants.
4. Initial assessments are made using biographical information (application blanks, resumes), and results of these assessments determine who will be interviewed.

EXHIBIT 6.15 Staffing Flowchart for Medium-Sized Printing Company: Company Perspective

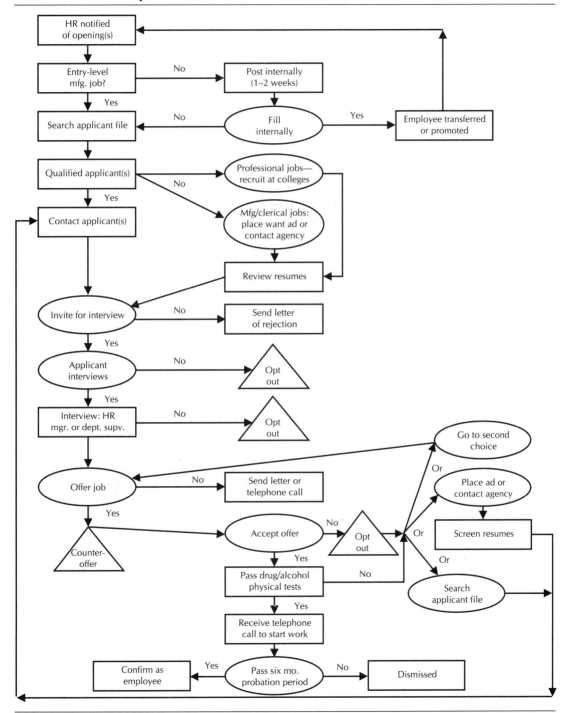

5. Substantive assessments are made through the interview(s) conducted by the HR manager and the hiring supervisor, and results of these assessments determine who receives the job offer.

6. The applicant may counteroffer, and acceptance by the applicant of the final offer is conditional upon passing drug/alcohol and physical tests.

7. The new hire undergoes a six-month probationary employment period before becoming a so-called permanent employee.

Applicant Staffing Flowchart   It is useful for an organization also to chart the staffing flow from the viewpoint of the job applicant. This helps the organization better understand what experiences their staffing system creates for the applicant, as well as potential applicant reactions to those experiences.

Using the preceding example of a printing and lithography company, and drawing upon its organizational staffing flowchart, the company's applicant staffing flowchart is developed as in Exhibit 6.16. Inspection of that flowchart reveals that the organization does not actively seek out external applicants for entry-level jobs; it waits for applicants to come to it. For higher-level jobs, resume submission in response to knowledge of vacancies gained through the internal posting or external recruitment sources is used by applicants. There are several identifiable decision points at which the applicant may self-select out of the staffing process. Occasionally, and outside the formal staffing process (as shown by the dotted line), the applicant may receive a plant tour. For the applicant, this tour may be very useful for learning more about both job requirements and rewards. If the applicant receives and accepts an offer, he or she may not be told a specific starting date, but must await a phone call to report to work as a new hire. Finally, the new hire knows that the first six months of employment are probationary, and that failure to pass the probationary period will result in dismissal.

LEGAL ISSUES

The major legal issue in HR and staffing planning is that of affirmative action plans and programs (AAPs). AAPs originate from many different sources—voluntary employer efforts, court-imposed remedies for discriminatory practices, conciliation or consent agreement, and requirements as a federal contractor. Regardless of source, all AAPs seek to rectify the effects of past employment discrimination by increasing the representation of certain groups (minorities, women, disabled) in the organization's workforce. This is to be achieved through establishing, and actively pursuing, hiring and promotion goals, and adhering to timetables for achieving those goals.

This section describes the general content of AAPs, discusses the affirmative action requirements for federal contractors under Revised Order No. 4, and pro-

EXHIBIT 6.16   Staffing Flowchart for Medium-Sized Printing Company: Applicant Perspective

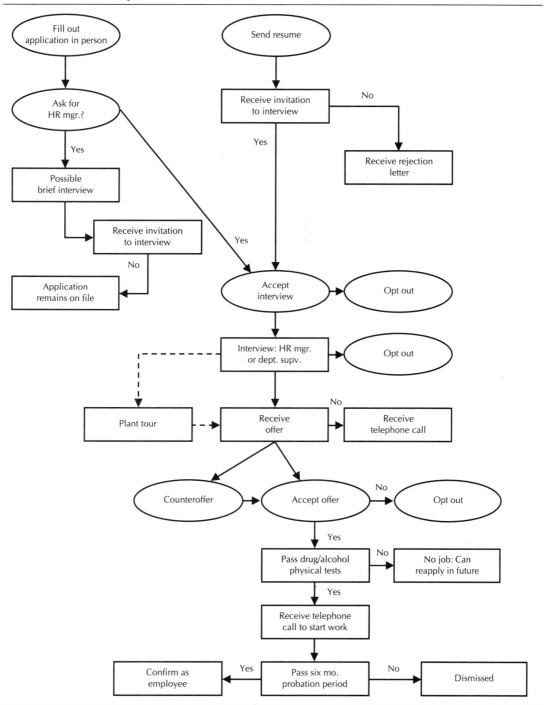

vides some general indications as to the legality of AAPs. Also, a brief presentation is made of so-called diversity programs, which can augment, and potentially increase, the effectiveness of AAPs.

Affirmative Action Plans (AAPs)

AAPs are organization-specific plans and thus their content varies across organizations. Nonetheless, all AAPs share three general components, namely *utilization analysis, staffing goals and timetables,* and *action plans.*[14]

An example of a partial AAP with these three general components is shown in Exhibit 6.17. The example draws from the general HR planning example in Exhibits 6.1 and 6.2. The AAP shown is for only one job category (sales) and for only one group (women).

Inspection of the exhibit reveals that the organization has a current sales force of n = 100, of whom n = 10 (10%) are women. A utilization analysis with accompanying stock statistics (see Chapter 3) shows that the current percentage of female salespeople (10%) is less than their estimated availability (20%), based on consideration of eight availability factors. A comparison of these two percentages suggests that there is underutilization of women in the sales job category.

Based on the identified underutilization, the organization sets an affirmative action goal of 20% utilization and sets an ambitious timetable of one year to achieve that goal. Action plans are now developed for achieving this goal. These involve staffing plans and other HR plans.

In terms of staffing plans, the organization first considers the results of its general HR forecast for the next year, which had predicted a shortage of 39 salespeople. New hires may be obtained from both external and internal (job transfer) sources, consistent with past staffing practices. Based on its affirmative action goal and timetable, the organization sets a staffing target of n = 24 men and n = 15 women, for a total of n = 39 new sales people. If, in fact, these targets are met, the organization will come close to its affirmative action goal of 20% women in the sales job category (the n = 15 new saleswomen plus whatever number of the n = 10 current saleswomen who remain in the job category, out of the total of n = 112 that were forecast in Exhibit 6.2).

Armed with this numerical staffing target, the organization can now develop specific plans for pursuing it. This involves development of detailed staffing plans, as discussed earlier in this chapter. It also involves consideration of other action plans to support the staffing plan. As shown in Exhibit 3.17, the development of an accelerated training program and the development of a child care program have been identified as two possible support plans.

This example illustrates the basics of an affirmative action plan (utilization analysis, staffing goals and timetables, and action plans). It is, however, a very simplified version of an AAP. It involves only one job category, one group

EXHIBIT 6.17 Example of Affirmative Action Plan (AAP): Essential Components

Job Category: Sales
Affirmative Action Plan: Women

Current Workforce			Utilization Analysis: Availability* (8 factors)		Utilization Analysis: Under-utilization (?)	Goals and Timetables: Goal	Goals and Timetables: Timetable	Forecast of Gap	Action Plan (one year): External Staffing		Action Plan (one year): Other Plans
Total	%M	%F	%M	%F		%F	%F		M	F	
100	90	10	80	20	Yes	20	1 year	−39 (shortage)	24	15	accelerated training program, day care program

* Availability determined on the basis of the eight factors contained in Revised Order No. 4. It includes both internal (current employees) and external (labor force) factors.

(women), and a one-year time frame. Specifics of the utilization analysis, and action plans, are ignored. AAPs are, in reality, much more complex than this example suggests. They involve all job categories, multiple underrepresented groups (women, minorities, disabled), multiple-year time frames, internal administration and enforcement mechanisms, and very detailed staffing plans. A consideration of the actual AAP requirements for federal contractors under Revised Order No. 4 shows the complexities involved in AAPs.

Revised Order No. 4

Revised Order No. 4 (Appendix B) spells out in detail the requirements a federal contractor must adhere to as it develops, implements, and administers an AAP. Three basic features of the order should be emphasized—its broad scope, utilization analysis requirements, and judgment of contractor compliance status.

Scope   AAPs are very broad in scope under the order, touching on virtually all HR policies and practices of the organization. This breadth comes from the order's statement regarding ''required ingredients of affirmative action programs.'' The order specifically requires

1. ''development or reaffirmation of the contractor's equal employment policy in all personnel actions
2. formal internal and external dissemination of the contractor's policy
3. establishment of responsibilities for implementation of the contractor's affirmative action program
4. identification of problem areas (deficiencies) by organizational units and job classifications
5. establishment of goals and objectives by organizational units and job classifications, including timetables for completion
6. development and execution of action oriented programs designed to eliminate problems and further designed to attain established goals and timetables
7. design and implementation of internal audit and reporting systems to measure effectiveness of the total program
8. compliance of personnel policies and practices with the Sex Discrimination Guidelines (41 CFR Part 60–20)
9. active support of local and national community action programs and community service programs designed to improve the employment opportunities of minorities and women
10. consideration of minorities and women not currently in the work force having requisite skills who can be recruited through affirmative action measures''

The content of Revised Order No. 4 is organized around these "required ingredients," all of which are amplified in detail in the order. A careful reading of these requirements in their entirety will show the breadth of their scope. To help cope with the sheer magnitude of the requirements, the organization should consult the EEO/AA information sources discussed in Chapter 3. Of particular usefulness are examples and samples of full-blown AAPs.[15]

Utilization Analysis   Utilization analysis is critical in an AAP because through it are derived the numerical standards (availability percentages for women and minorities) against which the representativeness of the organization's workforce is to be judged. In Exhibit 6.17, for example, an availability percentage of 20% for women in the sales job category is shown. It is against this figure that the current percentage of women in the job category (10%) is compared in order to help determine if there is underutilization of women.

Where do availability statistics come from? The example in Exhibit 6.17 indicates that the number is determined on the basis of the eight factors contained in Revised Order No. 4. Those factors for women (there are also very similar ones for minorities) are as follows:

1. "the size of the female unemployment force in the labor area surrounding the facility

2. the percentage of the female work force as compared with the total work force in the immediate labor area

3. the general availability of women having the requisite skills in the immediate labor area

4. the availability of women having requisite skills in an area in which the contractor can reasonably recruit

5. the availability of women seeking employment in the labor or recruitment area of the contractor

6. the availability of promotable and transferable female employees within the contractor's organization

7. the existence of training institutions capable of training persons in the requisite skills

8. the degree of training which the contractor is reasonably able to undertake as a means of making all job classes available to women"

These eight factors require the contractor to take many different considerations into account in determining availability statistics. These include requisite skills, general applicant availability, geographic recruitment area, training possibilities, and internal employees. Unfortunately, hard data for these factors are often difficult to come by; federal and state labor force statistics are of only limited usefulness. Hence, availability figures such as shown in Exhibit 6.17 should be treated as estimates, rather than precise indicators. Also, the organization should consult sources of assistance on the gathering and interpretation of availability statistics.[16]

Compliance Status   How is an organization's compliance with the order to be judged? Is failure to achieve affirmative action goals grounds for concluding there is noncompliance? The order makes clear that lack of goal attainment, by itself, does not constitute noncompliance. As long as the contractor sets reasonable, attainable goals and timetables, and then makes a good faith effort to achieve them, the contractor is meeting the requirements of the order. Specifically:

> The goals and timetables developed by the contractor should be attainable in terms of the contractor's analysis of his deficiencies and his entire affirmative action program. No contractor's compliance status shall be judged alone by whether or not he reaches his goals and meets his timetables. Rather, each contractor's compliance posture shall be reviewed and determined by reviewing the contents of his program, the extent of his adherence to the program, and his good faith efforts to make his program work toward the realization of the program's goals within the timetables set for completion.

The above statements make clear that AAPs under the order are not hiring quota ones.

Legality of AAPs

AAPs have been controversial since their inception, and there have been many challenges to their legality. Questions of legality are difficult to answer or provide guidance on because of complexities in the interpretations of the relevant laws, as well as complexities in the nature of AAPs themselves as adopted by organizations. Despite these problems, it is possible to provide several conclusions and recommendations regarding AAPs.

AAPs in general are legal in the eyes of the Supreme Court. However, to be acceptable, an AAP should be based on the following guidelines:[17]

1. The plan should have as its purpose the remedying of specific and identifiable effects of past discrimination.
2. There should be definite underutilization of women and/or minorities currently in the organization.
3. As regards nonminority and male employees, the plan should not unnecessarily interfere with their job interests and rights, not result in their discharge and replacement with minority or women employees, and not create an absolute bar to their promotion.
4. The plan should be temporary, and eliminated once affirmative action goals have been achieved (this occurred, for example, to the AAP for police officers in the city of Detroit).[18]

5. All candidates for positions should be qualified for those positions.
6. The plan should include organizational enforcement mechanisms, as well as a grievance procedure.

These recommendations, though quite general, do provide some measure of guidance to the organization and the design of AAP components of its staffing systems.

AAPs are not separate staffing systems, but rather integral parts of general staffing systems. As such, AAPs should be incorporated into more general HR and staffing planning. In this way, there is a single, unified staffing system to serve both broad organizational goals and more specific affirmative action ones.

Diversity Programs

Staffing focuses on the initial acquisition of people and creation of the initial person/job match. AAPs likewise have this focus. Once the initial match has occurred, however, the organization must be concerned about employee adaptation to the job and maintenance of the employment relationship over time. Without such a concern, the effectiveness of AAPs can be severely undercut. In particular, satisfaction and retention problems for those acquired through the AAP can arise, and these problems in turn will thwart any meaningful, permanent change in the race/sex composition of the organization's workforce.

Recently, organizations have begun experimenting with *diversity programs.* These programs arise out of a recognition that the labor force, and thus the organization's workforce, is becoming more demographically diverse. The focus of diversity programs is on the assimilation and adaptation of a diverse workforce once it has been acquired. Diversity programs thus pick up where affirmative action programs leave off, and indeed may be viewed as a logical continuation of them.

A diverse workforce is a heterogeneous one in terms of individuals' KSAOs and motivation. Such individual diversity requires a diversity in programs designed to facilitate an effective, long-term person/job match.[19] Examples of the types of content found in diversity programs include flexible work schedules, telecommuting, training programs to heighten employee awareness and acceptance of diversity, mentoring relationships, special career and credential-building assignments, child care, and team building. Other, more traditional HR programs, especially performance management and career development ones, may also be included in an organization's diversity initiative.

Though in their infancy, and without any specific legal basis or requirement, diversity programs can be of assistance to organization AAPs in two major ways. First, having a diversity program may aid in the recruitment and attraction of a diverse workforce, thus contributing directly to the achievement of affirmative action goals and timetables. Second, with a diversity program, the organization may increase the retention rates of those acquired through the AAP. As a consequence, underutilization of underrepresented groups will lessen over time and ideally lead to the elimination of the need for an AAP in the first place.

SUMMARY

Human resource planning (HRP) is a process and set of activities undertaken to forecast future HR requirements and availabilities, resulting in the identification of likely employment gaps (shortages and surpluses). Action plans are then developed for addressing the gaps. Before HRP begins, initial decisions must be made about its comprehensiveness, planning time frame, job categories and levels to be included, how to ''count heads,'' and the roles and responsibilities of line and staff (including HR) managers.

A variety of statistical and judgmental techniques may be used in forecasting. Those used in forecasting requirements are typically used in conjunction with business and organization planning. For forecasting availabilities, techniques must be used that take into account the movements of people into, within, and out of the organization, on a job-by-job basis. Here, Markov Analysis is particularly useful in jobs with relatively large numbers of employees. For other situations, executive reviews, succession planning, and vacancy analysis may be more useful.

External and internal environmental scanning occur after forecasting. Their results temper, and aid in interpretation of, identified employment gaps. Analysis of gaps requires determining likely reasons for them. Such reasons can serve as stimuli for, and inputs into, action planning.

Staffing planning is one outgrowth of action planning. It requires setting staffing objectives, generating alternative staffing activities, assessing those alternatives, and finally choosing from among alternatives. Once alternatives have been chosen, their implementation begins. Implementation sets in motion another round of staffing planning, one that is more specific and focused. It requires explicit consideration of the organization's staffing philosophy and helps shape the design and construction of actual staffing systems. Such systems must guide the flow of applicants from the point of initial contact to becoming a new hire. Development of staffing flow diagrams can be very useful in these endeavors.

Affirmative Action Plans (AAPs) are an extension and application of general HR and staffing planning. AAPs have three basic components, namely utilization analysis, staffing goals and timetables, and action plans. Revised Order No. 4, which applies to federal contractors, specifies requirements for each of these three components. The legality of AAPs has been clearly established, but the courts have fashioned limits to their content and scope. Diversity programs are organizational initiatives to help effectively manage a diverse workforce. Such programs have the potential for successfully working in tandem with AAPs by contributing to the attraction and retention of AAP-targeted people.

DISCUSSION QUESTIONS

1. What are the types of experiences, especially staffing-related ones, that an organization will be likely to have if it does not engage in HR and staffing planning?

2. Why are decisions about job categories and levels so critical to the conduct and results of HRP?

3. What are the differences between statistical and judgmental techniques for forecasting future availabilities?

4. What is meant by reconciliation, and why can it be so useful as an input to staffing planning?

5. What criteria would you suggest using for assessing the staffing alternatives shown in Exhibit 6.11?

6. Some people object to staffing flowcharts as making the staffing process too mechanical, impersonal, and cold. Do you agree? Why?

7. What problems might an organization encounter in doing an AAP that it might not encounter in regular staffing planning?

ENDNOTES

1. Major treatments of HRP are in: J. P. Begin, *Strategic Employment Policy* (Englewood Cliffs, NJ: Prentice-Hall, 1991); J. E. Butler, G. R. Ferris, and N. K. Napier, *Strategy and Human Resource Management* (Cincinnati: South-Western, 1991); L. Dyer (ed.), *Human Resource Planning: A Case Study Reference Guide to the Tested Practices of Five Major U.S. and Canadian Companies* (New York: Random House, 1986); H. G. Heneman III, D. P. Schwab, J. A. Fossum, and L. Dyer, *Personnel/Human Resource Management,* fourth ed. (Homewood, IL: Irwin, 1988); D. W. Jarrell, *Human Resource Planning* (Englewood Cliffs, NJ: Prentice-Hall, 1993); P. Osterman, "Internal Labor Markets in a Changing Environment," in D. Lewin, O. S. Mitchell, and P. D. Sherer (eds.), *Research Frontiers in Industrial Relations and Human Resources* (Madison, WI: Industrial Relations Research Association, 1992), pp. 273–308; G. T. Milkovich and T. M. Mahoney, "Human Resource Planning and PAIR Policy," in D. Yoder and H. G. Heneman, Jr. (eds.), *ASPA Handbook of Personnel and Industrial Relations* (Washington, D.C.: Bureau of National Affairs, 1979), pp. 2–1 to 2–28; S. E. Jackson and R. S. Schuler, "Human Resource Planning: Challenges for Industrial/Organizational Psychologists," *American Psychologist,* 1990, 45, pp. 223–239; J. W. Walker, *Human Resource Strategy* (New York: McGraw-Hill, 1992); R. Page and D. V. D. Voort, "Job Analysis and HR Planning," in W. F. Cascio (ed.), *Human Resource Planning* (Washington, D.C.: Bureau of National Affairs, 1989).

2. Heneman III, Schwab, Fossum, and Dyer, *Personnel/Human Resource Management,* pp. 201–243.

3. Heneman III, Schwab, Fossum, and Dyer, *Personnel/Human Resource Management,* pp. 205–209.

4. Jackson and Schuler, "Human Resource Planning: Challenges to Industrial/Organizational Psychologists," p. 225.

5. Heneman III, Schwab, Fossum, and Dyer, *Personnel/Human Resource Management,* p. 213; Walker, *Human Resource Strategy,* pp. 156–177.

6. Heneman III, Schwab, Fossum, and Dyer, *Personnel/Human Resource Management,* pp. 214–281; Jarrell, *Human Resource Planning,* pp. 256–281; L. T. Pinfield and M. Morishima, "Taking the Measure of Human Resource Management Flows," *Public Personnel Management,* 1991, 20, pp. 299–318.

7. H. G. Heneman III and M. H. Sandver, "Markov Analysis in Human Resource Administration: Applications and Limitations," *Academy of Management Review,* 1977, 2, pp. 535–542.

8. A. K. Deegan, *Succession Planning: Key to Corporate Excellence* (New York: Wiley, 1986).

9. C. R. Greer and T. C. Ireland, "Organizational and Financial Correlates of a Contrarian Human Resource Investment Strategy," *Academy of Management Review,* 1992, 35, pp. 956–984.

10. Heneman III, Schwab, Fossum, and Dyer, *Personnel/Human Resource Management,* pp. 227–233; Milkovich and Mahoney, "Human Resource Planning and PAIR Policy."

11. T. J. Atchison, "The Employment Relationship: Un-tied or Re-tied?", *Academy of Management Executive,* 1991, 5, pp. 52–62.

12. Olsten Corporation, *New Staffing Strategies for the 1990's* (Westbury, NY: author, 1992).

13. J. Breaugh, *Recruitment: Science and Practice* (Boston: PWS-Kent, 1992); J. Wanous, *Organizational Entry,* second ed. (Reading, MA: Addison-Wesley, 1992).

14. Bureau of National Affairs, *Fair Employment Practice Manual* (Washington, D.C.: author, periodically updated), pp. 403:499–507; 431:11–16.

15. Bureau of National Affairs, *Fair Employment Practice Manual,* pp. 443:465–632.

16. Bureau of National Affairs, *Fair Employment Practice Manual* pp. 443:201–208, 209–211, 9005–9010.

17. T. Johnson, "Affirmative Action as a Title VII Remedy: Recent U.S. Supreme Court Decisions, Racial Quotas and Preferences," *Labor Law Journal,* 1987, 38, pp. 574–581; T. Johnson, "The Legal Use of Racial Quotas and Gender Preferences by Public and Private Employers," *Labor Law Journal,* 1989, 40, pp. 419–425; G. P. Panaro, *Employment Law Manual* (Boston: Warren, Gorham, and Lamont, 1990), pp. 5–1 to 5–40; N. J. Sedmak and M. D. Levin-Epstein, *Primer on Equal Employment Opportunity* (Washington, D.C.: Bureau of National Affairs, 1991), pp. 135–140.

18. International Personnel Management Association, "Court Ends Affirmative Action Plan," *IPMA News,* June 1993, pp. 19–20.

19. S. E. Jackson and Associates, *Diversity in the Workplace* (New York: The Guilford Press, 1992); S. Caudron, "U.S. West Finds Strength in Diversity," *Personnel Journal,* 1992, March, pp. 40–44; B. Rosen and K. Lovelace, "Piecing Together the Diversity Puzzle," *HR Magazine,* 1991, June, pp. 78–84.

STAFFING ORGANIZATIONS MODEL

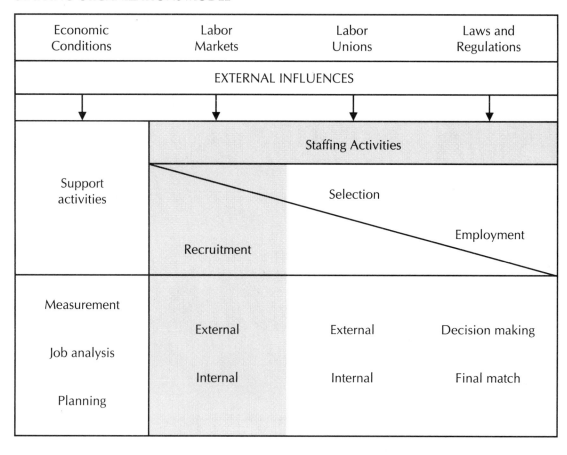

Economic Conditions	Labor Markets	Labor Unions	Laws and Regulations
EXTERNAL INFLUENCES			

Support activities	Staffing Activities		
	Recruitment	Selection	Employment
Measurement Job analysis Planning	External Internal	External Internal	Decision making Final match

PART THREE

Staffing Activities: Recruitment

CHAPTER SEVEN

External Recruitment

Recruitment Planning
Organizational Issues
Administrative Issues

Strategy Development
Where to Look
How to Look
When to Look

Searching
Communication Message
Communication Medium

Evaluation
Process
Applicant Reactions
Impact on Outcomes

Special Case: College Recruitment
Selecting Campuses to Visit
Organizing College Recruitment
Effective College Recruitment Practices

Legal Issues
Definition of Job Applicant
Disclaimers
Targeted Recruitment
Recruitment Sources
Job Advertisements
Fraud and Misrepresentation

Summary

The objective of the external recruitment process is to identify and attract job applicants from outside the organization. It is from among these applicants that hiring decisions are to be made. In order to meet this objective, organizations follow a systematic set of activities shown in Exhibit 7.1.

The recruitment process begins with a planning phase where both organizational and administrative issues regarding the identification and attraction of applicants are addressed. Organizational issues include in-house versus external recruitment locations, individual versus cooperative recruitment alliances, and centralized versus decentralized recruitment functions. Administrative issues include requisitions; number and types of contracts; the recruitment budget; selection, training, and rewarding of recruiters; and development of a recruitment guide.

Next, a recruitment strategy is formed in order to know where, how, and when to look for qualified applicants. Knowing where to look requires an understanding of the job requirements matrix, demographics, geographic area, recruitment sources, tradition, applicant interests and availability, and special availabilities. Knowing how to look requires an understanding of conventional recruitment sources (e.g., walk-ins and ads) and innovative recruitment sources (e.g., computerized resume services and churches). Knowing when to look requires an understanding of lead time concerns and time sequence concerns.

Following the formation of strategy, the message to be communicated to job applicants is established and it is decided which communication medium should be used to communicate the message. The message may be realistic, attractive, or targeted. It may be communicated with recruitment brochures, advertisements, and voice messages.

An evaluation of the recruitment process, applicant reactions to the process, and the impact on human resource outcomes is then conducted. Process measures include yield ratios, time lapse data, and cost figures. Applicant reactions include reactions to recruiters and recruitment activities.

Special consideration must be given to college recruitment, given the large costs with this type of recruitment. Issues to be considered include selecting campuses to visit, organizing college recruitment, and effective college recruitment practices. Close attention must also be given to legal issues. This includes consideration of the definition of job applicant, disclaimers, targeted recruitment, recruitment sources, job advertisements, and fraud and misrepresentation.

RECRUITMENT PLANNING

Before actually identifying and attracting applicants to the organization, two issues must be resolved. First, organizational plans must be made to coordinate the identification and attraction of applicants. Second, administrative issues, such as the number of contacts to be made, recruiters to be used, and the budget to be spent,

EXHIBIT 7.1   External Recruitment Process

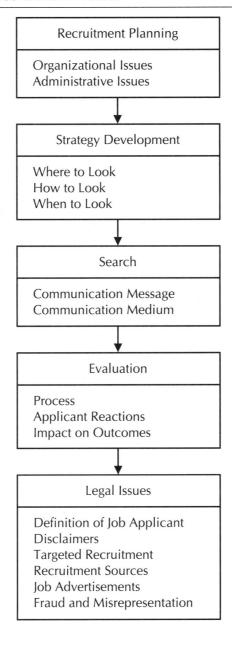

need to be considered to ensure that there are adequate resources to conduct a successful recruitment campaign.

Organizational Issues

The recruitment process in an organization can be organized in a variety of ways. It can be coordinated in-house or by an external recruitment agency. An organization can do its own recruiting or cooperate with other organizations in a recruitment alliance. Authority to recruit may be centralized or decentralized in the organization.

In-House versus External Recruitment Agency

Most organizational recruiting is done in-house. Smaller organizations may rely on external recruitment agencies rather than an in-house function to coordinate their recruitment efforts since smaller organizations may not have the staff or budget to run their own recruitment functions. Organizations with low turnover rates may also prefer to use external recruitment agencies because they recruit so infrequently it would not make sense to have a recruitment function of their own.

External recruitment agencies are growing in number. Some agencies, such as Elaine R. Shepherd Company, provide full-scale recruitment services ranging from identifying recruitment needs to advertising for applicants and checking references. Others, such as National Advertising Services, Inc., simply perform one recruitment activity. Although these services are expensive, the costs may be justified for organizations without a recruitment function or for employers with infrequent vacancies.

Large organizations and ones with frequent recruitment needs should have their own in-house recruitment function. An in-house function is needed to ensure that recruitment costs are minimized, recruitment searches are consistent from opening to opening, and the specific needs of the organization are being met.

Individual versus Cooperative Recruitment Alliances

Most organizations, especially ones that compete with one another in the same product and labor markets, do not cooperate with one another when recruiting. They do not cooperate because one organization's gain (a well-qualified hire) is another organization's loss (loss of a well-qualified candidate). Instead, they conduct their own recruitment programs to maintain a competitive advantage.

There are times, however, when even competitors may enter into cooperative recruitment alliances where arrangements are made to share recruitment resources.[1] Smaller organizations may gain from cooperating with one another in order to minimize recruitment costs. If there is an abundance of applicants in the labor market, with enough good applicants to go around, it may also make sense to cooperate. For example, a group called Hospital Personnel Exchange, in Melbourne, Florida, temporarily transfers personnel among hospitals to eliminate the problems of seasonal over- and understaffing for hospitals.

Even in a tight market it may make sense to cooperate when it comes to the spouses of job applicants. For example, the Personnel Association of Central Ohio (PACO) has a "trailing spouse network," where employers have a common pool of resumes from spouses following their partner's career move to central Ohio. All PACO members take from and contribute to the resume pool. By doing so, they are able to hire those job applicants who are unable to relocate unless their spouses find a job in the same area.

Centralized versus Decentralized Recruitment

The recruitment of external job applicants can be centralized or decentralized by an organization. A centralized recruitment function is one where recruitment activities are coordinated by a central group, usually human resource professionals in the corporate offices. A decentralized recruitment system is one where recruitment activities are coordinated by individual business units or individual managers. In most larger organizations, the recruitment function is centralized.[2] Although the ultimate hiring decision resides in the business unit, most organizations centralize the administrative activities associated with recruiting and screening applicants.

One advantage to a centralized recruitment function is that duplications of effort are eliminated. For example, when recruiting at a school, only one advertisement is placed rather than multiple ads for multiple business units. Another advantage to a centralized approach is that it ensures that policy is being consistently interpreted across business units. Along the same lines, a centralized function helps to ensure compliance with relevant laws and regulations.

Some organizations do have decentralized recruitment functions. One advantage to decentralized recruitment is that recruitment efforts may be undertaken in a more timely manner when there are fewer people to recruit than when a centralized approach is used. Also, the recruitment search may be more responsive to the business unit's specific needs because those involved with recruitment may be closer to the day-to-day operations of the business unit than their corporate counterparts.

Administrative Issues

In the planning stage of recruitment, attention must be given to administrative as well as organizational issues.

Requisitions

A requisition is a formal document that authorizes the filling of a job opening indicated by the signatures of top management.[3] Supervisors are not given discretion to authorize the filling of job openings. Top managers rather than supervisors are more likely to be familiar with staffing planning information for the entire organization, and their approval is needed instead to ensure that recruitment activities are coordinated with staffing planning activities.

An example of a requisition is shown in Exhibit 7.2. A well-developed requisition will specify clearly both the quantity and the quality (KSAOs) of labor to be hired. Hence, each requisition will list the number of openings per job and the minimum qualifications an applicant must have.[4] Qualifications should be based on the job requirements matrix.

Many smaller organizations do not have requisitions. They should, however, for two reasons. First, the procedure ensures that staffing activities are consistent with the business plan of the organization. Second, it ensures that the qualifications of the job are clearly detailed so that a good person/job match is made.

Number of Contacts

The pool of applicants to be selected almost always needs to be larger than the number of applicants that will be hired eventually. Some applicants who are contacted may not be interested in the position, and others may not be qualified.

It is very difficult to identify the exact number of contacts needed to fill a particular vacant position. However, historical data is very useful in establishing the targeted number of contacts. If careful records are kept, then *yield ratios* can be calculated to summarize the historical data and to guide decisions about the number of contacts to make. A yield ratio expresses the relationship of applicant inputs to outputs at various decision points. For example, if 90 people were contacted (as identified by the number of resumes submitted) to fill one position, then the yield ratio would be 90:1. To fill two identical positions, it would be necessary to contact 180 applicants, based on the historical yield ratio of 90:1.

Types of Contacts

The types of contacts to be made depend upon two factors. First, it is essential that the qualifications needed to perform the job be clearly established. This is done through the process of job analysis, which results in the job requirements matrix. The more clearly these requirements are specified, the fewer the number of applicants who must be contacted to yield a successful candidate and the narrower the recruitment search can be.

Second, consideration must be given to the job search and choice process used by applicants.[5] That is, the organization must be aware of where likely applicants search for employment opportunities and what it will take to attract them to the organization. One consistent finding in the research is that job seekers tend to rely upon informal rather than formal recruitment sources.[6] This means that applicants are more likely to find out about jobs through friends and family than they are through printed advertisements or through intermediaries (e.g., employment agencies).

EXHIBIT 7.2 Personnel Requisition

Position Title	Division	Department	Department #
Salary/Grade Level	Work Hours	Location	Reports to

Position eligible for the following incentive programs ☐ Sales Commission ☐ Key Contributor ☐ Production Incentive ☐ Other (specify) ☐ Management Incentive ☐ _____	Budgeted ☐ Replacement for:_____ ☐ Yes Transfer/Term Date_____ ☐ No ☐ Addition to staff

POSITION OVERVIEW

Instructions: (1) Complete Parts I, II, and III. (2) Attach Position Description Questionnaire (if available) or complete reverse side.

I. POSITION PURPOSE: Briefly state in one or two sentences the primary purpose of this position.

II. POSITION QUALIFICATIONS: List the *minimum* education, formal training, and experience required to perform this position.

III. SPECIAL SKILLS: List the specialized clerical, administrative, technical, or managerial skills needed to perform this position.

Do current or previous incumbents possess these qualifications and skills? If no, please describe the reason for these requirements when hiring for this position.

APPROVALS	**FOR HUMAN RESOURCES USE ONLY**
Party Responsible for Conducting Second Interview _____ Hiring Supervisor/Manager Date _____ Next Approval Level Date _____ Human Resources Approval Date	Posting Date_____Advertising Date_____ Req Number _____ Job Number _____ Acceptance Date _____ Start Date _____ New Employee _____ Source _____

Source: Reprinted with permission from United Health Care Corporation.

How proactive the organization should be in soliciting applicants is a policy issue that arises when deciding on the types of contacts the organization will make.[7] Some organizations spend very few resources identifying contacts and actively soliciting applicants from these sources. For example, many times grocery stores simply post a job opening in their store window to fill a vacancy. Other organizations, however, are very proactive in making their presence known in the community. For example, Spartan Stores in Michigan has formed a partnership with a local high school so that they will have higher quality applicants for entry-level positions in their grocery stores.[8] Many organizations are becoming involved with educational institutions through scholarships, adopt-a-school programs, mentorships, equipment grants, internships, and career planning services.[9] NASA has programs to help educate teachers, students, and administrators on the application of science and math.[10] These approaches are likely to build goodwill toward an organization in the community and, as a result, foster greater informal contacts with job applicants.

Research has shown that greater employer involvement with prospective applicants is likely to improve the image of the organization. In turn, a better image of the organization is likely to result in prospective applicants pursuing contact with the organization.[11]

Recruitment Budget

The recruitment process is a very expensive component of organizational staffing. The average cost per hire for exempt positions is $4,000, and the average cost per hire for nonexempt positions is $1,000.[12] As a result of these high costs, many organizations are currently using cost containment programs in their recruitment efforts. Examples here include the elimination of display advertising, greater reliance on state employment agencies, and the reduction of on-campus visits for college recruitment.[13] An example of a recruitment budget is shown in Exhibit 7.3. Due to pressures to contain costs, recruitment budgets have been reduced. In one survey, budgets were reduced in 61% of the surveyed organizations from 1991 to 1992.[14]

The high costs of recruitment also point to the importance of establishing a well-developed recruitment budget. Two issues need to be addressed in establishing a recruitment budget.[15] First, a top-down or bottom-up procedure can be used to gather the information needed to formulate the budget. With a top-down approach, the budget for recruitment activities is set by top management on the basis of the business plan for the organization and on the basis of projected revenues. With a bottom-up approach, the budget for recruitment activities is set up on the basis of the specific needs of each business unit. The former approach works well when the emphasis is on controlling costs. The latter approach works better when commitment to the budget by business unit heads is the goal. A cumbersome, yet useful, method is to combine these two approaches into program-oriented bud-

---

EXHIBIT 7.3   Example of a Recruitment Budget for 500 New Hires

---

Administrative Expenses

Staff	32,000
Supplies	45,000
Equipment	10,000
	$87,000

Recruiter Expenses

Salaries	240,000
Benefits	96,000
Expenses	150,000
	$486,000

Candidate Expenses

Travel	320,000
Lodging	295,000
Fees	50,000
Relocation	150,000
	$815,000

Total Recruitment Expenses

   87,000 + 486,000 + 815,000 = $1,388,000

Total Cost Per Hire

   $1,388,000/500 new hires = $2,776

---

geting where there is heavy involvement in the budgeting process by both top management and business unit leaders.

A second issue that needs to be addressed in establishing a well-developed recruitment budget is to decide whether to charge recruitment costs to business unit users. That is, should recruitment expenses be charged to human resources or to the business unit using human resources' services? Most organizations charge the human resources department for the costs of recruitment rather than the business unit users of recruitment activities.[16] Perhaps this is done in order to encourage each business unit to use the recruitment services of the human resources group. However, it should be recognized that this practice of not charging the business unit may result in the business unit users not being concerned about minimizing recruitment costs.

Selecting Recruiters

Many studies have been conducted to assess desirable characteristics of recruiters. Reviews of these studies indicate that an ideal recruiter would possess the following characteristics:[17] strong interpersonal skills; knowledge about the organization, jobs, and career-related issues; and enthusiasm about the organization and job candidates. These characteristics represent a start on developing a set of KSAOs to select recruiters.

These characteristics are only a start at developing a job requirements matrix due to limitations in the research to date.[18] For example, the results are based on the special case of college recruitment, and college recruitment is only one of many forms of recruitment. It remains to be seen if characteristics of ideal college recruiters are the same as the characteristics of recruiters in noncollege settings. Hence, care should be taken to develop a job requirements matrix for the position of recruiter just as should be done for the recruitment of people to any position in an organization.

Not only do characteristics of the ideal recruiter need to be considered in selecting recruiters, but the characteristics of the job of recruiter also need to be considered. The research to date has primarily focused on the recruiter's job in the initial campus interview, but the job itself entails much more.[19] The job may consist of any or all of the steps shown in this book, ranging from the identification of appropriate sources to recruiting candidates to extending job offers.

Training Recruiters

Many recruiters who come from areas outside human resources do not have any specialized training in human resources. Hence, the training of recruiters is essential. Unfortunately, very few recruiters ever receive any training. Based on current organizational practices, recruiters should receive training in the following areas:[20] interviewing skills, job analysis, interpersonal aspects of recruiting, laws and regulations, forms and reports, company and job characteristics, and recruitment targets. Important training aids for recruiter training are the job requirements matrix and the job rewards matrix.

Virtually no research has been conducted on the effectiveness of recruiter training. One exception is the well-documented effectiveness of rater error training.[21] This training is designed to eliminate rating errors such as halo effect in the interview. To do so, recruiters practice making ratings using the videotaped performance of employees. Feedback is given to recruiters on the accuracy of their ratings, and plans are drawn up to minimize their rating errors back on the job. The research has convincingly shown that this approach does eliminate rating errors.[22]

Rewarding Recruiters

In order to reinforce effective recruitment practices, it is essential that recruiter performance—both effective recruitment behaviors and end results—be monitored and rewarded. Measures of performance commonly used include being on time for appointments, favorable comments from students, meeting affirmative action goals, and feedback from line managers.[23] Unfortunately, very few organizations collect the data needed to make an objective assessment of these factors.

Rewards can be coupled with performance standards. For example, in one interesting study, it was shown that the efforts of Navy recruiters were substantially heightened when there was the promise of a monetary reward for meeting their recruitment quotas.[24] In addition to rewarding recruiters for the successful completion of results, rewards should also be provided for the demonstration of critical behaviors.[25] For example, although good public relations activities may not result in more hires, they may result in more customer satisfaction, which is a major goal of most business organizations today. Accordingly, both the successful attraction of candidates and successful publicity concerning the organization should be rewarded.

Development of a Recruitment Guide

A recruitment guide is a formal document that details the process to be followed to attract applicants to a job.[26] It should be based on the organization's staffing flowcharts, if available. Included in the guide are details such as the time, money, and staff required to fill the job as well as the steps to be taken to do so. An example of a recruitment guide is shown in Exhibit 7.4.

Although a recruitment guide takes time to produce—time that may be difficult to find in the face of an urgent requisition to be filled—it is an essential document. It clarifies expectations for both the recruiter and the requesting department as to what will be accomplished, what the costs are, and who will be held accountable for the results. It also clarifies the steps that need to be taken to ensure that they are all followed in a consistent fashion and in accordance with organization policy as well as relevant laws and regulations. In short, a recruitment guide safeguards the interests of the employer, applicant, and recruiter.

STRATEGY DEVELOPMENT

Once the recruitment planning phase is complete, the next phase is the development of a strategy. In essence, strategy development helps to assess those issues fundamental to the organization: where to look, how to look, and when to look. Each of these issues will be addressed in turn.

Where to Look

Once a requisition has been received, one of the most difficult aspects of recruitment is knowing where to look for applicants. In theory, the pool of potential job applicants is the eligible labor force (employed, unemployed, discouraged workers, new labor force entrants, and labor force reentrants). In practice, the organization must narrow down or target this vast pool into segments or strata of workers believed to be the most desirable applicants for the organization. Segmentation factors used to generate a manageable applicant pool include the job requirements

---

EXHIBIT 7.4   Recruitment Guide for Director of Claims

Position: Director, Claims Processing

Reports to: Senior Director, Claims Processing

Qualifications: 4-year degree in business;
8 years experience in health care, including 5 in claims, 3 of which
should be in management

Relevant labor market: Regional midwest

Time line: week of 1/17:   Conduct interviews with qualified applicants
        2/1/93:   Targeted hire date

Activities to undertake to source well-qualified candidates:

Regional newspaper advertising

Request employee referrals

Contact regional health and life insurance associations

Call HR departments of regional health and life insurance companies to see if any are
outplacing any middle managers.

Contact, if necessary, executive recruiter to further source candidates.

Staff members involved:

HR Recruiting Manager
Sr. Director, Claims Processing
V.P. Human Resources
Potential peers and direct reports

Budget:
$3,000–$5,000

---

matrix, demographics, geographic areas, recruitment sources, applicant interests
and availability, and special availabilities.

Segmentation Factors

Job Requirements Matrix   As with all aspects of staffing, the starting point for
knowing where to look for applicants is the job requirements matrix. By knowing
the KSAOs needed to perform the job, the applicant pool is narrowed. For example, the fact that a college degree is required to perform the job eliminates from
the population those candidates with a high school degree only. The fact that a
major in statistics is required eliminates from the sample the nonstatistics majors

with a college degree. This iterative process is followed for all the KSAOs specified in the job requirements matrix.

Demographics Demographics can also be used to target the applicant pools. Care must be taken not to use demographics to systematically exclude women and minorities from the applicant pool. Job-related demographics, as shown in the job requirements matrix, can and should be used. For example, some positions may require a certain number of years of experience.

Geographic Area In targeting the applicant pool, one can look on a local, county, regional, state, national, or international basis. In general, the lower the skill levels required to perform the job, the more employers narrow the pool down to close geographic proximity to the organization. This is done to minimize recruitment and selection costs. Chances are that with low-skill jobs, the availability of those people will be high in the local labor market. Hence, an employer will not have to pay for ads in national magazines, relocation costs, and so forth.

On the other hand, for high-skill jobs, the employer is more likely to broaden the search. Although more costly, this is done in order to locate people who have the requisite high level of KSAOs needed to perform the job.

Recruitment Sources A critical factor in narrowing down the applicant pool is an organization's previous successes and failures with alternative recruitment sources. Through previous searches, for example, an organization may find that the yield of high-quality candidates is best when applicants from professional societies, rather than applicants from placement agencies, are attracted.

Tradition Some organizations have a rich history of successful recruitment with various segments of the population. Through their affirmative action efforts, for example, some organizations have hired many successful minority individuals from schools with large minority enrollments. In turn, these schools provide excellent services to these companies for the placement of their students. As a result, there is a tradition of certain schools placing students with certain employers.

Applicant Interest and Availability Applicants self-select out of the potential applicant pool for a variety of reasons. Some are so-called discouraged workers who are no longer a part of the labor force. Others are gainfully employed and very happy to remain with a current employer. Another segment may be unwilling to relocate to a different geographic area. Many people, for example, have family constraints that prevent them from moving.

Special Availabilities Employers traditionally have limited themselves to applicants who are members of the labor force and are between the ages 18 and 65. This traditional approach has excluded many potential applicants who are fully capable of performing the job even though they do not fit this traditional description. Many organizations have been forced to break away from this traditional view in order to adequately fill jobs when there is a shortage of entry-level employees.[27] Examples of such potential applicants include teenagers, older workers, welfare recipients, people with disabilities, the homeless, veterans, and homemakers.

Teenagers are an excellent source of potential applicants for entry-level positions in service jobs, such as cashier. Although they may not be able to work as many hours as more senior employees, teenagers may be less costly to hire. And their initial employment experiences, if favorable, may lead them to pursue other jobs in the organization as they acquire additional skills and education.

Older people who have withdrawn from the labor force represent another group with special availabilities. The older worker may be inclined to return to the workforce in order to enhance retirement funds or to meet social needs by working with others. A recent study showed that turnover rates are lower for older workers than for younger workers.[28] This is a distinct advantage in jobs, such as cashier, where turnover rates can be over 100%.

America Works is a temporary employment agency on the East Coast. Its mission is to take people off welfare and find them gainful employment. So far the agency has been successful at placing over 2,000 people. Part of the success has been attributed to the training and follow-up the company provides along with its insistence on no tardiness as a requirement to remain in the program.[29]

It is estimated that in this country the number of people with disabilities is about 36 million. People with disabilities include not only those needing wheelchairs, but those with AIDS, lower-back pain, mental illness, and a whole host of other physically challenging conditions. Many organizations have taken advantage of this large population to fill vacant jobs on an ongoing basis. For example, the Friendly Restaurant Corporation has developed a systematic recruitment procedure to attract and hire people with disabilities.[30] As shown in Exhibit 7.5, there are many unwarranted stereotypes about individuals with disabilities that need to be overcome in order for the disabled to be included in an organization's applicant pool.

The homeless do not have normal access to the labor market. Through rehabilitation centers, churches, and shelters they may receive the training and assistance needed to hold a job. Days Inn, for example, has hired the homeless since 1988, and about half of those employed have turned out to be successful by company standards.[31] One stumbling block to hiring the homeless has been the inability of organizations to contact them. Organizations may not be able to contact the homeless because they may not have access to a phone. Fortunately, in several communities, such as Columbus, Cincinnati, and Seattle, this obstacle has been removed. Businesses and social service agencies in these communities are setting up voice mail boxes for the homeless so that they can be regularly contacted. It is estimated that 30 to 40 cities have these programs.[32]

EXHIBIT 7.5   Overcoming Objections About Applicants with Disabilities

---

Leonard describes a good case study of the process. "Our sales department needed to fill an opening. I was contacted by Lighthouse. I tried to get the manager to stop focusing on the problem and look at what the person has achieved. We had a meeting with a representative from the Lighthouse, the EEO manager and the sales manager, and walked the manager through each of his objections. When he saw the facts, he was still skeptical but open. We moved the manager from a rejection mode to a listening mode.

Next, we presented the candidate to the manager and discussed the line manager's concerns. The job candidate was well dressed, intelligent, articulate and confident. He uses a scanner attached to a voice box to read memos and other materials. He uses a cane to navigate around the room. He is pleasant and establishes relationships easily. He is good on the phone.

The manager went from a listening mode to a being-open mode. The candidate was hired, performed well and was eventually promoted."

Source: J. E. Peters, "How to Bridge the Hiring Gap," *HR Magazine,* October 1989, pp. 83–84. Reprinted with the permission of HR Magazine (formerly Personnel Administrator) published by the Society for Human Resource Management, Alexandria, VA.

The U.S. Department of Defense is downsizing and, in the process, is creating a rich source of potential job applicants. The source is rich because it consists of trained and experienced personnel. It is estimated that about 600,000 people will be released from the military over the next five years.[33] Many, but not all, of the skills learned in the military are transferable to the civilian sector of the economy.[34]

Many women are forced to enter the labor force because of the death of a spouse, a divorce, or an abusive home situation. Many of their skills as home-makers are transferable to jobs in the labor force.[35] A group that helps them meet their needs, including employment, is the Displaced Homemakers Network in Washington, DC.

Choice of Segmentation Factors

A decision needs to be made about the extent to which each of the preceding segmentation factors is to be used to target the applicants the organization seeks to attract. The decision for any given segmentation factor should depend upon the following criteria.

Attraction Outcomes   The goals or outcomes of the recruitment process may dictate the emphasis given to segmentation factors. For example, if a large quantity of labor is the goal, then the labor market search may need to be broadened to capture a large number of candidates. If the quality of labor is the goal, then multiple segmentation factors may need to be considered to pinpoint high-quality talent.

Job Requirements   If the requirements to perform a job as shown in the job requirements matrix are very general, then not a great deal of market segmentation is required. On the other hand, the more specific the requirements, the more the market needs to be segmented in order to locate applicants with these special KSAOs. A larger number of segmentation factors gives more precision in identifying applicants with specific qualifications.

Job Rewards   In order to attract some individuals to an organization, substantial job rewards are sometimes needed. For example, attracting someone from a national or international market may require a signing bonus and relocation assistance. Some organizations, especially during harsh economic times, may not have the budget to meet these demands. Hence, certain market segments may be precluded by the size of the job rewards required.

Labor Market Data   Sometimes it is not possible to segment the labor market due to the lack of labor market data necessary to do so. For example, organizations wishing to relocate plants to rural areas may find that there is a lack of data regarding employees with specialized KSAOs in the area.

Anticipated Subsequent Recruitment Costs   Initial segmentation attempts may be so specific (e.g., petroleum engineers in Venezuela) that cost makes recruitment prohibitive. When this happens, the amount of segmentation needs to be relaxed. Or the segmentation may be so general that the organization is flooded with applicants. In this case, additional segmentation is required to meet budgeting constraints.

How to Look

Fortunately for employers, when conducting a search for applicants they do not have to identify each possible job applicant. Instead, there are institutions in our economy where job seekers congregate. Moreover, these institutions often act as intermediaries between the applicant and employer to ensure that a match takes place. These institutions are called recruitment sources or methods in staffing. Some are very conventional and have been around for a long time. Others are more innovative and have less of a track record. Both will be considered.

Conventional Sources

Walk-Ins   It is a common practice for employers to accept applications from job applicants who physically walk into the organization to apply for a job. The usual point of contact for walk-ins is the receptionist in smaller organizations and the employment office in larger organizations.

Organizations that rely upon walk-ins must be prepared to deal with the physical demands created by this process. In order for walk-ins not to disrupt the normal work flow in an organization, a contact person who is responsible for processing walk-ins needs to be assigned. Space needs to be created for walk-ins to complete application blanks and preemployment tests. Hours need to be established when applicants can apply for jobs. Procedures must be in place to ensure that data from walk-ins are entered into the applicant flow process. If these steps are not taken, not only may the organizational work flow be disrupted, but the image of the organization may be tarnished as well. If walk-ins are treated as being unexpected intruders, they may communicate a very negative image about the organization in the community. In turn, this negative image may have a chilling effect on other recruitment efforts by the organization (e.g., advertising).

Employee Referrals   Employees currently working for an employer are a valuable source for finding job applicants. The employees can refer people they know to their employer for consideration. In some organizations, a cash bonus is given to employees who refer job candidates who prove to be successful on the job for a given period of time. In order to ensure that there are adequate returns on bonuses for employee referrals, it is essential that there be a good performance appraisal system in place to measure the performance of the referred new hire. There also needs to be a good applicant tracking system to ensure that new hire performance is maintained over time before a bonus is offered.

Advertisements   A convenient way to attract job applicants is to write an ad that can be placed in newspapers, trade journals, and the like. Advertisements can also be recorded and placed on radio or television. Cable television channels, for example, sometimes have "Job Shows." Advertisements can be very costly and need to be closely monitored for yield. Advertisements in some periodicals may yield more and better qualified candidates than others. By carefully monitoring the results of each ad, the organization can then make a more informed decision as to which ads should be run next time a position is vacant. To track ads, each ad should be coded to assess the yield. Then as resumes come into the organization in response to the ad, they can be recorded, and the yield for that ad can be calculated.

Coding an ad is a very straightforward process. For example, in advertising for a vice president of human resources, ads may be placed in a variety of human resources periodicals, such as *HR Magazine,* and business publications, such as the *Wall Street Journal.* To track responses sent, applicants for the vacant position are asked to respond to Employment Department A for *HR Magazine* and Employment Department B for the *Wall Street Journal.* (The other part of the return address is, of course, the same for each periodical.) As resumes arrive, those that are addressed to Department A are coded as responses from the *HR Magazine,* and those addressed to Department B are coded as responses from the *Wall Street Journal.*

Colleges and Placement Offices   Colleges are a source of people with specialized skills for professional positions. Most colleges have a placement office or officer who is in charge of ensuring that a match is made between the employer's interests and the graduating student's interests. Recruitment at colleges is usually performed at no cost to the employer. College recruitment is considered in more detail later on in this chapter.

Employment Agencies   A source of nonexempt employees and lower-level exempt employees is employment agencies or body shops, as they are sometimes called. These agencies collect, screen, and present applicants to employers for a fee. The fee is contingent upon successful placement of a candidate with an employer and is a percentage, around 25%, of the candidate's starting salary. During difficult economic periods, employers cut back on the use of these agencies and/ or attempt to negotiate lower fees in order to contain costs.[36]

Care must be exercised in selecting an employment agency. It is a good idea to check the references of employment agencies with other organizations that have used their services. Allegations abound regarding the shoddy practices of these agencies. They may, for example, flood the organization with resumes. Unfortunately, this flood may include both qualified and unqualified applicants. A good agency will screen out unqualified applicants and not attempt to dazzle the organization with a large volume of resumes. Poor agencies may misrepresent the organization to the candidate and the candidate to the organization. Misrepresentation may take place when the agency is only concerned about a quick placement (and fee) without regard to the costs of poor future relationships with clients. A good agency will be in business for the long run and not misrepresent information and invite turnover. Poor agencies may pressure managers to make decisions when they are uncertain or do not want to do so. Also, they may "go around" the human resources staff in the organization to negotiate "special deals" with individual managers. Special deals may result in paying higher fees than agreed upon with human resources and overlooking qualified minorities and women. A good agency will not pressure managers, make special deals, or avoid the human resources staff.

Executive Search Firms   For higher-level professional positions, or jobs with salaries of $100,000 and higher, executive search firms, or "headhunters," may be used. Like employment agencies, these firms collect, screen, and present resumes to employers. Unlike employment agencies, they operate on the basis of a retainer fee rather than a contingency fee. This means that they collect a fee from the employer regardless of whether a successful placement is made. Thus, their services are retained by a fee in advance of a placement. The fee is paid up front so that the search firm has the resources to conduct exhaustive searches and has a travel budget to help screen candidates.

Technical and Professional Meetings   Many technical and professional organizations have annual meetings around the country at least once a year. Many of these groups run a placement service for their members. There may be a fee to recruit at these meetings. This source represents a way to attract applicants with specialized skills or professional credentials. Also, some meetings represent a way to attract women and minorities. For example, the National Council of Black Engineers and Scientists holds an annual meeting.[37]

Professional Associations   In addition to having placement activities at annual conventions, professional associations also may have a placement function throughout the year. For example, it is a common practice in professional association newsletters to advertise both positions available and interested applicants. Others may also have a computerized job and applicant bank.

State Employment Services   All states have an employment or job service. These services are funded by employer-paid payroll taxes.[38] This service is provided by the states to help secure employment for those seeking employment, particularly those currently unemployed. Typically, these services refer low- to middle-level employees to employers. In order for jobs to be properly filled, the hiring organization must maintain a close relationship with the employment service. Job qualifications need to be clearly communicated to ensure that proper screening takes place by the agency. Positions that have been filled must be promptly reported to the agency so that resumes are not sent for closed positions.

Outplacement Firms   Outplacement services are funded by the organization letting the employee go and/or the employees losing their jobs. Outplacement firms usually offer job seekers assistance in the form of counseling and training to help facilitate a good person/job match. Most large outplacement firms have job banks, which are computerized listings of applicants and their qualifications. Registration by employers to use these job banks is usually free.

Community Agencies   Some agencies in local communities may also provide outplacement assistance for the unemployed who cannot afford outplacement services. The applicants who use these services may also be listed with a state employment service as well. Community agencies may also offer counseling and training.

Job Fairs   Professional associations, schools, employers, the military, and other interested organizations hold career or job fairs to attract job applicants.[39] Typically, the sponsors of a job fair will meet in a central location with a large facility in order to provide information, collect resumes, and screen applicants. Often, there is a fee for the employer to participate. Job fairs may provide both short- and long-term gains. In the short run, the organization may identify qualified applicants. In the long run, it may be able to enhance its visibility in the community, which, in turn, may improve its image and ability to attract applicants for jobs.

In order for a job fair to yield a large number of applicants, it must be advertised well in advance. Moreover, advertisements may need to be placed in specialized publications likely to attract minorities and women. In order for an organization to attract quality candidates from all of those in attendance, the organization must be able to differentiate itself from all the other organizations competing for applicants at the job fair. To do so, giveaways such as mugs and key chains, with company logos, can be distributed to remind the applicants of employment opportunities at a particular organization. An even better promotion may be to provide attendees at the fair with assistance in developing their resumes and cover letters.

Innovative Sources

Organizational Outplacement Offices   Larger organizations experiencing a downsizing may have their own internal outplacement function and perform the activities traditionally found in external outplacement agencies. They may also hold in-house job fairs. The reason for this in-house function is to save on the costs of using an external outplacement firm and to build the morale of those employees who remain with the organization and are likely to be affected by their friends' loss of jobs.

Co-ops and Internships   Students currently attending school are sometimes available for part-time work. Two part-time working arrangements are known as co-ops and internships. Under a co-op arrangement, the student works with one employer on an alternating quarter basis. In one quarter the student works full-time, and the next quarter, attends school full-time. Under an internship arrangement, the student has a continuous period of employment with an employer for a specified period of time. These approaches allow an organization to obtain services from a part-time employee for a short period of time, but they also allow the organization the opportunity to assess the person for a full-time position upon graduation. In turn, interns have better employment opportunities as a result of their experiences.[40]

Not only can the co-ops and interns themselves be a good source of candidates for full-time jobs, but they can also be a good referral source. Those with a favorable experience with an employer are more likely to refer others from their schools for jobs. In order for this to occur, the students' experiences must be favorable. To ensure this happens, students should not be treated as cheap commodities. Care must be taken to provide them with meaningful job experiences and with the training necessary to do a good job.

Contingent Workers   A very large and growing segment of our labor market is comprised of contingent workers. They include the self-employed, *temporary or leased employees* (those who work for an agency who provides temporary workers to employers), and *independent contractors* (those who work for themselves or for a firm specializing in providing a product or service to employers).[41] Contingent workers can be used when work is of limited duration, but may not always produce satisfactory results if they are not committed to the goals and objectives of the organization.[42] In response to this possible problem, some organizations, such as hospitals, have created in-house temporary pools to fill limited-term positions.

Computerized Resume Services   Many organizations now offer employers computerized resume services. A large bank of resumes is stored in a computer, and for a fee, the data base is searched for applicants who meet the employer's specifications. Organizations that provide this service include Job Bank USA, which has resumes for a large number of professions, and Connexion, which has an international data bank.[43]

Alumni Associations   Another source for experienced personnel are alumni associations at schools. Some schools, such as the Georgia Institute of Technology, offer placement services for past as well as current students.[44] A small fee is assessed for the service. Placement opportunities are made known, and training and career counseling are offered.

Unemployed Youth Services   Youth unemployment is very high relative to that of other demographic groups in the United States. In order to reach this group for entry-level positions, employers can use unemployed youth services, which provide placement opportunities for youths as well as counseling and training in some local communities.

Religious Organizations   These organizations (e.g., churches) provide another source of labor often overlooked. Such institutions typically have many senior and teenage human resources. Organizations can attract members by sponsoring events such as socials and by making donations to charitable causes endorsed by them.

Interest Groups   There are many associations that help facilitate the interests of their members. Two such groups are the American Association for Retired Persons (AARP) and the National Association for the Advancement of Colored People (NAACP). An example of how these groups provide for the employment interests of their members is the NAACP job fair conducted by BPI Tech Fair in Minneapolis.[45]

Realtors Some realtors now offer employment services for trailing partners. When one person in a relationship must relocate to further a career, the realtor may also help the trailing partner to find a new job.

Direct Mail Solicitations Drawing upon marketing tactics in business, some organizations now recruit by direct mail solicitations. Likely segments of the labor market are targeted and sent direct mail to inform them of employment opportunities. In addition to mailing letters, employers also communicate with potential applicants via door hangers, bargain shoppers, welcome wagons, point-of-sale messages, and talent scout cards.[46]

Choice of Source

There is no one best source for recruitment; each source has its strengths and weaknesses. The following criteria can be used to select which sources are most appropriate for each search.

Quantity of Labor Some sources, such as advertisements, produce a large number of applicants. Such a source is appropriate when a large head count is needed by the organization. When number of hours of work is the quantity indicator, temporary employee sources may be most beneficial.

Quality of Labor If a premium is to be paid for high-quality candidates in the recruitment process, then some sources are better than others. If a very high level of KSAOs is required, an executive search firm is helpful. If certain skills are needed, then some schools that emphasize these skills may be better sources of employees than others.

Availability of Sources Not all of the possible sources are available to a given organization. For example, one is unlikely to find temporary agencies in rural areas. Similarly, some jobs do not have members who belong to professional associations.

Past or Promised Experiences Many organizations have a past track record with various sources. Organizations who have not used a certain source in the past can look to the past experiences of other organizations, or the promises made by the source, for validation of its effectiveness. Issues to be considered in evaluating experiences with the source include its process and outcomes. Process issues to be considered include the types of services provided, the quality of services, and the timing and dependability of services offered. Outcomes of concern include not only the number of candidates, but the quality of candidates as well.

Budget Constraints   Some organizations have large enough budgets that they can perform many of the services offered by institutions who act as intermediaries in the labor market, such as employment agencies. Other organizations, due to a lack of resources, small size, or infrequency of search, cannot replicate these services in-house.

Contractual Obligations   In organizations where all or part of the workforce is organized by a union, the labor agreement may spell out the conditions under which external and internal sources can be used. Even in nonunion organizations, there may be an agreement between the employment function, where external recruitment is housed, and placement, where internal recruitment is housed, concerning when and which sources can be used to recruit externally.

Effectiveness

A considerable amount of research has been conducted on the effectiveness of some, but certainly not all, of the sources.[47] Summaries from the findings of this research are shown in Exhibit 7.6. Several criteria of effectiveness are used— frequency of use, perceived effectiveness, cost, impact on increased satisfaction, performance, and retention. Several observations may be made about the results shown in Exhibit 7.6.

Very little research has been conducted on innovative sources. As a result, caution should be exercised in placing heavy reliance on these sources compared with their more traditional ones with proven track records. The most effective recruitment sources are not necessarily the most expensive ones. For example, employee referrals are low cost, but have a sizeable impact on satisfaction, performance, and retention. There are also many myths about the effectiveness of various sources in organizations. For example, state employment services are often scoffed at because they supposedly have few qualified job candidates. As shown in Exhibit 7.6, however, this is not always the case. At least for one organizational outcome, performance, state employment agencies seem to provide qualified candidates. Another myth is the perceived ineffectiveness of walk-ins. Again, as shown in Exhibit 7.6, the large positive impact of walk-ins on performance and retention indicates that this can be an effective source of employees when used under the right circumstances.

It should also be noted that hard evidence on effectiveness is difficult to find for any source. Studies that look at hard criteria such as satisfaction, retention, and performance, rather than soft criteria like perceived effectiveness, have only been conducted for a few traditional sources and for none of the nontraditional sources. This suggests that organizations need to systematically collect their own data to gauge effectiveness and to guide their choice of recruitment sources.

EXHIBIT 7.6   Effectiveness of External Recruitment Sources

Source	Frequency of Use	Perceived Effectiveness	Cost	Impact on Increased		
				Satisfaction	Performance	Retention
Walk-ins	High	Moderate	Low	Small	Large	Large
Employee referrals	High	High	Low	Large	Large	Large
Advertisements	High	Moderate	Moderate	Small	Moderate	Moderate
Colleges and placement offices	Moderate	High	High	Small	?	?
Employment agencies	Low	High	High	?	?	Moderate
Executive search firms	Low	High	High	?	?	?
Technical and professional meetings	Moderate	?	?	?	?	?
Professional associates	?	Moderate	?	?	?	?
Employment services	Moderate	Low	Low	?	Large	?
Outplacement firms	?	Moderate	Low	?	?	?
Community agencies	Moderate	?	?	?	?	?
Job fairs	Moderate	Low	?	?	?	?
Organizational outplacement offices	Low	?	?	?	?	?
Coops and internships	Low	High	?	?	?	?
Temporary employees	Low	?	?	?	?	?
Computerized resume services	Low	?	?	?	?	?
Alumni associates	?	?	?	?	?	?
Unemployed youth services	?	?	?	?	?	?
Churches	?	?	?	?	?	?
Interest groups	?	?	?	?	?	?
Realtors	?	?	?	?	?	?
Direct mail solicitations	?	?	?	?	?	?

When to Look

Two factors that drive the decision of when to look for job applicants are lead time concerns and time sequence concerns.

Lead Time Concerns

Although managers would like to have each position filled immediately upon approval of requisitions, this goal is not possible. It is possible, however, to minimize the delay in filling vacancies by planning for openings well in advance of their actual occurrence. To do so requires consideration of a number of variables, as indicated next.[48]

Budget Filling a vacancy requires direct and indirect expenditures. Direct expenditures go toward compensating hired personnel, and indirect expenditures are required to cover the costs of the search. Both expenditures need to be budgeted for well in advance of the search. A lack of funds has delayed the search for many a manager with job vacancies.

Date of Hire Some vacancies need to be filled more immediately than do others. Vacancies need to be prioritized in order to establish reasonable lead times. Prioritization can be accomplished on the basis of work flow, the start of training and orientation classes, and the receipt of funding.

Seasonal Employment Given the institutions in our society and how they operate, there are natural employment cycles that must be taken into consideration. Due to family and religious commitments, many experienced people do not actively seek employment during the holiday period from Thanksgiving to New Year's. Most college graduates for entry-level positions are available in May and June. It is customary for employed persons to give their current employer two weeks' notice before beginning a new job.

Print Deadlines If advertising is to be a part of the search, then the lead times of publications must be observed. Advertisements must be received by the publications before a certain date in order to appear at a later date. The time required between submission and publication of an ad can range from days to weeks.

Applicant Availability Depending upon the supply of and demand for labor, some jobs will require more extensive searches than others. If the vacancy is in an occupation with strong demand and weak supply, then an intensive search may need to be conducted. When an intensive search is conducted, more lead time is needed in order to ensure that all of the necessary planning takes place.

Recruiter Availability   Busy recruiters will require more lead time to fill a vacancy than less busy recruiters. The average number of vacancies a recruiter must fill at any one time is about 17.[49] The availability of recruiters depends upon the number of vacancies that they are required to fill. Recruiters may also be busier during some times of the year than others due to the seasonal nature of employment.

Previous Searches   The successfulness of previous searches can be used in part to gauge the lead time needed in a current search. Less lead time is needed if the search is a replication of one that was previously conducted in a timely manner with a yield of successful candidates. Also, the advent of the computer now makes it possible to use the resumes generated in previous searches for current searches.[50] A computerized bank of resumes makes it possible to have an immediate source to begin the search. Most organizations, however, still have manual filing systems for resumes, and, as a result, most resumes are only retained for a short period of time.

Time Sequence Concerns

In a successful recruitment program, the steps involved in the process are clearly defined and sequenced in a logical order. A staffing flowchart should be used to organize all components of the recruitment process. The sequence of recruitment activities has a large bearing on the time that will be required to fill job vacancies. An extensive search, such as for entry-level professionals from college campuses, obviously requires more time than for cashiers from walk-in applicants.

A very useful set of indicators for time sequence concerns is known as *time-lapse statistics*. These statistics provide data on the average length of time that expires between various phases in the recruitment process. Organizations should routinely collect these data in order to assist managers in planning when vacancies are to be filled.

Time lapse data tend to vary by type of job. One survey, for example, indicates that it takes about 6.8 weeks on average to fill a supervisory and managerial position, while it takes about 2.7 weeks on average to fill a clerical position.[51] Time lapse data also vary by events in the recruitment process. The average number of days between when an employment requisition is opened and when a job offer is accepted is 31 days. On the other hand, the average number of days between the opening of an employment requisition and the start date for the new employee is 45 days.[52]

SEARCHING

Once the recruitment planning and strategy development phases are completed, then it is time to actively conduct the search. Searching for candidates first requires the development of a message and then the selection of a medium to communicate that message. Each of these phases is considered in turn.

Communication Message

Job Requirements and Rewards Matrices

Information presented by the organization to the job applicant is essential to the decision to accept or reject a job offer.[53] The starting point for all information presented by the organization should be the job requirements and job rewards matrices (or their equivalent). These matrices may be used in all forms of communications with job applicants, including advertisements, recruitment brochures, and face-to-face discussions. The job requirements matrix communicates to the applicant what is needed to perform the job. The job rewards matrix describes what rewards are offered to the applicant for performing the job. Both pieces of information are essential to the applicant in formulating a decision whether to become an applicant, to remain an applicant, and ultimately to join an organization.

Types of Messages

Traditional Messages   Information about the organization, also known as the message, varies by the amount of information presented and by the accuracy of that information.[54] With traditional recruitment procedures, the job applicant may be given relatively little concrete or accurate information. For example, it is common to see the phrase ''unlimited growth opportunities'' in job recruitment advertisements in the paper. This phrase may sound promising, but it is very vague and possibly misleading. Such information may cause applicants to shun the advertised position. It may also create retention problems for misled applicants who joined the organization.

Fortunately, some organizations are now presenting messages that are more specific and accurate than the traditional message. As a result, job applicants are able to make better informed decisions about their employment with an organization, and organizations gain more credibility in the eyes of the applicants.

Realistic Recruitment Message   A realistic recruitment message portrays the organization and job as it really is rather than describing what the organization thinks job applicants want to hear. Several different recruitment practices work well with this approach.

A very well researched recruitment message is known as a realistic job preview or RJP.[55] According to this practice, job applicants are given a ''vaccination'' by being told verbally, in writing, or on videotape what the actual job is like.[56] An example of the attributes that might be contained in an RJP is shown in Exhibit 7.7. It shows numerous attributes for the job of elementary school teacher. Note

EXHIBIT 7.7 Example of Job Attributes in an RJP for Elementary School Teachers

Positive Job Attributes

Dental insurance is provided
Innovative teaching strategies are encouraged
University nearby to take classes
Large support staff for teachers

Negative Job Attributes

Salary growth has averaged 2% in past three years
Class sizes are large
The length of the school day is long
Interactions with community have not been favorable

that the attributes are quite specific, and that they are both positive and negative. Information like this "tells it like it is" to job applicants.

After receiving the vaccination, job applicants can decide whether they want to work for the organization. The hope with the RJP is that job applicants will self-select into and out of the organization. By selecting into the organization, the applicant may be more committed than otherwise to working there. By selecting out, the organization does not face the costs associated with recruiting, selecting, training, and compensating employees, only to then have them leave because the job did not meet their expectations.

The research that has been conducted to date on the effectiveness of RJPs has yielded differing interpretations.[57] What seems clear is that RJPs, like any recruitment message, are more or less likely to be successful under certain conditions. These conditions will be reviewed shortly.

There are other possible ways to provide job applicants with a realistic look at their potential job. These approaches include work-site tours, work simulations or job try-outs, internships, co-op arrangements, part-time work, and summer jobs.[58] While employers may use these other recruitment practices more frequently than RJPs, they have not been explicitly developed for the purpose of communicating realism and they have not received much attention by researchers. As a result, this is a newer area of exploration for the development of realistic messages.

Attractive Messages   An attractive message portrays the organization in a manner such that applicants are induced to interview, join, or stay with the organization before they actually become employees. For example, most employers pay travel expenses for the applicant to interview. Some organizations go much further. For example, General Mills has wined and dined MBA students from Northwestern University aboard a yacht in hopes of getting them to sign up for an interview.[59]

Upon completion of the trip, General Mills also sent each prospective interviewee a Wheaties box with his or her picture and name on it.

Once interviews have been conducted, other attractive messages are used to induce the applicant to accept a job offer. Traditionally, this has meant paying for moving expenses. Some organizations go beyond moving expenses to help the person locate and pay for a new house, sell an old home, or assist a partner in finding a new job.

Organizations also try to induce job applicants to make a long-term commitment to the organization. To do so, organizations have traditionally offered basic benefits such as health care and the possibility of salary growth through merit pay. Some employers have expanded these inducements in order to be seen as family-friendly organizations. Johnson and Johnson offers family care leave and sick days, and child care. IBM offers flexible work hours, leaves of absence, work-at-home programs, and child care programs. Aetna Life and Casualty offers job sharing, part-time work, flexible hours, school-holiday program, and a work-at-home program. Corning offers child care, part-time work, summer camps, and after-school programs.[60]

Targeted Messages   One way to improve upon matching people with jobs is to target the recruitment message to a particular audience. Different audiences may be looking for different rewards from an employer.[61] This would appear to be especially true of special applicant populations such as teenagers, older workers, welfare recipients, people with disabilities, homeless individuals, veterans, and displaced homemakers, who may have special needs. Older workers, for example, may be looking for employers who can meet their financial needs (e.g., supplement social security), security needs (e.g., retraining), and social needs (e.g., place to interact with people).[62]

Contingency Approach to Message Selection

The four different types of messages—realistic, attractive, traditional, and targeted—are not likely to be equally effective under the same conditions. Which message to convey depends upon the labor market, vacancy characteristics, and applicant characteristics.

Labor Market   If the labor market is tight and applicants are difficult to come by, then realism may not be an effective message, because to the extent that applicants self-select out of the applicant pool, fewer are left for an employer to choose from during an already tight labor market. Hence, if the employment objective is to simply fill job slots in the short run and worry about turnover later, a realistic message will have counterproductive effects. Obviously then, when applicants are in abundance and turnover is an immediate problem, a realistic message is appropriate.

During a tight labor market, attractive and targeted messages are likely to be more effective in attracting job applicants. Attraction is strengthened as there are inducements in applying for a job. In addition, individual needs are more likely to be perceived as met by a prospective employer. Hence, the applicant is more motivated to apply for organizations with an attractive or targeted message than without. During loose economic times when applicants are plentiful, the attractive or targeted approaches may be more costly than necessary to attract an adequate supply of labor. Also, they may set up false expectations concerning what life will be like on the job, and thus lead to turnover.

Vacancy Characteristics[63]   Job applicants have better knowledge about the actual characteristics of some jobs than others. For example, service sector jobs, such as cashier, are highly visible to people. For these jobs, it may be redundant to give a realistic message. Other jobs, such as an outside sales position, are far less visible to people. They may seem very glamorous (e.g., sales commissions) to prospective applicants who fail to see the less glamorous aspects of the job (e.g., heavy travel and paperwork).

Some jobs seem to be better suited to special applicant groups, and, hence, a targeted approach may work well. For example, older employees may have social needs that can be met well by a job that requires lots of public contact. Organizations, then, can take advantage of the special characteristics of jobs to attract applicants.

The value of the job to the organization also has a bearing on the selection of an appropriate recruitment message. Inducements for jobs of higher value or worth to the organization are easier to justify in a budgetary sense than are jobs of lower worth. The job may be of such importance to the organization that it is willing to pay a premium through inducements to attract well-qualified candidates.

Applicant Characteristics   Some applicants are less likely than others to be influenced in their attitudes and behaviors by the recruitment message. In a recent study, for example, it was shown that a realistic message is less effective for those with considerable previous job experience.[64] A targeted message does not work very well if the source is seen as being not credible.[65] Inducements may not be particularly effective with applicants who do not have a family or have considerable wealth.

Communication Medium

Not only is the message itself an important part of the recruitment process; so, too, is the selection of a medium to communicate the message. Three of the most common recruitment media are recruitment brochures, advertisements, and voice messages.

Recruitment Brochures

A recruitment brochure is usually sent or given directly to job applicants. Information in the brochure may be very detailed, and, hence, the brochure may be lengthy. A brochure not only covers information about the job, but also communicates information about the organization and the location of the organization. It may include pictures in addition to written narrative in order to illustrate various aspects of the job, such as the city in which the organization is located and actual coworkers.

The advantages of a brochure are that the organization controls who receives a copy. Also, it can be more lengthy than an advertisement. A disadvantage is that it can be quite costly to develop this medium.

Developing a brochure can be done inside the organization or by outside media professionals. By developing a brochure in-house, the organization may be able to keep the cost down. However, in-house capabilities may not be very technically advanced, so that outside sources may be needed if advanced graphics, picture displays, or other technical advances are required.

Advertisements

Given the expense of advertising in business publications, ads are much shorter and to the point than are recruitment brochures. As a general rule, the greater the circulation of the publication, the greater the cost of advertising in it.

Ads appear in a variety of places other than business publications. Ads can be found in local, regional, and national newspapers; on television and radio; and in bargain shoppers, door hangers, direct mail, and welcome wagons. Advertisements can thus be used to reach a broad market segment. Although they are brief, there are many different types of ads:[66]

1. *Classified Advertisements.* These ads appear in alphabetical order in the "Help Wanted" section of the newspaper. Typically, they allow for very limited type and style selection and are usually only one newspaper column in width. These ads are used most often for the purpose of quick resume solicitation for low-level jobs at a low cost.

2. *Classified Display Ads.* A classified display ad allows more discretion in the type that is used, and its location in the paper. A classified display ad does not have to appear in alphabetical order and can appear in any section of the newspaper. The cost of these ads is moderate, and they are often used as a way to announce openings for professional and managerial jobs. An example of a classified display ad is shown in Exhibit 7.8.

3. *Display Ads.* These ads allow for freedom of design and placement in a publication. As such, they are very expensive and begin to resemble recruitment brochures. These ads are typically used when an employer is searching for a large number of applicants to fill multiple openings.

EXHIBIT 7.8   Classified Display Ad for Human Resource Generalist

---

HUMAN RESOURCE GENERALIST

ABC Health, a leader in the health care industry, currently has a position available for an experienced **Human Resource Generalist.**

This position will serve on the human resources team, which serves as a business partner with our operational departments. Our team prides itself on developing and maintaining progressive and impactful human resources policies and programs.

Qualified candidates for this position will possess a bachelor's degree in business with an emphasis on human resource management, or a degree in a related field, such as industrial psychology. In addition, a minimum of three years experience as a human resource generalist is required. This experience should include exposure to at least four of the following functional areas: compensation, employment, benefits, training, employee relations, and performance management.

In return for your contributions, we offer a competitive salary as well as comprehensive, flexible employee benefits. If you meet the qualifications and our opportunity is attractive to you, please forward your resume and salary expectations to:

Human Resource Department
ABC Health
P.O. Box 123
Pensacola, FL 12345

An Equal Opportunity/Affirmative Action Employer

---

4. *Blind Ad.* A blind ad is one where the identity of the employer is hidden from job applicants. Resumes are solicited and sent to a post office box. In most instances, these ads are to be avoided. Readers of these ads are likely to have negative reactions to them because they have no idea where their resume is being sent. Also, some applicants may fear that their employer is advertising with a blind ad to see who is thinking of leaving the organization. Due to these perceptions, it is unlikely that blind ads draw any applicants other than those who are desperate for a job.

How to Write an Ad   The State of Wisconsin published an excellent booklet on how to write advertisements.[67] Points to consider in writing advertising copy follow:

- A good ad should draw attention, create interest, screen candidates, and provide for easy responses.
- The headline should be used to draw attention.

- The body of the ad should be based on the job requirements matrix to create interest in the job through the job description and to allow applicants to self-screen through the job specification.
- The body of the ad should also be based on the job rewards matrix to provide basic information about job rewards.
- The writing style should be natural, enthusiastic, engaging, and easy to understand.
- The ad should close with detailed information about how to apply for the job.
- The best time of week to advertise in the newspaper is on Sunday.
- Advertising around the time of major holidays is ineffective.

Voice Messages

As a result of the latest advances in the telecommunications industry, the most recent development in advertising is voice messages. With this approach, the applicant hears information over the phone about job openings. The Dime National Bank of New York uses this relatively inexpensive approach.[68] At Dime Bank, calls are solicited through advertisements in the paper. Once an applicant calls, he or she is routed through the menu shown in Exhibit 7.9. Callers have access to each of the items on the menu by pressing keys on a Touch-Tone phone. If what they hear is of interest to them, they can leave a message in a voice mailbox. All applicants receive a return call, and if they appear to be qualified for a vacant position, they are invited in for an interview. Although the effectiveness of this procedure has not yet been researched, it appears to be a promising way to provide a more personable introduction to job applicants.

EVALUATION

It is essential that organizations evaluate the effectiveness of the recruitment process. By doing so, they can determine strengths and weaknesses in the recruitment process and undertake continuous efforts to improve upon the current effectiveness of their process. An evaluation consists of examining the process, its impact on outcomes, and application reactions.

Process

The recruitment process consists of the steps shown in Exhibit 7.1. Three measures that help identify the effectiveness of the process are yield ratios, time lapse data, and cost figures.[69]

EXHIBIT 7.9 Advertising by Voice Messages

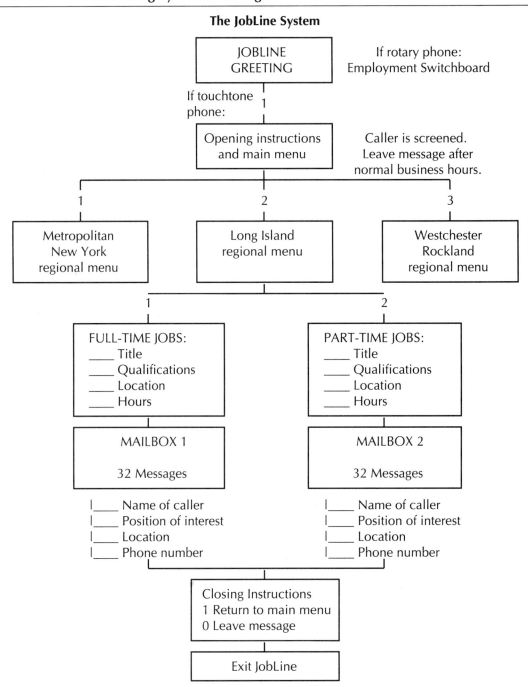

The JobLine System

JOBLINE GREETING

If rotary phone: Employment Switchboard

If touchtone phone: 1

Opening instructions and main menu

Caller is screened. Leave message after normal business hours.

1 — Metropolitan New York regional menu

2 — Long Island regional menu

3 — Westchester Rockland regional menu

1 —
FULL-TIME JOBS:
____ Title
____ Qualifications
____ Location
____ Hours

2 —
PART-TIME JOBS:
____ Title
____ Qualifications
____ Location
____ Hours

MAILBOX 1

32 Messages

MAILBOX 2

32 Messages

|____ Name of caller
|____ Position of interest
|____ Location
|____ Phone number

|____ Name of caller
|____ Position of interest
|____ Location
|____ Phone number

Closing Instructions
1 Return to main menu
0 Leave message

Exit JobLine

Source: A. M. Micola, "High-Tech Recruiting at Low Cost," *HR Magazine,* August 1991, pp. 49–52. Reprinted with the permission of HR Magazine (formerly Personnel Administrator) published by the Society for Human Resource Management, Alexandria, VA.

Yield Ratio

As indicated earlier in the chapter, a yield ratio is simply the number of applicants divided by the number of new hires. Yield ratios can be calculated at various stages in the recruitment process as well as at the end to find out the overall yield. Yield ratios can be calculated to see which recruitment source, recruitment methods, and type of recruiter produce the greatest yield and to identify areas where improvement is needed.

The calculation of the yield ratio can vary by stage in the applicant flow process. Not only can the number of hires be compared with the number of applicants, but the number of offers can be compared with the number of applicants. Also, the number of hires can be compared with the number of offers.

The ratio of applicants to offers may better capture those parts of the recruitment process under the organization's control than the ratio of applicants to hires. The reason this may be more amenable to control is that applicants may decide on their own volition not to accept a job offer. A ratio of applicants to hires may penalize the organization for matters out of their hands.

The ratio of offers to hires is a measure that provides feedback on whether the job offer process is working correctly. A high offer to hire ratio may indicate that while qualified applicants are being identified, they are not attracted to the organization. This feedback suggests that better offers need to be made rather than trying to identify more new hires in the recruitment process.

Time Lapse Data

Not only is yield an important part of the recruitment process, so, too, is the time it takes to yield a certain number of hires. This is typically assessed using time lapse data, which refers to the time between events in the recruiting process.

As with yield ratios, time lapse data can be collected for each recruitment source, method, and type of recruiter. Time lapse data can be calculated for the amount of time that expires between the identification of applicants and actual starting date, between the identification of applicants and the issuance of job offers, and between the issuance of job offers and actual starting date. These data are then used to diagnose where in the recruitment process additional speed and efficiency are needed.

Cost

A final process issue is the cost involved in the recruitment process. Cost refers to both the direct costs of recruitment (e.g., salaries of recruiters) and indirect costs (e.g., overhead expenses such as supplies and travel). An important measure is cost per hire. This measure can be used to assess if some sources, methods, or recruiters are more expensive than others. Calculation of recruitment costs and cost per hire may be guided by the recruitment budget calculations in Exhibit 7.3.

An important distinction that needs to be made is recruitment costs versus total costs.[70] Recruitment costs simply look at the direct and indirect costs involved in recruiting. Total costs looks at the total costs to the organization for a new hire. These two figures may yield very different results.

For example, the recruitment cost of a new hire may be $1,200 when using a local ad. The total cost, however, may be $2,200 if employees hired with ads have a high turnover rate that costs the organization an additional $1,000 per hire to replace them when they leave. This example illustrates the fact that some recruitment sources and methods that appear very inexpensive are actually quite costly to the organization in the long run. Organizations thus should pay more attention to total cost than to just recruitment cost.

A Practical Illustration

A recruiter is often faced with the issue of where to place an advertisement. Should it be placed in periodical A or B? If previous data on the process have been collected, a rational answer can be determined. If cost is no issue, then the ad with the best yield and time lapse should be used. If speed is of the essence, then the ad with the best time lapse should be used. If attaining a large number of hires is the objective, then the ad with the best yield should be placed. A similar logic can be applied by organizations when choosing among other recruitment alternatives.

Applicant Reactions

An important source of information in designing and implementing an effective recruitment system is applicant reactions to the system. Both attitudinal and behavioral reactions to components of the recruitment system are important. Components of this system that have been studied include the recruiter and the recruitment process. Each of these components will be reviewed, followed by a discussion of the measurement of applicant reactions.

Reactions to Recruiters

Considerable research has been conducted and carefully reviewed on the reactions of job applicants to the behavior and characteristics of recruiters.[71] The data that have been collected have been somewhat limited by the fact that they primarily focus on reactions to college rather than noncollege recruiters. Despite this limitation, several key themes emerge in the literature.

First, while the recruiter does indeed influence job applicant reactions, he or she does not have as much influence on them as do actual characteristics of the job. This indicates that the recruiter cannot be viewed as a substitute for a well defined and communicated recruitment message showing the actual characteristics of the job. It is not enough just to have good recruiters to attract applicants to the organization.

Second, the influence of the recruiter is more likely to be felt on the attitudes rather than the behaviors of the job applicant. That is, an applicant who has been exposed to a talented recruiter is more likely to walk away with a favorable impression of the recruiter than to accept a job on the basis of the interaction with a recruiter. This attitudinal effect is important, however, as it may lead to good publicity for the organization. In turn, good publicity may lead to a larger applicant pool to draw upon in the future.

Third, demographic characteristics of the recruiter do not have much impact on applicant reactions, with one exception. Recruiters who are human resource specialists do not fare as well in terms of applicant reactions as do line managers. Hence, the common practice of using line managers to recruit, and human resource people to coordinate recruitment activities, appears to be an appropriate strategy.

Fourth, two behaviors of the recruiter seem to have the largest influence on applicant reactions. The first behavior is the level of warmth that the recruiter shows toward the job applicant. Warmth can be expressed by being enthusiastic, personable, empathetic, and helpful in dealings with the candidate. The second behavior is being knowledgeable about the job. This can be conveyed by being well versed with the job requirements matrix and the job rewards matrix.

Reactions to the Recruitment Process

Only some administrative components of the recruitment process have been shown to have an impact on applicant reactions.[72] First, job applicants are more likely to have favorable reactions to the recruitment process when the screening devices that are used to narrow the applicant pool are seen as job-related. That is, the process that is used should be closely related to the content of the job as spelled out in the job requirements matrix.

Second, delay times in the recruitment process do indeed have a negative effect on applicants' reactions. In particular, when long delays take place between the applicant's expression of interest and the organization's response, negative reactions are formed by the applicant. The negative impression formed by the applicant is about the organization rather than the applicant him or herself. For example, with a long delay between an on-site visit and a job offer, an applicant is more likely to believe that something is wrong with the organization rather than with his or her personal qualifications. This is especially true of the better quality candidate who is also likely to act on these feelings by accepting another job offer.

Third, simply throwing money at the recruitment process is unlikely to result in any return. There is no evidence that increased expenditures on the recruitment process result in more favorable attitudes or behaviors by job applicants. In order for expenditures to pay dividends, they need to be specifically targeted to effective recruitment practices rather than indiscriminately directed to all practices.

Fourth, the influence of the recruiter on the applicant is more likely to occur in the initial rather than the latter stages of the recruitment process. In the latter stages, actual characteristics of the job carry more weight in the applicant's decision. At the initial screening interview, the recruiter may be the applicant's only contact with the organization. Later in the process, the applicant is more likely to have additional information about the job and company. Hence, the credibility of the recruiter is most critical upon initial contact with applicants.

Measurement of Reactions

Questionnaire items should be developed to assess the reaction of applicants to the process. Research has shown that applicant reactions are not only determined by the outcomes of recruitment (e.g., invitation for a second interview, job offer), but also by the procedure used by the organization to decide upon these outcomes.[73] Procedures that need to be assessed include the job-relatedness of procedures followed, interpersonal treatment during the assessment process, and explanation of the procedures followed. Gathering customer reactions, in this case the applicant's, is an important part of managing for quality in the recruitment process.

Impact on Outcomes

Outcomes of the recruitment process that are of ultimate interest to top-level decision makers in the organization are the job satisfaction, performance, and turnover of those who are recruited to join the organization. These outcomes should be tallied for each recruitment source and method. Results can then be compared among the various sources and methods to gauge their relative effectiveness, much as in Exhibit 7.6.

SPECIAL CASE: COLLEGE RECRUITMENT

One aspect of recruitment that deserves special attention is the recruitment of applicants from colleges and universities. This aspect deserves special consideration because of the huge costs associated with college recruitment.

Selecting Campuses to Visit

The cost of college recruitment is very high because of the expense of on-site visits to campuses and of bringing candidates to the hiring organization.

Given the large cost involved, it is essential that appropriate colleges and universities be selected for a visit. Fortunately, many sound guidelines have been written on how to select campuses to visit.[74] A summary of the recommended factors to consider in selecting campuses follows.

Curriculum

It is essential that schools have degree programs in the areas where job openings exist in the organization. To make the match between the curriculum and organizational needs, there must be careful assessment of the job requirements matrix as it relates to the specific classes offered on campus. Conversation with faculty members is often required to make this match as the description of courses in a course bulletin may be out of date.

School Reputation

Many surveys have been conducted on the quality of the educational setting. Each year, *Business Week* reports the results of a survey on top MBA programs in the country, and *Peterson's Guide* reports on the quality of undergraduate programs. Care must be exercised in reviewing these reports. Though helpful in establishing school reputation, they may fail to consider important criteria to judge reputation. For example, to ensure that students are being provided with state-of-the-art information, attention should be paid to the research quality of the faculty. Unfortunately, few surveys use faculty research quality as a criterion in the assessments.

Proximity

The closer the school is to the organization, the less the transportation cost involved in recruitment may be. Many organizations have found that turnover rates are decreased by recruiting locally. Job applicants already have a realistic idea of what it is like to live in the area.

Student Performance

The quality of applicants, as measured by both the performance of students while on campus and their subsequent performance on the job, must also be assessed. Hence, one should monitor student GPAs, work experience levels, and other KSAOs while on campus. Also, one should monitor the performance and turnover levels of new hires from various campuses.

Yield

Previous success at attracting applicants on various campuses should be considered. Indicators to pay attention to here include overall yield ratios, as well as specific ones for women and minorities.

Organizing College Recruitment

A uniform college recruitment program is destined to fail. Schools vary considerably on the criteria just reviewed as well as on other characteristics. Consequently, the organization must target its efforts to the specific characteristics of each school. With large schools, the organization may need to target its efforts at the program level as well. Issues to consider in targeting a college recruitment program are life cycle, quality, and structure.

Life Cycle

The relationship between college or university placement offices and organizations follows a life cycle. Just as individuals are born, grow, mature, and decline over time, so do relationships between placement offices and hiring organizations. Steps taken by hiring organizations need to be different depending upon the stage of the relationship.[75] For example, as an organization enters into a recruitment arrangement with a school or program for the first time, it is unlikely to recruit very many students because the new recruits are a somewhat unknown commodity. As a result, the organization is unlikely to offer scholarships to students at that school or program.

As its relationship to the school grows and matures, however, the organization is likely to recruit many more candidates and offer scholarships. More candidates are recruited because they are now a proven commodity, and scholarships are offered to maintain a steady flow of well-qualified candidates into the organization. Other recruitment activities, such as internships and advertising, also need to be considered in relation to the life cycle.

Quality

In order to establish high-quality relationships on campus, AT&T has developed a customer-supplier model to guide the relationship between career service offices on campus and the recruitment function in organizations.[76] The model is shown in Exhibit 7.10.

This model shows that both the organization (AT&T) and university serve as customers and suppliers to one another. In terms of being a customer, AT&T employs the services of students graduated by the university. The university is also a customer as it receives special services provided by AT&T. These special services include the training of university placement counselors on effective counseling techniques. In terms of being a supplier, AT&T supplies training services to university placement counselors. The university is also a supplier as it supplies AT&T with students for employment.

EXHIBIT 7.10   The Customer Supplier Model of College Recruitment at AT&T

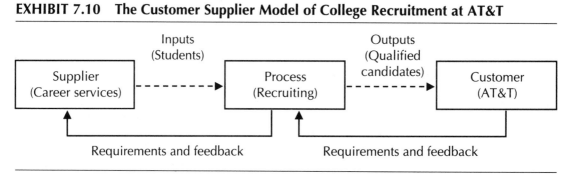

Source: Reprinted with permission from Gale Hiering Varma.

The key to arranging college recruitment activities according to this model is for both parties to clearly define their requirements of one another as customers and suppliers. Then, periodic feedback needs to be exchanged between the parties to ensure compliance with these requirements.

Structure

A college recruitment program can but does not have to be housed in a single location. A college recruitment program may have multiple structures depending upon the stage of its relationship with colleges and depending upon the requirements of the organization and program. Alternative structures follow:[77]

Full-Time College Recruiter These individuals work out of a central office on a full-time basis. They travel to schools to recruit and may recruit by region, size of school, program, or special characteristics of school.

Regional Approach Individuals in particular areas are assigned schools within their geographic area, where they recruit on a part-time basis.

Rotating Assignments A rotating schedule is used to have part-time people (e.g., executives or regional managers) recruit from certain schools.

Alma Mater System Individuals recruit at their own alma mater on a part-time basis.

Effective College Recruitment Practices

Many surveys have been conducted on the extent to which employers follow certain practices when recruiting on college and university campuses.[78] Of greater importance than mere usage of practices is how effective these practices are. A recent study begins to address these issues.[79] The results of this study are very consistent with many of the points made throughout this chapter. According to corporate human resource professionals, effective college recruitment practices include the communication of accurate job information to candidates, the selection of recruiters knowledgeable about the organization and jobs, and the collection of data about each college. Note that these practices are consistent with all forms of recruitment, not just college recruitment.

LEGAL ISSUES

External recruitment practices are subject to considerable legal scrutiny and influence. It is through external recruitment that job applicants first establish contact with the organization and then become more knowledgeable about job requirements and rewards. During this process, there is ample room for the organization to exclude certain applicant groups (e.g., minorities, women, and people with disabilities), as well as deceive in its dealings with applicants. Various laws and regulations seek to place limits on these exclusionary and deceptive practices.

Legal issues regarding several of the practices are discussed in this section. These include definition of job applicants and disclaimers (planning), targeted recruitment (where to look), recruitment sources (how to look), job advertisements (communication medium), and fraud and misrepresentation (communication message).

Definition of Job Applicant

Exactly what and who is a job applicant? Does the definition include unsolicited resumes, applications for any job opening, casual walk-ins, phone call inquiries, anyone who fills out an application blank? Any person who is considered an applicant by the organization must be reflected in its record keeping; all such people are also potential litigants against the organization.

The organization is required to keep records on numbers of applicants and use these in the calculation of applicant flow and selection rate statistics (see Chapter 4). The denominator of the selection rate is the number of applicants. Thus, who is counted as an applicant will have a direct bearing on selection rate statistics and subsequent determination of adverse impact through the comparison of selection rates for various groups. Presumably, the organization would like such statistics to reflect its real or serious applicants and not its casual and frivolous applicants. In a related vein, without any limitations on who is deemed an applicant, anyone who makes any effort at application might be considered an applicant legally and thus be a potential litigant in an EEO/AA case.

As these examples suggest, the organization needs to establish an explicit job applicant policy for guidance and protection in EEO/AA matters. The following are some suggestions for such a policy:[80]

1. Applicants should be accepted only when there is a job vacancy open and ready to be filled (any exception to this, such as for difficult-to-fill jobs, should also be included in the policy).

2. Applicants must specify the job being applied for.

3. There should be a limit on the number of people who will be considered applicants when there are likely to be large numbers of applicants (e.g., first 100 who apply).

4. Applications should be kept live and on file for only a limited time, such as 30 or 60 days.

5. All unsolicited applications should be returned via the mail.

The above suggestions apply to the private sector primarily. Public sector employers by law must be more lenient in defining job applicants. The state of Wisconsin, for example, counts as an applicant anyone who completes, and turns in, a simple machine-scorable application blank. Because of this, the state typically has large numbers of applicants for any specific job vacancy announcement.

Disclaimers

Disclaimers are statements (usually written) that provide or confer explicit rights to the employer as part of the employment contract, and that are shown to job applicants. During the recruitment planning stage, the organization needs to decide (or reevaluate) which rights it wants to retain and how these will be communicated to job applicants.

Three areas or rights are usually suggested for possible inclusion in a disclaimer policy. These are (a) employment-at-will (right to terminate the employment relationship at any time, for any reason); (b) verification consent (right to verify information provided by the applicant); and (c) false statement warning (right to not hire, terminate, or discipline prospective employee for providing false information to the employer). Usually, it is recommended that the organization have all three of these disclaimers as part of its planned policy toward job applicants.[81]

To communicate disclaimers, it is advisable that they be shown in writing to job applicants (often on the application blank), reviewed with the applicant if possible, and then signed by the applicant. It should be remembered that signed disclaimer statements will become part of the employment contract for those applicants who accept a job offer. Care should thus be exercised in the development and communication of disclaimers.

Targeted Recruitment

Targeted recruitment is a necessary part of EEO/AA programs designed to address problems of underutilization of minorities and women. Such recruitment refers to explicit attempts to identify and attract people from underutilized groups in areas where, and through sources from which, they are available.

Examples of targeted recruitment are numerous. Discussed previously, for example, were special availabilities of people outside the mainstream of labor force participation (teenagers, older workers, welfare recipients, and people with disabilities).

As another important example, under Revised Order No. 4 (see appendix B), federal contractors' AAPs must include targeted recruitment. The order gives contractors special recruitment sources to consider, suggests holding recruitment briefings with representatives from these sources, encourages employer use of employee referral systems for women and minority applicants, and requires active recruiting at schools with predominantly minority and female enrollment.

Other examples of targeted recruitment occur within the context of larger EEO/ AA programs at employers such as McDonald's, Kentucky Fried Chicken (KFC), and the California Department of Corrections.[82] McDonald's started its McJobs program for hiring people with disabilities back in 1981, and it has hired more than 9,000 mentally and physically challenged people since then. The program is a partnership between vocational rehabilitation (VR) agencies, local school systems and workshops, and family members. Individuals are recruited from these sources and then assigned a specific VR counselor to serve as a liaison between them and the company. Recruits then embark on a six- to eight-week training program to learn job skills, both in the classroom and on the job at a McDonald's restaurant.

KFC's targeted recruitment program, called the Designates Program, is intended to identify and attract female and minority executives from other companies. It seeks to place, or promote these recruits through the managerial ranks into senior-level management positions. To do this, it uses executive search firms owned by minority group members and women, as well as white men. In a given recruiting initiative, recruiters from these three differently owned search firms (all using the same KSAO job requirements) are asked to produce three different slates of candidates—all white men, all black men, and all women (minority and white). One person is then hired from all three slates.

The California Department of Corrections hires about 2,000 correctional officers each year. It tracks the ethnic composition of its workforce to identify emergent underutilization (recently, Hispanics, Asians, Filipinos, Pacific Islanders, Native Americans, and women). Its multiracial recruitment staff then implements a variety of recruitment initiatives. These include newspaper ads, TV and radio commercials, posters and billboards, mass mailings, job information workshops, and high school and college campus visits.

Recruitment Sources

Use of traditional or conventional recruitment sources can create EEO/AA problems for the organization. Often, the demographic pools available through these sources lack in diversity, and this leads to underutilization in the organization's workforce.

Several conventional recruitment sources are potentially tainted with possible discrimination effects, and they should be used cautiously by the employer.[83] Employee referral systems are often suspect because employees are most likely to advise only people like themselves about job opportunities. This is also a strong possibility with nepotism systems, in which only family members of current employees may be hired. Finally, it is illegal for employment agencies and executive firms to fail, or refuse, to refer members of protected groups for employment. Despite this, it is sometimes alleged that such refusals occur.

Any recruitment source can potentially lead to discrimination. The organization should carefully track the demographics of recruits from various sources, looking for possible adverse impact in the use of those sources. Where it is found, the organization must take steps to eliminate it. This may mean a halt in the use of the source, discussions with the source to rectify the problem, a shift to more demographically neutral sources, or use of targeted recruitment sources in order to address and correct workforce imbalances.

Job Advertisements

Some of the earliest, and most blatant, examples of discrimination come from job advertisements. Newspaper employment ads were once listed under separate "Help-Wanted Male" and "Help-Wanted Female" sections and the content of the ads contained statements such as "Applicant must be young and energetic." Such types of ads would obviously discourage certain potential applicants from applying because of their sex or age.

The EEOC has issued policy statements regarding age- and sex-referent language in advertising.[84] It bans the use of explicit age- or sex-based preferences. It also addresses more subtle situations, in which ads contain implicit age- or sex-based preferences, such as "junior executive," "recent college graduate," "me-termaid," and "patrolman." These are referred to in the policy statements as "trigger words," and their use may have the effect of deterring certain individuals from becoming applicants. The statements make clear that trigger words, in and of themselves in an advertisement, are not illegal. However, the total context of the ad in which trigger words appear must not be discriminatory, or the trigger words will be a violation of the law.

The EEOC provides the following as an example of an advertisement with a trigger word:

"Wanted: Individuals of all ages. Day and evening hours available. Full and part-time positions. All inquiries welcomed. Excellent source of secondary income for retirees."

Use of the trigger word "retiree" in this ad is considered permissible because the context of the ad makes it clear that applicants of all ages are welcomed to apply.

Fraud and Misrepresentation

Puffery, promises, half-truths, and even outright lies are all encountered in recruitment under the guise of selling the applicant on the job and the organization. Too much of this type of selling can be legally dangerous. When it occurs, under workplace tort law, applicants may file suit claiming fraud or misrepresentation.[85] Claims may cite false statements of existing facts (e.g., the nature and profitability of the employer's business), or false promises of future events (e.g., promises about terms and conditions of employment, regarding pay, promotion opportunities, and geographic location). It does not matter if the false statements were made intentionally (fraud) or negligently (misrepresentation). Both types of statements are a reasonable basis for a claim by the applicant or newly hired employee.

To be successful in such a suit, the plaintiff must demonstrate that

1. a misrepresentation occurred;
2. the employer knew, or should have known, about the misrepresentation;
3. the plaintiff relied on the information to make a decision or take action; and
4. the plaintiff was injured because of reliance placed on the statements made by the employer.[86]

While these four requirements appear to be a stiff set of hurdles for the plaintiff, they are by no means insurmountable, as many successful plaintiffs can attest.

Avoidance of fraud and misrepresentation claims in recruitment requires straightforward action by the organization and its recruiters. First, provide applicants with copies of the job requirements matrix and the job rewards matrix. They contain a wealth of specific, truthful information about the job. Second, be truthful about the nature of the business and its profitability. Third, avoid specific promises about future events, regarding terms and conditions of employment or business plans and profitability. Finally, make sure that all recruiters follow these suggestions when they recruit job applicants.

SUMMARY

The objective of the external recruitment process is to identify and attract qualified applicants. In order to meet this objective the organization must conduct recruitment planning. At this stage, attention must be given to both organizational issues (e.g., centralized versus decentralized recruitment function) and administrative issues (e.g., size of the budget). Particular care needs to be taken in the selection, training, and rewards of recruiters.

The next stage in external recruitment is the development of a strategy. The strategy should detail where to look, how to look, and when to look. In general, an organization should consider looking at a wide range of applicant groups to attract a well-qualified applicant pool. Consideration should be given to those with special availabilities, and the search should be guided by the job requirements matrix. Multiple sources, including innovative ones, should be used to identify specific applicant populations. There are trade-offs involved in using any source to identify applicants, which should be carefully reviewed prior to using it. When to look for applicants depends upon the lead time required to fill a vacancy and the time it took to fill previous vacancies.

The next stage is to develop a message to give to the job applicants and to select a medium to convey that message. The message may be traditional, realistic, attractive, or targeted. There is no one best message; it depends upon the characteristics of the labor market, the job, and the applicants. The message should, however, be based on the job requirements matrix and the job rewards matrix. The message can be communicated through brochures, advertisements, or voice messages, each of which has different strengths and weaknesses.

In order to ensure that a qualified applicant pool is finally formed using these procedures, attention must be given to evaluating the recruitment process. In evaluating the recruitment process, the process itself, applicant reactions to the process and recruiters, and the impact of recruitment on HR outcomes should be assessed. The process is evaluated by collecting yield, time lapse, and cost data. Reactions are assessed by measuring the perceived fairness of the process. HR outcomes that are measured include satisfaction, performance, and retention.

Recruitment at colleges and universities is a very costly procedure. Care needs to be taken to select programs likely to yield qualified applicants, and recruitment efforts should be targeted by school and program. As with other types of recruitment programs, college recruitment is more likely to be effective when accurate information is communicated to applicants, knowledgeable recruiters are selected, and data are collected about each recruitment source (i.e., program and campus).

Recruitment activities are highly visible and sensitive for employees. They raise a host of legal issues regarding potential exclusion of minority and female applicants, maintenance of employer rights, and truthful communication with job applicants. The organization should carefully define what it considers to be job applicants, as well as the rights it retains for itself through the issuance of disclaimers to those applicants. For enhanced representation of minorities and women in the applicant pool, targeted recruitment and possible changes in use of conventional recruitment sources should be undertaken. Consistent with this, job advertisements should not openly or implicitly express preferences for or against protected demographic characteristics of applicants. Finally, the organization should be truthful with applicants about the terms and conditions of employment, as well as the overall nature of the business, in order to avoid allegations of fraud and misrepresentation in recruitment.

DISCUSSION QUESTIONS

1. List and briefly describe each of the administrative issues that needs to be addressed in the planning stage of external recruiting.
2. List the nontraditional sources of applicants that organizations began to turn to in the 1980s. For each source, identify needs specific to the source, as well as pros and cons of using the source for recruitment.

3. This chapter discusses both traditional and innovative recruitment sources that can be used to identify applicants. List the criteria that should be considered in the selection of a recruitment source, describing the importance of each criterion.

4. In designing the communication message to be used in external recruiting, what kinds of information should be included?

5. What are the advantages of conveying a realistic recruitment message as opposed to one portraying the job in a way that the organization thinks that job applicants want to hear?

6. What nontraditional inducements are some organizations offering so that they are seen as family-friendly organizations? What result does the organization hope to realize as a result of providing these inducements?

7. In evaluating the effectiveness of external recruiting practices, certain outcomes are of ultimate interest to top-level decision makers in the organization. List and describe each of these outcomes, focusing on how the recruitment process influences each outcome.

ENDNOTES

1. A. S. Bargerstock and G. A. Swanson, "Four Ways to Build Cooperative Recruitment Alliances," *HR Magazine*, 1991, 36 (3), pp. 49–51, 79. L. S. Vines, "Recruiting Outlook," *Human Resource Executive,* 1992, 6 (10), pp. 47.

2. Personnel Policies Forum, *Recruiting and Selection Procedures* (PPF Survey No. 146) (Washington: The Bureau of National Affairs, Inc., 1988).

3. P. F. Wernimont, "Recruitment Policies and Practices," in D. Yoder and H. G. Heneman, Jr. (eds.), *ASPA Handbook of Personnel and Industrial Relations* (Washington, DC: Bureau of National Affairs, 1979), pp. 4–85 to 4–115.

4. J. S. Scott, "External and Internal Recruitment," in W. F. Cascio (ed.), *Human Resource Planning, Employment, and Placement* (Washington, DC: Bureau of National Affairs, 1989), pp. 2–73 to 2–134.

5. D. P. Schwab, "Recruiting and Organizational Participation," in K. M. Rowland and G. R. Ferris (eds.), *Personnel Management* (Boston: Allyn and Bacon, 1982), pp. 103–128.

6. D. P. Schwab, S. L. Rynes, and R. J. Aldag, "Theories and Research on Job Search and Choice," in K. M. Rowland and G. M. Ferris (eds.), *Research in Personnel and Human Resources Management,* 1987, 5, pp. 129–166; S. M. Bostnick and M. H. Ports, "Job Search Methods and Results: Tracking the Unemployed, 1991," *Monthly Labor Review,* Dec. 1992, pp. 29–35.

7. J. D. Olian and S. L. Rynes, "Organizational Staffing: Integrating Practice with Strategy," *Industrial Relations,* 1984, 23 (2), pp. 170–183; "10 Ways HR Can Take the Lead in Breaking Down Barriers to Employment," Special Report, *Personnel Journal,* Mar. 1993, pp. 47–99.

8. "Personnel Shop Talk," *BNA Bulletin to Management,* May 23, 1991, p. 154.

9. W. L. Bainbridge and S. M. Sundre, "Employment Objectives Increasingly Linked to School/Business Partnerships," *EMA Journal,* 1991, 6 (4), pp. 20–23.

10. I. J. Shaver, "Innovative Techniques Lure Quality Workers to NASA," *Personnel Journal,* Aug. 1990, pp. 100–106.

11. R. D. Gatewood, M. A. Gowen, and G. Lautenschlager, "Corporate Image, Recruitment Image, and Initial Job Choice Decisions," *Academy of Management Journal,* 1993, 36(2), pp. 414–427.

12. Coopers and Lybrand, *Employment Policies, Turnover, and Cost-Per-Hire* (New York: Coopers and Lybrand Compensation Resources, 1992).

13. Coopers and Lybrand, *Employment Policies, Turnover, and Cost-Per-Hire.*

14. Coopers and Lybrand, *Employment Policies, Turnover, and Cost-Per-Hire.*

15. R. D. Borgeson, "Planning the Human Resources Function Program and Budget," in J. J. Famularo (ed.), *Handbook of Human Resources Administration* (New York: McGraw-Hill, 1986), pp. 7–1 to 7–17.

16. Personnel Policies Forum, *Recruiting and Selection Procedures.*

17. J. A. Breaugh, *Recruitment: Science and Practice* (Boston: PWS-Kent, 1992); S. L. Rynes and J.W. Boudreau, "College Recruiting Practices in Large Organizations: Practice, Evaluation, and Research Implications," *Personnel Psychology,* 1986, 39 (3), pp. 286–310.

18. S. L. Rynes and A. E. Barber, "Applicant Attraction Strategies: An Organizational Perspective," *Academy of Management Review,* 1990, 15 (2), pp. 286–310.

19. M. S. Taylor and T. J. Bergmann, "Organizational Recruitment Activities and Applicant Reactions at Different Stages of the Recruitment Process," *Personnel Psychology,* 1987, 40, pp. 261–285.

20. Rynes and Boudreau, "College Recruiting Practices in Large Organizations: Practice, Evaluation, and Research Implications."

21. D. E. Smith, "Training Programs for Performance Appraisal: A Review," *Academy of Management Review,* 1985, 11, pp. 22–40.

22. G. P. Latham and K. N. Wexley, *Increasing Productivity through Performance Appraisal* (Reading, MA: Addison-Wesley, 1981).

23. Rynes and Boudreau, "College Recruiting Practices in Large Organizations: Practice, Evaluation, and Research Implications."

24. B. J. Asch, "Do Incentives Matter? The Case of Navy Recruiters," *Industrial and Labor Relations Review,* 43 (Special Issue), pp. 89–106.

25. R. L. Heneman, *Merit Pay: Linking Pay Increases to Performance Ratings* (Reading, MA: Addison-Wesley, 1992).

26. Department of Employment Relations, *Recruitment Planning* (Madison, WI: State Division of Personnel, 1981); R. H. Hawk, *The Recruitment Function* (New York: American Management Association, 1967).

27. "Alternative Recruitment Methods Take Center at Fall Conference," *EMA Reporter,* 1992, 18 (1), pp. 3–5.

28. B. Quirk, "Older Workers Prove Valuable," *Capital Times,* Oct. 29, 1991, p. 1.

29. B. Rogers, "From Welfare to Workforce," *HR Magazine,* 1991, 36 (7), pp. 36–38, 85.

30. J. E. Peters, "How to Bridge the Hiring Gap," *Personnel Administrator,* Oct. 1989, pp. 76–85.

31. "Alternative Recruitment Centers Take Center Stage at Fall Conference."

32. "Phone Message Service Helps Homeless Find Jobs," *Columbus Dispatch,* Feb. 16, 1993, p. 5B.

33. K. E. Larson and L. Davis, "Workforce 2000 Solutions: A Partnership with Armed Services," *EMA Journal*, 1991, 6 (4), pp. 2–8.

34. S. Mangum, "Transferability of Military Occupational Training in the Post Draft Era," *Industrial and Labor Relations Review*, 1989, 42 (2), pp. 230–245.

35. R. D. Arvey and M. E. Begella, "Analyzing the Homemaker Job Using the PAQ," *Journal of Applied Psychology*, 1975, 60, pp. 513–517.

36. G. A. Cluff, *1990 National Cost Per Hire Survey* (Raleigh, NC: Employment Management Association, 1990); Coopers and Lybrand, *Employment Policies, Turnover, and Cost-Per-Hire.*

37. Deutsch, Shea, and Evans, *Human Resources Manual* (New York: author, 1992–1993).

38. A. Bargerstock, "Low-Cost Recruiting For Quality," *HR Magazine*, 1990, 35 (9), pp. 68–70.

39. Deutsch, Shea, and Evans, *Human Resource Manual.*

40. M. S. Taylor, "Effects of College Internships on Individual Participants," *Journal of Applied Psychology*, 1988, 73 (3), pp. 393–401.

41. J. Ross, "Effective Ways to Hire Contingent Personnel," *HR Magazine*, Feb. 1991, pp. 52–54.

42. S. Drake, "Temporaries are Here to Stay," *Human Resource Executive*, 1992, 6 (2), pp. 27–30.

43. "High Tech Recruitment Solutions," *HR Magazine*, Feb. 1992, p. 54.

44. T. Lee, "Alumni Go Back to School to Hunt Jobs," *Wall Street Journal*, June 11, 1991, p. B1.

45. Deutsch, Shea, and Evans, *Human Resources Manual*, p. 24.

46. C. D. Fyock, "Ways to Recruit Top Talent," *HR Magazine*, 1991, 36 (7), pp. 33–35.

47. G. A. Cluff, *National Cost-Per-Hire Survey* (Raleigh, NC: Employment Management Association, 1990); Coopers and Lybrand, *Employment Policies, Turnover, and Cost-Per-Hire; Personnel Policies Forum, Recruiting and Selection Procedures* (Washington, DC: Bureau of National Affairs, Inc., May 1988); S. L. Rynes, "Recruitment, Job Choice and Post-Hire Decisions," in M. D. Dunnette and L. M. Hough (eds.), *Handbook of Industrial and Organizational Psychology*, Vol. 2, second ed. (Palo Alto, CA: Consulting Psychologists Press, 1991), pp. 399–444; D. P. Schwab, "Recruiting and Organizational Participation," in K. M. Rowland and G. R. Ferris (eds.), *Personnel Management* (Boston; Allyn and Bacon, 1982), pp. 103–128; D. P. Schwab, S. L. Rynes, and R. J. Aldag, "Theories and Research on Job Search and Choice," in K. M. Rowland and G. R. Ferris (eds.), *Research in Personnel and Human Resources Management*, 1987, 5, pp. 129–166; J. P. Wanous, *Organizational Entry*, second ed. (Reading, MA: Addison-Wesley, 1992); J. P. Wanous and A. Colella, "Organizational Entry Research: Current Status and Future Directions," in G. R. Ferris and K. M. Rowland (eds.), *Organizational Entry* (Greenwich, CT: JAI Press, 1990), pp. 253–313.

48. "Recruitment Planning," State Division of Personnel, State of Wisconsin, Department of Employment Relations, WPM-Staffing-Chapter 136, Sept. 1981; W. F. Cascio, *Applied Psychology in Personnel Management*, fourth ed. (Englewood Cliffs, NJ, 1991); R. H. Hawk, *The Recruitment Function* (New York: American Management Association, 1967).

49. G. A. Cluff, *National Cost-Per-Hire Survey* (Raleigh, NC: Employment Management Association, 1990).

50. "High Tech Recruitment Solutions," *HR Magazine*, Feb. 1992, p. 54.

51. G. A. Cluff, *National Cost-Per-Hire Survey.*

52. Personnel Policies Forum, *Recruiting and Selection Procedures.*

53. J. A. Breaugh, *Recruitment: Science and Practice* (Boston: PWS-Kent, 1992); S. D. Maurer, V. Howe, and T. W. Lee, ''Organizational Recruiting as Marketing Management: An Interdisciplinary Study of Engineering Graduates,'' *Personnel Psychology,* 1992, 45, pp. 807–833.

54. J. P. Wanous, *Recruitment, Selection, Orientation, and Socialization of Newcomers,* second ed. (Reading, MA: Addison-Wesley, 1992).

55. S. L. Premack and J. P. Wanous, ''A Meta-Analysis of Realistic Job Preview Experiments''; *Journal of Applied Psychology,* 1985, 70, pp. 706–719.

56. J. P. Wanous, *Recruitment, Selection, Orientation, and Socialization of Newcomers.*

57. S. L. Premack and J. P. Wanous, ''A Meta-Analysis of Realistic Job Preview Experiments''; S. L. Rynes, ''Recruitment, Job Choice, and Post-Hire Decisions.''

58. J. A. Breaugh, *Recruitment: Science and Practice.*

59. J. S. Hirsch, ''Companies Try Bolder Tactics to Win MBAs,'' *Wall Street Journal,* Nov. 29, 1989, pp. B1.

60. S. Shellenbarger, ''More Job Seekers Put Family Needs First,'' *Wall Street Journal,* Nov. 15, 1991, p. B1.

61. K. G. Connolly and P. M. Connolly, *Competing for Employees: Proven Marketing Strategies for Keeping and Hiring Exceptional People* (Lexington, MA: D. C. Heath, 1991); S. D. Maurer et al., ''Organizational Recruiting as Marketing Management: An Interdisciplinary Study of Engineering Graduates.''

62. C. D. Fyock, *America's Work Force is Coming of Age* (Lexington, MA: D.C. Heath, 1990).

63. J. P. Wanous, *Organizational Entry.*

64. R. J. Vandenberg and V. Scarpello, ''The Matching Model: An Examination of the Processes Underlying Realistic Job Previews,'' *Journal of Applied Psychology,* 1990, 75 (1), pp. 60–67.

65. D. R. Ilgen, C. D. Fisher, and M. S. Taylor, ''Consequences of Individual Feedback on Behavior in Organizations,'' *Journal of Applied Psychology,* 1979, 64, pp. 349–371.

66. P. F. Wernimont, ''Recruitment Policies and Practices,'' in D. Yoder and H. G. Heneman, Jr. (eds.), *ASPA Handbook of Personnel and Industrial Relations* (Washington, DC: Bureau of National Affairs), 1979, pp. 4–85 to 4–115.

67. *Recruitment Advertising: Writing and Placing in the Print Media* (Wisconsin State Government: State Division of Personnel, June 1980).

68. A. M. Micolo, ''High-Tech Recruiting at Low Cost,'' *HR Magazine,* Aug. 1991, pp. 49–52.

69. R. H. Hawk, *The Recruitment Function* (New York: The American Management Association, 1967); W. F. Cascio, *Applied Psychology in Personnel Management,* fourth ed. (Englewood Cliffs, NJ: Prentice-Hall, 1991).

70. D. J. B. Mitchell, *Human Resource Management: An Economic Approach* (Boston: PWS-Kent, 1989).

71. S. L. Rynes, ''Recruitment, Job Choice, and Post-Hire Decisions,'' in M. D. Dunnette and L. M. Hough (eds.), *Handbook of Industrial and Organizational Psychology,* Vol. 2, second ed. (Palo Alto, CA: Consulting Psychologists Press, 1991), pp. 399–444; J.P. Wanous, *Organizational Entry.*

72. S. L. Rynes, ''Who's Selecting Whom? Effects of Selection Practices in Applicant Attitudes and Behaviors,'' in N. Schmitt, W. Borman, and Associates, *Personnel Selection in Organizations* (San Francisco: Jossey-Bass, 1993), pp. 240–276; S. L. Rynes, ''Recruitment, Job Choice, and Post-Hire Decisions''; S. L. Rynes, R. D. Bretz, and B. Gerhart, ''The Importance of Recruitment and Job Choice: A Different Way of Looking,'' *Personnel Psychology,* 1991, 44, pp.

487–521; M. S. Taylor and T. J. Bergmann, "Organizational Recruitment Activities and Applicant Reactions to Different Stages of the Recruiting Process," *Personnel Psychology,* 40, pp. 261–285.

73. J. Greenberg, "A Taxonomy of Organizational Justice Theories," *Academy of Management Review,* 1987, 12, pp. 9–22; D. E. Eskew, *Fairness In Recruitment: Applying a Framework of Organizational Justice to Recruitment Perceptions* (unpublished doctoral dissertation, Ohio State University, Columbus, Ohio, 1993).

74. S. L. Rynes and J. W. Boudreau, "College Recruiting in Large Organizations: Practice, Evaluation, and Research Implications"; G. H. Varma and J. W. Smither, "Selecting Colleges and Universities for On-Campus Recruiting," *Journal of Career Planning and Employment,* Spring 1990, pp. 34–40; P. F. Wernimont, "Recruitment Policies and Practices."

75. W. J. Kucker, "Marketing Your Company on Campus," *Journal of Career Planning and Employment,* Spring 1987, pp. 34–38.

76. AT&T, "Customer-Supplier Discussion Guide: 'AT&T Driving Quality on Campus' For Use by AT&T Campus Leader with Career Services Offices," July 1992.

77. M. Tynes, "How to Set Up A College Recruitment Program That Pays Off," *Recruiting and Hiring Handbook* (Waterford, CT: Prentice-Hall, 1989), pp. 14–1 to 14–12.

78. V. R. Lindquist, "The Northwestern Lindquist-Endicott Report," *The Placement Center of Northwestern University* (Evanston, IL: Northwestern University, 1991); L. P. Scheetz, *Recruiting Trends 1989–1990* (East Lansing, MI: Career Development and Placement Services, Michigan State University); Personnel Policies Forum, *Recruiting and Selection Procedures.*

79. J. W. Boudreau and S. L. Rynes, "Giving It the Old College Try," *Personnel Administrator,* Mar. 1987, pp. 78–85; S. L. Rynes and J. W. Boudreau, "College Recruiting in Large Organizations: Practice, Evaluation, and Research Implications."

80. J. C. Cook, "Preparing for Statistical Battles Under the Civil Rights Act," *HR Focus,* May 1992, pp. 12–13; G. P. Panaro, *Employment Law Manual* (Boston: Warren, Gorham and Lamont, 1990), pp. I–24 to I–26.

81. G. P. Panaro, *Employment Law Manual,* pp. I–16 to I–20.

82. J. L. Laabs, "Affirmative Outreach," *Personnel Journal,* 1991, 70, pp. 86–93; J. L. Laabs, "The Golden Arches Provide Golden Opportunities," *Personnel Journal,* 1991, 70, pp. 52–57; J. E. Rigdon, "PepsiCo's KFC Scouts for Blacks and Women for its Top Echelons," *Wall Street Journal,* Nov. 13, 1991, p. A1.

83. Bureau of National Affairs, *Fair Employment Practices* (Washington, D.C.: author, periodically updated), pp. 421:101–104.

84. Bureau of National Affairs, *Fair Employment Practices,* pp. 405:4027–4033; and 405:6847–6848.

85. R. M. Green and R. J. Reibstein, *Employer's Guide to Workplace Torts* (Washington, D.C.: Bureau of National Affairs, 1992, pp. 40–61, 200, 254–255.

86. A. G. Feliu, *Primer on Individual Employee Rights* (Washington, D.C.: Bureau of National Affairs, 1992), p. 270.

CHAPTER EIGHT

Internal Recruitment

The objective of the internal recruitment process is to identify and attract applicants from among individuals already holding jobs within the organization. The process followed in meeting this objective parallels the external recruitment process and is shown in Exhibit 8.1.

The first step is recruitment planning, which addresses both organizational and administrative issues. Organizational issues include types of internal labor markets and mobility patterns within these internal labor markets. Administrative issues include rules and procedures, requisitions, number and types of contacts, budgets, and the recruitment guide.

The second step is strategy development. Attention here is directed to where, when, and how to look for qualified internal applicants. Knowing where to look requires an understanding of career paths, seniority systems, and skills inventories. Knowing how to look requires an understanding of the advantages and disadvantages of open, closed, and dual systems of internal recruitment. Knowing when to look requires an understanding of lead time and time sequencing concerns.

The third step is searching for internal applicants. It consists of the communication message and medium for notification and description of the job vacancy. The message can be realistic, attractive, or targeted. The medium for delivering the message can be a formal job posting system or a more informal system.

The fourth step is evaluation of recruitment activities. This step includes consideration of the recruitment process, applicant reactions, and impact on HR outcomes. Specific attention needs to be focused on the fairness of the internal recruitment system in terms of its procedural and distributive justice.

The fifth step is the consideration of legal issues. Specific issues to be addressed include Revised Order No. 4, bona fide seniority systems, and the glass ceiling. All three of these issues deal with mechanisms for enhancing the identification and attraction of minorities and women for higher-level jobs within the organization.

RECRUITMENT PLANNING

Prior to identifying and attracting internal applicants to vacant jobs, attention must be directed to organizational and administrative issues that facilitate the effective matching of internal applicants with vacant jobs.

Organizational Issues

Just as the external labor market can be divided into segments or strata of workers believed to be desirable job applicants, so, too, can the internal labor market of an organization. This is often done inside organizations on an informal basis. For example, managers might talk about the talented pool of managerial trainees this year. As another example, people in the organization talk about their ''techies''

EXHIBIT 8.1   Internal Recruitment Process

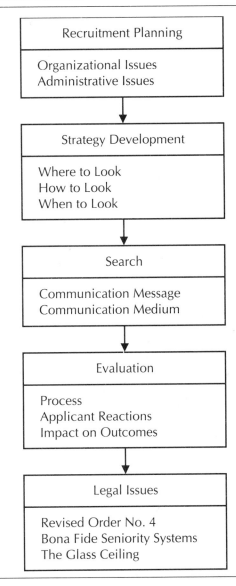

internal collection of employees with the technical skills needed to run the business.

At a more formal level, organizations must create a structured set of jobs for its employees and paths of mobility for them to follow as they advance in their careers. To do this, organizations create internal labor markets. Each internal labor market has two components—organizational and administrative. The organizational component deals with the hierarchical structure of jobs and the paths of mobility among them.[1] The administrative component (discussed later) contains the rules and procedures that govern internal labor mobility. Usually, an organization has several internal labor markets rather than just one.[2]

Internal labor markets are not only shaped by formal organizational and administrative components, but also by a set of norms or informal rules that bind the employee to the organization and the organization to the employee.[3] For example, the organization invests money in the employee through orientation, training, and rewards programs. If the organization dismisses the employee, the organization loses this investment. Similarly, the employee invests in learning organization-specific skills in order to work effectively for the organization. If the employee leaves the organization, the employee may not be able to use these skills in the marketplace. Consequently, internal labor markets order social relationships by explicitly and implicitly creating ties that bind organizations and employees together.

Types of Internal Labor Markets

Just as organizations may be characterized as having more than one external labor market, so, too, organizations may be characterized as having different types of internal labor markets.[4] *Task-based* internal labor markets are organized on the basis of tasks as defined in the job requirements matrix. Here, jobs are classified together due to the logical relationship between job descriptions. For example, the job of team leader, supervisor, manager, and executive all entail managerial responsibilities such as planning, organizing, directing, staffing, and controlling. Collectively, they are a task-based internal labor market known as management.

KSAO-based internal labor markets are organized by the KSAOs of the the job as defined in the job requirements matrix. Some jobs are classified together due to a common set of KSAOs. For example, a recruiter, compensation analyst, and trainer all share an understanding of the body of knowledge known as human resources. As a result, they are known as the human resource occupation, which comprises a KSAO-based internal labor market.

Mobility Patterns

Internal labor markets create and are influenced by paths of mobility in organizations.[5] Mobility patterns refer to the flow of human resources into, through, and out of the organization. Mobility into the organization is known as entry, upward mobility is known as promotion, downward mobility is known as demotion, lateral mobility is known as transfer, and exit from the organization is known as termination.

The hierarchy of jobs within an organization helps define the mobility patterns that employees can take. Mobility patterns can be followed using an organizational chart like the one shown in Exhibit 8.2. This exhibit depicts the partial organi-

EXHIBIT 8.2   Partial Organizational Structure for Human Resources

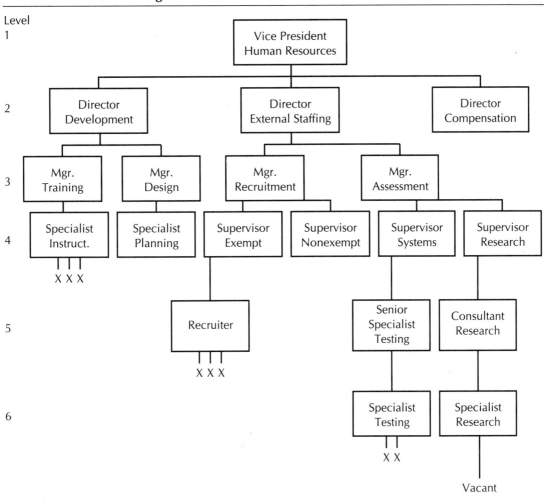

zational structure of a human resources group in an organization. Each box represents a job, and the jobs are listed by level within the organization. Each line depicts the subordinates reporting to a particular job. The lines thus depict one form of possible mobility, namely promotion within the functional areas of development, external staffing, and compensation. However, there are many other possible mobility paths for internal employees to follow. The best way to illustrate these paths is to describe possible paths that employees can take as they work their way up to the position of vice president of human resources from staff level positions.

In Exhibit 8.2, entry-level positions include those of testing specialist, research specialist, or recruiter. Some employees advance from these jobs to a supervisory level. Recruiters may directly advance to become supervisor of exempt or nonexempt recruitment. Because testing specialists and research specialists occupy lower-level jobs than the recruiter position, they may need to advance in their specialty areas—become senior testing specialists or research consultants—before taking on a supervisory position in systems or research. Alternatively, the testing and research specialists may become recruiters as their careers advance, and eventually they may supervise exempt or nonexempt recruitment rather than supervising systems or research.

At the supervisory level, many different mobility patterns are possible for internal employees as they advance to a managerial rank. For example, the supervisor of research may move directly up to become the manager of assessment, a position that includes responsibility for both research and systems. Alternatively, the supervisor of research may become supervisor of assessment for a period of time before advancing to become the manager of assessment. Or the supervisor of research may spend time as a supervisor of recruitment, or even as a specialist in planning, before ascending to a managerial position.

There are many alternative mobility paths from the position of manager to director and eventually to that of vice president. The manager of assessment may become director of staffing and then vice president of human resources. More likely, however, the employee is likely to need additional experience as director of compensation and director of development before becoming vice president. In most organizations today, employees need to have familiarity with many different facets of the business before advancing to the next level in the organization.

Administrative Issues

Not only must the structure of the internal labor market and mobility patterns be established as part of the planning process, but so, too, must administrative matters. Those administrative matters that must be included in the process are the rules and procedures of internal labor markets, requisitions, number and type of contracts, the budget, and the recruitment guide.

Rules and Procedures

The structure of the internal labor market shows the relationships among jobs, but it does not show the rules by which people move between jobs. Such rules are based on the operating efficiency of the organization and the needs of employees to determine who, what, when, where, and how movements take place.[6] Quite often, these rules are determined by the placement function in human resources, or by the terms of the collective bargaining agreement agreed to by the union. The rules themselves are usually KSAO-based, seniority-based, or both.

KSAO-Based Rules   An example of the organizational logic determining the rules that balance the needs of organizations and individuals is illustrated in Exhibit 8.3.[7] In this exhibit, three current employees (A, B, C) are moving into three vacant jobs (1, 2, 3). To move into a job, an employee has to take an aptitude test and there is a minimum qualification score that must be attained.

One KSAO-based rule that the organization could follow is a *vocational guidance* approach, where employees are placed according to their best talent. With this approach, each person is placed in the job for which he or she scored the highest. For example, employee B's highest test score was on the test for job one, so she is assigned to job 1. Although this approach may be desirable from the individual's point of view, it may not work well for the organization. For example, employee C is placed in job 2, where she does not meet the minimum qualification score. She received a score of 60, but the minimum score is 70.

Another KSAO-based rule that an organization may follow is a *pure selection* approach, where each job is filled with the most qualified person. In theory, this approach should maximize productivity as each job is filled with the person receiving the highest test score for that job. Unfortunately, this approach does not always work either. As shown in the exhibit, employee A received the highest score for all three jobs, but obviously, one person cannot hold three jobs at once. Thus, using this approach, two jobs are not filled.

Given the data presented in the exhibit, the most realistic approach is a *cut-and-fit* strategy where each job is filled by a person who has at least the minimum qualifications needed to perform the job. By assigning employee A to job 1, employee B to job 2, and employee C to job 3, all three jobs are filled adequately. More often than not, organizations must settle for a cut-and-fit approach to ensure

EXHIBIT 8.3   Internal Labor Market: KSAO-Based Rules Concerning Job Assignments

	Job		
Test Scores	**1**	**2**	**3**
Employee A	100	90	95
Employee B	80	70	65
Employee C	50	60	55
Minimum Qualification Score	90	70	50
Assignment Rule			
Vocational guidance	B	C	A
Pure selection	A	A	A
Cut and fit	A	B	C

Source: W. F. Cascio, *Applied Psychology in Personnel Management*, 4th edition, 1991, McGraw-Hill, Inc. Reprinted with permission of McGraw-Hill.

that its positions are staffed adequately. Operational decision rules are formed to ensure this staffing pattern for internal recruitment.

Seniority-Based Rules   Another example of a rule that allocates people to jobs in an internal labor market is a seniority clause. One example of a seniority clause from a labor contact is shown in Exhibit 8.4.

As can be seen, in the system in Exhibit 8.4, seniority is the primary determinant in assigning personnel to jobs. Section 10.4 (A) shows that divisional vacancies are to be filled strictly on the basis of seniority. Section 10.4 (B)(1) shows that "dependability" and "work performance" are also to be considered in filling departmental vacancies.

Seniority clauses usually spell out how seniority is to be determined, when it is to be used, and how it is to be used. Sections 10.1 and 10.2 in the system in Exhibit 8.4 show how seniority is to be measured in this organization. Sections 10.3 and 10.4 show when seniority is to be used. Note that different seniority measures are used to make different decisions. For example, under 10.3, seniority within one's present job classification is used to rank preferences for vacation dates. What this means is that an employee with a short employment record with the organization (as assessed by date of hire) may receive a preferred date over an employee with a long employment record if the former employee has been in the current job classification longer than the latter employee. If this is indeed the case, the former employee will have greater seniority under section 10.3.

Sections 10.5, 10.6, and 10.7 show how seniority is to be used. As can be seen, the ground rules governing when an employee can use seniority rights are detailed in Section 10.5. Sections 10.6 and 10.7 show the role that labor and management play in determining seniority.

Requisitions

A requisition or authorization to fill a position by higher-level management is essential to the internal recruitment process. Without a formal requisition, it is far too easy for managers to make promises or "cut deals" with employees that are contrary to organizational objectives. For example, managers may promote their employees into new job titles that have not been authorized by top management. In doing so, they may create perceptions of unfairness among those with similar backgrounds who were not promoted. This action thus runs contrary to the organizational goal of fair human resource systems. Formal requisitions thus should always be used in internal recruitment just as they are in external recruitment.

Number and Types of Contacts

As with external recruitment, the number of contacts to be made can be forecast using yield ratios. The types of contacts that need to be made are determined by the job requirements matrix and job rewards matrix. An additional consideration

---

EXHIBIT 8.4   Internal Labor Market: Seniority-Based Rules from Seniority Provision of a Labor Contract

---

ARTICLE 10
SENIORITY

10.1   New hires shall have no seniority during their probationary period of employment, but after completion of their probationary period, their seniority date shall be the date of hire which was used to compute their probationary period.

10.2   An employee who is unable to work because of a service connected disability shall accumulate seniority during this period of sickness or disability not to exceed two (2) years' duration. During this period of sickness or disability should circumstances warrant, the City may require a formal hearing to determine the employee's ability to perform the duties of his classification.

10.3   The determination of preferences for the purpose of scheduling vacations shall be based upon classification seniority within the operating unit.

10.4   Classification seniority rights may be exercised for filling vacancies (i.e., workweek, shift and transfers) within that classification as follows:

(A)   Divisional Vacancies

Vacancies within a division shall be filled on the basis of classification seniority from the original date of hire.

(B)   Departmental Vacancies

(1)   Vacancies within a department that are not filled at the divisional level shall be filled on the basis of an applicant's dependability and work performance.

(2)   Provided dependability and work performance factors are equal, classification seniority from the original date of hire, shall determine which applicant is given the vacancy in question.

10.5   An employee may exercise his classification seniority rights no more than once within a ninety (90) day period unless a new employee is hired.

10.6   The City will provide the Union with a seniority list of all members of the bargaining unit upon request. Seniority lists shall contain the name, job classification, division and date of classification entry of all members of the bargaining unit. The City shall meet with the Union to review the seniority list whenever necessary to correct any errors.

10.7   The classification seniority of employees in classifications which are merged by the Civil Service Commission shall be determined as provided herein. Where an employee has prior seniority in any of the merged classifications, the employee's new classification seniority shall be a combination of the total time spent in each of the merged classifications.

Collective Bargaining Contract Between The City of Columbus and American Federation of State, County and Municipal Employees, Ohio Council 8, Local 1632, April 1, 1993–March 31, 1996.

to be dealt with is the fact that internal and external recruitment efforts need to be coordinated and synchronized via the organization's staffing philosophy.

If this coordination is not done, disastrous results can occur. For example, if independent searches are conducted internally and externally, then two people may be hired for one open vacancy. If only an external recruitment search is conducted, the morale of existing employees may be reduced when they feel that they have been bypassed for a promotion. If only an internal recruitment search is conducted, the person hired may not be as qualified as someone from the external market. Because of these possibilities, internal *and* external professionals must work together with the line manager to coordinate efforts before the search for candidates begins.

In order to coordinate activities, two steps should be taken. First, internal staffing specialist positions should be designated to ensure that internal candidates are considered in the recruitment process. External staffing specialists are called recruiters; internal staffing specialists are often known as placement or classification professionals to acknowledge the fact that they are responsible for placing or classifying existing employees rather than bringing in or recruiting employees from outside the organization.

Second, policies need to be created that specify the number and types of candidates sought internally and the number and types of candidates sought externally. For example, at Honeywell's Systems and Research Center in Bloomington, Minnesota, a management team meets regularly as a part of the planning and development process to make these determinations.[8]

Budget

An organization's internal recruitment budgeting process should also closely mirror the budgeting process that occurs with external recruitment. The cost per hire may, however, differ between internal and external recruitment. The fact that internal recruitment targets candidates already working for the organization does not mean that the cost per hire is necessarily less than external recruitment. Sometimes internal recruitment can be more costly than external recruitment because some of the methods involved in internal recruitment can be quite costly. For example, when internal candidates are considered for the job but not hired, they need to be counseled on what to do to further develop their careers to become competitive for the position the next time it is vacant. When a candidate is rejected with external recruiting, a simple and less costly rejection letter usually suffices.

Recruitment Guide

As with external recruitment, internal recruitment activities involve the development of a recruitment guide, a formal document that details the process to be followed to attract applicants to a vacant job. Included in the plan are details such as the time, money, and staff activities required to fill the job, as well as the steps to be taken. An example of an internal recruitment guide is shown in Exhibit 8.5.

EXHIBIT 8.5   Internal Recruitment Guide

Position Reassignments into New Claims Processing Center

Goal: Transfer all qualified medical claims processors and examiners from one company subsidiary to the newly developed claims processing center. Terminate those who are not well qualified for the new positions and whose existing positions are being eliminated.

Assumptions: That all employees have been notified that their existing positions in company subsidiary ABC are being eliminated and they will be eligible to apply for positions in the new claims processing center.

Hiring responsibility: Manager of Claims Processing and Manager of Claims Examining.

Other resources: Entire human resource department staff.

Time frames:

Positions posted internally on April 2, 1993
Employees may apply until April 16, 1993
Interviews will be scheduled/coordinated during week of April 19, 1993
Interviews will occur during the week of April 26, 1993
Selections made and communicated by last week in May
Total number of available positions: 60

Positions available and corresponding qualification summaries:

6 claims supervisors—4-year degree with 3 years of claims experience, including 1 year of supervisory experience.

14 claims data entry operators—6 months data entry experience. Knowledge of medical terminology helpful.

8 hospital claims examiners—12 months claims data entry/processing experience. Knowledge of medical terminology necessary.

8 physician claims examiners—12 months claims data entry/processing experience. Knowledge of medical terminology necessary.

8 dental claims examiners—12 months claims data entry/processing experience and 6 months dental claims examining experience. Knowledge of dental terminology necessary.

8 mental health claims examiners—12 months claims data entry/processing experience and 6 months mental health claims experience. Knowledge of medical and mental health terminology necessary.
8 substance abuse claims examiners—12 months claims data entry/processing experience and 6 months substance abuse experience. Knowledge of medical terminology necessary.

Transfer request guidelines: Internal candidates must submit internal transfer requests and an accompanying cover page listing all positions for which they are applying, in order of preference.

Internal candidates may apply for no more than five positions.

Transfer requests must be complete and be signed by the employee and the employee's supervisor.
Candidate qualification review process: Transfer requests from internal candidates will be reviewed on a daily basis. Those not qualified for any positions for which they applied will be notified by phone that day, due to the large volume of requests.

(continued)

EXHIBIT 8.5 Continued

All transfer requests and accompanying cover pages will be filed by the position for which they applied. If internal candidates applied for more than one position, their transfer packet will be copied so that one copy is in each position folder.

Once all candidate qualifications have been received and reviewed, each candidate's transfer packet will be copied and transmitted to the managers for review and interview selection. Due to the large number of candidates, managers will be required only to interview those candidates with the best qualifications for the available positions. Managers will notify human resources with the candidates with whom they would like interviews scheduled. Whenever possible, the manager will interview the candidate during one meeting for all of the positions applied and qualified for.

Selection guidelines: Whenever possible, the best-qualified candidates shall be selected for the available positions.

The corporation has committed to attempting to place all employees whose positions are being eliminated.

Managers reserve the right to not select employees currently on disciplinary probationary periods.

Employees should be slotted in a position with a salary grade comparable to their current salary grade. Employees' salaries shall not be reduced due to the involuntary nature of the job reassignment.

Notification of nonselection: Candidates not selected for a particular position will be notified by electronic message.

Selection notifications: Candidates selected for a position will be notified in person by the human resource staff, and will be given a confirmation letter specifying starting date, position, reporting relationship, and salary.

STRATEGY DEVELOPMENT

After organizational and administrative issues have been covered in the planning phase of internal recruitment, an organization must develop a strategy to locate viable internal job applicants. It must consider where to look, how to look, and when to look.

Where to Look

Knowing where to look inside organizations requires a knowledge of career paths, seniority systems, and skills inventories.

Career Paths

A career path consists of employees' movements within the internal labor market structure. Career paths are determined by many factors, including workforce, organizational, labor union, and labor market characteristics.[9] Career paths are of two types—traditional and innovative.[10] Both types of career paths determine who is eligible for a new job in the organization.

Traditional Career Paths   Examples of traditional career paths are shown in Exhibit 8.6. As can be seen, the emphasis is primarily on upward mobility in the organization. Due to the upward nature of traditional career paths, they are often labeled promotion ladders. This label implies that each job is a step toward the top of the organization. Upward promotions in an organization are often seen by employees as prizes because of their desirable characteristics. They receive these prizes as they compete against one another for available vacancies.[11] For example, a promotion may lead to a higher rate of pay, and a transfer may result in a move to a better work location. Research has shown that these competitions may be hotly contested as opportunities for upward advancement are limited in most organizations.[12]

An exception to the primarily upward mobility in the promotion ladders in Exhibit 8.6 shows the lateral moves that sometimes occur for the staff member who has both generalist and specialist experiences as well as corporate and division experience. This staff member is considered more well-rounded and better able to work within the total organization. Experience as a specialist helps the person to be familiar with technical issues that arise. Experience as a generalist gives the employee a breadth of knowledge about many matters in the staff function. Corporate experience provides a policy and planning perspective, while division experience provides greater insight on day-to-day operational matters.

Traditional career paths make it very easy from an administrative vantage point to identify where to look for applicants in the organization. One looks at the next level down (for promotion) in the organizational hierarchy and over (for transfer). Although such a system is straightforward to administer, it is not very flexible and may inhibit the matching of the best person for the job. For example, the best person for the job may be at two job levels down and in another division from the vacant job. It is very difficult to locate such a person under a traditional career path.

Innovative Career Paths   Examples of innovate career paths are shown in Exhibit 8.7. The emphasis here is no longer simply on upward mobility. Instead, movement in the organization may be in any direction, including up, down, and from side to side. Employee movement is emphasized to ensure continuous learning by employees such that each can make the greatest contribution to the organization. This is in direct contrast to the traditional promotion ladder, where the goal is for each person to achieve a position with ever-higher status.

Parallel tracks allow for employees to specialize in technical work or management work and advance within either. Historically, technical specialists had to shift away from technical to managerial work if they wanted to continue to receive higher-status job titles and pay. In other words, being a technical specialist was a dead-end job. Under a parallel track system, both job titles and salaries of technical specialists are elevated to be commensurate with their managerial counterparts.

With a lateral track system, there may be no upward mobility at all. The individual's greatest contribution to the organization may be to stay at a certain level

EXHIBIT 8.6   Traditional Career Paths

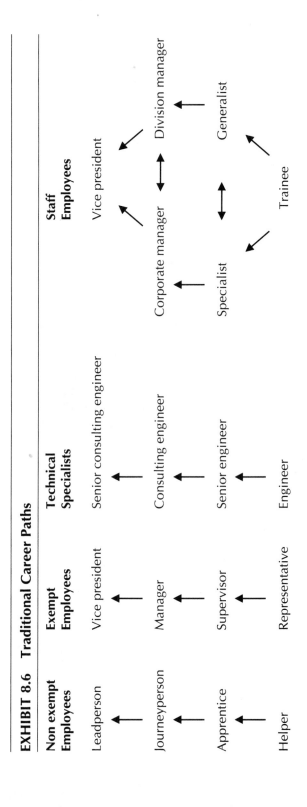

EXHIBIT 8.7   Innovative Career Paths

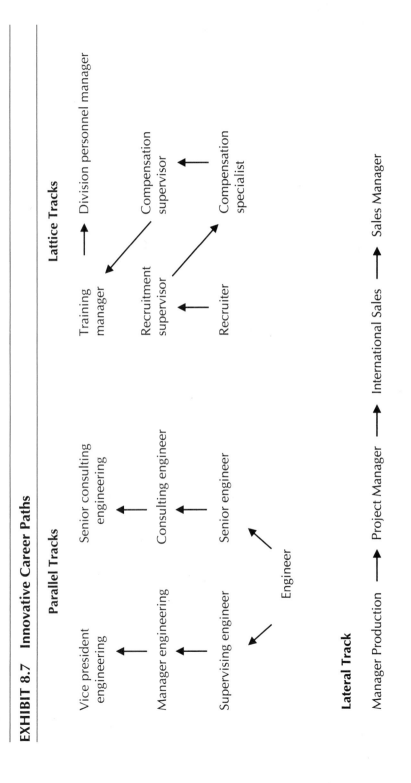

of the organization for an extended period of time while serving in a variety of capacities as shown in Exhibit 8.7.

A lattice mobility path has upward, lateral, and even downward movement. For example, a recruiter may be promoted to a recruitment supervisor position, but in order to continue to contribute to the organization, the person may need to take a lateral step to become knowledgeable about all the technical details in compensation. After mastering these details, the person may then become a supervisor again, this time in the compensation area rather than recruitment. From a previous company, the person may have experience in training and be ready to take the next move to training manager without training experience internal to the organization. Finally, the person may take a lateral move to manage all the human resource functions (recruitment, compensation, training) in a division as a division personnel manager.

The downside to innovative career paths, such as those discussed, is that it is very difficult to administer the system. Nice and neat categories of where to look do not exist to the same degree as with traditional career paths. On the positive side, however, talented inside candidates, who may not have been identified within a traditional system, are identified because the system is flexible enough to do so.

When upward mobility is limited in an organization, as with many organizations using innovative career paths, special steps need to be taken to ensure that work remains meaningful to employees. If steps are not taken, the organization with limited promotional opportunities risks turnover of good employees. Examples of steps to make work more meaningful include the following:[13]

1. *Alternative Reward Systems.* Rather than basing pay increases on promotions, pay increases can be based upon knowledge and skill acquisition and contribution to the organization as a team member and individual.

2. *Team Building.* Greater challenge and autonomy in the workplace can be created by having employees work in teams where they are responsible for all aspects of work involved in providing a service or product, including self-management.

3. *Counseling.* Workshops, self-directed workbooks, and individual advising can be used by organizations to ensure that employees have a well-reasoned plan for movement in the organization.

4. *Alternative Employment.* Arrangements can be made for employee leaves of absence, sabbaticals, and consulting assignments to ensure that they remain challenged and acquire new knowledge and skills.

Career Path Policies   Due to technology, the changing nature of products and services, and other factors, it is sometimes difficult to specify promotion and transfer opportunities in advance.[14] It is, however, possible to develop a sound policy regarding the procedures to be followed once there is an opening. A good promotion policy statement is needed for both traditional and innovative career paths and has the following characteristics:[15]

1. The intent of the policy is clearly communicated.
2. The policy is consistent with the philosophy and values of top management.
3. The scope of the policy, such as coverage by geographic region, employee groups, and so forth, is clearly articulated.
4. Employees' responsibilities and opportunities for development are clearly spelled out.
5. Supervisors' responsibilities for employee development are clearly spelled out.
6. Procedures are clearly described, such as how employees will be notified of openings, time deadlines, data to be supplied by the employee, how requirements and qualifications will be communicated, how the selection process will work, and the extension of job offers.
7. Rules regarding compensation and advancement are included.
8. Rules regarding benefits and benefit changes as they relate to advancement are included.

A well articulated and executed promotion and transfer policy is likely to be seen by employees as being fair. A poorly developed or nonexistent policy is likely to lead to employee claims of favoritism and discrimination.

Seniority Systems
In many organizations, both union and nonunion, seniority or time with the organization or job is applied as a standard to determine who will be eligible for advancement or transfer in the internal labor market. Sometimes seniority alone is used in making this determination, and at other times, seniority is used in conjunction with KSAOs. Usually a job posting and bidding system is used to facilitate advancements through seniority.

Union versus Nonunion Companies   In most unionized firms, heavy reliance is placed on seniority over other KSAOs for advancement.[16] Seniority is used because unions believe that more senior employees should be rewarded for their loyalty to the organization with first choice on more desirable jobs. Unions are also skeptical of the objectivity with which KSAOs can be measured. Seniority is hence viewed as a more quantitative and more objective measure with which to make advancement decisions.

   In policy, nonunion organizations claim to put less weight on seniority than other factors in making advancement decisions. In practice, however, at least one study shows that, regardless of the wording in policy statements, heavy emphasis is still placed on seniority in nonunion settings.[17]

Heavy reliance on seniority in both union and nonunion firms may be problematic. Recent research has shown that seniority is a good predictor of job performance during an individual's first 12 months or so on the job.[18] However, seniority has not proved to be a particularly good predictor of performance in the long run.[19] Hence, seniority should perhaps be used as a sign of immediate rather than long-term performance in the successive jobs. Unfortunately, most organizations appear to use it as a signal of long-term performance as well.

Types of Systems   Since there is a range of the degree to which seniority is used in advancement decisions, it logically follows that there are different types of seniority systems. In general, these systems break down into three categories:[20] (1) *pure seniority,* (2) *sufficient ability seniority,* and (3) *relatively equal seniority.* Under a pure seniority system, the person who has the most seniority advances before others. Under a sufficient ability seniority system, the senior person must be advanced first if minimally qualified, even if less senior employees are better suited to the job. Qualifications are determined on the basis of KSAOs. Under a relatively equal seniority system, the senior person must be advanced when that person's KSAOs are relatively equal to that of other candidates. If the KSAOs are not relatively equal, then a more qualified junior employee can bypass a less qualified senior employee for advancement.

As one moves from a pure to relatively equal seniority system, the system becomes more complex to administer because not only must seniority be calculated to make decisions, but KSAOs must be measured as well.

Job Posting and Bidding   The actual process whereby employees make their desires known under a seniority system involves job posting and bidding. The organization posts the job for all to see, and bids are taken from those who are interested in advancing. An example of a bidding form is shown in Exhibit 8.8. The value or worth of each bid depends upon one's seniority and/or other KSAOs. A good posting and bidding system posts the job for a long enough period of time for all qualified employees to see it, clearly articulates the qualifications needed to bid, and provides timely feedback to bidders.

Skills Inventories

KSAOs that are used in making advancement decisions are stored in skills inventories. These inventories consist of manual files or computer files for each employee. Examples of computer file screens for employees are shown in Exhibit 8.9. Unfortunately, many skills inventories are plagued by problems that make their usefulness suspect. One such problem is the very careful and tedious record keeping required to keep them up to date and useful. Qualified candidates may be bypassed if current files are not maintained. Another problem is that too much information is sometimes recorded. Variables having little relevance to advancement decisions are recorded, making them redundant with other files (e.g., pay-

---

EXHIBIT 8.8   Example of Bidding Form

INTERNAL APPLICATION FORM COVER SHEET

To apply for a posted position, interested employees should:

1. Look at the job posting notebook(s) or postings posted on the bulletin boards and choose the job or jobs that you are qualified for and interested in applying for. (Check the Qualifications section of the posting.) Make note of the deadline for applying for this position which is indicated on the posting.

2. Complete one Internal Application Form to apply for a position or positions. This form acts as a resume/application form. Obtain your direct supervisor's signature before turning the form into human resources.

3. Indicate below the priority of the jobs for which you would like to be given consideration.

   (Priority—1 = first choice, 2 = second choice, 3 = third choice)

Priority Job Title

_____   _____

_____   _____

_____   _____

_____   _____

_____   _____

4. Attach this cover sheet to the UHC Internal Application Form and turn both in to Karen in human resources by the application deadline appearing on the job posting.

5. Sign and date below:

_____   _____
Employee Signature   Date

Source: Reprinted with permission from United HealthCare Corporation and Physicians Health Plan of Ohio, Inc., Columbus, Ohio.

---

roll). Managers are often overwhelmed by the sheer volume in files and, as a result, may be resistant to using skills inventories.

A final problem that must be confronted in keeping skills inventories is that files must be user-friendly. Files must be understood and accepted by system users. To do so requires the participation of users in deciding which variables are to be retained. A user-friendly data base should also have the following attributes:[21]

1. simplicity of format for data collection
2. easy method for updating basic information on a scheduled basis
3. reasonable and efficient techniques for extracting information from the data base
4. provisions for varied formats for output
5. capability for statistical analysis using relational data bases
6. confidentiality of information
7. representativeness of data provided
8. accuracy of data by audit and verification procedures
9. simplicity in querying data bank
10. inclusive but not unwieldy detail
11. integration with other human resource files

EXHIBIT 8.9   Sample Elements in Skills Inventory

Screen 1:   Current employee data

Name:
SS #:
Department:
Position:
Supervisor:
Date in position:
Date of hire:

Screen 2:   Education data

	School Attended	**Degree**	**Major**	**GPA**	**Year(s)**
High school:					
Undergrad:					
Graduate:					
Doctorate:					

Additional course work:
Certifications/licenses:
Additional training:
Company training:

Additional training recommended:

(continued)

EXHIBIT 8.9   Continued

Screen 3:   Company employment data

	Title	Date in Job	Performance Ratings/Dates
Present position:			
Previous positions:			

Positions in company qualified for:

Screen 4:   Previous employment data

	Company	Title	From	To	Reference Quality
Prev. Empl.					
Prev. Empl.					
Prev. Empl.					
Prev. Empl.					

Screen 5:   Express interests/goals

Areas of company:
Positions:
Additional training/education:

How to Look

Once it is understood where in the organization qualified personnel are likely to be found, there are three major methods that can be used to decide how to look for them: closed, open, and dual.[22]

Closed Internal Recruitment System

Under a closed internal recruitment system, employees are not made aware of job vacancies. The only people made aware of promotion or transfer opportunities are those who oversee placement in the human resource department, line managers with vacancies, and contacted employees. The way a vacancy is typically filled under a closed system is shown in Exhibit 8.10.

A closed system is very efficient. There are only a few steps to follow, and the time and cost involved in employing it are minimal. However, a closed system is only as good as the files showing candidates' KSAOs. If inaccurate or out-of-date files are kept, qualified candidates may be overlooked.

Open Internal Recruitment System

Under an open internal recruitment system, employees are made aware of job vacancies. Usually this is accomplished by a job posting and bidding system. The

EXHIBIT 8.10   Closed Internal Recruitment System

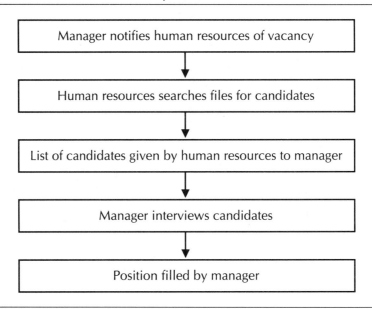

typical steps followed in filling a vacancy under an open internal recruitment system are shown in Exhibit 8.11.

An open system gives employees a chance to measure their qualifications against those required for advancement. It helps minimize the possibility of supervisors selecting only their favorite employees for promotion or transfer. Hidden talent is often uncovered.

An open system may, however, create unwanted competition among employees for limited advancement opportunities. It is a very lengthy and time-consuming process to screen all candidates and provide them with feedback. Employee morale may be decreased among those who are not advanced.

Dual System of Internal Recruitment

Under a dual system, both open and closed steps are followed at the same time. Jobs are posted, and the human resources department conducts a search outside the job posting system.

A dual system has three advantages: a thorough search is conducted, people have equal opportunity to apply for postings; and hidden talent is uncovered. The major disadvantages with a dual system are that it entails a very lengthy, time-consuming, and costly process.

EXHIBIT 8.11   Open Internal Recruitment System

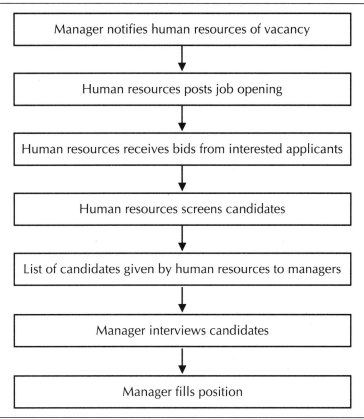

Criteria for Choice of System

In an ideal world, with unlimited resources, one would chose a dual system of internal recruitment. Resource constraints often make this choice impossible, so organizations must choose between open and closed systems. There are several criteria that need to be considered thoroughly before selecting an internal recruitment system.

Cost   A closed system is the least expensive in terms of search costs. However, it may lead to high legal costs if minorities and women do not have equal access to jobs. An open system is more costly; a dual system costs the most.

Time   Many managers want a person immediately when they have a vacancy; a closed system offers the quickest response.

Yield   An open system is more likely than a closed system to identify more candidates, and hidden talent is less likely to be overlooked.

Required KSAOs   Some openings may require a very narrow and specialized KSAO set. A closed system may be able to quickly identify these people. An open system may be very cumbersome when only a select few meet the minimum qualifications needed to perform the job.

Availability of Labor   An open system may motivate migration of labor from jobs that are critical and difficult to fill. If so, then employees may create vacancies in critical areas, which in turn may create new recruitment problems.

Labor Contract   A labor agreement or contract is a legally binding agreement. Whatever system is specified within it, it must be followed.

Fairness Perceptions   An open system, where rules and regulations are known, enhances perception of procedural justice.

When to Look

A final strategic consideration an organization must make is when to look for internal candidates. As with external recruitment, consideration involves calculation of lead time and time sequence concerns.

Lead Time Concerns
A major difference between internal and external recruitment is that internal recruitment not only fills vacancies, but creates them as well. Each time a vacancy is filled with an internal candidate, a new vacancy is created in the spot vacated by the internal candidate.

As a result of this difference, it is incumbent upon the organization to do human resource planning along with internal recruitment. This involves elements of succession planning (see Chapter 6). Such planning is essential for effective internal recruitment.[23]

Time Sequence Concerns
As previously noted, it is essential that internal and external recruitment activities be coordinated. This is especially true with the timing and sequencing of events that must be carefully laid out for both recruitment and placement personnel. Many organizations start with internal recruitment followed by external recruitment to fill a vacancy. Issues that need to be addressed include how long the internal search will take place, whether external recruitment can be done concurrently with internal recruitment, and who will be selected if both an internal and external candidate are identified with relatively equal KSAOs.

As with the external recruitment process, time lapse data should be kept to ensure the completion of the search in a timely manner. These data are valuable in helping to estimate how long it will take to fill similar vacancies from internal sources in the future. These data are also valuable in pointing out areas in which internal recruitment needs to be improved. For example, the data may indicate that some divisions are slower than others in releasing candidate lists to managers for interviews.

SEARCHING

Once the planning and strategy development phases are conducted, then it is time to conduct the search. As with external recruitment, the search for internal recruits is activated with a requisition. Once the requisition has been approved, then the message and medium must be developed to communicate the vacancy to applicants.

Communications

Message

As with external recruitment, the message to be communicated with internal recruitment can be realistic, can be targeted, or can offer an inducement. A realistic message, which uses a technique like the realistic job preview (RJP), could be employed. However, since it is being used for applicants who already likely have reasonably accurate information about the job, its effectiveness may be limited.[24]

Targeted messages along with inducements are likely to attract experienced internal employees. Targeted messages about the desirability of a position and the actual rewards should come directly from the job rewards matrix. Clearly the information in the job rewards matrix needs to be communicated by the hiring manager who hopes to catch an experienced employee, rather than offers of elaborate promises that the manager may not be able to keep.

Medium

The actual method or medium used to communicate job openings internally is usually a job posting. Other more informal methods are used as well.

Job Posting   A job posting is very similar to the advertisement used in external recruitment. It spells out the duties and requirements of the job and shows how applicants can apply. Its content should be based upon the job requirements matrix. An example of a detailed job posting is presented in Exhibit 8.12. An example of the procedures to be followed for a job posting system is shown in Exhibit 8.13.

An example of a well-developed job posting system comes from National SemiConductors in Santa Clara, California.[25] At National SemiConductors, it used to be easier to find a job through external recruitment than through internal recruitment! In response to this state of affairs, a new user-friendly job posting system was developed and put on the computer for access by internal employees. Not only does the new system contain traditional job posting data for each vacant position, it shows the user how the job fits into established career paths and what training, education, and experience are needed to become eligible for the job. Hence, the new system communicates information about jobs and also helps to further career development planning. The system is being used currently for exempt jobs only, but plans are to use it for hourly and salaried nonexempt jobs as well.

Not all job posting systems are this advanced, and even advanced job posting systems may have some problems in administration. Examples of difficulties include situations where employees believe that someone has been selected before

---

EXHIBIT 8.12   Job Posting Form

ANNOUNCEMENT NO.: 92-25   OPENING DATE 12-14-92   CLOSING DATE: APPLICATION MUST BE POSTMARKED BY:

POSITION: Loan Specialist (Commercial)
              GS-1165-9/11 (1 position)

SALARY: GS-9 = $26,798–$34,835 per annum
              GS-11 = $32,423–$42,152 per annum

LOCATION: Small Business Administration, 477 Michigan Ave., Room 515
              Detroit, MI

AREA OF CONSIDERATION: Regionwide

COMPETITIVE STATUS REQUIRED: _____ Yes   __X__ No

DUTIES: Incumbent performs loan processing activities such as interviewing and counseling of loan applicants, screening loan applications for eligibility, and processing applications. Makes professional analysis of loan applications and accompanying financial statements to assess the risk of granting the loan and the assurance of repayment. Determines eligibility and most beneficial type of assistance. Prescribes corrective financial or management changes to be accomplished by applicant as a prerequisite to loan approval. Prepares report of loan analysis including pro forma balance sheet, with recommendation for approval or decline. Analyzes requests for modification to loan authorizations on undisbursed loans and prepares report, with recommendation for appropriate actions. Screens applications on basis of eligibility, completeness and credit sufficiency. Counsels small business firms on SBA programs and requirements, financial needs, purchasing, profit margin, etc. Explains financing program requirements to financial institutions.

(continued)

EXHIBIT 8.12   Continued

OTHER PERTINENT FACTS: This position has promotion potential to the GS-12 level. Applicants who are considered under SBA merit promotion plan procedures are subject to time-in-grade requirements. Applicants who meet the time-in-grade requirements within 45 days of the closing date will be considered. No written test is required. PAYMENT OF RELOCATION EXPENSES IS NOT AUTHORIZED.

QUALIFICATIONS: Applicant must possess one year of experience demonstrating competence in commercial loan making. Experience may have been gained in such work as reviewing and passing upon applications for commercial loans; servicing a loan portfolio of a bank or other loan association; or performing financial analysis of commercial concerns for investment purposes. Experience must be of a scope and quality sufficient to give him/her the ability to handle technical assignments commensurate with the duties of the position.

SUBSTITUTION OF EDUCATION FOR EXPERIENCE: Two full academic years of graduate level education or master's or equivalent graduate degree or LL.B. or J.D. may be substituted for experience at the GS-9 level. Three full academic years of graduate level education or Ph.D. or equivalent doctoral degree may be substituted for experience at the GS-11 level. Education may be substituted provided major study was finance, business administration, economics, accounting, mathematics, banking and credit, law, real estate operations, statistics, or other fields related to the position.

KNOWLEDGE, SKILLS, AND ABILITIES (KSA'S) USED IN THE RATING PROCESS:

To aid us in more closely matching your work experience and/or education with the actual job requirements, provide a narrative self-assessment as a supplement to your SF-171, concisely describing work you have performed which addresses the knowledge, skills and abilities described below. Include relevant paid or volunteer public or private sector experience and the dates. Do not send position descriptions, manuscripts, personal endorsements or other unsolicited materials. Please address each KSA in the following order:

1) Skill in analyzing business-related financial statements such as statements of assets and liabilities, statements of earning for the purpose of determining repayment risks.

2) Knowledge of laws and customs governing negotiable instruments, transfer of title to chattels and realty, contracts and assignment of collateral.

3) Knowledge of economic-related factors and trends and their impact on business.

4) Knowledge of business financial structures and management practices.

APPLICANTS WILL BE EVALUATED ON THE FOLLOWING CRITERIA:

1. Experience Documented on Application

2. Narrative Self-assessment of KSA's Listed Above

3. Education (Merit promotion procedures only)

4. Training (within last 5 years) (Merit promotion procedures only)

5. Awards (within last 5 years) (Merit promotion procedures only)

6. Annual Performance Appraisal (Merit promotion procedures only)

(continued)

EXHIBIT 8.12   Continued

APPLICATION REQUIREMENTS

Applicants should submit the following materials:

1. Standard Form 171—Application for Federal Employment

2. Narrative response to knowledge, skills and abilities listed above

3. Copy of last appraisal under an annual performance rating system (only for consideration under merit promotion procedures)

4. Standard Form 15—Application for 10-Point Veteran Preference, if applicable (only for consideration under competitive examining procedures)

Candidates will NOT routinely be contacted to provide missing information concerning their experience, education, veteran's preference, citizenship, etc. Application materials will be retained in the merit promotion file or competitive examining case file and will not be returned to applicant.

The evaluation procedures used to evaluate applications depend upon whether or not the applicant has competitive status. Applicants who have competitive status (current Federal employees serving on career or career-conditional appointments, or former employees eligible for reinstatement to the federal service) may be considered under both government-wide competitive examining procedures and SBA merit promotion plan procedures. Applicants with competitive status who wish to be considered under both procedures MUST submit two complete applications. When only one application is received from a status applicant, it will be considered under SBA merit promotion procedures only, unless a clear and unequivocal statement is received from the applicant that he or she wishes to be considered under competitive examining procedures only.

COMPLETED APPLICATION MATERIALS SHOULD BE SUBMITTED TO:

U.S. Small Business Administration
230 S. Dearborn Street, Room 580
Chicago, IL 60604
ATTN: Kay Yount

For information call (312) 353-4695.

IMPORTANT INFORMATION—READ CAREFULLY.

The use of U.S. Government postage-paid envelopes for the filing of job applications is a violation of the Office of Personnel Management and Postal Service regulations. Penalties include fines of up to $300 and/or disciplinary action under SBA regulations.

The Defense Authorization Act of 1986 requires all males born after 12/31/59 to register under the Military Selective Service Act. Failure to register may prohibit appointment in this agency.

Any individual eligible for consideration under special hiring authorities, e.g., handicapped, and VRA, etc. may apply for this position. Please indicate on SF 171 if you are in one of these categories.

SBA—AN EQUAL OPPORTUNITY EMPLOYER

SBA FORM 534 (1-90)

Source: U.S. Small Business Administration, Chicago, 1993.

EXHIBIT 8.13 Recruiting and Selection Procedures—Job Posting Procedure for Small North-Central Hospital

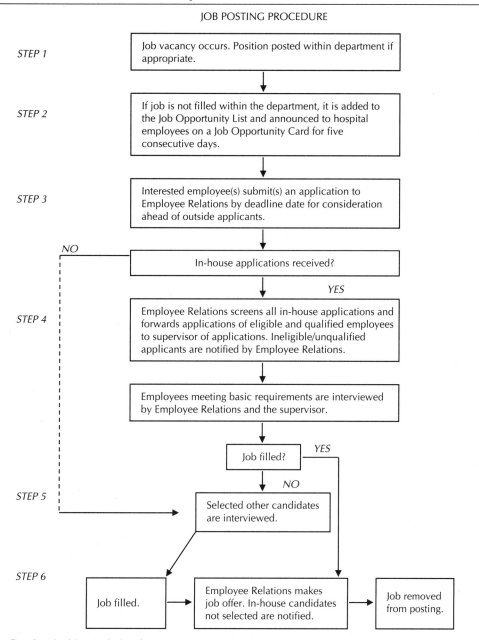

JOB POSTING PROCEDURE

STEP 1 — Job vacancy occurs. Position posted within department if appropriate.

STEP 2 — If job is not filled within the department, it is added to the Job Opportunity List and announced to hospital employees on a Job Opportunity Card for five consecutive days.

STEP 3 — Interested employee(s) submit(s) an application to Employee Relations by deadline date for consideration ahead of outside applicants.

In-house applications received? — NO / YES

STEP 4 — Employee Relations screens all in-house applications and forwards applications of eligible and qualified employees to supervisor of applications. Ineligible/unqualified applicants are notified by Employee Relations.

Employees meeting basic requirements are interviewed by Employee Relations and the supervisor.

Job filled? — YES / NO

STEP 5 — Selected other candidates are interviewed.

STEP 6 — Job filled. → Employee Relations makes job offer. In-house candidates not selected are notified. → Job removed from posting.

Source: Reprinted with permission from *Recruiting and Selection Procedures,* Personnel Policies Forum Survey No. 146, p. 34 (May 1988). Copyright 1988 by the Bureau of National Affairs, Inc. (800-372-1033).

the job was posted (a "bagged" job), cumbersome systems where managers and human resources personnel are overwhelmed with resumes of unqualified candidates, and criticisms that the human resources department is not doing an effective job of screening candidates for positions.[26]

Some of these problems again point to the critical importance of the job requirements matrix. A good job posting system will clearly define the requisite KSAOs needed to perform the job. By having a job requirements matrix, employees, human resources staff, and managers can do a more effective and efficient job of screening.

Another important issue with posting systems is feedback. Not only do employees need to know whether they receive the job or not, but those who do not receive the job need to be made aware *why* they did not. Providing this feedback serves two purposes. First, it makes job posting a part of the career development system of the organization. Second, it invites future bidding on postings by candidates. If employees are not given feedback, they may be less likely to bid again for a job because they feel that their bidding attempts are futile.

An empirical study showed the characteristics of job posting systems that led to high satisfaction by users.[27] Key characteristics include the adequacy of job descriptions, the adequacy of job notification procedures, the treatment received during the interview, the helpfulness of counseling, and the fairness of the job posting system. These characteristics should be treated as requirements of a good posting policy.

As indicated, job posting can be done traditionally by physically posting job openings in a convenient location. Such an approach, however, can be very slow and inefficient, and create a large amount of paperwork. A faster and more efficient way to post jobs is to put them on personal computers, which also gives employees 24-hour-a-day access to job postings. Phones can be used when not all employees have access to personal computers.[28]

Informal Systems

Along with formal job posting systems, informal systems exist in organizations where organizational members communicate to one another about job vacancies to be filled internally. The problem with "word of mouth," the "grapevine," and "hall talk" is that it can be a highly selective, inaccurate, and haphazard method of communicating information. It is selective because, by accident or design, not all employees hear about vacant jobs. Talented personnel, including minorities and women, may thus be overlooked. It is inaccurate because it relies on second- or third-hand information, and important details, such as actual job requirements and job rewards, are omitted or distorted as they are passed from person to person. Informal methods are also haphazard in that there is no regular communication channel specifying set times for communicating job information. As a result of these problems, informal systems are not to be encouraged.

EVALUATION

As with external recruitment, it is essential to evaluate the effectiveness of the internal recruitment process. Just because people are already employed by an organization does not mean that it is easier to be successful at identifying and attracting candidates to job vacancies by internal as compared with external recruitment. The federal government, for example, employs millions of employees, so it is no easy task to identify qualified internal candidates. Moreover, if an employee is identified and eventually selected, this creates a new vacancy to be filled. Employees may become very comfortable in their positions and be reluctant to leave for other openings. Likewise, supervisors may be reluctant to let good performers go to other jobs in the organization. As a result, it can be just as much or more of a challenge to attract internal as compared with external candidates. Given these considerations, internal recruitment should not be assumed to be effective. Instead, an evaluation of the process, applicant reactions, and organizational outcomes needs to be conducted.

Process

Yield ratios, time lapse data, and cost figures used in external recruitment are also relevant to the internal recruitment process. Unfortunately, unlike the external recruitment process, where these data are routinely reported in surveys so that an employer can gauge the results of its process against others in their industry, the reporting of benchmark data is not a common practice with internal recruitment. As a result, organizations need to monitor these measures over time in their own organizations so that the data can be compared to historical standards to assess effectiveness.

Applicant Reactions

A glaring omission in the research literature is a lack of attention paid to studying the reactions of applicants to the internal recruitment process. This lapse stands in stark contrast to the quantity of research conducted on reactions to the external recruitment process. Two areas of the internal recruitment process that have been studied, fairness and job posting, are considered in turn.

Fairness

Given limited opportunities for promotion and transfer, issues of fairness often arise over promotion decisions within an organization. Issues of fairness can be broken down into the categories of distributive and procedural justice.[29]

Distributive Justice   This concept refers to how fair the employee perceives the actual decision (e.g., promote or not promote). This particular aspect of fairness is very salient today because there are a large number of baby boomers competing for the few positions at the top of organizational hierarchies. At the same time, many organizations are eliminating middle management positions.

Procedural Justice   This concept refers to how fair the employee perceives the process (e.g., policies and procedures) to be that leads to the promotion or transfer decision.[30] Reviews of the evidence suggest that procedures may be nearly as great a source of dissatisfaction to employees as are outcomes.[31] In some organizations, dissatisfaction arises as a result of the fact that there is no formal policy regarding promotion and transfer opportunities. In other organizations, there may be a formal policy, but it may not be followed. In yet other organizations, it may be who you know, rather than what you know, that serves as the criterion that determines advancement. Finally, in some organizations there is outright discrimination against women and minorities. All of these examples are violations of procedural justice and likely to be seen as unfair.

The concepts of procedural and distributive justice indicate that organizations should routinely survey the reactions of organizational members to determine the effectiveness of the internal recruitment process. This has been done for one aspect of internal recruitment, namely job posting, and will now be described.

Job Posting

The results of a study that examines application reactions to job posting is shown in Exhibit 8.14. The first step in this study was to generate a list of questionnaire items showing characteristics of a job posting system. As can be seen, these items closely mirror the concepts of procedural and distributive justice. Next, the questionnaire items were passed out to employees to gather their reactions. These reactions were tallied and summarized as shown in Exhibit 8.14 according to the percentage of employees who had "favorable," "neutral," or "unfavorable" reactions to each of the characteristics of the job posting system listed in the items. It can be seen that applicants had diverse reactions to the system. Though not shown, applicants' reactions to characteristics of the job posting system were also correlated with overall satisfaction with the system. The three largest correlations with satisfaction involved the fairness of the job posting system, effect on job mobility, and treatment during the interview.

This is a good illustration of how applicant reactions can be measured for job posting. The same steps can be followed to evaluate applicant reactions to other steps in the internal recruitment process.

Impact on Outcomes

The impact of the internal recruitment process upon outcomes should be evaluated using the standardized measures of organizational outcomes discussed in the pre-

---

EXHIBIT 8.14   Evaluation of a Job Posting System

		Applicants' Response (Percent)		
Item	**N**	**Favorable**	**Neutral**	**Unfavorable**
Adequacy of job description	382	39.7	35.9	24.3
Adequacy of job notification procedures	390	42.0	36.9	21.0
Difficulty of completing application	197	87.3	9.1	3.5
Quality of handbook	155	76.8	18.7	4.5
Treatment during interview	152	61.8	18.4	19.7
How well reasons for nonacceptance were explained	87	23.0	17.2	59.8
How well job requirements match those in job description	79	60.8	24.1	15.2
How well worker met job demands	76	94.8	3.9	1.3
Helpfulness of counseling	52	28.8	26.9	44.2
Effect on job mobility	362	65.2	24.9	9.9
Fairness of job posting system	367	35.8	28.0	34.6
Satisfaction with job posting system	378	28.8	26.9	36.2
Was handbook read?	403	38.6	—	61.4
Did applicant receive a job offer?	173	44.5	—	55.5
Was counseling sought?	403	12.5	—	87.5
Was applicant considered for position?	183	82.5	—	17.5
Average number of times interviewed	153	Mean = 1.83		

Source: L. W. Kleinman and K. J. Clark, "Users' Satisfaction With Job Posting," *HR Magazine,* 1984, 29(9) pp. 104–110. Reprinted with the permission of HR Magazine (formerly Personnel Administrator) published by the Society for Human Resource Management, Alexandria, VA.

vious chapter. Unfortunately, this appears to be done very infrequently by organizations, and there is little published research available to draw upon. The available research indicates that promotional opportunities are related to satisfaction, performance, and turnover. The strength and direction of these relationships, however, is subject to dispute.[32] Moreover, almost no research has been conducted on the effectiveness of various stages in the internal recruitment process. It remains for individual organizations to ascertain, for example, whether better performing internal applicants are identified through seniority clauses, formal career paths, skills inventories, or other members of the organization. Also, individual organizations need to assess the impact of innovative career paths on organizational outcomes such as satisfaction and performance.

In order to make these assessments, organizations should track the levels of performance, satisfaction, and turnover associated with various components of the internal staffing process. Also, as new procedures, such as innovative career paths, are implemented, evaluation research needs to be conducted. To do so, organizational outcomes should be assessed before and after the new procedures to see if organizational outcomes improved. If possible, the procedure should be pilot tested to ensure its effectiveness. When a pilot test is run on a segment of the workforce, the results can be compared with those of a comparable group of employees operating under similar circumstances to determine if any changes are really due to the new procedure rather than other events taking place at the same time.

LEGAL ISSUES

The mobility of people within the organization, particularly upward, has long been a matter of EEO/AA concern. The workings of the internal labor market rely heavily on internal recruitment activities. As with external recruitment, internal recruitment activities can operate in exclusionary ways, resulting in unequal promotion opportunities, rates, and results for certain groups of employees, particularly women and minorities. Revised Order No. 4 specifically addresses internal recruitment as a part of the federal contractor's AAP. Seniority systems are likewise subject to legal scrutiny, particularly regarding the determination of what constitutes a bona fide system under the law. More recently, promotion systems have been studied as they relate to the "glass ceiling" effect and the kinds of barriers that have been found to stifle the rise of minorities and women upward in organizations.

Revised Order No. 4

Revised Order No. 4 (see Appendix B) treats internal recruitment as a part of an AAP in some detail, since an AAP addresses both seniority systems and promotion. Regarding seniority systems, the order requires the organization to make an in-depth analysis of several facets of HR programs that may lead to underutilization. One such facet is seniority practices and seniority provisions in labor contracts and applies to all seniority-based internal staffing systems, regardless of whether or not they are governed by the provisions of a labor contract. Unfortunately, the order is silent on what constitutes an in-depth examination of a seniority system.

For promotion systems specifically, the order is explicit in its suggestions for the organization. Most of these pertain to recruitment, though some also spill over into selection. According to the order:

The contractor should ensure that minority and female employees are given equal opportunity for promotion. Suggestions for achieving this result include:

1. Post or otherwise announce promotion opportunities;
2. Make an inventory of current minority and female employees to determine academic, skill and experience level of individual employees;
3. Initiate necessary remedial job training and workstudy programs;
4. Develop and implement formal employee evaluation programs;
5. Make certain ''worker specifications'' have been validated on job performance related criteria (neither minority nor female employees should be required to possess higher qualifications than those of the lowest qualified incumbent);
6. When apparently qualified minority or female employees are passed over for upgrading, require supervisory personnel to submit written justification;
7. Establish formal career counseling programs to include attitude development, education aid, job rotation, buddy systems and similar programs;
8. Review seniority practices and seniority clauses in union contracts to ensure such practices or clauses are nondiscriminatory and do not have a discriminatory effect.

As can be seen, the order contains a broad range of suggestions for reviewing and improving promotion systems. In terms of recruitment itself, the order appears to favor developing KSAO-based information about employees as well as an open promotion system characterized by job posting and cautious use of seniority as a basis for governing upward mobility. The order itself, however, says little else about seniority systems and their permissible characteristics.

Bona Fide Seniority Systems

The law (see Chapter 3) explicitly permits the use of ''bona fide'' seniority systems, as long as they are not the result of an intention to discriminate. This position confronts the organization with a serious dilemma. Past discrimination in external staffing may have resulted in a predominantly white male workforce. A change to a nondiscriminatory external staffing system may increase the presence of women and minorities within an organization, but they will have less seniority there than the white males. If eligibility for promotion is based on seniority and/or if seniority is an actual factor considered in promotion decisions, then those with less seniority will have a lower incidence of promotion. Thus, the seniority system will have an adverse impact on women and minorities, even though there is no current intention to discriminate. Is such a seniority system a bona fide one?

Two points are relevant here. First, the law never defines the term seniority system. Generally, however, any practice that uses length of employment as a basis for making decisions, such as promotion decisions, is interpreted as a seniority system. Thus, seniority systems can and do occur outside the context of a collective bargaining agreement.[33]

Second, current interpretation is that, in the absence of a discriminatory intent, virtually any seniority system is likely to be bona fide, even if it causes adverse impact.[34] This interpretation creates an incentive for the organization not to change its current seniority-based practices or systems. Other pressures, such as Revised Order No. 4 or a voluntary AAP, create an incentive to change in order to eliminate the occurrence of adverse impact in promotion. The organization thus must carefully consider exactly what its posture will be toward seniority practices and systems within the context of its overall AAP.

The Glass Ceiling

The glass ceiling is a term that was coined to characterize strong but invisible barriers to promotion in an organization. Those barriers include both organizational and administrative characteristics of the internal labor market, as well as attitudes such as occur through sex-role stereotyping. While originally applied to barriers for women, the term now encompasses minorities as well. The term has also been adapted to apply to aspects of the overall diversity programs of an organization.[35]

Evidence demonstrating the existence of a glass ceiling is overwhelming. Labor market and other types of surveys convincingly show a statistical domination of white males in managerial occupations, and that domination becomes even greater at higher levels of the managerial ranks. For example, while the overall labor force is about 46% female, 41% of managers are female and only 3% of top executives are female.[36] There is also an occupational crowding of women and minorities in staff functions such as advertising, human resources, and legal services; white males dominate the line positions and are usually found in production and sales.[37] White males thus dominate the managerial jobs, at all levels, that most directly effect the organization's "bottom line." Concentration statistics such as these suggest the strong possibility that it is the organization's own internal staffing practices, in conjunction with entry-level external staffing practices, that are responsible for creating and maintaining such demographic imbalances in the workforce.

The Glass Ceiling Initiative

In 1991, the Department of Labor reported the results of the Glass Ceiling Initiative, which was a very thorough study of the promotion practices of nine anonymous Fortune 500 companies.[38] The study found evidence of the glass ceiling for minorities and women in all companies, with minorities having a lower promotional plateau or ceiling than women. Staffing practices in the companies were characterized by (a) a lack of corporate ownership for EEO/AA principles, as well as a lack of accountability for EEO/AA results by managers; (b) placement patterns indicating occupational crowding of women and minorities in staff functions, even at the highest levels; (c) lack of monitoring of performance appraisal and compensation systems by management; and (d) inadequate recording and monitoring of EEO/AA activities.

Three major barriers to upward mobility were also suggested in the study. The first of these was recruitment activities involving recruitment sources that had exclusionary effects on women and minorities—for example, practices based upon word-of-mouth, employee referral, and executive search sources. The other two barriers were lack of opportunity to participate in meaningful corporate training and credential-building development experiences, and a lack of understanding that EEO/AA is a part of every manager's job, rather than just a job for the head of EEO/AA.

The DOL continued to study these companies and published follow-up results. These results indicate that the companies had undertaken changes to remove the promotion barriers, and that those changes were showing some positive results. The study also reported, however, that these changes required considerable time and effort, suggesting that shattering the glass ceiling will be a long and painstaking process.[39]

To help encourage organizations to start the change process, and to provide role models for this, The DOL, through the OFCCP, has implemented the EVE (Exemplary Voluntary Efforts) Awards program for federal contractors. The awards are presented annually to contractors who have undertaken exemplary programs to enhance workforce diversity and shatter the glass ceiling. Brief descriptions of the programs for some of the 13 award winners in 1992 are shown in Exhibit 8.15.

Internal Recruitment Implications

Barriers to upward mobility can be addressed and removed, at least in part, through internal recruitment activities. Internal recruitment planning needs to involve the design and operation of internal labor markets that facilitate the identification and flows of people to jobs throughout the organization. This may very well conflict with seniority-based practices or seniority systems, both of which are likely to be well entrenched. Organizations simply have to make hard and clear choices about the role(s) that seniority will play in promotion systems.

In terms of recruitment strategy, where to look for employees looms as a major factor in potential change. The organization must increase its scanning capabilities and horizons to identify candidates to promote throughout the organization. In particular, this requires looking across functions for candidates, rather than merely promoting within an area (from sales to sales manager to district sales manager, for example). Candidates should thus be recruited through both traditional and innovative career paths.

EXHIBIT 8.15   Examples of Award Winning Programs to Increase Workforce Diversity and Shatter the Glass Ceiling

---

SOME OF THE 1992 EXEMPLARY VOLUNTARY EFFORT (EVE) AWARD WINNERS

Wisconsin Gas Company—Milwaukee, Wis.

Recruits, trains and promotes women into nontraditional occupations; through its Mentoring Program, teams senior employees with less experienced women and minorities to prepare them for advancement; identifies talented women and minorities for development for future managerial and executive positions; hires and trains up to 20 minority students each year for trade positions; and participates in "Set-Up," a year-round achievement, regular attendance and good behavior reward program.

McNeil Pharmaceutical Company—Dorado, Puerto Rico

Trains women and minorities for managerial and executive careers; creates employment opportunities for individuals with disabilities; and assists students in two local schools, through counseling and a company sponsored library.

Motorola, Inc.—Schaumburg, Ill.

Trains women and minorities for executive positions; trains employees through Motorola University courses ranging from basic skills to advanced engineering; and the Minority Scholarship/Internship Investment Program recruits women, minorities, and individuals with disabilities.

Saturn Corporation—Spring Hill, Tenn.

Recruits women and minorities for all levels of its workforce, resulting in a significant increase in the number of minorities and women at the new facility; and encourages workforce diversity through its video, "The New South 89," depicting women and minorities working for Saturn.

Society Corporation—Cleveland, Ohio

Recruits, trains and promotes women and minorities for professional, managerial, and upper-level executive positions; and its Corporate Minority Program develops skills of talented minorities.

Source: U.S. Department of Labor, *News*, 9/17/92.

Recruitment sources have to be more open and accessible to far-ranging sets of candidates. Informal, word-of-mouth, and "good old boy" sources do not suffice. Job posting and other recruitment strategies that encourage openness of vacancy notification and candidate application will become necessary.

The timing of internal recruitment has to be carefully integrated with overall business plans. Promotions may have to be speeded up or slowed down in order to fit the business plan. With business downturns, for example, care must be taken to ensure that the upward mobility of women and minorities is not adversely thwarted.

Finally, it should be recognized, and acted upon, that recruitment activities do not suffice to bring about the desired changes. They must be supported by a myriad of other HR activities, especially in the compensation, and training and development, areas. In addition, the organization has to make its managers responsible and accountable for the desired demographics in promotion results.

SUMMARY

The steps involved in the internal recruitment process closely parallel those in the external recruitment process. These steps include planning, strategy development, and communication of the message. The search is conducted inside rather than outside the organization. Where both internal and external searches are conducted, they need to be coordinated with one another.

Identifying the applicant population in the internal recruitment process requires a knowledge of internal labor markets, promotion and transfer policies, seniority systems, and skills inventories of employees. All of these topics relate the operational rules that govern the movement of employees within the internal labor market structure. Some internal labor market structures are formed on the basis of tasks, and others are formed on the basis of KSAOs.

Without the reward of promotions, organizations must place greater reliance on alternative reward systems, team building, counseling, lateral moves, and alternative employment arrangements. Seniority systems place different weights on seniority as a factor in hiring, depending upon whether the system is one of pure seniority, sufficient ability seniority, or relatively equal seniority. Employees' skills inventories need to contain relevant information and be user-friendly to be effectively used by managers.

In deciding how to recruit applicants, organizations must consider the trade-offs between open and closed internal recruitment systems. Increasingly, organizations are shifting from closed to open systems. Which system is most advantageous to an organization depends upon its position relative to factors of cost, time, yield, required skills, availability of labor, the labor contract, and fairness perceptions.

The communication of internal vacancies is usually done via job posting. In order for job postings to be seen as effective by employees, they need to be based on the job requirements matrix, spell out fair procedures, and provide adequate time for a bid. The organization needs to provide counseling and feedback.

Evaluation of internal recruitment is an essential, yet often overlooked, procedure. The process itself can be evaluated using yield ratios, time lapse data, and cost figures. Applicant reactions can be monitored by questionnaire items designed to assess the fairness of each phase of the internal recruitment process. The impact of the internal recruitment process can be assessed using standardized measures of performance, satisfaction, and turnover.

Internal recruitment activities have been the object of close legal scrutiny. Beginning with Revised Order No. 4, which contains specific provisions about seniority-based practices and labor contract provisions, as well as several suggestions regarding promotion systems, the relevant laws permit ''bona fide'' seniority systems, as long as they are not intentionally used to discriminate. Seniority systems may have the effect of impeding promotions for women and minorities because these groups have not had the opportunity to accumulate an equivalent amount of seniority to that of white males. The glass ceiling refers to invisible barriers to upward advancement, especially to the top levels, for minorities and women. Studies of promotion systems indicate that internal recruitment practices contribute to this barrier. Changes are now being experimented with to open up internal recruitment as a portion of an overall strategy to shatter the glass ceiling.

DISCUSSION QUESTIONS

1. Traditional career paths strictly emphasize upward mobility within an organization. How does mobility differ in organizations with innovative career paths? List three innovative career paths discussed in this chapter, describing how mobility occurs in each.

2. A sound policy regarding promotion is important. List the characteristics necessary for an effective promotion policy.

3. Compare and contrast a closed internal recruitment system with an open internal recruitment system.

4. What information should be included in the targeted internal communication message?

5. Applicant reactions and perceptions of the fairness of the internal recruitment process are an important consideration when evaluating the effectiveness of the process. Describe the two categories of fairness that are discussed in this chapter.

6. Describe the three major barriers to upward mobility for women and minorities that were suggested in the Glass Ceiling Initiative, conducted by the Department of Labor.

7. How can organizations change where they are looking for internal applicants in an effort to remove barriers to upward mobility for women and minorities?

ENDNOTES

1. R. D. Connor and R. L. Fjersted, ''Internal Personnel Maintenance,'' in D. Yoder and H. G. Heneman, Jr. (eds.), *ASPA Handbook of Personnel and Industrial Relations* (Washington, DC: Bureau of National Affairs), pp. 4–203 to 4–234; P. M. Osterman, ''Internal Labor Markets in a Changing Environment: Models and Evidence,'' in D. Lewin, O. S. Mitchell, and P. Sherer

(eds.), *Research Frontiers in Industrial Relations and Human Resources* (Madison, WI: Industrial Relations Research Association), 1992, pp. 273–308.

2. P. D. Sherer, "Labor Market Balkanization Revisited: Variation in Internal Labor Markets and Employment Arrangements," *IRRA Proceedings*, 1990, Washington, DC, pp. 458–466.

3. M. L. Wachter and R. D. Wright, "The Economics of Internal Labor Markets," *Industrial Relations*, 1990, 29 (2), pp. 240–262.

4. P. Doeringer and M. Piore, *Internal Labor markets and Manpower Analysis* (Lexington: Heath, 1971); R. P. Althauser and A. L. Kalleberg, "Firms, Occupations, and the Structure of Labor Markets," in I. Berg (ed.), *Sociological Perspectives on Labor Markets* (New York: Academic Press, 1981), pp. 119–149.

5. J. C. Anderson, G. T. Milkovich, and A. Tsui, "A Model of Intra-Organizational Mobility," *Academy of Management Review*, 1981, 6 (4), pp. 529–538.

6. M. D. Dunnette, *Personnel Selection and Placement* (Belmont, CA: Wadsworth, 1966); E. E. Ghiselli and C. W. Brown, *Personnel and Industrial Psychology*, second ed. (New York: McGraw Hill, 1955).

7. W. F. Cascio, *Applied Psychology in Personnel Management*, fourth ed. (Englewood Cliffs, NJ: Prentice-Hall, 1991).

8. "The Need for Hiring: A Second Look," *Employee Relations and Human Resources Bulletin* (Waterford, CT: National Foreman's Institute), Feb. 21, 1993, Report No. 1778, Section 1, p. 7.

9. J. C. Anderson, G. T. Milkovich, and A. Tsui, "A Model of Intra-Organizational Mobility"; J. N. Baron, "Organizational Perspectives on Stratification," in R. F. Turner and J. F. Short, Jr. (eds.), *Annual Review of Sociology* (Palo Alto, CA: Annual Reviews, 1985), pp. 37–69.

10. C. Harkin, "Boost Morale to Gain Productivity: Lattice Rather Than Ladder Career Paths Keep Morale High in Flatter Organizations," *HR Magazine*, Feb. 1993, pp. 46–49; G. Fuchsberg, "Parallel Lines: Companies Create New Ways to Promote Employees Without Making Them Bosses," *Wall Street Journal*, Apr. 21, 1993, pp. R4–R7; R. W. Goddard, "Lateral Moves Enhance Careers," *HR Magazine*, Dec. 1990, pp. 69–74; S. Shellenberger, "Allowing Fast Trackers to Stay in One Place," *Wall Street Journal*, Jan. 7, 1992, p. B1; B. Nussbaum, "A Career Survival Kit," *Business Week*, Oct. 7, 1991, pp. 98–99.

11. J. E. Rosenbaum, "Tournament Mobility: Career Patterns in a Corporation," *Administrative Science Quarterly*, 1979, 24, pp. 220–241.

12. W. T. Markham, S. L. Harlan, and E. J. Hackett, "Promotion Opportunity in Organizations: Causes and Consequences," in K. M. Rowland and G. R. Ferris (eds.), *Research in Personnel and Human Resources Management*, 1987, 5, pp. 223–287.

13. "Farewell, Fast Track: Promotions and Raises are Scarcer: So What Will Energize Managers?" *Business Week*, Dec. 10, 1990, pp. 192–198.

14. J. N. Baron, A. Davis-Blake, and W. T. Bielby, "The Structure of Opportunity: How Promotion Ladders Vary Within and Among Organizations," *Administrative Science Quarterly*, 1986, 31, pp. 248–273; M. Granovetter, "Labor Mobility, Internal Markets, and Job Matching: A Comparison of the Sociological and Economic Approaches," in R. V. Robinson (ed.), *Research in Social Stratification and Mobility* (Greenwich, CT: JAI Press, 1986), pp. 3–39.

15. F. K. Foulkes, *Personnel Policies in Large Nonunion Companies* (Englewood Cliffs, NJ: Prentice-Hall, 1980); R. D. Connor and R. L. Fjersted, "Internal Personnel Maintenance," 1979.

16. R. D. Connor and R. L. Fjersted, "Internal Personnel Maintenance," 1979.

17. F. K. Foulkes, *Personnel Policies in Large Nonunion Companies*, 1980.

18. F. L. Schmidt, J. E. Hunter, A. N. Outerbridge, and S. Goff, "Joint Relations of Experience and Ability with Job Performance: Test of Three Hypotheses," *Journal of Applied Psychology*, 1988, 73, pp. 46–57.

19. M. E. Gordon and W. A. Johnson, ''Seniority: A Review of Its Legal and Scientific Standing,'' *Personnel Psychology,* 1982, 35, pp. 255–280.

20. R. R. Cerbone and J. Walsh, ''Management Judgment vs. Seniority-Grist for the Arbitration Mill,'' *Employee Law Journal,* 1988, 14 (3), pp. 429–437.

21. R. D. Connor and R. L. Fjersted, ''Internal Personnel Maintenance,'' 1979.

22. L. E. Albright, ''Staffing Policies and Strategies,'' in D. Yoder and H. G. Heneman, Jr. (eds.), *ASPA Handbook of Personnel and Industrial Relations* (Washington, DC: Bureau of National Affairs, 1979); pp. 4–1 to 4–34; F. K. Foulkes, *Personnel Policies in Large Nonunion Companies,* 1980.

23. C. Borwick, ''Integrating Succession Planning and Employment: A Necessary Step,'' *EMA Journal,* 1992, 7 (4), pp. 24–29.

24. R. J. Vandenberg and V. Scarpello, ''The Matching Model: An Examination of the Processes Underlying Realistic Job Previews,'' *Journal of Applied Psychology,* 1990, 75 (1), pp. 60–67.

25. M. Moravec, ''Effective Job Posting Fills Dual Needs,'' *HR Magazine,* Sept. 1990, pp. 76–80.

26. F. K. Foulkes, *Personnel Policies in Large Nonunion Companies,* 1980.

27. L. W. Kleinman and K. J. Clark, ''Users' Satisfaction with Job Posting,'' *Personnel Administrator,* 1984, 29 (9), pp. 104–110.

28. W. C. DeLone, ''Telephone Job Posting Cuts Costs,'' *Personnel Journal,* Apr. 1993, pp. 115–118.

29. J. Greenberg, ''A Taxonomy of Organizational Justice Theories,'' *Academy of Management Review,* 1987, 12, pp. 9–22.

30. R. Folger and J. Greenberg, ''Procedural Justice: An Interpretive Analysis of Personnel Systems,'' in K. M. Rowland and G. R. Ferris (eds.), *Research in Personnel and Human Resources Management,* 1985, 3 (Greenwich, CT: JAI Press, pp. 141–183.

31. F. K. Foulkes, *Personnel Policies in Large Non Union Companies* (Englewood Cliffs, NJ: Prentice-Hall, 1985); M. London and S. A. Stumpf, *Managing Careers* (Reading, MA: Addison Wesley, 1982); W. T. Markham, S. L. Harlan, and E. J. Hackett, ''Promotion Opportunities in Organizations: Causes and Consequences''; S. A. Stumpf and M. London, ''Management Promotions: Individual and Organizational Factors Influencing the Decision Process,'' *Academy of Management Review,* 1981, 6 (4), pp. 539–549.

32. W. T. Markham, S. L. Harlan, and E. J. Hackett, ''Promotional Opportunities in Organizations: Causes and Consequences,'' 1987.

33. Bureau of National Affairs, *Fair Employment Practices* (Washington, D.C.: author, periodically updated), pp. 421:161–166.

34. Bureau of National Affairs, *Fair Employment Practices,* pp. 421:161–166.

35. Bureau of Business Practice, *Workplace Diversity: Shattering the Glass Ceiling* (Waterford, CT: author, 1993); B. Rosen and K. Lovelace, ''Piecing Together the Diversity Puzzle,'' *HR Magazine,* 1991, 36 (9), pp. 78–84; B. Rosen and S. Rynes, ''Diversity Management is a Culture Change, Not Just Training,'' Commerce Clearing House Survey, May 20, 1993.

36. A. T. Segal and W. Zellner, ''Corporate Women,'' *Business Week,* June 8, 1992, pp. 74–78; S. Harlan, ''Women Face Barriers in Top Management'' (SUNY-Albany, NY: Center for Women in Government, 1992).

37. A. T. Segal and W. Zellner, ''Corporate Women,'' pp. 74–78.

38. U.S. Department of Labor, *Labor Department Report on the Glass Ceiling Initiative* (Washington, D.C.: author, 1991).

39. U.S. Department of Labor, *Pipelines of Progress* (Washington, D.C.: author, 1992).

STAFFING ORGANIZATIONS MODEL

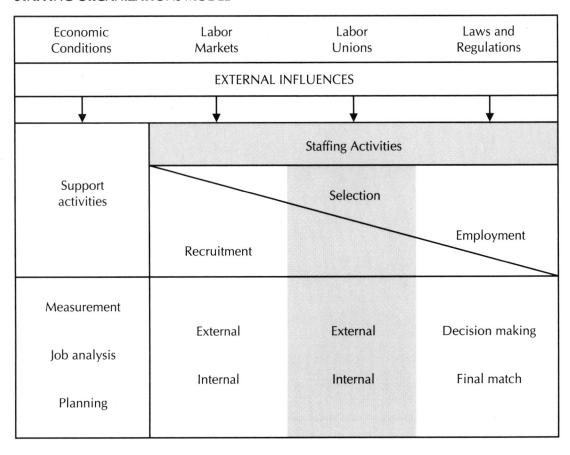

Economic Conditions	Labor Markets	Labor Unions	Laws and Regulations
EXTERNAL INFLUENCES			

Staffing Activities

Support activities		Selection	Employment
	Recruitment		
Measurement	External	External	Decision making
Job analysis			
	Internal	Internal	Final match
Planning			

PART FOUR

Staffing Activities: Selection

CHAPTER NINE

External Selection

Preliminary Issues
    The Logic of Prediction
    The Nature of Predictors
    Development of the Selection Plan
    Selection Sequence

Initial Assessment Methods
    Application Blanks
    Biographical Data
    Reference Reports
    Resumes and Cover Letters
    Initial Interview
    Handwriting Analysis
    Genetic Screening
    Literacy Testing
    Integrity Testing
    Choice of Initial Assessment Methods

Substantive Assessment Methods
    Personality Tests
    Ability Tests
    Performance Tests and Work Samples
    Interest, Values, and Preference Inventories
    Achievement History Questionnaires
    Structured Interview
    Clinical Assessments
    Drug Testing
    Physical Health Tests
    Team Assessment
    Choice of Substantive Assessment Methods

Discretionary Assessment Methods

Collection of Assessment Data

Legal Issues
    Uniform Guidelines on Employee Selection Procedures
    Selection Under the ADA

External selection refers to the assessment and evaluation of external job applicants. A variety of different assessment methods are used. Preliminary issues that guide the use of these assessment methods include the logic of prediction, the nature of predictors, development of the selection plan and the selection sequence.

Initial assessment methods are used to select candidates from among the initial job applicants. These assessment methods are application blanks, biographical data, reference reports, resumes and cover letters, initial interviews, handwriting analysis, literacy testing, and integrity testing.

Substantive assessment methods are used to select finalists from among candidates. These assessment methods are personality tests; ability tests; performance tests and work samples; interest, values, and preference inventories; achievement history questionnaires; structured interviews; clinical assessments; drug testing; physical health tests; and team assessments. The choice of initial and substantive assessment methods should be guided by several factors. These factors are frequency of use, cost, reliability, validity, utility, applicant reactions, and adverse impact.

Discretionary assessment methods are used to select offer receivers from among finalists. These decisions may be based on factors such as projected organizational citizenship behavior and the EEO/AA philosophy of the organization.

The use of assessment methods requires the collection of a large amount of data. In order to make sure that accurate data are collected in a fair manner, attention must be given to support services, the required expertise needed to administer and interpret predictors, security, privacy and confidentiality, and the standardization of procedures.

The use of assessment methods also requires a firm understanding of legal issues. In particular, attention must be paid to the Uniform Guidelines on Employee Selection Procedures, and the selection requirements under the Americans With Disabilities Act. In addition, the organization must comply with the numerous constraints on the use of preemployment inquiries. Finally, the organization must exercise caution in the use of bona fide occupational qualifications claims.

PRELIMINARY ISSUES

Many times selection is equated with one event, namely, the interview. Nothing could be further from the truth if the best possible person/job match is to be made. In order for the best possible match to take place, a series of well-thought-out activities needs to take place. Hence, selection is a process rather than an event. It is guided by a logic that determines the steps that need to be taken. The logic applies to all predictors that might be used, even though they differ in terms of several characteristics. Actual implementation of the logic of prediction requires that predictors be chosen through development of a selection plan. Implementation also requires creation of a selection sequence, which is an orderly flow of people through the stages of applicant, candidate, finalist, and offer receiver.

The Logic of Prediction

In Chapter 1, the selection component of staffing was defined as the process of assessing and evaluating people for purposes of determining the likely fit between the person and the job. This process is based on the logic of prediction, which says that indicators of a person's degree of success in past situations should be predictive of how successful he or she will likely be in new situations. Application of this logic to selection is illustrated in Exhibit 9.1.

A person's KSAOs and motivation are the product of experiences of past job, current job, and nonjob situations. During selection, samples of these KSAOs and motivation are identified, assessed, and evaluated by the organization. The results constitute the person's overall qualifications for the new situation or job. These qualifications are then used to predict how successful the person is likely to be in that new situation or job in terms of the HR outcomes. The logic of prediction works in practice if the organization accurately identifies and measures qualifications relative to job requirements, and if those qualifications remain stable over time so that they are carried over to the new job and used on it.

An example of how this logic can be followed in practice comes from a national communications organization with sales volume in the billions of dollars.[1] They were very interested in improving upon the prediction of job success (sales volume) for sales people, whose sales figures had stagnated. To do so, they constructed what they labeled a "sales competency blueprint," or selection plan, to guide development of a new selection process. The blueprint depicted the KSAOs that needed to be sampled from previous jobs in order to predict sales success in a telemarketing sales job. The blueprint was established on the basis of a thorough job analysis in which subject matter experts identified the KSAOs thought nec-

---

EXHIBIT 9.1   The Logic of Prediction

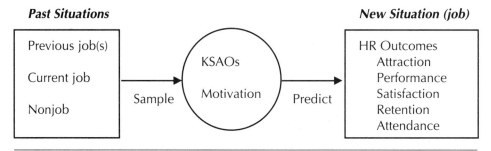

essary to be a successful telemarketer (e.g., knowledge of the product, how it was developed, and how it compared to the competitors' products). Then a structured interview was developed to sample the extent to which applicants for sales jobs in telemarketing had acquired the KSAOs required. In turn, the interview was used in selection to predict the likely success of applicants for the job.

The logic of prediction shown in Exhibit 9.1 demonstrates how critical it is to carefully scrutinize the applicant's past situation when making selection decisions. For example, in selecting someone for a police officer position, the successfulness of the applicant in a previous security guard position might be considered a relevant predictor of the likelihood that the applicant will succeed in the new police officer position. Alternatively, the fact that the person was previously successful as a homemaker might be viewed as totally irrelevant to the new job of police officer. Surprisingly, considering the homemaker role to be irrelevant might well be an incorrect assessment. A study showed that there is a close correspondence between the homemaker and the police officer position.[2] Specifically, thorough job analysis showed that both jobs rely heavily upon troubleshooting and emergency handling skills. Hence, in the absence of a sound job analysis, many qualified applicants may inadvertently be overlooked even though they have some of the characteristics needed to perform the job. Nonjob experience in the home, in the community, and in other institutions may be as valuable or more valuable than previous employment experiences.

Job titles, such as homemaker, are not nearly specific enough to make selection decisions. Similarly, the fact that someone has a certain number of years experience is usually not sufficient detail to make selection decisions. What counts, and what is revealed through job analysis, is the specific types of experiences required and the level of successfulness at each. Similarly, the fact that someone was paid or not paid for employment is not relevant. What counts is the quality of their experiences as it relates to success on the new job. Thus, for example, someone who volunteered to serve as an arbitrator of disputes in the community may have more relevant experience to become a labor relations representative than someone who was paid as a bookkeeper. In short, the logic of prediction indicates that a point-to-point comparison needs to be made between requirements of the job to be filled and the qualifications that applicants have acquired from a variety of past situations.

Not only is the logic of prediction important to selection, but it is important to recruitment as well. A recent study shows that applicant reactions to selection procedures are determined in part by the job-relatedness of the selection procedure. If applicants see the selection process as job-related, which should occur if the logic of prediction is used, then they are more likely to view the selection process as being fair.[3] It would be expected that applicants who view the selection procedure as fair are more likely to accept a job offer and/or encourage others to apply for a job at the organization.

The Nature of Predictors

As will be seen shortly, there is a wide variety of different types of predictors, ranging from interviews to genetic screening. These types can be differentiated from one another in terms of their content and their form.

Content

The substance or content of what is being assessed with a predictor varies considerably and may range from a sign to a sample to a criterion.[4] A *sign* is a predisposition of the person that is thought to relate to performance on the job. Personality as a predictor is a good example here. If personality is used as a predictor, the prediction is that someone with a certain personality (e.g., "abrasive") will demonstrate certain behaviors (e.g., "rude to customers") leading to certain results on the job (e.g., "failure to make a sale"). As can be seen, a sign is very distant from the actual on-the-job results. A *sample* is closer than a sign to actual on-the-job results. Observing a set of interactions between a sales applicant and customer to see if sales are made provides an example of a sample. The *criterion* is very close to the actual job performance, such as sales during a probationary period for a new employee.

Form

The form or design of the predictor may vary along a number of different lines.

Speed versus Power A person's score on some predictors is based upon the number of responses completed within a certain time frame. One event in a physical abilities test may, for example, be the number of bench presses completed in a given period of time. This is known as a *speed test*. If a person's score on some predictor is the number of correct items, then the test is a *power test*. A speed test is used when speed of work is an important part of the job, and a power test is used when the correctness of the response is essential to the job.[5]

Paper and Pencil versus Performance Many predictors are of the paper-and-pencil variety; applicants are required to fill out a form, write out an answer, or complete multiple choice items. Other predictors are *performance tests* where the applicant is asked to manipulate an object or equipment. Testing running backs for the NFL on their time in the 40-yard dash is a performance test. Paper-and-pencil tests are frequently used when cognitive abilities are required to perform the job, and performance tests are used when physical and social skills are required to perform the job.[6]

Objective versus Essay An *objective* paper-and-pencil predictor is one where multiple choice questions or true/false questions are used. These tests should be used to measure specific knowledge in specific areas. Another form of a predictor is an *essay,* where a written answer is required of the respondent. Essays are best used to assess written communication, problem solving, and analytical skills.[7]

Oral versus Written versus Computer   Responses to predictor questions can be spoken, written, or entered into the computer. For example, when conducting interviews, some organizations listen to oral responses, read written responses, or read computer printouts of typed-in responses to assess applicants. As with all predictors, the appropriate form depends upon the nature of the job. If the job requires a high level of verbal skill, then oral responses should be solicited. If the job requires a large amount of writing, then written responses should be required. If the job requires constant interaction with the computer, then applicants should enter their responses into the computer.[8]

Development of the Selection Plan

In order to translate the results of a job analysis into the actual predictors to be used for selection, a selection plan must be developed. A selection plan describes which predictor(s) will be used to assess the KSAOs required to perform the job. The recommended format for a selection plan and an example of such a plan for the job of secretary is shown in Exhibit 9.2. In order to establish a selection plan, three steps are followed. First, a listing of KSAOs is written in the left-hand column. This list comes directly from the job requirements matrix. Second, for each KSAO, a "yes" or "no" is written to show whether this KSAO needs to be assessed in the selection process. Sometimes the answer is no because it is a KSAO the applicant will acquire (e.g., knowledge of company policies and procedures) once on the job. Third, possible methods of assessment are listed for the required KSAOs, and the specific method to be used for each of these KSAOs is then indicated.

Although costly and time-consuming to develop, organizations are increasingly finding that the benefits of developing a selection plan outweigh the cost. As a result, it is and should be a required step in the selection process. For example, a selection plan or "niche testing" was used to select tellers and customer service representatives by the Barnett Bank in Jacksonville, Florida.[9] They found that an essential KSAO for both positions is the ability to make judgments when interacting with the public. For this KSAO, a niche test was developed in which applicants watch actual dealings with the public on video and then decide upon the appropriate course of action. Their responses are graded and used to predict their likelihood of success in either position.

Selection Sequence

Usually a series of decisions is made about job applicants before they are selected. These decisions are depicted in Exhibit 9.3. The first decision that is reached is

EXHIBIT 9.2   Selection Plan Format and Example for Secretarial Position

Major KSA Category	Necessary for Selection? (Y/N)	WP	CT	DB	LTR	TEF	ML	EM	TM	Interview
					Method of Assessment					
1. Ability to follow oral directions/listening skills	Y							X	X	
2. Ability to read and understand manuals/guidelines	Y	X	X	X	X	X	X	X		
3. Ability to perform basic arithmetic operations	Y			X		X				
4. Ability to organize	Y			X			X			
5. Judgments/priority setting/decision making ability	Y			X		X		X		
6. Oral communication skills	Y									X
7. Written communication skills	Y		X		X			X	X	
8. Interpersonal skills	Y									X
9. Typing skills	Y	X	X		X					
10. Knowledge of word processing, graphics, database, and spreadsheet software	Y	X	X	X	X	X				
11. Knowledge of company policies and procedures	N									
12. Knowledge of basic personal computer operations	Y	X	X	X	X	X		X		
13. Knowledge of how to use basic office machines	N									
14. Flexibility in dealing with changing job demands	Y						X	X	X	
15. Knowledge of computer software	Y	X	X	X	X	X	X	X		
16. Ability to attend to detail and accuracy	Y	X	X	X	X	X	X	X	X	

WP = Word processing test, CT = Correction test, DB = Data base exam, LTR = Letter, TEF = Travel expense form, ML = Mail log, EM = Electronic mail messages, and TM = Telephone messages.

Source: Adapted from N. Schmitt, S. Gilliland, R. L. Landis, and D. Devine, "Computer-Based Testing Applied to Selection of Secretarial Positions," *Personnel Psychology*, 1993, 46, pp. 149–165.

EXHIBIT 9.3 Assessment Methods by Applicant Flow Stage

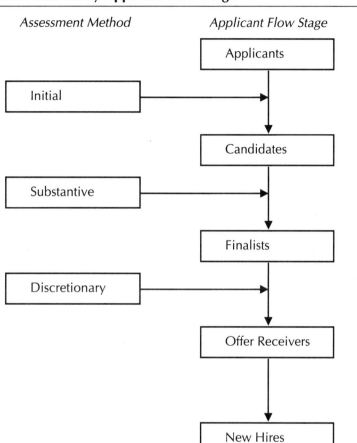

Assessment Method   *Applicant Flow Stage*

Applicants

Initial

Candidates

Substantive

Finalists

Discretionary

Offer Receivers

New Hires

---

whether initial *applicants* who have applied for the job become candidates or are rejected. A *candidate* is someone who has not yet received an offer but who possesses the minimum qualifications to be considered for further assessment. Initial assessment methods are used to choose candidates. The second decision made is which candidates become *finalists*. A finalist is someone who meets all the minimum qualifications and whom the organization is willing to consider further. Substantive assessment methods are used to select finalists. The third decision made is which finalist receives the actual job offer. *Offer receivers* are those finalists who are extended an offer of employment. Discretionary methods are used to select finalists. Finally, some offer receivers become *new hires* when they decide to join the organization.

INITIAL ASSESSMENT METHODS

In this section, initial assessment methods are covered. These methods are also referred to generally as *preemployment inquiries* and are used to minimize the costs associated with substantive assessment methods by narrowing the number of people assessed. Predictors typically used to screen candidates from applicants include application blanks, biodata, background testing, reference reports, initial interviews, handwriting analysis, genetic screening, literacy testing, and honesty or integrity tests. Each of these initial assessment methods will be described in turn. Then, a general evaluation will be presented to help guide decisions about which initial assessment methods to use.

Application Blanks

Most application blanks request in written form the applicant's background with regard to educational experiences, training, and job experiences. This information is also often on the resume and may seem unnecessarily duplicated. This is not the case. An application can be used to verify the data presented on the resume and can also be used to obtain data omitted on the resume, such as employment dates. The major advantage of application blanks over resumes is that the organization, rather than the applicant, dictates what information is presented. As a result, information critical to success on the job is less likely to be omitted by the applicant or overlooked by the reviewer of the resume. The major issue with application blanks is to make sure that information requested is critical to job success, following the logic of prediction discussed earlier.

Educational Requirements
Special care needs to be taken in wording items on an application blank to solicit information about educational experiences and performance.[10]

Level of Education   Level of education or degree is one element of educational performance used to predict job performance. Often, level of education is measured by the attainment of a degree. The degree should be assessed in conjunction with other educational requirements. A high-level degree from a nonaccredited school may be an indication of a lesser accomplishment than a lower-level degree from an accredited school, for example.

A recent report indicates that the high school degree may no longer be as good a predictor as it once was, because the attainment of a GED (high school equivalency) is often used as a substitute for a diploma on an application form, and does not predict as well.[11] Hence, in designing the application form, an item separate from high school degree should be used for high school equivalency.

Grade Point Average (GPA) Classroom grades are measured using a grade point average. Care should be exercized in the interpretation of GPA information. For example, a GPA in one's major in college may be different (usually higher) than one's GPA for all classes. Also, a GPA of 3.5 may be good at one school, but not another. For example, GPAs are calculated on a 4-point scale at some schools, while they are calculated on a 5-point scale at other schools. Some schools do not report GPAs. Some schools have grade inflation (e.g., at Princeton University 80% of undergraduates receive As and Bs).[12] Graduate students receive higher grades on average than do undergraduates.[13] In short, GPA may be influenced by many factors in addition to the applicant's KSAOs and motivation.

Quality of School In recent times, much has been said and written about the quality of various educational programs. For example, *U.S. News and World Report* annually publishes the results of a survey showing the ratings of school quality. Care should be taken to critically examine on what basis school quality ratings are made and their relevance to the job for which selection is to occur.

Major Field of Study The more specialized the knowledge requirements of a particular position, the more important is an applicant's major field of study likely to be as a predictor. An English major may do very well as a managerial trainee, but may be unsuccessful as a physician. It should also be noted that a major does not guarantee that a certain number or type of classes have been taken. The number and type of classes needed for a major or minor varies from school to school and needs to be carefully scrutinized to ensure comparability across majors.

Extracurricular Activities The usefulness of extracurricular activities as a predictor depends upon the job. Being an ice or field hockey player may have little relevance to being a successful manager. However, being elected captain of a hockey team may be a sign of leadership qualities needed to be a successful manager. Information about extracurricular activities taken from an application blank must be relevant to the job in question.

Training and Experience Requirements

Many past experiences predictive of future performance do not take place in a classroom. Instead, these experiences come from life experiences in other institutions, which, fortunately, can also be captured on an application blank. A great deal of weight is often put on training and experience requirements on the theory that "actions speak louder than words." The drawback of putting too much emphasis on previous work experience, however, is that the amount of experience and training an applicant has may be overstated. Also, applicants with high potential may be overlooked because they have not had the opportunity to gain the training or experience needed. Finally, though various methods can be used to measure training and experience, these methods are rarely used.[14]

Licensing, Certification, and Job Knowledge

Many professions and occupations require or encourage people to demonstrate mastery of a certain body of knowledge. A *license* is required of people by law to perform an activity, whereas a *certification* is voluntarily acquired.[15] The purpose of a license is to protect the public interest, while the purpose of a certification is to identify those people who have met a minimum standard of proficiency. Licensing exams and certification exams are usually developed by subject matter experts in conjunction with testing specialists.

Approximately 800 occupations in the United States are regulated by state government boards. Many others are monitored by professional associations. For example, in human resources, there are seven certifications offered by five certifying agencies. Certifications offered are the Professional in Human Resources, Senior Professional in Human Resources, Certified Compensation Professional, Certified Employee Benefit Specialist, Associate Safety Professional, Certified Safety Professional, and Occupational Health and Safety Technologist.[16]

Certification helps guard against the misuse of job titles in human resource selection. For example, anyone could adopt the title of safety consultant, but a certification from the Board of Certified Safety Professionals and/or American Board of Industrial Hygiene guarantees that the person has mastered a certain amount of technical knowledge in the safety area.

While licensure and certification demonstrate mastery of a general body of knowledge applicable to many organizations, job knowledge tests assess a specific body of knowledge within a particular organization. Job knowledge tests are usually used in the public sector as an initial screening device. In the private sector, they are used primarily for promotion purposes. Although mentioned here, job knowledge tests will be covered in detail in Chapter 10.

Weighted Application Blanks

Not all of the information contained on an application blank is of equal value to the organization in making selection decisions. Depending on the organization and job, some information better predicts success on the job than other information. Procedures have been developed that help to weight application blank information by the degree to which the information differentiates between high- and low-performing individuals.[17] This scoring methodology is referred to as a *weighted application blank* (WAB) and is useful not only in making selection decisions, but in developing application blanks as well. The statistical procedures involved help the organization to discern which items should be retained for use in the application blank and which should be excluded on the basis of how well they predict performance.

Biographical Data

A more elaborate method of collecting data on people in previous situations than application blanks is collecting biographical information or biodata. The technique that is most often used to do so is known as a *biographical information blank* (BIB). It not only asks applicants to record previous experiences, but may also ask them to express their attitudes, beliefs, and feelings about these experiences.[18] Having this additional information, organizations may be able to better interpret how these experiences are likely to guide applicants' behaviors in future situations.[19] Examples of BIB items that request very specific information are shown in Exhibit 9.4.

The development of a BIB should be based on job analysis and theory.[20] Unfortunately, this is not always the case, as many employers continue to use a "seat-

---

EXHIBIT 9.4   Examples of Biodata Items

When working with a group of people on a project of some kind, how often was it obvious to you that one of the group members was not "pulling his/her own weight"?

How often have you made speeches in front of a group of adults?

How often have you had to work one-on-one with an adult in or out of school?

How often have you been a member of a group or "team" that you thought needed more cooperation and team work?

How often have you been responsible for equipment and/or supplies as part of some group activity?

How often have you set aside personal differences in order to "get the job done"?

How often have you felt proud of an accomplishment because you achieved it on your own with no help from anyone?

How often have you had to teach or instruct someone how to do something?

How often have you set long-term (more than a year) objectives or goals for yourself?

How often have you worked in a group on some activity where teamwork was the only way anything could be achieved?

How often have you been in a situation where an adult had to interview you and decide something about you?

How often have you set a goal to do better than anyone else on something?

How often have you worked at an activity for which the only reward was self-satisfaction (no grades, no pay, no outcomes of any value to anyone other than yourself)?

How often have other students come to you for advice?

How often have you had to persuade someone to do what you wanted?

How often have you given a speech that was particularly well received?

Source: C. J. Russell, J. Mattson, S. E. Devlin, and D. Atwater, "Predictive Validity of Biodata Items Generated From Retrospective Life Experience Essays," *Journal of Applied Psychology*, 1990, 75, pp. 569–580. Copyright 1990 by the American Psychological Association. Adapted by permission.

of-the-pants'' approach in hopes of predicting future performance. For example, A-Plus Flooring Service in Madison, Wisconsin, asks applicants for entry-level jobs the following yes/no question: ''Could you tell me in 50 pages or more what your full potential is in every area of life?''[21]

When job analysis and theory are used to develop the items on a BIB, then this instrument is likely to better predict success than is a WAB. The reason once again has to do with the logic of prediction (see Exhibit 9.1). The more carefully the organization can pinpoint which characteristics of an applicant's past situation are important to success on the applied-for job, the more likely successful prediction is to take place.

The possibility of faking responses to biodata is an issue of concern, especially with highly subjective items looking into the future or not requiring verification. With these items, applicants may supply a socially desirable response. That is, applicants can respond in the manner they think is most likely to get them a job. While faking does occur with biodata, it does not appear to substantially alter the validity of this selection device.[22] Also, it is possible to guard against some attempts to fake responses with certain methods of scoring the results.[23] Faking can also be guarded against by using other predictors to verify information presented on the BIB.

Reference Reports

Background information about job applicants can come not only from the applicant, but also from people familiar with the applicant in previous situations (e.g., employers, creditors, neighbors).[24] Organizations often solicit this information on their own or use the services of agencies specializing in investigating applicants. Background information solicited from others is called reference reports and consist of letters of recommendation, reference checks, and background testing. Reference reports can be used to verify information presented by the applicant on the resume, application form, and BIB.

Letters of Recommendation

A very common selection procedure in some settings (e.g., academic institutions) is to ask applicants to have letters of recommendation written for them. There are two major problems with this approach. First, they may do little to help the organization to discern more qualified from less qualified applicants. The reason for this is that only very poor applicants are unable to arrange for positive letters about their accomplishments. Second, most letters are not structured or standardized. What this means is that the organization receives data from letter writers that are not consistent across organizations. For example, one applicant may send letters about his educational qualifications, while another applicant may send letters sent about her work experience. Comparing the qualifications of applicant A and B under these circumstances is like comparing apples and oranges.

The problem with letters of recommendation is demonstrated dramatically in one study that showed there was a stronger correlation between two letters written by one person for two different applicants than between two different people writing letters for the same person.[25] This finding indicates that letters of recommendation have more to do with the letter writer than the person being written about.[26]

Such problems indicate that organizations should downplay the weight given to letters unless a great deal of credibility and accountability can be attached to the letter writer's comments. Also, a structured form should be provided so that each writer provides the same information about each applicant.

Another way to improve upon letters of recommendation is to use a standardized scoring key. An example of one is shown in Exhibit 9.5. Using this method, categories of KSAOs are established and become the scoring key (shown at the bottom of the exhibit). Then the adjectives in the actual letter are underlined and classified into the appropriate category. The number of adjectives used in each category constitute the applicant's score.

Reference Checks

With this form of reference report, a check is made (e.g., over the phone) on the applicant's background. Usually the person contacted is the immediate supervisor of the applicant or is in the human resource department of current or previous organizations with which the applicant has contact. Both of the problems that occur with letters of recommendation take place with reference checks as well. Additionally, organizations are reluctant to give out the requested data over the phone because they fear a lawsuit due to invasion of privacy or defamation of character.[27] Most organizations will now only verify dates of employment over the phone and refuse to answer questions about the persons' character or performance.[28]

A summary of a survey showing specific employer practices regarding reference checks is shown in Exhibit 9.6.

Background Testing

How would you feel if you found out that the organization you had hoped to join was having your court record and moral character investigated? How would you feel if an organization did *not* investigate the court record and moral character of guards to be selected for the gun storage depot of the U.S. military near your home?

Although it may seem to be a very invasive procedure, background investigations are routinely conducted on matters such as these and are sometimes needed to protect the public's interests. Some organizations do background testing on their own, while others employ agencies such as Pinkerton to do so.[29] As with any predictor, the reasonableness of this procedure depends upon how related the factors being investigated are to the requirements of the job.[30]

EXHIBIT 9.5   Scoring Letters of Recommendation

Dear Personnel Director:

Mr. John Anderson asked that I write this letter in support of his application as assistant manager and I am pleased to do so. I have know John for six years as he was my assistant in the accounting department.

John always had his work completed <u>accurately</u> and <u>promptly</u>. In his years here, he <u>never missed a deadline</u>. He is very <u>detail</u> oriented, <u>alert</u> in finding errors, and <u>methodical</u> in his problem solving approach. Interpersonally, John is a very <u>friendly</u> and <u>helpful</u> person.

I have great confidence in John's ability. If you desire more information, please let me know.

MA __0__   CC __2__   DR __6__   U __0__   V __0__

Dear Personnel Director:

Mr. John Anderson asked that I write this letter in support of his application as assistant manager and I am pleased to do so. I have know John for six years as he was my assistant in the accounting department.

John was one of the most <u>popular</u> employees in our agency as he is a <u>friendly, outgoing, sociable</u> individual. He has a great sense of <u>humor</u>, is <u>poised</u>, and is very <u>helpful</u>. In completing his work, he is <u>independent, energetic, and industrious</u>.

I have great confidence in John's ability. If you desire more information, please let me know.

MA __0__   CC __2__   DR __0__   U __5__   V __3__

Key *MA = mental ability*
     CC = consideration-cooperation
     DR = dependability-reliability
     U = urbanity
     V = vigor

Source: M. G. Aumodt, D. A. Bryan, and A. J. Whitcomb, "Predicting Performance with Letters of Recommendation," *Public Personnel Management*, 1993, 22, pp. 81–90. Reprinted with permission of *Public Personnel Management*, published by the International Personnel Management Association.

At a general level, background testing is concerned with the reliability of applicants' behavior, their integrity, and their personal adjustment. These factors are often used as requirements for the selection of people in occupations such as law enforcement, private security, and nuclear power, and in positions requiring government-issued security clearances.[31]

Measures used include criminal history (convictions), civil litigation (both plaintiff and defendant history), financial history (credit reports, bankruptcies, tax liens, civil judgments, and defaults), driving record (citations, accidents, and

EXHIBIT 9.6   Policy on Reference Disclosure by Size of Organization (in Percent)

Policy on Disclosure*	Very Small	Small	Medium	Large	Very Large	Average All Firms
Refuse disclosure completely	6.4	10.0	11.3	12.2	11.4	10.5
Refuse disclosure by telephone	16.4	22.8	37.0	39.5	38.0	30.2
Disclose only if inquirer known	31.2	27.8	28.3	30.5	26.4	28.5
Require employee's written release	32.8	49.2	57.0	64.1	59.8	53.4
Require all requests in writing	25.8	33.7	47.5	48.1	55.4	42.0
Verify all disclosed information	63.5	45.4	43.3	39.0	49.0	46.5
Use telephone "call back" to verify	25.8	22.5	17.4	14.2	17.1	19.5

*Combines respondents who always or frequently resort to this particular mode of operation.

Source: C. W. Langdon and W. P. Galle, Jr. "And What Was the Reason for Departure," *Personnel Administrator,* 1989, 34 (3), pp. 62–70. Reprinted with the permission of HR Magazine (formerly Personnel Administrator) published by the Society for Human Resource Management, Alexandria, VA.

DUIs), education verification (degree awarded), earnings history, and workers' compensation claims.[32] Extreme care needs to be taken in the use of such measures because of the limited validity reports available to date, as well as legal constraints on preemployment inquiries (see "Legal Issues" in this chapter).

Resumes and Cover Letters

The first introduction of the applicant to the organization is often a cover letter and resume. This introduction is controlled by the applicant as to the amount, type, and accuracy of information provided. As a result, resumes and cover letters always need to be verified with other predictors such as application blanks to ensure that there is accurate and complete data across all job applicants with which to make informed selection decisions.

One major issue with resumes as a selection tool is the volume of resumes that organizations must process. It is very difficult for many organizations to store resumes for any extended period of time and to accurately read them. Fortunately, the computer has resolved this issue for some companies such as Nike.[33] Resumes from previous searches can be stored on disk so that when a new vacancy arises, a new recruitment search does not have to take place. Optical scanners now make it possible to machine read resumes. According to Resumix, Inc., a maker of resume tracking software, these scanners require resumes not to be ornate or elaborate (e.g., exotic typeface, colored paper). While the costs of these innovations are high, they may pay for themselves rapidly given the reduced time spent generating and screening resumes.

A well-documented problem with resumes and cover letters is fraud.[34] Consider the extreme case of Eugene Roscoe.[35] Not only did he lie about his degree and experiences, but he also lied in his cover letter about interviews. He made over $100,000 in reimbursements for expenses incurred during interviews that he never made. Although most cases are not nearly this extreme, the falsification of credentials does occur.

A computer does not guard against the falsification of credentials. Resumes need to be verified by other predictors and carefully reviewed. Warning labels that should throw up a red flag include gaps in employment dates, a lack of any employment history, a preponderance of former employers listed who are out of business, and a lack of location for previous employers.[36] Vague expressions that sound impressive may not be. Phrases to be on guard for include "was thoroughly involved in . . . ," "steered the company through. . . ," "worked closely with . . . ," "had deep involvement in . . . ," "was active in the planning and implementation of . . . ," and "quickly responded to . . . "[37]

Initial Interview

The initial interview occurs very early in the initial assessment process, and is often the applicant's first personal contact with the organization and its staffing system. At this point, applicants are relatively undifferentiated to the organization in terms of KSAOs. The initial interview will begin the process of necessary differentiation, a "rough cut" of sorts.

The purpose of the initial interview is, and should be, to screen out the most obvious cases of person/job mismatches. To do this, the interview should focus on an assessment of KSAOs that are absolute requirements for the applicant. Examples of such minimum levels of qualifications for the job include certification and licensure requirements, and necessary (not just preferred) training and experience requirements.

These assessments may be made on the basis of information gathered from written means (e.g., application blank or resume), as well as the interview per se. Care should be taken to ensure that the interviewer focuses on only this information as a basis for decision making. Personal characteristics of the applicant (e.g., race, sex), as well as personality characteristics (e.g., she seems so outgoing and just "right" for this job), are to be avoided. Indeed, to ensure that this focus happens, some organizations (e.g., civil service agencies) have basically eliminated the initial interview altogether and make the initial assessment only on the basis of written information provided by the applicant.

Handwriting Analysis

An extremely distant sign of job performance is handwriting analysis or graphology.[38] Yet, some employers use this type of analysis to predict job performance. In fact, it is used fairly frequently in western European countries as a predictor.

The theory behind graphology as a selection device is that handwriting is a measure of personality. So, for example, the height of the bar used to cross your t's is a measure of your approach to achievement. The higher the level that you use the bar to cross your lowercase t's, the stronger your willpower. The lower that you cross your t with a bar, the less self-confidence you have. In turn, personality is believed to have an impact on job performance.

An advantage of this predictor over other predictors measuring personality is that it is difficult to fake. The problem with this approach is that the link between handwriting, personality, and HR outcomes is tenuous at best. One would expect to find virtually no relationship between handwriting analysis and a distant outcome like job performance.

Genetic Screening

Due to the advances in medical technology, it is now possible for employers to screen people on the basis of their genetic code. The testing is done to screen out people who are susceptible to certain diseases (e.g., sickle-cell anemia) due to exposure to toxic substances at work.[39] Screening people out is one way to ensure that workers do not become ill. Another way to do so is to eliminate the toxic substances. Although the use of genetic screening is not widespread, companies such as DuPont and Dow Chemical have experimented with it to protect their employees.[40] Organizations have also experimented with genetic screening because of the huge costs associated with work-related diseases and illnesses.[41]

Genetic screening has been and will continue to be very controversial. It is not at all clear at this stage whether it is legal under current laws or regulations.[42] Labor unions and others disfavor screening some employees rather than creating a safe work environment for all employees. Employers who are now considering the use of this predictor to screen out people with AIDS raise a myriad of moral, legal, and ethical issues.[43] Organizations considering the use of this predictor need to proceed cautiously and with legal counsel.[44]

Literacy Testing

Most jobs require that employees possess reading and writing skills. In some jobs, the need for these skills is obvious. In others, while the need is not obvious, these skills are nevertheless critical to successful on-the-job performance. A good example here is the position of custodian. Reading skills do not at first seem important for this position. However, reading skills may be very important for custodians, as witnessed by the authors of this book in a small school district in Ohio, where an illiterate night custodian mistakenly used what he thought was a cleaning compound for toilets. The substance turned out to have a large amount of an acid compound, as shown on the label. He then used it to clean the toilet seats. Fortunately, no one was hurt in this incident. The incident emphasizes the importance of carefully identifying all relevant USAOs when developing the job requirements matrix and selection plan.

Illiteracy is a big problem in our country. It is estimated that over 30 million Americans are functionally illiterate. Historically, this was not a selection issue in industries where people's physical skills were much more important than their mental skills. Today, all that has changed. Ford, Chrysler, and GM have invested almost $100 million dollars in literacy programs.[45] These dollars have gone toward providing training for those presently employed workers who cannot read or write up to the standards required by new jobs in the auto industry.

Another way for employers to address the issue of illiteracy is to select in advance those people who already have the required reading and writing skills. A great deal of theory and research has gone into developing standardized reading tests.[46] In addition, companies are developing their own tests. For example, Southern California Gas Company has developed a writing test for its sales position that assesses writing mechanics, written content, and ability to follow exercise directions.[47] It has been well received by the company, and by the union as well, because of the detailed feedback it gives to applicants.

Integrity Testing

Dishonesty by employees is a subtle and expensive problem for employers. It is subtle because it can take place in occupations where one would not expect it to take place. For example, one unpublished study indicates that 50 percent of police officer applicants lied when taking a personality test for employment purposes.[48] It is an expensive problem as well. One form of dishonesty, theft, can result in large losses to employers. This is true even if relatively inexpensive items (e.g., pencils) are stolen by a large number of people and at a frequent rate.

Not all theft, however, leads to large expenses for employers. In some cases, the cost of testing may outweigh the cost of theft. So, as a general rule, honesty tests should only be used if serious theft is suspected.[49] Places where this is likely to occur include retail stores, financial institutions, and warehouse operations. In these institutions, some employees are likely to have access to cash and merchandise. Even in these types of institutions, not all employees are likely to have equal access to cash and merchandise. Hence, only certain occupations, such as clerks, tellers, cashiers, and security guards, may need to be singled out for the use of this predictor in selection.[50]

Measurers of honesty are sometimes called *integrity tests*. Examples of integrity test items are shown in Exhibit 9.7.

The content of these tests is of two types.[51] Overt integrity tests contain items that measure admissions of theft and other illegal activities (e.g., item 2 in Exhibit 9.7). They may also contain items concerning one's attitudes toward theft and other forms of dishonesty (e.g., items 1, 3, 6, 7 in Exhibit 9.7). Personality-based integrity tests do not contain direct references to theft. Instead, personality items believed to be related to theft are used (e.g., items 4 and 5 in Exhibit 9.7).

Integrity tests can be one of three types. A polygraph test is an electronic device used to detect lying. It is also often illegal for purposes of selection under the Employee Polygraph Protection Act (see Chapter 3). As a result, most integrity tests are of a pencil-and-paper format where the respondent answers questions like those shown in Exhibit 9.7. At least one testing group now has an interview format that assesses verbal and nonverbal indications of dishonesty.[52]

Honesty tests are not without problems. Almost everyone has been dishonest on some of the items mentioned on the test some of the time. The legal, moral, and ethical issue then becomes, How dishonest must one be before being rejected from a job?[53]

Another issue is faking. Who would admit to stealing outright on an honesty test? For the person who routinely steals, it may be normal to report thefts. In fact, some may even view it as an opportunity to boast.[54] Even people who are trying to fake it may be screened out due to inconsistencies in their responses from item to item. Another issue that pertains to honesty tests is the questionable sales techniques used to market them. In one review of the literature, instances were found where the test publishers overstated the value of their test and the qualifications of those who developed the test.[55]

A final issue to consider is the reactions of job applicants to honesty tests. Some job applicants, even qualified ones, may simply refuse to take such a test. They

---

EXHIBIT 9.7   Examples of Integrity Test Items

---

1. Do you ever think about cheating people?
2. How many dollars worth of merchandise have you taken from your current employer?
3. Do you think that most people like to steal?
4. Do you consider yourself a trustworthy person?
5. Are you loyal?
6. Would you turn in your boss if you caught him stealing?
7. Are there times when it is okay to be dishonest?

---

may be offended that their honesty would be questioned. In one study, where people were already employed, 10% refused to take the test.[56]

Choice of Initial Assessment Methods

As has now been described, there is a wide range of initial assessment methods available to organizations to help reduce the applicant pool to bona fide candidates. These predictors range from signs (e.g., personality-based honesty tests) to samples (e.g., licensing). A range of formats is available as well. Fortunately, with so many choices available to organizations, research results are available to help guide choices of methods to use. This research has been reviewed many times and is summarized in Exhibit 9.8.[57]

In Exhibit 9.8, each initial assessment method is rated according to several criteria. Use refers to how frequently surveyed organizations use each predictor. Cost refers to expenses incurred in using the predictor. Reliability refers to consistency of measurement. Validity refers to the strength of the relationship between the predictor and job performance. Low validity refers to validity in the range of about .00 to .15. Moderate validity corresponds to validity in the range of about .16 to .30, and high validity is .31 and above. Utility refers to the monetary return associated with using the predictor, relative to its cost. Reactions refers to the favorability of applicants' reactions to the predictor. Adverse impact refers to the possibility that a disproportionate number of women and minorities may be rejected using this predictor.

As can be seen in Exhibit 9.8, the data available to make a decision as to which initial assessment method to use are sporadic. In particular, not much is known about the economic and social impact of many of these predictors, as indicated by the large number of question marks for cost, utility, reactions, and adverse impact. This is due in large part to the newness of many of these procedures. The lack of data with which to make judgments indicates that organizations need to exercise care in selecting an initial assessment method. Organizations need to collect their own data to evaluate the effectiveness of initial assessment methods as well as relying on previous research.

What becomes very evident from a review of Exhibit 9.8 is that the closer the sampling of past situations to the requirements of job success, the higher is the validity of the method. For example, level of education has low validity because it is a very general and vague description of a past situation that does not closely correspond to the specific requirements for success on the job. On the other hand, biographical data has high validity because there is a very close correspondence between what is asked about the applicant's past situation and what is required to succeed on the applied-for job. This result is very consistent with the logic of prediction in Exhibit 9.1.

EXHIBIT 9.8   Evaluation of Initial Assessment Methods

Predictors	Use	Cost	Reliability	Validity	Utility	Reactions	Adverse Impact
Level of education	High	Low	?	Low	Low	?	Moderate
Grade point average	Moderate	Low	?	Low	?	?	?
Quality of school	?	Low	?	Low	?	?	Moderate
Major field of study	?	Low	?	Moderate	?	?	?
Extracurricular activity	?	Low	?	Moderate	?	?	?
Training and experience	High	Low	?	Moderate	Moderate	?	Moderate
Licensing and certification	Low	Low	?	?	?	?	?
Weighted application blanks	Low	Moderate	Moderate	Moderate	?	?	?
Biographical data	Low	Moderate	High	High	High	?	Moderate
Letters of recommendation	Low	Low	?	Low	?	?	?
Reference checks	High	Moderate	?	Moderate	Moderate	?	Low
Background testing	Low	High	?	?	?	?	?
Resumes and cover letters	High	Low	?	?	?	?	?
Initial interview	High	Moderate	Low	Low	?	?	Moderate
Handwriting analysis	Low	Moderate	Low	Low	?	Negative	?
Genetic screening	Low	High	Moderate	?	?	?	High
Literary testing	Low	Moderate	?	Low	?	?	?
Integrity testing	Low	Moderate	Moderate	High	?	Neutral	?

SUBSTANTIVE ASSESSMENT METHODS

Initial assessment methods are used to reduce the applicant pool to candidates. Substantive assessment methods are used to reduce the candidate pool to finalists for the job. As with initial assessment methods, substantive assessment methods are developed using the logic of prediction outlined in Exhibit 9.1 and the selection plan shown in Exhibit 9.2. Predictors typically used to select finalists from the candidate pool include personality tests; ability tests; performance tests and work samples; achievement history questionnaires; interest, values, and preference inventories; depth interviews; clinical assessment; physical health tests; and team assessments. Each of these predictors is described next.

Personality Tests

Personality tests are methods used to assess people's disposition to function in certain ways. As such, they are used to determine the unique set of characteristics that define an individual and determine that person's pattern of interaction with the environment. These characteristics of the person are known as personality traits. The major categories of traits that have been used and investigated over the years are the "big five": extroversion, emotional stability, agreeableness, conscientiousness, and openness to experience.[58] Personality tests are used to predict both behaviors (e.g., performance and turnover) and attitudes (e.g., job satisfaction) in the work environment.

An example of a personality test is the Employee Reliability Inventory. It is used to predict which candidates are likely to quit or be fired. The test is used to pick out those with a likelihood of being fired and those with a likelihood of quitting. People with a higher likelihood of being fired share the following constellation of personality traits: "pronounced feelings of bitterness and alienation, cynical view of others and their motivations, enjoyment of being loud and outspoken, and claiming to be calm, cool, and collected under any circumstances." People with a higher likelihood of quitting the job share the following constellation of traits: "personal feelings of dullness and a lack of involvement in one's own life and society, a hedonistic outlook (living for the pleasure of the moment), and avoidance of personal involvement, challenge, or complexity." These traits were identified in a study of 43,000 job applicants.[59]

Personality tests come in a variety of formats. There are *inventories,* where candidates respond to written items on a page or computer screen by choosing a multiple choice answer. There are *projective tests,* where the candidate responds to a visual stimulus with a written statement or by completing a word in a sentence. The results of interviews and work sample tests can also be used to infer traits on the basis of what people say or do.

The results of these tests can be analyzed using the computer. Programmed into the computer is a decision support system. This system takes the predictions of subject matter experts and forms judgments about the job candidate. Thus, the system takes a set of traits and interprets these traits in terms of likely job performance.[60] An example of a computerized report is shown in Exhibit 9.9.

This report is based on a paper-and-pencil measure of Ms. Sample's personality as it relates to supervisory work. Traits that are assessed include emotional intensity, initiative, recognition motivation, sensitivity, assertiveness, trust, good impression, ego drive, interpersonal warmth, stability, empathy, objectivity, independence, aggressiveness, decisiveness, tolerance, and efficiency. A report similar to the one here for emotional intensity is developed for each of these traits. The report summarizes the meaning and implications of the score that the candidate receives for each trait.

The administration of personality items is of critical importance. Personality tests are susceptible to faking by job candidates; they respond in the manner in which they believe the hiring organization wants them to respond rather than according to their own beliefs. Fortunately, the impact of faking on validity is not

---

EXHIBIT 9.9   Summary Report on the Trait "Emotional Intensity" for a Job Candidate

EMOTIONAL INTENSITY

- GENERAL STATEMENT

Ms. Sample is typically energetic and oriented toward goals rather than methods. She places emphasis on the results and typically does not get bored with the methods. Ms. Sample has a tendency to take on more responsibility than she can handle.

- STRENGTHS

Ms. Sample is quick-starting and highly motivated toward goals or challenges. Her high degree of goal-oriented energy provides her with an uncanny ability to turn monotonous procedures into creative challenges. It is similar to an idling speed of an automobile. Her idling speed is typically high, even when she is in neutral or reverse.

- IMPROVEMENT OPPORTUNITIES

Ms. Sample's high energy level can create definite problems if it is not directed properly toward efficiency and productivity. She can get too involved in too many different activities at one time. It may be difficult to maintain her interest for any extended period of time, unless variety and change are part of the job.

- SUPERVISORY RECOMMENDATIONS

Short-term goals are more important to Ms. Sample than long-term goals such as increasing earnings, company seniority, or management opportunities. If management emphasizes both short-term and long-term goals, interest and persistency can be achieved.

Source: Reprinted with permission from Wonderlic Personnel Test, Inc. *Comprehensive Personality Profile*, Libertyville, IL: Author, 1992.

large.[61] Organizations can use certain scales to detect faking applicants and can minimize faking by warning job candidates against doing it.[62]

Ability Tests

Ability tests are mechanisms for assessing an individual's capacity to function in a certain way. There are two major types of ability tests: aptitude and achievement. Aptitude tests look at a person's innate capacity to function, while achievement tests look at a person's learned capacity to function.

Organizations rely heavily upon ability tests because they assess a key determinant of employee performance. Without a certain level of ability, be it innate or learned, performance is unlikely to be at an acceptable level, regardless of motivation. Someone may try extremely hard to do well in a very difficult class (e.g., calculus), but will not succeed unless they have the ability (e.g., mathematical aptitude).

There are four major classes of ability tests: cognitive abilities, psychomotor abilities, physical abilities, and sensory/perceptual abilities.[63] Cognitive abilities refer to abilities involved in thinking, including perception memory, reasoning, and the expression of ideas. Examples of paper-and-pencil test items that measure cognitive ability are shown in Exhibit 9.10.

Psychomotor abilities refer to the correlation of thought with bodily movement. Involved here are processes such as reaction time, arm-hand steadiness, control precision, and manual and digital dexterity. An example of testing for psychomotor abilities is a test used by the City of Columbus, Ohio, to select firefighters. The test mimics coupling a hose to a fire hydrant, and it requires a certain level of processing with psychomotor abilities to achieve a passing score.

Physical abilities refer to strength, balance, and stamina. An example of a test that requires all three again comes from the City of Columbus. The test mimics carrying firefighting equipment (e.g., hose, fan, oxygen tanks) up flights of stairs in a building. Equipment must be brought up and down the stairs as quickly as possible in the test. The equipment is heavy, so strength is required. The climb is steep, so balance is required. The trips up the flights of stairs are lengthy, so stamina is required.

Sensory/perceptual abilities include the detection and recognition of stimuli. An example of a sensory/perceptual ability test is the paper folding test. A sample item from this test is shown in Exhibit 9.11. Items on this test, which is used to select air traffic controllers, are designed to test for spatial visualization.[64]

Most ability tests are paper-and-pencil tests, administered in a group with time limits. There are numerous ability tests available commercially.[65] Before deciding which test to use, organizations are advised to seek out a reputable testing firm. An association of test publishers is now being formed with bylaws to help ensure this process.[66] It is also advisable to seek out the advice of a testing specialist.

EXHIBIT 9.10 Sample Cognitive Ability Test Items

Look at the row of numbers below. What number should come next?

| 8 | 4 | 2 | 1 | 1/2 | 1/4 | ? |

Assume the first 2 statements are true. Is the final one: (1) true, (2) false, (3) not certain?

The boy plays baseball. All baseball players wear hats. The boy wears a hat.

One of the numbered figures in the following drawing is most different from the others. What is the number in that drawing?

 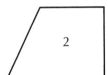

A train travels 20 feet in 1/5 second. At this same speed, how many feet will it travel in three seconds?

How many of the six pairs of items listed below are exact duplicates?

3421	1243
21212	21212
558956	558956
10120210	10120210
612986896	612986896
356471201	356571201

The hours of daylight and darkness in SEPTEMBER are nearest equal to the hours of daylight and darkness in

(1) June   (2) March   (3) May   (4) November

Source: Reprinted with permission from C. F. Wonderlic Personnel Test, Inc. *1992 Catalog: Employment Tests, Forms, and Procedures* (Libertyville, IL: Author-Charles F. Wonderlic, 1992).

Many specialists are members of the American Psychological Association or the American Psychological Society.

Performance Tests and Work Samples

These tests are mechanisms to assess actual performance rather than underlying capacity or disposition. As such, they are more akin to samples rather than signs, of work performance. For example, at Domino's Pizza Distribution, job candidates for the positions of dough maker, truck driver, and warehouse worker are given performance tests to ensure that they can safely perform the job.[67] This sample is taken rather than using drug testing as a sign, because candidates may not be able

EXHIBIT 9.11   Paper Folding Test

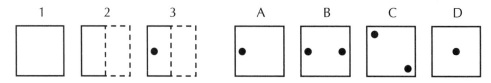

Visualize what happens when a piece of paper is folded, has a hole punched in it, and then is unfolded.

Source: Reprinted by permission from P. L. Ackerman and R. Kanfer. "Integrating Laboratory and Field Study for Improving Selection: Development of a Battery for Predicting Air Traffic Controller Success." *Journal of Applied Psychology*, 1993, 78, pp. 413–432. Copyright 1993 by the American Psychological Association. Reprinted by permission.

to safely perform the job for a variety of reasons, in addition to drug and alcohol abuse.

Types of Tests

Performance Test versus Work Sample   A *performance test* measures what the person actually does on the job. The best examples of performance tests are internships, job tryouts, and probationary periods. A *work sample* is designed to capture parts of the job, for example, a drill press test for machine operators and a programming test for computer programmers.[68] A performance test is more costly to develop than a work sample, but it is usually a better predictor of job performance.

Motor versus Verbal Work Samples   A *motor work sample* test involves the physical manipulation of things. Examples include a driving test and a clothes making test. A *verbal work sample* test involves a problem situation requiring language skills and interaction with people. Examples include role-playing tests that simulate contacts with customers and an English test for foreign teaching assistants.[69]

High-versus Low-Fidelity Tests   A *high-fidelity* test uses very realistic equipment and scenarios to simulate the actual tasks of the job. As such, they elicit actual responses encountered in performing the task.[70] A good example of a high-fidelity test is one being developed to select truck drivers in the petroleum industry. The test is on the computer and mimics all the steps taken to load and unload fuel from a tanker to a fuel reservoir at a service station.[71] It is not a test of perfect high fidelity, because fuel is not actually unloaded. It is, however, a much safer test because the dangerous process of fuel transfer is simulated rather than taking place.

A *low-fidelity* test is one that simulates the task in a written or verbal description and elicits a written or verbal response rather than an actual response.[72] An example of a low-fidelity test is describing a work situation to job applicants and asking them what they would do in that particular situation. This was done in writing in a study by seven companies in the telecommunications industry for the position of manager.[73]

Computer Interaction Performance Tests versus Paper-and-Pencil Tests

The computer has made it possible to measure aspects of work not possible to measure with a paper-and-pencil test. The computer can capture the complex and dynamic nature of work. This is especially true in work where perceptual and motor performance is required.[74]

An example of how the computer can be used to capture the dynamic nature of service work comes from Connecticut General Life Insurance Company. Fact-based scenarios are presented to candidates on the computer. The candidates' reactions to the scenarios, both mental (e.g., comprehension, coding, calculation) and motor (e.g., typing speed and accuracy), are assessed as the job candidate processes the claim.[75]

The computer can also be used to capture the complex and dynamic nature of management work. AccuVision shows the candidate actual job situations likely to be encountered on the job on videotape. In turn, the candidate selects a behavioral option in response in each situation. The response is entered in the computer and scored according to what it demonstrates of the skills needed to successfully perform as a manager.[76]

Administrative Concerns

The costs of realism are high. The closer a predictor comes to simulating actual job performance, the more expensive it becomes to use it. Actually having the people perform the job, as with an internship, may require paying a wage. Using videotapes and the computer adds cost as well.

The importance of safety must also be considered the more that realism is used in the selection procedure. If actual work is performed, care must taken so that the candidate's and employer's safety are ensured. When working with dangerous objects or procedures, the candidate must have the knowledge to follow the proper procedures. For example, in selecting nurse's aides for a long-term health care facility, it would not be wise to have candidates actually move residents in and out of their beds. Both the untrained candidate and resident may suffer physical harm if proper procedures are not followed.

Interest, Values, and Preference Inventories

Interest, values, and preference inventories examine what job candidates want to do on the job. This is in comparison with predictors that measure whether the person can do or is willing to do the job. However, just because a person can and is willing to do a job does not guarantee success on the job. If the person does not want to do the job as well, that individual may fail at it. Although wants seem important, they have not been used very much in human resource selection.

One interesting example of the use of these tests in business is found in the study of selection procedures for attorneys. An interest and opinion survey was developed based on applicants' interests as shown by academic and extracurricular activities during high school and college.[77] Standardized tests of interests, values, and preferences are also available.[78]

Achievement History Questionnaires

Achievement history questionnaires assess the past accomplishments of job candidates as they relate to dimensions of work that are part of performing effectively at a particular job. These questionnaires have been labeled as accomplishment records, achievement records, and retrospective life essays.[79] Information that is solicited from each candidate includes a written statement of the accomplishment, when it took place, any recognition for the accomplishment, and verification of the accomplishment.[80] The emphasis is on achievements rather than activities only, and it is in this regard that achievement history questionnaires differ from application blanks that solicit data on activities. Interestingly, this procedure may replace the traditional paper-and-pencil tests used by the Federal government to select new college graduates.[81]

An example of an accomplishment record scoring key, developed to select attorneys, is shown in Exhibit 9.12. Specifically, it is used to evaluate the candidate's research and investigation skills. The scale is used to score the accomplishment record submitted by the candidate. Similar scales are used to score other aspects of the candidate's skills. The scale is anchored with behavioral benchmarks. These benchmarks are illustrative of what candidates would have to present in their essay to earn a certain score, which can range from 1 to 6.

Structured Interview

The structured interview is a very standardized, job-related method of assessment. It requires careful and thorough construction, as described in the sections that follow. It is instructive to compare the structured job interview with what might be described generically as an unstructured interview. This comparison will serve to highlight the difference between the two.

A typical unstructured interview has the following sorts of characteristics:

1. It is unplanned (e.g., just sit down and "wing it" with the candidate).
2. It is "quick and dirty" (e.g., 10–15 minutes).

EXHIBIT 9.12   Scoring Key Excerpt for an Accomplishment Record

Dimensions: Researching/Investigating

General Definition: Obtaining all information, facts, and materials that are important, relevant, or necessary for a case, project, or assignment; gathering accurate information from all possible sources (i.e., persons both within and outside, interviews, journals, publications, company records, etc.); being thorough and overcoming all obstacles in gathering the required information.

Guidelines for Ratings: In RESEARCHING/INVESTIGATING, accomplishments at the lower levels are characterized by projects which require a minimal amount of research or research that is mundane in nature, e.g., routine interviews or journal reviews. At progressively higher levels, the accomplishments describe information gathered from multiple sources or information that would require considerable expertise to collect. The research projects may be part of a case or procedure which is novel or of substantial import. The projects generally demand increasingly complex interpretation of the information gathered. At the highest levels of achievement, awards or commendations are likely.

Scale:

6 =   I assumed major responsibility for conducting an industry-wide investigation of the industry and for preparation of a memorandum in support of complaints against the three largest members of the industry. A complaint was issued unanimously by the Commission and a consent settlement was obtained subsequently from all three respondents. I obtained statistical data from every large and medium industry in the U.S. and from a selection of small ones. I obtained and negotiated subpoenas with, and obtained statistical information from numerous other members of the industry. I deposed *many* employees of manufacturers and renters. I received a Meritorious Service award.

5 =   I obtained crucial evidence in Docket, which was used as the basis for obtaining consent orders against more than 25 companies. I personally conducted more than 30 Investigational Hearings by subpoena. I did much outside research and reading to become familiar with technology. I handled all investigational and research work in the Northeastern United States. I obtained documentary material from many sources and obtained the files upon which the matter was finally based.

4 =   As a lead attorney in a major investigation at the _____ , I performed all of the tasks described in this category. I supervised the investigation and brought it to its ultimate conclusion, which was to recommend that the matter be closed with no official action. I interviewed witnesses, including interviews on official record, subpoenaed documents from target sources, and spoke with numerous experts about scientific and technical information related to the case.

(continued)

EXHIBIT 9.12   Continued

3 =   In the investigation, I helped to develop and gather the evidence necessary to pursue litigation. I prepared several complex subpoenas and negotiated them with industry counsel from three major corporations. The subpoenas requested detailed information on activities of major _____ .

2 =   I interviewed potential witnesses and compiled evidence that was relevant to the case against Corporation. I analyzed documents submitted pursuant to subpoenas, interviewed witnesses, and wrote admission of fact.

1 =   My research involved checking reference books, LEXIS, and telephone interviews with various people—individuals, state officials, etc.

Source: L. M. Hough, M. A. Keyes, and M. D. Dunnette, "An Evaluation of Three 'Alternative' Selection Procedures," *Personnel Psychology*, 1983, 36, p. 265.

3. It consists of casual questioning (e.g., "Tell me a little bit about yourself").
4. It has obtuse questions (e.g., "What type of animal would you most like to be, and why?").
5. It has highly speculative questions (e.g., Where do you see yourself ten years from now?").
6. The interviewer is unprepared (e.g., forgot to review job description and specification before the interview).
7. The interviewer makes a quick, and final, evaluation of the candidate (e.g., often in the first couple of minutes).

The unstructured interview, and the accompanying examples of it, are all too common in actual interview practice. Research shows that organizations clearly pay a price for the use of the unstructured interview, namely very low reliability and validity.[82] Interviewers using the unstructured interview: (a) are unable to have high interrater agreement in their evaluation of job candidates, and (b) cannot predict the job success of candidates with any degree of consistent accuracy.

Fortunately, research has begun to unravel the reasons why the unstructured interview works so poorly and what factors need to be changed in order to improve reliability and validity. These factors are shown in Exhibit 9.13.[83]

The interview process shown in the exhibit depicts the interviewer as a decision maker who makes judgments about applicants based on the applicant's fit to the job. That process involves

1. interviewer's preinterview impressions
2. interviewer's conduct of the interview
3. candidate's interview behavior and statements
4. interviewer's information processing

EXHIBIT 9.13   Interviewer Information Processing and Decision Making

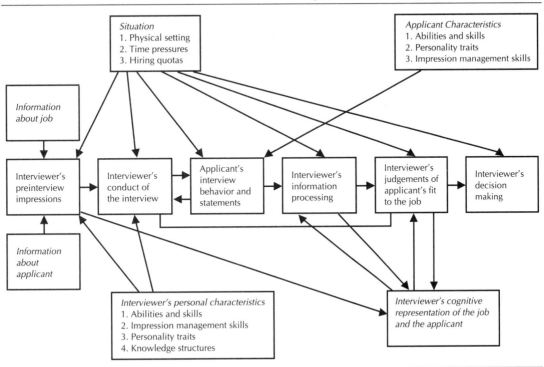

Source: R. L. Dipboye and B. B. Gaugler, ''Cognitive and Behavioral Processes in the Selection Interview,'' in N. Schmitt, W. C. Borman, and Associates, *Personnel Selection in Organizations* (San Francisco: Jossey-Bass, 1993), p. 144. Copyright 1993 by Jossey-Bass, Inc., Publishers. Code 9274.

5. interviewer's judgments about applicant fit to the job
6. interviewer's decision making

As shown in Exhibit 9.13, there are numerous sources of influence on the interviewer during this process. These sources are information about the candidate and the job, situational characteristics, candidate's characteristics, interviewer's personal characteristics, and interviewer's cognitive representation of the job and the candidate. All of these sources affect the interviewer during various portions of the interview process. Ultimately, these sources converge to shape the interviewer's final judgment of and decision about the candidate. In turn, these sources also affect the reliability and validity of the interviewer's decisions.

The structured interview is one that, by design and conduct, standardizes and controls for sources of influence on the interview process and the interviewer. The goal here is to improve interview reliability and validity beyond that of the unstructured interview. Research shows that this goal can be achieved. Doing so requires following each of these steps: consult the job requirements matrix, develop the selection plan, develop the structured interview plan, train interviewers, and evaluate effectiveness. Each of these steps is elaborated on next.

The Job Requirements Matrix

The starting point for the structured interview is the job requirements matrix. It identifies the tasks and KSAOs that define the job requirements around which the structured interview is constructed and conducted.

The Selection Plan

As previously described, the selection plan flows from the KSAOs identified in the job requirements matrix. The selection plan addresses which KSAOs it is necessary to assess during selection, and whether the structured interview is the preferred method of assessing them.

Is the KSAO Necessary?   Some KSAOs must be brought to the job by the candidate, and others can be acquired on the job (through training and/or job experience). The bring-it/acquire-it decision must be made for each KSAO. This decision should be guided by the importance indicator(s) for the KSAOs in the job requirements matrix.

Is the Structured Interview the Preferred Method?   It must be decided if the structured interview is the preferred method of assessing each KSAO necessary for selection. Several factors should be considered when making this decision. First, job knowledges are usually best assessed through other methods, such as a written job knowledge test or specific training and experience requirements. The structured interview thus should focus more on skills and abilities. Second, many methods are available for assessing these skills and abilities, as discussed throughout this chapter. Third, the structured interview is probably best suited for assessing only some of these skills and abilities, such as verbal, interpersonal, adaptability, and flexibility skills and abilities.

An example of a selection plan for the job of sales associate in a retail clothing store is shown in Exhibit 9.14. While there were five task dimensions for the job in the job requirements matrix (customer service, use of machines, use of customer service outlets, sales and departmental procedures, and cleaning and maintenance), the selection plan is shown only for the dimension customer service.

Note in the exhibit that the customer service dimension has several required KSAOs. However, only some of these will be assessed during selection, and only some of those will be assessed by the structured interview. The method of assessment is thus carefully targeted to the KSAO to be assessed.

Developing the Structured Interview Plan

Development of the structured interview plan proceeds along three sequential steps—construction of interview questions, construction of benchmark responses

EXHIBIT 9.14   Partial Selection Plan for Job of Retail Store Sales Associate

Task Dimension: Customer Service

KSAO	Necessary for Selection?	Method of Assessment
1. Ability to make customer feel welcome	Yes	Interview
2. Knowledge of merchandise to be sold	Yes	Written test
3. Knowledge of location of merchandise in store	No	– – – –
4. Skill in being cordial with customers	Yes	Interview
5. Ability to create and convey ideas to customers	Yes	Interview

for the questions, and weighting of the importance of the questions. The output of this process for the sales associate job is shown in Exhibit 9.15, and is referred to in the discussion that follows.

Constructing Questions   One or more questions must be constructed for each KSAO targeted for assessment by the structured interview. Many different types of questions have been experimented with and researched, including situational interviewing, behavior description interviewing, job content interviewing, and structured behavioral interviewing.[84] Despite differences, there is a major underlying characteristic common to all.

That characteristic is sampling of the candidate's behavior, as revealed by past situations and what the candidate reports would be his or her behavior in future situations. The questions ask in essence, "What have you done in this situation?" and "What would you do if you were in this situation?"

The key to constructing both types of questions is to create a scenario relevant to the KSAO in question and to ask the candidate to respond to them by way of answering a question. Situations may be drawn from past job experiences, as well as nonjob experiences. Inclusion of nonjob experiences is important for applicants who have not had similar previous job experience, or have not had any previous job experience at all.

The "what would you do if" type questions should be constructed around important scenarios or events that the person is likely to encounter on the job. The candidate may draw upon both previous job and nonjob situations, as well as more general behavioral intentions, in fashioning a response.

Exhibit 9.15 shows three questions for the KSAOs to be assessed by the interview, as determined by the initial selection plan for the job of sales associate in a retail store. As can be seen, all three questions present very specific situations that a sales associate is likely to encounter. The content of all three questions is clearly job-relevant, a logical outgrowth of the process that began with the development of the job requirements matrix.

EXHIBIT 9.15 Structured Interview Questions, Benchmark Responses, Rating Scale, and Question Weights

Job: Sales Associate
Task Dimension: Customer Service

	Rating Scale					Rating	X	Weight	=	Score
	1	2	3	4	5					
Question No. One (KSAO 1) A customer walks into the store. No other salespeople are around to help the person, and you are busy arranging merchandise. What would you do if you were in this situation?	Keep on arranging merchandise		Keep working but greet the customer		Stop working, greet customer, and offer to provide assistance	5		1		5
Question No. Two (KSAO 4) A customer is in the fitting room and asks you to bring her some shirts to try on. You do so, but by accident bring the wrong size. The customer becomes irate and starts shouting at you. What would you do if you were in this situation?	Tell customer to "keep her cool"		Go get correct size		Apologize, go get correct size	3		1		3
Question No. Three (KSAO 5) A customer is shopping for the "right" shirt for her 17-year-old granddaughter. She asks you to show her shirts that you think would be "right" for her. You do this, but the customer doesn't like any of them. What would you do if you were in this situation?	Tell customer to go look elsewhere		Explain why you think your choices are good ones		Explain your choices, suggest gift certificate as alternative	5		2		10
										18

Benchmark Responses and Rating Scales The interviewer must somehow evaluate or judge the quality of the candidates' response to the interview questions. Prior development of benchmark responses and corresponding rating scales is the method for providing firm guidance to the interviewer in doing this task. Benchmark responses represent qualitative examples of the types of candidate response that the interviewer may encounter. They are located on a rating scale (usually 1–5, or 1–7, rating scale points) to represent the level or ''goodness'' of the response.

Exhibit 9.15 contains benchmark responses, positioned on 1–5 rating scales, for each of the three interview questions. Note that all the responses are quite specific, and they clearly suggest that some answers are better than others. These responses represent judgments on the part of the organization as to the desirable and not so desirable behaviors it would like its employees to engage in.

Weighting Responses Each candidate will receive a total score for the structured interview. It thus must be decided whether each question is of equal importance in contributing to the total score. If so, the candidates' total interview scores are simply the sum of the scores on the individual rating scales.

If some questions are more important than others in assessing candidates, then those questions receive greater weight. The more important the question, the greater its weight relative to the other questions.

Exhibit 9.15 shows the weighting decided upon for the three interview questions. As can be seen, the first two questions receive a weight of 1, and the third question receives a weight of 2. The candidate's assigned ratings are multiplied by their weights and then summed to determine a total score for this particular task dimension. In the exhibit, the candidate receives a score of 18 ($5 + 3 + 10 = 18$) for customer service. The candidate's total interview score would be the sum of the scores on all the dimensions.

Training Interviewers

It is likely that interviewers will need training in the structured interview process. The process is probably quite different from what they have encountered and/or used, and training becomes a way of introducing them to the process. The little available research suggests that interviewers are generally receptive to training attempts.[85] Logical program content areas to be covered as part of the training are

1. problems with the unstructured interview
2. advantages of the structured interview
3. development of the structured interview
4. use of probe questions and note taking
5. elimination of rating errors
6. actual practice in conducting the structured interview

Evaluating Effectiveness

As noted, research on the effectiveness of the structured interview is quite favorable, though sparse. As with any assessment device, there is a constant need to learn more about its reliability, validity, and utility. This is particularly so because of the complexity of the interview process. Thus, evaluation of the structured interview's effectiveness should be built directly into the process itself.[86]

Clinical Assessments

A clinical assessment is a mechanism whereby a trained psychologist makes a judgment about the suitability of a candidate for a job. Typically, such assessments are used for selecting people for middle- and upper-level management positions. A typical assessment takes about a half day. Judgments are formed on the basis of an interview, personal history form, ability tests, and personality tests. Feedback to the organization usually includes a narrative description of the candidate, with or without a stated recommendation.[87]

Scott Paper Company has taken this approach in an effort to improve its selection for 50 management positions in the manufacturing operations of the company. In particular, Scott was very interested in shifting the orientation of its management staff away from an autocratic, hierarchical system of decision making to one where the participation and the development of subordinates was emphasized. To do so, selection of individuals with this management style was emphasized rather than the training of managers to acquire this style. Clinical assessments were made to ensure that this selection procedure worked.[88] This example nicely demonstrates the role that clinical assessments can play in the selection process. They can be useful when making decisions about criteria in the job requirements matrix that are difficult to quantify. In the case of many companies, as with Scott, management style is one such KSAO.

Drug Testing

The cost of alcohol and drug abuse in our country is estimated to be $60 billion per year.[89] As shown in a recent study, substance abuse is associated with psychological (e.g., daydreaming, spending work time on personal matters) and physical (e.g., falling asleep at work, extra long lunch and rest breaks, theft) withdrawal behaviors at work.[90] Additionally, substance abuse leads to higher utilization of benefits, such as sick time and health care. As a result of these costs, drug testing is used by 63% of U.S. corporations, according to a study of 1,633 human resource managers.[91]

Drug testing is a procedure used by organizations to assess those who abuse alcohol and drugs. By identifying abusers, employers can potentially select them out of the organization before they engage in negative work behaviors and cost the organization large sums of money. Typical substances that are screened for by employers include alcohol, cocaine, amphetamines, marijuana, heroin, and PCP. Screening usually takes place at a laboratory away from the company premises.[92]

Large-scale testing programs for preemployment purposes can be found with many employers. Some of these organizations are conducting research on the deleterious effects of substance abuse. For example, the U.S. Postal Service recently conducted an evaluation of their drug testing program. They found higher absenteeism and turnover rates for substance abusers than for nonabusers.[93]

Types of Tests
There are a variety of tests to ascertain substance abuse. A description of the major categories of tests follows.[94]

Body Fluids   Both urine and blood tests can be used. Urine tests are by far the most frequently used method of detecting substance abuse.[95] There are different types of measures for each test. For example, urine samples can be measured using the enzyme multiplied immunoassay technique or the gas/chromatography/spectrometry technique.[96]

Hair Analysis   Samples of hair are analyzed using the same techniques as are used to measure urine samples. Chemicals remain in the hair as it grows.

Pupillary Reaction Test   The reaction of the pupil to light is assessed. Applicants' pupils will react differently when under the influence of drugs than when drug-free.

Performance Tests   Hand-eye coordination is assessed to see if there is impairment compared with the standard drug-free reactions.

Administration
In order for the results of drug tests to be accurate, care must be taken to ensure that precautions are taken in their administration. When collecting samples to be tested, care must be taken in ensure that the sample is authentic and not contaminated. To do so, the U.S. Department of Health and Human Procedures has established specific guidelines to be followed.[97]

The testing itself must be carefully administered as well. Labs may process up to 3,000 samples a day. Hence, human error can occur in the detection process. Also, false-positive results can be generated due to cross reactions. What this means is that a common compound (e.g., poppy seeds) may interact with the antibodies and mistakenly identify a person as a substance abuser. Prescription medications may also affect drug test results.

In order for the testing to be carefully administered, two steps need to be taken. First, care must be taken in the selection of a reputable drug testing firm. Various certification programs, such as the College of American Pathologists, exist to ensure quality services. Second, positive drug tests should always be verified by a second test to ensure reliability.

Physical Health Tests

Physical exams are often used to identify potential health risks in job candidates. Their use is strictly regulated by the Americans With Disabilities Act (discussed later in this chapter). Although many organizations use physical exams, they are not particularly valid because the procedures performed vary from doctor to doctor.[98] Also, physical exams are not always job-related.[99] Finally, the emphasis is usually on short-term rather than long-term health.[100]

A promising new development has recently taken place in physical exams. This development is known as job-related medical standards.[101] Under this procedure, physical health standards have been developed that are highly job-related. Physicians' manuals have been developed that provide information on the specific diseases and health conditions that prohibit adequate functioning on specific jobs or clusters of tasks. Not only should this procedure improve content validity because it is job-related, but it should also improve reliability because it standardizes diagnosis across physicians. Along with the manuals, useful data-gathering instruments have been developed to properly assess applicants' actual medical conditions. Again, this helps to standardize assessments by physicians, which should improve reliability.

Team Assessment

In order to be responsive to a rapidly changing business environment, some organizations are decentralizing decision making. In some cases, this decentralized decision making has resulted in self directed or managed work teams. Employees are responsible for decisions usually made by managers in centralized organizations. One set of decisions that employees may be responsible for is hiring decisions.

In making hiring decisions, team assessments are made by members of the self-directed work team in deciding who becomes a member of the group. An example of an organization following this procedure is South Bend, Indiana-based I/N Tek, a billion dollar steel-finishing mill established in a joint venture between the United States' Inland Steel and Japan's Nippon Steel. Employees in self-directed work teams, along with managers and human resource professionals, interview candidates as a final step in the selection process. This approach is felt to lead to greater satisfaction with the results of the hiring process because employees have a say in which person is selected to be part of the team.[102]

Choice of Substantive Assessment Methods

As with the choice of initial assessment methods, there has been research conducted on substantive assessment methods that can help guide organizations on the appropriate method to use. Reviews of this research, using the same criteria that were used to evaluate initial assessment methods, are shown in Exhibit 9.16.[103]

A comparison of Exhibits 9.8 and 9.16 is instructive. In general, both the validity and the cost of substantive assessment procedures are higher than those of initial assessment procedures. As with the initial assessment procedures, the economic and social impact of substantive assessment procedures is not well understood. Many organizations rely upon initial assessment methods to make substantive assessment decisions. This is unfortunate because, with the exception of biographical data, the validity of substantive assessment methods is higher. This is especially true of the initial interview relative to the structured interview. At a minimum, organizations need to supplement the initial interview with structured interviews. Better yet, organizations should strongly consider using ability, performance, and work sample tests along with either interview.

DISCRETIONARY ASSESSMENT METHODS

Discretionary assessment methods are used to separate those who receive job offers from the list of finalists. Sometimes discretionary methods are not followed because all finalists may receive job offers. When used, discretionary assessment methods are typically very subjective and rely heavily on the intuition of the decision maker. Thus, factors other than KSAOs per se may be assessed.

One interesting method of discretionary assessment is the selection of people on the basis of likely organizational citizenship behavior.[104] With this approach, finalists not only must fulfill all of the requirements of the job, but also are expected to fulfill some roles outside the requirements of the job, called organizational citizenship behaviors. These behaviors include things like doing extra work, helping others at work, covering for a sick coworker, and being courteous.

Discretionary assessments should involve use of the organization's staffing philosophy regarding EEO/AA commitments. Here, the commitment may be to enhance the representation of minorities and women in the organization's workforce, either voluntarily or as part of an organization's affirmative action plan. At this point in the selection process, the demographic characteristics of the finalists may be given weight in the decision about to whom the job offer will be extended. Regardless of how the organization chooses to make its discretionary assessments,

EXHIBIT 9.16 Evaluation of Substantive Assessment Methods

Predictors	Use	Cost	Reliability	Validity	Utility	Reactions	Adverse Impact
Personality tests	Low	Moderate	Moderate	Moderate	?	?	?
Ability tests	Low	Moderate	High	High	High	?	High
Performance tests and work samples	Moderate	High	High	High	High	?	?
Interest, value, and preference inventories	Low	Moderate	Moderate	?	?	?	?
Achievement history questionnaires	Low	Moderate	High	Moderate	?	?	?
Structured interviews	Low	Moderate	Moderate	Moderate	?	?	?
Clinical assessments	Low	High	Moderate	Moderate	?	?	?
Drug testing	Moderate	Moderate	Moderate	Moderate	?	Neutral	?
Physical health tests	Moderate	Moderate	Low	Low	?	?	?
Team assessments	Low	Moderate	?	?	?	Positive	?

they should never be used without being preceded by initial and substantive methods.

COLLECTION OF ASSESSMENT DATA

Any of the predictors discussed requires the collection of data about people. Several issues must be addressed to ensure that the data are properly and fairly collected and used.

If a predictor is purchased, then support services are needed as well. Helpful support, especially for smaller organizations, includes computerized scoring of tests and quick turnaround time. Also necessary is legal support to ensure compliance with laws and regulations. Validity studies are important to ensure the effectiveness of the tests. Training on how to administer the predictor is also needed.[105]

Predictors cannot always be purchased by any firm that wants to use them; many test publishers require the purchaser to have certain expertise to properly use the test. For example, they may require the user to hold a Ph.D. in a field of study related to the test and its use. For smaller organizations, this means that they need to hire the consulting services of a specialist in order to use a particular test.

Care must be taken to ensure that correct answers for predictors are not shared with job applicants in advance of administration of the predictor. Any person who has access to the predictor answers should be fully trained and sign a predictor security agreement. Also a regular inventory procedure needs to be established to ensure that predictor materials are not inappropriately dispersed. Should a breach of security take place, use of the predictor should be abandoned, and a new one should be used.[106]

Not only should the predictor itself be kept secure, but so, too, should the results of the predictor in order to ensure the privacy of the individual. The results of the predictor should only be used for the intended purposes and by persons qualified to interpret them. While feedback can be given to the candidate on results, the individual should not be given a copy of the predictor or the scoring key.[107]

Finally, it is imperative that all applicants be assessed using standardized procedures. This means that not only should the same or a psychometrically equivalent predictor be used, but individuals should take the test under the same circumstances. The purpose of the predictor should be explained to applicants, and they should be put at ease, held to the same time requirements to complete the predictor, and take the predictor in the same location.

LEGAL ISSUES

The legal issues surrounding external selection are substantial in number and complexity. Some of these issues are general and involve concepts and processes that apply to virtually any selection device or system. Other issues are quite specific, often focusing on usage of a particular method of assessment, such as drug testing or reference checks. Indeed, each of the methods of assessment discussed in this chapter has specific legal overtones.

Only general issues, and, particularly, only issues dealing with EEO/AA, are discussed in this section. With the field thus narrowed considerably, the following four issues are discussed: (a) the Uniform Guidelines on Employee Selection Procedures (UGESP), (b) selection under the Americans With Disabilities Act, (c) preemployment inquiries, and (d) bona fide occupational qualifications, (BFOQs).

Uniform Guidelines on Employee Selection Procedures

The UGESP are a comprehensive set of federal regulations specifying requirements for the selection systems of organizations covered under the Civil Rights Acts and under E.O. 11246. (see Appendix A for the full text of the UGESP). There are four major sections to the UGESP, namely, general principles, technical standards, documentation of impact and validity evidence, and definitions of terms. Each of these sections is summarized next. An excellent review of the UGESP in terms of court cases and examples of acceptable and unacceptable practices is available and should be consulted.[108]

General Principles

Summary   The organization must keep records that allow it to determine if its selection procedures are causing adverse impact in employment decisions. If no adverse impact is found, the remaining provisions of the UGESP generally do not apply. If adverse impact is found, the organization must either validate the selection procedure(s) causing the adverse impact or take steps to eliminate the adverse impact (such as using an alternative selection procedure that has less adverse impact).

Scope   The scope of the UGESP is very broad in that the guidelines apply to selection procedures that are used as the basis for any employment decisions. Employment decisions include hiring, promotion, demotion, and retention. A selection procedure is defined as ''any measure, combination of measures, or procedure used as a basis for any employment decision.'' The procedures include ''the full range of assessment techniques from traditional paper and pencil tests, performance tests, training programs, or probationary periods and physical, educational, and work experience requirements through informal or casual interviews and unscored application forms.''

Discrimination Defined Any selection procedure that has an adverse impact is discriminatory unless it has been validated. There is a separate section (described later in this chapter) for procedures that have not been validated.

Suitable Alternative Selection Procedures When a selection procedure has adverse impact, consideration should be given to the use of suitable alternative selection procedures that have lesser adverse impact.

Information on Adverse Impact The organization must keep impact records by race, sex, and ethnic group for each of the job categories shown on the EEO-1 form.

Evaluation of Selection Rates For each job or job category, the organization should evaluate the results, also known as the "bottom line," of the total selection process. The purpose of the evaluation is to determine if there are differences in selection rates that indicate adverse impact. If adverse impact is not found, the organization usually does not have to take additional compliance steps, such as validation of each step in the selection process. If overall adverse impact is found, the individual components of the selection process should be evaluated for adverse impact.

Adverse Impact and the Four-Fifths Rule The organization should compute and compare selection rates for race, sex, and ethnic groups. A selection rate that is less than 4/5 (or 80%) of the rate for the group with the highest rate is generally regarded as evidence of adverse impact. There are exceptions to this general rule, based on sample size (small sample) considerations, and on the extent to which the organization's recruitment practices have discouraged applicants disproportionately on grounds of race, sex, or ethnic group.

General Standards for Validity Studies There are three types of acceptable validity studies—criterion-related, content, and construct. There are numerous provisions pertaining to standards governing these validity studies, as well as the appropriate use of selection procedures.

Procedures That Have Not Been Validated This section discusses the use of alternative selection procedures to eliminate adverse impact. It also discusses instances in which validation studies cannot or need not be performed.

Affirmative Action Use of validated selection procedures does not relieve the employer of any affirmative action obligation it may have. The employer is encouraged to adopt and implement voluntary affirmative action plans.

Technical Standards

This section contains a lengthy specification of the minimum technical standards that should be met when conducting a validation study. There are separate standards given for each of the three types of validity (criterion-related, content, construct).

Documentation of Impact and Validity Evidence

For each job or job category, the employer is required to keep detailed records on adverse impact, and where adverse impact is found, evidence of validity. Detailed record keeping requirements are provided.

There are two important exceptions to these general requirements. First, a small employer (fewer than 100 employees) does not have to keep separate records for each job category, but only for its total selection process across all jobs. Second, records for race or national origin do not have to be kept for groups constituting less than 2% of the labor force in the relevant labor area.

Definitions

This section provides definitions of terms (25 in total) used throughout the UGESP.

As is evident, the UGESP makes substantial demands of an organization and its staffing systems. Those demands exist to ensure organizational awareness of the possibility of adverse impact in employment decisions. When adverse impact is found, the UGESP provides mechanisms (requirements) for coping with it. The UGESP thus should occupy a place of prominence in any covered organization's EEO/AA policies and practices.

Selection Under the ADA

The Americans With Disabilities Act, as interpreted by the EEOC, creates substantial requirements (Appendix C) and suggestions for compliance pertaining to external selection.[109] The general nature of these is identified and commented upon next.

General Principles

There are two major, overarching principles pertaining to selection. The first principle is that it is unlawful to screen out individuals with disabilities, unless the selection procedure is job-related and consistent with business necessity. The second principle is that a selection procedure must accurately reflect the KSAOs being measured, and not impaired sensory, manual, or speaking skills, unless those impaired skills are the ones being measured by the procedure.

The first principle is obviously very similar to principles governing selection generally under federal laws and regulations. The second principle is important because it cautions the organization to be sure that its selection procedures do not inadvertently and unnecessarily screen out applicants with disabilities.

Access to Job Application Process

The organization's job application process must be accessible to individuals with disabilities. Reasonable accommodation must be provided to enable all persons to apply, and applicants should be provided assistance (if needed) in completing the application process. Applicants should also be told about the nature and content of the selection process. This allows them to request reasonable accommodation, if needed, in advance.

Background and Reference Checks

Before making a conditional job offer (upon satisfactory background or reference check), the organization is limited in its use of background and reference checks. Specifically, it may not ask previous employers or other sources about the applicant's disability, illness, or workers' compensation history. Also, the organization may not ask any questions that the organization itself would not ask the applicant.

Pre-Employment Inquiries

There are definite restrictions on making preemployment inquiries. These are explained in a separate section that follows, as part of a more general discussion of the issue.

Testing

In general, the organization may use any kind of test in assessing job applicants. These tests must be administered consistently to all job applicants for any particular job.

A very important provision of testing pertains to the requirement to provide reasonable accommodation, if requested, by an applicant to take the test. The purpose of this requirement is to ensure that the test accurately reflects the KSAO being measured, rather than an impairment of the applicant. Reasonable accommodation, however, is not required for a person with an impaired skill if the purpose of that test is to measure that skill. For example, the organization does not have to provide reasonable accommodation on a manual dexterity test to a person with arthritis in the fingers and hands, if the purpose of the test is to measure manual dexterity.

There are numerous types of reasonable accommodation that can be made, and there is organizational experience and research in providing reasonable accommodation.[110] Examples of what might be done to provide reasonable accommodation include substituting an oral test for a written one (or vice versa), providing extra time to complete a test, scheduling rest breaks during a test, and administering tests in large print, in Braille, or by reader.

Medical Examinations

There are substantial regulations surrounding medical exams, both before and after a job offer. Prior to the offer, the organization may not make medical inquiries or require medical exams of an applicant. The job offer, however, may be conditional, pending the results of a medical exam.

Post-offer, the organization may conduct a medical exam. The exam must be given to all applicants for a particular job, not just individuals with a known or suspected disability. While the content of the exam is not restricted to being only job-related, the reasons for rejecting an applicant on the basis of the exam must be job-related. A person may also be rejected if exam results indicate a direct threat to health and safety. Results of medical exams are to be kept confidential, held separate from the employee's personnel file, and released only under very specific circumstances.

Drug Testing

Drug testing is permitted to detect the use of illegal drugs. The law, however, is neutral as to its encouragement.

UGESP

The UGESP do not apply to the ADA or its regulations. This means that the guidance and requirements for employers' selection systems under the Civil Rights Act may or may not be the same as those that end up being required for compliance with the ADA.

Pre-Employment Inquiries

The term *pre-employment inquiry* (PI), as used here, pertains to both content and method of assessment. Regarding content, PI refers to applicants' personal and background data. These data cover demographics (race, color, religion, sex, national origin, age), physical characteristics (disability, height, weight), family and associates, residence, economic status, and education. The information may be gathered by any method; most frequently, it will be gathered with an initial assessment method, particularly the application blank or preliminary interview. At times, PIs may also occur as part of an unstructured interview.

PIs have been singled out for particular legal (EEO/AA) attention at both the federal and state levels. The reason for this is that PIs have great potential for use in a discriminatory manner early on in the selection process.[111] Moreover, research continually finds that organizations make inappropriate and illegal PIs. One study, for example, found that out of 46 categories of application blank items, there was an average of 7.4 inadvisable items used by employers on their application blanks.[112] It is thus critical to understand the laws and regulations surrounding the use of PIs.

Federal Laws and Regulations

The laws and their interpretation indicate that it is illegal to use PI information that has a disparate impact on the basis of a protected characteristic (race, color, etc.), unless such disparate impact can be shown to be job-related and consistent with business necessity. The emphasis here is on the potentially illegal use of the information, rather than its collection per se.

The EEOC makes the following points generally about PIs:[113]

> It is reasonable to assume that all information on an application form or in a pre-employment interview are for some purpose and that selection or hiring decisions are being made on the basis of the answers given. In an investigation of charges of discrimination, the burden of proof is on the employer to show that answers to all questions on application forms or in oral interviews are not used in making hiring and placement decisions in a discriminatory manner prohibited by law.
>
> To seek information other than that which is essential to effectively evaluate a person's qualifications for employment is to make oneself vulnerable to charges of discrimination and consequent legal proceedings.
>
> It is, therefore, in an employer's own self-interest to carefully review all procedures used in screening applicants for employment, eliminating or altering any not justified by business necessity.

These principles are reflected in two sets of regulations and guidelines.

EEOC Guide to Pre-Employment Inquiries   This guide provides the principles just given. It then provides specific guidance (dos and don'ts) on PIs regarding the following: race, color, religion, sex, national origin, age, height and weight, marital status, number of children, provisions for child care, English language skill, educational requirements, friends or relatives working for the employer, arrest records, conviction records, discharge from military service, citizenship, economic status, and availability for work on weekends or holidays.[114]

ADA Regulations   These regulations (see Appendix C) prohibit PIs or preemployment medical examinations in order to determine if an applicant is disabled, or the nature or severity of a disability. Despite this seemingly strict prohibition, the regulations also specifically permit PIs and medical exams as follows:

> Acceptable pre-employment inquiry—a covered entity may make pre-employment inquiries into the ability of an applicant to perform job-related functions, and/or ask an applicant to describe or to demonstrate how, with or without reasonable accommodation, the applicant will be able to perform job related functions.
>
> Employment entrance examination—a covered entity may require a medical examination (and/or inquiry) after making an offer of employment to a job applicant and before the applicant begins his or her employment duties, and may condition an offer of employment on the results of such examination (and/

or inquiry), if all employees in the same job category are subjected to such an examination (and/or inquiry) regardless of disability.[115]

There appears to be a fine line between permissible and impermissible information that may be gathered, and between appropriate and inappropriate methods for gathering it, under the ADA. To help employers, the EEOC has developed specific assistance and recommendations on these matters. Examples of this for the application form and interview are shown in Exhibit 9.17. Shown first are examples of what may not be asked. These are followed by an example of what may be asked, and the appropriate way of doing so.

EXHIBIT 9.17 Pre-Employment Inquiries Under the Americans With Disabilities Act

---

A. **Some Examples of Questions that May Not be Asked on Application Forms or in Job Interviews:**

- Have you ever had or been treated for any of the following conditions or diseases? (Followed by a checklist of various conditions and diseases.)
- Please list any conditions or diseases for which you have been treated in the past 3 years.
- Have you ever been hospitalized? If so, for what condition?
- Have you ever been treated by a psychiatrist or psychologist? If so, for what condition?
- Have you ever been treated for any mental condition?
- Is there any health-related reason you may not be able to perform the job for which you are applying?
- Have you had a major illness in the last 5 years?
- How many days were you absent from work because of illness last year?
- Do you have any physical defects which preclude you from performing certain kinds or work? If yes, describe such defects and specific work limitations.
- Do you have any disabilities or impairments which may affect your performance in the position for which you are applying?
- Are you taking any prescribed drugs?

B. **Information that May be Requested on Application Forms or in Interviews**

An employer may ask questions to determine whether an applicant can perform specific job functions. The questions should focus on the applicant's *ability* to perform the job, not on a disability.

> **For example:** An employer could attach a job description to the application form with information about specific job functions. Or the employer may describe the functions. This will make it possible to ask whether the applicant can perform these functions. It also will give an applicant with a disability needed information to request any accommodation required to perform a task. The applicant could be asked:

- **Are you able to perform these tasks with or without an accommodation?**

> If the applicant indicates that s/he can perform the tasks with an accommodation, s/he may be asked:

(continued)

EXHIBIT 9.17   Continued

- **How would you perform the tasks, and with what accommodation(s)?**

However, the employer must keep in mind that it cannot refuse to hire a qualified individual with a disability because of this person's need for an accommodation that would be required by the ADA.

An employer may inform applicants on an application form that they may request any needed accommodation to participate in the application process. **For example:** accommodation for a test, a job interview, or a job demonstration.

The job interview should focus on the *ability* of an applicant to perform the job, not on disability.

> **For example:** If a person has only one arm and an essential function of a job is to drive a car, the interviewer should not ask if or how the disability would affect this person's driving. The person may be asked if s/he has a valid driver's license, and whether s/he can perform any special aspect of driving that is required, such as frequent long-distance trips, with or without an accommodation.

> The interviewer also could obtain needed information about an applicant's ability and experience in relation to specific job requirements through statements and questions such as: "Eighty-percent of the time of this sales job must be on the road covering a three-state territory. What is your outside selling experience? Do you have a valid driver's license? What is you accident record?"

Where an applicant has a visible disability (for example, uses a wheelchair or a guide dog, or has a missing limb) or has volunteered information about a disability, the interviewer may *not* ask questions about:

- the nature of the disability;
- the severity of the disability;
- the condition causing the disability;
- any prognosis or expectation regarding the condition or disability; or
- whether the individual will need treatment or special leave because of the disability.

The interview may describe or demonstrate the specific functions and tasks of the job and ask whether an applicant can perform these functions with or without a reasonable accommodation.

> **For example:** An interviewer could say: "The person in this mailroom clerk position is responsible for receiving incoming mail and packages, sorting the mail, and taking it in a cart to many offices in two buildings, one block apart. The mailclerk also must receive incoming boxes of supplies up to 50 pounds in weight, and place them on storage shelves up to 6 feet in height. Can you perform these tasks? Can you perform them with or without a reasonable accommodation?"

As suggested above [see 55(d)], the interviewer also may give the applicant a copy of a detailed position description and ask whether s/he can perform the functions described in the position, with or without a reasonable accommodation.

Source: Equal Employment Opportunity Commission, *Technical Assistance Manual of the Employment Provisions (Title 1) of the Americans With Disabilities Act* (Washington, D.C.: author, 1992), pp. 67–71.

State Laws and Regulations

There is a vast cache of state laws and regulations pertaining to PIs.[116] These requirements vary substantially among the states. They are often more stringent and inclusive than federal laws and regulations. The organization thus must become familiar with and adhere to the laws for each state in which it is located.

An example of Ohio state law regarding PIs is shown in Exhibit 9.18. Notice how the format of the example points out both lawful and unlawful ways of gathering PI information.

Bona Fide Occupational Qualifications

Title VII of the Civil Rights Act explicitly permits discrimination on the basis of sex, religion, or national origin (but not race or color) if it can be shown to be a bona fide occupational qualification (BFOQ) ''reasonably necessary to the normal operation'' of the business. The ADEA contains a similar provision regarding age. These provisions thus permit outright rejection of applicants because of their sex, religion, national origin, or age, as long as the rejection can be justified under the ''reasonably necessary'' standard. Exactly how have BFOQ claims by employers fared? When are BFOQ claims upheld as legitimate? Several points are relevant to understanding the BFOQ issue.

The burden of proof is on the employer to justify any BFOQ claim, and it is clear that the BFOQ exception is to be construed narrowly. Thus, it does not apply to the following:[117]

1. refusing to hire women because of a presumed difference in comparative HR outcomes (e.g., women are lower performers, have higher turnover rates)
2. refusing to hire women because of personal characteristic stereotypes (e.g., women are less aggressive than men)
3. refusing to hire women because of the preferences of others (customers or fellow workers)

To amplify on the above points, an analysis of BFOQ claims involving sex reveals four types of justifications usually presented by the employer. These involve inability to perform the work, personal contact with others requires the same sex, customers have a preference for dealing with one sex, and pregnancy or fertility protection concerns.[118]

Inability to Perform The general employer claim here is that one sex (usually women) is unable to perform the job, due to job requirements such as lifting heavy weight, being of a minimum height, or long hours of work. The employer must be able to show that the inability holds for most, if not all, members of the sex. Moreover, if it is possible to test the required abilities for each person, then that must be done rather than having a blanket exclusion from the job based on sex.

EXHIBIT 9.18 Ohio Pre-Employment Inquiry Guide

INQUIRIES BEFORE HIRING	LAWFUL	UNLAWFUL*
1. NAME	Name	Inquiry into any title which indicates race, color, religion, sex, national origin, handicap, age or ancestry.
2. ADDRESS	Inquiry into place and length at current address.	Inquiry into any foreign addresses which would indicate national origin.
3. AGE	Any inquiry limited to establishing that applicant meets any minimum age requirement that may be established by law.	A. Requiring birth certificate or baptismal record before hiring. B. Any inquiry which may reveal the date of high school graduation. C. Any other inquiry which may reveal whether applicant is at least 40 and less than 70 years of age.
4. BIRTHPLACE, NATIONAL ORIGIN, OR ANCESTRY		A. Any inquiry into place of birth. B. Any inquiry into place of birth of parents, grandparents or spouse. C. Any other inquiry into national origin or ancestry.
5. RACE OR COLOR		Any inquiry which would indicate race or color.
6. SEX		A. Any inquiry which would indicate sex. B. Any inquiry made of members of one sex, but not the other.

(continued)

EXHIBIT 9.18   Continued

7. HEIGHT AND WEIGHT	Inquiries as to ability to perform actual job requirements.	Being a certain height or weight will not be considered to be a job requirement unless the employer can show that no employee with the ineligible height or weight could do the work.
8. RELIGION—CREED		A. Any inquiry which would indicate or identify religious denomination or custom. B. Applicant may not be told any religious identity or preference of the employer. C. Request pastor's recommendation or reference.
9. HANDICAP	Inquiries necessary to determine applicant's ability to substantially perform specific job without significant hazard.	A. Any inquiry into past or current medical conditions not related to position applied for. B. Any inquiry into Worker's Compensation or similar claims.
10. CITIZENSHIP	A. Whether a U.S. citizen B. If not, whether applicant intends to become one. C. If U.S. residence is legal. D. If spouse is citizen. E. Require proof of citizenship after being hired. F. Any other requirement mandated by the Immigration Reform and Control Act of 1986, as amended.	A. If native-born or naturalized. B. Proof of citizenship before hiring. C. Whether parents or spouse are native-born or naturalized.
11. PHOTOGRAPHS	May be required after hiring for identification.	Require photograph before hiring.
12. ARREST AND CONVICTIONS	Inquiries into *conviction* of specific crimes related to qualifications for the job applied for.	Any inquiry which would reveal arrests without convictions.

(continued)

EXHIBIT 9.18 Continued

13. EDUCATION	A. Inquiry into nature and extent of academic, professional or vocational training. B. Inquiry into language skills such as reading and writing of foreign languages, if job related.	A. Any inquiry which would reveal the nationality or religious affiliation of a school. B. Inquiry as to what mother tongue is or how foreign language ability was acquired.
14. RELATIVES	Inquiry into name, relationship, and address of person to be notified in case of emergency.	Any inquiry about a relative which would be unlawful if made about the applicant.
15. ORGANIZATIONS	Inquiry into membership in professional organizations and offices held, excluding any organization, the name or character of which indicates the race, color, religion, sex, national origin, handicap, age, or ancestry of its members.	Inquiry into every club and organization where membership is held.
16. MILITARY SERVICE	A. Inquiry into service in U.S. Armed Forces when such service is a qualification for the job. B. Require military discharge certificate after being hired.	A. Inquiry into military service in armed service of any country but U.S. B. Request military service records. C. Inquiry into type of discharge.
17. WORK SCHEDULE	Inquiry into willingness or ability to work required work schedule.	Any inquiry into willingness or ability to work any particular religious holidays.
18. MISCELLANEOUS	Any question required to reveal qualifications for the job applied for.	Any non-job related inquiry which may elicit or attempt to elicit any information concerning race, color, religion, sex, national origin, handicap, age, or ancestry of an applicant for employment or membership.

(continued)

EXHIBIT 9.18   Continued

19. REFERENCES	General personal and work references which do not reveal the race, color, religion, sex, national origin, handicap, age, or ancestry of the applicant.	Request references specifically from clergymen or any other persons who might reflect race, color, religion, sex, national origin, handicap, age, or ancestry of applicant.

I. Employers acting under bona fide Affirmative Action Programs or acting under orders of Equal Employment law enforcement agencies of federal, state, or local governments may make some of the prohibited inquiries listed above to the extent that these inquiries are required by such programs or orders.

II. Employers having Federal defense contracts are exempt to the extent that otherwise prohibited inquiries are required by Federal Law for security purposes.

III. Any inquiry is prohibited although not specifically listed above, which elicits information as to, or which is not job related and may be used to discriminate on the basis of, race, color, religion, sex, national origin, handicap, age, or ancestry in violation of law.

*Unless bona fide occupational qualification is certified in advance by the Ohio Civil Rights Commission.

Source: Ohio Civil Rights Commission, 1989.

Same-Sex Personal Contact   Due to a job requirement of close personal contact with other people, the employer may claim that employees must be the same sex as those people with whom they have contact. This claim has often been made, but not always successfully defended, for the job of prison guard. Much will depend on an analysis of just how inhospitable and dangerous the work environment is (e.g., minimum security versus maximum security prisons). Same-sex personal contact claims have been made successfully for situations involving personal hygiene, health care, and rape victims. In short, the permissibility of these claims depends on a very specific analysis of the job requirements matrix (including the job context portion).

Customer Preference   The claim here is that customers prefer members of one sex, and this preference must be honored in order to serve and maintain the continued patronage of the customer. This claim might occur, for example, for the job of salesperson in women's sportswear. Usually, customer preference claims cannot be successfully defended by the employer.

Pregnancy or Fertility   Nonpregnancy could be a valid BFOQ claim, particularly in jobs where the risk of sudden incapacitation due to pregnancy poses threats to public safety (e.g., airline attendant). Threats to fertility of either sex generally cannot be used as a basis for sustaining a BFOQ claim. For example, an employer's fetal protection policy that excluded women from jobs involving exposure to lead in the manufacture of batteries was held to not be a permissible BFOQ.[119]

The discussion and examples here should make clear that BFOQ claims involve complex situations and considerations. The organization should remember that the burden of proof is on it to defend BFOQ claims. BFOQ provisions in the law are and continue to be construed vary narrowly. The employer thus must have an overwhelming preponderance of argument and evidence on its side in order to make and successfully defend a BFOQ claim.

SUMMARY

The selection process is used to narrow down the size of the initial applicant pool to candidates, then finalists, and, eventually, job offer receivers. The distinction between applicants and candidates is made using initial assessment methods. The distinction between candidates and finalists is made using substantive assessment methods. Discretionary methods are used to distinguish between finalists and job offer receivers.

Assessment methods should always be based on the logic of prediction and the use of selection plans. The logic of prediction indicates that there must be a close correspondence between elements in the applicants past situations and KSAOs critical to success on the job applied for. Job analysis helps to ensure that the appropriate KSAOs in previous situations are identified. The selection plan is the link between job analysis and predictors. It details the required KSAOs and in-dicates which selection methods will be used to assess each KSAO.

Initial assessment methods, which are typically low in cost, are used extensively for selection purposes. Unfortunately, with the notable exception of biodata, their levels of reliability and validity are usually low to moderate. As a result, the common practice of using only initial assessment methods for selection should not be followed. Instead, initial assessment methods should be used only to screen candidates from applicants. Substantive methods should then be used to separate out finalists from candidates.

Substantive assessment methods show a marked improvement in reliability and validity over initial assessment methods. This is probably due to the stronger relationship between the sampling of the applicant's previous situations with the requirements for success on the job. Ability, performance, and work sample tests predict performance quite well. The validity of the initial interview can be sub-stantially improved upon by following it up with structured interviews.

Regardless of predictor type, attention must be given to the proper collection and use of predictor information. In particular, support services need to be estab-lished, administrators with the appropriate credentials need to be hired, data need to be kept private and confidential, and administration procedures must be standardized.

Along with administrative issues, legal issues need to be considered as well. Particular attention needs to be paid to regulations that govern permissible activities by organizations. Regulations reviewed included those in the Uniform Guidelines on Employee Selection Procedures and the Americans With Disabilities Act. Two areas of external selection that require special attention are pre-employment inquiries and bona fide occupational qualifications.

DISCUSSION QUESTIONS

1. A selection plan describes which predictor(s) will be used to assess the KSAOs required to perform the job. Describe the three steps to follow to establish a selection plan.

2. Describe when initial assessment methods are used versus when substantive assessment methods are used.

3. One substantive assessment method is personality tests, which attempt to assess personality traits. Why should caution be exercised in relying on personality tests to predict potential success on the job?

4. Describe the structured interview, noting the characteristics that improve upon the shortcomings of unstructured interviews.

5. Describe the issues that must be addressed to ensure that predictors are properly administered and fair.

6. What types of preemployment inquiries are acceptable for organizations who are covered by the Americans with Disabilities Act to make?

ENDNOTES

1. G. J. Myszkowski and S. Sloan, "Hiring by Blueprint," *HR Magazine,* May 1991, pp. 55–58.
2. R. D. Arvey and M.E. Begella, "Analyzing the Homemaker Job Using the Position Analysis Questionnaire (PAQ)," *Journal of Applied Psychology,* 1975, 160, pp. 513–517.
3. J. W. Smither, R. R. Reilly, R. E. Millsap, K. Pearlman, and R. Stoffey, "Applicant Reactions to Selection Procedures," *Personnel Psychology,* 1993, 46, pp. 49–76.
4. P. F. Wernimont and J. P. Campbell, "Signs, Samples, and Criteria," *Journal of Applied Psychology,* 1968, 52, pp. 372–376.
5. P. M. Muchinsky, *Psychology Applied to Work,* third ed. (Pacific Grove, CA: Brook/Cole, 1990).
6. P. M. Muchinsky, *Psychology Applied to Work,* 1990.
7. State of Wisconsin, Chapter 134, *Evaluating Job Content for Selection,* Undated.
8. State of Wisconsin, *Evaluating Job Content for Selection,* Undated.
9. B. Kelley, "The Right Niche," *Human Resource Executive,* Jan. 1993, pp. 32–34.
10. A. Howard, "College Experiences and Managerial Performance," *Journal of Applied Psychology,* 1986, 71(3), pp. 530–552; R. Merritt-Halston and K. Wexley, "Educational Requirements: Legality and Validity," *Personnel Psychology,* 1983, 36, pp. 743–753.

11. Wonderlic Personnel Testing, Inc., "New Employment Standards Needed as Meaning of Diploma Changes," *Human Resource Measurements,* Fall 1992, pp. 1–2.

12. S. Alexander, "Trophy Transcript Hunters are Finding Professors Have Become an Easy Mark," *Wall Street Journal,* Apr. 27, 1993, pp. B1, B10.

13. L. E. Briggs, "Administrators Disagree Over Role of Grades," *Ohio State University Lantern Commencement Issue,* June 2, 1993, p. 16.

14. R. A. Ash and E. L. Levine, "Job Applicant Training and Work Experience Evaluation: An Empirical Comparison of Four Methods," *Journal of Applied Psychology,* 1985, 70(3), pp. 572–576; M. E. Griffin, "Learning from Personnel Research," *Public Personnel Management,* 1989, 8(2), pp. 127–137; M. A. McDaniel, F. L. Schmidt, and J. E. Hunter, "A Meta-Analysis of the Validity of Methods for Rating Training and Experience in Personnel Selection," *Personnel Psychology,* 1988, 44, pp. 283–309.

15. B. Shimberg, "Testing for Licensure and Certification," *American Psychologist,* 1981, 36(10), pp. 1138–1146.

16. C. Wiley, "The Certified HR Professional," *HR Magazine,* Aug. 1992, pp. 77–84.

17. G. W. England, *Development and Use of Weighted Application Blanks* (Dubuque, IA: W. M. C. Brown, 1961).

18. R. D. Gatewood and H. S. Feild, *Human Resource Selection,* second ed. (Chicago: The Dryden Press, 1990); W. A. Owens, "Background Data," in *Handbook of Industrial and Organizational Psychology,* M. Dunnette (ed.) (Chicago: Rand McNally, 1976).

19. F. S. Mael, "A Conceptual Rationale for the Domain of Biodata Items," *Personnel Psychology,* 1991, 44, pp. 763–792.

20. J. A. Breaugh and D. L. Dossett, "Rethinking the Use of Personnel History Information: The Value of Theory Based Biodata for Predicting Turnover," *Journal of Business and Psychology,* 1989, 3(4), pp. 371–385.

21. B. Lueders, "Down on Your Knees," *Isthmus,* Apr. 12–23, 1992.

22. T. E. Becker and A. L. Colquitt, "Potential Versus Actual Faking of a Biodata Form: An Analysis Along Several Dimensions of Item Type," *Personnel Psychology,* 1992, 45, pp. 389–406.

23. A. N. Kluger, R. R. Reilly, and C. J. Russell, "Faking Biodata Tests: Are Option Keyed Instruments More Resistant?" *Journal of Applied Psychology,* 1991, 76(6), pp. 889–896.

24. P. M. Muchinsky, "The Use of Reference Reports in Personnel Selection: A Review and Evaluation," *Journal of Occupational Psychology,* 1979, 52, pp. 287–297.

25. J. C. Baxter, B. Brock, P. C. Hill, and R. M. Rozelle, "Letters of Recommendation: A Question of Value," *Journal of Applied Psychology,* 66, pp. 296–301.

26. M. G. Aamodt, D. A. Bryan, and A. J. Whitcomb, "Predicting Performance with Letters of Recommendation," *Public Personnel Management,* 1993, 22, pp. 81–90; S. H. Peres and J. R. Garcia, "Validity and Dimensions of Descriptive Adjectives Used in Reference Letters for Engineering Applicants," *Personnel Psychology,* 1962, 15, pp. 279–296.

27. C. S. White and L. S. Kleiman, "The Cost of Candid Comments," *HR Magazine,* Aug. 1991, pp. 54–56.

28. C. W. Langdon and W. P. Galle, Jr., ". . . And What Was the Reason for Your Departure?" *Personnel Administrator,* 1989, 34(3), pp. 62–70.

29. Pinkerton Investigation Services, *The 1991 Employers Guide to Investigation Services* (Atlanta: Pinkerton Information Resources Center, 1991).

30. J. M. Hahn, "Pre-Employment Information Services: Employers Beware?" *Employee Relations Law Journal,* 1991, 17(1), pp. 45–69.

31. M. A. McDaniel, "Biographical Construct for Predicting Employee Suitability," *Journal of Applied Psychology,* 1989, 74(6), pp. 964–970.

32. M. S. Olson, "Security Issues of the 90's Addressed at San Diego Conference," *EMA Reporter,* 1992, 18(3), p. 4.

33. M. Mannix, "Writing a Computer-Friendly Resume," *U.S. News and World Report,* Oct. 26, 1992, pp. 90–93; G. A. Cluff, "To Scan or Not to Scan," *The EMA Journal,* 1992, 7(1), pp. 2–3; L. Stevens, "Resume Scanning Simplifies Tracking," *Personnel Journal,* Apr. 1993, pp. 77–79; J. Perry, "Resume-Sorting Computer Helps Clinton Team Screen Thousands Seeking Administrative Jobs," *Wall Street Journal,* Jan. 11, 1993, p. B1.

34. J. E. Rigdon, "Deceptive Resumes Can Be Door-Openers, But Can Become an Employees Undoing," *Wall Street Journal,* July 17, 1992, pp. B1, B11; A. A. Sloane, "Countering Resume Fraud Within and Beyond Banking: No Excuse for Not Doing More," *Labor Law Journal,* May 1991, pp. 303–310; W. Yu, "Firms Tighten Resume Checks of Applicants," *Wall Street Journal,* Aug. 20, 1985, p. 27.

35. C. Harlan, "He Apparently Succeeded Better Than Most of Us at Avoiding Work," *Wall Street Journal.*

36. M. Brown, "Checking the Facts on a Resume," *Human Resource Measurements* (Supplement to the January 1993 *Personnel Journal*), pp. 6–7.

37. K. W. Moore, "The Most Important Things to Know About an Applicant," *Recruiting and Hiring Handbook* (Waterford, CT: Prentice Hall, 1989), pp. 4–1 to 4–8.

38. "Handwriting Analysis," *Bulletin to Management* (Washington, DC: Bureau of National Affairs, May 8, 1986).

39. Office of Technology Assessment, *Genetic Monitoring and Screening in the Workplace* (Washington: US Congress, 1990).

40. S. Dentzer, B. Cohn, G. Raine, G. Carroll, and V. Quade, "Can You Pass This Job Test?" *Newsweek,* May 5, 1986, pp. 46–53.

41. J. D. Olian, "Genetic Screening for Employment Purposes," *Personnel Psychology,* 1984, 37, pp. 423–438.

42. J. D. Olian, "Genetic Screening for Employment Purposes," 1984.

43. S. Dentzer et al., "Can You Pass This Job Test?", 1986.

44. Office of Technology Assessment, *Genetic Monitoring and Screening in the Workplace,* 1990.

45. K. Miller, "At GM, the Three R's Are the Big Three," *Wall Street Journal,* July 3, 1992, p. D1.

46. S. Schwartz (ed.), *Measuring Reading Competence: A Theoretical Prescriptive Approach* (New York: Praeger, 1985).

47. "Assessing Writing Skills," *The Industrial/Organizational Psychologist,* 1992, 30(2), pp. 27–28.

48. "Poor Quality of Applicants Raises Hiring Concerns," 1992.

49. J. W. Townsend, "Is Integrity Testing Useful?", *HR Magazine,* July 1992, p. 96.

50. P. R. Sackett and M. M. Harris, "Honesty Testing for Personnel Selection: A Review and Critique, *Personnel Psychology,* 1984, 37, pp. 221–245.

51. P. R. Sackett et al., "Integrity Testing for Personnel Selection: An Update," 1989.

52. John E. Reid and Associates, "The Integrity Interview," Chicago, IL, 1989.

53. "The Honesty Test: Everyone's Guilty at Least Some of the Time," *Newsweek,* May 5, 1986, pp. 49.

54. E. Bean, "More Firms Use 'Attitude Tests' to Keep Thieves Off the Payroll," *Wall Street Journal,* Feb. 27, 1987, p. 33.

55. P. R. Sackett, L. R. Burris, and C. Callahan, "Integrity Testing for Personnel Selection: An Update," *Personnel Psychology,* 1989, 42, pp. 491–529.

56. A. M. Ryan and P. R. Sackett, "Pre–employment Honesty Testing: Fakability, Reactions of Test Takers, and Company Image," *Journal of Business and Psychology,* 1987, 1, pp. 248–256.

57. R. D. Arvey and R. H. Faley, *Fairness in Selecting Employees,* second ed. (Reading, MA: Addison-Wesley, 1988); E. Bean, ''More Firms Use 'Attitude Tests' to Keep Thieves Off the Payroll,'' *Wall Street Journal,* Feb. 27, 1987, p. 33; G. Ben-Shakhar, M. Bar-Hillel, Y. Bilu, E. Ben-Abba, and A. Flug, ''Can Graphology Predict Occupational Success? Two Empirical Studies and Some Methodological Ruminations,'' *Journal of Applied Psychology,* 1986, 71(4), pp. 645–653; J. A. Cox, D. W. Schlueter, K. K. Moore, and D. Sullivan, ''A Look Behind Corporate Doors,'' *Personnel Administrator,* Mar. 1989, pp. 56–59; R. M. Guion, and W. M. Gibson, ''Personnel Selection and Placement,'' *Annual Review of Psychology,* 39, pp. 349–374; ''Handwriting Analysis,'' *Bulletin to Management* (Washington, DC: Bureau of National Affairs, May 8, 1986); A. Howard, ''College Experiences and Managerial Performance,'' *Journal of Applied Psychology,* 1986, 71(3), pp. 530–552; J. E. Hunter, and R. F. Hunter, ''Validity and Utility of Alternative Predictors of Job Performance,'' *Psychological Bulletin,* 96(1), pp. 72–98; C. W. Langdon and W. P. Galle, Jr., ''. . . And What Was the Reason for Departure?'' *Personnel Administrator,* 1989, 34(3), 62–70; V. R. Lindquist, ''The Northwestern Lindquist-Endicott Report-1991,'' *The Placement Center of Northwestern University* (Evanston, IL: Northwestern University); M. A. McDaniel, ''Biographical Constructs for Predicting Employee Suitability,'' *Journal of Applied Psychology,* 1989, 74(6), pp. 964–970; R. Meritt-Halston and K. N. Wexley, ''Educational Requirements: Legality and Validity,'' *Personnel Psychology,* 1983, 36, pp. 743–753; Office of Technology Assessment, *Genetic Monitoring and Screening in the Workplace,* 1991, Congress of the United States; J. D. Olian, ''Genetic Screening for Employment Purposes,'' *Personnel Psychology,* 1984, 37, pp. 423–438; Personnel Policies Forum, *Recruiting and Selection Procedures* (Washington, DC: Bureau of National Affairs, Inc., May 1988); R. R. Reilly and G. T. Chao, ''Validity and Fairness of Some Alternative Selection Procedures,'' *Personnel Psychology,* 1982, 35, pp. 1–62; P. R. Sackett, L. R. Burris, and C. Callahan, ''Integrity Testing for Personnel Selection: An Update,'' *Personnel Psychology,* 42, pp. 491–529; P. R. Sackett and M. M. Harris, ''Honesty Testing for Personnel Selection: A Review and Critique,'' *Personnel Psychology,* 1984, 37, pp. 221–245; P. R. Sackett and M. M. Harris, ''Honesty Testing for Personnel Selection: A Review and Critique,'' in H. J. Bernardin and D. A. Bownas, *Personality Assessment in Organizations* (New York: Praeger, 1985), pp. 236–276; F. L. Schmidt, D. S. Ones, and J. E. Hunter, ''Personnel Selection,'' *Annual Review of Psychology,* 43, 627–670; N. Schmitt, R. Z. Gooding, R. A. Noe, and M. Kirsch, ''Meta-Analyses of Validity Studies Between 1964 and 1982 and the Investigation of Study Characteristics,'' *Personnel Psychology,* 1984, 37, pp. 407–422; M. S. Singer and C. Bruhns, ''Relative Effect of Applicant Work Experience and Academic Qualifications on Selection Interview Decisions: A Study of Between-Sample Generalizability,'' *Journal of Applied Psychology;* ''Testing Report,'' *HR Magazine,* 1992, 6(5), pp. 46–47; J. William Townsend, ''Is Integrity Testing Useful?'' *HR Magazine,* July 1992, p. 96; D. S. Ones, C. Viswesvaran, and F. L. Schmidt, ''Comprehensive Meta-Analysis of Integrity Test Validities: Findings and Implications for Personnel Selection and Theories of Job Performance,'' *Journal of Applied Psychology,* 1993, 78, pp. 531–537.

58. M. R. Barrick and M. K. Mount, ''The Big Five Personality Dimensions and Job Performance: A Meta-Analysis,'' *Personnel Psychology,* 1991, 44, pp. 1–26.

59. ''New Behavioral Study Defines Typical Turnover Personality,'' *Human Resource Measurements* (Northfield, IL: Wonderlic Personnel Test, Inc., Spring 1992), p. 4.

60. C. D. Vale, L. S. Keller, and V. J. Bentz, ''Development and Validation of a Computerized Interpretation System for Personnel Tests,'' *Personnel Psychology,* 1986, 39, pp. 525–542.

61. L. M. Hough, N. K. Eaton, M. D. Dunnette, J. D. Kamp, and R. A. McCloy, ''Criterion-Related Validities of Personality Constructs and the Effects of Response Distortions on Those Validities,'' *Journal of Applied Psychology,* 1990, 75(5), pp. 581–595.

62. L. M. Hough et al., "Criterion-Related Validities of Personality Constructs and the Effects of Response Distortions on Those Validities," 1990.

63. E. A. Fleishman and M. E. Reilly, *Handbook of Human Abilities* (Palo Alto, CA: Consulting Psychologists Press, 1992).

64. P. L. Ackerman and R. Kanfer, "Integrating Laboratory and Field Study for Improving Selection: Development of a Battery for Predicting Air Traffic Controller Success," *Journal of Applied Psychology,* 1993, 78, pp. 413–432.

65. "Test Byers Guide," *Human Resource Executive,* 1992, 6(13), pp. 43–47.

66. C. F. Wonderlic, Jr., "Test Publishers Form Association," *Human Resource Measurements* (Supplement to the January 1993 *Personnel Journal*), p. 3.

67. L. McGinley, "Fitness Exams Help to Measure Worker Activity," *Wall Street Journal,* Apr. 21, 1992, p. B1.

68. J. J. Asher and J. A. Sciarrino, "Realistic Work Sample Tests: A Review," *Personnel Psychology,* 1974, 27, pp. 519–533.

69. J. J. Asher and J. A. Sciarrino, "Realistic Work Sample Tests: A Review," 1974.

70. S. J. Motowidlo, M. D. Dunnette, and G. Carter, "An Alternative Selection Procedure: A Low-Fidelity Simulation," *Journal of Applied Psychology,* 1990, 75(6), pp. 640–647.

71. W. Arthur, Jr., G. V. Barrett, and D. Doverspike, "Validation of an Information Processing-Based Test Battery Among Petroleum-Product Transport Drivers," *Journal of Applied Psychology,* 1990, 75(6), pp. 621–628.

72. S. J. Motowidlo et al., "An Alternative Selection Procedure: A Low-Fidelity Simulation," 1990.

73. S. J. Motowidlo et al., "An Alternative Selection Procedure: A Low-Fidelity Simulation," 1990.

74. E. A. Fleishman, "Some New Frontiers in Personnel Selection Research," *Personnel Psychology,* 1988, 41, pp. 679–699.

75. S. Sillup, "Applicant Screening Cuts Turnover Costs," *Personnel Journal,* May 1992, pp. 115–116.

76. Electronic Selection Systems Corporation, *AccuVision: Assessment Technology for Today, Tomorrow, and Beyond* (Maitland, FL: Electronic Selection Systems, Inc., 1992).

77. L. M. Hough, M. A. Keyes, and M. D. Dunnette, "An Evaluation of Three 'Alternative' Selection Procedures," *Personnel Psychology,* 1983, 36, pp. 261–276.

78. R. V. Dawis, "Vocational Interests, Values, and Preferences," in M. D. Dunnette and L. M. Hough (eds.), *Handbook of Industrial and Organizational Psychology,* Vol. 2, second ed. (Palo Alto, CA: Consulting Psychologists Press, 1991), pp. 833–872.

79. L. M. Hough, M. A. Keyes, and M. D. Dunnette, "An Evaluation of Three 'Alternative' Selection Procedures," *Personnel Psychology,* 1983; S. Landers, "PACE to be Replaced with Biographical Test," *The APA Monitor,* 1989, 20(4), p. 14; C. J. Russell, J. Mattson, S. E. Devlin, and D. Atwater, "Predictive Validity of Biodata Items Generated from Retrospective Life Experience Essays," *Journal of Applied Psychology,* 1990, 75(5), pp. 569–580.

80. F. L. Schmidt, J. R. Caplan, S. E. Bemis, R. Decuir, L. Dunn, and L. Antone, *The Behavioral Consistency Method of Unassembled Testing* (Washington, DC: U.S. Office of Personnel Management, 1979).

81. S. Landers, "PACE to be Replaced with Biographical Test," 1989.

82. R. L. Dipboye, *Selection Interviews: Process Perspectives* (Cincinnati, OH: South-Western, 1992), pp. 150–180; R. L. Dipboye and B. B. Gaugler, "Cognitive and Behavioral Processes in the Selection Interview," in N. Schmitt, W. C. Borman, and Associates, *Personnel Selection in Organizations* (San Francisco: Jossey-Bass, 1993), pp. 135–170; R. D. Gatewood and H. S. Feild, *Human Resource Selection,* second ed. (Chicago: Dryden, 1990), pp. 461–504; S. J. Motowidlo, G. W. Carter, M. D. Dunnette, N. Tippins, S. Werner, J. R. Burnett, and M. J. Vaughn,

"Studies of the Structured Behavioral Interview," *Journal of Applied Psychology,* 1992, 77, pp. 571–587.

83. R. L. Dipboye and B. B. Gaugler, "Cognitive and Behavioral Process in the Selection Interview."

84. See the references in endnote 82.

85. R. L. Dipboye, *Selection Interviews: Process Perspectives,* pp. 214–217; R. L. Dipboye and B. B. Gaugler, "Cognitive and Behavioral Process in the Selection Interview," p. 142; R. D. Gatewood and H. S. Feild, *Human Resource Selection,* pp. 479–482.

86. R. L. Dipboye, *Selection Interviews: Process Perspectives,* pp. 150–179.

87. A. M. Ryan and P. R. Sackett, "A Survey of Industrial Assessment Practices by I/O Psychologists," *Personnel Psychology,* 1987, 40, pp. 455–488.

88. R. J. Stahl, "Succession Planning Drives Plant Turnaround," *Personnel Journal,* Sept. 1992, pp. 67–70.

89. S. Dentzer, B. Cohn, G. Raine, G. Carroll, and V. Quade, "Can You Pass This Job Test?" *Newsweek,* May 5, 1986, pp. 46–53.

90. W. E. K. Lehman and D. D. Simpson, "Employee Substance Abuse and On-the-Job Behaviors," *Journal of Applied Psychology,* 1992, 77(3), pp. 309–321.

91. "Employee Drug Testing Escalates," *BNA Bulletin to Management,* May 23, 1991, p. 154.

92. V. C. Smith, "Fighting Back," *Human Resource Executive,* Sept. 1992, pp. 38–39.

93. J. Normand, S. D. Salyards, and J. J. Mahoney, "An Evaluation of Pre-employment Drug Testing," *Journal of Applied Psychology,* 1990, 75(6), pp. 629–639.

94. J. A. Segal, "To Test or Not To Test," *HR Magazine,* Apr. 1992, pp. 40–43.

95. V. C. Smith, "Fighting Back," 1992.

96. J. Normand, S. D. Salyards, and John J. Mahoney, "An Evaluation of Pre-employment Drug Testing," 1990.

97. M. D. Urich, "Are You Positive the Test is Positive?" *HR Magazine,* Apr. 1992, pp. 44–48.

98. E. A. Fleishman, "Some New Frontiers in Personnel Selection Research," 1988.

99. M. A. Campion, "Personnel Selection for Physically Demanding Jobs: Review and Recommendations," *Personnel Psychology,* 1983, 36, pp. 527–550.

100. J. C. Hogan, "Physical Abilities," in M. D. Dunnette and L. M. Hough (eds.), *Handbook of Industrial & Organizational Psychology,* second ed. (Palo Alto, CA: Consulting Psychologists Press), pp. 753–832.

101. E. A. Fleishman, "New Research Frontiers in Personnel Selection," 1988.

102. M. Levinson, "When Workers Do the Hiring," *Newsweek,* June 21, 1993, p. 48; S. M. Colarelli and A. L. Boos, "Sociometric and Ability-Based Assignment to Work Groups: Some Implications for Personnel Selection," *Journal of Organizational Behavior Management,* 1992, 13, pp. 187–196.

103. R. D. Arvey and R. H. Faley, *Fairness in Selecting Employees,* second ed. (Reading, MA: Addison-Wesley, 1988); M. R. Barrick and M. K. Mount, "The Big Five Personality Dimensions and Job Performance: A Meta-Analysis," *Personnel Psychology,* 1991, 44, pp. 1–26; M. A. Campion, "Personnel Selection for Physically Demanding Jobs: Review and Recommendations," *Personnel Psychology,* 1983, 36, pp. 527–550; E. T. Cornelius, III, "The Use of Projective Tests in Personnel Selection," in G. R. Ferris and K. M. Rowland, *Organizational Entry* (Greenwich, CT: JAI Press, 1990), pp. 73–114; J. A. Cox, D. W. Schlueter, K. K. Moore, and D. Sullivan, "A Look Behind Corporate Doors," *Personnel Administrator,* Mar. 1989, pp. 56–59; R. V. Dawis, "Vocational Interests, Values, and Preferences," in M. D. Dunnette and L. M. Hough (eds.), *Handbook of Industrial and Organizational Psychology,* Vol. 2, second ed. (Palo Alto, CA: Consulting Psychologists Press, 1991), pp. 833–872; "Employee Drug

Testing Escalates," *BNA Bulletin to Management,* May 23, 1991, p. 154; R. M. Guion, and W. M. Gibson, "Personnel Selection and Placement," *Annual Review of Psychology,* 39, pp. 349–374; J. C. Hogan, "Physical Abilities," in M. D. Dunnette and L. M. Hough (eds.), *Handbook of Industrial & Organizational Psychology,* second ed. (Palo Alto, CA: Consulting Psychologists Press), pp. 753–832; R. T. Hogan, "Personality and Personality Measurement," in M. D. Dunnette and L. M. Hough (eds.), *Handbook of Industrial & Organizational Psychology,* Vol. 2, second ed. (Palo Alto, CA: Consulting Psychologists Press); R. T. Hogan, B. N. Carpenter, S. R. Briggs, and R. O. Hansson, "Personality Assessment and Personnel Selection," in H. J. Bernardin and D. A. Bounds, *Personality Assessment in Organizations* (New York: Praeger, 1985), pp. 21–52; L. M. Hough, M. A. Keyes, and M. D. Dunnette, "An Evaluation of Three 'Alternative' Selection Devices," *Personnel Psychology,* 1983, 36 pp. 261–277; J. E. Hunter, and R. F. Hunter, "Validity and Utility of Alternative Predictors of Job Performance," *Psychological Bulletin,* 96(1), pp. 72–98; V. R. Lindquist, "The Northwestern Lindquist-Endicott Report-1991," *The Placement Center of Northwestern University* (Evanston, IL: Northwestern University); K. R. Murphy, G. C. Thornton III, and D. H. Reynolds, "College Students' Attitudes Towards Drug Testing Programs," *Personnel Psychology,* 1990, 43, pp. 615–631; J. Normand, S. D. Salyards, and John J. Mahoney, "An Evaluation of Pre-employment Drug Testing," *Journal of Applied Psychology,* 1990, 75(6), pp. 629–639; M. R. Potsfall and N. R. Feimer, "The Role of Person-Environment Fit in Job Performance and Satisfaction," in H. J. Bernardin and D. A. Bownas (eds.), *Personality Assessment in Organizations* (New York: Praeger, 1985), pp. 53–81; "Pay Now, Fly Later," *Newsweek,* Nov., 1991; Personnel Policies Forum, *Recruiter and Selection Procedures* (Washington, DC: Bureau of National Affairs, Inc., May 1988); R. R. Reilly and G. T. Chao, "Validity and Fairness of Some Alternative Selection Procedures," *Personnel Psychology,* 1982, 35, pp. 1–62; C. J. Russell, J. Mattson, S. E. Devlin, and D. Atwater, "Predictive Validity of Biodata Items Generated from Retrospective Life Experience Essays," *Journal of Applied Psychology,* 1990, 75(5), pp. 569–580; A.M. Ryan and P. R. Sackett, "A Survey of Industrial Assessment Practices by I/O Psychologists," *Personnel Psychology,* 1987, 40, pp. 455–488; S. L. Rynes, "Who's Selecting Whom? Effects of Selection Practices on Applicant Attitudes and Behaviors," in N. Schmitt, W. Borman, and Associates, *Personnel Selection in Organizations* (San Francisco: Jossey-Bass, 1993), pp. 240–276; P. R. Sackett, L. R. Burris, and C. Callahan, "Integrity Testing for Personnel Selection: An Update," *Personnel Psychology,* 42, pp. 491–529; "Satisfaction With the Quality of New Hires is 50% Higher for Companies who Test," *Human Resource Measurements* (Northfield, IL: Wonderlic Personnel Test, Inc., Spring 1992), pp. 1–2; F. L. Schmidt, D. S. Ones, and J. E. Hunter, "Personnel Selection," *Annual Review of Psychology,* 43, 627–670; N. Schmitt, R. Z. Gooding, R. A. Noe, and M. Kirsch, "Meta–Analyses of Validity Studies Between 1964 and 1982 and the Investigation of Study Characteristics," *Personnel Psychology,* 1984, 37, pp. 407–422; V. C. Smith, "Fighting Back," *Human Resource Executive,* Sept. 1992, pp. 38–39; "Testing Report," *HR Magazine,* 1992, 6(5), pp. 46–47; R. T. Tett, D. N. Jackson, and M. Rothstein, "Personality Measures as Predictors of Job Performance: A Review," *Personnel Psychology,* 44, pp. 703–742; S. Zedeck, and W. F. Cascio, "Psychological Issues in Personnel Decisions," *Annual Review of Psychology,* 1984, 35, pp. 461–518; S. M. Colarelli and A. L. Boos, "Sociometric and Ability-Based Assignment to Work Groups: Some Implications for Personnel Selection," *Journal of Organizational Behavior,* 1992, 13, pp. 187–196.

104. D. Organ, *Organizational Citizenship Behavior: The Good Soldier Syndrome* (Lexington, MA: D. C. Heath, 1988); W. C. Borman and S. J. Motowidlo, "Expanding the Criterion Domain to Include Elements of Contextual Performance," in N. Schmitt, W. Borman, and Associates, *Personnel Selection in Organizations* (San Francisco: Jossey-Bass, 1993) pp. 71–98.

105. Division of Merit Recruitment and Selection, *An Introduction to Wisconsin State Civil Service Test Development* (State of Wisconsin: Department of Employment Relations, 1986).

106. R. M. Guion, *Personnel Testing* (New York: McGraw-Hill, 1965).

107. N. W. Schmitt and R. L. Klimoski, *Research Methods in Human Resources Management* (Cincinnati: South-Western, 1991).

108. G. P. Panaro, *Employment Law Manual* (Boston: Warren, Gorham, and Lament, 1990), pp. 3–10 to 3–52.

109. See Appendix C; Equal Employment Opportunity Commission, *Technical Assistance Manual of the Employment Provisions (Title 1) of the Americans With Disabilities Act* (Washington, D.C.: author, 1992), pp. 51–88; J. G. Frierson, *Employer's Guide to the Americans With Disabilities Act* (Washington, D.C.: Bureau of National Affairs, 1992).

110. L. Daley, M. Dolland, J. Kraft, M.A. Nester, and R. Schneider, *Employment Testing of Persons With Disabling Conditions* (Alexandria, VA: International Personnel Management Association, 1988).

111. R. D. Arvey and R. H. Faley, *Fairness in Selecting Employees,* second ed. (Reading, MA: Addison-Wesley, 1988), pp. 251–310.

112. S. J. Vodanovich and R. H. Lowe, "They Ought to Know Better: The Incidence and Correlates of Inappropriate Application Blank Inquiries," *Public Personnel Management,* 1992, 21, 363–370.

113. Bureau of National Affairs, "EEOC Guide to Pre-Employment Inquiries," *Fair Employment Practices* (Washington, D.C.: author, periodically updated), pp. 443:65–80.

114. Bureau of National Affairs, "EEOC Guide to Pre-Employment Inquiries," pp. 443:65–80.

115. See Appendix C.

116. Bureau of National Affairs, *Fair Employment Practices,* 454:whole section.

117. Bureau of National Affairs, *Fair Employment Practices* (Washington, D.C.: author, periodically updated), pp. 421:352–356.

118. N. J. Sedmak and M. D. Levin-Epstein, *Primer on Equal Employment Opportunity* (Washington, D.C.: Bureau of National Affairs, 1991), pp. 36–40.

119. Bureau of National Affairs, *Fair Employment Practices,* pp. 405:6941–6943.

CHAPTER TEN

Internal Selection

Preliminary Issues
The Logic of Prediction
Types of Predictors
Selection Plan

Initial Assessment Methods
Skills Inventories
Peer Assessments
Self-Assessments
Managerial Sponsorship
Informal Discussions and Recommendations
Leader-Member Exchange
Choice of Initial Assessment Methods

Substantive Assessment Methods
Seniority
Job Knowledge Tests
Performance Appraisal
Promotability Ratings
Assessment Centers
Interview Simulations
Promotion Panels and Review Boards
Choice of Substantive Assessment Methods

Discretionary Assessment Methods

Collection of Assessment Data

Legal Issues
Uniform Guidelines on Employee Selection Procedures
Revised Order No. 4
The Glass Ceiling

Summary

Internal selection refers to the assessment and evaluation of employees from within the organization as they move from job to job via transfer and promotion systems. Many different assessment methods are used to make internal selection decisions. Preliminary issues that should guide the use of these assessment methods include the logic of prediction, the nature of predictors, and the development of a selection plan.

Initial assessment methods are used to select internal candidates from among the internal applicants. Methods that may be used are skills inventories, peer assessments, self-assessments, managerial sponsorship, informal discussions and recommendations, and leader-member exchange. Substantive assessment methods are used to select internal finalists from among internal candidates. Various methods may be used, specifically seniority, job knowledge, performance appraisal, promotability ratings, assessment centers, interview simulations, and promotion panel and review boards. The choice of initial and substantive assessment methods to use should be guided by several factors. These factors are frequency of use, cost, reliability, validity, utility, applicant reactions, and possible adverse impact.

Discretionary assessment methods are used to select offer receivers from among the finalists. These decisions may be based on several factors, such as EEO/AA concerns, whether the finalist had previously been a finalist, and second opinions about the finalist by others in the organization.

All of these assessment methods require the collection of a large amount of data. In order to be sure that accurate data are collected in a fair manner, attention must be given to support services, the required expertise needed to administer and interpret predictors, security, privacy and confidentiality, and the standardization of procedures.

The use of assessment methods also requires a firm understanding of legal issues. In particular, attention must be paid to the Uniform Guidelines on Employee Selection Procedures, Revised Order No. 4, and the glass ceiling.

PRELIMINARY ISSUES

The Logic of Prediction

The logic of prediction described in Chapter 9 is equally relevant to the case of internal selection. Specifically, indicators of internal applicants' degree of success in past situations should be predictive of their likely success in new situations. Past situations importantly include previous jobs, as well as the current one, held by the applicant with the organization. The new situation is the internal vacancy the applicant is seeking via the organization's transfer or promotion system.

Although the logic of prediction is similar for external and internal selection, in practice there are several potential advantages of internal over external selection. In particular, the data collected on internal applicants in their previous jobs often offer greater depth, relevance, and verifiability than the data collected on external applicants. This is because organizations usually have much more detailed and in-depth information about internal candidates' previous job experiences. In this age of computers, where organizations can store large amounts of data on employees' job experiences, this is especially true. It is far more difficult to access data in a reliable manner when external candidates are used. As indicated in Chapter 9 previous employers are often hesitant to release data on previous employees due to legal concerns, such as potential invasion of privacy. As a result, employers often have to rely upon reports by external candidates of their previous experiences, and the candidates may not always present the whole picture or an accurate picture of their past experiences.

In terms of the relevance of past experiences, organizations may also have better data with which to make selection decisions on internal than external candidates. The experiences of insiders may more closely mirror the experiences likely to be encountered on the new job than the experiences of outsiders. For example, organizations often worry about whether some candidate will be willing to live in a certain geographic area. The answer may be obvious with an internal candidate who already lives in that location. As another example, organizations often wonder about the transferability of skills learned in another organization to their own. Hence, when a new CEO is brought to a computer company from a tobacco company, many will comment on whether he will make it in this new environment.

Along with depth and relevance, another positive aspect of the nature of predictors for internal selection is verifiability. Rather than simply relying on the opinion of one person as to the suitability of an internal candidate for the job, multiple assessments may be solicited. Opinions about the suitability of the candidate can also be solicited from other supervisors and peers as well. By pooling opinions, it is possible to get a more complete and accurate picture of a candidate's qualifications.

Types of Predictors

The distinctions made between types of predictors used in external selection are also applicable to types of internal predictors. One important difference to note between internal and external predictors pertains to content. There is usually greater depth and relevance to the data available on internal candidates. As a result, greater emphasis can be placed on samples and criteria rather than signs in selection. This is possible because the data on previous situations are more readily available with internal candidates. That is, the organization can go to their own files or managers to get reports on the applicants' previous experiences.

Selection Plan

Often it seems that internal selection is done on the basis of who you know rather than relevant KSAOs. Managers tend to rely heavily upon the subjective opinions of previous managers who supervised the internal candidate for a job. When asked why they rely on these subjective assessments, the answer is often, "Because the candidate has worked here for a long time and I trust his supervisor's feel for the candidate."

Decision errors often occur when relying upon subjective feelings for internal selection decisions. For example, in selecting managers to oversee engineering and scientific personnel in organizations, it is sometimes felt that those internal job candidates with the best technical skills will be the best managers. This is not always the case. Some technical wizards are poor managers and vice versa. Sound internal selection procedures need to be followed to guard against this error. A sound job analysis will show that both technical and managerial skills need to be assessed with well-crafted predictors.

Feel, hunch, gut instinct, intuition, and the like do not substitute for well-developed predictors. Relying solely on others' "feelings" about the job may result in the lowering of hiring standards for some employees, discrimination against protected class employees, and decisions with low validity. As a result, it is imperative that a selection plan be used for internal as well as external selection. As described in the previous chapter, a selection plan lists the predictors to be used for assessment of each KSAO.

INITIAL ASSESSMENT METHODS

The internal recruitment process may generate a large number of applications for vacant positions. This is especially true when an open rather than closed recruitment system is used—where jobs are posted for employees to apply. Given the time and cost of rigorous selection procedures, organizations use initial assessment methods to screen out applicants who do not meet the minimum qualifications needed to become a candidate. Initial assessment methods for internal recruitment typically include the following predictors: skills inventories, peer evaluations, self-assessments, managerial sponsorship, and informal discussions and recommendations. Each of these predictors will be described in turn, followed by a general evaluation of them all.

Skills Inventories

An immediate screening device in applicant assessment is to rely upon existing data on employee skills. These data can be found in personnel files, which are usually on the computer in larger organizations and in file drawers in smaller organizations. The level of sophistication of the data kept by organizations varies considerably, depending upon the method used. Methods used include traditional skills inventories, upgraded skills inventories, and customized skills assessments.

Traditional Skills Inventories

A traditional skills inventory is a listing of the KSAOs held by each employee in the organization. Usually the system records a small number of skills listed in generic categories such as education, experience, and supervisory training received. A sound traditional system should be systematically updated on a periodic basis by the human resources group. Unfortunately, the maintenance of the data base is often a low-priority project, and, as a result, traditional skills inventories often do not reflect current skills held by employees.

Upgraded Skills Inventories

In an upgraded skills inventory, managers systematically enter the latest skills acquired by employees into the data base as soon as they occur. The system may also include a listing of the skill sets held by external job candidates who were not hired. Members of the human resources group systematically record and enter the skills of people whose resume they receive. Thus, even though some individuals were not hired for an initial position, their resumes can be drawn upon for future positions where they match the qualifications. In essence, human resources is enlarging the existing internal applicant pool with external applicants' files.

Customized Skill Inventory

Both the traditional and upgraded skills inventory rely upon broadly defined skill categories. As has been indicated repeatedly throughout the book, the more specific the KSAOs required for the job, the more likely is a good person/job match. A customized skills assessment (CSA) moves in this direction.[1] With a CSA, specific skill sets are recorded for specific jobs. Skills are not included simply because they are relevant to all jobs or because they happen to match a particular computer software package. Instead, subject matter experts (e.g., managers and experienced job incumbents) identify skills that are critical to job success.

An example of a customized skills inventory is shown in Exhibit 10.1. As can be seen, each job requires increasing numbers of KSAOs. The associate position requires technical skills only; the team leader position requires technical skills plus coaching, counseling, and teamwork skills. The manager position requires all of these skills plus strategic management skills as well. An inventory like this is kept for each employee. As the person gains skills, they are entered into the appropriate boxes. Once a column of boxes is completed, the person then becomes eligible for the appropriate position when a vacancy exists.

Peer Assessments

Assessments by peers or coworkers can be used to evaluate the promotability of an internal applicant. A variety of methods can be used, including peer ratings,

EXHIBIT 10.1 Customized Skill Inventory

Name: _____

Skills Required for Future Position

KSAO Dimension	Associate	Team Leader	Manager
Technical knowledge	1. _____ 2. _____ 3. _____	1. _____ 2. _____ 3. _____	1. _____ 2. _____ 3. _____
Coaching, counseling, teamwork		1. _____ 2. _____ 3. _____	1. _____ 2. _____ 3. _____
Strategic management			1. _____ 2. _____ 3. _____

peer nominations, and peer rankings.[2] Examples of all three are shown in Exhibit 10.2.

As can be seen in Exhibit 10.2, while peers are used to make promotion decisions in all three methods of peer assessments, the format of each is different. With peer ratings, readiness to be promoted is assessed for each peer using a rating scale. The person with the highest ratings is deemed most promotable. On the other hand, peer nominations rely on voting for the most promotable candidates. Peers receiving the greatest number of "votes" are the most promotable. Finally,

---

EXHIBIT 10.2 Peer Assessments Methods

Peer Rating

Please consider each of the following employees and rate them using the following scale for the position of manager described in the job requirements matrix:

	Not Promotable 1	2	Promotable in One Year 3	4	Promotable Now 5
Jean	1	2	3	4	5
John	1	2	3	4	5
Andy	1	2	3	4	5
Herb	1	2	3	4	5

Peer Nominations

Please consider each of the following employees and mark an X for the one employee who is most promotable to the position of manager as described in the job requirements matrix:

Jeff   _____
Carolyn   _____
Jeffrey   _____
Shelly   _____
Renee   _____

Peer Ranking

Please rank order the following employees from the most promotable (1) to the least promotable (5) for the position of manager as described in the job requirements matrix:

Ila   _____
Karen   _____
Phillip   _____
Rebecca   _____
Buster   _____

peer nominations rely upon a rank ordering of peers. Those peers with the highest rankings are the most promotable.

Peer assessments have been used extensively in the military over the years and to a lesser degree in industry. A virtue of peer assessments is that they rely upon raters who presumably are very knowledgeable of the applicants' KSAOs due to their day-to-day contact with them. A possible downside to peer assessments, however, is that they may encourage friendship bias. Also, they may undermine morale in a work group by fostering a very competitive environment.

Another possible problem with peer assessment is that the criteria by which assessments are made are not always made clear. For peer assessments to work, care should be taken in advance to carefully spell out the KSAOs needed for successful performance in the position the peer is being considered for. In order to do so, a job requirements matrix should be used.

A probable virtue of peer assessments is that peers are more likely to feel that the decisions reached are fair ones, because they had an input into the decision. The decision is thus not seen as a ''behind the backs'' maneuver by management. As such, peer assessments are used more often with open rather than closed systems of internal recruitment.

Self-Assessments

Job incumbents can be asked to evaluate their own skills as a basis for determining promotability. This procedure is sometimes used with open recruitment systems. An example of this approach is shown in Exhibit 10.3. Caution must be exercised in using this process for selection as it may raise the expectations of those rating themselves that they will be selected. Also, this approach should be coupled with other internal selection procedures as employees may have a tendency to overrate themselves.

Managerial Sponsorship

Increasingly, organizations are relying upon higher-ups in the organization to identify and develop the KSAOs of those at lower levels in the organization. Historically, the higher-up has been the person's immediate supervisor. Today, however, the higher-up may be a person at a higher level of the organization who does not have direct responsibility for the person being rated. Higher-ups are sometimes labeled coaches, sponsors, or mentors, and their roles are defined in Exhibit 10.4. In some organizations, there are formal mentorship programs where employees are assigned coaches, sponsors, and mentors. In other organizations, these matches may just naturally occur, often progressing from coach to sponsor to mentor as the relationship matures. Regardless of the formality of the relationship, these individuals are often given considerable weight in promotion decisions. Their

---

EXHIBIT 10.3   Self-Assessment Form Used for Application in Job Posting System

---

SUPPLEMENTAL QUESTIONNAIRE

This supplemental will be the principle basis for determining whether or not you are highly qualified for this position. You may add information not identified in your SF-171 or expand on that which is identified. You should consider appropriate work experience, outside activities, awards, training, and education for each of the items listed below.

---

1. Knowledge of the Bureau of Indian Affairs' mission, organization, structure, policies, and functions, as they relate to Real Estate.

2. Knowledge of technical administrative requirements to provide technical guidance in administrative areas, such as personnel regulations, travel regulations, time and attendance requirements, budget documents, Privacy Act, and Freedom of Information Act, etc.

3. Ability to work with program directors and administrative staff and ability to apply problem solving techniques and management concepts; ability to analyze facts and problems and develop alternatives.

4. Ability to operate various Computer programs and methodology in the analysis and design of automated methods for meeting the information and reporting requirements for the Division.

5. Knowledge of the Bureau Budget process and statistical Profile of all field operations that impact in the Real Estate Services program.

On a separate sheet of paper, address the above items in narrative form. Identify the vacancy announcement number across the top. Sign and date your Supplemental Questionnaire.

Source: Department of the Interior, Bureau of Indian Affairs. Form BIA-4450 (4/22/92).

---

weight is due to their high organizational level and in-depth knowledge of the employee's KSAOs. Not only is the judgment of these advocates important, but so, too, are their behaviors. Mentors, for example, are likely to put employees in situations where they receive high visibility. That visibility may increase the applicants' chances of promotion.

Informal Discussions and Recommendations

Not all promotion decisions are made on the basis of formal human resource policy and procedures. Much of the decision process occurs outside normal channels through informal discussions and recommendations. These discussions are difficult to characterize because some are simply idle hall talk, while others are directly job-related. For example, a lawyer who is expected to be a rainmaker (someone who brings in clients and possible revenue) may be assessed by his contacts in the community. An assessment of the person's qualifications for rainmaking may be done by an informal conversation between a senior partner and a previous

---

EXHIBIT 10.4   Employee Advocates

Coach

- Provides day to day feedback
- Diagnoses and resolves performance problems
- Creates opportunities for employees using existing training programs and career development programs

Sponsor

- Actively promotes person for advancement opportunities
- Guides person's career rather than simply informing them of opportunities
- Creates opportunities for people in decision making capacities to see the skills of the employee (e.g., lead a task force)

Mentor

- Becomes personally responsible for the success of the person
- Available to person on and off the job
- Lets person in on "insider" information
- Solicits and values person's input

Source: Reprinted with permission from Dr. Janina Latack, PhD, Nelson O'Connor & Associates/Outplacement International, Phoenix/Tucson.

client of the supposed rainmaker at a board meeting. Unfortunately, many informal discussions are suspect in terms of their relevance to actual job performance.

Leader-Member Exchange

Leaders in an organization may also exert influence over the internal selection process. Sometimes this is consciously done through formal human resource programs where leaders' opinions are solicited about job applicants. Other times, it may occur as a result of the leaders' behavior toward subordinates. In either event, subordinates are sometimes characterized as in- or out-group members as shown in Exhibit 10.5. In-group members are much more likely to receive favorable treatment, including promotion recommendations, than are out-group members, regardless of their actual performance levels.[3]

Choice of Initial Assessment Methods

As was discussed, there are several formal and informal methods of initial assessment available to screen internal applicants in order to produce a list of can-

EXHIBIT 10.5   Leader-Member Exchange Theory

Characteristics of In-Group Members

Highly trusted by supervisor
Frequently consulted by supervisor
High degree of support from supervisor
High level of rewards from supervisor
Depended on by the supervisor to get things done
Suggestions are welcomed by the supervisor
Helps supervisor problem solve

Characteristics of Out-Group Members

Little trust by supervisor
Seldom consulted by supervisor
Little support from supervisor
Few rewards from supervisor
Seldom depended on to get things done
Suggestions are seldom welcomed by supervisor
Little opportunity to help supervisor solve problems

didates. Research has been conducted on the effectiveness of each method, which will now be presented to help determine which initial assessment methods should be used.[4] The reviews of this research are summarized in Exhibit 10.6.

In Exhibit 10.6, the same criteria are applied to evaluating the effectiveness of these predictors as were used to evaluate the effectiveness of predictors for external selection. Cost refers to expenses incurred in using the predictor. Reliability refers to the consistency of measurement. Validity refers to the strength of the relationship between the predictor and job performance. Low validity refers to validity in the range of about .00 to .15, moderate validity corresponds to validity in the range of about .16 to .30, and high validity is .31 and above. Utility refers to the monetary return, minus costs, associated with using the predictor. Adverse impact refers to the possibility that a disproportionate number of women and minorities are rejected using this predictor. Finally, reaction refers to the likely impact on applicants.

Two points should be made about the effectiveness of initial internal selection methods. First, skills inventories and informal methods are used extensively. This suggests that many organizations continue to rely upon closed rather than open internal recruitment systems. Certainly this is a positive procedure when administrative ease is of importance. However, it must be noted that these approaches may result in the overlooking of talented applicants for candidate status. Also, there may be a discriminatory impact on women and minorities.

The second point to be made is that peer assessment methods are very promising in terms of reliability and validity. They are not frequently used, but need to be

EXHIBIT 10.6   Evaluation of Initial Assessment Methods

Predictors	Use	Cost	Reliability	Validity	Utility	Reactions	Adverse Impact
Self-nominations	Low	Low	Moderate	Moderate	?	Mixed	?
Skills inventories	High	High	Moderate	Moderate	?	?	?
Peer assessments	Low	Low	High	High	?	Negative	?
Managerial sponsorship	Low	Moderate	?	?	?	Positive	?
Informal methods	High	Low	?	?	?	Mixed	?
Leader-member exchange	High	Low	?	?	?	Mixed	?

given more consideration by organizations as a screening device. Perhaps this will take place as organizations continue to decentralize decision making and empower employees to make business decisions historically made only by the supervisor.

SUBSTANTIVE ASSESSMENT METHODS

The internal applicant pool is narrowed down to candidates using the initial assessment methods. A decision as to which internal candidates will become finalists is usually made using the following substantive assessment methods: seniority, job knowledge tests, performance appraisal, promotability ratings, assessment centers, interview simulations, and review boards. After each of these methods is discussed, an evaluation of them is made.

Seniority

At first blush, the concept of seniority seems to be a relatively straightforward one. It refers to one's length of continuous employment in one organization. The concept of seniority becomes, however, very complicated when one asks the following questions: "Which months, days, or years should be measured?" "What about other qualifications that predict HR outcomes?" and "In what unit of the organization is seniority awarded?"[5]

Measurement of Seniority
In response to the first question, distinctions need to be made between tenure and experience. *Tenure* simply looks at the amount of time one has been an employee with an organization. Usually tenure is measured as the amount of time with the organization since one's date of hire. The problem with using tenure as a predictor of performance is that it says nothing about the types of experience one has had during one's tenure with an organization. For example, just because a person has worked five years with an organization does not guarantee that he or she is promotable. Five years of sales experience does not mean one has had the experience needed to be a production manager.

Another way to measure seniority is *experience,* which considers not only time with the organization, but relevant experiences as well. For example, experience measures may gauge the amount of time a person has spent in a particular job. As such, it is likely to be more specific and job-related than tenure. As another example, experience may be measured by participation or nonparticipation in certain events, such as a training program or a committee assignment.

The amount of seniority that is held by an employee is adjusted in some organizations to account for factors other than date of hire. For example, some organizations award superseniority to union officials. In other organizations, seniority is not granted to probationary employees. Other times, special exceptions may be arranged such that employees receive additional seniority for experience outside their seniority unit. For example, a clause in the policy may stipulate that employees get a partial departmental seniority count for experience in the same department in a different organization.

Seniority and Other KSAOs

In response to the second question, tenure and/or experience must be considered in the context of KSAOs required. This may be done, as described in Chapter 7, with pure seniority, sufficient ability seniority, and relatively equal seniority systems. Which system to use should depend on the relative importance the organization wishes to attach to seniority as compared with other KSAOs in predicting candidates' likely success on the new job.

Seniority Unit

In response to the third question, the places in an organization where seniority can be earned are known as seniority units. Examples of such places include plantwide, departmental, divisionwide, occupational group or job classifications. The collective bargaining agreement or policy and procedure manual needs to clearly spell out what the seniority unit is so that employees know when seniority is earned.[6] For example, it needs to be clear whether the seniority unit is the department or the entire organization. If the appropriate unit for calculating seniority is the department, then someone with 5 years departmental seniority and 8 years organizational seniority will be promoted over someone with 3 years department seniority and 25 years organizational seniority. If the appropriate seniority unit is the entire organization, then the latter rather than former employee in the example will be promoted.

Sometimes seniority units are eliminated through mergers and acquisitions. When this happens, seniority lists may need to be merged together. That is, the two previous seniority lists must be merged together so that internal selection decisions can be made in the newly formed unit. To do so, several rules can be followed, which are described in Exhibit 10.7.

Job Knowledge Tests

Job knowledge measures one's mastery of the concepts needed to perform certain work. Job knowledge is a complex concept that includes elements of both ability (capacity to learn) and seniority (opportunity to learn). It is usually measured with a paper-and-pencil test. In order to develop a paper-and-pencil test to assess job knowledge, the content domain from which test questions will be constructed must be clearly identified. For example, a job knowledge test used to select sales managers from among salespeople must identify the specific knowledges necessary for being a successful sales manager.

EXHIBIT 10.7   Methods to Merge Seniority Lists

1. *The surviving-group principle.* Here when one company purchases or acquires another company, the employees of the purchasing or acquiring company receive seniority preference over the employees of the purchased or acquired company. The seniority lists are merged by adding the names of the employees of the acquired company to the bottom of the list of the acquiring company.

2. *The length-of-service principle.* Here a combined seniority list is prepared by placing employees on the new list in the order of their length of service regardless of which company or plant the employee worked for prior to the merger or consolidation. All employees are thus treated as if they had always been employed by the same company or plant.

3. *The follow-the-work principle.* Here when companies merge or when plants or departments within a company are consolidated, the employees are given the opportunity to follow their work (if it still can be adequately identified) with the seniority rights to such work protected by continuation of the separate seniority lists. If the work becomes merged or its identity is otherwise lost, the seniority lists may be integrated into a single list on a ratio basis representing the amount of work brought to the consolidation by each group of employees.

4. *The absolute-rank principle.* Here employees are placed on the merged seniority list on the basis of the rank they held on their respective prior lists. Thus, the two employees who were first on the two original lists are given the first two places on the merged list (the employee with the longer service gets the first place and the other employee gets the second); the two employees who were second on the two original lists are given the third and fourth places on the merged list; and so on. The ratio-rank principle, noted below, is much more popular than the absolute-rank principle since the ratio-rank method gives due consideration to the rank factor without producing the serious distortions which can occur under the absolute-rank method, as where the groups to be merged are of different size.

5. *The ratio-rank principle.* Here integration of seniority lists may be accomplished by establishing a ratio from the number of employees in each of the groups to be merged and assigning the places on the new seniority list according to this ratio. Thus, if seniority list A has 200 employees and seniority list B has only 100 employees, the ratio is two to one. Therefore, of the first three places on the new seniority list, two are allocated to the first two employees on the A list and one is allocated to the first employee on the B list (as among the three employees, length of service may be used to determine which employees get each of the first three places); then places 4, 5 and 6 on the new list are allocated to the third and fourth employees on the A list and the second employee on the B list; and so on, until all the A and B employees are placed on the new list.

Source: Reprinted with permission excerpts from pp. 608–609, of *How Arbitration Works, Fourth Edition,* by Frank and Edna Elkouri. Copyright © 1985 by the Bureau of National Affairs, Inc., Washington, DC 20037.

Although job knowledge is not a well-researched method of either internal or external employee selection, it holds great promise as a predictor of job performance. This is because it reflects an assessment of previous experiences of an applicant and an important KSAO, namely cognitive ability.[7]

Performance Appraisal

One possible predictor of future job performance is past job performance. This assumes, of course, that elements of the future job are similar to the past job. Data on employees' previous performance is routinely collected as a part of the performance appraisal process and thus available for use in internal selection.

One advantage of performance appraisals over other internal assessment methods is that they are readily available in many organizations. Another desirable feature of performance appraisals is that they likely capture both ability and motivation. Hence, they offer a very complete look at the person's qualifications for the job. Care must still be taken in using performance appraisals because there is not always a direct correspondence between the requirements of the current job and the requirements of the position applied for. Performance appraisals should only be used as predictors when job analysis indicates a close relationship between the current job and position applied for.

For example, performance in a highly technical position (e.g., scientists/engineers) may require certain skills (e.g., quantitative skills) that are required in both junior- and senior-level positions. As a result, using the results of the performance appraisal of the junior position is appropriate in predicting the performance in the senior position. It is not, however, appropriate to use the results of the performance appraisal for the junior-level technical job to predict performance in a job, such as manager, requiring a different set of skills (e.g., planning, organizing, staffing).

Although there are some advantages to using performance appraisal results for internal selection, they are far from perfect predictors. They are subject to many influences that have nothing to do with the likelihood of success in a future job.[8]

EXHIBIT 10.8   Examples of Extraneous Factors Influencing Performance Appraisals

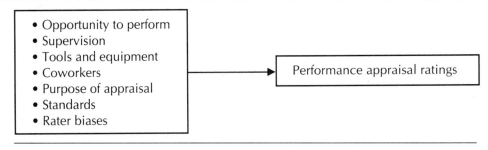

Exhibit 10.8 shows some of these extraneous factors influencing performance appraisal ratings.

Promotability Ratings

In many organizations, an assessment of promotability (assessment of potential for higher-level job) is made at the same time that performance appraisals are conducted. An example of a form to be used for such an assessment is shown in Exhibit 10.9.

Promotability ratings are useful not only from a selection perspective, but from a recruitment perspective as well. By discussing what is needed to be promotable, employee development may be encouraged as well as coupled with organizational sponsorship of the opportunities needed to develop. In turn, the development of new skills in employees increases the internal recruitment pool for promotions.

Caution must be exercised in using promotability ratings as well. If employees receive separate evaluations for purposes of performance appraisal, promotability, and pay, the possibility exists of mixed messages going out to employees that may be difficult for them to interpret. For example, it is difficult to understand why one receives an excellent performance rating and a solid pay raise, but at the same time is rated as not promotable. Care must be taken to show employees the relevant judgements that are being made in each assessment. In the example presented, it must be clearly indicated that promotion is not only based upon past performance, but is also based on skill acquisition and opportunities for advancement.

Assessment Centers

An elaborate method of employee selection, primarily used internally, is known as an assessment center. An assessment center is a collection of predictors used to forecast success primarily in higher-level jobs. It is used for higher-level jobs because of the high costs involved in conducting the center. The assessment center can be used to select employees for lower-level jobs as well, though this is rarely done.

The theory behind assessment centers is relatively straightforward. Concern is with the prediction of an individual's behavior and effectiveness in critical roles, usually managerial ones. Since these roles require complex behavior, multiple KSAOs will predict those behaviors. Hence, there is a need to carefully identify and assess those KSAOs. This will require multiple methods of assessing the KSAOs, as well as multiple assessors. The result should be higher validity than could be obtained from a single assessment method or assessor.

As with any sound selection procedure, the assessment center predictors are based on job analysis to identify KSAOs and aid in the construction of content valid methods of assessment for those KSAOs. As a result, a selection plan must

EXHIBIT 10.9   Promotability Rating Form

Form BIA-4450	DEPARTMENT OF THE INTERIOR	44 BIAM335
(4/22/92)	BUREAU OF INDIAN AFFAIRS	Illustration 4
		Page 1 of 2

SUPERVISORY APPRAISAL OF DEMONSTRATED
PERFORMANCE OF POTENTIAL

ANNOUNCEMENT NO. CO-92-125

PLEASE HAVE THIS APPRAISAL COMPLETED BY YOUR
SUPERVISOR AND SUBMIT WITH YOUR APPLICATION.
SF-171 (If the appraisal is submitted directly by the
Supervisor, the Applicant will be permitted to review
and/or obtain a copy of the appraisal upon request.)

Name of Applicant: _____   Position: _Program Specialist_____

Basis of Appraisal					Level of Performance			
Check One								
Outside Activities	On-the-job Performance	Formal Training	Unable to Appraise	RANKING FACTORS (Knowledge, Skills, Abilities, and Personal Characteristics)	Check as appropriate: 4 – Exceptional 3 – Above average 2 – Average/Satisfactory 1 – Rarely Satisfactory			
					4	3	2	1
				1. Knowledge of the Bureau of Indian Affairs' mission, organizaton, structure, policies, and functions, as they relate to Real Estate.				
				2. Knowledge of technical administrative requirements to provide technical guidance in administrative areas, such as personnel regulations, travel regulations, time and attendance requirements, budget documents, Privacy Act, and Freedom of Information Act, etc.				
				3. Ability to work with program directors and administrative staff and ability to apply problem solving techniques and management concepts; ability to analyze facts and problems and develop alternatives.				
				4. Ability to operate various Computer programs and methodology in the analysis and design of automated methods for meeting the information and reporting requirements for the Division.				
				5. Knowledge of the Bureau Budget process and statistical Profile of all field operations that impact in the Real Estate Services program.				

44 BIAM, 335, REL. 127, 4/22/92

(continued)

EXHIBIT 10.9   Continued

Form BIA-4450   DEPARTMENT OF THE INTERIOR   44 BIAM 335
(Rev. 4/22/92)   BUREAU OF INDIAN AFFAIRS   Illustration 4
                                                                              Page 2 of 2

SUPERVISORY APPRAISAL OF DEMONSTRATED
PERFORMANCE OF POTENTIAL

ANNOUNCEMENT NO.: <u>CO-92-125</u>

NARRATIVE: BRIEFLY EVALUATE THE CANDIDATE'S OVERALL ABILITY TO PERFORM THE
DUTIES AND RESPONSIBILITIES OF THE POSITION. NARRATIVE COMMENTS ARE REQUIRED
FOR ALL EVALUATIONS.

IN WHAT CAPACITY ARE YOU MAKING THIS APPRAISAL? (Please ✓ as appropriate)

( ) Present Immediate Supervisor   ( ) Present 2nd Level Supervisor   ( ) Other
                                                                              (Specify)
( ) Former Immediate Supervisor   ( ) Former 2nd Level Supervisor

Period during which you supervised the Applicant:
                                        From: To:

Appraiser:

            (Signature)   (Date)   (Phone No.)

Source: Department of the Interior, Bureau of Indian Affairs, Form BIA-4450 (4/22/92).

be developed when using assessment centers. An example of such a selection plan is shown in Exhibit 10.10.

Characteristics of Assessment Centers

While specific characteristics vary from situation to situation, assessment centers generally have some common characteristics.[9] Job candidates usually participate in an assessment center for a period of days rather than hours. Most assessment centers last two to three days, but some may be as long as five days. Participants take part in a series of simulations and work sample tests known as exercises. The participants may also be assessed with other devices, such as interviews and biographical information blanks. As they participate in the exercises, trained assessors evaluate participants' performance. Assessors are usually line managers, but sometimes psychologists are used as well.

The participants in the center are usually managers who are being assessed for higher-level managerial jobs. Normally, they are chosen to participate by other organizational members, such as their supervisor.

At the conclusion of the assessment center, the participants are evaluated by the assessors. Typically, this involves the assessor examining all of the information gathered about each participant. The information is then translated into a series of ratings on several dimensions of managerial jobs. Typical dimensions assessed include communications (written and oral); leadership and human relations; and planning, problem solving, and decision making. In evaluating these dimensions, assessors are trained to look for critical behaviors that represent highly effective or ineffective responses to the exercise situations in which participants are placed. There may also be an overall assessment rating (OAR) that represents the bottom line evaluation for each participant.

A variety of different exercises are used at a center, but those most frequently used are the in-basket exercise, leaderless group discussions, and case analysis. Each of these exercises will be briefly described.

In-Basket Exercise   An element common to most higher-level positions is an in-basket. The in-basket usually contains memoranda, reports, phone calls, and letters that require a response. In an assessment center, a simulated in-basket is presented to the candidate. The candidate is asked to respond to the paperwork in the in-basket by prioritizing items, drafting memos, scheduling meetings, and so forth. It is a timed exercise, and usually the candidate has two to three hours to respond.

Leaderless Group Discussion   In a leaderless group discussion, a small group of candidates is given a problem to work on. The problem is one they would likely encounter in the higher-level position for which they are applying. As a group, they are asked to resolve the problem. As they work on the problem, assessors sit around the perimeter of the group and evaluate how each candidate behaves in an unstructured setting. They look for skills such as leadership and communication.

EXHIBIT 10.10   Selection Plan for an Assessment Center

KSAO	Writing Exercise	Speech Exercise	Analysis Problem	In-Basket		Leadership Group Discussion	
				Tent.	Final	Management Problems	City Council
Oral communications					X	X	X
Oral presentation		X				X	
Written communications	X		X	X	X		
Stress tolerance				X	X	X	X
Leadership					X	X	
Sensitivity			X	X	X	X	X
Tenacity				X	X	X	
Risk taking			X	X	X	X	X
Initiative			X	X	X	X	X
Planning & organization			X	X	X	X	X
Management control				X	X		
Delegation				X	X		
Problem analysis			X	X	X	X	X
Decision making			X	X	X	X	X
Decisiveness			X	X	X	X	X
Responsiveness			X	X	X	X	X

Source: Department of Employment Relations, State of Wisconsin.

Case Analysis Cases of actual business situations can also be presented to the candidates. Each candidate is asked to provide a written analysis of the case, describing the nature of the problem, likely causes, and recommended solutions. Not only are the written results evaluated, but the candidate's oral report is scored as well. The candidates may be asked to give an oral presentation to a panel of managers and to respond to their questions, comments, and concerns.

Validity and Effective Practices

In a study of 50 different assessment centers, their overall validity was very favorable (an average of $r = .37$). This study showed that the validity of the assessment center was higher when multiple predictors were used, when assessors were psychologists rather than managers, and when peer evaluations as well as assessor evaluations were used. The latter results question the common practice of using only managers as assessors. It suggests that multiple assessors be used, including psychologists and peers as well as managers. Such usage provides a different perspective on participants' performance, one which may be overlooked by managers.[10]

Interview Simulations

An interview simulation simulates the oral communication required on the job. It is sometimes used in an assessment center, but it is used less frequently than in-baskets, leaderless group discussions, and case analysis. It is also used as a predictor separate from the assessment center. There are several different forms of interview simulations.[11]

Role-Play

With a role-play, the job candidate is placed in a simulated situation where she must interact with a person at work, such as the boss, a subordinate, or a customer. The interviewer or someone else plays one role, and the job candidate plays the role of the person in the position for which she has applied. So, for example, in selecting someone to be promoted to a supervisory level, the job candidate may be asked to role-play dealing with a difficult employee.

Fact Finding

In a fact-finding interview, the job candidate is presented with a case or problem with incomplete information. It is the job of the candidate to solicit from the interviewer or a resource person the additional facts needed to resolve the case. If one was hiring someone to be an equal employment opportunity manager, one might present him with a case where adverse impact is suggested, and then evaluate the candidate according to what data he solicits to confirm or disconfirm adverse impact.

Oral Presentations

In many jobs, presentations need to be made to customers, clients, or even boards of directors. To select someone to perform this role, an oral presentation can be required. This approach would be useful, for example, to see what sort of "sales pitch" a consultant might make or to see how an executive would present his or her proposed strategic plan to a board of directors.

Given the importance of interpersonal skills in many jobs, it is unfortunate that not many organizations use interview simulations. This is especially true with internal selection where the organization knows if the person has the right credentials (e.g., company experiences, education, and training), but may not know if the person has the right interpersonal "chemistry" to fit in with the work group. Interview simulations allow for a systematic assessment of this chemistry rather than relying upon the instinct of the interviewer. To be effective, these interviews need to be structured and evaluated according to observable behaviors identified in the job analysis as necessary for successful performance.

Promotion Panels and Review Boards

In the public sector, it is a common practice to use a panel or board of people to review the qualifications of candidates. Frequently, a combination of both internal and external candidates are being assessed. Typically, the panel or board consists of job experts, human resource professionals, and representatives from constituencies in the community that the board represents. Having a board such as this hire public servants, such as school superintendents or fire and police officials, offers two advantages. First, as with assessment centers, there are multiple assessors with which to ensure a complete and accurate assessment of the candidate's qualifications. Second, by participating in the selection process, constituents are likely to be more committed to the decision reached. This "buy-in" is particularly important for community representatives with whom the job candidate will interact. It is hoped that by having a voice in the process, they will be less likely to voice objectives once the candidate is hired.

Choice of Substantive Assessment Methods

Along with research on initial assessment methods, there has also been research conducted on substantive assessment methods.[12] The reviews of this research are summarized in Exhibit 10.11. The same criteria are applied to evaluating the effectiveness of these predictors as were used to evaluate the effectiveness of initial assessment methods.

An examination of Exhibit 10.11 indicates that there is no one best method of narrowing down the candidate list to finalists. What is suggested, however, is that some predictors are more likely to be effective than are others. In particular,

EXHIBIT 10.11 Evaluation of Substantive Assessment Methods

Predictors	Use	Cost	Reliability	Validity	Utility	Reactions	Adverse Impact
Seniority	High	Low	High	High	?	?	?
Job knowledge tests	Low	Moderate	High	High	?	?	?
Performance appraisal	Moderate	Moderate	?	?	?	?	?
Promotability ratings	Low	Low	High	High	?	?	?
Assessment center	Low	High	High	High	?	?	?
In-basket exercise	Low	Moderate	Moderate	Moderate	?	?	?
Leaderless group discussion	Low	Low	?	?	?	?	?
Case analysis	Low	Low	?	?	?	?	?
Interview simulations	Low	Low	?	?	?	?	?
Panels and review boards	Low	?	?	?	?	?	?

seniority, job knowledge, promotability ratings, and assessment centers have a strong record in terms of reliability and validity in choosing candidates. A very promising development for internal selection is use of job knowledge tests. The validity of these tests appears to be substantial, but, unfortunately, few organizations use them for internal selection purposes.

The effectiveness of several internal selection predictors (case analysis, interview simulations, panels and review boards) is not known at this stage. Interview simulations appear to be a promising technique for jobs requiring public contact skills. All of them need additional research. Other areas in need of additional research are the utility, reactions, and adverse impact associated with all of the substantive assessment methods.

DISCRETIONARY ASSESSMENT METHODS

Discretionary methods are used to narrow down the list of finalists to those who will receive job offers. Sometimes all finalists will receive offers, but other times, there may not be enough positions to fill for each finalist to receive an offer. As with external selection, discretionary assessments are sometimes made on the basis of organizational citizenship behavior and staffing philosophy regarding EEO/AA.

There are two areas of discretionary assessment that differ from external selection and need to be considered in deciding job offers. First, previous finalists who do not receive job offers do not disappear. They may remain with the organization in hopes of securing an offer next time the position is open. At the margin, this may be a factor in decision making because being bypassed a second time may create a disgruntled employee. As a result, a previous finalist may be given an offer over a first-time finalist, all other things being equal.

Second, multiple assessors are generally used with internal selection. That is, not only can the hiring manager's opinion be used to select who will receive a job offer, but so can the opinions of others (e.g., previous manager, top management) who are knowledgeable about the candidate's profile and the requirements of the current position. As a result, in deciding which candidates will receive job offers, evaluations by people other than the hiring manager may be accorded substantial weight in the decision-making process.

COLLECTION OF ASSESSMENT DATA

As with external selection, the careful administration of internal selection predictors is crucial for measurement, legal, and motivation reasons. Attention must be given to support services, required expertise, security, privacy and confidentiality, and standardization (see Chapter 9). With internal selection, a premium must be placed on security. Unlike with external selection, where applicants are physically outside the organization, applicants in internal selection are physically inside the organization. As a result, internal applicants potentially have far greater access to private and confidential selection materials. Computer files regarding internal selection must be carefully set up so that only authorized personnel have access to them. Clerks, secretaries, and anyone having access to manual files must be trained and held accountable to procedures designed to safeguard manual files.

LEGAL ISSUES

From a legal perspective, methods and processes of internal selection are to be viewed in the same ways as external selection ones. The laws and regulations make no major distinctions between them. Consequently, most of the legal influences on internal selection have already been treated in Chapter 9 (External Selection). There are, however, some brief comments to be made about internal selection as it is affected by three previously discussed legal influences. Those influences are the Uniform Guidelines on Employee Selection Procedures (UGESP), Revised Order No. 4, and the glass ceiling.

Uniform Guidelines on Employee Selection Procedures

It should be remembered that the UGESP (see Appendix A) defines a ''selection procedure'' in such a way that virtually any selection method, be it used in an external or internal context, is covered by the requirements of the UGESP. It should also be remembered that the UGESP applies to any ''employment decision,'' which explicitly includes promotion decisions.

When there is adverse impact in promotions, the organization is given the option of justifying it through the conduct of validation studies. These are primarily criterion-related or content validity studies. Ideally, criterion-related studies with predictive validation designs will be used, as has been partially done in the case of assessment centers. Unfortunately, this places substantial administrative and research demands on the organization that are difficult to fulfill most of the time. Consequently, content validation appears a better bet for validation purposes.

Many of the methods of assessment used in internal selection attempt to gauge KSAOs and behaviors directly associated with a current job that are felt to be related to success in higher-level jobs. Examples include seniority, performance appraisals, and promotability ratings. These are based on current, as well as past, job content. Validation of these methods, if necessary legally, likely occurs along content validation lines. The organization thus should pay particular and close attention to the validation and documentation requirements for content validation in the UGESP.

Revised Order No. 4

The order (see Appendix B) explicitly covers AAP requirements for both external and internal staffing systems, including promotion systems. A careful reading of the order shows that it also speaks specifically to selection methods. Most salient are the following statements:

1. The contractor should evaluate the total selection process to ensure freedom from bias, and, thus aid the attainment of goals and objectives.
2. The contractor should validate worker specifications by division, department, location or other organizational unit and by job category using job performance criteria. Special attention should be given to academic, experience and skill requirements to ensure that the requirements in themselves do not constitute inadvertent discrimination. Specifications should be consistent for the same job classification in all locations and should be free from bias as regards to race, color, religion, sex, or national origin, except where sex is a bona fide occupational qualification. Where requirements screen out a disproportionate number of minorities or women, such requirements should be professionally validated to job performance.

These requirements, coupled with those in the UGESP, provide firm guidance as to the use and validation of internal selection methods.

The Glass Ceiling

In Chapter 7, the nature of the glass ceiling was discussed, as well as staffing steps to remove it from organizational promotion systems. Most of that discussion centered on internal recruitment and supporting activities that could be undertaken. Surprisingly, selection methods used for promotion assessment are rarely mentioned in literature on the glass ceiling.

This is a major oversight. While the internal recruitment practices recommended may enhance the identification and attraction of minority and women candidates for promotion, effectively matching them to their new jobs requires application of internal selection processes and methods. What might this require of an organization committed to shattering the glass ceiling?

The first possibility is for greater use of selection plans. As discussed in Chapter 9, these plans lay out the KSAOs required for a job, which KSAOs are necessary to bring to the job (as opposed to being acquired on the job), and of those necessary, the most appropriate method of assessment for each. Such a plan forces an organization to conduct job analysis, construct career ladders or KSAO lattices, and consider alternatives to many of the traditional methods of assessment used in promotion systems.

A second suggestion is for the organization to back away from use of these traditional methods of assessment as much as possible, in ways consistent with the selection plan. This means a move away from casual, subjective methods, such as supervisory recommendation, typical promotability ratings, quick reviews of personnel files, and informal recommendations. In their place should come more formal, standardized, and job-related assessment methods. Examples here include assessment centers, promotion review boards or panels, and interview simulations.

A final suggestion is for the organization to pay close attention to the types of KSAOs necessary for advancement, and undertake programs to impart these KSAOs to aspiring employees. These developmental actions might include key job and committee assignments, participation in conferences and other networking opportunities, mentoring and coaching programs, and skill acquisition in formal training programs. Internal selection methods would then be used to assess proficiency on these newly acquired KSAOs, in accordance with the selection plan.

SUMMARY

The selection of internal candidates follows a process very similar to the selection of external candidates. The logic of prediction is applied and a selection plan is developed and implemented.

One important area where internal and external selection methods differ is in the nature of the predictor. Predictors used for internal selection tend to have greater depth and more relevance, and are better suited for verification. As a result, there are often different types of predictors used for internal than for external selection decisions.

Initial assessment methods are used to narrow down the applicant pool to a qualified set of candidates. Approaches used are skills inventories, peer assessments, self-assessments, managerial sponsorship, informal discussions and recommendations, and leader-member exchange. Of these approaches, no one approach is particularly strong in predicting future performance. Hence, consideration should be given to using multiple predictors to verify the accuracy of any one method. These results also point to the need to use substantive as well as initial assessment methods in making internal selection decisions.

Substantive assessment methods are used to select finalists from the list of candidates. Predictors used to make these decisions include seniority, job knowledge tests, performance appraisals, promotability ratings, the assessment center, interview simulations, and panels and review boards. Of this set of predictors, ones that work well are seniority systems, job knowledge tests, promotability ratings, and assessment centers. Organizations need to give greater consideration to the latter three predictors to supplement traditional seniority systems.

Although very costly, the assessment center seems to be very effective. The reason that it is so effective is that it is grounded in behavioral science theory and the logic of prediction. In particular, samples of behavior are analyzed, multiple assessors and predictors are used, and predictors are developed on the basis of job analysis.

Internal job applicants have the potential for far greater access to selection data than do external job applicants due to their physical proximity to the data. As a result, procedures must be implemented to ensure that manual and computer files with sensitive data are kept private and confidential.

Three areas of legal concern for internal selection decisions are the Uniform Guidelines on Employee Selection Procedures (UGESP), Revised Order No. 4, and the glass ceiling. In terms of the UGESP, particular care must be taken to ensure that internal selection methods are valid if adverse impact is occurring. Revised Order No. 4 needs to be carefully consulted as it offers explicit guidelines regarding the use and validation of internal selection methods. In order to minimize glass ceiling effects, organizations should make greater use of selection plans and more objective internal assessment methods, as well as help impart the KSAOs necessary for advancement.

DISCUSSION QUESTIONS

1. Explain how internal selection decisions differ from external selection decisions.
2. What are the differences between peer ratings, peer nominations, and peer rankings?
3. Explain the theory behind assessment centers.
4. Describe the three different types of interview simulations.
5. Evaluate the effectiveness of seniority, assessment centers, and job knowledge as substantive internal selection procedures.
6. What steps should be taken by an organization that is committed to shattering the glass ceiling?

ENDNOTES

1. K. Ludwan, ''Customized Skills Assessments,'' *HR Magazine,* July 1991, pp. 67–69, 85.
2. J. J. Kane and E. E. Lawler, ''Methods of Peer Assessment,'' *Psychological Bulletin,* 1978, 85, 555–586.
3. G. Green, M. Novak, and P. Sommerkamp, ''The Effects of Leader-Member Exchange and Job Design on Productivity and Job Satisfaction: Testing a Dual Attachment Model,'' *Organizational Behavior and Human Performance,* 1982, 30, pp. 109–131; R. L. Heneman, D. B. Greenberger, and C. Anonyuo, ''Attributions and Exchanges: The Effects of Interpersonal Factors on the Diagnosis of Employee Performance,'' *Academy of Management Journal,* 1989, 32, pp. 466–472.
4. R. R. Reilly and G. T. Chao, ''Validity and Fairness of Some Alternative Selection Procedures,'' *Personnel Psychology,* 1982, 35, pp. 1–62.
5. R. R. Cerbone and J. Walsh, ''Management Judgment vs. Seniority—Grist for the Arbitration Mill,'' *Employee Relations Law Journal,* 1988, 14(3), pp. 429–437; M. E. Gordon and W. A. Johnson, ''Seniority: A Review of Its Legal and Scientific Standing,'' *Personnel Psychology,* 1982, 35, pp. 255–279; R. C. Liden and G. M. Kromm, ''Testing Standards in Grievance Ar-

bitration: A Case Review and Critique,'' *Employee Relations Law Journal,* 1987, 13, pp. 287–303.

6. The remainder of the discussion on seniority draws heavily from F. Elkouri and E. Elkouri, *How Arbitration Works,* third ed. (Washington, DC: BNA, 1973), pp. 551–609.

7. F. L. Schmidt and J.E. Hunter, ''Development of a Causal Model of Processes Determining Job Performance,'' *Current Directions in Psychological Science,* 1992, 1(3), pp. 89–92.

8. K. R. Murphy and J. M. Cleveland, *Performance Appraisal: An Organizational Perspective* (Boston: Allyn and Bacon, 1991).

9. S. B. Keel, D. S. Cochran, K. Arnett, and D. R. Arnold, ''AC's are not Just for the Big Guys,'' *Personnel Administrator,* May 1989, pp. 100–101; G. C. Thornton, *Assessment Centers in Human Resource Management* (Reading, MA: Addison-Wesley, 1992).

10. B. B. Gaugler, D. B. Rosenthal, G. C. Thornton, III, and C. Bentson, ''Meta-Analysis of Assessment Center Validity,'' *Journal of Applied Psychology,* 1987, 72(3), pp. 493–511.

11. G. C. Thornton, *Assessment Centers,* 1992.

12. R. D. Arvey and R. H. Faley, *Fairness in Selecting Employees,* second ed. (Reading, MA: Addison-Wesley, 1988); B. B. Gaugler, D. B. Rosenthal, G. C. Thornton III, and C. Bentson, ''Meta-Analysis of Assessment Center Validity,'' *Journal of Applied Psychology,* 1987, 72(3), pp. 493–511; J. R. Hinrichs, ''An Eight-year Follow-up of a Management Assessment Center,'' *Journal of Applied Psychology,* 1978, 63(5), pp. 596–601; J. E. Hunter and R. F. Hunter, ''Validity and Utility of Alternative Predictors of Job Performance,'' *Psychological Bulletin,* 96(1), pp. 72–98; S. B. Keel, D. S. Cochran, K. Arnett, and D. R. Arnold, ''AC's are not Just for the Big Guys,'' *Personnel Administrator,* May 1989, pp. 98–100; R. C. Liden and G. M. Kromm, ''Testing Standards in Grievance Arbitration: A Case Review and Critique,'' *Employee Relations Law Journal,* 13, pp. 287–303; J. E. Pynes and H. J. Bernardin, ''Predictive Validity of an Entry-Level Police Officer Assessment Center,'' *Journal of Applied Psychology,* 1989, 74(5), 831–833; R. R. Reilly and G. T. Chao, ''Validity and Fairness of Some Alternative Selection Procedures,'' *Personnel Psychology,* 1982, 35, pp. 1–62; J. S. Schippman, E. P. Prien, and J. A. Katz, ''Reliability and Validity of In-Basket Performance Measures,'' *Personnel Psychology,* 1990, 43, pp. 837–859; F. L. Schmidt, D. S. Ones, and J. E. Hunter, ''Personnel Selection,'' *Annual Review of Psychology,* 43, 627–670; F. L. Schmidt, J. E. Hunter, A. N. Outerbridge, and S. Goff, ''Joint Relation of Experience and Ability with Job Performance: Test of Three Hypotheses,'' *Journal of Applied Psychology,* 1988, 73(1), pp. 46–57; F. L. Schmidt and J. E. Hunter, ''Development of a Causal Model of Processes Determining Job Performance,'' *Current Directions in Psychological Science,* 1992, 1(3), pp. 89–92; N. Schmitt, R. Z. Gooding, R. A. Noe, and M. Kirsch, ''Meta-Analyses of Validity Studies Between 1964 and 1982 and the Investigation of Study Characteristics,'' *Personnel Psychology,* 1984, 37, pp. 407–422; J. Schwarzwald, M. Koslowsky, & B. Shalit, ''A Field Study of Employees' Attitudes and Behaviors After Promotion Decisions,'' *Journal of Applied Psychology,* 1992, 77(4), pp. 511–514; G. C. Thornton, *Assessment Centers in Human Resource Management* (Reading, MA: Addison-Wesley, 1992).

STAFFING ORGANIZATIONS MODEL

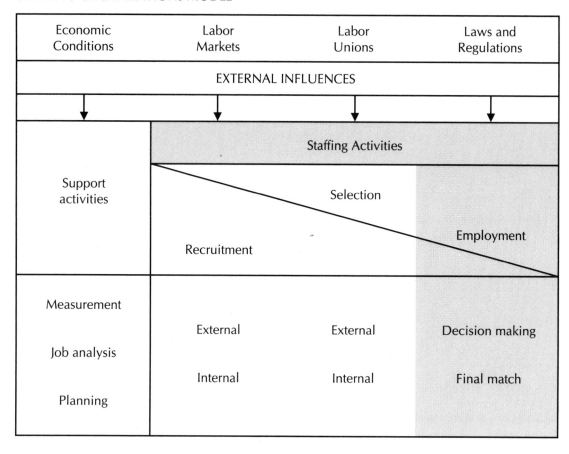

Economic Conditions	Labor Markets	Labor Unions	Laws and Regulations

EXTERNAL INFLUENCES

Support activities	Staffing Activities		
	Recruitment	Selection	Employment
Measurement	External	External	Decision making
Job analysis			
Planning	Internal	Internal	Final match

PART FIVE

Staffing Activities: Employment

CHAPTER ELEVEN
Decision Making

CHAPTER TWELVE
Final Match

CHAPTER ELEVEN

Decision Making

Choice of Assessment Method
Validity Coefficient
Correlation with Other Predictors
Adverse Impact
Utility

Hiring Standards and Cut Scores
Description of the Process
Consequences of Cut Scores
Methods to Determine Cut Scores

Using Multiple Predictors
Compensatory Model
Multiple Hurdles
Combined Method

Methods of Final Choice
Random Selection
Ranking
Grouping

Decision Makers
Human Resource Professionals
Managers
Employees

Legal Issues
Uniform Guidelines on Employee Selection Procedures
Choices Among Finalists

Summary

Individuals flow through the staffing process, passing through several stages: applicant, candidate, finalist, offer receiver, and new hire. To implement and manage this flow, key decisions must be made in several areas. First, attention must be given to the choice of assessment methods to be used. This decision should be guided by consideration of validity, the correlation of one assessment method with other methods, likely adverse impact, and the utility of the method.

Hiring standards and cut scores must be established to determine passing scores on each predictor that has been chosen for use. This requires an understanding of the process used, the consequences of cut scores, and methods to determine cut scores. Methods to choose from include norm-referenced, content-related, and criterion-related methods.

If multiple assessment methods are used, methods to combine predictor scores need to be considered. Methods that can be used are a compensatory model, multiple hurdles, or a combined approach. Each has distinct strengths and weaknesses.

Methods of final choice must be considered to determine who from among the finalists will receive a job offer. Methods of final choice include random selection, ranking, and grouping. Each method may be advantageous, depending upon one's objectives.

For all of the preceding decisions, consideration must be given to who should be involved in the decision process. Decision makers include human resource professionals, line managers, and employees. In general, decisions about the staffing procedures to be followed are determined by HR professionals. Actual hiring decisions are usually made by managers. Increasingly, employees are being involved in both decisions.

Finally, legal issues should also guide the decision making. Particular attention must be given to the Uniform Guidelines on Employee Selection Procedures. Of special concern are the use of cutoff scores, and choices from among finalists.

CHOICE OF ASSESSMENT METHOD

Several factors affect which predictor(s) to use. These factors include the validity coefficient, correlation with other predictors, likely adverse impact, and utility. They can be used to determine which initial assessment methods, which substantive assessment methods, and which discretionary assessment methods should be used. These factors are discussed in the sections that follow.

Validity Coefficient

Validity refers to the relationship between predictor and criterion scores. Often this relationship is assessed using a correlation (see Chapter 4). The correlation between predictor and criterion scores is known as a *validity coefficient*. For example, the validity coefficient for an ability test may be $r = .40$ when scores on the test (predictor) are correlated with performance ratings (criterion). The usefulness of a predictor is determined on the basis of the practical significance and statistical significance of its validity coefficient.

Practical Significance

Practical significance refers to the extent to which the predictor adds value to the prediction of job success. It is assessed by examining the sign and the magnitude of the validity coefficient.

Sign The sign of the validity coefficient refers to the direction of the relationship between the predictor and criterion. A useful predictor is one where the sign of the relationship is positive or negative and is consistent with the logic or theory behind the predictor.

A positive or negative sign in and of itself, however, says nothing about the usefulness of a predictor. A positive sign does not mean a good predictor and a negative sign does not mean a poor predictor. The signs should not be considered independent of the theory because a positive sign may be desirable in one situation, but not another. A useful predictor is one where the sign is consistent with the theory. For example, if an ability test is used to predict job performance, then the test would probably be most useful when there is a positive sign. This is because theory suggests that ability is positively related to how well people perform on the job.

Magnitude The magnitude of the validity coefficient refers to the size of the coefficient. It can range from 0 to 1.00, with a coefficient of 0 being the least desirable and a coefficient of 1.00 being the most desirable. The closer the validity coefficient is to 1.00, the more useful is the predictor. Predictors with validity coefficients of 1.00 are not to be expected with predictors. Instead, as shown in Chapters 9 and 10, validity coefficients for current assessment methods range from 0 to about .60. Any validity coefficient above 0 is better than random selection and is somewhat useful. Validities above .15 are of moderate usefulness and validities above .30 are of high usefulness.

Statistical Significance

Statistical significance, as assessed by probability or p values (see Chapter 4) is another factor that should be used to interpret the validity coefficient. If a validity coefficient has a reasonable p value, it indicates that chances are good that, if the same predictor were used with different sets of job applicants, it would yield a similar validity coefficient. That is, a reasonable p value indicates that the method of prediction rather than chance produced the observed validity coefficient.

Convention has it that a reasonable level of significance is $p < .05$. This means there are fewer than 5 chances in 100 of concluding there is a relationship in the population of job applicants, when, in fact, there is not. In most cases, this is a reasonable level of certainty indicating that the validity coefficient is statistically significant. Other times, a smaller p value, such as .001, is chosen for statistical significance. This may be the case, for example, when selecting people for a hazardous occupation, such as firefighting, and using a nonvalid predictor may have many disastrous and expensive consequences.

It should be pointed out that caution must be exercised in using statistical significance as a way to gauge the usefulness of a predictor. Research has clearly shown that nonsignificant validity coefficients may simply be due to the small samples of employees used to calculate the validity coefficient. Rejecting the use of a predictor solely on the basis of a small sample may lead to the rejection of a predictor that would have been quite acceptable had a larger sample of employees been used to test for validity.[1]

Correlation with Other Predictors

If a predictor is to be considered useful, it must add value to the prediction of job success. In order to add value, it must add to the prediction of success above and beyond the forecasting powers of current predictors. In general, a predictor is more useful the smaller the correlation it has with other predictors and the higher the correlation it has with the criterion.

In order to assess whether the predictor adds anything new to forecasting, a matrix showing all the correlations between the predictors and the criteria should always be generated. If the correlations between the new predictor and existing predictors are higher than the correlations between the new predictor and criterion, then the new predictor is not adding much that is new.

Predictors are likely to be highly correlated with one another when their domain of content is similar. For example, both biodata and application blanks may focus on previous training received. Thus, using both biodata and application blanks as predictors may be redundant, and neither one may augment the other much in predicting job success.

Adverse Impact

A predictor discriminates between people in terms of the likelihood of their success on the job. A predictor may also discriminate by screening out a disproportionate number of minorities and women. To the extent that this happens, the predictor has adverse impact and it may result in legal problems. As a result, when the validity of alternative predictors is the same and one predictor has less adverse impact than the other predictor, then the predictor with less adverse impact should be used.

A very difficult judgement call arises when one predictor has high validity and high adverse impact while another predictor has low validity and low adverse impact. From the perspective of accurately predicting job performance, the former predictor should be used. From an EEO/AA standpoint, the latter predictor is preferable. Balancing the trade-offs is difficult and requires use of the organization's staffing philosophy regarding EEO/AA.[2]

Utility

Utility refers to the expected gains to be derived from using a predictor. Expected gains are of two types: hiring success and economic.

Hiring Success Gain

Hiring success refers to the proportion of new hires who turn out to be successful on the job. Hiring success gain refers to the increase in the proportion of successful new hires that is expected to occur as a result of adding a new predictor to the selection system. If the current staffing system yields a success rate of 75% for new hires, how much of a gain in this success rate will occur by adding a new predictor to the system? The greater the expected gain, the greater the utility of the new predictor. This gain is influenced not only by the validity of the new predictor (as already discussed), but also by the selection ratio and base rate.

Selection Ratio   The *selection ratio* is simply the number of people hired divided by the number of applicants (sr = number hired/number of applicants). The lower the selection ratio, the more useful the predictor. When the selection ratio is low, the organization is more likely to be selecting successful employees.

If the selection ratio is low, then the denominator is large or the numerator is small. Both conditions are desirable. A large denominator means that the organization is reviewing a large number of applicants for the job. The chances of identifying a successful candidate are much better in this situation than when an organization hires the first available person or only reviews a few applicants. A small numerator indicates that the organization is being very stringent with its hiring standards. The organization is hiring people likely to be successful rather than hiring anyone who meets the most basic requirements for the job; it is using high standards to ensure that the very best are selected.

Base Rate   The *base rate* is defined as the proportion of current employees who are successful on some criterion or HR outcome (br = number of successful employees/number of employees). A high base rate is desired for obvious reasons. A high base rate may come about from the organization's staffing system alone, or in combination with other HR programs such as training and compensation.

When considering possible use of a new predictor, one issue is whether the proportion of successful employees (i.e., the base rate) will increase as a result of using the new predictor in the staffing system. This is the matter of hiring success gain. Dealing with it requires simultaneous consideration of the organization's current base rate and selection ratio, as well as the validity of the new predictor.

The Taylor-Russell Tables provide the necessary assistance for addressing this issue.[3] An excerpt from the Taylor-Russell Tables is shown in Exhibit 11.1.

The Taylor-Russell Table shows in each of its cells the percentage of new hires who will turn out to be successful. This is determined by a combination of the validity coefficient for the new predictor, the selection ratio, and the base rate. The top matrix (A) shows the percentage of successful new hires when the base rate is low (.30), the validity coefficient is low (.20) or high (.60), and the selection ratio is low (.10) or high (.70). The bottom matrix (B) shows the percentage of successful new hires when the base rate is high (.80), the validity coefficient is low (.20) or high (.60), and the selection ratio is low (.10) or high (.70). Two illustrations show how these tables may be used.

The first illustration has to do with the decision whether or not to use a new test to select computer programmers. Assume that the current test used to select programmers has a validity coefficient of .20. Also assume that a consulting firm has approached the organization with a new test that has a validity coefficient of .60. Should the organization purchase and use the new test?

At first blush, the answer might seem to be affirmative, since the new test has a substantially higher level of validity. This initial reaction, however, must be gauged in the context of the selection ratio and the current base rate. If the current base rate is .80 and the current selection ratio is .70, then, as can be seen in the lower matrix (B) of Exhibit 11.1, the new selection procedure will only result in

---

EXHIBIT 11.1   Excerpts from the Taylor-Russell Tables

A.

	Base Rate = .30 Selection Ratio	
Validity	**.10**	**.70**
.20	43%	33
.60	77	40

B.

	Base Rate = .80 Selection Ratio	
Validity	**.10**	**.70**
.20	89%	83
.60	99	90

Source: H. C. Taylor and J. T. Russell, "The Relationship of Validity Coefficients to the Practical Effectiveness of Tests in Selection," *Journal of Applied Psychology*, 1939, 23, pp. 565–578.

a hiring success gain from 83% to 90%. The organization may already have a very high base rate due to other facets of human resource management it does quite well (e.g., training, rewards). Hence, even though it has validity of .20, the base rate of its current predictor is already .80.

On the other hand, if the existing base rate of the organization is .30 and the existing selection ratio is .10, then it should strongly consider use of the new test. As shown in the top matrix (A) in Exhibit 11.1, the hiring success gain will go from 43% to 77% with the addition of the new test.

A second illustration using the Taylor-Russell Tables has to do with recruitment in conjunction with selection. Assume that the validity of the organization's current predictor, a cognitive ability test, is .60. Also assume that a new college recruitment program has been very aggressive. As a result, there is a large swell in the number of applicants, and the selection ratio has decreased from .70 to .10. The decision the organization faces is whether to continue this new college recruitment program.

An initial reaction may be that the program should be continued because of the large increase in applicants generated. As shown in the top matrix of Exhibit 11.1, this answer would be correct if the current base rate is .30. By decreasing the selection ratio from .70 to .10, the hiring success gain increases from 40% to 77%. On the other hand, if the current base rate is .80, the correct decision may be to not continue the programs. The hiring success increases from only 90% to 99%, which may not justify the very large expense associated with aggressive college recruitment campaigns.

The point of these illustrations is that when confronted with the decision whether or not to use a new predictor, the decision depends upon the validity coefficient, base rate, and selection ratio. They should not be considered independent of one another. Human resource professionals should carefully record and monitor base rates and selection ratios. Then, when asked by management whether they should be using a new predictor, they can respond appropriately. Fortunately, the Taylor-Russell Tables are for any combination of validity coefficient, base rate, and selection ratio values. The values shown in Exhibit 11.1 are excerpts for illustration only. When other values need to be considered, then the original tables should be consulted to provide the appropriate answers.

Economic Gain
Economic gain refers to the bottom line or monetary impact of a predictor on the organization. A predictor is more useful the greater the economic gain it produces. Considerable work has been done over the years on assessing the economic gain associated with predictors.[4] The basic utility formula used to estimate economic gain is shown in Exhibit 11.2.

At a general level, the economic gain formula shown in Exhibit 11.2 works as follows. Economic gains derived from using a valid predictor versus random selection (the left-hand side of the equation) depend upon two factors (the right-

---

EXHIBIT 11.2   Economic Gain Formula

$$\Delta U = N_s TrSDy\bar{Z}_s - NC$$

Where:

ΔU = expected dollar value increase to the organization using the predictor versus random selection

T = tenure of selected group

N_s = number of applicants selected

r = correlation between predictor and job performance

SDy = standard deviation of job performance

$\bar{Z}_s$ = average standard predictor score of selected group

N = number of applicants

C = cost per applicant

Source: Wayne F. Cascio, *Applied Psychology in Personnel Management*, 4e, © 1991, p. 300. Adapted by permission of Prentice-Hall, Englewood Cliffs, New Jersey.

hand side of the equation). The first factor (the entry before the subtraction sign) is the revenue generated by hiring productive employees using the new predictor. The second factor (the entry after the subtraction sign) is the costs associated with using the new predictor. Positive economic gains are achieved when revenues are maximized and costs are minimized. Revenues are maximized by using the most valid selection procedures. Costs are minimized by using the predictors with the least costs. In order to estimate actual economic gain, values are entered into the equation for each of the variables shown. Values are usually generated by experts in human resource research relying upon the judgments of experienced line managers.

Several variations on the economic gain (utility) formula shown in Exhibit 11.2 have been developed. For the most part, these variations require consideration of additional factors, such as assumptions about tax rates and applicant flows. In all of these models, the most difficult factor to estimate is the standard deviation of job performance (SDy), which represents the difference between productive and nonproductive employees in dollar value terms. These must be estimated using judgmental procedures. Despite this difficulty, economic gain formulas represent a significant way of estimating the economic gains that may be anticipated with the use of a new (and valid) predictor.

HIRING STANDARDS AND CUT SCORES

Hiring standards or cut scores address the issue of what constitutes a passing score on any one predictor. To address this, a description of the process and the consequences of cut scores are presented. Then, methods that may be used to establish the actual cut score are described.

Description of the Process

Once a predictor has been chosen for use, a decision must be made as to who advances further in the selection process. This decision requires that a cut score be established. A *cut score* is the score that separates those who advance further in the process (e.g., applicants who become candidates) from those who are rejected. For example, assume a test is used on which scores may range from 0 to 100 points. A cut score of 70 would mean that those applicants with a 70 or more would advance, while all others would be rejected for employment purposes.

Consequences of Cut Scores

The setting of a cut score is a very important process as it has consequences for the organization and the applicant. The consequences of cut scores can be shown using Exhibit 11.3, which contains a summary of a scatterdiagram of predictor and criterion scores. The horizontal line shows the criterion score at which the organization has determined whether an employee is successful or unsuccessful— for example, a 3 on a 5-point performance appraisal scale where 1 is the low

---

EXHIBIT 11.3   Consequences of Cut Scores

Criterion	Predictor Cut Score	
	D	A
Successful	False negative	True positive
	C	B
Unsuccessful	True negative	False positives
	No hire	Hire

Predictor

performance and 5 is the high performance. The vertical line is the cut score for the predictor—for example, a 3 on a 5-point interview rating scale where 1 reveals no chance of success and 5 a high chance of success.

The consequences of setting the cut score at a particular level are shown in each of the quadrants. Quadrants A and C represent correct decisions, which have positive consequences to the organization. Quadrant A applicants are called *true positives* because they were assessed as having a high chance of success using the predictor and would have succeeded if hired. Quadrant C applicants are called *true negatives* because they were assessed as having little chance for success and, indeed, would not be successful if hired.

Quadrants D and B represent incorrect decisions, which have negative consequences to the organization and affected applicants. Quadrant D applicants are called *false negatives* because they were assessed as not being likely to succeed, but had they been hired, they would have been successful. Not only was an incorrect decision reached, but a person who would have done well was not hired. Quadrant B applicants are called *false positives*. They were assessed as being likely to succeed, but would have ended up being unsuccessful performers. Eventually, these people would need to receive remedial training, be transferred to a new job, or even be terminated.

How high or low a cut score is set has a large impact on the consequences shown in Exhibit 11.3, and trade-offs are always involved. Compared with the moderate cut score in Exhibit 11.3, a high cut score results in fewer false positives, but a larger number of false negatives. Is this a good, bad, or inconsequential set of outcomes for the organization? The answer depends upon the job open for selection and the costs involved. If the job is an astronaut position for NASA, then it is essential that there be no false positives. The cost of a false positive may be the loss of a human life.

Now consider the consequences of a low cut score, relative to the one shown in Exhibit 11.3. There are fewer false negatives and more true positives, but more false positives are hired. In organizations that gain competitive advantage in their industry by hiring the very best, this set of consequences may be unacceptable. Alternatively, for EEO/AA purposes it may be desirable to have a low cut score so that the number of false negative minorities and women is minimized.

In short, when setting a cut score, attention must be given to the consequences. As indicated, these consequences can be very serious. As a result, different methods of setting cut scores have been developed to guide decision makers. These will now be reviewed.[5]

Methods to Determine Cut Scores

Norm-Referenced Methods

One method of determining at what level the cut score should be set is to simply examine the distribution of predictor scores for applicants and set the cut score at the level that best meets the demands of the organization. Demands of the organization may include the number of vacancies to be filled and EEO/AA requirements. The advantage of this approach is that it is a system that is easy to administer. It also minimizes judgment required because the cut score is determined on the basis of the demand for labor. The big drawback to this approach is that validity has often not been established prior to the use of the predictor. Also, there may be overreliance on the use of a single predictor and cut score, while other potentially useful predictors are ignored.

Content-Related Methods

While norm-referenced methods are established on the basis of the organization's demand for labor, content-related methods are established on the basis of labor supply. In particular, the cut score is set on the basis of the minimum qualifications deemed necessary to perform the job. This approach is often needed in situations where the first step in the hiring process is the demonstration of minimum skill requirements. The downside to this approach, like norm-referenced methods, is that knowledge of the validity of the predictor is not used to help establish the cutoff score. Also, it fails to account for the demand for labor or the number of positions needed to be filled.

A well-known example of a content-related method is the Angoff method.[6] According to this approach, subject matter experts are used to set the minimum cut scores needed to proceed in the selection process. These experts go through the content of the predictor (e.g., test items) and determine which items the minimally qualified person should be able to pass. Usually seven to ten subject matter experts (e.g., job incumbents, managers) are used who must agree upon the items to be passed. The cutoff score is the sum of the number of items that must be answered correctly.

There are several problems with this particular approach and subsequent modifications to it. First, it is a time-consuming procedure. Second, the results are dependent upon the subject matter experts. It is a very difficult matter to get members of the organization to agree upon who are ''the'' subject matter experts. Which set of subject matter experts are selected may have a bearing on the actual cut scores developed. Finally, it is unclear how much agreement there must be among subject matter experts when they evaluate test items.

Criterion-Related Methods

Validity is explicitly factored into setting cut scores with criterion-related methods. The KSAOs needed to perform the job are specified through the job analysis and are each linked to performance on the job. This is done in two ways. First, subject matter experts can be used to assess the degree to which the KSAO must be demonstrated to show adequate job performance. Second, empirical techniques can be used to establish the necessity of each KSAO as determined by its relationship to the actual performance and monetary outcomes associated with good performance. Although it does address validity, an advantage over norm-based and content-based approaches, it is a costly and administratively complex process to undertake.

Professional Guidelines

Much more research is needed on systematic procedures that are effective in setting optimal cut scores. In the meantime, a sound set of professional guidelines for setting cut scores is shown in Exhibit 11.4.

USING MULTIPLE PREDICTORS

Given the less-than-perfect validities of predictors, most organizations use multiple predictors in making selection decisions. With multiple predictors, decisions must be made about combining the resultant scores. These decisions can be addressed through consideration of compensatory, multiple hurdles, and combined approaches.

Compensatory Model

With a compensatory model, scores on one predictor are simply added to scores on another predictor to yield a total score. What this means is that high scores on

---

EXHIBIT 11.4   Professional Guidelines for Setting Cutoff Scores

1. It is unrealistic to expect that there is a single "best" method of setting cutoff scores for all situations.
2. The process of setting a cutoff score (or a critical score) should begin with a job analysis that identifies relative levels of proficiency on critical knowledge, skills, abilities, or other characteristics.
3. The validity and job relatedness of the assessment procedure are crucial considerations.
4. How a test is used (criterion-referenced or norm-referenced) affects the selection and meaning of a cutoff score.
5. When possible, data on the actual relation of test scores to outcome measures of job performance should be considered carefully.
6. Cutoff scores or critical scores should be set high enough to ensure that minimum standards of job performance are met.
7. Cutoff scores should be consistent with normal expectations of acceptable proficiency within the workforce.

Source: W. F. Cascio, R. A. Alexander, and G. V. Barrett, "Setting Cutoff Scores: Legal, Psychometric, and Professional Issues and Guidelines," *Personnel Psychology*, 1988, 41, pp. 21–22.

one predictor can compensate for low scores on another predictor. For example, if an employer is using an interview and GPA to select a person, an applicant with a low GPA, who does well in the interview, may still get the job.

The advantage of a compensatory model is that it recognizes that people have multiple talents and that many different constellations of talents may produce success on the job. The disadvantage to a compensatory model is that, at least for some jobs, level of proficiency for specific talents cannot be compensated for by other proficiencies. For example, a firefighter requires a certain level of strength that cannot be compensated for by intelligence.

In terms of making actual decisions using the compensatory model, there are four procedures that may be followed: clinical prediction, unit weighting, rational weighting, and multiple regression. The four methods differ from one another in terms of the manner in which predictor scores (raw or standardized) are weighted before being added together for a total or composite score.

The following example will be used to illustrate these procedures. In all four procedures, raw scores are used to determine a total score. Standard scores (see Chapter 4) may need to be used rather than raw scores if each predictor variable uses a different method of measurement or is measured under different conditions.[7] Differences in weighting methods are shown in part A of Exhibit 11.5. In Part B of Exhibit 11.5, there is a selection system consisting of interviews, application blanks, and recommendations. For simplicity, assume that scores on each predictor range from 1 to 5. Scores on these three predictors are shown for three applicants.

Clinical Prediction

Returning to Exhibit 11.5, note that with a clinical prediction, managers use their expert judgment to arrive at a total score for each applicant. That final score may or may not be a simple addition of the three predictor scores shown in Exhibit 11.5. Hence, applicant A may be given a higher total score than applicant B even though simple addition shows that applicant B had one point more (4 + 3 + 4 = 11) than did applicant A (3 + 5 + 2 = 10).

The advantage to this approach is that it draws upon the expertise of managers to weight and combine predictor scores. In turn, managers may be more likely to accept the selection decisions than if a mechanical scoring rule (e.g., add up the points) were used. The problem with this approach is that the reasons for the weightings are known only to the manager. Also, clinical predictions have generally been shown to be less accurate than mechanical decisions.[8]

Unit Weighting

With unit weighting, each predictor is weighted the same at a value of 1.00. What this means is shown in Exhibit 11.5 (Part A): the predictor scores are simply added together to get a total score. So, in Exhibit 11.5 (Part B), the total scores for applicants A, B, and C are 10, 11, and 12, respectively. The advantage to unit weighting is that it is a simple and straightforward process to follow and makes

---

EXHIBIT 11.5 Four Compensatory Model Procedures for Three Predictors

---

A. Models

Clinical Prediction

$P_1 \rightarrow P_2 \rightarrow P_3 \rightarrow$ Total Score

Unit Weighting

$P_1 + P_2 + P_3 =$ Total Score

Rational Weighting

$w_1 P_1 + w_2 P_2 + w_3 P =$ Total Score

Multiple Regression

$a + b_1 P_1 + b_2 P_2 + b_3 P_3 =$ Total Score

Where: P = predictor score
   w = rational weight
   a = intercept
   b = statistical weight

B. Raw Scores for Applicants on Three Predictors

	Predictors		
Applicant	Interview	Application Blank	Recommendation
A	3	5	2
B	4	3	4
C	5	4	3

---

the importance of each predictor explicit to decision makers. The problem with this approach is that it assumes that each predictor contributes equally to the prediction of job success, which may not always be the case.

Rational Weighting

With rational weighting, each predictor receives a differential rather than equal weighting. Managers and other subject matter experts establish the weights for each predictor according to degree to which each is believed to predict job success. These weights (w) are then multiplied times each raw score (P) to yield a total score as shown in Exhibit 11.5 (Part A).

For example, the predictors in Exhibit 11.5 (Part B) may be weighted .5, .3, and .2 for the interview, application blank, and recommendation. Each applicant's raw score in Exhibit 11.5 (Part B) is multiplied times the appropriate weight to yield a total score. For example, the total score for applicant A is (.5) 3 + (.3) 5 + (.2) 2 = 3.4.

The advantage to this approach is that it considers the relative importance of each predictor and makes this assessment explicit. The downside, however, is that it is an elaborate procedure that requires managers and subject matter experts to agree upon the differential weights to be applied.

Multiple Regression

Multiple regression is similar to rational weighting in that the predictors receive different weights. With multiple regression, however, the weights are established on the basis of statistical procedures rather than on the basis of judgments by managers or other subject matter experts. The statistical weights are developed on the basis of (a) the correlation of each predictor with the criterion, and (b) the correlations among the predictors.[9]

The calculations result in a multiple regression formula like the one shown in Exhibit 11.5 (Part A). A total score for each applicant is obtained by multiplying the statistical weight (b) for each predictor by the predictor (P) score, and summing these along with the intercept value (a). As an example, assume the statistical weights are .9, .6, and .2 for the interview, application blank, and recommendation, respectively, and that the intercept is .09. Using these values, the total score for applicant A is $(.9)3 + (.6)5 + (.2)2 = 6.1$.

Multiple regression offers the possibility of a much higher degree of precision in the prediction of criterion scores than do the other methods of weighting. Unfortunately, this level of precision is only realized under a limited set of circumstances. In particular, for multiple regression to be more precise than unit weighting, there must be a small number of predictors, low correlations between predictor variables, and a large sample.[10] Most selection settings do not meet these criteria, so consideration should be given to unit or rational weighting instead. Another reason to consider these alternatives is the high levels of resources and expertise required to conduct multiple regression.

Multiple Hurdles

With a multiple hurdles approach, an applicant must earn a passing score on each predictor before advancing in the selection process. Such an approach is taken when each requirement measured by a predictor is critical to job success. Passing scores are set using the methods to determine cut scores previously discussed. With multiple hurdles, unlike the compensatory model, a high score on one predictor cannot compensate for a low score on another predictor. An example of a multiple hurdles approach is shown in Exhibit 11.6 for the position of pyrotechnician.

As can be seen in Exhibit 11.6, a pyrotechnician must pass a multiple set of hurdles to be hired. A pyrotechnician is the person responsible for the demolition of high-powered explosives and fireworks. This is a highly hazardous endeavor,

EXHIBIT 11.6   Multiple Hurdles for Pyrotechnician Position

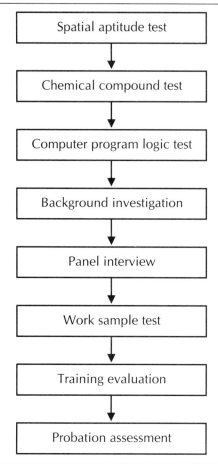

and false positive errors must be absolutely minimized. If this is not done, then the safety of the public may be jeopardized. For example, at the annual Fourth of July celebrations in Columbus or Boston, tons of explosives are detonated in fairly close proximity to hundreds of thousands of spectators. A misdirected explosive could result in a disaster. To adequately perform this job, one must be well versed in many areas, including computers. The timing and detonation of the explosives, as well as modeling of the entire program, is done by computer.

Multiple hurdles are used to prevent false-positive errors. They are costly and time-consuming to set up. As a result, they are used to select people for jobs where the occupational hazards are great (e.g., astronaut) or the consequences of poor performance have a great impact upon the public at large (e.g., police officers and firefighters).

Combined Method

For jobs where some, but not all requirements, are critical to job success, a combined method may be used in which the compensatory and multiple hurdles models are combined together. The process starts with the multiple hurdles and ends with the compensatory method.

An example of the combined approach for the position of recrutiment manager is shown in Exhibit 11.7. The selection process for recruitment manager starts with two hurdles that must be passed, in succession, by the applicant. These are the application blank and the job knowledge test. Failure to clear either hurdle results in rejection. Having passed them, applicants take an interview and have their references checked. Information from the interview and the references is combined in a compensatory manner. Those who pass are offered the job, and those who do not pass are rejected.

METHODS OF FINAL CHOICE

The discussion thus far has been on decision rules that can be used to narrow down the list of people to successively smaller groups who advance in the selection

EXHIBIT 11.7 Combined Model for Recruitment Manager

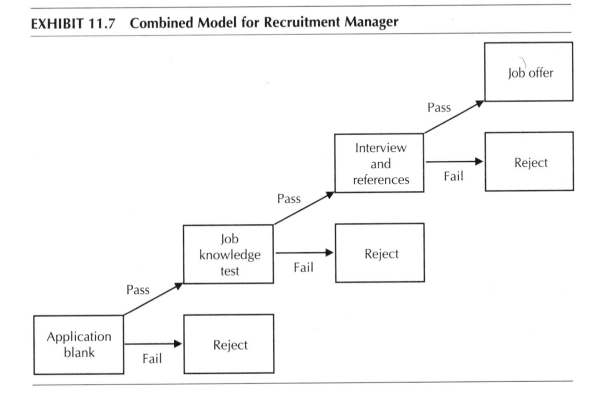

process from applicant to candidate to finalist. How can the organization now choose from among the finalists to decide which of them will receive job offers? Discretionary assessments about the finalists must be converted into final choice decisions. The methods of final choice are the mechanisms by which discretionary assessments are translated into job offer decisions.

Methods of final choice include random selection, ranking, and grouping. Examples of each of these methods of final choice are shown in Exhibit 11.8 and are here discussed.

Random Selection

With random selection, each finalist has an equal chance of being selected. The only rationale for the selection of a person is the "luck of the draw." For example, the six names from Exhibit 11.8 could be put in a hat and the finalist drawn out. The one drawn out would be the person selected and made a job offer. This approach has the advantage of being quick. Also, with random selection, one cannot be accused of favoritism because everyone has an equal chance of being selected. The disadvantage to this approach is that discretionary assessments are simply ignored.

Ranking

With ranking, finalists are ordered from the most desirable to the least desirable based on results of discretionary assessments. As shown in Exhibit 11.8, the person ranked 1 (Goldie) is the most desirable, and the person ranked 6 (Harold) is the least desirable. It is important to note that desirability should be viewed in the context of the entire selection process. When this is done, persons with lower levels of desirability (e.g., ranks of 3, 4, 5) should not be viewed necessarily as

---

EXHIBIT 11.8   Methods of Final Choice

Random	Ranking	Grouping
Casey Goldie Buster Abby — Pick one Roxie Harold	1. Goldie 2. Roxie 3. Buster 4. Abby 5. Casey 6. Harold	Goldie Roxie] Top choices Buster Abby] Acceptable Casey Harold] Last resorts

failures. Job offers are extended to people on the basis of their rank ordering, with the person ranked 1 receiving the first offer. Should that person turn down the job offer, or suddenly withdraw from the selection process, then the finalist ranked 2 receives the offer, and so on.

The advantage to ranking is that it provides an indication of the relative worth of each finalist for the job. It also provides a set of backups should one or more of the finalists withdraw from the process.

It should be remembered that backup finalists may decide to withdraw from the process to take a position elsewhere. Although ranking does give the organization a cushion should the top choices withdraw from the process, it does not mean that the process of job offers can proceed at a leisurely pace. Immediate action needs to be taken with the top choices in case they decide to withdraw and there is a need to go to backups. This is especially true in tight labor markets where there is a strong demand for the services of people on the ranking list.

Grouping

With the grouping method, finalists are banded together into rank-ordered categories. For example, in Exhibit 11.8, the finalists are grouped according to whether they are top choices, acceptable, or last resorts. The advantage of this method is that is permits ties among finalists, thus avoiding the need to assign a different rank to each person. The disadvantage is that choices still have to be made from among the top choices. These might be made on the basis of factors such as probability of each person accepting the offer.

DECISION MAKERS

A final consideration in decision making for selection is who should participate in the decisions. That is, who should determine the process to be followed (e.g., establishing cut scores) and who should determine the outcome (e.g., who gets the job offer)? The answer is that both human resource professionals and line managers must play a role. Although the two roles are different, both are critical to the organization. Employees may play certain roles as well.

Human Resource Professionals

As a general rule, human resource professionals should have a high level of involvement in the processes used to design and manage the selection system. They should be consulted in matters such as which predictors to use and how to use them best. In particular, they need to orchestrate the development of policies and procedures in the staffing areas covered. These professionals have or know where to find the technical expertise needed to develop sound selection decisions. Also, they have the knowledge to ensure that relevant laws and regulations are being followed. Finally, they can also represent the interests and concerns of employees to management.

Although the primary role to be played by human resource professionals is in terms of process, they should also have some involvement in determining who receives job offers. One obvious area where this is true is with staffing the human resource function. A less obvious place where human resource professionals can play an important secondary role is in terms of providing input into selection decisions made by managers.

Human resource professionals may be able to provide some insight on applicants that is not always perceived by line managers. For example, they may be able to offer some insight on the applicants' people skills (e.g., communications, teamwork). Human resource professionals are sensitive to these issues because of their training and experience. They may have data to share on these matters as a result of their screening interviews, knowledge of how to interpret paper-and-pencil instruments (e.g., personality test), and interactions with internal candidates (e.g., serving on task forces with the candidates).

The other area where human resource professionals may make a contribution to outcomes is in terms of initial assessment methods. Many times, human resource professionals are and should be empowered to make initial selection decisions such as who gets invited into the organization for administration of the next round of selection. Doing so they save managers time to carry out their other responsibilities. Also, human resource professionals can ensure that minorities and women applicants are actively solicited and not excluded from the applicant pool for the wrong reasons.

Managers

As a general rule, a manager's primary involvement in staffing is in determining who is selected for employment. Managers are the subject matter experts of the business, and, thus, they are held accountable for the success of the people hired. They are far less involved in determining the processes followed to staff the organization because they often do not have the time or expertise to do so.

Although they may not play a direct role in establishing process, managers can and should periodically be consulted by human resource professionals on process issues. They should be consulted because they are the consumers of human resource services. As such, it is important to provide them input into the staffing process to ensure that it is meeting their needs in making the best possible person/ job matches.

There is an additional benefit to allowing management a role in process issues. As a result of their involvement, managers may develop a better understanding of why certain practices are prescribed by human resource professionals. When they are not invited to be a part of the process to establish staffing policy and procedures, line managers may view human resource professionals as an obstacle to hiring the right people for the job.

It should also be noted that the degree of managers' involvement usually depends on the type of assessment decisions made. Decisions made using initial assessment methods are usually delegated to the human resource professional, as just discussed. Decisions made using substantive assessment methods usually involve some degree of input from the manager. Decisions made using discretionary methods are usually the direct responsibility of the manager. As a general rule, the extent of managerial involvement in determining outcomes should only be as great as management's knowledge of the job. If managers are involved in hiring decisions for jobs with which they are not familiar, then legal, measurement, and morale problems are likely to be created.

Employees

Traditionally, employees are not considered part of the decision-making process in staffing. Slowly this tradition is changing. For example, in team assessment approaches (see Chapter 9), employees may have a voice in both process and outcomes. That is, they may have ideas about how selection procedures are established and make decisions about or provide input into who gets hired. Employee involvement in the team approach is encouraged because it may give a sense of ownership of the work process and help employees to better identify with organizational goals. Also, it may result in the selection of members who are more compatible with the goals of the work team. In order for employee involvement to be effective, employees need to be provided with staffing training just as managers do (see Chapter 9).

LEGAL ISSUES

The legal issue of major importance in decision making is that of cutoff scores or hiring standards. These scores or standards regulate the flow of individuals from applicant to candidate to finalist. Throughout this flow, adverse impact may occur. When it does, the Uniform Guidelines on Employee Selection Procedures (UGESP) come into play. At the finalist stage, decisions about to whom to offer the job are made, and the UGESP has less direct relevance.

Uniform Guidelines on Employee Selection Procedures

If there is no adverse impact in decision making, the UGESP (see Appendix A) are essentially silent on the issue of cutoff scores. The discretion being exercised by the organization as it makes its selection decisions is thus unconstrained legally. If there is adverse impact occurring, however, then the UGESP become directly applicable to decision making.

Recall that under conditions of adverse impact, the UGESP requires the organization to either eliminate its occurrence or justify it through the conduct of validity studies. As part of the general standards for such validity studies, the UGESP says the following about cutoff scores:

> Where cutoff scores are used, they should normally be set as to be reasonable and consistent with normal expectations of acceptable proficiency within the workforce. Where applicants are ranked on the basis of properly validated selection procedures and those applicants scoring below a higher cutoff score than appropriate in light of such expectations have little or no chance of being selected for employment, the higher cutoff score may be appropriate, but the degree of adverse impact should be considered.

This provision suggests that the organization should be cautious in general about setting cutoff scores that are above those necessary to achieve acceptable proficiency among those hired. In other words, even with a valid predictor, the organization should be cautious that its hiring standards are not so high that they create needless adverse impact. This is particularly true with ranking systems. Use of random, or to a lesser extent grouping, methods would help overcome this particular objection to ranking systems.

Whatever cutoff score procedure is used, the UGESP also requires that the organization be able to document its establishment and operation. Specifically, the UGESP says that "if the selection procedure is used with a cutoff score, the user should describe the way in which normal expectations of proficiency within the workforce were determined and the way in which the cutoff score was determined."

The preceding validation and cutoff score approach is one option for dealing with problems of adverse impact. The UGESP also suggests two other options, both of which seek to eliminate adverse impact rather than justify it as in the validation and cutoff score approach. The next option is the "alternative procedures" one. Here, the organization must consider using an alternative selection procedure that causes less adverse impact (e.g., work sample instead of a written test), but has roughly the same validity as the procedure it replaces.

The final selection option is that of affirmative action. The UGESP do not relieve the organization of any affirmative action obligations it may have. Also, the UGESP strive to "encourage the adoption and implementation of voluntary affirmative action programs" for organizations that do not have any affirmative action obligations.

Choices Among Finalists

Where there is more than one finalist for a job, a decision must be made as to which will receive the job offer. There is little legal influence on this finalist decision. Presumably, if the steps in the selection process leading up to this point have been within legal bounds, the finalist choice is a legal matter of relative indifference. Despite this, the organization should once again review its EEO/AA commitments, policies, and results to date. Such a review may prove instructive as final choices are made. It represents the organization's "last chance" concerning selection, and the organization should be sure that its decision is consistent with its affirmative action objectives.

SUMMARY

The selection component of a staffing system requires that decisions be made in several areas. These include deciding which predictors to use, how to set cut scores, how to use scores when there are multiple predictors, considering who within the organization should help make selection decisions, and determining who fills the vacancy.

In deciding which predictors to use, consideration should be given to the validity coefficient, correlation with other predictors, adverse impact, and utility. Ideally, a predictor would have a validity coefficient with large magnitude and significance, low correlations with other predictors, little adverse impact, and high utility.

In deciding who earns a passing score on a predictor, cut scores must be set. Recognition must be given to the consequences of setting different levels of cut scores, especially assessing some applicants as false positives and false negatives. Methods to determine cutoff scores include norm-referenced, criterion-related, and content-related methods. Professional guidelines were offered on how best to set cut scores.

Deciding how to use multiple predictors requires an understanding of compensatory, multiple hurdles, and combined approach models. A compensatory model allows a person to compensate for a low score on one predictor with a high score on another predictor. A multiple hurdles approach requires that a person achieve a passing score on each predictor. A combined approach uses elements of both the compensatory and the multiple hurdles approaches.

Methods for choosing among finalists are random selection, ranking, and grouping. Each has advantages and disadvantages.

Resources to consider in making selection decisions include others within the organization and the Uniform Guidelines on Employee Selection Procedures. Human resource professionals primarily play a role in determining the selection process to be used and in making selection decisions based on initial assessment results. Managers primarily play a role in deciding whom to select during the final choice stage. Employees are becoming part of the decision-making process in team assessment approaches. The Uniform Guidelines on Employee Selection Procedures should be consulted in setting cut scores in ways that help minimize adverse impact and allow the organization to fulfill its EEO/AA obligations.

DISCUSSION QUESTIONS

1. Your boss is considering using a new predictor. The base rate is high, the selection ratio is low, and the validity coefficient is high for the current predictor. What would you advise your boss and why?

2. What are the positive consequences associated with a high predictor cutoff score? What are the negative consequences?

3. Under what circumstances should a compensatory model be used? When should a multiple hurdles model be used?

4. What are the advantages of ranking as a method of final choice over random selection?

5. What roles should human resource professionals play in staffing decisions? Why?

6. What guidelines do the Uniform Guidelines on Employee Selection Procedures offer to organizations when it comes to setting cutoff scores?

ENDNOTES

1. F. L. Schmidt and J. E. Hunter, "Moderator Research and the Law of Small Numbers," *Personnel Psychology,* 1978, 31, pp. 215–232.

2. L. Gottfredson and J. C. Sharf (eds.), "Fairness in Employment Testing," *A Special Issue of the Journal of Vocational Behavior,* 1988, 33, pp. 225–490.

3. H. C. Taylor and J. T. Russell, "The Relationship of Validity Coefficients to the Practical Effectiveness of Tests in Selection," *Journal of Applied Psychology,* 1939, 23, pp. 565–578.

4. H. E. Brogden, "When Testing Pays Off," *Personnel Psychology,* 1949, 2, pp. 171–183; L. J. Cronbach and G. C. Gleser, *Psychological Tests and Personnel Decisions,* second ed. (Urbana, IL: University of Illinois Press, 1965); F. L. Schmidt, J. E. Hunter, R. C. McKenzie, and T. W. Muldrow, "Impact of Valid Selection Procedures on Work-Force Productivity," *Journal of Applied Psychology,* 1979, 64, pp. 609–626; J. W. Boudreau and C. J. Berger, "Decision Theoretic Utility Analysis Applied to Employee Separations and Acquisitions," *Journal of Applied Psychology,* 1985, 70, pp. 581–612.

5. Except where noted this discussion draws very heavily upon W. F. Cascio, R. A. Alexander, and G. V. Barrett, "Setting Cutoff Scores: Legal, Psychometric, and Professional Issues and Guidelines," *Personnel Psychology,* 1988, 41, pp. 1–24.

6. W. H. Angoff, "Scales, Norms, and Equivalent Scores," in R. L. Thorndike (ed.), *Educational Measurement* (Washington, DC: American Council on Education, 1971), pp. 508–600; R. E. Biddle, "How to Set Cutoff Scores for Knowledge Tests Used in Promotion, Training, Certification, and Licensing," *Public Personnel Management,* 1993, 22 (1), pp. 63–79.

7. E. E. Ghiselli, J. P. Campbell, and S. Zedeck, *Measurement Theory for the Behavioral Sciences* (San Francisco: W. H. Freeman, 1981).

8. J. Sawyer, "Measurement and Predictions, Clinical and Statistical," *Psychological Bulletin,* 1966, 66, pp. 178–200.

9. For an applied perspective on regression with human resources examples, see N. W. Schmitt and R. J. Klimoski, *Research Methods in Human Resources Management* (Cincinnati: South-Western, 1991).

10. F. L. Schmidt, ''The Relative Efficiency of Regression and Sample Unit Predictor Weights in Applied Differential Psychology,'' *Educational and Psychological Measurement,* 1971, 31, pp. 699–714.

CHAPTER TWELVE

Final Match

In the previous chapter, the focus was on organizational aspects of decision making regarding the likely match or fit between an individual and an organization. The emphasis was on reducing the initial applicant pool to a smaller set of candidates, and identifying one or more job finalists from that candidate set to whom to offer employment.

A final match occurs when the offer receiver and the organization have determined that the probable overlap between the person's KSAOs/motivation and the job's requirements/rewards is sufficient to warrant entering into the employment relationship. Once this decision has been made, the organization and the individual become legally bound to each other through mutual agreement on the terms and conditions of employment. They thus enter into an employment contract, and each expects the other to abide by the terms of the contract. Failure to do so constitutes a breach of contract, which may lead to litigation between the parties as well as potential recovery of damages for the breach.

The formation of, and agreement upon, the employment contract occurs in both external and internal staffing. Any time the matching process is set in motion, either through external or internal staffing, the goal is establishment of a new employment relationship.

Knowledge of employment contract concepts and principles is central to understanding the final match. This chapter begins with an overview of such material, emphasizing the essential requirements for establishing a legally binding employment contract, as well as some of the nuances in doing so. Major components of a job offer, and points to address in it, are suggested. As is apparent, staffing organizations effectively demands great skill and care by the employer as it enters into employment contracts. The employer and offer receiver are accorded great freedom in the establishment of terms and conditions of employment; both parties have much to decide and agree upon pertaining to job offer content.

Through the job offer process, these terms and conditions are proposed, discussed, negotiated, modified, and, ultimately, agreed upon. The job offer process thus is frequently complex, requiring planning by those responsible for it. Elements and considerations in this process are discussed next.

Once agreement on the terms and conditions of employment has been reached, the final match process is completed, and the formal employment relationship is established. In a sense, staffing activities end at this point. In another sense, however, it is important to phase these activities into initial postemployment activities that help the new employee adapt and adjust to the new job. Employee orientation and socialization activities are of particular importance to such adaptation, and are briefly explored.

The chapter concludes with a discussion of specific legal issues that pertain not only to the establishment of the employment contract, but to potential long-run consequences of that contract that must be considered at the time it is established.

EMPLOYMENT CONTRACTS

The establishment and enforcement of employment contracts is a very complex, and constantly changing, undertaking. Touched on next are some very basic, yet subtle, issues associated with this undertaking. It is crucial to understand the elements that comprise a legally enforceable contract and to be able to identify the parties to the contract (employees or independent contractors, third-party representatives), the form of the contract (written, oral), disclaimers, fulfillment of other conditions, reneging on an offer or acceptance, and other sources (e.g., employee handbooks) that may also constitute a portion of the total employment contract.

Requirements for an Enforceable Contract

There are three basic elements required for a contract to be legally binding and enforceable: *offer, acceptance,* and *consideration.*[1] If any one of these is missing, there is no binding contract.

Offer

The offer is usually made by the employer. It is composed of the terms and conditions of employment desired and proposed by the employer. The terms must be clear and specific enough to be acted on by the offer receiver. Vague statements and offers are unacceptable (e.g., ''Come to work for me right now; we'll work out the details later''). The contents of newspaper ads for the job, or general written employer material such as a brochure describing the organization, probably are also too vague to be considered offers. Both the employer and the offer receiver should have a definite understanding of the specific terms being proposed.

Acceptance

To constitute a contract, the offer must be accepted on the terms as offered. Thus, if the employer offers a salary of $25,000 per year, the offer receiver must either accept or reject that term. Acceptance of an offer on a contingency basis does not constitute an acceptance. If the offer receiver responds to the salary offer of $25,000 by saying, ''Pay me $27,500, and I'll come to work for you,'' this is not an acceptance. Rather it is a counteroffer, and the employer must now either formally accept or reject it.

The offer receiver must also accept the offer in the manner specified in the offer. If the offer requires acceptance in writing, for example, the offer receiver must accept it in writing. Or, if the offer requires acceptance by a certain date, it must be accepted by that date.

Consideration

Consideration entails the exchange of something of value between the parties to the contract. Usually, it involves an exchange of promises. The employer offers or promises to provide compensation to the offer receiver in exchange for labor, and the offer receiver promises to provide labor to the employer in exchange for compensation. Usually, establishment of consideration is quite straightforward. Occasionally, consideration can become an issue. For example, if the employer makes an offer to a person that requires a response by a certain date, and then does not hear from the person, there is no contract, even though the employer thought that they "had a deal."

Parties to the Contract

Two issues arise regarding the parties to the contract—whether the employer is entering into a contract with an "employee" or with an "independent contractor,"[2] and whether an outsider or "third party" can execute or otherwise play a role in the employment contract.[3]

Employee or Independent Contractor

Individuals are hired as either *employees* or *independent contractors*; both of these terms have definite legal meaning (though the distinction between the two is vague at times). Generally, an employee is one who is hired by the employer to work on an ongoing basis, and who is subject to direct control (e.g., supervision and evaluation of work performance) by the employer. An independent contractor, on the other hand, is hired to perform only specific tasks at a specific price, furnishes the tools and equipment necessary for the work, and is not under the direct control of the employer in performing those tasks. Common examples of independent contractors include plumbers, consultants, and lawyers.

The practical staffing implications of the distinction between employee and independent contractor are important. Independent contractors may be less expensive than employees, and may not represent a fixed labor cost. The reason for this is that the employer is not legally required to withhold federal income taxes, contribute to social security, or secure workers' compensation insurance for an independent contractor. In addition, the federal laws and regulations detailed in Chapter 3 apply to employers and their employees, but not their independent contractors. Independent contractors are thus out of the scope of legal coverage from the employer's perspective. Finally, independent contractors are almost invariably employed only at-will, and thus may be terminated as such without threat of legal recourse by the contractor. As will be discussed later, employment-at-will issues are more complicated in the case of employees.

Third Parties

Often times, someone other than the employer or offer receiver speaks on their behalf in the establishment or modification of employment contracts. These people serve as *agents* for the employer and offer receiver. For the employer, this may mean the use of outsiders such as employment agencies, executive recruiters, or search consultants; it also usually means the use of one or more employees, such as the HR department representative, the hiring manager, higher-level managers, and other managers within the organization. For the offer receiver, it may mean the use of a special agent, such as a professional agent for a sports player or executive. These possibilities raise three important questions for the employer.

First, who if anyone speaks for the offer receiver? This is usually a matter of checking with the offer receiver as to whether any given person is indeed authorized by the offer receiver to be a spokesperson, and what, if any, limits have been placed on that person regarding terms that may discussed and agreed upon with the employer.

Second, who is the spokesperson for the employer? In the case of its own employees, the employer must recognize that, from a legal standpoint, any of them could be construed as speaking for the employer. Virtually anyone could thus suggest and agree to contract terms, knowingly or unknowingly. This means that the employer should formulate and enforce explicit policies as to who is authorized to speak on its behalf.

Third, exactly what is that person authorized to say? Here, the legal concept of *apparent authority* is relevant. If the offer receiver believes that a person has the authority to speak for the employer, and there is nothing to indicate otherwise, that person has the apparent authority to speak for the employer. In turn, the employer may be bound by what that person says and agrees to, even if the employer did not grant express authority to do so to this person. It is thus important for the organization to clarify to both the offer receiver and designated spokespersons what the spokesperson is authorized to discuss and agree to without approval from other organizational members.

Form of the Contract

Employment contracts may be written, oral, or even a combination of the two.[4] All may be legally binding and enforceable. Within this broad parameter, however, are numerous caveats and considerations.

Written Contracts

As a general rule, the law favors written contracts over oral ones. This alone should lead an organization to use only written contracts whenever possible.

A written contract may take many forms, and all may be legally enforceable. Examples of a written document that may be construed as a contract include a letter of offer and acceptance (the usual example), a statement on a job application blank (such as an applicant voucher to the truthfulness of information provided), internal job posting notices, and statements in employee handbooks or other personnel manuals. The more specific the information and statements in such documents, the more likely they are to be considered employment contracts.

Unintended problems may arise with these documents. They may become interpreted as enforceable contracts, even though that was not their intent (perhaps the intent was merely informational). Or, statements on a given term or condition of employment may contradict each other in various documents.

An excellent illustration of these kinds of problems involves the issue of employment-at-will. Assume an employer wishes to be, as a matter of explicit policy, a strict at-will employer. That desire may be unintentionally undercut by written documents that imply something other than an employment-at-will relationship. For example, correspondence with an applicant may talk of ''continued employment after you complete your probationary period.'' This statement might be legally interpreted as creating something other than a strict at-will employment relationship. To further muddy the waters, the employee handbook may contain an explicit at-will statement, thus contradicting the policy implied in the correspondence with the applicant.

Care must thus be taken to ensure that all written documents accurately convey only the intended meanings regarding terms and conditions of employment. To this end, the following suggestions should be heeded:[5]

1. Before putting anything in writing, ask, Does the company mean to be held to this?
2. Choose words carefully; where appropriate avoid using words that imply binding commitment.
3. Make sure all related documents are consistent with each other.
4. Always have a second person review what another has written.
5. Form the habit of looking at the entire hiring procedure and consider any writings within that context.

Oral Contracts

While oral contracts may be every bit as binding as written contracts, there are two notable exceptions that support placing greater importance on written contracts.

The first exception is the one-year rule, which comes about in what is known as the *statute of frauds*.[6] Under this rule, a contract that cannot be performed or fulfilled within a one-year interval is not enforceable unless it is in writing. Thus, oral agreements for any length greater than one year are not enforceable. Because of this rule, the organization should not make oral contracts that are intended to last more than one year.

The second exception involves the concept of *parole evidence*, which pertains to oral promises that are made about the employment relationship.[7] Legally, parole evidence (e.g., the offer receiver's claim that ''I was promised that I wouldn't have to work on weekends'') may not be used to enforce a contract if it is inconsistent with the terms of a written agreement. Thus, if the offer receiver's letter of appointment explicitly stated that weekend work was required, the oral promise of not having to work weekends would not be enforceable.

Note, however, in the absence of written statements to the contrary, oral statements may indeed be enforceable. In the preceding example, if the letter of appointment was silent on the issue of weekend work, then the oral promise of no weekend work might well be enforceable.

More generally, oral statements are more likely to be enforceable as employment contract terms:[8]

1. when there is no written statement regarding the term (e.g., weekend work) in question;
2. when the term is quite certain ("You will not have to work on weekends," as opposed to, "Occasionally, we work weekends around here");
3. when the person making the oral statement is in a position of authority to do so (e.g., the hiring manager as opposed to a coworker);
4. the more formal the circumstances in which the statement was made (the manager's office as opposed to around the bar or dinner table as part of a recruiting trip); and
5. the more specific the promise ("You will work every other Saturday from 8:00 to 5:00," as opposed to, "You may have to work from 8:00 to the middle of the afternoon on the weekends, but we'll try to hold that to a minimum").

As this discussion makes clear, oral statements are a potential mine field in establishing employment contracts from the legal perspective. They obviously cannot be avoided (employer and applicant have to speak to each other), and they may serve other legitimate and desired outcomes such as providing realistic recruitment information to job applicants. Nonetheless, the organization should use oral statements with extreme caution, and alert all members to its policies regarding their use.

Disclaimers

A *disclaimer* is a statement (oral or written) that explicitly limits an employee right and reserves that right for the employer.[9] Disclaimers are often used in letters of appointment, job application blanks, and employee handbooks.

A common, and increasingly important, employee "right" that is being limited through the use of disclaimer is that of job security. Here, through its policy of employment-at-will, the employer explicitly makes no promise of any job security and reserves the right to terminate the employment relationship at its own will. The following is an example of such a disclaimer:

In consideration of my employment, I agree to conform to the rules and regulations of Sears, Roebuck and Company, and recognize that employment and compensation can be terminated, with or without cause, and with or without notice, at any time, at the option of either the company or myself. I understand that no store manager or representative of Sears, Roebuck and Company, other than the president or vice-president of the company, has any authority to enter into any agreement for employment for any specified period of time, or to make any agreement contrary to the foregoing.[10]

Disclaimers are generally enforceable (the preceding one has successfully survived court challenge). They can thus serve as an important component of employment contracts. Their use should be guided by the following set of recommendations:[11]

1. They should be clearly stated and conspicuously placed in appropriate documents.
2. The employee should acknowledge receipt and review of the document and the disclaimer.
3. The disclaimer should state that it may be modified only in writing, and by whom.
4. The terms and conditions of employment, including the disclaimer, as well as limits on their enforceability, should be reviewed with offer receivers and employees.

Fulfillment of Further Conditions

Often, the employer may wish to make a job offer that is contingent upon certain other conditions being fulfilled by the offer receiver.[12] Examples of such *contingencies* include (a) passage of a particular test, such as a licensure exam (e.g., CPA or bar exam); (b) passage of a medical exam, including alcohol/drugs/AIDS screening tests; (c) satisfactory background and reference checks; and (d) proof of employability under the Immigration Reform and Control Act.

While contingencies to a contract are generally enforceable, contingencies to an employment contract (especially those involving any of the preceding examples) are exceedingly complex and may only be made within defined limits. For this reason, contingencies should not be used in employment contracts without prior legal counsel.

Reneging

At times, the employer may wish to withdraw an offer that has already been made to an offer receiver. Or, the offer receiver may wish to withdraw from an offer that has already been extended and accepted. These withdrawals are known as *reneging.* Though reneging is usually an unfortunate event, and one that may invoke ill-feelings, it generally may be done without legal recourse or penalty by either party. This is a logical extension of the employment-at-will concept.

An important exception to this conclusion regarding reneging involves the doctrine of *promissory estoppel.*[13] This doctrine covers the situation where the offer receiver relied on the employer's job offer with good faith, the offer was subsequently withdrawn by the employer, and the withdrawal had a detrimental effect on the offer receiver. Examples of these effects include resigning from one's current employer, passing up other job opportunities, relocating geographically, and incurring expenses associated with the job offer. When the offer receiver experiences such detrimental reliance, the person may sue the employer for damages; actual hiring of the offer receiver is rarely sought or required in such suits.

Other Employment Contract Sources

As alluded to previously, employment contract terms may be established through multiple sources, not just the letters of job offer and acceptance. Such establishment may be the result of both intentional and unintentional acts by the employer. Moreover, these terms may come about not only when the employment relationship is first established, but also during the course of the employment relationship.[14]

The employer thus must constantly be alert to the fact that terms and conditions of employment may come into being, and be modified, through a variety of employment contract sources. Sources worth reiterating here are employee handbooks (and other written documents) and oral statements made by employer representatives.

In the case of employee handbooks, the employer must consider whether statements in them are legally enforceable or merely informational. While there is legal opinion on both sides of this question, handbooks are being considered increasingly as a legally enforceable part of the employment contract. To avoid this occurrence, the employer may wish to place an explicit disclaimer in the handbook that states the intent to provide only information to employees, and that it will not be bound by any of the statements contained in the handbook.

In the case of oral statements, their danger and the need for caution in their use has already been addressed. It should be remembered that oral statements may present legal problems and challenges when made not only at the time of the initial employment contract, but throughout the course of the employment relationship as well. Of particular concern here are oral promises made to employees regarding future events such as job security ("Don't worry, you will always have a place with us") or job assignments ("After training, you will be assigned as the assistant manager at our new store"). With oral statements, there is thus a constant need to be careful regarding the messages being delivered to employees, as well as who delivers those messages.

JOB OFFERS

A *job offer* is an attempt by the organization to induce the offer receiver into the establishment of an employment relationship. Assuming that the offer is accepted and that consideration is met, the organization and offer receiver will have established their relationship in the form of a legally binding employment contract. That contract is the culmination of the staffing process. The contract also signifies that the person/job match process has concluded and that the person/job match is now about to become a reality. That reality, in turn, becomes the start of, and foundation for, subsequent employee effectiveness on the various HR outcomes. For these reasons, the content and extension of the job offer become critical final parts of the overall staffing process.

This section focuses on several job offer issues. First, it discusses job offers as part of an overall applicant attraction strategy. Second, it relates the job rewards matrix to the making of job offers. Third, the content of job offers is discussed, with a dual emphasis on what is normally required by way of content, and some of the complexities often associated with determining job offer content.

Applicant Attraction Strategies

A basic theme of this book has been that applicants are exposed and subjected to numerous forces throughout the staffing process. These forces include labor markets, laws and regulations, recruitment and selection activities, and knowledge of likely job requirements and rewards. The job offer is the final confluence of these forces and must be crafted and extended within them. It is the organization's attempt to "make it all happen"—to realize the person/job match within this set of forces. Doing this requires thinking of the job offer in strategic terms.

A helpful model for these purposes is the applicant attraction strategy model shown in Exhibit 12.1.[15] This model shows that there are three basic attraction strategy components—recruitment activities, inducements, and applicant pools. The inducements component is of most interest here, for it represents the job rewards (pecuniary or extrinsic, nonpecuniary or intrinsic) that become part and parcel of the job offer. Recruitment activities and applicant pool characteristics are also important components.

The three attraction strategy components combine to influence pre- and post-employment outcomes. The pre-employment outcomes are those that occur either before or at the point of job offer acceptance. They include applicant quantity (e.g., number of applicants, percent of vacancies filled), applicant quality (e.g., KSAOs), and spillover effects (e.g., applicants' reports of their recruitment experiences to other people, such as customers or potential future applicants).

Post-employment outcomes represent long-term effects of the attraction strategy, and are also expressed in terms of quantity, quality, and spillover. A quantity indicator might be the one-year retention rate for new hires. For quality, indicators

EXHIBIT 12.1   Model of the Applicant Attraction Process

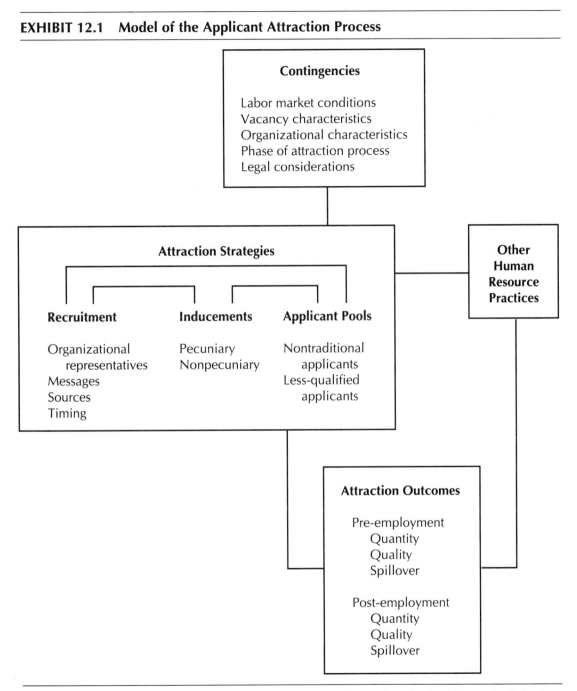

Source: S. L. Rynes and A. E. Barber, ''Applicant Attraction Strategies: An Organizational Perspective,'' *Academy of Management Review*, 1990, 15, pp. 286–310.

might be such things as KSAOs of new hires, their success in entry-level training programs, their performance ratings, and their promotion rates over time. Spillover effects might include the impact of the new hires on other employees, such as their socialization with other employees and acceptance into work groups.

The model suggests that the three recruitment strategy components have definite links to or impact upon the attraction outcomes. These linkages are conditioned, however, by various contingencies such as labor markets and legal influences. The linkages also depend on the operation and effectiveness of other HR activities, such as training and compensation.

The applicant attraction strategy model thus shows that job offers (inducements) do not occur in a vacuum, but in a much broader strategic context. This means that job offers must be synchronized and meshed with other attraction activities and external forces for purposes of achieving effectiveness on the attraction outcomes. For example, the desirability of job offers from the offer receiver's perspective may depend upon the credibility of the organizational representative who delivers it. Or, the content of job offers may have to vary according to characteristics of the recipients. Higher salaries may have to be offered to certain persons, for example, to make their daily transportation needs affordable.

Despite these interactions of the job offer content with other forces, it is ultimately the content of the job offer itself that is likely the most important force influencing offer receivers and thus determines the effectiveness of the attraction process. It is through the job offer, more than anything else, that the organization seeks to provide the types and amounts of rewards that are sufficient to induce acceptance of the offer by the offer receiver. A yes to an offer is explicit recognition by the receiver that the person/job match is sufficiently promising to warrant formally entering into it via an employment contract.

Job Rewards Matrix

The nature of the job rewards matrix was discussed in Chapter 5. The matrix specifies the extrinsic and intrinsic rewards associated with the job. For each such reward it also shows three reward characteristics—its level or amount, the amount of variability present in the reward among employees, and the reward's stability or frequency of change. An example of the matrix for the job of administrative assistant, taken from Chapter 5, is shown in Exhibit 12.2.

Several points need to be made about the matrix as it pertains to job offers. First, it provides an overall snapshot of the rewards that, on average or in general, are associated with the job. Such information is extremely important to communicate to applicants as part of a realistic recruitment campaign (see Chapters 7 and 8). The matrix, however, should not be construed or presented by the organization as part of a job offer to anyone. Rather, it should be emphasized to each person that the matrix is informational only, and that the terms and conditions that count

EXHIBIT 12.2   Portion of Job Rewards Matrix for Job of Administrative Assistant

Reward	Dimension	Reward Characteristics		
		Amount	Differential	Stability
1. Starting pay	A. Individual pay (extrinsic)	$2,000/month minimum	May exceed minimum, depending on KSAOs	Changes according to market conditions
2. Pay raises	A. Individual pay (extrinsic)	Typically, 2–3%	Across the board (same % for all)	Ranged from 0% to 10%, annually
3. Bonuses	A. Individual pay (extrinsic)	2.5% average	Range from 0% to 10%, depending on performance	Will vary each year, depending on size of bonus pool
4. Doing different tasks	B. Skill variety (intrinsic)	$\bar{x} = 4.8$*	SD = .73*	Frequent change
5. Using complex skills	B. Skill variety (intrinsic)	$\bar{x} = 3.9$*	SD = 1.54*	No recent changes; none anticipated
6. Simple and repetitive tasks	B. Skill variety (intrinsic)	$\bar{x} = 5.4$*	SD = .37*	Will continue to be part of job

*Rating scale (1–7) values, based on the three skill variety items from the Job Diagnostic Survey (JDS).

are those contained in the formal job offer. Failure to do this may mean that the job rewards matrix becomes interpreted as part of the actual employment contract.

Second, it is almost impossible to address the intrinsic rewards of the job in a job offer. Such rewards, and their characteristics, cannot be handed to people; they are very personal rewards that may or may not be experienced by a given applicant. Consider the reward "skill variety" in Exhibit 12.2. The average level of skill variety, as expressed by job incumbents on a rating scale, is shown in the matrix. The organization obviously cannot offer, or guarantee, that each offer receiver would experience that level of skill variety as an employee. Thus, it is best to confine the formal job offer to extrinsic terms and conditions being offered.

Third, the matrix only provides an overall framework and set of parameters for constructing a job offer for any particular person. Consider the compensation rewards shown in Exhibit 12.2. In the case of starting pay, only the minimum for the job is shown ($2,000 per month); this is the minimum amount that must be in the offer, although a higher amount could certainly be offered. In the case of pay raises and bonuses, what is reported in the matrix is general information about their availability and what has happened historically. At best, the job offer can only promise participation in pay raise and bonus plans to the offer receiver; it cannot promise the amount of those raises and bonuses.

Job Offer Content

As the preceding discussion suggests, the organization has latitude in the terms and conditions of employment that it may offer to people. That latitude, of course, should be exercised within the organization's particular applicant attraction strategy, as well as the rewards generally available and shown in the job rewards matrix.

With some degree of latitude in terms and conditions offered for almost any job, it is apparent that job offers should be carefully constructed. There are definite rewards that can, and for the most part should, be addressed in any job offer. Moreover, the precise terms or content of the offer to any given finalist requires careful forethought. What follows is a discussion of the types of rewards to address, as well as some of their subtleties and complexities.

Starting Date

Normally, the organization desires to control when the employment relationship begins. To do so, it must provide a definite starting date in its offer. If it does not, acceptance and consideration of the offer occurs at the time the new hire actually begins work. Normally, the starting date is one that allows the offer receiver at least two weeks to provide notification of the resignation date to a current employer.

Duration of Contract

As noted in Chapter 3, employment contracts may be of a fixed term (i.e., have a definite ending date) or indeterminate term (i.e., have no definite ending date). The decision about duration is intimately related to the employment-at-will issue.

A fixed-term contract provides certainty to both the new hire and organization regarding the length of the employment relationship. Both parties decide to and must abide by an agreed-upon term of employment. The organization can then (according to common law) terminate the contract prior to its expiration date for "just cause" only. Determination and demonstration of just cause can be a complicated legal problem for the organization.[16]

Most organizations are unwilling to provide such employment guarantees. They much prefer an employment-at-will relationship, in which either party may terminate the employment relationship at any time, without having to demonstrate just cause.[17] Of course, there are exceptions to this, as the example describing Northern Telecom's employment guarantee program in Exhibit 12.3, amply demonstrates. This example clearly shows how the company had strategically considered whether to offer such an employment guarantee based on its likely impact upon attraction outcomes such as acceptance of offers and employee retention.

Should the organization decide to have indeterminate term employment contracts, it should carefully state in its written offer that the duration is indeterminate, and that it may be terminated by either party at any time, for any reason. Because of the overriding importance of this issue, all wording should be approved at the highest organizational level.

EXHIBIT 12.3 Example of Employment Guarantee for New Hires

CANADIAN FIRM GIVES NEW HIRES JOB GUARANTEES

Northern Telecom, Ltd., in a move that could spark a recruiting war among companies seeking young technical talent, is adding something extra to lure new graduates: a three-year employment guarantee.

The Toronto-based telecommunications company will announce today that it will make that offer to between 600 and 700 graduates it plans to hire over the next year from several dozen universities in the U.S. and Canada.

The strategy, coming amid tough economic times, represents a rare corporate commitment to new employees. Even Northern Telecom has slashed hundreds of jobs lately. Meanwhile, legions of students graduated into the swelling ranks of the unemployed this year.

But some positions, particularly those demanding hard-to-find technical skills, remain hard to fill. So even in a recession, certain graduates in fields such as electrical engineering and computer science are getting multiple job offers. And many employers, though trimming back, are still scrambling to attract and retain these top young talents.

(continued)

EXHIBIT 12.3   Continued

"For us to compete for these students, we decided we needed to change the way we recruit them," said Gary R. Donahee, Northern Telecom's senior vice president, human resources. "Even though we've had to trim the workforce, if we stopped the on-campus recruitment effort, we'd be shooting ourselves in the foot."

The job guarantee likely will raise the stakes among big companies competing for top technical students. "There will be all sorts of one-upmanship," said Noel M. Tichy, professor of human resources management at the University of Michigan. "I can just see the young engineers saying to Hewlett Packard and AT&T, 'Northern Telecom gave me this. What are you going to give me?' "

Several competitors said they would study Northern Telecom's plan but didn't envision copying it immediately. At Bell Laboratories, a research arm of American Telephone & Telegraph Co., Lloyd L. Friend, director of university relations, said, "This is something that in this day and age we could not do."

Because Bell Labs has halved the number of graduates it hires annually to about 300, "We have not been having trouble finding the good students that we've needed," Mr. Friend added. But he said a plan such as Northern Telecom's "might not be outside the realm of our considering" because it would hold great appeal for students worried about job security.

US West, Inc. "will continually be monitoring the market to keep us competitive," said Marti Hamlen, one of four new recruiters hired in the past year to step up the regional phone company's campus-scouting efforts. "This seems like a very innovative plan."

Though job guarantees are common in Japan and once were a tradition among some big American companies, Northern Telecom's three-year commitment is apparently unique in the U.S. today, university job counselors said.

Electronic Data Systems Corp., a Dallas-based unit of General Motors Corp., offers three-year contracts to about 2,000 graduates accepted annually into an entry-level technical-development program. But there's a catch. If the graduates bail out early, they may have to reimburse EDS for as much as $8,500 of their $100,000-plus training costs, a spokesman said.

By contrast, graduates hired under Northern Telecom's plan won't face any liability. "We're not going to hold it against someone or force them to remain if they're unhappy," Mr. Donahee said. And if Northern Telecom becomes unhappy? Mr. Donahee said that problem employees would be handled on a case-by-case basis, but that he didn't envision high turnover. One reason: a more careful screening of candidates set to accompany the job guarantee program.

Still, there are risks in promising jobs for any length of time. Northern Telecom could be burdened with "minimal performers—people who don't pull their weight and create morale problems," warned Maury Hanigan, a New York-based consultant to companies on campus recruiting strategies.

Northern Telecom's guarantee will apply mostly to positions in areas requiring technical skills, such as manufacturing and engineering, as well as jobs in human relations, marketing, finance and product development. College graduates are expected to be hired for roughly 60% of the positions. Holders of advanced degrees, including M.B.A.s and Ph.D.s, will fill the rest.

Compensation

Compensation terms of the job offer are often straightforward. For example, there may be a standard, fixed pay rate and benefit package that is offered, and offer receivers either accept or reject the terms. Often, however, compensation portions of the offer become more complicated. This arises in particular when the organization departs from standard offers and embarks on offers that are more custom- or tailor-made to each finalist.

Starting Pay: Flat Rate   In flat rate job offers, all persons are offered an identical rate of pay, and variance from this is not permitted. Starting pay is thus offered on a "take it or leave it" basis.

Use of flat rates is appropriate in many circumstances. Examples of these include

1. jobs for which there is a plentiful supply of job applicants
2. where applicants are of quite similar KSAO quality
3. where there is a desire to avoid creating potential inequities in starting pay among new employees

It should also be noted that under some circumstances use of flat rates may be mandatory. Examples here include pay rates under many collective bargaining agreements, and for many jobs covered by civil service laws and regulations.

Starting Pay: Differential Rates   Organizations often opt out of flat rates, despite their simplicity, and choose differential starting pay rates. In general, this occurs under two sets of circumstances.

First, there are situations where the organization thinks there are clear qualitative (KSAO) differences among finalists. Some finalists are thus felt to be worth more than others, and starting pay differentials are used in recognizing this. A good example here involves new college graduates. Research clearly shows that differences in major and previous work experience lead to starting pay differentials among them.[18]

The second situation occurs when the organization is concerned about attraction outcomes, almost regardless of applicant KSAO differences. Here, the organization is under intense pressure to acquire new employees and fill vacancies promptly. To accomplish these outcomes, flexibility in starting pay rate offers is used to be responsive to finalists' demands, to sweeten offers, and otherwise impress applicants with an entrepreneurial spirit of wheeling and dealing. Hence, the organization actively seeks to strike a bargain with the offer receiver, and differential starting pay rates are a natural part of the attraction package.

Whenever differential rates of starting pay are to be used, there is the need for the organization to carefully consider what is permissible and within bounds. At times, the organization may choose to provide minimal guidance to managers making the offers. Often, however, there is a need for some constraints on managers. These constraints may specify when differential starting pay offers may be made, and where within a pay range starting pay rates must fall. Exhibit 12.4 contains examples of such starting pay policies.

Pay Incentives and Bonuses   Pay incentives and bonuses may be available on jobs, and, if so, the organization should address this in the job offer.

Prior to the job offer itself, the organization should give serious thought to whether there should be an incentive or bonus plan in the first place. This is a major issue that far transcends staffing per se, but it does have important implications for the likely effectiveness of staffing activities.

Consider an organization with sales jobs, a classic example of a situation in which incentive or commission pay systems might be used. The mere presence/absence of such a pay plan will likely affect the motivation/job rewards part of the matching process. Such likely effects will carry over to the staffing processes of the organization. Retailers such as Sears and Dayton-Hudson, for example, are cutting back on the use of sales commission plans because of difficulties in attracting and retaining employees. These difficulties come from employees' desire for a straight salary, a revulsion for the pressure of commission selling, a lack of training to provide them the KSAOs necessary for selling success, and a lack of promotion into the managerial ranks for successful salespeople.[19] In short, different "breeds of cat" may be attracted to jobs providing incentive plans from those that do not.

EXHIBIT 12.4   Example of Starting Pay Policies

The Wright Company

The following policies regarding starting pay must be adhered to:

1. No person is to be offered a salary that is below the minimum, or above the midpoint, of the salary range for the job.
2. Generally, persons with reasonable qualifications should be offered a salary within the first quartile (bottom 25%) of the salary range for the job.
3. Salary offers above the first quartile, but not exceeding the midpoint, may be made for exceptionally well qualified persons, or when market conditions dictate.
4. Salary offers should be fair in relation to other offers made and to the salaries paid to current employees.
5. Salary offers below the first quartile may be made without approval; offers at or above the first quartile must be approved in advance by the Manager of Compensation.
6. Counteroffers may not be accepted without approval of the Manager of Compensation.

If there are to be incentive or bonus pay plans, the organization should communicate this in the offer letter. Beyond that, the organization should give careful consideration to how much detail about such plans, including payout formulas and amounts, it wants to include in the job offer. The more specific the information, the less flexibility the organization will have in the operation or modification of the plan.

Benefits   Normally there is a fixed benefit package for a job, and it is offered as such to all offer receivers. Occasionally, however, differential benefit packages and/or custom-made benefit packages enter into the job offer picture. The classic example here involves the pay package for high-level executives, which normally has a detailed benefit component to it. That component is usually tailored to the individual executive, and it arises from negotiations as to its contents. The issues involve both regular benefits as well as *perquisites* (or "perks") to be provided. These run the gamut from life insurance to kidnapping insurance, severance packages (also called "golden parachutes") to stock option plans, country club memberships to corporate planes, and so forth.

Less rarified and more recent examples of benefits that are being offered on a personalized basis are what is generically referred to as "stuff."[20] What is stuff made up of? The answer is a vast list of perks, goodies, and assorted services. Examples include a car phone, personal computer and fax machine, take-home food from the company cafeteria, adoption assistance, and student loan assistance. Other examples of stuff, and an attempt to place perceived monetary value on it, are shown in Exhibit 12.5.

In terms of job offers, both executive perks and stuff raise questions about whether, and how, they should be represented in the content of the offer. By not mentioning them, the organization does not commit itself to formally providing them as a term and condition of employment. Doing this, however, may diminish the potential recruitment and attraction value of stuff. Conversely, mentioning them in the job offer heightens awareness of them, but also commits the organization to providing them over the course of the contract. Also, the offer receiver may insist that the offer deal with these items, and then the organization may have little choice but to do so. This is particularly the case with executive perks, and may well become the case with certain stuff that has high perceived value to the offer receiver.

Hours

Statements regarding hours of work should be carefully thought out and worded. For the organization, such statements will affect staffing flexibility and cost. In terms of flexibility, a statement such as, "Hours of work will be as needed and scheduled," provides maximum flexibility. Designation of work as part-time, as opposed to full-time, may affect cost because the organization may provide re-

EXHIBIT 12.5   Differential Benefit Possibilities or "Stuff"

PUTTING A PRICE ON STUFF

As companies increasingly offer a range of "soft," non-monetary benefits, a question arises: How much are they worth? Can a price be put on the right to work at home one day a week—or having a dry-cleaning service at the office? And how does the actual cost of providing such a benefit vary from its value, as perceived by different employees?

We asked a panel of compensation specialists to use their expert judgment—and best guessing skills—to help us complete the following "price list" of soft benefits. For each benefit, we sought four estimates—the annual dollar value as *perceived* by three hypothetical employees, as well as the *actual cost* to the company. We asked our respondents to assume a standard benefits package for each employee that includes health insurance, vacation and a pension plan. And we asked them to assume no co-payment by the employees. The results—averaged and rounded—aren't scientific, but they may help you figure out where you fit into one of the fastest growing of all pay schemes.

	Clerk/Secretary, age 25, male, single	Middle mgr., 37, female, divorced, 5-year-old child	Senior mgr., 49, male, married, 2 children in college	Actual cost
SALARY	$28,000	$55,000	$90,000	—
On-site child care (per child)	$ 10	$ 4,100	$ 0	$4,100
Telecommute two days weekly	800	3,333	1,583	300
Month-long paid leave every four years	739	2,274	3,187	—[1]
Title upgrade; no more pay or authority	142	242	842	20[2]
Flexible schedule; work any eight hours in 12-hour period	550	1,717	642	0
Free use of fitness center at office (per person)	392	533	658	410
Week in Barbados for professional meeting (in Feb.)	1,050	1,270	1,517	2,400

EXHIBIT 12.5   Continued

Yearly meeting with personal financial planner	100	408	875	673
Cellular car phone for business (with some personal use)	121	642	658	980
Option to wear informal clothes on summer Fridays	59	53	12	0
Membership on corporate panel on customer service	17	150	8	0
Reserved parking near entrance	243	225	350	212
On-site grocery shopping and dry-cleaning service	33	213	8	—³
Annual stress test and cholesterol screening on-site	10	64	125	112

[1]Cost equals one month's pay for each employee; [2]Cost of printing new business cards; [3]Could be a profit center, with revenue from vendors.

Source: G. Fuchsberg, "What is Pay, Anyway," *Wall Street Journal*, 4/22/93, p. R3. Reprinted by permission of *The Wall Street Journal*, © 1992 Dow Jones & Company, Inc. All Rights Reserved Worldwide.

stricted, if any, benefits to part-time employees. This restriction is clearly the norm nationwide, as the data in Exhibit 12.6 show.

Factors other than just number of hours may also need to be addressed in the job offer. If there are to be any special, tailor-made hours of work arrangements, these need to be clearly spelled out. Examples include "Weekend work will not be required of you," and "Your hours of work will be from 7:30 to 11:30 a.m., and 1:30 to 5:30."

Special Hiring Inducements
At times, the organization may want or need to offer special inducements to increase the likelihood that an offer will be accepted. Two common examples of these inducements are hiring bonuses and relocation assistance.

Hiring Bonuses   Hiring, signing, or "up-front" bonuses are one-time payments offered and subsequently paid upon acceptance of the offer. Typically, the bonus

EXHIBIT 12.6   Benefit Availability in Medium and Large Industries—1991

Employee Benefit Program	All Full-Time Employees	All Part-Time Employees
Paid time off		
Holidays	92	47
Vacations	96	55
Personal leave	21	10
Lunch period	8	2
Rest period	67	56
Funeral leave	80	39
Jury duty leave	86	45
Military leave	54	14
Sick leave	67	30
Maternity leave	2	1
Paternity leave	1	(3)
Unpaid time off		
Maternity leave	37	19
Paternity leave	26	14
Insurance		
Sickness and accident insurance	45	19
Long-term liability insurance	40	3
Medical care	83	28
Dental care	60	18
Life insurance	94	31

(continued)

EXHIBIT 12.6   Continued

Employee Benefit Program	All Full-Time Employees	All Part-Time Employees
Retirement		
All retirement	78	40
Defined benefit pension	59	28
Defined contribution	48	20
Uses of funds:		
Retirement	39	18
Capital accumulation	10	2
Types of plans:		
Savings and thrift	29	8
Deferred profit sharing	16	10
Employee stock ownership	3	(3)
Money purchase pension	7	4
Stock bonus	(5)	—
Other		
Flexible benefits plans	10	2
Reimbursement accounts	36	11
Employer-subsidized child care	8	5
Employee assistance programs	56	31
Wellness programs	35	16
Long-term care insurance	4	1
Eldercare	9	4

Source: U.S. Department of Labor, Bureau of Labor Statistics, "BLS Reports on Employee Benefits in Medium and Large Private Industry Establishments" (Washington, D.C.: author, 1992).

is in the form of an outright cash grant; the bonus may also be in the form of a cash advance against future expected earnings.

One example of hiring bonuses is that employed by brokerage firms, who have long used them as a way of luring applicants away from competitors. Bonuses up to $100,000 are not uncommon. The bonus is usually a combination of cash grant and cash advance against future sales commissions.[21]

Relocation Assistance   Acceptance of the offer may require a geographic move and entail relocation costs for the offer receiver. The organization may want to provide assistance to conduct the move, as well as totally or partially defray moving costs. Thus, a relocation package may include assistance with house hunting, guaranteed purchase of the applicant's home, a mortgage subsidy, and actual moving cost reimbursement.

Recently, relocation has become even more difficult in dual career circumstances.[22] With both people working, it may be necessary to move both the offer receiver and the accompanying partner. Such a move may entail employing both people, or providing job search assistance to the accompanying partner. The problem is likely to grow in magnitude.

Other Terms and Conditions

Job offers are by no means restricted to the terms and conditions discussed so far. Virtually any terms and conditions may be covered and presented in a job offer, provided they are legally permissible. Hence, the organization should carefully and creatively think of other terms it may wish to offer. None of these other possible terms should be offered, however, unless the organization is truly willing to commit itself to them as part of a legally binding contract.

The organization should also give careful thought to the possible use of contingencies, which, as mentioned previously, are terms and conditions that the applicant must fulfill before the contract becomes binding (e.g., passage of a medical exam). As was noted, inclusion of these contingencies should not be done without prior knowledge and understanding of their potential legal ramifications (e.g., in the case of a medical exam, potential factors to consider under the Americans With Disabilities Act).

Acceptance Terms

The job offer should specify terms of acceptance required of the offer receiver. For reasons previously noted regarding oral contracts, acceptances should normally be required in writing only. The receiver should be required to accept or reject the offer in total, without revision. Any other form of acceptance is not an acceptance, but merely a counteroffer. Finally, the offer should specify the date, if any, by which it will lapse. A lapse date is recommended so that certainty and closure are brought to the offer process.

Sample Job Offer Letter

A sample job offer letter is shown in Exhibit 12.7 that summarizes and illustrates the previous discussion and recommendations regarding job offers. This letter should be read and analyzed for purposes of becoming familiar with job offer letters, as well as gaining an appreciation for the many points that need to be addressed in such a letter. Remember that normally whatever is put in the job offer letter, once accepted by the receiver, becomes a binding employment contract.

JOB OFFER PROCESS

Besides having a knowledge of the types of issues to address in a job offer, it is equally important to have an understanding of the total job offer process. The

EXHIBIT 12.7   Example of Job Offer Letter

The Wright Company

Mr. Laverne Markowski
152 Legion Lane
Clearwater, Minnesota

Dear Mr. Markowski:

We are pleased to offer you the position of Human Resource Specialist, beginning March 1, 1994. Your office will be located here in our main facility at Silver Creek, Minnesota.

This offer is for full-time employment, meaning you will be expected to work a minimum of 40 hours per week. Weekend work is also expected, especially during peak production periods.

Your starting pay will be $2,100 per month. Should you complete one year of employment, you will then participate in our managerial performance review and merit pay process.

Should you choose to relocate to the Silver Creek area, we will reimburse you for one house/apartment hunting trip for up to $1,000. We will also pay reasonable and normal moving expenses up to $7,500 with receipts required.

It should be emphasized that we are an employment-at-will employer. This means that we, or you, may terminate our employment relationship at any time, for any reason. Only the president of the Wright Company is authorized to provide any modification to this arrangement.

This offer is contingent upon (a) your receiving certification as a Professional in Human Resources (PHR) from the Human Resource Certification Institute prior to March 1, 1994, and (b) your passing a company-paid and approved medical exam prior to March 1, 1994.

We must have your response to this offer by February 1, 1994, at which time the offer will lapse. If you wish to accept our offer as specified in this letter, please sign and date at the bottom of the letter and return it to me (a copy is enclosed for you). Should you wish to discuss these or any other terms prior to February 1, 1994, please feel free to contact me.

Sincerely yours,

Mary Kaiser
Senior Vice President-Human Resources

I accept the employment offer, and its terms, contained in this letter.

_____   _____
Signed   Date

content of any specific job offer must be formulated within a broad context of considerations. Once these have been taken into account, the specific offer must be developed and presented to the finalist. Following this, there will be matters to address in terms of either acceptance or rejection of the offer. Finally, there will be an occasional need to deal with the unfortunate issue of reneging, either by the organization or by the offer receiver.

Formulation of the Job Offer

When the organization puts together a job offer, several factors should be explicitly considered. These factors are knowledge of the terms and conditions offered by competitors, applicant truthfulness about KSAO and reward information provided, the receiver's likely reaction to the offer, and policies on negotiation of job offer content with the offer receiver.

Knowledge of Competitors

As discussed in Chapter 2, the organization competes for labor within labor markets. The job offer must be sensitive to the labor demand and supply forces operating, for these forces set the overall parameters for job offers to be extended.

On the demand side, this requires becoming knowledgeable about the terms and conditions of job contracts offered and provided by competitors. Here, the organization must confront two issues: exactly who are the competitors, and exactly what terms and conditions are they offering for the type of job for which the hiring organization is staffing?

Assume the hiring organization is a national discount retailer, and it is hiring recent (or soon-to-be) college graduates for the job of management trainee. It may identify as competitors other retailers at the national level (e.g., Sears), as well as national discount retailers (e.g., Target, Wal-Mart, and K-Mart). There may be fairly direct competitors in other industries as well (e.g., banking, insurance) that typically place new college graduates in training programs.

Once such competitors are identified, the organization needs to determine, if possible, what terms and conditions they are offering. This may be done through formal mechanisms such as performing salary surveys, reading competitors' ads, or consulting with trade associations. Information may be gathered informally as well, such as through telephone contacts with competitors and conversations with actual job applicants who have first-hand knowledge of competitors' terms.

Through all of these mechanisms, the organization becomes "marketwise" regarding its competitors. Invariably, however, the organization will discover that, for any given term or condition, there will be a range of values offered. For example, starting pay might range from $24,000 per year to $34,500, and the length of the training program may vary from three months to two years. The organization will thus need to determine where within these ranges its wishes to position itself in general, as well as for each particular offer receiver.

On the labor supply side, the organization will need to consider its needs concerning both labor quantity and quality (KSAOs and motivation). Offers in general need to be attractive enough that they yield the head count required. Moreover, offers need to take into account the KSAOs each specific receiver possesses, and what these specific KSAOs are worth in terms and conditions offered the person. This calculation is illustrated in Exhibit 12.4, which shows an example of an organization's policies regarding differential starting pay offers among offer receivers. Such differential treatment, and all the issues and questions it raises, applies to virtually any other term or condition as well.

Applicant Truthfulness

Throughout the recruitment and selection process, information about KSAOs and other factors (e.g., current salary) is being provided by the applicant. Initially, this information is being gathered as part of the assessment process, whose purpose is to determine which applicants are most likely to provide a good fit with job requirements and rewards. For applicants who pass the hurdles and are to receive job offers, the information that has been gathered may very well be used to decide the specific terms and conditions to include in a job offer. Just how truthful or believable is this information? The content and cost of job offers depends on how the organization answers this question.

Solid evidence on the degree of applicant truthfulness is lacking in general. However, there are some anecdotal indications that lack of truthfulness by applicants may be a problem.

Consider the case of starting pay. Quite naturally, the organization may wish to base its starting pay offer on knowledge of what the offer receiver's pay is currently. Will the person be truthful or deceitful in reporting current salary? Indications are that deceit may be common. People may embellish or enhance not only their reported salaries, but their KSAOs as well, in order to provide an artificially high base or starting point for the organization as it prepares its job offer. A production analyst earning $55,000 did this and obtained a new job at $150,00, with a company car and a country club membership also included in the package.[23]

To combat such deceit by applicants, organizations are becoming increasingly prone to pursue verification of all applicant information, including salary, and may go to extremes to do so. At the executive level, for example, some organizations now require people to provide copies of their W-2 income forms that are used for reporting to the Internal Revenue Service. The organization should not act on finalist-provided information in the preparation of job offers unless it is willing to assume, or has verified, that the information is accurate.

Likely Reactions of Offer Receivers

Naturally, the terms and conditions to be presented in an offer should be based on some assessment of the receiver's likely reaction to it. Will the receiver jump at it or laugh at it, or something in between?

One way to gauge likely reactions to the offer is to gather information about various preferences from the offer receiver during the recruitment/selection process. Such preliminary discussions and communications will help the organization construct an offer that is likely to be acceptable. At the extreme, the process may lead to almost simultaneous presentation and acceptance of the offer.

Another way to assess likely reactions to offers from offer receivers is to conduct research on why they accept or decline job offers. An example of this is a study of finalists for entry-level jobs in a broad range of occupations (e.g., accounting, mathematics, biologist, immigration inspection) in the federal civil service.[24] While all finalists had been certified as qualified and thus eligible to receive a job offer, some accepted the offer and others declined to even receive the offer. Results of the study are shown in Exhibit 12.8.

EXHIBIT 12.8   Comparison of Job Offer Acceptors and Decliners in Federal Government

---

A.   SURVEY METHODOLOGY

We obtained hiring data from the Office of Personnel Management for June through November 1990. This data was the most recent available. During this period, 78 people accepted offers and were hired for entry-level professional and administrative positions from OPM job registers; 132 people declined those same jobs.

Because of the limited hiring and timing period, the conclusions that can be drawn from our survey data are limited. The data represent only the 52 acceptors and 94 decliners who responded to our survey questionnaires. Nevertheless, we believe the information is important because it sheds light on some of the reasons for the government's recruiting difficulties.

B.   SURVEY RESULTS

Financial considerations dominated the decliners' reasons for their decisions. Two-thirds or more said low salaries or the high cost of living in the job locations caused them to lose interest in federal employment. A comment one of the decliners wrote on her questionnaire reflected a typical concern: ''To the best of my knowledge, this job offered below $20,000 per year. With the cost of living anywhere, much less New York City, I don't know how anyone could make it.''

Two-thirds of the 61 decliners who were in permanent jobs or self-employed said they would have suffered pay cuts if they had taken the federal jobs. For 24 decliners (39 percent), the loss would have been more than $6,000 a year.

In contrast, most of the acceptors said salaries were not the driving force behind their decisions. Over three-fourths said opportunities for career advancement or a chance to apply their education and skills were of great or very great importance in selecting federal employment. Sixteen acceptors (31 percent) said salary was an important factor. The location of the job was influential with about half of the acceptors.

Unlike the decliners, the majority of the 19 acceptors who were self-employed or in permanent jobs said they received pay increases when they joined the government. For five acceptors, the increase was more than $6,000.

(continued)

EXHIBIT 12.8   Continued

Another important difference between acceptors and decliners related to their employment status. Compared to the decliners, a larger proportion of acceptors were unemployed at the time they were offered a federal job. Thus, the need for a better paying job, or a job of any kind, appears to have been a major factor in many of the acceptors' decisions.

Fifty-six decliners (65 percent) said the location of the job was a great or very great factor in their decisions to reject federal employment.

The next highest factors related to the decliners' perceptions of the nature and quality of federal work. Thirty-nine decliners (45 percent) thought they would be unable to apply their education and skills, while the same number thought there would be few opportunities for career advancement.

The length of the hiring process was a great or very great consideration to 35 decliners (42 percent). In fact, 47 decliners (56 percent) said they had accepted other jobs while waiting to hear the results of their federal job applications. One candidate wrote the following in her questionnaire:

> "... I declined because it was too far to travel for an interview and I had already found a full-time job. However, I have applied for several other federal government jobs and the hiring process is worse than any I have encountered.... In the length of time it takes to start, I imagine that most of the good candidates have already found other jobs."

Thirty-three decliners (38 percent) said they turned down federal employment because they believed the work would not be challenging.

Source: U.S. Government Accounting Office, "Survey of Applicants Who Accepted or Declined Federal Job Offers" (Washington, D.C.: author, March 20, 1992, B-243207).

The results show that several terms and conditions were responsible for the split between acceptors and decliners. The most important were starting pay and cost of living in the relevant location. Also important were other extrinsic and intrinsic rewards, such as opportunities for advancement and quality of work (i.e., utilization of KSAOs). Note also that, rewards aside, the excessive length of the recruitment process itself also played a role in decliners' decisions.

How would such results be used in the formulation of job offers? There seems to be a clear need for higher starting pay to be offered. This may not only address low pay and high cost of living issues, but help compensate for deficiencies in intrinsic rewards. Steps will also have to be taken to shorten the recruitment process. More generally, there is probably a need to examine the total applicant attraction strategy used (i.e., recruitment practices, extrinsic and intrinsic rewards, and applicant pools). Once this examination has been completed, then the narrower issue of job offer formulation can be more thoughtfully addressed.

Policies on Negotiations and Initial Offers

Prior to making job offers, the organization should decide whether or not it will negotiate on them. In essence, the organization must decide whether its first offer to a person will also be its final offer.

Presumably, each term or condition contained in an offer is a mini-offer itself. For each term or condition, therefore, the organization must decide

1. whether it will negotiate on this term or condition; and
2. if it negotiates, what are its lower and (especially) upper bounds.

Once these questions have been answered, the organization may determine its posture regarding the presentation of the initial offer to the receiver. There are three basic strategies to choose from: low ball, competitive, and best shot.

Low Ball   This strategy involves offering the lower bounds of terms and conditions to the receiver. Advantages to this strategy include getting acceptances from desperate or unknowledgeable receivers, minimizing initial employment costs, and leaving plenty of room to negotiate upward. Dangers to the low-ball strategy are failing to get any acceptances, driving people away from and out of the finalist pool, developing an unsavory reputation among future potential applicants, and creating inequities and hard feelings that the reluctant accepter may carry into the organization and may then influence postemployment attraction outcomes, such as retention.

Competitive   With a competitive strategy, the organization prepares an offer that it feels is ''on the market,'' neither too high nor too low. The competitive strategy should yield a sufficient number of job offer acceptances overall, though not all of the highest-quality (KSAO) applicants. This strategy leaves room for subsequent negotiation, should that be necessary. Competitive offers are unlikely to either offend or excite the receiver. They probably will not have negative consequences for postemployment outcomes either.

Best Shot   With this strategy, the organization ''goes for broke'' and gives a high offer, one right at the upper bounds of feasible terms and conditions. Accompanying this offer is usually a statement to the receiver that this is indeed the organization's ''best shot,'' thus leaving little or no room for negotiation. These offers should enhance both preemployment attraction outcomes (e.g., filling vacancies quickly) and postemployment outcomes (e.g., job satisfaction). Best shot offers obviously increase employment costs. They also leave little or no room for negotiation or for ''sweetening'' the offer. Finally, they may create feelings of inequity or jealousy among some current employees.

None of these initial offer strategies is inherently superior. But the organization does need to make some choices as to which to generally use. It could also choose to tailor-make the strategy used to the finalist pursued, as well as other circumstances. For example, the best shot strategy may be chosen (a) for high-quality finalists, (b) when there are strong competitive hiring pressures from competitors, (c) when the organization feels great pressure to fill vacancies quickly, and (d) as part of an aggressive EEO/AA recruitment program.

Presentation of the Job Offer

Presentation of the offer may proceed along many different paths. The precise path chosen depends upon the content of the offer, as well as factors considered in formulating the offer. To illustrate, two extreme approaches to presenting the job offer—the mechanical and the sales approaches—are detailed.

Mechanical Approach

The mechanical approach is a dry, sterile one that relies on simple one-way communication from the organization to the offer receiver. Little more than a standard, or "form," written offer is sent to the person. The organization then awaits a response. Little or no input about the content of the offer is received from the person, and after the offer has been made, there is no further communication with the person. If the person rejects the offer, another form letter acknowledging receipt of the rejection is sent. Meanwhile, the offer process is repeated anew, without modification, for a different receiver.

Sales Approach

The sales approach treats the job offer as a product that must be developed and sold to the customer (i.e., receiver). There is active interaction between the organization and the receiver as the terms and conditions are developed and incorporated into an offer package. There is informal agreement that unfolds between the receiver and organization, and reduction of that agreement into an actual job offer is a mere formality. After the formal offer has been presented, the organization continues to have active communication with the receiver. In this way, the organization can be alert to possible glitches that occur in the offer process, and continue to sell the job to the receiver.

An excellent example of the sales approach is shown in Exhibit 12.9. This example is based on two premises:

1. The offer is not a gift. Instead, it must be sold to the receiver. Extending the job offer is a sales job and should be treated as such.
2. If possible, an offer should not be left open awaiting a response, since this generally precludes making an offer to another person.[25]

As the mechanical and sales approaches to job offer presentation make clear, the organization has considerable discretion in choosing how it delivers the offer. When it develops its job offer presentation process, it should be ever mindful of the applicant attraction strategy (Exhibit 12.1), and its emphasis on both the recruitment process and job offer content, as factors affecting applicant attraction outcomes.

EXHIBIT 12.9   Example of a Sales Approach to Job Offers

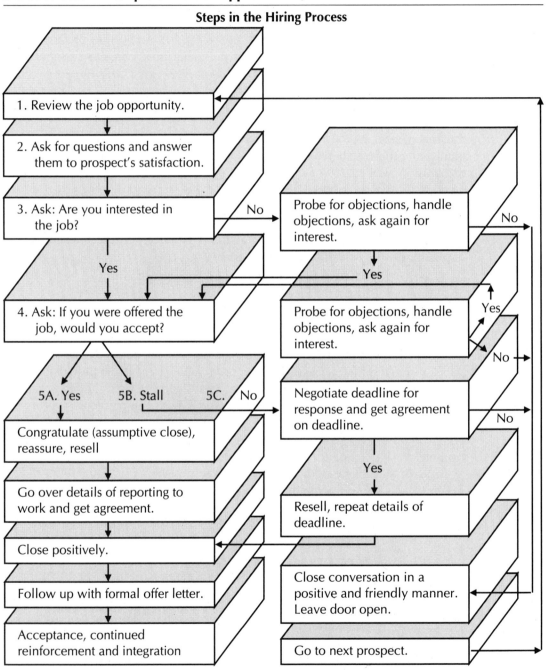

Steps in the Hiring Process

1. Review the job opportunity.

2. Ask for questions and answer them to prospect's satisfaction.

3. Ask: Are you interested in the job?

   No → Probe for objections, handle objections, ask again for interest. → No

   Yes

   Yes

4. Ask: If you were offered the job, would you accept?

   Probe for objections, handle objections, ask again for interest. → Yes / No

   5A. Yes   5B. Stall   5C. No

   Congratulate (assumptive close), reassure, resell

   Negotiate deadline for response and get agreement on deadline. → No

   Yes

   Go over details of reporting to work and get agreement.

   Resell, repeat details of deadline.

   Close positively.

   Follow up with formal offer letter.

   Close conversation in a positive and friendly manner. Leave door open.

   Acceptance, continued reinforcement and integration

   Go to next prospect.

Source: R. Goddard, J. Fox, and W. E. Patton, "The Job-Hire Sale," *Personnel Administrator,* 1989, 34(6), p. 121. Reprinted with the permission of HR Magazine (formerly Personnel Administrator) published by the Society for Human Resource Management, Alexandria, VA.

Job Offer Acceptance and Rejection

Ultimately, of course, job offers are accepted and rejected. How this happens, and how it is handled, are often as important as the outcomes themselves.

There is very little solid data about how organizations actually handle the ending stage of the final match process. An exception to this involves college recruiting. Survey data reveal some indications about the acceptance and rejection process for new college graduates.[26] Results of that survey are shown in Exhibit 12.10.

It is clear from the exhibit that the surveyed companies differ in how they handle the acceptance/rejection process. As an interesting exercise, the reader should examine those results and ask two questions about them. First, why do these differences in practice exist? Second, how might these differences in practice affect the attraction outcomes?

Provided next are some general suggestions and recommendations about acceptances and rejections. These are intended to serve as advice about additional practices and issues involved in the job offer process.

Acceptance

When the offer receiver accepts a job offer, the organization should do two important things. First, it should check the receiver's actual acceptance to ensure that it has been accepted as required in the offer. Thus, the acceptance should not come in the form of a counteroffer or with any other contingencies attached to it. Also, the acceptance should occur in the manner required (normally, writing), and it should arrive on or before the date specified.

The second thing the organization must do is maintain contact with the new hire. Initially, this means acknowledging receipt of the acceptance. Additional communication may also be appropriate to further "cement the deal" and build commitment to the new job and organization. Examples of such continued communication include soon-to-be coworkers calling and offering congratulations to the new hire, sending work materials and reports to the new hire to help phase the person into the new job, and inviting the new hire to meetings and other activities prior to that person's starting date.

Rejection

The organization may reject the finalist, and the finalist may reject the organization.

By the Organization   Depending on the decision-making process used, the acceptance of an offer by one person means that the organization will now have to reject others. This should be done promptly and courteously. Moreover, the organization should keep records of those it rejects. This is necessary for legal purposes (e.g., applicant flow statistics), and for purposes of building and main-

---

EXHIBIT 12.10   College Recruitment Practices Regarding Job Offers

Process: Rejection to Acceptance

. . . The campus interviewee is notified of your interest or rejection:
   at the close of the campus interview 2%
   later by letter or telephone 91%
   only notified if company is interested by phone or letter 7%

. . . The second or follow-up interview is usually conducted:
   the same day or in next few days on campus 4%
   later at a corporate office or plant 95%
   later by a third-party contractor off campus 1%

. . . After the campus interview, the second interview will likely occur:
   within two weeks 5%
   within one month 44%
   within three months 23%
   any time that is mutually convenient 28%

. . . If the candidate is rejected after the second interview is completed, she/he will be notified:
   on-site—in person and immediately 2%
   later by letter or phone 98%

. . . If an offer of employment is extended, it will usually be made:
   after the first interview, by the on-campus interviewer in person 0%
   after a single on-campus interview, but later by letter or phone 1%
   after a second on-campus interview 1%
   in person at the conclusion of the second interview(s) conducted on-site 5%
   after the second on-site interview and usually within:
      one week .... 40%   within 3 days 5%
      one month .... 35%   later 5%

. . . Once a job offer is extended, the candidate is usually expected to accept or reject it:
      immediately .... 2%   within 3 days 4%
      within 1 week .... 15%   within 2 weeks 24%
      within 1 month .... 15%   within 2 months 3%
      within the quarter or semester .... 3%   at candidate's convenience 1%
      open—but mutually agreeable 33%

. . . Do you think your procedures are "forcing" the candidate into an early decision?
      Yes .... 3%   No 97%

. . . Do you feel that you as a recruiter are under pressure, given present market conditions, to meet your hiring goals early?
   Yes, significantly 5%
   Yes, some 37%
   Not at all 58%

Source: V. R. Lindquist, *Trends in the Employment of College and University Graduates in Business and Industry,* 1992, p. 10. The Lindquist-Endicott Report-1992 by Victor R. Lindquist, Published by The Northwestern University Placement Center, Evanston, IL.

taining a pool of potential applicants that the organization may wish to contact about future vacancies.

The content of the rejection message (usually a letter) is up to the discretion of the organization. Most organizations opt for short and vague content that basically mentions a lack of fit between applicant and job characteristics. Providing more specific reasons for rejection should only be done with caution. The reasons provided should be candid and truthful, and they should match with the reasons recorded and maintained on other documents by the organization.

By the Offer Receiver   When the receiver rejects the job offer, the organization must first decide whether it wants to accept the rejection or extend a new offer to the person. If the organization's position on negotiations has already been determined, as ideally it should, then there is little reason to reconsider the position chosen on negotiations.

When the rejection is accepted, it should be done so promptly and courteously. Moreover, records should also be kept of these rejections, for the same reasons they are kept when rejection by the organization occurs.

Reneging

Occasionally, and unfortunately, reneging occurs. Organizations renege on offers extended, and receivers renege on offers accepted. Solid evidence on reneging, and exactly why it occurs, is lacking.

Some feeling for reneging is available from studies of college recruitment. One survey of 489 employers of college graduates found that a total of 1,159 students had reneged on acceptances in one year. These same employers also reported there were 379 instances in which they had reneged on job offers they had made to graduating students.[27]

Another recent survey of college recruiting practices and experiences also studied the reneging phenomenon. Results of that study are shown in Exhibit 12.11.[28]

Sometimes reneging is unavoidable. The organization may experience a sudden downturn in business conditions, so that planned-on jobs evaporate. Or, the offer receiver may experience sudden changes in circumstances requiring reneging, such as a change in health status. For the most part, however, reneging is probably avoidable, and steps should be taken by both parties to minimize its occurrence.

The organization should maintain high ethical standards regarding the extension of job offers. First and foremost, this requires extending offers only for positions that are known to exist and are vacant. Second, the organization should ensure that it has done a thorough and satisfactory assessment of all applicants, including verification of necessary applicant information. In this way, hidden surprises about offer receivers will be minimized. Finally, the organization should have a review

---

EXHIBIT 12.11   Organization Experiences with College Student Reneging on Job Offers

---

Student Reneging

. . . . .   Has your organization experienced any ''student reneging'' on accepted employment offers?

Yes . . . . . 49%   No 51%

. . . . .   Do you think this has increased in the last couple of years?

Yes . . . . . 22%   No . . . . . 44%   About same 34%

Comments:

''Students are placed in the undesirable position of feeling pressure to accept an offer before they have completed their selection process. Firms that force an early decision are making a mistake.''

''Most is based on pressure from company to make an early decision to fill needs.''

''Some companies continue to make offers to students even with the knowledge that they have accepted other positions.''

''This has gone up a little, but it is not unexpected.''

''Placement Centers should conduct programs on ethics for students.''

''Companies are starting to renege so students must protect themselves. Ethics have deteriorated on both sides. If a company pressured me unrealistically, I would accept and make my decision later.''

Source: V. R. Lindquist, *Trends in the Employment of College and University Graduates in Business and Industry,* 1992, p. 11. The Lindquist-Endicott Report-1992 by Victor R. Lindquist, Published by The Northwestern University Placement Center, Evanston, IL.

---

procedure in which decisions to renege are subject to approval by higher levels of management.

For the offer receiver, high ethical standards are also required. The receiver should not be a frivolous one, just going through the application process ''for the experience.'' Nor should the receiver accept an offer as a way of extracting a counteroffer out of his or her current employer. Indeed, organizations should be aware of the fact that some of the people to whom they make job offers will receive such counteroffers, and this should be taken into account during the time the offer is initially formulated and presented.[29] Finally, the receiver should do a careful assessment of probable fit for the person/job match prior to accepting an offer.

NEW EMPLOYEE ORIENTATION AND SOCIALIZATION

Establishment of the employment relationship through final match activities does not end a concern with the person/job match. Rather, that relationship must now be nurtured and maintained over time to ensure that the intended match becomes and remains an effective one. The new hires become newcomers, and their initial entry into the job and organization should be guided by orientation and socialization activities.[30]

Orientation

Orientation of the newcomer should begin immediately upon establishment of the employment relationship. The orientation may even begin before the newcomer officially reports to work for the first time (e.g., by sending the newcomer work materials and reports). The typical orientation period is quite brief, lasting from a few hours the first day on the job to a week or so.

The focus of the orientation should be on the person/job match and making it become an effective reality. At the same time, it should be recognized that the newcomer will experience apprehension and stress as the new job begins. Starting an effective match, and minimizing stress while doing so, is probably best accomplished by paying explicit attention to both the KSAO-job requirements and motivation/job rewards portions of the matching model.

The organization should be sure that the newcomer understands the requirements of the job. A good way to accomplish this is to have the newcomer's supervisor review and discuss the job requirements matrix (or its equivalent) with the newcomer. That discussion should begin with a review of task requirements, which presumably have already been communicated to the newcomer as part of a realistic recruitment program by the organization. The review, however, allows the organization to once again establish a clear understanding of task expectations and provides the newcomer an opportunity to clarify misunderstandings.

From there, the discussion should turn to KSAOs. The supervisor should emphasize to the newcomer that there appears to be a good fit between KSAOs required on the job and those of the newcomer. In addition, where there are KSAO requirements that the newcomer does not (and was not expected to) meet, these should be clearly noted. Then, clear plans for how to cope with these deficiencies, such as attendance at initial training programs, should be outlined.

For the motivation/job rewards portion of the match, the supervisor should review the job rewards matrix (or its equivalent) with the newcomer. The supervisor should review extrinsic rewards and seek to clarify any questions about them. The supervisor should also inform the newcomer where additional information about external rewards may be obtained (e.g., employee handbook, HR department).

For intrinsic rewards, there is less that is concrete to discuss. The supervisor should emphasize that the intrinsic rewards will occur and be experienced on a more personal basis. The supervisor should also caution the newcomer to be patient about these experiences that often depend on the newcomer's rate of learning and mastery of the job.

Socialization

Like orientation, socialization is concerned with the person/job fit, both the KSAO/ job requirements and the motivation/job rewards components. There are, however, two major differences between orientation and socialization. These pertain to time-frame, and to organizational norms and values.

Regarding time frame, orientation activities focus on the initial and immediate adaptation of the newcomer to the job. Socialization, alternatively, focuses on helping the newcomer adapt to the organization over time. The emphasis is on establishing a person/job match that lasts over the long haul. Here, HR activities other than staffing become prominent, such as training and development, performance appraisal, and internal mobility systems.

Organizational norms and values consist of issues that are related to, but transcend, the person/job match per se. In addition to immediate job rewards, norms and values touch upon ways of "doing business." It becomes important for these to be communicated to, and inculcated in, employees, beginning when they are newcomers and then carrying forward through their organizational careers. The intent is to achieve employee conformance with these norms and values.

One example of this is a norm that emphasizes an entrepreneurial spirit among employees, or a "work hard/play hard" mentality. Through socialization, the newcomer hears and reads of this norm and learns how to exhibit this norm behaviorally. Often, this learning takes place through observation of others' entrepreneurial actions. Working late, working on weekends, taking special initiatives to find new customers and clients, suggesting improvements in production techniques as a member of a work team are all examples of specific actions that are consistent with the norm of being entrepreneurial.

Another important organizational norm or value that can be addressed through socialization is that of workforce diversity.[31] Diversity is a value that emphasizes the importance and acceptance of employee differences. Such differences may be demographic (race, sex, age, national origin, and so forth), physical (such as disability), religious, and so on. The organization must formulate and communicate its norms and values regarding diversity. But it must also then engage in actions that are consistent with these.

Consider the case of demographic diversity and affirmative action. The organizational value might be to have a workforce whose diversity matches that found in the relevant external labor market. This then becomes translated into practice through an affirmative action hiring plan, using utilization analysis, hiring goals and timetables, targeted recruitment, and the like. Both newcomers and more seasoned employees can learn from these actions that the organization values and seeks to practice diversity in the workforce.

LEGAL ISSUES

The employment contract establishes the actual employment relationship and the terms and conditions that will govern it. In the process of establishing it, there are certain obligations and responsibilities that the organization must reckon with. These pertain to (a) employing only those people who meet the employment requirements under the Immigration Reform and Control Act (IRCA), (b) avoiding the negligent hiring of individuals, and (c) maintaining the organization's posture toward employment-at-will. Each of these is discussed in turn.

Authorization to Work

Under the IRCA (see Chapter 3), the organization is prohibited from hiring, or continuing to employ, an alien who is not authorized to work in the United States. Moreover, the organization must verify such authorization for any person hired (after November 6, 1986, only), and it must not discriminate against individuals on the basis of national origin or citizenship status. There are specific federal regulations detailing the requirements and methods of compliance.[32]

Compliance with these means the following for the organization.[33] First, the organization must verify the employability status of each new employee (not just aliens). This is accomplished through the completion of the I-9 verification form, which in turn requires documents that verify the new employee's identity and eligibility. Both identity and eligibility must be verified. Some documents (e.g., U.S. passport) verify both identity and eligibility; other documents verify only identity (e.g., state-issued driver's license or ID card) or employment eligibility (e.g., original social security card or birth certificate).

Second, verification must occur within three days of being hired. Note, therefore, that verification need not have occurred at the time of the extension of the job offer. For offers extended without verification, they should contain a contingency clause making the offer contingent upon satisfactory employment verification.

Finally, to avoid possible national origin or citizenship discrimination, it is best not to ask for proof of employment eligibility prior to making the offer. The reason for this is that many of the identity and eligibility documents contain personal information that pertain to national origin and citizenship status, and such personal information might be used in a discriminatory manner. As a further matter of caution, the organization should not refuse to make a job offer to a person based on that person's foreign accent or appearance.

Negligent Hiring

Negligent hiring is a workplace torts issue (see Chapter 3) involving claims by an injured plaintiff (e.g., customer or employee) that the plaintiff was harmed by an unfit employee who was negligently hired by the organization. The employer is claimed to have violated its common-law duty to protect its employees and customers from injury by hiring an employee it knew (or should have known) posed a threat of risk to them.[34] For example, a newly hired drug addict who subsequently attacks other employees, or steals money from them, may cause those employees to becomes plaintiffs in a negligent hiring lawsuit against the employer. Punitive monetary penalties may be levied against the employer if the plaintiffs are successful in their suit.

To have a successful suit, there are several things that the plaintiff must prove:

1. The person was, in fact, an employee of the organization.
2. The employee was, in fact, incompetent, as opposed to being a competent employee who acted in a negligent manner.
3. The employer knew, or should have known, of the employee's incompetence.
4. The employer had a legal duty to select competent employees.
5. The injury or harm was a foreseeable consequence of hiring the unfit employee.
6. The hiring of the unfit employee was the proximate cause of the injury or harm.

Examples of negligent hiring cases abound, particularly extreme ones involving violence, bodily injury, physical damage, and death. There is some suggestion that the incidence of such cases, along with the monetary damages awarded plaintiffs, is increasing. Accordingly, the organization should seek to ensure that its new hires will not become negligent hires.

Doing this, however, is no small task. There are many intricacies to consider, far too numerous to consider here. Despite this, there are several straightforward recommendations that can be made on the basis of staffing concepts discussed throughout this book. First, staffing any job should be preceded by a thorough job analysis that identifies all the KSAOs required by the job. Failure to identify, or otherwise consider, KSAOs prior to the final match is not likely to be much of a defense in a negligent hiring lawsuit.

Second, particular attention should be paid to the O's part of KSAOs, such as licensure requirements, criminal records, references, unexplained gaps in employment history, and alcohol and illegal drug usage. Of course, these should be derived separately for each job, rather than applied identically to all jobs.

Third, methods for assessing these KSAOs that are valid and legal must be used. This is difficult to do in practice because of lack of knowledge about the validity of some predictors, or their relatively low levels of validity. Also, difficulties arise because of legal constraints on the acquisition and use of pre-employment inquiries, as explained in Chapter 9.

Fourth, require all applicants to sign disclaimer statements allowing the employer to check references and otherwise conduct background investigations. In addition, have the applicant sign a statement indicating that all provided information is true, and that the applicant has not withheld requested information.

Fifth, apply utility analysis to determine whether it is worthwhile to engage in the preceding recommendations in order to try to avoid the (usually slight) chance of a negligent hiring lawsuit. Such an analysis will undoubtedly indicate great variability among jobs in terms of how many resources the organization wishes to invest in negligent hiring prevention.

Finally, when in doubt about a finalist and whether to extend a job offer, do not extend it until those doubts have been resolved. Acquire more information from the finalist, verify more thoroughly existing information, and seek the opinions of others on whether or not to proceed with the job offer.

Employment-at-Will

As discussed in this chapter and Chapter 3, employment-at-will involves the right of either the employer or employee to unilaterally terminate the employment relationship at any time, for any legal reason. In general, the employment relationship is an at-will one, and usually the employer wishes it to remain that way. Hence, during the final match (and even before) the employer must take certain steps to ensure that its job offers in fact clearly establish the at-will relationship. These steps are merely a compilation of points already made regarding employment contracts and employment-at-will.

The first thing to be done is ensure that job offers are for an indeterminate time period, meaning that they have no fixed-term or specific ending date. Second, include in the job offer a specific disclaimer stating that the employment relationship will be strictly at-will. Third, review all written documents (e.g., employee handbook, application blank) to ensure that they do not contain any language that implies anything but a strictly at-will relationship. Finally, take steps to ensure that organizational members do not make any oral statements or promises that would serve to create something other than a strictly at-will relationship.[35]

SUMMARY

During the final match, the offer receiver and the organization move toward each other through the job offer/acceptance process. They seek to enter into the employment relationship and become legally bound to each other through an employment contract.

Knowledge of employment contract principles is central to understanding the final match. The most important principle pertains to the requirements for a legally enforceable employment contract (offer, acceptance, and consideration). Other important principles focus on the identity of parties to the contract, the form of the contract (written or oral), disclaimers by the employer, fulfillment of other conditions by the offer receiver, reneging by the organization or offer receiver, and other sources (e.g., employee handbooks) that may also specify terms and conditions of employment.

Job offers are designed to induce the offer receiver to join the organization. Offers should be viewed and used in the context of an applicant attraction strategy by the organization. In that strategy, job offers, recruitment activities, and applicant characteristics all interact to exert forces on applicants that will have positive impacts on recruitment outcomes (preattraction, postattraction, and spillover). Use of the job rewards matrix may be helpful in the preparation and communication of the job offer.

Job offers may contain virtually any legal terms and conditions of employment. Generally, the offer addresses terms pertaining to starting date, duration of contract, compensation, hours, special hiring inducements (if any), other terms such as contingencies, and acceptance of the offer.

The process of making job offers can be a complicated one, involving a need to think through multiple issues prior to the making of formal offers. Offers should take into account the content of competitors' offers, potential problems with applicant truthfulness, likely reactions of the offer receiver, and the organization's policies on negotiating offers. Presentation of the offer can range from a mechanical process all the way to a major sales job. Ultimately, offers are accepted and rejected, and all offer receivers should receive prompt and courteous attention during these events. Steps should be taken to minimize reneging by either the organization or the offer receiver.

Acceptance of the offer marks the beginning of the employment relationship. To help ensure that the initial person/job match starts out, and continues to be, an effective one, the organization should undertake both orientation and socialization activities for newcomers. These are profitably meshed with the organization's workforce diversity programs and initiatives.

From a legal perspective, the organization must be sure that the offer receiver is employable according to provisions of the Immigration Reform and Control Act. Both identity and eligibility for employment must be verified. The potential negligent hiring of individuals who, once on the job, cause harm to others (employees or customers) is also of legal concern. Those so injured may bring suit against the organization. There are certain steps the organization can take in an attempt to minimize the occurrence of negligent hiring lawsuits. There are limits on these steps, however, such as other legal constraints on the gathering of background information about applicants. Finally, the organization should have its posture, policies, and practices regarding employment-at-will firmly developed and aligned. There are numerous steps that can be taken to help achieve this.

DISCUSSION QUESTIONS

1. If you were the HR staffing manager for an organization, what guidelines might you recommend regarding oral and written communication with job applicants by members of the organization?

2. Using the applicant attraction strategy model (Exhibit 12.1), what are some examples of how the same job offer has different effects on pre- and post-attraction outcomes?

3. What are the advantages and disadvantages to the sales approach in the presentation of the job offer?

4. What are examples of orientation experiences you have had as a new hire that have been particularly effective (or ineffective) in helping to make the person/job match happen?

5. What are the steps an employer should take to develop and implement its policy regarding employment-at-will?

ENDNOTES

1. C. J. Bakaly, Jr. and J. M. Grossman, *The Modern Law of Employment Relationships* (Englewood Cliffs, NJ: Prentice-Hall, 1992), pp. 25–43; A. G. Feliu, *Primer on Individual Employee Rights* (Washington, D.C.: Bureau of National Affairs, 1992), pp. 9–13; G. P. Panaro, *Employment Law Manual* (Boston, MA: Warren, Gorham and Lamont, 1990), pp. 4–2 to 4–4.

2. C. J. Bakaly, Jr. and J. M. Grossman, *The Modern Law of Employment Relationships*, pp. 15–23; G. C. Pierson, ''Independent Contractor v. Employees: Guess Who's Coming to Work,'' *SHRM Legal Report,* Summer 1993, pp. 1–4.

3. G. P. Panaro, *Employment Law Manual*, pp. 4–23 to 4–26.

4. C. J. Bakaly, Jr. and J. M. Grossman, *The Modern Law of Employment Relationships*, pp. 61–74; A. G. Feliu, *Primer on Individual Employee Rights*, pp. 37–38; G. P. Panaro, *Employment Law Manual*, pp. 4–4 to 4–22.

5. G. P. Panaro, *Employment Law Manual*, pp. 4–12 to 4–13.

6. C. J. Bakaly, Jr. and J. M. Grossman, *The Modern Law of Employment Relationships*, pp. 61–74; A. G. Feliu, *Primer on Individual Employee Rights*, pp. 23–25; G. P. Panaro, *Employment Law Manual*, pp. 4–13 to 4–17.

7. A. G. Feliu, *Primer on Individual Employee Rights*, pp. 25–26.

8. A. G. Feliu, *Primer on Individual Employee Rights*, pp. 43–47.

9. A. G. Feliu, *Primer on Individual Employee Rights*, pp. 20–23.

10. A. G. Feliu, *Primer on Individual Employee Rights*, pp. 21–22.

11. A. G. Feliu, *Primer on Individual Employee Rights*, p. 23.

12. G. P. Panaro, *Employment Law Manual*, pp. 4–27 to 4–45.

13. A. G. Feliu, *Primer on Individual Employee Rights*, pp. 15–17.

14. C. J. Bakaly, Jr. and J. M. Grossman, *The Modern Law of Employment Relationships*, pp. 47–60; A. G. Feliu, *Primer on Individual Employee Rights*, pp. 39–50.

15. S. L. Rynes and A. E. Barber, ''Applicant Attraction Strategies: An Organizational Perspective,'' *Academy of Management Review*, 1990, 15, pp. 286–310.

16. A. G. Feliu, *Primer on Individual Employee Rights*, pp. 52–55.

17. C. J. Bakaly, Jr. and J. M. Grossman, *The Modern Law of Employment Relationships*, pp. 141–182.

18. V. R. Lindquist, *Trends in the Employment of College and University Graduates in Business and Industry* (Evanston, IL: Northwestern University Placement Center, 1992); S. L. Rynes and J. W. Boudreau, "College Recruiting in Large Organizations: Practice, Evaluation, and Research Implications," *Personnel Psychology,* 1986, 39, pp. 729–757.

19. G. A. Patterson, "Distressed Shoppers, Disaffected Workers Prompt Stores to Alter Sales Commission," *Wall Street Journal,* July 1, 1992, p. B1.

20. G. Fuchsberg, "What is Pay, Anyway?", *Wall Street Journal,* April 22, 1993, p. R3.

21. W. Power and M. Siconolfi, "Wall Street Sours on Up-Front Bonuses," *Wall Street Journal,* June 13, 1991, p. C1.

22. J. S. Lubin, "As More Men Become 'Trailing Spouses,' Firms Help Them Cope," *Wall Street Journal,* April 13, 1993, p. A1.

23. J. A. Lopez, "The Big Lie," *Wall Street Journal,* April 21, 1993, pp. R6–R8.

24. U.S. Government Accounting Office, "Survey of Applicants Who Accepted or Declined Federal Job Offers" (Washington, D.C.: author, 1992, B-243207).

25. R. Goddard, J. Fox, and W. E. Patton, "The Job-Hire Sale," *The Personnel Administrator,* 1989, 34(6), pp. 119–122.

26. V. R. Lindquist, *Trends in the Employment of College and University Graduates in Business and Industry.*

27. L. P. Scheetz, *Recruiting Trends 1989–90* (East Lansing, MI: Michigan State University, Career Development and Placement Services, 1990).

28. V. R. Lindquist, *Trends in the Employment of College and University Graduates in Business and Industry.*

29. J. A. Lopez and J. S. Lubin, "Bosses Seek Ways to Hold Onto Workers as Recovery Encourages Job Hopping," *Wall Street Journal,* Jan. 5, 1993, pp. B1, B4; L. Reibstein, "Offers and Counteroffers: Attitudes Change in Executive Search Game," *Wall Street Journal,* May 5, 1986, p. 21.

30. J. P. Wanous, *Organizational Entry,* second ed. (Reading, MA: Addison-Wesley, 1992), pp. 155–234.

31. S. E. Jackson and Associates, *Diversity in the Workplace* (New York: Guilford Press, 1992); D. Jamieson and J. O'Mara, *Managing Workforce 2000* (San Francisco: Jossey-Bass, 1991).

32. Bureau of National Affairs, *Fair Employment Practices Manual* (Washington, D.C.: author, periodically updated), pp. 403:5937–5941, 6169–6191.

33. G. P. Panaro, *Employment Law Manual,* pp. 1–48 to 1–54.

34. A. G. Feliu, *Primer on Individual Employee Rights,* pp. 258–263; R. M. Green and R. J. Reibstein, *Employers Guide to Workplace Torts* (Washington, D.C.: Bureau of National Affairs, 1992), pp. 1–18, 198–200, 245–250; A. M. Ryan and M. Lasek, "Negligent Hiring and Defamation: Areas of Liability Related to Preemployment Inquiries," *Personnel Psychology,* 1991, 44, pp. 293–319; W. J. Woska, "Negligent Employment Practices," *Labor Law Journal,* 1991, pp. 603–610.

35. N. K. Kubasek and M. Neil Browne, "Recruiter Beware: The Oral Promise of Lifetime Employment May Be More Than a Mere Inducement," *Labor Law Journal,* 1991, pp. 273–285.

APPENDIX A

Uniform Guidelines on Employee Selection Procedures (EEOC)

GENERAL PRINCIPLES

§1607.1 *Statement of purpose.*

A. *Need for uniformity–Issuing agencies.* The Federal government's need for a uniform set of principles on the question of the use of tests and other selection procedures has long been recognized. The Equal Employment Opportunity Commission, the Civil Service Commission, the Department of Labor, and the Department of Justice jointly have adopted these uniform guidelines to meet that need, and to apply the same principles to the Federal Government as are applied to other employers.

B. *Purpose of guidelines.* These guidelines incorporate a single set of principles which are designed to assist employers, labor organizations, employment agencies, and licensing and certification boards to comply with requirements of Federal law prohibiting employment practices which discriminate on grounds of race, color, religion, sex, and national origin. They are designed to provide a framework for determining the proper use of tests and other selection procedures. These guidelines do not require a user to conduct validity studies of selection procedures where no adverse impact results. However, all users are encouraged to use selection procedures which are valid, especially users operating under merit principles.

C. *Relation to prior guidelines.* These guidelines are based upon and supersede previously issued guidelines on employee selection procedures. These guidelines have been built upon court decisions, the previously issued guidelines of the agencies, and the practical experience of the agencies, as well as the standards of the psychological profession. These guidelines are intended to be consistent with existing law.

§1607.2 *Scope.*

A. *Application of guidelines.* These guidelines will be applied by the Equal Employment Opportunity Commission in the enforcement of title VII of the Civil Rights Act of 1964, as amended by the Equal Employment Opportunity Act of 1972 (hereinafter "Title VII"); by the Department of Labor, and the contract compliance agencies until the transfer of authority contemplated by the President's Reorganization Plan No. 1 of 1978, in the administration and enforcement of Executive Order 11246, as amended by Executive Order 11375 (hereinafter "Executive Order 11246"); by the Civil Service Commission and other Federal agencies subject to section 717 of Title VII; by the Civil Service Commission in exercising its responsibilities toward State and local governments under section 208(b)(1) of the Intergovernmental-Personnel Act; by the Department of Justice in exercising its responsibilities under Federal law; by the Office of Revenue Sharing of the Department of the Treasury under the State and Local Fiscal Assistance Act of 1972, as amended; and by any other Federal agency which adopts them.

B. *Employment decisions.* These guidelines apply to tests and other selection procedures which are used as a basis for any employment decision. Employment decisions include but are not limited to hiring, promotion, demotion, membership (for example, in a labor organization), referral, retention, and licensing and certification, to the extent that licensing and certification may be covered by Federal equal employment opportunity law. Other selection decisions, such as selection for training or transfer, may also be considered employment decisions if they lead to any of the decisions listed above.

C. *Selection procedures.* These guidelines apply only to selection procedures which are used as a basis for making employment decisions. For example, the use of selection procedures designed to attract members of a particular race, sex, or ethnic group, which were previously denied employment opportunities or which are currently underutilized, may be necessary to bring an employer into compliance with Federal law, and is frequently an essential element of any effective affirmative action program; but recruitment practices are not considered by these guidelines to be selection procedures. Similarly, these guidelines do not pertain to the question of the lawfulness of a seniority system within the meaning of section 703(h), Executive Order 11246 or other provisions of Federal law or regulation, except to the extent that such systems utilize selection procedures to determine qualifications or abilities to perform the job. Nothing in these guidelines is intended or should be interpreted as discouraging the use of a selection procedure for the purpose of determining qualifications or for the purpose of selection on the basis of relative qualifications, if the selection procedure had been validated in accord with these guidelines for each such purpose for which it is to be used.

D. *Limitations.* These guidelines apply only to persons subject to Title VII, Executive Order 11246, or other equal employment opportunity requirements of Federal law. These guidelines do not apply to responsibilities under the Age Discrimination in Employment Act of 1967, as amended, not to discriminate on the basis of age, or under sections 501, 503, and 504 of the Rehabilitation Act of 1973, not to discriminate on the basis of handicap.

E. *Indian preference not affected.* These guidelines do not restrict any obligation imposed or right granted by Federal law to users to extend a preference in employment to Indians living on or near an Indian reservation in connection with employment opportunities on or near an Indian reservation.

§1607.3 *Discrimination defined: Relationship between use of selection procedures and discrimination.*

A. *Procedure having adverse impact constitutes discrimination unless justified.* The use of any selection procedure which has an adverse impact on the hiring, promotion, or other employment or membership opportunities of members of any race, sex, or ethnic group will be considered to be discriminatory and inconsistent with these guidelines, unless the procedure has been validated in accordance with these guidelines, or the provisions of section 6 below are satisfied.

B. *Consideration of suitable alternative selection procedures.* Where two or more selection procedures are available which serve the user's legitimate interest in efficient and trustworthy workmanship, and which are substantially equally valid for a given purpose, the user should use the procedure which has been demonstrated to have the lesser adverse impact. Accordingly, whenever a validity study is called for by these guidelines, the user should include, as a part of the validity study, an investigation of suitable alternative selection procedures and suitable alternative methods of using the selection procedure which have as little adverse impact as possible to determine the appropriateness of using or validating them in accord with these guidelines. If a user has made a reasonable effort to become aware of such alternative procedures and validity has been demonstrated in accord with these guidelines, the use of the test or other selection procedure may continue until such time as it should reasonably be reviewed for currency. Whenever the user is shown an alternative selection procedure with evidence of less adverse impact and substantial evidence of validity for the same job in similar circumstances, the user should investigate it to determine the appropriateness of using or validating it in accord with these guidelines. This subsection is not intended to preclude the combination of procedures into a significantly more valid procedure, if the use of such a combination has been shown to be in compliance with the guidelines.

§1607.4 *Information on impact.*

A. *Records concerning impact.* Each user should maintain and have available for inspection records or other information which will disclose the impact which its tests and other selection procedures have upon employment opportunities of persons by identifiable race, sex, or ethnic group as set forth in subparagraph B below in order to determine compliance with these guidelines. Where there are large numbers of applicants and procedures are administered frequently, such information may be retained on a sample basis, provided that the sample is appropriate in terms of the applicant population and adequate in size.

B. *Applicable race, sex, and ethnic groups for recordkeeping.* The records called for by this section are to be maintained by sex, and the following races and ethnic groups: Blacks (Negroes), American Indians (including Alaskan Natives), Asians (including Pacific Islanders), Hispanic (including persons of Mexican, Puerto Rican, Cuban, Central or South American, or other Spanish origin or culture regardless of race), whites (Caucasians) other than Hispanic, and totals. The race, sex, and ethnic classifications called for by this section are consistent with the Equal Employment Opportunity Standard Form 100, Employer Information Report EEO-1 series of reports. The user should adopt safeguards to ensure that the records required by this paragraph are used for appropriate purposes such as determining adverse impact, or (where required) for developing and monitoring affirmative action programs, and that such records are not used improperly. See sections 4E and 17(4), below.

C. *Evaluation of selection rates. The "bottom line."* If the information called for by sections 4A and B above shows that the total selection process for a job has an adverse impact, the individual components of the selection process should be evaluated for adverse impact. If this information shows that the total selection process does not have an adverse impact, the Federal enforcement agencies, in the exercise of their administrative and prosecutorial discretion, in usual circumstances, will not expect a user to evaluate the individual components for adverse impact, or to validate such individual components, and will not take enforcement action based upon adverse impact of any component of that process, including the separate parts of a multipart selection procedure or any separate procedure that is used as an alternative method of selection. However, in the following circumstances, the Federal enforcement agencies will expect a user to evaluate the individual components for adverse impact and may, where appropriate, take enforcement action with respect to the individual components: (1) where the selection procedure is a significant factor in the continuation of patterns of assignments of incumbent employees caused by prior discriminatory employment practices; (2) where the weight of court decisions or administrative interpretations hold that a specific procedure (such as height or weight requirements or no-arrest records) is not job related in the same or similar circumstances. In unusual circumstances, other than those listed in (1) and (2) above, the Federal enforcement agencies may request a user to evaluate the individual components for adverse impact and may, where appropriate, take enforcement action with respect to the individual component.

D. *Adverse impact and the "four-fifths rule."* A selection rate for any race, sex, or ethnic group which is less than four-fifths (4/5) (or eighty percent) of the rate for the group with the highest rate will generally be required by the Federal enforcement agencies as evidence of adverse impact, while a greater than four-fifths rate will generally not be regarded by Federal enforcement agencies as evidence of adverse impact. Smaller differences in selection rate may nevertheless constitute adverse impact, where they are significant in both statistical and practical terms or where a user's actions have discouraged applicants disproportionately on grounds of race, sex, or ethnic group. Greater differences in selection rate may not constitute adverse impact where the differences are based on small numbers and are not statistically significant, or where special recruiting or other programs cause the pool of minority or female candidates to be atypical of the normal pool of applicants from that group. Where the user's evidence concerning the impact of a selection procedure indicates adverse impact but is based upon numbers which are too small to be reliable, evidence concerning the impact of the procedure over a longer period of time and/or evidence concerning the impact which the selection procedure had when used in the same manner in similar circumstances elsewhere may be considered in determining adverse impact. Where the user has not maintained data on adverse impact as required by the documentation section of applicable guidelines, the Federal enforcement agencies may draw an inference of adverse impact of the selection process from the failure of the user to maintain such data, if the user has an underutilization of a group in the job category, as compared to the group's representation in the relevant labor market or, in the case of jobs filled from within, the applicable workforce.

E. *Consideration of user's equal employment opportunity posture.* In carrying out their obligations, the Federal enforcement agencies will consider the general posture of the user with respect to equal employment opportunities for the job or group of jobs in question. Where a user has adopted an affirmative action program, the Federal enforcement agencies will consider the provisions of that program, including the goals and timetables which the user has adopted and the progress which the user has made in carrying out that program and in meeting the goals and timetables. While such affirmative action programs may in design and execution be race, color, sex, or ethnic conscious, selection procedures under such programs should be based upon the ability or relative ability to do the work.

§1607.5 *General standards for validity studies.*

A. *Acceptable types of validity studies.* For the purposes of satisfying these guidelines, users may rely upon criterion-related validity studies, content validity studies or construct validity studies, in accordance with the standards set forth in the technical standards of these guidelines, section 14 below. New strategies for showing the validity of selection procedures will be evaluated as they become accepted by the psychological profession.

B. *Criterion-related, content, and construct validity.* Evidence of the validity of a test or other selection procedure by a criterion-related validity study should consist of empirical data demonstrating that the selection procedure is predictive of or significantly correlated with important elements of job performance. See section 14B below. Evidence of the validity of a test or other selection procedure by a content validity study should consist of data showing that the content of the selection procedure is representative of important aspects of performance on the job for which the candidates are to be evaluated. See section 14C below. Evidence of the validity of a test or other selection procedure through a construct validity study should consist of data showing that the procedure measures the degree to which candidates have identifiable characteristics which have been determined to be important in successful performance in the job for which the candidates are to be evaluated. See section 14D below.

C. *Guidelines are consistent with professional standards.* The provisions of these guidelines relating to validation of selection procedures are intended to be consistent with generally accepted professional standards for evaluating standardized tests and other selection procedures, such as those described in the Standards for Educational and Psychological Tests prepared by a joint committee of the American Psychological Association, the American Educational Research Association, and the National Council on Measurement in Education (American Psychological Association, Washington, D.C., 1974) (hereinafter ''A.P.A. Standards'') and standard textbooks and journals in the field of personnel selection.

D. *Need for documentation of validity.* For any selection procedure which is part of a selection process which has an adverse impact each user should maintain and have available such documentation as is described in section 15 below.

E. *Accuracy and standardization.* Validity studies should be carried out under conditions which assure insofar as possible the adequacy and accuracy of the research and the report. Selection procedures should be administered and scored under standardized conditions.

F. *Caution against selection on basis of knowledges, skills, or ability learned in brief orientation period.* In general, users should avoid making employment decisions on the basis of measures of knowledges, skills, or abilities which are normally learned in a brief orientation period, and which have an adverse impact.

G. *Method of use of selection procedures.* The evidence of both the validity and utility of a selection procedure should support the method the user chooses for operational use of the procedure, if that method of use has a greater adverse impact than another method of use. Evidence which may be sufficient to support the use of a selection procedure on a pass/fail (screening) basis may be insufficient to support the use of the same procedure on a ranking basis under these guidelines. Thus, if a user decides to use a selection procedure on a ranking basis, and that method of use has a greater adverse impact than use on an appropriate pass/fail basis (see section 5H below), the user should have sufficient evidence of validity and utility to support the use on a ranking basis. See sections 3B, 14B (5) and (6), 14C (8) and (9).

H. *Cutoff scores.* Where cutoff scores are used, they should normally be set so as to be reasonable and consistent with normal expectations of acceptable proficiency within the workforce. Where applicants are ranked on the basis of properly validated selection procedures and those applicants scoring below a higher cutoff score than appropriate in light of such expectations have little or no chance of being selected for employment, the higher cutoff score may be appropriate, but the degree of adverse impact should be considered.

I. *Use of selection procedures for higher-level jobs.* If job progression structures are so established that employees will probably, within a reasonable period of time and in a majority of cases, progress to a higher level, it may be considered that the applicants are being evaluated for a job or jobs at the higher level. However, where job progression is not so nearly automatic, or the time span is such that higher level jobs or employees' potential may be expected to change in significant ways, it should be considered that applicants are being evaluated for a job at or near the entry level. A ''reasonable period of time'' will vary for different jobs and employment situations but will seldom be more than 5 years. Use of selection procedures to evaluate applicants for a higher level job would not be appropriate:

(1) If the majority of those remaining employed do not progress to the higher level job;

(2) If there is a reason to doubt that the higher level job will continue to require essentially similar skills during the progression period; or

(3) If the selection procedures measure knowledges, skills, or abilities required for advancement which would be expected to develop principally from the training or experience on the job.

J. *Interim use of selection procedures.* Users may continue the use of a selection procedure which is not at the moment fully supported by the required evidence of validity, provided: (1) the user has available substantial evidence of validity, and (2) the user has in progress, when technically feasible, a study which is designed to produce the additional evidence required by these guidelines within a reasonable time. If such a study is not technically feasible, see section 6B. If the study does not demonstrate validity, this provision of these guidelines for interim use shall not constitute a defense in any action, nor shall it relieve the user of any obligations arising under Federal law.

K. *Review of validity studies for currency.* Whenever validity has been shown in accord with these guidelines for the use of a particular selection procedure for a job or group of jobs, additional studies need not be performed until such time as the validity study is subject to review as provided in section 3B above. There are no absolutes in the area of determining the currency of a validity study. All circumstances concerning the study, including the validation strategy used, and changes in the relevant labor market and the job should be considered in the determination of when a validity study is outdated.

§1607.6 *Use of selection procedures which have not been validated.*

A. *Use of alternate selection procedures to eliminate adverse impact.* A user may choose to utilize alternative selection procedures in order to eliminate adverse impact or as part of an affirmative action program. See section 13 below. Such alternative procedures should eliminate the adverse impact in the total selection process, should be lawful, and should be as job related as possible.

B. *Where validity studies cannot or need not be performed.* There are circumstances in which a user cannot or need not utilize the validation techniques contemplated by these guidelines. In such circumstances, the user should utilize selection procedures which are as job related as possible and which will minimize or eliminate adverse impact, as set forth below.

(1) *Where informal or unscored procedures are used.* When an informal or unscored selection procedure which has an adverse impact is utilized, the user should eliminate the adverse impact, or modify the procedure to one which is a formal, scored or quantified measure or combination of measures and then validate the procedure in accord with these guidelines, or otherwise justify continued use of the procedure in accord with Federal law.

(2) *Where formal and scored procedures are used.* When a formal and scored selection procedure is used which has an adverse impact, the validation techniques contemplated by these guidelines usually should be followed if technically feasible. Where the user cannot or need not follow the validation techniques anticipated by these guidelines, the user should either modify the procedure to eliminate adverse impact or otherwise justify continued use of the procedure in accord with Federal law.

§1607.7 *Use of other validity studies.*

A. *Validity studies not conducted by the user.* Users may, under certain circumstances, support the use of selection procedures by validity studies conducted by other users or conducted by test publishers or distributors and described in test manuals. While publishers of selection procedures have a professional obligation to provide evidence of validity which meets generally accepted professional standards (see section 5C above), users are cautioned that they are responsible for compliance with these guidelines. Accordingly, users seeking to obtain selection procedures from publishers and distributors should be careful to determine that, in the event the user becomes subject to the validity requirements of these guidelines, the necessary information to support validity has been determined and will be made available to the user.

B. *Use of criterion-related validity evidence from other sources.* Criterion-related validity studies conducted by one test user, or described in test manuals and the professional literature, will be considered acceptable for use by another user when the following requirements are met:

(1) *Validity evidence.* Evidence from the available studies meeting the standards of section 14B below clearly demonstrates that the selection procedure is valid;

(2) *Job similarity.* The incumbents in the user's job and the incumbents in the job or group of jobs on which the validity study was conducted perform substantially the same major work behaviors, as shown by appropriate job analyses both on the job or group of jobs on which the validity study was performed and on the job for which the selection procedure is to be used; and

(3) *Fairness evidence.* The studies include a study of test fairness for each race, sex, and ethnic group which constitutes a significant factor in the borrowing user's relevant labor market for the job or jobs in question. If the studies under consideration satisfy (1) and (2) above but do not contain an investigation of test fairness, and it is not technically feasible for the borrowing user to conduct an internal study of test fairness, the borrowing user may utilize the study until studies conducted elsewhere meeting the requirements of these guidelines show test unfairness, or until such time as it becomes technically feasible to conduct an internal study of test fairness and the results of that study can be acted upon. Users obtaining selection procedures from publishers should consider, as one factor in the decision to purchase a particular selection procedure, the availability of evidence concerning test fairness.

C. *Validity evidence from multiunit study.* If validity evidence from a study covering more than one unit within an organization satisfies the requirements of section 14B below, evidence of validity specific to each unit will not be required unless there are variables which are likely to affect validity significantly.

D. *Other significant variables.* If there are variables in the other studies which are likely to affect validity significantly, the user may not rely upon such studies, but will be expected either to conduct an internal validity study or to comply with section 6 above.

§1607.8 *Cooperative studies.*

A. *Encouragement of cooperative studies.* The agencies issuing these guidelines encourage employers, labor organizations, and employment agencies to cooperate in research, development, search for lawful alternatives, and validity studies in order to achieve procedures which are consistent with these guidelines.

B. *Standards for use of cooperative studies.* If validity evidence from a cooperative study satisfies the requirements of section 14 below, evidence of validity specific to each user will not be required unless there are variables in the user's situation which are likely to affect validity significantly.

§1607.9 *No assumption of validity.*

A. *Unacceptable substitutes for evidence of validity.* Under no circumstances will the general reputation of a test or other selection procedures, its author or its publisher, or casual reports of its validity be accepted in lieu of evidence of validity. Specifically ruled out are: assumptions of validity based on a procedure's name or descriptive labels; all forms of promotional literature; data bearing on the frequency of a procedure's usage; testimonial statements and credentials of sellers, users, or consultants; and other nonempirical or anecdotal accounts of selection practices or selection outcomes.

B. *Encouragement of professional supervision.* Professional supervision of selection activities is encouraged but is not a substitute for documented evidence of validity. The enforcement agencies will take into account the fact that a thorough job analysis was conducted and that careful development and use of a selection procedure in accordance with professional standards enhance the probability that the selection procedure is valid for the job.

§1607.10 *Employment agencies and employment services.*

A. *Where selection procedures are devised by agency.* An employment agency, including private employment agencies and State employment agencies, which agrees to a request by an employer or labor organization to devise and utilize a selection procedure should follow the standards in these guidelines for determining adverse impact. If adverse impact exists, the agency should comply with these guidelines. An employment agency is not relieved of its obligation herein because the user did not request such validation or has requested the use of some lesser standard of validation than is provided in these guidelines. The use of an employment agency does not relieve an employer or labor organization or other user of its responsibilities under Federal law to provide equal employment opportunity or its obligations as a user under these guidelines.

B. *Where selection procedures are devised elsewhere.* Where an employment agency or service is requested to administer a selection procedure which has been devised elsewhere and to make referrals pursuant to the results, the employment agency or service should maintain and have available evidence of the impact of the selection and referral procedures which it administers. If adverse impact results the agency or service should comply with these guidelines. If the agency or service seeks to comply with these guidelines by reliance upon validity studies or other data in the possession of the employer, it should obtain and have available such information.

§1607.11 *Disparate treatment.*

The principles of disparate or unequal treatment must be distinguished from the concepts of validation. A selection procedure—even though validated against job performance in accordance with these guidelines—cannot be imposed upon members of a race, sex, or ethnic group where other employees, applicants, or members have not been subjected to that standard. Disparate treatment occurs where members of a race, sex, or ethnic group have been denied the same employment, promotion, membership, or other employment opportunities as have been available to other employees or applicants. Those employees or applicants who have been denied equal treatment, because of prior discriminatory practices or policies, must at least be afforded the same opportunities as had existed for other employees or applicants during the period of discrimination. Thus, the persons who were in the class of persons discriminated against during the period the user followed the discriminatory practices should be allowed the opportunity to qualify under the less stringent selection procedures previously followed, unless the user demonstrates that the increased standards are required by business necessity. This section does not prohibit a user who has not previously followed merit standards from adopting merit standards which are in compliance with these guidelines; nor does it preclude a user who has previously used invalid or unvalidated selection procedures from developing and using procedures which are in accord with these guidelines.

§1607.12 *Retesting of applicants.*

Users should provide a reasonable opportunity for retesting and reconsideration. Where examinations are administered periodically with public notice, such reasonable opportunity exists, unless persons who have previously been tested are precluded from retesting. The user may however take reasonable steps to preserve the security of its procedures.

§1607.13 *Affirmative action.*

A. *Affirmative action obligations.* The use of selection procedures which have been validated pursuant to these guidelines does not relieve users of any obligations they have to undertake affirmative action to assure equal employment opportunity. Nothing in these guidelines is intended to preclude the use of lawful selection procedures which assist in remedying the effects of prior discriminatory practices, or the achievement of affirmative action objectives.

B. *Encouragement of voluntary affirmative action programs.* These guidelines are also intended to encourage the adoption and implementation of voluntary affirmative action programs by users who have no obligation under Federal law to adopt them; but are not intended to impose any new obligations in that regard. The agencies issuing and endorsing these guidelines endorse for all private employers and reaffirm for all governmental employers the Equal Employment Opportunity Coordinating Council's "Policy Statement on Affirmative Action Programs for State and Local Government Agencies" (41 FR 38814, September 13, 1976). That policy statement is attached hereto as appendix, section 17.

TECHNICAL STANDARDS

§1607.14 *Technical standards for validity studies.*

The following minimum standards, as applicable, should be met in conducting a validity study. Nothing in these guidelines is intended to preclude the development and use of other professionally acceptable techniques with respect to validation of selection procedures. Where it is not technically feasible for a user to conduct a validity study, the user has the obligation otherwise to comply with these guidelines. See sections 6 and 7 above.

A. *Validity studies should be based on review of information about the job.* Any validity study should be based upon a review of information about the job for which the selection procedure is to be used. The review should include a job analysis except as provided in section 14B(3) below with respect to criterion-related validity. Any method of job analysis may be used if it provides the information required for the specific validation strategy used.

B. *Technical standards for criterion-related validity studies.*

(1) *Technical feasibility.* Users choosing to validate a selection procedure by a criterion-related validity strategy should determine whether it is technically feasible (as defined in section 16) to conduct such a study in the particular employment context. The determination of the number of persons necessary to permit the conduct of a meaningful criterion-related study should be made by the user on the basis of all relevant information concerning the selection procedure, the potential sample and the employment situation. Where appropriate, jobs with substantially the same major work behaviors may be grouped together for validity studies, in order to obtain an adequate sample. These guidelines do not require a user to hire or promote persons for the purpose of making it possible to conduct a criterion-related study.

(2) *Analysis of the job.* There should be a review of job information to determine measures of work behavior(s) or performance that are relevant to the job or group of jobs in question. These measures or criteria are relevant to the extent that they represent critical or important job duties, work behaviors or work outcomes as developed from the review of job information. The possibility of bias should be considered both in selection of the criterion measures and their application. In view of the possibility of bias in subjective evaluations, supervisory rating techniques and instructions to raters should be carefully developed. All criterion measures and the methods for gathering data need to be examined for freedom from factors which would unfairly alter scores of members of any group. The relevance of criteria and their freedom from bias are of particular concern when there are significant differences in measures of job performance for different groups.

(3) *Criterion measures.* Proper safeguards should be taken to ensure that scores on selection procedures do not enter into any judgments of employee adequacy that are to be used as criterion measures. Whatever criteria are used should represent important or critical work behavior(s) or work outcomes. Certain criteria may be used without a full job analysis if the user can show the importance of the criteria to the particular employment context. These criteria include but are not limited to production rate, error rate, tardiness, absenteeism, and length of service. A standardized rating of overall work performance may be used where a study of the job shows that it is an appropriate criterion. Where performance in training is used as a criterion, success in training should be properly measured and the relevance of the training should be shown either through a comparison of the content of the training program with the critical or important work behavior(s) of the job(s), or through a demonstration of the relationship between measures of performance in training and measures of job performance. Measures of relative success in training include but are not limited to instructor evaluations, performance samples, or tests. Criterion measures consisting of paper and pencil tests will be closely reviewed for job relevance.

(4) *Representativeness of the sample.* Whether the study is predictive or concurrent, the sample subjects should insofar as feasible be representative of the candidates normally available in the relevant labor market for the job or group of jobs in question, and should insofar as feasible include the races, sexes, and ethnic groups normally available in the relevant job market. In determining the representativeness of the sample in a concurrent validity study, the user should take into account the extent to which the specific knowledges or skills which are the primary focus of the test are those which employees learn on the job.

Where samples are combined or compared, attention should be given to see that such samples are comparable in terms of the actual job they perform, the length of time on the job where time on the job is likely to affect performance, and other relevant factors likely to affect validity differences; or that these factors are included in the design of the study and their effects identified.

(5) *Statistical relationships.* The degree of relationship between selection procedure scores and criterion measures should be examined and computed, using professionally acceptable statistical procedures. Generally, a selection procedure is considered related to the criterion, for the purposes of these guidelines, when the relationship between performance on the procedure and performance on the criterion measure is statistically significant at the 0.05 level of significance, which means that it is sufficiently high as to have a probability of no more than one (1) in twenty (20) to have occurred by chance. Absence of a statistically significant relationship between a selection procedure and job performance should not necessarily discourage other investigations of the validity of that selection procedure.

(6) *Operational use of selection procedures.* Users should evaluate each selection procedure to assure that it is appropriate for operational use, including establishment of cutoff scores or rank ordering. Generally, if other factors remain the same, the greater the magnitude of the relationship (e.g., correlation coefficient) between performance on a selection procedure and one or more criteria of performance on the job, and the greater the importance and number of aspects of job performance covered by the criteria, the more likely it is that the procedure will be appropriate for use. Reliance upon a selection procedure which is significantly related to a criterion measure, but which is based upon a study involving a large number of subjects and has a low correlation coefficient will be subject to close review if it has a large adverse impact. Sole reliance upon a single selection instrument which is related to only one of many job duties or aspects of job performance will also be subject to close review. The appropriateness of a selection procedure is best evaluated in each particular situation and there are no minimum correlation coefficients applicable to all employment situations. In determining whether a selection procedure is appropriate for operational use, the following considerations should also be taken into account: The degree of adverse impact of the procedure, the availability of other selection procedures of greater or substantially equal validity.

(7) *Overstatement of validity findings.* Users should avoid reliance upon techniques which tend to overestimate validity findings as a result of capitalization on chance unless an appropriate safeguard is taken. Reliance upon a few selection procedures or criteria of successful job performance when many selection procedures or criteria of performance have been studied, or the use of optimal statistical weights for selection procedures computed in one sample, are techniques which tend to inflate validity estimates as a result of chance. Use of a large sample is one safeguard; cross-validation is another.

(8) *Fairness.* This section generally calls for studies of unfairness where technically feasible. The concept of fairness or unfairness of selection procedures is a developing concept. In addition, fairness studies generally require substantial numbers of employees in the job or group of jobs being studied. For these reasons, the Federal enforcement agencies recognize that the obligation to conduct studies of fairness imposed by the guidelines generally will be upon users or groups of users with a large number of persons in a job class, or test developers; and that small users utilizing their own selection procedures will generally not be obligated to conduct such studies because it will be technically infeasible for them to do so.

(a) *Unfairness defined.* When members of one race, sex, or ethnic group characteristically obtain lower scores on a selection procedure than members of another group, and the differences in scores are not reflected in differences in a measure of job performance, use of the selection procedure may unfairly deny opportunities to members of the group that obtains the lower scores.

(b) *Investigation of fairness.* Where a selection procedure results in an adverse impact on a race, sex, or ethnic group, identified in accordance with the classifications set forth in section 4 above, and that group is a significant factor in the relevant labor market, the user generally should investigate the possible existence of unfairness for that group if it is technically feasible to do so. The greater the severity of the adverse impact on a group, the greater the need to investigate the possible existence of unfairness. Where the weight of evidence from other studies shows that the selection procedure predicts fairly for the group in question and for the same or similar jobs, such evidence may be relied on in connection with the selection procedure at issue.

(c) *General considerations in fairness investigations.* Users conducting a study of fairness should review the A.P.A. Standards regarding investigation of possible bias in testing. An investigation of fairness of a selection procedure depends on both evidence of validity and the manner in which the selection procedure is to be used in a particular employment context. Fairness of a selection procedure cannot necessarily be specified in advance without investigating these factors. Investigation of fairness of a selection procedure in samples where the range of scores on selection procedures or criterion measures is severely restricted for any subgroup sample (as compared to other subgroup samples) may produce misleading evidence of unfairness. That factor should accordingly be taken into account in conducting such studies and before reliance is placed on the results.

(d) *When unfairness is shown.* If unfairness is demonstrated through a showing that members of a particular group perform better or more poorly on the job than their scores on the selection procedure would indicate through comparison with members of other groups, the user may either revise or replace the selection instrument in accordance with these guidelines, or may continue to use the selection instrument operationally with appropriate revisions in its use to assure compatibility between the probability of successful job performance and the probability of being selected.

(e) *Technical feasibility of fairness studies.* In addition to the general conditions needed for technical feasibility for the conduct of a criterion-related study (see section 16, below) an investigation of fairness requires the following:

(i) An adequate sample of persons in each group available for the study to achieve findings of statistical significance. Guidelines do not require a user to hire or promote persons on the basis of group classifications for the purpose of making it possible to conduct a study of fairness; but the user has the obligation otherwise to comply with these guidelines.

(ii) The samples for each group should be comparable in terms of the actual job they perform, length of time on the job where time on the job is likely to affect performance, and other relevant factors likely to affect validity differences; or such factors should be included in the design of the study and their effects identified.

(f) *Continued use of selection procedures when fairness studies not feasible.* If a study of fairness should otherwise be performed, but is not technically feasible, a selection procedure may be used which has otherwise met the validity standards of these guidelines, unless the technical infeasibility resulted from discriminatory employment practices which are demonstrated by facts other than past failure to conform with requirements for validation of selection procedures. However, when it becomes technically feasible for the user to perform a study of fairness and such a study is otherwise called for, the user should conduct the study of fairness.

C. *Technical standards for content validity studies.*

(1) *Appropriateness of content validity studies.* Users choosing to validate a selection procedure by a content validity strategy should determine whether it is appropriate to conduct such a study in the particular employment context. A selection procedure can be supported by a content validity strategy to the extent that it is a representative sample of the content of the job. Selection procedures which purport to measure knowledges, skills, or abilities may in certain circumstances be justified by content validity, although they may not be representative samples, if the knowledge, skill, or ability measured by the selection procedure can be operationally defined as provided in section 14C(4) below, and if that knowledge, skill, or ability is a necessary prerequisite to successful job performance. A selection procedure based upon inferences about mental processes cannot be supported solely or primarily on the basis of content validity. Thus, a content strategy is not appropriate for demonstrating the validity of selection procedures which purport to measure traits or constructs, such as intelligence, aptitude, personality, common sense, judgment, leadership, and spatial ability.

Content validity is also not an appropriate strategy when the selection procedure involves knowledges, skills, or abilities which an employee will be expected to learn on the job.

(2) *Job analysis for content validity.* There should be a job analysis which includes an analysis of the important work behavior(s) required for successful performance and their relative importance and, if the behavior results in work product(s), an analysis of the work product(s). Any job analysis should focus on the work behavior(s) and the tasks associated with them. If work behavior(s) are not observable, the job analysis should identify and analyze those aspects of the behavior(s) that can be observed and the observed work products. The work behavior(s) selected for measurement should be critical work behavior(s) and/or important work behavior(s) constituting most of the job.

(3) *Development of selection procedures.* A selection procedure designed to measure the work behavior may be developed specifically from the job and job analysis in question, or may have been previously developed by the user, or by other users or by a test publisher.

(4) *Standards for demonstrating content validity.* To demonstrate the content validity of a selection procedure, a user should show that the behavior(s) demonstrated in the selection procedure are a representative sample of the behavior(s) of the job in question or that the selection procedure provides a representative sample of the work product of the job. In the case of a selection procedure measuring a knowledge, skill, or ability, the knowledge, skill, or ability being measured should be operationally defined. In the case of a selection procedure measuring a knowledge, the knowledge being measured should be operationally defined as that body of learned information which is used in and is a necessary prerequisite for observable aspects of work behavior of the job. In the case of skills or abilities, the skill or ability being measured should be operationally defined in terms of observable aspects of work behavior of the job. For any selection procedure measuring a knowledge, skill, or ability, the user should show that (a) the selection procedure measures and is a representative sample of that knowledge, skill, or ability; and (b) that knowledge, skill, or ability is used in and is a necessary prerequisite to performance of critical or important work behavior(s). In addition, to be content valid, a selection procedure measuring a skill or ability should either closely approximate an observable work behavior, or its product should closely approximate an observable work product. If a test purports to sample a work behavior or to provide a sample of a work product, the manner and setting of the selection procedure and its level and complexity should closely approximate the work situation. The closer the content and the context of the selection procedure are to work samples or work behaviors, the stronger is the basis for showing content validity. As the content of the selection procedure less resembles a work behavior, or the setting and manner of the administration of the selection procedure less resemble the work situation, or the result less resembles a work product, the less likely the selection procedure is to be content valid, and the greater the need for other evidence of validity.

(5) *Reliability.* The reliability of selection procedures justified on the basis of content validity should be a matter of concern to the user. Whenever it is feasible, appropriate statistical estimates should be made of the reliability of the selection procedure.

(6) *Prior training or experience.* A requirement for or evaluation of specific prior training or experience based on content validity, including a specification of level or amount of training or experience, should be justified on the basis of the relationship between the content of the training or experience and the content of the job for which the training or experience is to be required or evaluated. The critical consideration is the resemblance between the specific behaviors, products, knowledges, skills, or abilities in the experience or training and the specific behaviors, products, knowledges, skills, or abilities required on the job, whether or not there is close resemblance between the experience or training as a whole and the job as a whole.

(7) *Content validity of training success.* Where a measure of success in a training program is used as a selection procedure and the content of a training program is justified on the basis of content validity, the use should be justified on the relationship between the content of the training program and the content of the job.

(8) *Operational use.* A selection procedure which is supported on the basis of content validity may be used for a job if it represents a critical work behavior (i.e., a behavior which is necessary for performance of the job) or work behaviors which constitute most of the important parts of the job.

(9) *Ranking based on content validity studies.* If a user can show, by a job analysis or otherwise, that a higher score on a content valid selection procedure is likely to result in better job performance, the results may be used to rank persons who score above minimum levels. Where a selection procedure supported solely or primarily by content validity is used to rank job candidates, the selection procedure should measure those aspects of performance which differentiate among levels of job performance.

D. *Technical standards for construct validity studies.*

(1) *Appropriateness of construct validity studies.* Construct validity is a more complex strategy than either criterion-related or content validity. Construct validation is a relatively new and developing procedure in the employment field, and there is at present a lack of substantial literature extending the concept to employment practices. The user should be aware that the effort to obtain sufficient empirical support for construct validity is both an extensive and arduous effort involving a series of research studies, which include criterion-related validity studies and which may include content validity studies. Users choosing to justify use of a selection procedure by this strategy should therefore take particular care to assure that the validity study meets the standards set forth below.

(2) *Job analysis for construct validity studies.* There should be a job analysis. This job analysis should show the work behavior(s) required for successful performance of the job, or the groups of jobs being studied, the critical or important work behavior(s) in the job or group of jobs being studied, and an identification of the construct(s) believed to underlie successful performance of these critical or important work behaviors in the job or jobs in question. Each construct should be named and defined, so as to distinguish it from other constructs. If a group of jobs is being studied, the jobs should have in common one or more critical or important work behaviors at a comparable level of complexity.

(3) *Relationship to the job.* A selection procedure should then be identified or developed which measures the construct identified in accord with subparagraph (2) above. The user should show by empirical evidence that the selection procedure is validly related to the construct and that the construct is validly related to the performance of critical or important work behavior(s). The relationship between the construct as measured by the selection procedure and the related work behavior(s) should be supported by empirical evidence from one or more criterion-related studies involving the job or jobs in question which satisfy the provisions of section 14B above.

(4) *Use of construct validity study without new criterion-related evidence.* (a) *Standards for use.* Until such time as professional literature provides more guidance on the use of construct validity in employment situations, the Federal agencies will accept a claim of construct validity without a criterion-related study which satisfies section 14B above only when the selection procedure has been used elsewhere in a situation in which a criterion-related study has been conducted and the use of a criterion-related validity study in this context meets the standards for transportability of criterion-related validity studies as set forth above in section 7. However, if a study pertains to a number of jobs having common critical or important work behaviors at a comparable level of complexity, and the evidence satisfies subparagraphs 14B (2) and (3) above for those jobs with criterion-related validity evidence for those jobs, the selection procedure may be used for all the jobs to which the study pertains. If construct validity is to be generalized to other jobs or groups of jobs not in the group studied, the Federal enforcement agencies will expect at a minimum additional empirical research evidence meeting the standards of subparagraphs section 14B (2) and (3) above for the additional jobs or groups of jobs.

(b) *Determination of common work behaviors.* In determining whether two or more jobs have one or more work behavior(s) in common, the user should compare the observed work behavior(s) in each of the jobs and should compare the observed work product(s) in each of the jobs. If neither the observed work behavior(s) in each of the jobs nor the observed work product(s) in each of the jobs are the same, the Federal enforcement agencies will presume that the work behavior(s) in each job are different. If the work behaviors are not observable, then evidence of similarity of work products and any other relevant research evidence will be considered in determining whether the work behavior(s) in the two jobs are the same.

DOCUMENTATION OF IMPACT AND VALIDITY EVIDENCE

§1607.15 *Documentation of impact and validity evidence.*

A. *Required information.* Users of selection procedures other than those users complying with section 15A(1) below should maintain and have available for each job information on adverse impact of the selection process for that job and, where it is determined a selection process has an adverse impact, evidence of validity as set forth below.

(1) *Simplified recordkeeping for users with less than 100 employees.* In order to minimize recordkeeping burdens on employers who employ one hundred (100) or fewer employees, and other users not required to file EEO-1, et seq., reports, such users may satisfy the requirements of this section 15 if they maintain and have available records showing, for each year:

(a) The number of persons hired, promoted, and terminated for each job, by sex, and where appropriate by race and national origin;

(b) The number of applicants for hire and promotion by sex and where appropriate by race and national origin; and

(c) The selection procedures utilized (either standardized or not standardized).

These records should be maintained for each race or national origin group (see section 4 above) constituting more than two percent (2%) of the labor force in the relevant labor area. However, it is not necessary to maintain records by race and/or national origin (see § 4 above) if one race or national origin group in the relevant labor area constitutes more than ninety-eight percent (98%) of the labor force in the area. If the user has reason to believe that a selection procedure has an adverse impact, the user should maintain any available evidence of validity for that procedure (see sections 7A and 8).

(2) *Information on impact.* (a) *Collection of information on impact.* Users of selection procedures other than those complying with section 15A(1) above should maintain and have available for each job records or other information showing whether the total selection process for that job has an adverse impact on any of the groups for which records are called for by sections 4B above. Adverse impact determinations should be made at least annually for each such group which constitutes at least 2 percent of the labor force in the relevant labor area or 2 percent of the applicable workforce. Where a total selection process for a job has an adverse impact, the user should maintain and have available records or other information showing which components have an adverse impact. Where the total selection process for a job does not have an adverse impact, information need not be maintained for individual components except in circumstances set forth in subsection 15A(2)(b) below. If the determination of adverse impact is made using a procedure other than the "four-fifths rule," as defined in the first sentence of section 4D above, a justification, consistent with section 4D above, for the procedure used to determine adverse impact should be available.

(b) *When adverse impact has been eliminated in the total selection process.* Whenever the total selection process for a particular job has had an adverse impact, as defined in section 4 above, in any year, but no longer has an adverse impact, the user should maintain and have available the information on individual components of the selection process required in the preceding paragraph for the period in which there was adverse impact. In addition, the user should continue to collect such information for at least two (2) years after the adverse impact has been eliminated.

(c) *When data insufficient to determine impact.* Where there has been an insufficient number of selections to determine whether there is an adverse impact of the total selection process for a particular job, the user should continue to collect, maintain, and have available the information on individual components of the selection process required in section 15(A)(2)(a) above until the information is sufficient to determine that the overall selection process does not have an adverse impact as defined in section 4 above, or until the job has changed substantially.

(3) *Documentation of validity evidence.* (a) *Types of evidence.* Where a total selection process has an adverse impact (see section 4 above) the user should maintain and have available for each component of that process which has an adverse impact, one or more of the following types of documentation evidence:

(i) Documentation evidence showing criterion-related validity of the selection procedure (see section 15B, below).

(ii) Documentation evidence showing content validity of the selection process (see section 15C, below).

(iii) Documentation evidence showing construct validity of the selection procedure (see section 15D, below).

(iv) Documentation evidence from other studies showing validity of the selection procedure in the user's facility (see section 15E, below).

(v) Documentation evidence showing why a validity study cannot or need not be performed and why continued use of the procedure is consistent with Federal law.

(b) *Form of report.* This evidence should be compiled in a reasonably complete and organized manner to permit direct evaluation of the validity of the selection procedure. Previously written employer or consultant reports of validity, or reports describing validity studies completed before the issuance of these guidelines are acceptable if they are complete in regard to the documentation requirements contained in this section, or if they satisfied requirements of guidelines which were in effect when the validity study was completed. If they are not complete, the required additional documentation should be appended. If necessary information is not available, the report of the validity study may still be used as documentation, but its adequacy will be evaluated in terms of compliance with the requirements of these guidelines.

(c) *Completeness.* In the event that evidence of validity is reviewed by an enforcement agency, the validation reports completed after the effective date of these guidelines are expected to contain the information set forth below. Evidence denoted by use of the word "essential" is considered critical. If information denoted essential is not included, the report will be considered incomplete unless the user affirmatively demonstrates either its unavailability due to circumstances beyond the user's control or special circumstances of the user's study which make the information irrelevant. Evidence not so denoted is desirable, but its absence will not be a basis for considering a report incomplete. The user should maintain and have available the information called for under the heading "Source Data" in sections 15B(11) and 15D(11). While it is a necessary part of the study, it need not be submitted with the report. All statistical results should be organized and presented in tabular or graphic form to the extent feasible.

B. *Criterion-related validity studies.* Reports of criterion-related validity for a selection procedure should include the following information:

(1) *User(s), location(s), and date(s) of study.* Dates and location(s) of the job analysis or review of job information, the date(s) and location(s) of the administration of the selection procedures and collection of criterion data, and the time between collection of data on selection procedures and criterion measures should be provided (essential). If the study was conducted at several locations, the address of each location, including city and State, should be shown.

(2) *Problem and setting.* An explicit definition of the purpose(s) of the study and the circumstances in which the study was conducted should be provided. A description of existing selection procedures and cutoff scores, if any, should be provided.

(3) *Job analysis or review of job information.* A description of the procedure used to analyze the job or group of jobs, or to review the job information should be provided (essential). Where a review of job information results in criteria which may be used without a full job analysis (see section 14B(3)), the basis for the selection of these criteria should be reported (essential). Where a job analysis is required, a complete description of the work behavior(s) or work outcome(s), and measures of their criticality or importance should be provided (essential). The report should describe the basis on which the behavior(s) or outcome(s) were determined to be critical or important, such as the proportion of time spent on the respective behaviors, their level of difficulty, their frequency of performance, the consequences of error, or other appropriate factors (essential). Where two or more jobs are grouped for a validity study, the information called for in this subsection should be provided for each of the jobs, and the justification for the grouping (see section 14B(1)) should be provided (essential).

(4) *Job titles and codes.* It is desirable to provide the user's job title(s) for the job(s) in question and the corresponding job title(s) and code(s) from U.S. Employment Service's Dictionary of Occupational Titles.

(5) *Criterion measures.* The bases for the selection of the criterion measures should be provided, together with references to the evidence considered in making the selection of criterion measures

(essential). A full description of all criteria on which data were collected, and means by which they were observed, recorded, evaluated, and quantified, should be provided (essential). If rating techniques are used as criterion measures, the appraisal form(s) and instructions to the rater(s) should be included as part of the validation evidence, or should be explicitly described and available (essential). All steps taken to insure that criterion measures are free from factors which would unfairly alter the scores of members of any group should be described (essential).

(6) *Sample description.* A description of how the research sample was identified and selected should be included (essential). The race, sex, and ethnic composition of the sample, including those groups set forth in section 4A above, should be described (essential). This description should include the size of each subgroup (essential). A description of how the research sample compares with the relevant labor market or workforce, the method by which the relevant labor market or workforce was defined, and a discussion of the likely effects on validity of differences between the sample and the relevant labor market or workforce, are also desirable. Descriptions of educational levels, length of service, and age are also desirable.

(7) *Description of selection procedures.* Any measure, combination of measures, or procedure studied should be completely and explicitly described or attached (essential). If commercially available selection procedures are studied, they should be described by title, form, and publisher (essential). Reports of reliability estimates and how they were established are desirable.

(8) *Techniques and results.* Methods used in analyzing data should be described (essential). Measures of central tendency (e.g., means) and measures of dispersion (e.g., standard deviations and ranges) for all selection procedures and all criteria should be reported for each race, sex, and ethnic group which constitutes a significant factor in the relevant labor market (essential). The magnitude and direction of all relationships between selection procedures and criterion measures investigated should be reported for each relevant race, sex, and ethnic group and for the total group (essential). Where groups are too small to obtain reliable evidence, the magnitude of the relationship need not be reported separately. Statements regarding the statistical significance of results should be made (essential). Any statistical adjustments, such as for less than perfect reliability or for restriction of score range in the selection procedure or criterion, should be described and explained; and uncorrected correlation coefficients should also be shown (essential). Where the statistical technique categorizes continuous data, such as biserial correlation and the phi coefficient, the categories and the bases on which they were determined should be described and explained (essential). Studies of test fairness should be included where called for by the requirements of section 14B(8) (essential). These studies should include the rationale by which a selection procedure was determined to be fair to the group(s) in question. Where test fairness or unfairness has been demonstrated on the basis of other studies, a bibliography of the relevant studies should be included (essential). If the bibliography includes unpublished studies, copies of these studies, or adequate abstracts or summaries, should be attached (essential). Where revisions have been made in a selection procedure to assure compatibility between successful job performance and the probability of being selected, the studies underlying such revisions should be included (essential). All statistical results should be organized and presented by relevant race, sex, and ethnic group (essential).

(9) *Alternative procedures investigated.* The selection procedures investigated and available evidence of their impact should be identified (essential). The scope, method, and findings of the investigation, and the conclusions reached in light of the findings, should be fully described (essential).

(10) *Uses and applications.* The methods considered for use of the selection procedure (e.g., as a screening device with a cutoff score, for grouping or ranking, or combined with other procedures in a battery) and available evidence of their impact should be described (essential). This description should include the rationale for choosing the method for operational use, and the evidence of the validity and utility of the procedure as it is to be used (essential). The purpose for which the procedure is to be used (e.g., hiring, transfer, promotion) should be described (essential). If weights are assigned to different parts of the selection procedure, these weights and the validity of the weighted composite should be reported (essential). If the selection procedure is used with a cutoff score, the user should describe the way in which normal expectations of proficiency within the workforce were determined and the way in which the cutoff score was determined (essential).

(11) *Source data.* Each user should maintain records showing all pertinent information about individual sample members and raters where they are used, in studies involving the validation of selection procedures. These records should be made available upon request of a compliance agency. In the case of individual sample members, these data should include scores on selection procedure(s), scores on criterion measures, age, sex, race, or ethnic group status, and experience on the specific job on which the validation study was conducted, and may also include such things as education, training, and prior job experience, but should not include names and social security numbers. Records should be maintained which show the ratings given to each sample member by each rater.

(12) *Contact person.* The name, mailing address, and telephone number of the person who may be contacted for further information about the validity study should be provided (essential).

(13) *Accuracy and completeness.* The report should describe the steps taken to assure the accuracy and completeness of the collection, analysis, and report of data and results.

C. *Content validity studies.* Reports of content validity for a selection procedure should include the following information:

(1) *User(s), location(s) and date(s) of study.* Dates and location(s) of the job analysis should be shown (essential).

(2) *Problem and setting.* An explicit definition of the purpose(s) of the study and the circumstances in which the study was conducted should be provided. A description of existing selection procedures and cutoff scores, if any, should be provided.

(3) *Job analysis—Content of the job.* A description of the method used to analyze the job should be provided (essential). The work behavior(s), the associated tasks, and, if the behavior results in a work product, the work products should be completely described (essential). Measures of criticality and/or importance of the work behavior(s) and the method of determining these measures should be provided (essential). Where the job analysis also identified the knowledges, skills, and abilities used in work behavior(s), an operational definition for each knowledge in terms of a body of learned information, and for each skill and ability in terms of observable behaviors and outcomes, and the relationship between each knowledge, skill, or ability and each work behavior, as well as the method used to determine this relationship, should be provided (essential). The work situation should be described, including the setting in which work behavior(s) are performed, and where appropriate, the manner in which knowledges, skills, or abilities are used, and the complexity and difficulty of the knowledge, skill, or ability as used in the work behavior(s).

(4) *Selection procedure and its content.* Selection procedures, including those constructed by or for the user, specific training requirements, composites of selection procedures, and any other procedure supported by content validity, should be completely and explicitly described or attached (essential). If commercially available selection procedures are used, they should be described by title, form, and publisher (essential). The behaviors measured or sampled by the selection procedure should be explicitly described (essential). Where the selection procedure purports to measure a knowledge, skill, or ability, evidence that the selection procedure measures and is a representative sample of the knowledge, skill, or ability should be provided (essential).

(5) *Relationship between the selection procedures and the job.* The evidence demonstrating that the selection procedure is a representative work sample, a representative sample of the work behavior(s), or a representative sample of a knowledge, skill, or ability as used as a part of a work behavior and necessary for that behavior should be provided (essential). The user should identify the work behavior(s) which each item or part of the selection procedure is intended to sample or measure (essential). Where the selection procedure purports to sample a work behavior or to provide a sample of a work product, a comparison should be provided of the manner, setting, and the level of complexity of the selection procedure with those of the work situation (essential). If any steps were taken to reduce adverse impact on a race, sex, or ethnic group in the content of the procedure or in its administration, these steps should be described. Establishment of time limits, if any, and how these limits are related to the speed with which duties must be performed on the job, should be explained. Measures of central tendency (e.g., means) and measures of dispersion (e.g., standard deviations) and estimates of reliability should be reported for all selection procedures if available. Such reports should be made for relevant race, sex, and ethnic subgroups, at least on a statistically reliable sample basis.

(6) *Alternative procedures investigated.* The alternative selection procedures investigated and available evidence of their impact should be identified (essential). The scope, method, and findings of the investigation, and the conclusions reached in light of the findings, should be fully described (essential).

(7) *Uses and applications.* The methods considered for use of the selection procedure (e.g., as a screening device with a cutoff score, for grouping or ranking, or combined with other procedures in a battery) and available evidence of their impact should be described (essential). This description should include the rationale for choosing the method of operational use, and the evidence of the validity and utility of the procedure as it is to be used (essential). The purpose for which the procedure is to be used (e.g., hiring, transfer, promotion) should be described (essential). If the selection procedure is used with a cutoff score, the user should describe the way in which normal expectations of proficiency within the workforce were determined and the way in which the cutoff score was determined (essential). In addition, if the selection procedure is to be used for ranking, the user should specify the evidence showing that a higher score on the selection procedure is likely to result in better job performance.

(8) *Contact person.* The name, mailing address, and telephone number of the person who may be contacted for further information about the validity study should be provided (essential).

(9) *Accuracy and completeness.* The report should describe the steps taken to assure the accuracy and completeness of the collection, analysis, and report of data and results.

D. *Construct validity studies.* Reports of construct validity for a selection procedure should include the following information:

(1) *User(s), location(s), and date(s) of study.* Date(s) and location(s) of the job analysis and the gathering of other evidence called for by these guidelines should be provided (essential).

(2) *Problem and setting.* An explicit definition of the purpose(s) of the study and the circumstances in which the study was conducted should be provided. A description of existing selection procedures and cutoff scores, if any, should be provided.

(3) *Construct definition.* A clear definition of the construct(s) which are believed to underlie successful performance of the critical or important work behavior(s) should be provided (essential). This definition should include the levels of construct performance relevant to the job(s) for which the selection procedure is to be used (essential). There should be a summary of the position of the construct in the psychological literature, or in the absence of such a position, a description of the way in which the definition and measurement of the construct was developed and the psychological theory underlying it (essential). Any quantitative data which identify or define the job constructs, such as factor analyses, should be provided (essential).

(4) *Job analysis.* A description of the method used to analyze the job should be provided (essential). A complete description of the work behavior(s) and, to the extent appropriate, work outcomes and measures of their criticality and/or importance should be provided (essential). The report should also describe the basis on which the behavior(s) or outcomes were determined to be important, such as their level of difficulty, their frequency of performance, the consequences of error or other appropriate factors (essential). Where jobs are grouped or compared for the purposes of generalizing validity evidence, the work behavior(s) and work product(s) for each of the jobs should be described, and conclusions concerning the similarity of the jobs in terms of observable work behaviors or work products should be made (essential).

(5) *Job titles and codes.* It is desirable to provide the selection procedure user's job title(s) for the job(s) in question and the corresponding job title(s) and code(s) from the United States Employment Service's dictionary of occupational titles.

(6) *Selection procedure.* The selection procedure used as a measure of the construct should be completed and explicitly described or attached (essential). If commercially available selection procedures are used, they should be identified by title, form and publisher (essential). The research evidence of the relationship between the selection procedure and the construct, such as factor structure, should be included (essential). Measures of central tendency, variability and reliability of the selection procedure should be provided (essential). Whenever feasible, these measures should be provided separately for each relevant race, sex, and ethnic group.

(7) *Relationship to job performance.* The criterion-related study(ies) and other empirical evidence of the relationship between the construct measured by the selection procedure and the related work behavior(s) for the job or jobs in question should be provided (essential). Documentation of the criterion-related study(ies) should satisfy the provisions of section 15B above or section 15E(1) below, except for studies conducted prior to the effective date of these guidelines (essential). Where a study pertains to a group of jobs, and, on the basis of the study, validity is asserted for a job in the group, the observed work behaviors and the observed work products for each of the jobs should be described (essential). Any other evidence used in determining whether the work behavior(s) in each of the jobs is the same should be fully described (essential).

(8) *Alternative procedures investigated.* The alternative selection procedures investigated and available evidence of their impact should be identified (essential). The scope, method, and findings of the investigation, and the conclusions reached in light of the findings should be fully described (essential).

(9) *Uses and applications.* The methods considered for use of the selection procedure (e.g., as a screening device with a cutoff score, for grouping or ranking, or combined with other procedures in a battery) and available evidence of their impact should be described (essential). This description should include the rationale for choosing the method for operational use, and the evidence of the validity and utility of the procedure as it is to be used (essential). The purpose for which the procedure is to be used (e.g., hiring, transfer, promotion) should be described (essential). If weights are assigned to different parts of the selection procedure, these weights and the validity of the weighted composite should be reported (essential). If the selection procedure is used with a cutoff score, the user should describe the way in which normal expectations of proficiency within the workforce were determined and the way in which the cutoff score was determined (essential).

(10) *Accuracy and completeness.* The report should describe the steps taken to assure the accuracy and completeness of the collection, analysis, and report of data and results.

(11) *Source data.* Each user should maintain records showing all pertinent information relating to its study of construct validity.

(12) *Contact person.* The name, mailing address, and telephone number of the individual who may be contacted for further information about the validity study should be provided (essential).

E. *Evidence of validity from other studies.* When validity of a selection procedure is supported by studies not done by the user, the evidence from the original study or studies should be compiled in a manner similar to that required in the appropriate section of this section 15 above. In addition, the following evidence should be supplied:

(1) *Evidence from criterion-related validity studies.*—a. *Job information.* A description of the important job behavior(s) of the user's job and the basis on which the behaviors were determined to be important should be provided (essential). A full description of the basis for determining that these important work behaviors are the same as those of the job in the original study (or studies) should be provided (essential).

(b) *Relevance of criteria.* A full description of the basis on which the criteria used in the original studies are determined to be relevant for the user should be provided (essential).

(c) *Other variables.* The similarity of important applicant pool or sample characteristics reported in the original studies to those of the user should be described (essential). A description of the comparison between the race, sex and ethnic composition of the user's relevant labor market and the sample in the original validity studies should be provided (essential).

(d) *Use of the selection procedures.* A full description should be provided showing that the use to be made of the selection procedure is consistent with the findings of the original validity studies (essential).

(e) *Bibliography.* A bibliography of reports of validity of the selection procedure for the job or jobs in question should be provided (essential). Where any of the studies included an investigation of test fairness, the results of this investigation should be provided (essential). Copies of reports published in journals that are not commonly available should be described in detail or attached (essential). Where a user is relying upon unpublished studies, a reasonable effort should be made to obtain these studies. If these unpublished studies are the sole source of validity evidence, they should be described in detail or attached (essential). If these studies are not available, the name and address of the source, an adequate abstract or summary of the validity study and data, and a contact person in the source organization should be provided (essential).

(2) *Evidence from content validity studies.* See section 14C(3) and section 15C above.

(3) *Evidence from construct validity studies.* See sections 14D(2) and 15D above.

F. *Evidence of validity from cooperative studies.* Where a selection procedure has been validated through a cooperative study, evidence that the study satisfies the requirements of sections 7, 8 and 15E should be provided (essential).

G. *Selection for higher-level job.* If a selection procedure is used to evaluate candidates for jobs at a higher level than those for which they will initially be employed, the validity evidence should satisfy the documentation provisions of this section 15 for the higher-level job or jobs, and in addition, the user should provide: (1) a description of the job progression structure, formal or informal; (2) the data showing how many employees progress to the higher-level job and the length of time needed to make this progression; and (3) an identification of any anticipated changes in the higher-level job. In addition, if the test measures a knowledge, skill, or ability, the user should provide evidence that the knowledge, skill, or ability is required for the higher-level job and the basis for the conclusion that the knowledge, skill, or ability is not expected to develop from the training or experience on the job.

H. *Interim use of selection procedures.* If a selection procedure is being used on an interim basis because the procedure is not fully supported by the required evidence of validity, the user should maintain and have available (1) substantial evidence of validity for the procedure, and (2) a report showing the date on which the study to gather the additional evidence commenced, the estimated completion date of the study, and a description of the data to be collected (essential).

DEFINITIONS

§1607.16 *Definitions.*

The following definitions shall apply throughout these guidelines:

A. *Ability.* A present competence to perform an observable behavior or a behavior which results in an observable product.

B. *Adverse impact.* A substantially different rate of selection in hiring, promotion, or other employment decision which works to the disadvantage of members of a race, sex, or ethnic group. See section 4 of these guidelines.

C. *Compliance with these guidelines.* Use of a selection procedure is in compliance with these guidelines if such use has been validated in accord with these guidelines (as defined below), or if such use does not result in adverse impact on any race, sex, or ethnic group (see section 4, above), or, in unusual circumstances, if use of the procedure is otherwise justified in accord with Federal law. See section 6B, above.

D. *Content validity.* Demonstrated by data showing that the content of a selection procedure is representative of important aspects of performance on the job. See section 5B and section 14C.

E. *Construct validity.* Demonstrated by data showing that the selection procedure measures the degree to which candidates have identifiable characteristics which have been determined to be important for successful job performance. See section 5B and section 14D.

F. *Criterion-related validity.* Demonstrated by empirical data showing that the selection procedure is predictive of or significantly correlated with important elements of work behavior. See sections 5B and 14B.

G. *Employer.* Any employer subject to the provisions of the Civil Rights Act of 1964, as amended, including State or local governments and any Federal agency subject to the provisions of section 717 of the Civil Rights Act of 1964, as amended, and any Federal contractor or subcontractor or federally assisted construction contractor or subcontractor covered by Executive Order 11246, as amended.

H. *Employment agency.* Any employment agency subject to the provisions of the Civil Rights Act of 1964, as amended.

I. *Enforcement action.* For the purposes of section 4, a proceeding by a Federal enforcement agency such as a lawsuit or an administrative proceeding leading to debarment from or withholding, suspension, or termination of Federal Government contracts or the suspension or withholding of Federal Government funds; but not a finding of reasonable cause or a conciliation process or the issuance of right to sue letters under title VII or under Executive Order 11246 where such finding, conciliation, or issuance of notice of right to sue is based upon an individual complaint.

J. *Enforcement agency.* Any agency of the executive branch of the Federal Government which adopts these guidelines for purposes of the enforcement of the equal employment opportunity laws or which has responsibility for securing compliance with them.

K. *Job analysis.* A detailed statement of work behaviors and other information relevant to the job.

L. *Job description.* A general statement of job duties and responsibilities.

M. *Knowledge.* A body of information applied directly to the performance of a function.

N. *Labor organization.* Any labor organization subject to the provisions of the Civil Rights Act of 1964, as amended, and any committee subject thereto controlling apprenticeship or other training.

O. *Observable.* Able to be seen, heard, or otherwise perceived by a person other than the person performing the action.

P. *Race, sex, or ethnic group.* Any group of persons identifiable on the grounds of rate, color, religion, sex, or national origin.

Q. *Selection procedure.* Any measure, combination of measures, or procedure used as a basis for any employment decision. Selection procedures include the full range of assessment techniques from traditional paper and pencil tests, performance tests, training programs, or probationary periods and physical, educational, and work experience requirements through informal or casual interviews and unscored application forms.

R. *Selection rate.* The proportion of applicants or candidates who are hired, promoted, or otherwise selected.

S. *Should.* The term ''should'' as used in these guidelines is intended to connote action which is necessary to achieve compliance with the guidelines, while recognizing that there are circumstances where alternative courses of action are open to users.

T. *Skill.* A present, observable competence to perform a learned psychomotor act.

U. *Technical feasibility.* The existence of conditions permitting the conduct of meaningful criterion-related validity studies. These conditions include: (1) An adequate sample of persons available for the study to achieve findings of statistical significance; (2) having or being able to obtain a sufficient range of scores on the selection procedure and job performance measures to produce validity results which can be expected to be representative of the results if the ranges normally expected were utilized; and (3) having or being able to devise unbiased, reliable, and relevant measures of job performance or other criteria of employee adequacy. See section 14B(2). With respect to investigation of possible unfairness, the same considerations are applicable to each group for which the study is made. See section 14B(8).

V. *Unfairness of selection procedure.* A condition in which members of one race, sex, or ethnic group characteristically obtain lower scores on a selection procedure than members of another group, and the differences are not reflected in differences in measures of job performance. See section 14B(7).

W. *User.* Any employer, labor organization, employment agency, or licensing or certification board, to the extent it may be covered by Federal equal employment opportunity law, which uses a selection procedure as a basis for any employment decision. Whenever an employer, labor organization, or employment agency is required by law to restrict recruitment for any occupation to those applicants who have met licensing or certification requirements, the licensing or certifying authority to the extent it may be covered by Federal equal employment opportunity law will be considered the user with respect to those licensing or certification requirements. Whenever a State employment agency or service does no more than administer or monitor a procedure as permitted by Department of Labor regulations, and does so without making referrals or taking any other action on the basis of the results, the State employment agency will not be deemed to be a user.

X. *Validated in accord with these guidelines or properly validated.* A demonstration that one or more validity study or studies meeting the standards of these guidelines has been conducted, including investigation and where appropriate, use of suitable alternative selection procedures as contemplated by section 3B, and has produced evidence of validity sufficient to warrant use of the procedure for the intended purpose under the standards of these guidelines.

Y. *Work behavior.* An activity performed to achieve the objectives of the job. Work behaviors involve observable (physical) components and unobservable (mental) components. A work behavior consists of the performance of one or more tasks. Knowledge, skills, and abilities are not behaviors, although they may be applied in work behaviors.

APPENDIX

§1607.17 *Policy statement on affirmative action* (see section 13B).

The Equal Employment Opportunity Coordinating Council was established by act of Congress in 1972, and charged with responsibility for developing and implementing agreements and policies designed, among other things, to eliminate conflict and inconsistency among the agencies of the Federal Government responsible for administering Federal law prohibiting discrimination on grounds of race, color, sex, religion, and national origin. This statement is issued as an initial response to the requests of a number of State and local officials for clarification of the Government's policies concerning the role of affirmative action in the overall equal employment opportunity program. While the Coordinating Council's adoption of this statement expresses only the views of the signatory agencies concerning this important subject, the principles set forth below should serve as policy guidance for other Federal agencies as well.

(1) Equal employment opportunity is the law of the land. In the public sector of our society, this means that all persons, regardless of race, color, religion, sex, or national origin shall have equal access to positions in the public service limited only by their ability to do the job. There is ample evidence in all sectors of our society that such equal access frequently has been denied to members of certain groups because of their sex, racial, or ethnic characteristics. The remedy for such past and present discrimination is twofold.

On the other hand, vigorous enforcement of the laws against discrimination is essential. But equally, and perhaps even more important are affirmative, voluntary efforts on the part of public employers to assure that positions in the public service are genuinely and equally accessible to qualified persons, without regard to their sex, racial, or ethnic characteristics. Without such efforts equal employment opportunity is no more than a wish. The importance of voluntary affirmative action on the part of employers is underscored by title VII of the Civil Rights Act of 1964, Executive Order 11246, and related laws and regulations—all of which emphasize voluntary action to achieve equal employment opportunity.

As with most management objectives, a systematic plan based on sound organizational analysis and problem identification is crucial to the accomplishment of affirmative action objectives. For this reason, the Council urges all State and local governments to develop and implement results-oriented affirmative action plans which deal with the problems so identified.

The following paragraphs are intended to assist State and local governments by illustrating the kinds of analyses and activities which may be appropriate for a public employer's voluntary affirmative action plan. This statement does not address remedies imposed after a finding of unlawful discrimination.

(2) Voluntary affirmative action to assure equal employment opportunity is appropriate at any stage of the employment process. The first step in the construction of any affirmative action plan should be an analysis of the employer's workforce to determine whether percentages of sex, race, or ethnic groups in individual job classifications are substantially similar to the percentages of those groups available in the relevant job market who possess the basic job-related qualifications.

When substantial disparities are found through such analyses, each element of the overall selection process should be examined to determine which elements operate to exclude persons on the basis of sex, race, or ethnic group. Such elements include, but are not limited to, recruitment, testing, ranking certification, interview, recommendations for selection, hiring, promotion, etc. The examination of each element of the selection process should at a minimum include a determination of its validity in predicting job performance.

(3) When an employer has reason to believe that its selection procedures have the exclusionary effect described in paragraph 2 above, it should initiate affirmative steps to remedy the situation. Such steps, which in design and execution may be race, color, sex, or ethnic "conscious," include, but are not limited to, the following:

(a) The establishment of a long-term goal, and short-range, interim goals and timetables for the specific job classifications, all of which should take into account the availability of basically qualified persons in the relevant job market;

(b) A recruitment program designed to attract qualified members of the group in question;

(c) A systematic effort to organize work and redesign jobs in ways that provide opportunities for persons lacking "journeyman" level knowledge or skills to enter and, with appropriate training, to progress in a career field;

(d) Revamping selection instruments or procedures which have not yet been validated in order to reduce or eliminate exclusionary effects on particular groups in particular job classifications;

(e) The initiation of measures designed to assure that members of the affected group who are qualified to perform the job are included within the pool of persons from which the selecting official makes the selection;

(f) A systematic effort to provide career advancement training, both classroom and on-the-job, to employees locked into dead end jobs; and

(g) The establishment of a system for regularly monitoring the effectiveness of the particular affirmative action program, and procedures for making timely adjustments in this program where effectiveness is not demonstrated.

(4) The goal of any affirmative action plan should be achievement of genuine equal employment opportunity for all qualified persons. Selection under such plans should be based upon the ability of the applicant(s) to do the work. Such plans should not require the selection of the unqualified, or the unneeded, nor should they require the selection of persons on the basis of race, color, sex, religion, or national origin. Moreover, while the Council believes that this statement should serve to assist State and local employers, as well as Federal agencies, it recognizes that affirmative action cannot be viewed as a standardized program which must be accomplished in the same way at all times in all places.

Accordingly, the Council has not attempted to set forth here either the minimum or maximum voluntary steps that employers may take to deal with their respective situations. Rather, the Council recognizes that under applicable authorities, State and local employers have flexibility to formulate affirmative action plans that are best suited to their particular situations. In this manner, the Council believes that affirmative action programs will best serve the goal of equal employment opportunity.

APPENDIX
B

Affirmative Action Guidelines—Revised Order No. 4 (OFCCP)

PART 60-2—AFFIRMATIVE ACTION PROGRAMS

Subpart A—General

Subpart B—Required Contents of Affirmative Action Programs

Subpart C—Methods of Implementing the Requirements of Subpart B

Subpart D—Miscellaneous
   AUTHORITY: 5 U.S.C. 553(a)(3)(B); 29 CFR 2.7; Section 201, E.O. 11246, 30 FR 12319, and E.O. 11375, 32 FR 14303, as amended by E.O. 12086.

SUBPART A—GENERAL

§60-2.1. Title, Purpose and Scope
(a) This part shall also be known as "Revised Order No. 4" and shall cover nonconstruction contractors. Section 60-1.40 of this chapter, affirmative action compliance programs, requires that within 120 days from the commencement of a contract each prime contractor or subcontractor with 50 or more employees and (1) a contract of $50,000 or more; or (2) Government bills of lading which, in any 12-month period, total or can reasonably be expected to total $50,000 or more; or (3) who serves as a depository of Government funds in any amount; or (4) who is a financial institution which is an issuing and paying agent for U.S. savings bonds and savings notes in any amount, develop a written affirmative action compliance program for each of its establishments. A review of compliance surveys indicates that many contractors do not have affirmative action programs on file at the time an establishment is visited by a compliance investigator. This part details the review procedure and the results of a contractor's failure to develop and maintain an affirmative action program and then sets forth detailed guidelines to be used by the contractors and Government in developing and judging these programs as well as the good faith effort required to transform the programs from paper commitments to equal employment opportunity. Subparts B and C of this part are concerned with affirmative action plans only.

(b) Relief, including back pay where appropriate, for members of an affected class who by virtue of past discrimination continue to suffer the present effects of that discrimination, shall be provided in the conciliation agreement entered into pursuant to §60-60.6 of this title. An "affected class" problem must be remedied in order for a contractor to be considered in compliance. Section 60-2.2 herein pertaining to an acceptable affirmative action program is also applicable to the failure to remedy discrimination against members of an "affected class."

§60-2.2. Agency Action

(a) Any contractor required by §60-1.40 of this chapter to develop an affirmative action program at each of its establishments who has not complied fully with that section is not in compliance with Executive Order 11246, as amended (30 FR 12319). Until such programs are developed and found to be acceptable in accordance with the standards and guidelines set forth in §§60-2.10 through 60-2.32, the contractor is unable to comply with the equal employment opportunity clause. An affirmative action plan shall be deemed to have been accepted by the Government at the time the appropriate OFCCP field, area, regional, or national office has accepted such plan unless within 45 days thereafter the Director has disapproved such plan.

(b) If, in determining such contractor's responsibility for an award of a contract it comes to the contracting officer's attention, through sources within his agency or through the Office of Federal Contract Compliance Programs or other Government agencies, that the contractor has no affirmative action program at each of its establishments, or has substantially deviated from such an approved affirmative action program, or has failed to develop or implement an affirmative action program which complies with the regulations in this chapter, the contracting officer shall declare the contractor/bidder nonresponsible and so notify the contractor, and the Director, unless he can otherwise affirmatively determine that the contractor is able to comply with its equal employment obligations. Any contractor/bidder which has been declared nonresponsible in accordance with the provisions of this section may request the Director to determine that the responsibility of the contractor/bidder raises substantial issues of law or fact to the extent that a hearing is required. Such request shall set forth the basis upon which the contractor/bidder seeks such a determination. If the Director, in his/her sole discretion, determines that substantial issues of law or fact exist, an administrative or judicial proceeding may be commenced in accordance with the regulations contained in §60-1.26; or the Director may require the investigation or compliance review be developed further or additional conciliation be conducted: *Provided,* That during any preaward conferences, every effort shall be made through the processes of conciliation, mediation and persuasion to develop an acceptable affirmative action program meeting the standards and guidelines set forth in §§60-2.10 through 60-2.32 so that, in the performance of its contract, the contractor is able to meet its equal employment obligations in accordance with the equal employment clause and applicable rules, regulations, and orders: *Provided further,* That a contractor/bidder may not be declared nonresponsible more than twice due to past noncompliance with the equal employment clause at a particular establishment or facility without receiving prior notice and an opportunity for a hearing.

(c)(1) Immediately upon finding that a contractor has no affirmative action program, or has deviated substantially from an approved affirmative action program, or has failed to develop or implement an affirmative action program which complies with the requirements of the regulations in this chapter, that fact shall be recorded in the investigation file. Whenever administrative enforcement is contemplated, the notice to the contractor shall be issued giving him 30 days to show cause why enforcement proceedings under section 209(a) of Executive Order 11246, as amended, should not be instituted. The notice to show cause should contain:

(i) An itemization of the sections of the Executive Order and of the regulations with which the contractor has been found in apparent violation, and a summary of the conditions, practices, facts or circumstances which give rise to each apparent violation;

(ii) The corrective actions necessary to achieve compliance or, as may be appropriate, the concepts and principles of an acceptable remedy and/or the corrective action results anticipated;

(iii) A request for a written response to the findings, including commitments to corrective action or the presentation or opposing facts and evidence; and

(iv) A suggested date for the conciliation conference.

(2) If the contractor fails to show good cause for his failure or fails to remedy that failure by developing and implementing an acceptable affirmative action program within 30 days, the case file shall be processed for enforcement proceedings pursuant to §60-1.26 of this chapter. If an administrative complaint is filed, the contractor shall have 20 days to request a hearing. If a request for hearing has not been received within 20 days from the filing of the administrative complaint, the matter shall proceed in accordance with Part 60-30 of this chapter.

(3) During the "show cause" period of 30 days, every effort will be made through conciliation, mediation, and persuasion to resolve the deficiencies which led to the determination of nonresponsibility. If satisfactory adjustments designed to bring the contractor into compliance are not concluded, the case shall be processed for enforcement proceedings pursuant to §60-1.26 of this chapter.

(d) During the "show cause" period and formal proceedings, each contracting agency must continue to determine the contractor's responsibility in considering whether or not to award a new or additional contract.

SUBPART B—REQUIRED CONTENTS OF AFFIRMATIVE ACTION PROGRAMS

§60-2.10. Purpose of Affirmative Action Program

An affirmative action program is a set of specific and result-oriented procedures to which a contractor commits itself to apply every good faith effort. The objective of those procedures plus such efforts is equal employment opportunity. Procedures without effort to make them work are meaningless; and effort, undirected by specific and meaningful procedures, is inadequate. An acceptable affirmative action program must include an analysis of areas within which the contractor is deficient in the utilization of minority groups and women, and further, goals and timetables to which the contractor's good faith efforts must be directed to correct the deficiencies and, thus to achieve prompt and full utilization of minorities and women, at all levels and in all segments of its workforce where deficiencies exist.

§60-2.11. Required Utilization Analysis

Based upon the Government's experience with compliance reviews under the Executive order program and the contractor reporting system, minority groups are most likely to be underutilized in departments and jobs within departments that fall within the following Employer's Information Report (EEO-1) designations: officials and managers, professionals, technicians, sales workers, office and clerical and craftsmen (skilled). As categorized by the EEO-1 designations, women are likely to be underutilized in departments and jobs within departments as follows: officials and managers, professionals, technicians, sales workers (except over-the-counter sales in certain retail establishments), craftsmen (skilled and semiskilled). Therefore, the contractor shall direct special attention to such jobs in its analysis and goal setting for minorities and women. Affirmative action programs must contain the following information:

(a) Workforce analysis which is defined as a listing of each job title as appears in applicable collective bargaining agreements or payroll records (not job group) ranked from the lowest paid to the highest paid within each department or other similar organizational unit including departmental or unit supervision. If there are separate work units or lines of progression within a department, a separate list must be provided for each such work unit, or line, including unit supervisors. For lines of progression, there must be indicated the order of jobs in the line through which an employee could move to the top of the line. Where there are no formal progression lines or usual promotional sequences, job titles should be listed by department, job families, or disciplines, in order of wage rates or salary ranges. For each job title, the total number of incumbents, the total number of male and female incumbents, and the total number of male and female incumbents in each of the following groups must be given: Blacks, Spanish-surnamed Americans, American Indians, and Orientals. The wage rate or salary range for each job title must be given. All job titles, including all managerial job titles, must be listed.

(b) An analysis of all major job groups at the facility, with explanation if minorities or women are currently being underutilized in any one or more job groups (''job groups'' herein meaning one or a group of jobs having similar content, wage rates and opportunities). ''Underutilization'' is defined as having fewer minorities or women in a particular job group than would reasonably be expected by their availability. In making the utilization analysis, the contractor shall conduct such analysis separately for minorities and women.

(1) In determining whether minorities are being underutilized in any job group, the contractor will consider at least all of the following factors:

(i) The minority population of the labor area surrounding the facility;

(ii) The size of the minority unemployment force in the labor area surrounding the facility;

(iii) The percentage of the minority workforce as compared with the total workforce in the immediate labor area;

(iv) The general availability of minorities having requisite skills in the immediate labor area;

(v) The availability of minorities having requisite skills in an area in which the contractor can reasonably recruit;

(vi) The availability of promotable and transferable minorities within the contractor's organization;

(vii) The existence of training institutions capable of training persons in the requisite skills; and

(viii) The degree of training which the contractor is reasonably able to undertake as a means of making all job classes available to minorities.

(2) In determining whether women are being underutilized in any job group, the contractor will consider at least all of the following factors:

(i) The size of the female unemployment force in the labor area surrounding the facility;

(ii) The percentage of the female workforce as compared with the total workforce in the immediate labor area;

(iii) The general availability of women having requisite skills in the immediate labor area;

(iv) The availability of women having requisite skills in an area in which the contractor can reasonably recruit;

(v) The availability of women seeking employment in the labor or recruitment area of the contractor;

(vi) The availability of promotable and transferable female employees within the contractor's organization;

(vii) The existence of training institutions capable of training persons in the requisite skills; and

(viii) The degree of training which the contractor is reasonably able to undertake as a means of making all job classes available to women.

§ 60-2.12. Establishment of Goals and Timetables

(a) The goals and timetables developed by the contractor should be attainable in terms of the contractor's analysis of its deficiencies and its entire affirmative action program. Thus, in establishing the size of its goals and the length of its timetables, the contractor should consider the results which could reasonably be expected from its putting forth every good faith effort to make its overall affirmative action program work. In determining levels of goals, the contractor should consider at least the factors listed in §60-2.11.

(b) Involve personnel relations staff, department and division heads, and local and unit managers in the goal setting process.

(c) Goals should be significant, measurable, and attainable.

(d) Goals should be specific for planned results, with timetables for completion.

(e) Goals may not be rigid and inflexible quotas which must be met, but must be targets reasonably attainable by means of applying every good faith effort to make all aspects of the entire affirmative action program work.

(f) In establishing timetables to meet goals and commitments, the contractor will consider the anticipated expansion, contraction, and turnover of and in the workforce.

(g) Goals, timetables and affirmative action commitments must be designed to correct any identifiable deficiencies.

(h) Where deficiencies exist and where numbers or percentages are relevant in developing corrective action, the contractor shall establish and set forth specific goals and timetables separately for minorities and women.

(i) Such goals and timetables, with supporting data and the analysis thereof shall be a part of the contractor's written affirmative action program and shall be maintained at each establishment of the contractor.

(j) A contractor or subcontractor extending a publicly announced preference for Indians as authorized in 41 CFR 60-1.5(a)(6) may reflect in its goals and timetables the permissive employment preference for Indians living on or near an Indian reservation.

(k) Where a contractor has not established a goal, his written affirmative action program must specifically analyze each of the factors listed in 60-2.11 and must detail its reason for a lack of a goal.

(l) In the event it comes to the attention of the Office of Federal Contract Compliance Programs that there is a substantial disparity in the utilization of a particular minority group or men or women of a particular minority group, OFCCP may require separate goals and timetables for such minority group and may further require, where appropriate, such goals and timetables by sex for such group for such job classifications and organizational units specified by the OFCCP.

(m) Support data for the required analysis and program shall be compiled and maintained as part of the contractor's affirmative action program. This data will include but not be limited to progression line charts, seniority rosters, applicant flow data, and applicant rejection ratios indicating minority and sex status.

(n) Copies of affirmative action programs and/or copies of support data shall be made available to the Office of Federal Contract Compliance Programs, upon request, for such purposes as may be appropriate to the fulfillment of its responsibilities under Executive Order 11246, as amended.

§60-2.13. Additional Required Ingredients of Affirmative Action Programs

Effective affirmative action programs shall contain, but not necessarily be limited to, the following ingredients:

(a) Development of reaffirmation of the contractor's equal employment opportunity policy in all personnel actions.

(b) Formal internal and external dissemination of the contractor's policy.

(c) Establishment of responsibilities for implementation of the contractor's affirmative action program.

(d) Identification of problem areas (deficiencies) by organizational units and job group.

(e) Establishment of goals and objectives by organizational units and job groups, including timetables for completion.

(f) Development and execution of action oriented programs designed to eliminate programs and further designed to attain established goals and objectives.

(g) Design and implementation of internal audit and reporting systems to measure effectiveness of the total program.

(h) Compliance or personnel policies and practices with the Sex Discrimination Guidelines (41 CFR Part 60-20).

(i) Active support of local and national community action programs and community service programs, designed to improve the employment opportunities of minorities and women.

(j) Consideration of minorities and women not currently in the workforce having requisite skills who can be recruited through affirmative action measures.

§60-2.14. Program Summary

The affirmative action program shall be summarized and updated annually. The program summary shall be prepared in a format which shall be prescribed by the Director and published in the FEDERAL REGISTER as a notice before becoming effective. Contractors and subcontractors shall submit the program summary to OFCCP each year on the anniversary date of the affirmative action program (Added, eff. Jan. 28, 1980).

§60-2.15. Compliance Status

No contractor's compliance status shall be judged alone by whether or not it reaches its goals and meets its timetables. Rather, each contractor's compliance posture shall be reviewed and determined by reviewing the contents of its program, the extent of its adherence to this program, and its good faith efforts to make its program work toward the realization of the program's goals within the timetable set for completion. There follows an outline of examples of procedures that contractors and federal agencies should use as a guideline for establishing, implementing, and judging an acceptable affirmative action program (Sec. 60-2.15 was renumbered from old Sec. 60-2.14, eff. Jan. 28, 1980).

SUBPART C—METHODS OF IMPLEMENTING THE REQUIREMENTS OF SUBPART B

§60-2.20. Development or Reaffirmation of the Equal Employment Opportunity Policy

(a) The contractor's policy statement should indicate the chief executive officer's attitude on the subject matter, assign overall responsibility, and provide for a reporting and monitoring procedure. Specific items to be mentioned should include, but are not limited to:

(1) Recruit, hire, train, and promote persons in all job titles, without regard to race, color, religion, sex, or national origin, except where sex is a bona fide occupational qualification. (The term ''bona fide occupational qualification'' has been construed very narrowly under the Civil Rights Act of 1964. Under Executive Order 11246 as amended and this part, this term will be construed in the same manner.)

(2) Base decisions on employment so as to further the principle of equal employment opportunity.

(3) Ensure that promotion decisions are in accord with principles of equal employment opportunity by imposing only valid requirements for promotional opportunities.

(4) Ensure that all personnel actions such as compensation, benefits, transfers, layoffs, return from layoff, company sponsored training, education, tuition assistance, social and recreation programs, will be administered without regard to race, color, religion, sex, or national origin.

§60-2.21. Dissemination of the Policy

(a) The contractor should disseminate his policy internally as follows:

(1) Include it in contractor's policy manual.

(2) Publicize it in company newspaper, magazine, annual report, and other media.

(3) Conduct special meetings with executive, management, and supervisory personnel to explain intent of policy and individual responsibility for effective implementation, making clear the chief executive officer's attitude.

(4) Schedule special meetings with all other employees to discuss policy and explain individual employee responsibilities.

(5) Discuss the policy thoroughly in both employee orientation and management training programs.

(6) Meet with union officials to inform them of policy, and request their cooperation.

(7) Include nondiscrimination clauses in all union agreements, and review all contractual provisions to ensure they are nondiscriminatory.

(8) Publish articles covering EEO programs, progress reports, promotions, etc., of minority and female employees, in company publications.

(9) Post the policy on company bulletin boards.

(10) When employees are featured in product or consumer advertising, employee handbooks or similar publications, both minority and nonminority men and women should be pictured.

(11) Communicate to employees the existence of the contractor's affirmative action program and make available such elements of its program as will enable such employees to know of and avail themselves of its benefits.

(b) The contractor should disseminate its policy externally as follows:

(1) Inform all recruiting sources verbally and in writing of company policy, stipulating that these sources actively recruit and refer minorities and women for all positions listed.

(2) Incorporate the equal opportunity clause in all purchase orders, leases, contracts, etc., covered by Executive Order 11246, as amended, and its implementing regulations.

(3) Notify minority and women's organizations, community agencies, community leaders, secondary schools and colleges of company policy, preferably in writing.

(4) Communicate to prospective employees the existence of the contractor's affirmative action program and make available such elements of its program as will enable such prospective employees to know of and avail themselves of its benefits.

(5) When employees are pictured in consumer or help wanted advertising, both minority and nonminority men and women should be shown.

(6) Send written notification of company policy to all subcontractors, vendors and suppliers requesting appropriate action on their part.

§60-2.22. Responsibility for Implementation

(a) An executive of the contractor should be appointed as director or manager of company equal opportunity programs. Depending upon the size and geographical alignment of the company, this may be his or her sole responsibility. He or she should be given the necessary top management support and staffing to execute the assignment. His or her identity should appear on all internal and external communications on the company's equal opportunity programs. His or her responsibilities should include, but not necessarily be limited to:

(1) Developing policy statements, affirmative action programs, internal and external communication techniques.

(2) Assisting in the identification of problem areas.

(3) Assisting line management in arriving at solutions to problems.

(4) Designing and implementing audit and reporting systems that will:

(i) Measure effectiveness of the contractor's programs.

(ii) Indicate need for remedial action.

(iii) Determine the degree to which the contractor's goals and objectives have been attained.

(5) Serve as liaison between the contractor and enforcement agencies.

(6) Serve as liaison between the contractor and minority organizations, women's organizations, and community action groups concerned with employment opportunities of minorities and women.

(7) Keep management informed of latest developments in the entire equal opportunity area.

(b) Line responsibilities should include, but not be limited to the following:

(1) Assistance in the identification of problem areas and establishment of local and unit goals and objectives.

(2) Active involvement with local minority organizations, women's organizations, community action groups, and community service programs.

(3) Periodic audit of training programs, hiring and promotion patterns to remove impediments to the attainment of goals and objectives.

(4) Regular discussions with local managers, supervisors, and employees to be certain the contractor's policies are being followed.

(5) Review of the qualifications of all employees to ensure that minorities and women are given full opportunities for transfers and promotions.

(6) Career counseling for all employees.

(7) Periodic audit to ensure that each location is in compliance in areas such as:

(i) Posters are properly displayed.

(ii) All facilities, including company housing, which the contractor maintains for the use and benefit of his employees, are in fact desegregated, both in policy and use. If the contractor provides facilities such as dormitories, locker rooms, and rest rooms, they must be comparable for both sexes.

(iii) Minority and female employees are afforded a full opportunity and are encouraged to participate in all company sponsored educational, training, recreational and social activities.

(8) Supervisors should be made to understand that their work performance is being evaluated on the basis of their equal employment opportunity efforts and results, as well as other criteria.

(9) It shall be a responsibility of supervisors to take actions to prevent harassment of employees placed through affirmative action efforts.

§60-2.23. Identification of Problem Areas by Organizational Units and Job Groups

(a) An in-depth analysis of the following should be made, paying particular attention to trainees and those categories listed in §60-2.11(b).

(1) Composition of the workforce by minority group status and sex.

(2) Composition of applicant flow by minority group status and sex.

(3) The total selection process including position descriptions, position titles, worker specifications, application forms, interview procedures, test administration, test validity, referral procedures, final selection process, and similar factors.

(4) Transfer and promotion practices.

(5) Facilities, company sponsored recreation and social events, and special programs such as educational assistance.

(6) Seniority practices and seniority provisions of union contracts.

(7) Apprenticeship programs.

(8) All company training programs, formal and informal.

(9) Workforce attitude.

(10) Technical phases of compliance, such as poster and notification to labor unions, retention of applications, notification to subcontractors, etc.

(b) If any of the following items are found in the analysis, special corrective action should be appropriate.

(1) An "underutilization" of minorities and women in specific job groups.

(2) Lateral and/or vertical movement of minority or female employees occurring at a lesser rate (compared to workforce mix) than that of nonminority or male employees.

(3) The selection process eliminates a significantly higher percentage of minorities or women than nonminorities or men.

(4) Application and related preemployment forms not in compliance with Federal legislation.

(5) Position descriptions inaccurate in relation to actual functions and duties.

(6) Formal or scored selection procedures not validated as required by the OFCCP Uniform Guidelines on Employee Selection procedures.

(7) Test forms not validated by location, work performance and inclusion of minorities and women in sample.

(8) Referral ratio of minorities or women to the hiring supervisor or manager indicates a significantly higher percentage are being rejected as compared to nonminority and male applicants.

(9) Minorities or women are excluded from or are not participating in company sponsored activities or programs.

(10) De facto segregation still exists at some facilities.

(11) Seniority provisions contribute to overt or inadvertent discrimination, i.e., a disparity by minority group status or sex exists between length of service and types of job held.

(12) Nonsupport of company policy by managers, supervisors, or employees.

(13) Minorities or women underutilized or significantly underrepresented in training or career improvement programs.

(14) No formal techniques established for evaluating effectiveness of EEO programs.

(15) Lack of access to suitable housing inhibits recruitment efforts and employment of qualified minorities.

(16) Lack of suitable transportation (public or private) to the work place inhibits minority employment.

(17) Labor unions and subcontractors not notified of their responsibilities.

(18) Purchase orders do not contain EEO clause.

(19) Posters not on display.

§60-2.24.   Development and Execution of Programs

(a) The contractor should conduct detailed analyses of position descriptions to ensure that they accurately reflect position functions, and are consistent for the same position from one location to another.

(b) The contractor should validate worker specifications by division, department, location, or other organizational unit, and by job title, using job performance criteria. Special attention should be given to academic, experience, and skill requirements to ensure that the requirements in themselves do not constitute inadvertent discrimination. Specifications should be consistent for the same job title in all locations and should be free from bias as regards to race, color, religion, sex, or national origin, except where sex is a bona fide occupational qualification. Where requirements screen out a disproportionate number of minorities or women, such requirements should be professionally validated to job performance.

(c) Approved position descriptions and worker specifications, when used by the contractor, should be made available to all members of management involved in the recruiting, screening, selection, and promotion process. Copies should also be distributed to all recruiting sources.

(d) The contractor should evaluate the total selection process to ensure freedom from bias and, thus, aid the attainment of goals and objectives.

(1) All personnel involved in the recruiting, screening, selection, promotion, disciplinary, and related processes should be carefully selected and trained to ensure elimination of bias in all personnel actions.

(2) The contractor shall observe the requirements of the OFCCP *Uniform Guidelines on Employee Selection Procedures. (See 401:2231.)*

(3) Selection techniques other than tests may also be improperly used so as to have the effect of discriminating against minority groups and women. Such techniques include, but are not restricted to, unscored interviews, unscored or casual application forms, arrest records, credit checks, considerations of marital status or dependency or minor children. Where there exist data suggesting that such unfair discrimination or exclusion of minorities or women exists, the contractor should analyze his unscored procedures and eliminate them if they are not objectively valid.

(e) Suggested techniques to improve recruitment and increase the flow of minority or female applicants follow:

(1) Certain organizations such as the Urban League, Job Corps, Equal Opportunity Programs, Inc., Concentrated Employment programs, Neighborhood Youth Corps, Secondary Schools, Colleges, and City Colleges with high minority enrollment, the State Employment Service, specialized employment agencies, Aspira, LULAC, SER, the G.I. Forum, the Commonwealth of Puerto Rico are normally prepared to refer minority applicants. Organizations prepared to refer women with specific skills are: National Organization for Women, Welfare Rights organizations, Women's Equity Action League, Talent Bank from Business and Professional Women (including 26 women's organizations), Professional Women's Caucus, Intercollegiate Association of University Women, Negro Women's sororities and service groups such as Delta Sigma Theta, Alpha Kappa Alpha, and Zeta Phi Beta; National Council of Negro Women, American Association of University Women, YWCA, and sectarian groups such as Jewish Women's Groups, Catholic Women's Groups, and Protestant Women's Groups, and women's colleges. In addition, community leaders as individuals shall be added to recruiting sources.

(2) Formal briefing sessions should be held, preferably on company premises, with representatives from these recruiting sources. Plant tours, presentations by minority and female employees, clear

and concise explanations of current and future job openings, position descriptions, worker specifications, explanations of the company's selection process, and recruiting literature should be an integral part of the briefings. Formal arrangements should be made for referral of applicants, follow-up with sources, and feedback on disposition of applicants.

(3) Minority and female employees, using procedures similar to subparagraph (2) of this paragraph, should be actively encouraged to refer applicants.

(4) A special effort should be made to include minorities and women on the Personnel Relations staff.

(5) Minority and female employees should be made available for participation in Career Days, Youth Motivation Programs, and related activities in their communities.

(6) Active participation in "Job Fairs" is desirable. Company representatives so participating should be given authority to make on-the-spot commitments.

(7) Active recruiting programs should be carried out at secondary schools, junior colleges, and colleges with predominant minority or female enrollments.

(8) Recruiting efforts at all schools should incorporate special efforts to reach minorities and women.

(9) Special employment programs should be undertaken whenever possible. Some possible programs are:

(i) Technical and nontechnical coop programs with predominantly Negro and women's colleges.

(ii) "After school" and/or workstudy jobs for minority youths, male and female.

(iii) Summer jobs for underprivileged youth, male and female.

(iv) Summer work-study programs for male and female faculty members of the predominantly minority schools and colleges.

(v) Motivation, training and employment programs for the hard-core unemployed, male and female.

(10) When recruiting brochures pictorially present work situations, the minority and female members of the workforce should be included, especially when such brochures are used in school and career programs.

(11) Help wanted advertising should be expanded to include the minority news media and women's interest media on a regular basis.

(f) The contractor should ensure that minority and female employees are given equal opportunity for promotion. Suggestions for achieving this result include:

(1) Post or otherwise announce promotional opportunities.

(2) Make an inventory of current minority and female employees to determine academic, skill and experience level of individual employees.

(3) Initiate necessary remedial, job training and workstudy programs.

(4) Develop and implement formal employee evaluation programs.

(5) Make certain "worker specifications" have been validated on job performance related criteria. (Neither minority nor female employees should be required to possess higher qualifications than those of the lowest qualified incumbent.)

(6) When apparently qualified minority or female employees are passed over for upgrading, require supervisory personnel to submit written justification.

(7) Establish formal career counseling programs to include attitude development, education aid, job rotation, buddy system, and similar programs.

(8) Review seniority practices and seniority clauses in union contracts to ensure such practices or clauses are nondiscriminatory and do not have a discriminatory effect.

(g) Make certain facilities and company-sponsored social and recreation activities are desegregated. Actively encourage all employees to participate.

(h) Encourage child care, housing and transportation programs appropriately designed to improve the employment opportunities for minorities and women.

§60-2.25. Internal Audit and Reporting Systems

(a) The contractor should monitor records of referrals, placements, transfers, promotions, and terminations at all levels to ensure nondiscriminatory policy is carried out.

(b) The contractor should require formal reports from unit managers on a scheduled basis as to degree to which corporate or unit goals are attained and timetables met.

(c) The contractor should review report results with all levels of management.

(d) The contractor should advise top management of program effectiveness and submit recommendations to improve unsatisfactory performance.

§60-2.26. Support of Action Programs

(a) The contractor should appoint key members of management to serve on merit employment councils, community relations boards, and similar organizations.

(b) The contractor should encourage minority and female employees to participate actively in National Alliance of Businessmen programs for youth motivation.

(c) The contractor should support vocational guidance institutes, vestibule training programs and similar activities.

(d) The contractor should assist secondary schools and colleges in programs designed to enable minority and female graduates of these institutions to compete in the open employment market on a more equitable basis.

(e) The contractor should publicize achievements of minority and female employees in local and minority news media.

(f) The contractor should support programs developed by such organizations as National Alliance of Business, the Urban Coalition and other organizations concerned with employment opportunities for minorities or women.

SUBPART D—MISCELLANEOUS

§60-2.30. Use of Goals

The purpose of a contractor's establishment and use of goals is to ensure that it meets its affirmative action obligation. It is not intended and should not be used to discriminate against any applicant or employee because of race, color, religion, sex, or national origin.

§60-2.31. Preemption

To the extent that any State or local laws, regulations or ordinances, including those which grant special benefits to persons on account of sex, are in conflict with Executive Order 11246, as amended, or with requirements of this part, we will regard them as preempted under the Executive Order.

§60-2.32. Supersedure

All orders, instructions, regulations, and memoranda of the Secretary of Labor, other officials of the Department of Labor and contracting agencies are hereby superseded to the extent that they are inconsistent herewith, including a previous "Order No. 4" from this office dated January 30, 1970. Nothing in this part is intended to amend 41 CFR 60-3 or 41 CFR 60-20.

APPENDIX C

Employment Regulations for the Americans With Disabilities Act (EEOC)

PART 1630—REGULATIONS TO IMPLEMENT THE EQUAL EMPLOYMENT PROVISIONS OF THE AMERICANS WITH DISABILITIES ACT

Appendix to Part 1630—Interpretive Guidance on Title I of the Americans with Disabilities Act

Authority: 42 U.S.C. 12116.

§1630.1 Purpose, applicability, and construction.

(a) *Purpose.* The purpose of this part is to implement title I of the Americans with Disabilities Act (42 U.S.C. 12101, *et seq.* (ADA), requiring equal employment opportunities for qualified individuals with disabilities, and sections 3(2), 3(3), 501, 503, 506(e), 508, 510, and 511 of the ADA as those sections pertain to the employment of qualified individuals with disabilities.

(b) *Applicability.* This part applies to "covered entities" as defined at §1630.2(b).

(c) *Construction.*—(1) *In general.* Except as otherwise provided in this part, this part does not apply a lesser standard than the standards applied under title V of the Rehabilitation Act of 1973 (29 U.S.C. 790-794a), or the regulations issued by Federal agencies pursuant to that title.

(2) *Relationship to other laws.* This part does not invalidate or limit the remedies, rights, and procedures of any Federal law or law of any State or jurisdiction that provides greater or equal protection for the rights of individuals with disabilities than are afforded by this part.

§1630.2 Definitions.

(a) *Commission* means the Equal Employment Opportunity Commission established by section 705 of the Civil Rights Act of 1964 (42 U.S.C. 2000e-4).

(b) *Covered Entity* means an employer, employment agency, labor organization, or joint labor management committee.

(c) *Person, labor organization, employment agency, commerce, and industry affecting commerce* shall have the same meaning given those terms in section 701 of the Civil Rights Act of 1964 (42 U.S.C. 2000e).

(d) *State* means each of the several States, the District of Columbia, the Commonwealth of Puerto Rico, Guam, American Samoa, the Virgin Islands, the Trust Territory of the Pacific Islands, and the Commonwealth of the Northern Mariana Islands.

(e) *Employer.*—(1) *In general.* The term employer means a person engaged in an industry affecting commerce who has 15 or more employees for each working day in each of 20 or more calendar weeks in the current or preceding calendar year, and any agent of such person, except that, from July 26, 1992 through July 25, 1994, an employer means a person engaged in an industry affecting commerce who has 25 or more employees for each working day in each of 20 or more calendar weeks in the current or preceding year and any agent of such person.

(2) *Exceptions.* The term employer does not include—

(i) The United States, a corporation wholly owned by the government of the United States, or an Indian tribe; or

(ii) A bona fide private membership club (other than a labor organization) that is exempt from taxation under section 501(c) of the Internal Revenue Code of 1986.

(f) *Employee* means an individual employed by an employer.

(g) *Disability* means, with respect to an individual—

(1) A physical or mental impairment that substantially limits one or more of the major life activities of such individual;

(2) A record of such an impairment; or

(3) being regarded as having such an impairment.

(See §1630.3 for exceptions to this definition.)

(h) *Physical or mental impairment* means:

(1) Any physiological disorder, or condition, cosmetic disfigurement, or anatomical loss affecting one or more of the following body systems: neurological, musculoskeletal, special sense organs, respiratory (including speech organs), cardiovascular, reproductive, digestive, genito-urinary, hemic and lymphatic, skin, and endocrine; or

(2) Any mental or psychological disorder, such as mental retardation, organic brain syndrome, emotional or mental illness, and specific learning disabilities.

(i) *Major Life Activities* means functions such as caring for oneself, performing manual tasks, walking, seeing, hearing, speaking, breathing, learning, and working.

(j) *Substantially limits*—(1) The term *substantially limits* means:

(i) Unable to perform a major life activity that the average person in the general population can perform; or

(ii) Significantly restricted as to the condition, manner, or duration under which an individual can perform a particular major life activity as compared to the condition, manner, or duration under which the average person in the general population can perform that same major life activity.

(2) The following factors should be considered in determining whether an individual is substantially limited in a major life activity:

(i) The nature and severity of the impairment;

(ii) The duration or expected duration of the impairment; and

(iii) The permanent or long term impact, or the expected permanent or long term impact of or resulting from the impairment.

(3) With respect to the major life activity of *working*—

(i) The term *substantially limits* means significantly restricted in the ability to perform either a class of jobs or a broad range of jobs in various classes as compared to the average person having comparable training, skills, and abilities. The inability to perform a single, particular job does not constitute a substantial limitation in the major life activity of working.

(ii) In addition to the factors listed in paragraph (j)(2) of this section, the following factors may be considered in determining whether an individual is substantially limited in the major life activity of "working":

(A) The geographical area to which the individual has reasonable access;

(B) The job from which the individual has been disqualified because of an impairment, and the number and types of jobs utilizing similar training, knowledge, skills, or abilities, within that geographical area, from which the individual is also disqualified because of the impairment (class of jobs); and/or

(C) The job from which the individual has been disqualified because of an impairment, and the number and types of other jobs not utilizing similar training, knowledge, skills, or abilities, within that geographical area, from which the individual is also disqualified because of the impairment (broad range of jobs in various classes).

(k) *Has a record of such impairment* means has a history of, or has been misclassified as having, a mental or physical impairment that substantially limits one or more major life activities.

(l) *Is regarded as having such an impairment* means:

(1) Has a physical or mental impairment that does not substantially limit major life activities but is treated by a covered entity as constituting such limitation;

(2) Has a physical or mental impairment that substantially limits major life activities only as a result of the attitudes of others toward such impairment; or

(3) Has none of the impairments defined in paragraphs (h) (1) or (2) of this section but is treated by a covered entity as having a substantially limiting impairment.

(m) *Qualified individual with a disability* means an individual with a disability who satisfies the requisite skill, experience, education, and other job related requirements of the employment position such individual holds or desires, and who, with or without reasonable accommodation, can perform the essential functions of such position. (See §1630.3 for exceptions to this definition.)

(n) *Essential functions.*—(1) *In general.* The term *essential functions* means the fundamental job duties of the employment position the individual with a disability holds or desires. The term "essential functions" does not include the marginal functions of the position.

(2) A job function may be considered essential for any of several reasons, including but not limited to the following:

(i) The function may be essential because the reason the position exists is to perform that function;

(ii) The function may be essential because of the limited number of employees available among whom the performance of that job function can be distributed; and/or

(iii) The function may be highly specialized so that the incumbent in the position is hired for his or her expertise or ability to perform the particular function.

(3) Evidence of whether a particular function is essential includes, but is not limited to:

(i) The employer's judgment as to which functions are essential;

(ii) Written job descriptions prepared before advertising or interviewing applicants for the job;

(iii) The amount of time spent on the job performing the function;

(iv) The consequences of not requiring the incumbent to perform the function;

(v) The terms of a collective bargaining agreement;

(vi) The work experience of past incumbents in the job; and/or

(vii) The current work experience of incumbents in similar jobs.

(o) *Reasonable accommodation.*—(1) The term *reasonable accommodation* means:

(i) Modifications or adjustments to a job application process that enable a qualified applicant with a disability to be considered for the position such qualified applicant desires; or

(ii) Modifications or adjustments to the work environment, or to the manner or circumstances under which the position held or desired is customarily performed, that enable a qualified individual with a disability to perform the essential functions of that position; or

(iii) Modifications or adjustments that enable a covered entity's employee with a disability to enjoy equal benefits and privileges of employment that are enjoyed by its other similarly situated employees without disabilities.

(2) *Reasonable accommodation* may include but is not limited to:

(i) Making existing facilities used by employees readily accessible to and usable by individuals with disabilities; and

(ii) Job restructuring; part-time or modified work schedules; reassignment to a vacant position; acquisition or modifications of equipment or devices; appropriate adjustment or modifications of examinations, training materials, or policies; the provision of qualified readers or interpreters; and other similar accommodations for individuals with disabilities.

(3) To determine the appropriate reasonable accommodation it may be necessary for the covered entity to initiate an informal, interactive process with the qualified individual with a disability in need of the accommodation. This process should identify the precise limitations resulting from the disability and potential reasonable accommodations that could overcome those limitations.

(p) *Undue hardship*—(1) *In general. Undue hardship* means, with respect to the provision of an accommodation, significant difficulty or expense incurred by a covered entity, when considered in light of the factors set forth in paragraph (p)(2) of this section.

(2) *Factors to be considered.* In determining whether an accommodation would impose an undue hardship on a covered entity, factors to be considered include:

(i) The nature and net cost of the accommodation needed under this part, taking into consideration the availability of tax credits and deductions, and/or outside funding;

(ii) The overall financial resources of the facility or facilities involved in the provision of the reasonable accommodation, the number of persons employed at such facility, and the effect on expenses and resources;

(iii) The overall financial resources of the covered entity; the overall size of the business of the covered entity with respect to the number of its employees; and the number, type, and location of its facilities;

(iv) The type of operation or operations of the covered entity, including the composition, structure, and functions of the workforce of such entity, and the geographic separateness and administrative or fiscal relationship of the facility or facilities in question to the covered entity; and

(v) The impact of the accommodation upon the operation of the facility, including the impact on the ability of other employees to perform their duties and the impact on the facility's ability to conduct business.

(q) *Qualification standards* means the personal and professional attributes including the skill, experience, education, physical, medical, safety and other requirements established by a covered entity as requirements which an individual must meet in order to be eligible for the position held or desired.

(r) *Direct threat* means a significant risk of substantial harm or the health or safety of the individual or others that cannot be eliminated or reduced by reasonable accommodation. The determination that an individual poses a ''direct threat'' shall be based on an individualized assessment of the individual's present ability to safely perform the essential functions of the job. This assessment shall be based on a reasonable medical judgment that relies on the most current medical knowledge and/or on the best available objective evidence. In determining whether an individual would pose a direct threat, the factors to be considered include:

(1) The duration of the risk;

(2) The nature and severity of the potential harm;

(3) The likelihood that the potential harm will occur; and

(4) The imminence of the potential harm.

§1630.3 Exceptions to the definitions of "Disability" and "Qualified Individual with a Disability."

(a) The terms *disability* and *qualified individual with a disability* do not include individuals currently engaging in the illegal use of drugs, when the covered entity acts on the basis of such use.

(1) *Drug* means a controlled substance, as defined in schedules I through V of Section 202 of the Controlled Substances Act (21 U.S.C. 812).

(2) *Illegal use of drugs* means the use of drugs, the possession or distribution of which is unlawful under the Controlled Substances Act, as periodically updated by the Food and Drug Administration. This term does not include the use of a drug taken under the supervision of a licensed health care professional, or other uses authorized by the Controlled Substances Act or other provisions of Federal law.

(b) However, the terms *disability* and *qualified* individual with a disability may not exclude an individual who:

(1) Has successfully completed a supervised drug rehabilitation program and is no longer engaging in the illegal use of drugs, or has otherwise been rehabilitated successfully and is no longer engaging in the illegal use of drugs; or

(2) Is participating in a supervised rehabilitation program and is no longer engaging in such use; or

(3) Is erroneously regarded as engaging in such use, but is not engaging in such use.

(c) It shall not be a violation of this part for a covered entity to adopt or administer reasonable policies or procedures, including but not limited to drug testing, designed to ensure that an individual described in paragraph (b)(1) or (2) of this section is no longer engaging in the illegal use of drugs. (See §1630.16(c) Drug testing).

(d) *Disability* does not include:

(1) Transvestism, transsexualism, pedophilia, exhibitionism, voyeurism, gender identity disorders not resulting from physical impairments, or other sexual behavior disorders;

(2) Compulsive gambling, kleptomania, or pyromania; or

(3) Psychoactive substance use disorders resulting from current illegal use of drugs.

(e) *Homosexuality and bisexuality* are not impairments and so are not disabilities as defined in this part.

§1630.4 Discrimination prohibited.

It is unlawful for a covered entity to discriminate on the basis of disability against a qualified individual with a disability in regard to:

(a) Recruitment, advertising, and job application procedures;

(b) Hiring, upgrading, promotion, award of tenure, demotion, transfer, layoff, termination, right of return from layoff, and rehiring;

(c) Rates of pay or any other form of compensation and changes in compensation;

(d) Job assignments, job classifications, organizational structures, position descriptions, lines of progression, and seniority lists;

(e) Leaves of absence, sick leave, or any other leave;

(f) Fringe benefits available by virtue of employment, whether or not administered by the covered entity;

(g) Selection and financial support for training, including: apprenticeships, professional meetings, conferences and other related activities, and selection for leaves of absence to pursue training;

(h) Activities sponsored by a covered entity including social and recreational programs; and

(i) Any other term, condition, or privilege of employment.

The term *discrimination* includes, but is not limited to, the acts described in §§1630.5 through 1630.13 of this part.

§1630.5 Limiting, segregating, and classifying.

It is unlawful for a covered entity to limit, segregate, or classify a job applicant or employee in a way that adversely affects his or her employment opportunities or status on the basis of disability.

§1630.6 Contractual or other arrangements.

(a) *In general.* It is unlawful for a covered entity to participate in a contractual or other arrangement or relationship that has the effect of subjecting the covered entity's own qualified applicant or employee with a disability to the discrimination prohibited by this part.

(b) *Contractual or other arrangement defined.* The phrase *contractual or other arrangement or relationship* includes, but is not limited to, a relationship with an employment or referral agency; labor union, including collective bargaining agreements; an organization providing fringe benefits to an employee of the covered entity; or an organization providing training and apprenticeship programs.

(c) *Application.* This section applies to a covered entity, with respect to its own applicants or employees, whether the entity offered the contract or initiated the relationship, or whether the entity accepted the contract or acceded to the relationship. A covered entity is not liable for the actions of the other party or parties to the contract which only affect that other party's employees or applicants.

§1630.7 Standards, criteria, or methods of administration.

It is unlawful for a covered entity to use standards, criteria, or methods of administration, which are not job related and consistent with business necessity, and;

(a) That have the effect of discriminating on the basis of disability; or

(b) That perpetuate the discrimination of others who are subject to common administrative control.

§1630.8 Relationship or association with an individual with a disability.

It is unlawful for a covered entity to exclude or deny equal jobs or benefits to, or otherwise discriminate against, a qualified individual because of the known disability of an individual with whom the qualified individual is known to have a family, business, social, or other relationship or association.

§1630.9 Not making reasonable accommodation.

(a) It is unlawful for a covered entity not to make reasonable accommodation to the known physical or mental limitations of an otherwise qualified applicant or employee with a disability, unless such covered entity can demonstrate that the accommodation would impose an undue hardship on the operation of its business.

(b) It is unlawful for a covered entity to deny employment opportunities to an otherwise qualified job applicant or employee with a disability based on the need of such covered entity to make reasonable accommodation to such individual's physical or mental impairments.

(c) A covered entity shall not be excused from the requirements of this part because of any failure to receive technical assistance authorized by section 506 of the ADA, including any failure in the development or dissemination of any technical assistance manual authorized by that act.

(d) A qualified individual with a disability is not required to accept an accommodation, aid, service, opportunity, or benefit which such qualified individual chooses not to accept. However, if such individual rejects a reasonable accommodation, aid, service, opportunity or benefit that is necessary to enable the individual to perform the essential functions of the position held or desired, and cannot, as a result of that rejection, perform the essential functions of the position, the individual will not be considered a qualified individual with a disability.

§1630.10 Qualification standards, tests, and other selection criteria.

It is unlawful for a covered entity to use qualification standards, employment tests or other selection criteria that screen out or tend to screen out an individual with a disability or a class of individuals with disabilities, on the basis of disability, unless the standard, test, or other selection criteria, as used by the covered entity, is shown to be job related for the position in question and is consistent with business necessity.

§1630.11 Administration of tests.

It is unlawful for a covered entity to fail to select and administer tests concerning employment in the most effective manner to ensure that, when a test is administered to a job applicant or employee who has a disability that impairs sensory, manual, or speaking skills, the test results accurately reflect the skills, aptitude, or whatever other factor of the applicant or employee that the test purports to measure, rather than reflecting the impaired sensory, manual, or speaking skills of such employee or applicant (except where such skills are the factors that the test purports to measure).

§1630.12 Retaliation and coercion.

(a) *Retaliation.* It is unlawful to discriminate against any individual because that individual has opposed any act or practice made unlawful by this part or because that individual made a charge, testified, assisted, or participated in any manner in an investigation, proceeding, or hearing to enforce any provision contained in this part.

(b) *Coercion, interference or intimidation.* It is unlawful to coerce, intimidate, threaten, harass or interfere with any individual in the exercise or enjoyment of, or because that individual aided or encouraged any other individual in the exercise of, any right granted or protected by this part.

§1630.13 Prohibited medical examinations and inquiries.

(a) *Pre-employment examination or inquiry.* Except as permitted by §1630.14, it is unlawful for a covered entity to conduct a medical examination of an applicant or to make inquiries as to whether an applicant is an individual with a disability or as to the nature or severity of such disability.

(b) *Examination or inquiry of employees.* Except as permitted by §1630.14, it is unlawful for a covered entity to require a medical examination of an employee or to make inquiries as to whether an employee is an individual with a disability or as to the nature of severity of such disability.

§1630.14 Medical examinations and inquiries specifically permitted.

(a) *Acceptable pre-employment inquiry.* A covered entity may make pre-employment inquiries into the ability of an applicant to perform job related functions, and/or may ask an applicant to describe or to demonstrate how, with or without reasonable accommodation, the applicant will be able to perform job related functions.

(b) *Employment entrance examination.* A covered entity may require a medical examination (and/or inquiry) after making an offer of employment to a job applicant and before the applicant begins his or her employment duties, and may condition an offer of employment on the results of such examination (and/or inquiry), if all entering employees in the same job category are subjected to such an examination (and/or inquiry) regardless of disability.

(1) Information obtained under paragraph (b) of this section regarding the medical condition or history of the applicant shall be collected and maintained on separate forms and in separate medical files and be treated as a confidential medical record, except that:

(i) Supervisors and managers may be informed regarding necessary restrictions on the work or duties of the employee and necessary accommodations;

(ii) First aid and safety personnel may be informed, when appropriate, if the disability might require emergency treatment; and

(iii) Government officials investigating compliance with this part shall be provided relevant information on request.

(2) The results of such examination shall not be used for any purpose inconsistent with this part.

(3) Medical examinations conducted in accordance with this section do not have to be job related and consistent with business necessity. However, if certain criteria are used to screen out an employee or employees with disabilities as a result of such an examination or inquiry, the exclusionary criteria must be job related and consistent with business necessity, and performance of the essential job functions cannot be accomplished with reasonable accommodation as required in this part. (See §1630.15(b) Defenses to charges of discriminatory application of selection criteria.)

(c) *Examination of employees.* A covered entity may require a medical examination (and/or inquiry) of an employee that is job related and consistent with business necessity. A covered entity may make inquiries into the ability of an employee to perform job related functions.

(1) Information obtained under paragraph (c) of this section regarding the medical condition or history of any employee shall be collected and maintained on separate forms and in separate medical files and be treated as a confidential medical record, except that:

(i) Supervisors and managers may be informed regarding necessary restrictions on the work or duties of the employee and necessary accommodations;

(ii) First aid and safety personnel may be informed, when appropriate, if the disability might require emergency treatment; and

(iii) Government officials investigating compliance with this part shall be provided relevant information on request.

(2) Information obtained under paragraph (c) of this section regarding the medical condition or history of any employee shall not be used for any purpose inconsistent with this part.

(d) *Other acceptable examinations and inquiries.* A covered entity may conduct voluntary medical examinations and activities, including voluntary medical histories, which are part of an employee health program available to employees at the work site.

(1) Information obtained under paragraph (d) of this section regarding the medical condition or history of any employee shall be collected and maintained on separate forms and in separate medical files and be treated as a confidential medical record, except that:

(i) Supervisors and managers may be informed regarding necessary restrictions on the work or duties of the employee and necessary accommodations;

(ii) First aid and safety personnel may be informed, when appropriate, if the disability might require emergency treatment; and

(iii) Government officials investigating compliance with this part shall be provided relevant information on request.

(2) Information obtained under paragraph (d) of this section regarding the medical condition or history of any employee shall not be used for any purpose inconsistent with this part.

§1630.15 Defenses.

Defenses to an allegation of discrimination under this part may include, but are not limited to, the following:

(a) *Disparate treatment charges.* It may be a defense to a charge of disparate treatment brought under §§1630.4 through 1630.8 and 1630.11 through 1630.12 that the challenged action is justified by a legitimate, nondiscriminatory reason.

(b) *Charges of discriminatory application of selection criteria—*(1) *In general.* It may be a defense to a charge of discrimination, as described in §1630.10, that an alleged application of qualification standards, tests, or selection criteria that screens out or tends to screen out or otherwise denies a job or benefit to an individual with a disability has been shown to be job related and consistent with business necessity, and such performance cannot be accomplished with reasonable accommodation, as required in this part.

(2) *Direct threat as a qualification standard.* The term "qualification standard" may include a requirement that an individual shall not pose a direct threat to the health or safety of the individual or others in the workplace. (See §1630.2(r) defining direct threat.)

(c) *Other disparate impact charges.* It may be a defense to a charge of discrimination brought under this part that a uniformly applied standard, criterion, or policy has a disparate impact on an individual with a disability or a class of individuals with disabilities that the challenged standard, criterion, or policy has been shown to be job related and consistent with business necessity, and such performance cannot be accomplished with reasonable accommodation, as required in this part.

(d) *Charges of not making reasonable accommodation.* It may be a defense to a charge of discrimination, as described in §1630.9, that a requested or necessary accommodation would impose an undue hardship on the operation of the covered entity's business.

(e) *Conflict with other Federal laws.* It may be a defense to a charge of discrimination under this part that a challenged action is required or necessitated by another Federal law or regulation, or that another Federal law or regulation prohibits an action (including the provision of a particular reasonable accommodation) that would otherwise be required by this part.

(f) *Additional defenses.* It may be a defense to a charge of discrimination under this part that the alleged discriminatory action is specifically permitted by §§1630.14 or 1630.16.

§1630.16 Specific activities permitted.

(a) *Religious entities.* A religious corporation, association, educational institution, or society is permitted to give preference in employment to individuals of a particular religion to perform work connected with the carrying on by that corporation, association, educational institution, or society of its activities. A religious entity may require that all applicants and employees conform to the religious tenets of such organization. However, a religious entity may not discriminate against a qualified individual, who satisfies the permitted religious criteria, because of his or her disability.

(b) *Regulation of alcohol and drugs.* A covered entity:

(1) May prohibit the illegal use of drugs and the use of alcohol at the workplace by all employees;

(2) May require that employees not be under the influence of alcohol or be engaging in the illegal use of drugs at the workplace;

(3) May require that all employees behave in conformance with the requirements established under the Drug-Free Workplace Act of 1988 (41 U.S.C. 701 et seq.);

(4) May hold an employee who engages in the illegal use of drugs or who is an alcoholic to the same qualification standards for employment or job performance and behavior to which the entity holds its other employees, even if any unsatisfactory performance or behavior is related to the employee's drug use or alcoholism;

(5) May require that its employees employed in an industry subject to such regulations comply with the standards established in the regulations (if any) of the Departments of Defense and Transportation, and of the Nuclear Regulatory Commission, regarding alcohol and the illegal use of drugs; and

(6) May require that employees employed in sensitive positions comply with the regulations (if any) of the Departments of Defense and Transportation and of the Nuclear Regulatory Commission that apply to employment in sensitive positions subject to such regulations.

(c) *Drug testing*—(1) *General policy.* For purposes of this part, a test to determine the illegal use of drugs is not considered a medical examination. Thus, the administration of such drug tests by a covered entity to its job applicants or employees is not a violation of §1630.13 of this part. However, this part does not encourage, prohibit, or authorize a covered entity to conduct drug tests of job applicants or employees to determine the illegal use of drugs or to make employment decisions based on such test results.

(2) *Transportation Employees.* This part does not encourage, prohibit, or authorize the otherwise lawful exercise by entities subject to the jurisdiction of the Department of Transportation of authority to:

(i) Test employees of entities in, and applicants for, positions involving safety sensitive duties for the illegal use of drugs or for on-duty impairment by alcohol; and

(ii) Remove from safety-sensitive positions persons who test positive for illegal use of drugs or on-duty impairment by alcohol pursuant to paragraph (c)(2)(i) of this section.

(3) *Confidentiality.* Any information regarding the medical condition or history of any employee or applicant obtained from a test to determine the illegal use of drugs, except information regarding the illegal use of drugs, is subject to the requirements of §1630.14(b) (2) and (3) of this part.

(d) *Regulation of smoking.* A covered entity may prohibit or impose restrictions on smoking in places of employment. Such restrictions do not violate any provision of this part.

(e) *Infectious and communicable diseases; food handling jobs*—(1) *In general.* Under title I of the ADA, section 103(d)(1), the Secretary of Health and Human Services is to prepare a list, to be updated annually, of infectious and communicable diseases which are transmitted through the handling of food. (Copies may be obtained from Center for Infectious Diseases, Centers for Disease Control, 1600 Clifton Road, NE., Mailstop C09, Atlanta, GA 30333.) If an individual with a disability is disabled by one of the infectious or communicable diseases included on this list, and if the risk of transmitting the disease associated with the handling of food cannot be eliminated by reasonable accommodation, a covered entity may refuse to assign or continue to assign such individual to a job involving food handling. However, if the individual with a disability is a current employee, the employer must consider whether he or she can be accommodated by reassignment to a vacant position not involving food handling.

(2) *Effect on State or other laws.* This part does not preempt, modify, or amend any state, county, or local law, ordinance, or regulation applicable to food handling which:

(i) Is in accordance with the list, referred to in paragraph (e)(1) of this section, of infectious or communicable diseases and the modes of transmissibility published by the Secretary of Health and Human Services; and

(ii) Is designed to protect the public health from individuals who pose a significant risk to the health or safety of others, where that risk cannot be eliminated by reasonable accommodation.

(f) *Health insurance, life insurance, and other benefit plans*—(1) An insurer, hospital, or medical service company, health maintenance organization, or any agent or entity that administers benefit plans, or similar organizations may underwrite risks, classify risks, or administer such risks that are based on or not inconsistent with State law.

(2) A covered entity may establish, sponsor, observe or administer the terms of a bona fide benefit plan that are based on underwriting risks, classifying risks, or administering such risks that are based on or not inconsistent with State law.

(3) A covered entity may establish, sponsor, observe, or administer the terms of a bona fide benefit plan that is not subject to State laws that regulate insurance.

(4) The activities described in paragraphs (f) (1), (2), and (3) of this section are permitted unless these activities are being used as a subterfuge to evade the purposes of this part.

NAME INDEX

SUBJECT INDEX

A

Ability tests, 69, 358–59
Achievement history questionnaires, 362
Adverse impact predictors, 436–37
Advertisements, recruiting, 69, 70, 264–67
Affirmative Action, 50–51, 510–11, 524–25
  basic issues, 57–61
  and diversity programs, 227–28
  guidelines, 527–38
  information sources, 75–76
  laws, 61–66
  quotas, 58
  regulations, 74–75
  requirements, 58
  and selection, 377–78
  staffing provisions, 66–74
  See also Affirmative Action Plans;
    Discrimination, employment;
    Equal Employment Opportunity;
    Revised Order No. 4; Uniform
    Guidelines on Employee Selection
    Procedures
Affirmative Action Plans (AAPs), 220–28
Age Discrimination in Employment Act (1967), 61, 70
Agencies
  employment, 510
  governmental, 56–57
Americans With Disabilities Act (1990), 61, 64, 71–73, 378–80, 382–83
  employment regulations for, 539–49
Applications, employment, 304–7, 342–44
Assessment centers, 415–20
Authorization to work, 497

B

Benefits, 477, 478–79, 480–81
Bidding, job, 304
Biographical data, 344–46

Bona Fide Occupational Qualifications (BFOQ), 68, 70, 384, 388–89
Bona fide seniority systems, 321–22
Bonuses, 476–77

C

Career paths and recruiting, 298–303
Civil Rights Acts of 1964 and 1991, 61, 64, 66–70, 384
Civil Service laws and regulations, 79–82
Clinical assessment, 370
Common law, 55–56
Compensation, 475–77
Competitive advantages, 25–26
Consent decree, 65
Constitutional law, 56
Contingencies, employment, 466
Contracts
  disclaimers, 465–66
  enforceable, 461–62
  employment, 51–53, 461–67
  fulfillment of, 466
  form of, 463–65
  labor, 41–42, 42–45
  legal issues concerning, 496–99
  Office of Federal Contract
    Compliance Programs, 57, 64–66, 527–38
  oral, 464–65
  parties to, 462–63
  reneging, 466–67
  sources of, 467
Correlations, 103–8, 436
Cover letters, resume, 349–50
Cut scores, 440–44, 508

D

Disabilities
  discrimination, 71–73
Disclaimers, 465–66
Discrimination, employment
  in advertising jobs, 69, 70

age, 61, 70
bona fide occupational qualifications, 68, 70
disabilities, 71–73
and disparate impact, 59–61, 68, 131–33
and disparate treatment, 59, 68
employment advertising, 69
glass ceiling, 322–25
and medical exams, 73
and mixed motives, 68
national origin, 73–74
preferential treatment, 69
quotas, 69–70
race, 73–74
religion, 73–74
seniority and merit systems, 44, 69, 70
sex, 73–74
testing, 69
unlawful employment practices, 67
See also Age Discrimination in
  Employment Act; Americans With
  Disabilities Act; Civil Rights Acts
  of 1964 and 1991; Equal
  Employment Opportunity and
  Affirmative Action; Uniform
  Guidelines on Employee Selection
  Procedures
Disparate impact, 59–61, 68, 131–33
Disparate treatment, 59, 68, 510
Drug testing, 370–72, 380

E

Economic conditions, 22–24
  and competitive advantage, 25–26
  and human resources, 14
  and labor markets, 26–41
  and labor unions, 41–45
  orientation, 494–495
  private sector, 24–25
  public sector, 25
Employee Polygraph Protection Act, 76, 77–78
Employees